A HISTORY

OF

THE STATE TEACHERS COLLEGE

AT

RADFORD, VIRGINIA

1910 - 1930

BY

M'LEDGE MOFFETT, PH. D.

Transcribed and Typed, 1932
by Zella Blackard

FOREWORD

The early days of many institutions are shrouded in mystery and the lost story of the past. The facts in regard to these institutions could have been preserved had the actors then foreseen the many qyestions which the succeeding generations would raise and had the energy and foresight necessary to preserve the facts preceding and attending the origin and development of the institution.

The Radford State Teachers College has been unusually fortunate in having, from its earliest days, a remarkably complete record of all that preceded, attended, and characterized this institution. Doctor Moffett came to the institution in the early fall of 1913 and has been identified with it in very satisfactory and intimate capacities from that day to this. She had been looking forward to taking up her duties at the institution which was in the process of building through the days preceding the opening of the college in 1913. Having an inquisitive mind, great energy, and a keen sense of the worth of historical facts she assiduously began early in her life here to collect material having anything to do directly or indirectly with the new institution. She had had as a student, not as a professor, at the Harrisonburg State Teachers College which opened four years before this institution rare opportunity to study the early life of another higher educational institution. This intimate connection with the early days of that college gave her a peculiar preparation for preserving the facts in connection with Radford College, and in clearly understanding the drama of institutional organization and development that was being enacted daily. She was a very intelligent and observing actor in this drama. She was employed as a teacher of Home Economics. In addition she soon became identified with the official administrative life of the college. She had not been in this institution many weeks when it was found that a matron of the old Norwood home, used as a dormitory at that time, was needed. In the judgment of the President, she was the most suitable person for this trying position, this she filled with great satisfaction to all concerned. This was the beginning of her official duties in the college. These have so expanded in the last two decades that she had an intimate personal knowledge and contact with every phase of the institutional life and its development. Her association with the President and the administrative officers has given her a knowledge of the personality of the President, members of the faculty, and other officials of the institution that is absolutely unique. These contacts have prepared her for the production of the history of the institution in a fullness and accuracy that no other person associated with the college during the last two decades can approach in understanding, and in the accurateness of the facts.

As the second decade approached completion, at the request of President John Preston McConnell, Doctor Moffett undertook the laborious task of preparing this colossal history of the institution. In the midst of her other duties, this was indeed an arduous and trying task which was cheerfully assumed and which she has carried through with great enthusiasm and to the satisfaction of all concerned.

So far as I know no other college in the State of Virginia has been so fortunate in finding as discriminating or industrious chronicler of the material and intellectual development of its ideals and its ambition to serve the commonwealth. Therefore Moffett's history of this college tells its own story so well that a longer foreward is unnecessary.

Doctor Moffett, in the production of this history, has placed the friends of this institution and the friends of education in Virginia under lasting obligation to herself.

I, as President of this College from its earliest days, wish to place here on record my keen appreciation of the service Doctor Moffett has rendered me, this college, and the cause of education in Virginia by writing this History of the Radford State Teachers College, 1910 to 1930.

--JOHN PRESTON McCONNELL

PREFACE

This history of the first two decades (1910-1930) of the State Teachers College at Radford, Virginia, was written at the request of Doctor J. P. McConnell. As a historian Doctor McConnell realizes the importance of having some formal written record of the "beginnings" of the policies and activities of an institution established to serve people for many generations. He, therefore, commissioned the author, in addition to her duties for the academic session of 1930-31, to prepare the history.

It has taken practically two years to collect the data and prepare the manuscript. The task has involved:

First: the collection of all available documentary evidence, which includes:

    a. Acts of the General Assembly of Virginia, 1910 to 1930.
    b. Minutes of boards of trustees.
    c. Reports of President to the boards of trustees.
    d. Bound volumes of catalogs and other publications of the school.
    e. Personal and professional correspondence as shown in letters.
    f. Record books of student organizations.
    g. The Beehives and files of the Grapurchat and Rural School Messages.
    h. Published newspaper reports, complete since 1923.
    i. Memory books owned by various students.
    j. Prepared reports for the Southern Association of Secondary Schools and Colleges and for the American Association of Teachers Colleges.
    k. Copies of programs given in College.
    l. State Superintendents of Public Instruction reports.
    m. Educational Surveys of Virginia
    n. Minutes of the Faculty as a whole and of various committees.
    o. Books and other records of the Business office.
    p. Virginia Communities in War Time by Davis.
    q. Heatwole's History of Virginia.

Second: Extended correspondence and personal interviews with various board members, State officials, outstanding students, and faculty members.

Third: The circulation of a questionnaire to all Faculty members; tabulation of returns and interpretation of these data.

Fourth: The circulation of a questionnaire to all graduates of the college; tabulation of returns and interpretation of these data.

Much of the above documentary evidence has been collected, classified, filed and placed in the College Library for reference purposes. Summaries of the data compiled from the records and questionnaires are shown in the Appendix of the history.

The major portion of the story has been written from the memory of the author, who fortunately has had contact and first hand knowledge of the major events, development of policies and activities of the College since June 1913. The facts as given from memory have been verified as far as possible from the questionnaire returns and many conversations with others who were identified with the particular event.

Practically the entire manuscript has been read to Doctor McConnell (while he posed for his portrait May 1931), and he concurs in the accuracy of the account.

Although the history has been written to recount the story of the Radford College, the material has been so organized that certain sections are also a history of the development of some of the policies in teacher training for the entire State of Virginia. The account has been kept impersonal except in so far as personalities are essential to the record of real contribution and service. Much personal data is shown in the Appendix.

The author has been most ably assisted in the preparation of the manuscript by Miss Zella Blackard to whom the entire work was dictated and who has made three separate transcriptions and corrected copies; and by Miss Alma Mitchell who compiled much of the data from the source materials and tabulated all of the returns from the Alumnae survey. To these the Author extends heartfelt thanks and appreciation.

To Doctor McConnell the author expresses appreciation for the opportunity to prepare these volumes and for his generosity in providing stenographic help and for his patience and forbearance in an apparently never ending assignment.

M'LEDGE MOFFETT.

May 25, 1932.

TABLE OF CONTENTS

CONTENTS

Section III

PART III.   ADMINISTRATION OF THE COLLEGE

Section I

Section II

Section III

CONTENTS

CONTENTS

PART IV. INSTRUCTION

Section I

Appointment of Faculty, Qualifications of Faculty Members, Faculty for the Summer Schools, Faculty Organization, Professional organization of faculty, Faculty meetings, Faculty committees, American Association of University Women, Radford Chapter of University Professors, Extra-mural activities of the faculty, Social life of the faculty, Contributions of the faculty to educational literature, Service of the faculty to education in Virginia, Non-professional activities of the faculty, College publications, College publicity, Annual catalog, The Radford Normal Bulletin, The Normal School Glimpse, Rural School Messages, State Teachers College Bulletin, Student Publications.

Section II

Entrance requirements, Entrance requirements in 1913, Entrance requirements, 1930; Student records and registration, Student reports, Registration, The Daily schedule, Academic distinctions and honors.

Section III

Course of study committee, The professional high school period, The industrial courses, Two-year professional curricula, Influence of certification standards, Requirement for an elementary certificate or first-year Normal course, Courses for the Summer quarter, Four-year collegiate professional courses, Special courses, Physical education, The West Law, Sex Education, Expression, Special Music, Fine Arts, Organization of content material, Evaluation and numbering of courses, Methods of instruction, Tests and examinations.

CONTENTS

CONTENTS

CONTENTS

Section VI

The matron system, Some early regulations, Some
early cases of discipline, Creating spirit, The
problem of dress, The flapper period, Honor system, Student Government Association, Minor and
major calls, Black list, Forms of trial, The summer councils, The student association, Installation service, The system in vogue, 1930, Open
Forum, Electoral Board, Rules and regulations,
Student Council Room, Publications, Southern
Inter-Collegiate Student Government Association.

PART II. STUDENT ORGANIZATIONS

Section I

Regulations for control of student activities,
Student election day, Standards for student officers, Nominations, Student nomination committee, Voting.

Section II

Organization of Ingles and Pocahontas Societies,
The Ingles Creed, adapted 1920, Membership, Special
patrons of the society, Ingles Mother, Mrs. Mary S.
Moffett, "Grandpa" McCassell, Indian Allies, Society
Emblems, Red Skin Maid, Ingles emblems, Ingles Pep
song, The Ingles Girl, the Ingles tree, Society
buildings, Society bulletins, Time of meeting, Some
typical programs, the First Debate, Ingles Pilgrimage, May 27, 1927, Open programs, Society plays, Inter-Society basketball games, Society spirit, Society home project, Roll call and Pow Wow.

Section III

CONTENTS

CONTENTS

CONTENTS

Radford State Teachers College, Celebration program
was of a reminiscent nature, Inspection of buildings
and grounds, Alumnae reception, Founder's program,
The chief event, Twentieth Anniversary of the Establishment, Twentieth Anniversary of the Presidency of
Doctor John Preston McConnell.

Section III

State Conference of Charities and Corrections, Health
Committee of League of Nations, Fifth District Bankers, Virginia Press Association, Woman's Christian
Temperance Union Annual Meeting, Meetings of Scien-
tists, State Association of Funeral Directors, Public
Health Nurses, Virginia Federation of Women's Clubs,
Student Conventions, Motorcades, State Chamber of Commerce Good Will Tour, Atlanta Delegation, Boosters
from other sections of Virginia, Distinguished visitors, National Political leaders, Distinguished
ministers, Commencement speakers, Distinguished out-of-
State Educators, Governors as Visitors, Ohter State
Officials, Literary authors and poets.

Section I

First Alumnae Association, Local alumnae chapter,
Virginia Inter-Collegiate Alumnae Association,
National Inter-Collegiate Association, Full time
Alumnae secretary, Alumnae association committee
of Radford State Teachers College, Out-of-school
activities in connection with Literary Societies
Home Building Project, Duties of the Faculty Advisory Committee, Cooperation with Administrative
offices, Thanksgiving meeting, An analytical study
of the "After College Life" of 970 Graduates of the
State Teachers College, East Radford, Virginia,
Professional service, Teaching experience, Type of
service, Place of service, Salary of two-year
graduates, salary of four-year graduates, Educational professions, Degrees earned, Types of additional study, Professional affiliations, Travel,

CONTENTS

Forms of economic employment other than teaching
followed by Radford graduates, Married alumnae,
Family of married alumnae, Husbands, Children, Professional work, other employment outside the home,
Subjective reactions.

CONTENTS

- The End -

ESTABLISHMENT AND LEGAL ACTS CONTROLLING THE COLLEGE

SECTION I

A RESUME OF TEACHER TRAINING IN VIRGINIA PRIOR TO 1910
_____

Teacher training in Virginia became a legalized State function by the constitution adopted July 6, 1869. In the general plan for the inauguration of a public school system in the State a clause authorized the general assembly to establish, as soon as practicable, Normal schools.[1]

The Legislature of 1869 acting upon this authority given by the constitution appointed Reverend William H. Ruffner of Lexington, Virginia, State Superintendent of Public Instruction. Doctor Ruffner's plan for the organization of the system of public schools was adopted July 11, 1870. Many public schools were opened throughout the State in the fall of the same year. In three months' time 1400 county superintendents and district trustees were appointed. To these was intrusted the employment of the teachers. No uniform standards or qualifications were required. By the close of the scholastic year 1870, 3,000 teachers were employed in the public schools of the State.

In his first report Doctor Ruffner advised that provision be made whereby normal schools for the training of teachers be established. In support of this proposition he presented an array of statistics based upon the growth of normal schools in the Eastern and Central States.

The first normal schools of the United States had been established in Massachusetts in 1838 and 1839. The movement had spread rapidly throughout the New England States, New York State, and the Central States. Doctor Ruffner had watched the development of teacher training in these States and was thus prepared to sustain his argument to improve the quality of the public schools by trained teachers. No action, however, was taken upon his proposal and nothing was done by the State of Virginia for the training of teachers until 1880. At this time a summer school for white teachers was held at the University of Virginia and one for the colored teachers at Lynchburg. Prior to these schools there had been several private summer institutes, running from four to six weeks, conducted in various counties of the State, none of these however, were supported by the State. Their funds came largely from the "Peabody Fund" from which Virginia received $233,000.00 during the Ruffner administration. In 1881 during the Administration of Superintendent Farr

1. Heatwole's History of Education of Virginia. Page 216, Art. 5.

the State used $100,000.00 to establish the Normal and Industrial Institute for colored youth at Petersburg. This school has since been the chief State supported institution for the training of colored teachers.

Establishment of the School at Farmville

In 1884 the Legislature provided that a school for the "Training of Female Teachers for the Public Schools" be located at Farmville, Virginia. This school was established by a board appointed by the Governor. Doctor W. H. Ruffner was elected President. It was located on the site and on the property of the Farmville Female College, a small Methodist institution whose property was given to the State. The Legislature made an appropriation of five thousand dollars for the equipment of the school and ten thousand dollars for the running expenses.

The State later established a connection with William and Mary College whereby the men teachers of the State were given professional education.

For the next twenty years no effort was made to increase the training facilities for teachers in the State of Virginia. It was not until the public school system had become fairly well established and popularly accepted that an active demand began for additional educational facilities for the better training of teachers. In 1901 and 1902 Senator LeCato of Accomac County was co-author of a joint resolution requesting the appointment of a committee of five persons to be chosen by the President of the Senate and the Speaker of the House of Delegates to gather information bearing upon the establishment of an additional normal school which would also provide industrial training.[1] This resolution was approved by the House of Delegates and a committee composed of Senator A. D. Watkins, of Prince Edward, John M. Opey of Staunton, and Delegates F. T. West of Louisa, George Settle of Rappahannock, and M. K. Lowry of Stafford, was appointed. This committee reported on December 7, 1903 and favored the establishment of a Normal School with industrial training. Senator Keezell quotes this report thus: "The civilization of today has no place for the ignorant and incompetent man. There are 6,871 teachers in the public schools of Virginia; 1,671 are males, and 5,200 are females, thus we find that nine-tenths of the teachers in the white schools of the State are females. Not withstanding this ratio of female teachers, there are four institutions, William and Mary, Virginia Military Institute, Virginia Polytechnic Institute and University of Virginia for the equip-

1. From a report by Senator George B. Keezell, Daily News Record, Harrisonburg, Virginia, March 15, 1928.

ment of the sons of the State. There is only the Farmville Normal School for the equipment of the daughters of the State. Industrial training is no longer a fad or an experiment. We recommend the establishment of another Normal School for females with industrial training."

Immediately the various sections of Virginia became interested in securing the new normal school for their respective locality, however no action was taken upon these requests.

The Legislature of 1904, acting upon a resolution of Frank T. West of Louisa, appointed a committee to investigate and determine the best location for the school. This committee visited twenty-eight of the thirty places making propositions and demands for the location of the new school. So acute and pressing were these demands that the committee decided that the State needed more than one new normal school. It therefore, recommended to the Legislature of 1906 the establishment of three additional normal schools. One to be located in the Valley of Northern Virginia, one in Southwestern, and one in Tidewater, Virginia. The committee unanimously agreed and so reported the location of Radford as the most suitable place for the normal school proposed for Southwestern Virginia. The committee was not agreed upon the location of the other institutions. Immediately upon the report of this committee an active political fight started in the Legislature to secure the location of the school or schools which resulted in no action being taken by the Legislature of 1906.

ESTABLISHMENT OF THE SCHOOLS AT HARRISONBURG AND FREDERICKSBURG

The Legislature of 1908 met with the establishment of the new schools as one of the chief items of its agenda. By this time the pressure from the various localities of the State through their respective representatives had become so keen that it was practically impossible to secure action on any of the bills which called for the establishment of a normal school in any specific locality. The most active leaders in this contest were Senator George B. Keezell, advocating the location of the school at Harrisonburg; O'Conner Goolrich for Fredericksburg, and Charles A. Johnson of Christiansburg for Radford. This contest resulted in a division in the Senate and House on the locations of the schools. In order to bring about a settlement the question was referred to a conference committee. This committee recommended that two normal schools be established; one in Harrisonburg and one in Fredericksburg.

This resolution, carried as a rider to the appropriation bill of 1908, was passed. This bill provided for an appropriation of fifty thousand dollars. For the Harrisonburg school, and twenty-five thousand dollars for the Fredericksburg School. The acts of establishment of these two institutions called for the appointment of separate boards of trustees.[1]

On March 14, 1908, the Governor appointed a board of trustees for the Harrisonburg school. This board organized immediately, selected a site, perfected an organization and erected two buildings. The school opened September 28, 1909, under the presidency of Julian A. Burruss with an enrollment of one hundred and fifty students. The Fredericksburg school opened September 1911 under the presidency of E. H. Russell with an enrollment of one hundred and thirty-two students.

In 1908 a popular interest in industrial training probably accounts for the fact that the new State Normal Schools as established by the Legislature of 1908 were called State Normal and Industrial Schools. Just what was the full implication of the term "industrial" was never clearly stated in any of the Legislative Acts. In the first catalog of the Harrisonburg school the Administrators of that institution interpret "industrial" as follows:

"The most potent influence in modern educational thought is the awakening of educators and the public generally to the necessity of bringing the school into closer touch with the life of the people, their work, and their interests. It is properly expected of our schools supported by public funds that they train for good citizenship and it is generally recognized that this implies productive efficiency on the part of the individual so that he may be a self supporting and contributing unit in the social whole. In fulfillment of this expectation the public school education of the future must be brought close to the lives of the people, it must result in industry and thrift, it must make homes more sanitary and attractive, it must have the way to productive work with skilled hands, clear minds and pure hearts. In our cities our boys and girls must be put into possession of the elements of handcraft and in our rural districts they must be given the elements of agriculture and kindred subjects. To meet these demands of the new education it is obvious that the work of the normal school can no longer

1. From personal letters of Charles A. Johnson and George B. Keezell addressed to Dr. John Preston McConnell under the date of October 24, 1927 and October 13, 1927.

be confined to theory and books, but must seek its material in real things, in nature, in the practical activities of industry and commerce, in the business,
civic, and social interests of life. Without deprecia-
ting the limitless stores of useful knowledge bound up
in printed volumes, it must also draw from the outside
world the home, the farm, the workshop, the office, and
the marts of trade. The complete normal school must be
equipped to train teachers in agriculture and other
rural arts, in cooking and sewing and other household
arts and in drawing and other manual arts."

Summer Normals and High School Normal Training Classes

Contemporary with the legislative manoeuvers relative to the
location of the additional Normal Schools there was a general renaissance in public education in Virginia. Beginning with the organization of the Virginia Cooperative Educational Association in
1904 there was a rapid growth of public interest in the improvement of education. Throughout the entire State every civic organization devoted itself to a discussion of educational problems.
Striking through this general discussion and argument for general
improvement there was a plea for better trained teachers. The Legislative Acts which paralleled this general educational discussion indicate the political recognition of the need for trained teachers
which finally culminated in the establishment of the three State
Normal and Industrial Schools at Harrisonburg, Fredericksburg and
Radford.

Throughout the first decade of the twentieth century, however
many substitute and temporary measures were used for the training
of teachers. The old summer institutes which had been started in
the seventies greatly increased. Ten or twelve such institutes
were held in various sections of the State each summer. At first
these schools migrated from place to place, later they became more
permanently located. For a number of summers institutes were held
at Covington, Martinsville, Galax, and other places in the State.
These were conducted four weeks and were known as Summer Normal
Schools. Their primary purpose was the preparation of candidates
for the state examinations for the teachers certificates.

Of first importance among these summer institutes was the
School of Methods held under the direction of Superintendent E.
C. Glass of Lynchburg at the University of Virginia. This school
was the most largely attended, had the most able faculty and had
the most far-reaching effect upon teacher training in the State.

The school was conducted for six weeks each summer. Among its
faculty it had some of the most able teachers of Virginia and
many from other States. The chief emphasis of its work was upon
the methods of teaching in addition to the usual review courses
in elementary subjects as a preparation for the State examination.
A model school was held in the Midway School at Charlottesville
where popular educational theories were demonstrated. With the
development of professional education throughout the State the
School of Methods at the University was gradually converted into
the Summer Quarter of that institution and through its influence
upon the policies of the University led ultimately to the establishment of a year-around School of Education.

Certification of Teachers By Examination

Following the revision of the constitution of 1901 the State
Board of Public Instruction was given increased authority over the
public schools of the State. One of the chief changes made about
this time was in certification of teachers. The power to license
teachers was removed from the county superintendent and entrusted
to the State Board as a state function. The Board set up a plan
for examining teachers on the elementary school subjects with a
short examination on the theory and practice of teaching. These
examinations were held twice each year in the early spring and the
latter part of July. This led to the revival of the old summer institutes supported from the State Funds. These assumed the responsibility of coaching the candidates for the uniform examinations.

Throughout the State there were private training schools conducted during the spring. One of the most active of these was held
by Mrs. Mary S. Moffett in Rockbridge County, a woman who had been
trained in the Cincinnati Normal School and was teaching a model
school in that county. In other sections of the State the better
trained and educated teachers coached classes to prepare candidates
for the State examinations. The State examinations were held under
the auspices of the county superintendents in each of the counties
of the State. The questions were prepared under the direction of
the State Board of Education. The State Board authorized three
types of certificates, first, second and third grade certificates.
Any one who passed the examination won a certificate according to
his ability. Many of the people who successfully passed the State
examination had not completed the elementary schools and very few
of them had had any high school training. This latter condition
was due to the lack of public high schools in the State.

Agricultural and Normal Training High Schools

One of the chief results of the May Campaign of 1905 was an increase in the establishment of high schools. About this time there was a growing interest in vocational education throughout the United States. In many sections of the country agricultural high schools were established in the rural districts. Home Economics commonly called "domestic science" and industrial training called "manual arts" or "manual training" was introduced into the city and larger rural high schools. The National Educational meetings devoted much time to the discussion of the value of these courses. The leaders of education in Virginia became imbued with this idea of vocational education which in 1908 resulted in the establishment of agricultural high schools in each of the ten congressional districts of the State. Normal training classes were established in many of these high schools. Teacher training in high school had become very popular in the North Central States with the result that Virginia adopted this plan to meet her emergency in teacher training. Courses in pedagogy, school management and in some cases observation and practice teaching was added to the high school curriculum. High School Normal Training in Virginia continued for about ten years. With the establishment of the additional normal schools and the raising of professional standards they were gradually abolished.

SECTION II.

THE ESTABLISHMENT OF THE STATE NORMAL AND INDUSTRIAL SCHOOL FOR WHITE WOMEN, RADFORD, VIRGINIA

Almost immediately upon the announcement that the Legislature was considering the establishment of an additional normal school in the State the citizens of Radford became active in their efforts to secure this institution for Southwestern Virginia and to locate it within the City of Radford. A local committee composed of Judge George Cassell, W. T. Baldwin, Robert J. Noell, George A. Sullivan, and Robert L. Jordan, was self-appointed with the approval of other prominent citizens of Radford to go to Richmond and lobby for the establishment of the new school in this locality. This committee, backed by a strong appeal from the citizens of Radford, through its representative Honorable Charles A. Johnston of Christiansburg, made an appeal to the Legislative Committee on location of the school in behalf of Radford. As a result of the investigation of the commission appointed by the Legislature to study the sites proposed for the new institution, the city of Radford received a unanimous vote and was the only city definitely named in the report of this committee to the Legislature of 1906 as the location for one of the new schools proposed by the commission. The report of this committee failed of adoption in 1906 and was carried over to the Legislature of 1908.

During the interim the desire for the location of the school at Radford had increased and Honorable Charles A. Johnston of Christiansburg was charged with the responsibility of securing the new school for Radford. The records of the legislative committees show Mr. Johnston made a strenuous fight for the Radford location, however, largely due to the strategic position held by Senator George A. Keezell on the appropriation committee the Radford resolution was lost and in the final passage of the appropriation bill the Harrisonburg and Fredericksburg Schools were established. In order, however, to secure the support of Mr. Johnston for this appropriation bill, the first passage of which he had prevented, a Gentleman's Agreement was reached by the leaders of the various factions contending for the establishment of the schools, that a third normal school would be established without opposition, by the 1910 Legislature and that this school should be located at Radford. Accordingly the State Normal and Industrial School for Women at Radford was established by an Act of General Assembly of Virginia in 1910 as follows:

> 1. Be it enacted by the general assembly of Virginia that there is hereby established within the corporate limits of the city of Radford, Virginia, upon what is known as the "Adams Site" consisting of about forty acres or upon such other site within the corporate limits of the city of Radford as may be selected by the board of trustees, provided for in this act, a State normal and industrial school for white women.

> First: The said school shall be under the supervision, management and government of a board of trustees, which shall consist of ten members, to be appointed by the Governor, by and with the consent of the senate, to hold office for the term of four years: provided, that at the first appointment five shall be appointed for a term of two years, and five for a term of four years. The superintendent of public instruction shall be ex-officio member of said board of trustees, and any vacancy in the said board that shall be caused by death, resignation or otherwise, shall be filled by the governor, with the approval of the senate.

> Second: The said trustees shall be a body corporate under the name and style of State Normal and Industrial

School for Women at Radford, with the right as such to plead and be impleaded in the courts to receive all subscriptions, gifts, and donations, real or personal from any source whatsoever, the same by them to be held, invested, distributed or expended for the best use and benefit of the said school, and to exercise such other powers and do such other acts as are necessary and are proper to accomplish the end for which said school is created. Said trustees shall from time to time make all needful rules and regulations for the government and management of said school fix the number and compensation of teachers and employees of said school, and of said board, and prescribe the preliminary examinations and conditions upon which students shall be received therein. The board of trustees may appoint an executive committee of which the superintendent of public instruction shall be a member for the care, management and government of the said school, under the rules and regulations prescribed as aforesaid.

Third: The said trustees shall, annually, make and file with the said board of education a full report of their proceedings under this act, together with a report of the progress and condition of said school.

Fourth: Each county and city in the State shall be entitled to one pupil in the said school, who shall be nominated by the division superintendent of schools, and if any vacancy occur shall be filled by a like nomination, and each county and city in the State shall be entitled to one additional pupil for each additional representative in the house of delegates above one, to be nominated in a similar manner; provided, that the board of trustees may increase the number of pupils if they deem it expedient, said pupils to be selected as above. The said pupils so appointed shall be exempt from the charge of tuition. The board of trustees shall prescribe rules for the selection of said pupils, their examinations, and shall require of each pupil selected satisfactory evidence of an intention to teach in the public schools of this State for at least four years after leaving said normal school.

Fifth: The establishment of the said school within the corporate limits of the city of Radford, Virginia, is conditioned upon the city of Radford giving the tract of land known as the "Adams Site" consisting of forty acres of land, more or less, heretofore selected by the joint commission from the Legislature, or such other site of equal value as the "Adams Site" that might be available

10

to the city of Radford and acceptable to the board of
trustees, or, in lieu of a site, the city of Radford
may appropriate a sum of not less than twenty thousand
dollars. The plans for the building shall be submitted to inspection and approved by the board of education.

Sixth: It shall not be lawful for the board of trustees of the said school to contract any debt whatever
on account of said school without the consent of the
general assembly previously obtained.

SECTION III.
SUBSEQUENT LEGISLATIVE ACTS AFFECTING THE NAME AND POWER
OF TEACHER TRAINING INSTITUTIONS

The State female normal school at Farmville and each of the three
State normal and industrial schools established by the Legislative Acts
of 1908-1910 empowered the Governor to appoint a separate board   of
trustees. Each of these schools was administered by its respective
board until 1914. The Legislature of 1914 abolished the separate board
of trustees of the four State normal schools and established in its
place the Virginia Normal School Board.   This act also changed the
name of each of the four schools from State Normal and Industrial
School to The State Normal School for Women at Farmville, The State
Normal School for Women at Harrisonburg, The State Normal School for
Women at Fredericksburg and the State Normal School for Women at Radford. This act was approved by Governor Henry C. Stuart on March 27,
1914.

1. Be it enacted by the general assembly of Virginia, That a
board of visitors for the State Normal Schools for white women
of Virginia be, and is hereby created, which shall be and remain a corporation and be known as the "Virginia Normal School
Board."

1. The said board shall be composed of twelve members, one from
each congressional district, and two from the State at large, appointed by the governor, subject to confirmation by the senate.
Each member shall hold office for a term of four years, provided
that at the first appointment one-half of the members shall be
appointed for two years and one-half for four years. Thereafter
all appointments shall be for four years, except in case of a vacancy in which event the appointment shall be for the unexpired
term. Members of the said board shall serve without compensation,
but all expense incurred on account of services on said board
shall be paid by the State. The superintendent of public instruction of the State shall be ex-officio a member of the said
board. The governor of the State in his discretion, shall have
all the rights and privileges of a member of the said board. Six
members shall constitute a quorum.

2. The said board shall succeed to all the property, property rights, duties, contracts and agreements now controlled by
and vested in the board of trustees of the State female normal
school at Farmville, the State normal and industrial school for
women at Harrisonburg; the State normal and industrial school
for women at Fredericksburg; and the State normal and industrial school for women at Radford. The State female normal
school at Farmville shall hereafter be called "The State nor-

mal school for women at Farmville." The State normal and industrial school for women at Fredericksburg shall hereafter
be called "The State normal school for women at Fredericksburg."
The State normal and industrial school for women at Radford
shall hereafter be called "The State normal school for women
at Radford."

The "Virginia normal school board" shall have full authority
to manage and control the four said state institutions of
learning located at Farmville, Harrisonburg, Fredericksburg
and Radford, respectively. The said board shall safeguard
the State funds of the said schools and distribute all appropriations by the State in a careful and economical manner,
and shall appoint, subject to the limitations of its funds
and appropriations made by the State, such officers, teachers
and employees as it may deem necessary, and may remove any
one of them at any time for cause.

It shall be the duty of the said board to prevent, as far as
possible, unnecessary duplication of work in said schools, to
provide for the correlation of the work of said schools with
each other and with the primary and grammar grades and high
schools of the State. It shall have power to grant certificates of graduation and shall fix the necessary entrance requirements and courses of study, and shall provide proper facilities for carrying on the work of the said schools. It
shall be the duty of the said board to prepare all budgets to
be presented to the general assembly, and to make recommendations for maintenance and enlargement as the needs of the
schools demand. The said board is further empowered to appoint such committees of its members and employees, as, in
the said schools, separately or collectively. If in its judgment it seems best, the said board may appoint the presidents
of the respective schools as an executive council, which shall
constitute a proper correlation of the work of the said schools
with each other and with the public school system of the State.
When requested by the board to do so, the presidents of the
respective schools shall meet and confer with the said board
in an advisory capacity, and they may be appointed on any of
its committees, but shall have no vote in the meetings of the
said board.

3. All acts and parts of acts inconsistent herewith, are hereby repealed, and the boards of trustees of the State female normal school at Farmville; the State normal and industrial school for

women at Harrisonburg; the State normal and industrial school for women at Fredericksburg and the State normal and industrial school for women at Radford are hereby abolished.[1]

The new board assumed the control of the normal schools and held its first meeting July 10, 1914 at the office of the governor in Richmond. An amendment to the act establishing the State Normal School Board was made by the Legislature of 1916 and approved on March 21, 1916. This amendment empowered the new board to confer degrees in education. The act as amended reads as the one quoted above with the exception of the fourth paragraph which reads:

"It shall be the duty of the said board to prevent, as far as practicable, unnecessary, duplication of work in said schools, to provide for the correlation of the work of said schools with each other and with the primary and grammar grades and high schools of the State. It shall have the power to grant certificates of graduation; and to confer appropriate degrees in education upon students, completing courses in the institutions under their charge. It shall fix the necessary entrance requirements and courses of study, and shall provide proper facilities for carrying on the work of the said schools.[2]

Through the efforts of the Virginia Normal School Board and the presidents of the four normal schools an act was passed by the 1924 Legislature which changed the name of each of the four normal schools to State Teachers Colleges and changed the incorporate name of the board to The Board of Virginia Teachers Colleges.

1. Be it enacted by the general assembly of Virginia, that sections nine hundred and thirty-nine, nine hundred and forty, nine hundred and forty-two, nine hundred and forty-three, nine hundred and forty-six of the Code of Virginia of nineteen hundred and nineteen, be amended and reenacted so as to read as follows:

Section 939. The state normal schools for women continued.---The State normal schools for the training and education of white female teachers for public schools established at Farmville, in the county of Prince Edward, at Harrisonburg, in the county of Rockingham, at Fredericksburg in the county of Spotsylvania; and at Radford, in the county of Montgomery, shall be continued as now provided by law, and under the supervision and management and government of the

[1]Acts of Assembly 1914. Pages 567-568.
[2]Acts of Assembly 1916. Page 750.

14

board of the Virginia teachers Colleges as provided for in
this chapter.

Section 940. Virginia normal school board continued.------
The board of visitors for the State normal schools for white
women of Virginia is continued and shall be and remain a
corporation known as the "board of the Virginia teachers colleges."

Section 942. Property rights of board; names of institutions.----The said board shall succeed to all the property,
property rights, duties, contracts and agreements formerly
controlled by and vested in the board of trustees of the
State female normal school for women at Farmville, the State
normal and industrial school for women at Harrisonburg, the
State normal and industrial school for women at Fredericksburg, and the State normal and industrial school for women
at Radford and the Virginia normal school board. The State
female normal school at Farmville shall hereafter be called
the "State teachers college at Farmville." The State normal
and industrial school for women at Harrisonburg shall hereafter be called "The State teachers college at Harrisonburg".
The State normal and industrial school for women at Fredericksburg shall hereafter be called "The State teachers college at Fredericksburg." The State normal and industrial
school for women at Radford shall hereafter be called "The
State teachers college at Radford."

Section 943. Authority of board to control; to prevent duplication of work.---The board of the Virginia teachers college
shall have full authority to manage and control the four said
institutions of learning, located at Farmville, Harrisonburg,
Fredericksburg, and Radford, respectively.   The said board
shall safeguard the State funds of the said schools and distribute all appropriations by the State in a careful and economical manner, and shall appoint, subject to the limitations
of its funds and appropriations made by the State, such officers, teachers and employees as it may deem necessary and may
remove any one of them at any time for cause.

It shall be the duty of the said board to prevent, as far as
practicable, unnecessary duplication of work in said schools,
to provide for the correlation of the work of said schools
with each other and with the primary and grammar grades and
high schools of the State. It shall have the power to grant
certificates of graduation; and to confer appropriate degrees
in education upon students completing courses in the institutions under their charge. It shall fix the necessary entrance

requirements and courses of study, and shall provide proper facilities for carrying on the work of the said schools.

Section 945. Number of pupils each county and city may send free---Each county and city in the State shall be entitled to one pupil, and one for each additional representative in the house of delegates above one, in each of the State teachers colleges for white women, who shall receive gratuitous instruction. The board shall prescribe rules for the selection of such pupils and for their examination, and shall require each pupil selected to give satisfactory evidence of an intention to teach in the public schools of the State for at least two years after leaving the said school.

Section 946. Annual appropriations--For the support of the State teachers colleges there shall be paid out of the public treasury from time to time, such sums as may be appropriated therefor by the general assembly, to pay incidental expenses, the salaries of officers and teachers, and to maintain the efficiency of the schools; but the Commonwealth shall not in any instance be responsible for any debt contracted or expenditure made by the institutions in excess of the appropriations made.

By reason of the confusion which may arise in the appropriation for the support of the institutions affected by this act, unless this act be put into force and effect at once, an emergency is hereby declared to exist and this act shall go into force and effect, from the date of its passage.[1]

CERTAIN ACTS OF THE LEGISLATURE PASSED FROM TIME TO TIME WHICH AFFECT
THE CONTROL AND ACTIVITIES OF THE VARIOUS COLLEGES

Acts Affecting Business and Financial Management

An act of the Legislature approved March 20, 1924 provided for the centralized purchase of all the material and equipment of every description for all the State Institutions. The section of this act which affects the business management of the State Teachers Colleges is quoted in section four as:

Section 4. Except as hereinafter provided, every State officer, board, commission and institution, hereinafter called the using agency, shall, from and after July first, nineteen hundred and twenty-four, purchase through the State purchasing agent all materials, equipment and supplies of every description, the whole or a part of the costs whereof is to be paid out of the State

[1]
Acts of Assembly 1924, Pages 14-15.

treasury; and, under the supervision and control of the
State purchasing commission, and in conformity with this act,
it shall be the duty of the State purchasing agent to make
such purchases.

The State purchasing commission shall prescribe and enforce
rules and regulations, under which estimates of the needs of
the using agencies shall be submitted and requisitions made,
and under which contracts for purchases may be made. Estimates
of the amount and quality of materials, equipment and supplies
needed by the using agencies shall be submitted at such periods
as may be prescribed by the commission.

The State purchasing agent shall, when the amount of materials,
equipment and supplies needed exceeds one thousand dollars, and
in all other cases may advertise for bids on State purchases in
such manner and for such lengths of time as may be approved by
the State purchasing commission. When purchases are made through
competitive bidding, the contract shall be let to the lowest responsible bidder taking into consideration the qualities of the
articles proposed to be supplied, their conformity with specifications, the purposes for which required, and the times of delivery. Bids shall be received only in accordance with the
standards and standard specifications, if any, adopted by the
State purchasing commission. All bids may be rejected. Each bid
with the name of the bidder shall be entered on record and each
record, with the successful bid indicated, shall, after the letting of the contract, be open to public inspection. When any
bids shall have been accepted, the State purchasing agent may,
in his discretion, require of the successful a bond payable to
the Commonwealth, with good an sufficient surety, in the sum of
not less than one-third of the amount of the bid, conditioned
that he will fully, faithfully and accurately execute the terms
of the contract into which he has entered. The bond shall be
filed in the office of the Secretary of the Commonwealth. All
contracts entered into by the State purchasing agent shall be
executed in the name of the Commonwealth of Virginia by him as
State purchasing agent.

Section 5. So far as practicable all materials, equipment and
supplies, the purchase of which through the State purchasing
agent is made mandatory, shall be standardized by the State
purchasing commission, and no variation shall be allowed from
an established standard without the written approval of the
commission. Such standards shall be determined upon the needs
of all using agencies, so far as their needs are in common, and
for groups of using agencies or single using agencies so far as
their needs differ. Where changes or alteration in equipment are

necessary in order to permit the application of any standard, such changes and alterations shall be made as rapidly as possible.

And in order best to carry out the provisions of this section, there shall be established an advisory standardization board, consisting of the State purchasing agent as its head and such representatives (not exceeding nine) of the several institutions, offices and commissions affected by this act as shall be designated by the governor. The representatives so designated may be removed by the governor at his pleasure and others appointed in their stead. Said board shall consider and advise as to the needs of the various State activities and how far they can be reasonably harmonized and covered by standard specifications.

Section 6. The State purchasing commission shall have power, by general rule or special order, to permit purchases of any material, equipment or supplies whatsoever to be made by any using agency directly, and not through the State purchasing agent, whenever it shall appear to the satisfaction of the commission that by reason of the excess transportation costs, a lower price with equal quality can be obtained by the using agency, or for any other reason, which, in the judgment of the commission, warrants such exception. The commission shall give preference to State and local communities when materials, equipment and supplies can be purchased at the same price for the same quality as elsewhere.[1]

This act was amended in 1926 but such amendments did not affect the State Teachers Colleges. Another amendment of this act was affected under the re-organization of the business management of the State. This act of the Legislature approved March 10, 1928 reads:

1. Be it enacted by the general assembly of Virginia, That section six of chapter three hundred and ninety-two of the acts of assembly of nineteen hundred and twenty-four known as the centralized purchasing law, as amended, be amended and re-enacted so as to read as follows:

Section 6. The division of purchase and printing shall have power, by general rule or special order, to permit purchases of any material, equipment or supplies whatsoever to be made by any using agency directly, and not through the direction of said division, whenever it shall appear to the satisfaction of the division that by reason of the excess transportation costs, a lower price with equal quality can be obtained by the using agency, or for any other reason, which in the judgment of the commission, warrants such exemption. The

[1]The full account can be found in the Acts of Assembly of 1924. P.565-66.

division shall, in the purchase of materials, equipment and supplies, give preference so far as may be practicable, to materials, equipment and supplies produced in Virginia and are sold by Virginia persons, firms and corporations, and only soft winter wheat flour shall be purchased for, or used at State supported institutions. Except that the three sanatoriums for tuberculosis, the University hospital at Charlottesville, and the Memorial hospital at Richmond may use fifty per cent of spring wheat flour.

But it is expressly provided that unless otherwise ordered by the governor, the purchasing of materials, equipment and supplies through the division of purchase and printing is not mandatory in the following cases:

First--Telephone and telegraph service, and electric light and power service, and such materials, equipment and supplies as are incident to the performance of a contract for labor or for labor and material.

Second--Technical instruments and supplies, and technical books and other printed matter on technical subjects; also manuscripts, maps, books, pamphlets and periodicals purchased for the use of the Virginia State library or any other library in the State supported in whole or in part by the State appropriation.

Third--Perishable articles, such as fresh vegetables, fresh fish, eggs and milk; provided, that no other article shall be considered perishable within the meaning of this clause, unless so classified by the division of purchase and printing.

Fourth--Emergency purchases for immediate delivery to meet exigencies arising from unforeseen causes, including delays by contractors, delays in transportation and unforeseen volume of work in the department affected.

Fifth--Automobile license number plates.

Sixth--Materials, equipment and supplies needed by the State highway commission.

The several State institutions, in the purchase of all materials and supplies in excess of one hundred dollars, shall be subject to the provisions of this act as follows:

Provided, however, that the institution may submit bids together with samples from local concerns under the same rules and regulations as promulgated by the division of purchase and

printing for the submission of other competitive bids, and
should the same be of equal value, grade, quality and price,
then the division of purchase and printing shall accept such
local bids.

Nothing in this act contained shall be construed as intend-
ing to alter or repeal existing laws concerning the public
printing and binding.[1]

A general revision of the financial management of all the State
institutions was affected by the acts of legislature of 1926 and the
constitutional amendment approved by popular vote during that year.
These acts created a central control of the finances, both income
and expenditure, of the various institutions.

1. Be it enacted by the general assembly of Virginia, That
section ten, subsection (b) of section eleven and section
thirteen of an act entitled an act to reorganize the administration of the State government, in order to secure better
service, and through coordination and consolidation to promote economy and efficiency in the work of the government; to
create and establish or continue certain departments, divisions, offices, officers and other agencies, and to prescribe
their powers and duties; to abolish certain offices, boards,
commissions and other agencies, and to repeal all acts and
parts of acts, inconsistent with this act to the extent of
such inconsistency, approved April eighteenth, nineteen hundred and twenty-seven, be amended and re-enacted so as to
read as follows:

Section 10. Division of accounts and control and division of
the treasury--(a) The director of the division of accounts
and control shall be known as the comptroller. Before entering upon the discharge of his duties, he shall take an oath
that he will faithfully and honestly execute the duties of
his office during his continuance therein, and he shall give
bond in such penalty as may be fixed by the governor (but such
penalty shall not be less than twenty-five thousand dollars),
conditioned upon the faithful discharge of his duties, the pre-
mium on which bond shall be paid out of the State treasury.
The comptroller shall receive such annual compensation for his
services as may be appropriated by law for the purpose. Except
as otherwise provided in this act all the powers heretofore conferred and all the duties heretofore imposed by law upon the auditor of public accounts and the second auditor are hereby transferred to, vested in, and shall be exercised or performed by, the
comptroller. The office of second auditor is hereby abolished.

[1] Acts of Assembly, Pages 546-547-548. 1928.

Such of the employees in the office of the comptroller as, in
the opinion of the governor, should be bonded, shall be bonded
and the penalties of such bonds, respectively, shall be fixed
by the comptroller, subject to the approval of the governor.
The premiums on such bonds shall be paid out of the State treasury.

(b) Unified financial accounting and control shall be established through the department of finance, in the manner herein prescribed.

(c) Every State department, division, officer, board, commission,
institution or other agency owned or controlled by the State,
whether at the seat of government or not, collecting or receiving public funds, or moneys from any source whatever, belonging to
or for the use of the State, or for the use of any State agency,
shall hereafter pay the same promptly into the treasury of the
State, without any deductions on account of salaries, fees, costs,
charges, expenses, refunds, or claims of any description whatever,
and all balances of funds on March first, nineteen hundred and
twenty-eight in the possession or to the credit of any State Department, division, officer, board, commission, institution or
other agency owned or controlled by the State whether at the
seat of government or not, shall be then immediately paid into
the treasury of the State; provided, however, that any State
department, division, officer, board, commission, institution or
other agency at the seat of government may deposit such moneys
to the credit of the treasurer of Virginia upon communicating with
him and receiving the instructions from him as to what State depository may be used for the purpose, and in every such case such
depositor shall send a certificate of the deposit certified by
the bank receiving said deposit for every such deposit to the
State treasurer; and provided, further that any State department,
division, officer, board, commission, institution or other agency
not at the seat of government (other than county and city treasurers and clerks of courts) heretofore depositing such moneys to
its or his credit in local banks may hereafter deposit such moneys
to the credit of the treasurer of Virginia in a local State depository duly designated in pursuance of law as such, and in
every such case such depositor shall send a certificate of the
deposit certified by the bank receiving said deposit for every
such deposit to the State treasurer; but in no case shall a
State depository receive a larger sum to the credit of the
treasurer of Virginia than the amount covered by surey bond and
securities held by the treasurer of Virginia to protect State
funds on deposit in such depository; and provided, further, that
moneys paid into the State treasury which are not now payable into the general fund of the treasury shall be placed to the credit

of the respective accounts which are required by law to be kept on the books of the comptroller or to the credit of new accounts to be opened on the books of the comptroller with such agencies so paying such moneys into the treasury, respectively; and provided, further, that this act shall not apply to the endowment funds or gifts to institutions owned or controlled by the State, or to the income from such endowment funds or gifts, or to private funds belonging to the students or inmates of State institutions. Appropriations made by the government of the United States to or for the benefit of any State institution or agency, however shall be paid into the State treasury and used for the purposes for which such appropriations were made. The cash as well as the notes of student loan funds shall be held by the respective institution.

All county and city treasurers and clerks of courts receiving State moneys shall, on or before the tenth day of each month, or oftener, if the comptroller directs, report to the comptroller the total of each class of State revenue or State moneys received or collected for the previous calendar month unless otherwise directed, and at the same time pay into the State treasury the total amount so reported thereof received or collected from all sources.

Every State department division, officer, board, commission, institution or other agency owned or controlled by the State whether at the seat of government or not, including county and city treasurers and clerks of courts, collecting or receiving public funds, or moneys from any source whatever, belonging to or for the use of the State, or for the use of any State agency, and paying the same to the State treasurer, or depositing the same to his credit in pursuance of law, shall, on or before the tenth day of each month, or oftener, if directed by the comptroller, report to the comptroller in such a manner as he may direct, the amount collected or received and paid into the treasury for the preceding calendar month or other period designated by the comptroller, such report to show also the dates of payments to or deposits to the credit of the treasurer.

No State department, division, officer, board, commission, institution or other agency owned or controlled by the State, at the seat of government, except the State Treasurer, shall hereafter deposit any State funds to its, his or their credit in any bank.

(d) Any public officer, or any firm or corporation, or any

other person having to pay money into the treasury may make
such payment by delivering to the treasurer of Virginia a
check, draft or certificate of deposit, drawn or endorsed,
payable to the treasurer of Virginia, or his order, or may
make such payment by delivering to the treasurer of Virginia the proper amount of lawful money. Should any check,
draft, or certificate of deposit not be paid on presentation, the amount thereof, with all costs, shall be charged
to the person on whose account it was received, and his lia-
bility and that of his sureties, except the additional lia-
bility for costs, shall be as if he had never offered any
such check, draft, or certificate of deposit.

(e) The treasurer shall keep a record of every such check,
draft or certificate of deposit, and of all such money received by him, and upon receipt thereof, forthwith cause
the same to be placed to the credit of the Commonwealth
with some State depository. If any check, draft, or certificate of deposit not be paid on presentation, the treasurer shall immediately notify the comptroller and shall
proceed to collect the amount thereof from the person depositing the same. The treasurer shall daily transmit to
the comptroller a record of all receipts, giving the details thereof.

(f) It shall not be lawful for the treasurer to collect
any money on such check, draft, or certificate of deposit;
but the same shall, in every case, be by him properly endorsed and deposited, as aforesaid, with some State depository for the credit of the Commonwealth.

(g) The bond of the State treasurer shall be in the penalty
of two hundred and fifty thousand dollars. Such of the employees in the office of the State treasurer, as, in the
opinion of the governors, should be bonded, shall be bonded,
and the penalties of such bonds, respectively, shall be fixed
by the State treasurer, subject to the approval of the governor. The premiums on the bonds mentioned in this paragraph
shall be paid out of the State treasury.

(h) The Commonwealth shall not be liable for any loss resulting from lack of diligence on the part of any depository
in forwarding, or in failing to collect, any such check,
draft, or certificate of deposit, or for the loss of any such
check, draft, or certificate of deposit in transmission through
the mails or otherwise.

(i) The State treasurer shall be charged with the custody of
all investments and invested funds of the State or in posses-

sion of the State in a fiduciary capacity, and with the keeping of the accounts of such investments. The State treasurer shall also be charged with the custody of all bonds and certificates of the State debt, whether unissued or cancelled, and with the receipt and delivery of State bonds and certificates for transfer, registration or exchange.

(j) No money shall be paid out of the State treasury except in pursuance of appropriations made by law, and there shall be established in the division of accounts and control by the comptroller a complete system of general accounting to comprehend the financial transactions of every State department, division, officer, board, commission, institution or other agency owned or controlled by the State, whether at the seat of government or not. All transactions in public funds shall clear through the comptroller's office. All State moneys in a State depository shall stand on the books of such depository to the credit of the treasurer of Virginia. But the treasurer shall have no authority to draw any of the said money except by his check, drawn upon a warrant issued by the comptroller. If any money to his credit, as aforesaid, shall be knowingly paid otherwise than upon his check drawn upon such warrant, the payment shall not be valid against the Commonwealth.

(k) The comptroller shall not issue any disbursement warrant unless and until he shall have audited the bill, invoice, account, payroll or other evidence of the claim, demand or charge and satisfied himself as to the regularity, legality, and correctness of the expenditure or disbursement and that the claim, demand or charge has not been previously paid. If he, be so satisfied, he shall approve the same; otherwise, he shall withold his approval. In order that such regularity and legality may appear, the comptroller may, by general rule or special order, require such certification or such evidence as the circumstances may demand. Lump-sum transfers of appropriations to State departments, divisions, officers, boards, commissions, institutions and other agencies owned or controlled by the State, whether at the seat of government or not, are prohibited; but nothing in this sentence shall be construed as preventing the payment to or distribution among the political subdivisions of the State of any appropriations made to them by law. A reasonable petty cash fund shall be allowed each State department, institution, board, commission, or other agency, the amount of which petty cash fund shall be fixed by the comptroller in each case, but these funds shall be reimbursed only upon vouchers audited by the comptroller. No appropriation to any department, institution or other agency of the State government, except the general assembly and the judiciary, shall become available for expenditure until the agency shall submit to the director of the division of the budget quarterly estimates of the amount required for each activity to be carried on, and such estimates shall have been approved by the governor.

(1) The foregoing is subject to the qualification that, upon warrant of the comptroller, the State treasurer shall be authorized to advance amounts of cash as working funds to the division engineers of the department of highways, to be disbursed by them solely for the payment of laborer's wages and for emergency purchases; but the amounts of these funds shall be fixed by the comptroller and the disbursements therefrom shall be audited by the comptroller after payment. The State finance board shall designate the depositories in which such funds shall be placed.

(m) The comptroller shall prescribe what accounts shall be kept by each State agency in addition to the system of general accounting maintained in the comptroller's office, and in prescribing what accounts shall be kept by each State agency the comptroller shall take care that there shall be no unnecessary duplication.

(n) All the powers conferred and all the duties imposed by law upon the State fee commission are hereby transferred to, vested in, and shall be exercised or performed by the comptroller, and the State fee commission is hereby abolished. The board, known as the board of indemnity, and the board, known as the surety bond board, are hereby severally abolished.

(o) The finance board shall hereafter consist of the governor, the comptroller and the State treasurer, and the commissioners of the sinking fund shall hereafter consist of the comptroller and the State treasurer.

(p) The comptroller and the State treasurer shall each make an annual report to the governor on or before the first day of August, and shall make such other reports at such times as the governor may require.

(q) Sections twenty-one hundred and fifty-five, twenty-one hundred and sixty-three, twenty-one hundred and sixty-four, twenty-one hundred and sixty-five, as amended by an act approved March nineteenth, nineteen hundred and twenty-six twenty-one hundred and sixty-six, twenty-one hundred and sixty-seven, twenty-one hundred and sixty-eight, twenty-one hundred and sixty-nine, twenty-one hundred and seventy, twenty-one hundred and seventy-one, twenty-one hundred and eighty-two, twenty-one hundred and eighty-three, twenty-one hundred and ninety-three, twenty-one hundred and ninety-five, twenty-one hundred and ninety-seven, twenty-one hundred and ninety-eight, twenty-two hundred, twenty-two hundred and two, twenty-two hundred and three and twenty-two hundred and four of the Code of Virginia are hereby repealed.

Section 11 (b) Such director shall transfer surplus supplies or equipment from one State institution or agency to another, and sell surplus supplies or equipment which may accumulate in the possession of any State institution or agency and pay the proceeds derived therefrom into the State treasury; provided, however, that no such surplus supplies or equipment shall be transferred or sold without the consent of the head of the institution or agency having them in possession, or unless ordered by the governor. No such supplies or equipment shall be sold or exchanged except as provided herein.

Section 13. Auditor of public accounts.--An officer, to be known as the auditor of public accounts, shall be elected by the joint vote of the two houses of the general assembly, as provided in section eighty-two of the Constitution, and he shall receive such compensation as may be appropriated by law for the purpose; but such officer shall not perform any of the duties nor exercise any of the powers imposed or conferred upon the officer heretofore known as the auditor of public accounts, by any statute ennacted prior to March sixteenth, nineteen hundred and twenty-seven, all such duties and powers being by this act imposed or conferred upon the comptroller, except as otherwise herein provided. The auditor of public accounts shall perform such duties and exercise such powers as have been heretofore imposed or conferred by law upon the State accountant, and the office of State accountant is hereby abolished. In addition thereto, the auditor of public accounts shall audit all of the accounts kept in the department of finance and all accounts of every State department, officer, board, commission, institution or other agency in any manner handling State funds and in the performance of such duties and the exercise of such powers he may employ the services of certified public accountants, provided the cost thereof shall not exceed such sums as may be available out of the appropriation provided by law for the conduct of his office.

The auditor of public accounts shall be the chief auditor and accountant of the auditing committee of the general assembly. If the auditor of public accounts should at any time discover any unauthorized, illegal, irregular, or unsafe handling or expenditure of State funds contemplated but not consummated, in either case he shall forthwith lay the facts before the governor, the members of the auditing committee of the general assembly, and the comptroller.

The penalty of the bond of the auditor of public accounts shall be fixed by the governor, but the same shall not be less than five thousand dollars. Such of the employees in the office of the auditor of public accounts as, in the opinion of the governor, should be bonded, shall be bonded, and the penalties of such bonds, respectively, shall be fixed by the auditor of public accounts, subject to the approval of the governor. The premiums on the bond mentioned in this paragraph shall be paid out of the State treasury.

2. An emergency existing, this act shall be force on and after the first day of March, nineteen hundred and twenty-eight.[1]

An act was approved March 2, 1926 providing that the salary of no State officer can be changed without the consent of the governor.

1. Be it enacted by the general assembly of Virginia, That the salary of no State officer or employee which is payable by the State and which is not specifically fixed by law, and the salary of no officer or employee of any State institution, board, commission or agency which is not specifically fixed by law, shall be hereafter increased, or authorized to be increased, without prior authorization of said board or commission and the consent of the governor first obtained in writing in each case. Any violation of this act shall constitute misfeasance in office. Provided, however, that nothing herein contained shall apply to teachers in the elementary or high schools of the Commonwealth, or to employees receiving compensation not in excess of one hundred dollars per month.[2]

1. Be it enacted by the general assembly of Virginia, That it shall be lawful for the board of the Virginia teachers colleges, to accept any gift donation or benefaction offered by any person for any proper use by, or in connection with any or either of the State teachers colleges under the management and control of said board, and to apply the same directly to the use for which it was intended by the donor, and at, and in connection with the college, or colleges for whose benefit the gift, donation or benefaction was made; and if it be real estate, deed therefor shall be taken in the name of the Said

[1] Acts of Assembly 1928 - Pages 342-348.
[2] Acts of Assembly 1926 - Pages 86-87.

board.

Chapter 489.--An ACT to authorize the governing boards of certain State institutions of higher education to issue and sell, through the commissioners of the sinking fund, and subject to the approval of the State Board of Education, certificates of indebtedness in the names and on behalf of their institutions, respectively, to raise funds for dormitory construction purposes, subject to the conditions and limitations contained in this act; to provide for the payment of the interest thereon and the principal thereof at maturity, and to authorize the State Board of Education to sell any State bonds held as a part of the Literary Fund and to invest the proceeds derived from the sale of such bonds in the certificates of indebtedness issued under the provisions of this act, such certificates so purchased to become a part of the Literary Fund.

Approved March 25, 1926.

Be it enacted by the general assembly of Virginia, as follows:
1. Subject to the approval of the State board of education first obtained, the governing boards of the University of Virginia, the Virginia Agricultural and Mechanical College and Polytechnic Institute, the College of William and Mary in Virginia, the State Teachers Colleges at Farmville, Radford, Harrisonburg, and Fredericksburg, the Virginia Military Institute, and the Virginia Normal and Industrial Institute are hereby severally authorized, through the commissioners of the sinking fund, to issue and sell certificates of indebtedness in the names and on behalf of their institutions, respectively, to raise funds for dormitory construction purposes, subject to the conditions and limitations hereinafter set out.

2. The amount of certificates of indebteness which may be issued on behalf of each of the institutions herein named shall be as agreed upon by the governing board of each institution and the State board of education; but the aggregate amount of certificates issued on behalf of all the institutions herein named shall not exceed the sum of one million dollars.

The attention of the State Board of education is hereby directed to the message of the governor of Virginia to the general assembly dated January 13, 1926, in so far as such message deals with the needs of the several institutions mentioned in this act.

3. The certificates of indebtedness issued under the provisions

of this act shall be signed on behalf of the institutions
in the names of which they are issued, by the presiding
officers of their governing boards, respectively, and shall
be countersigned by the second auditor, who shall keep an
account thereof in his office. The certificates of indebtedness issued under this act are the certificates of the institutions issuing them, respectively, and not the certificates
of the State.

4. The said certificates of indebtedness shall bear interest
payable semi-annually January first and July first of each
year, at a rate to be fixed by the commissioners of the sinking fund with the approval of the State board of education,
but not exceeding four per centum annum. The said certificates
shall be issued in such denominations and shall mature at such
time or times, not exceeding twenty-two years from their date,
as may be prescribed by the State board of education, and shall
be in such form not inconsistent with the provisions of this
act, as may be approved by such board. The governing board of
each such institution on behalf of which such certificates are
issued may secure the payment of the interest thereon and the
principal thereof at maturity by giving a deed of trust upon
the property of such institution.

5. The commissioners of the sinking fund with the approval of
the State board of education, shall from time to time, sell
the said certificates of indebtedness for cash at such prices,
not less than par, as may be approved by them.

6. The sums of money received from the sale of the certificates of indebtedness issued and sold under the provisions of
this act shall be paid into the State treasury by the commissioners of the sinking fund to the credit of the institutions
on behalf of which such certificates are issued and sold, respectively, and such amounts so paid in to the credit of such
institutions, respectively, are hereby appropriated to any may
be expended by their governing boards, respectively, for the
construction of dormitories for the use of students of the re-
spection institutions, and for no other purposes whatsoever.
But all payments out of the treasury shall be made upon the
order of the second auditor. All plans, bids and costs of the
buildings shall be acted upon by the governing board of the
respective institutions and the State board of education. The
idea of the utility of the said buildings shall be paramount
and adhered to in their design for the purposes intended, and
the consumption of space for any non-essential purpose shall be
avoided. In constructing a dormitory at the State Teachers College at Radford, the general design of the present dormitory

shall be adhered to and it shall also harmonize with the original building plan.

7. The State board of education is hereby authorized, in its discretion, to sell any bonds of the State held as a part of the literary fund and to invest the proceeds derived from the sale of such bonds in the certificates of indebtedness issued under the provisions of this act, such certificates so purchased to become a part of the literary fund.

8. In order to provide for the payment of the interest on the certificates issued under this act and the creation of a sinking fund to retire them at maturity, the governing boards of each of the institutions on behalf of which such certificates are issued, shall cause to be paid quarterly into the State treasury to the credit of special accounts to be opened on the books of the second auditor for each of such institutions, all net rents and fees received from students or other persons for the use of the dormitories constructed with funds derived from the issuance of such certificates of indebtedness. The rents charged for the use of such dormitories shall not be less than six dollars per month for each student occupying a room therein, and on the basis of not less than two students to a room, and the same price for each student in excess of two to a room who may occupy any of the rooms.

The term "net rents and fees", as herein used, shall be construed to mean the gross rents and fees received for the use of such dormitories, including insurance premiums, which cost of operation and maintenance including insurance premiums shall not exceed twenty-four hundred dollars each per annum, on the basis of a dormitory costing one hundred and fifty thousand dollars, nor shall such cost exceed twenty-eight hundred dollars in the case of a dormitory costing two hundred thousand dollars, and a proportionate cost for less sums expended in building construction. It shall be the duty of the State accountant semi-annually to audit the accounts of the rents and fees received and disbursed by each institution, and if it shall come to his knowledge that such accounts are not being kept properly, or that any of such rents and fees are being devoted to purposes not authorized by this act, he shall report the facts to the governor.

9. If at any time any default should be made by any institution in the payment into the State treasury of the moneys hereby required so to be paid in for interest and sinking fund requirements, the commissioners of the sinking fund shall direct the second auditor to make requisition on the auditor of public

accounts who shall draw his warrant upon the then current
annual State appropriation of such institution for the a-
mount estimated to be due. Such warrant shall thereupon
be honored and such amount disposed of in the same manner
as if it had been paid into the State treasury by such institution as required by section eight of this act.

10. The moneys so received into the State treasury to be
placed to the credit of the special accounts mentioned in
section eight of this act shall be used by the commissioners
of the sinking fund, first to pay the interest on such certificates of indebtedness issued on behalf of such institutions,
respectively, when and as it becomes due and payable, and the
balance shall constitute a sinking fund in each instance to
retire the certificates of indebtedness at maturity. Each
of such sinking funds may be used by the commissioners of
the sinking fund to purchase and retire certificates of indebtedness for which such sinking funds are provided in which
case such certificates so purchased shall be cancelled and
not re-issued. To the extent that each of such sinking funds
is not used to purchase such certificates, as aforesaid, the
moneys belonging to it shall be invested by the commissioners
of the sinking fund in safe securities at the highest rate
of interest obtainable, and all interest received on such investments shall become a part of the sinking fund out of the
sinking funds respectively provided for that purpose. All
moneys disbursed by the commissioners of the sinking fund under this act shall be paid out by the State treasurer on
warrants of the second auditor issued on the order of such
commissioners.

11. All buildings constructed with funds derived from such
certificates of indebtedness shall be practically fireproof.
They shall be kept adequately insured by the respective governing boards of such institutions.

12. The moneys made available by this act to the institutions
named in this act shall be used only for the construction of
dormitories. All such dormitories shall be furnished by donations, gifts, or otherwise and shall be so kept furnished
until the certificates issued have been retired.

13. No purchasers of any certificate of indebtedness issued
under this act shall be required to see to the application of
the purhcase money.[1]

1 Acts of Assembly 1926. Pages 829, 830, 831, 832.

Approved March 18, 1926.

Chap. 184--An Act requiring the governing boards or heads of
State departments and institutions to provide for the regis-
tration of officers and employees when absent from duty.
(S B 12)

1. Be it enacted by the general assembly of Virginia, That
the governing boards or heads of all State departments and
institutions shall hereafter cause to be kept in the main
office of such department or institution, respectively, a
blank book to be known as the registration record or proper
alphabetical card system in which it shall be the duty of
all officers and salaried employees of such departments and
institutions, respectively, to register upon leaving the department or institution to be absent from duty for more than
one day whether on official or personal business. Such registration shall state the date of leaving, the reason for
such absence, and the probable date of return. Upon their
return they shall likewise register the date thereof, the
reason for such absence, and, if delayed in returning the
reason for such delay; but whenever any such officer or employee shall have been absent from duty on account of sick-
ness or otherwise, and has had no opportunity to so register
before leaving, his registration upon his return shall be
sufficient compliance with this act. The registration record
herein required to be kept shall be public records. Any officer or employee refusing or failing to comply with this act
shall be subject to a fine of five dollars for each offense.

Also a record of absence from duty shall be transmitted with
the annual report of the department and institutions.

This act shall not interfere with the time clock system, used
by the State highway departments, or used by any other department; nor the departments or employees at the capitol, nor to
the employees of the State forrestry department engaged in
field work, a check on whose time and service shall be prescribed or managed by the governor.[1]

[1]Registration Book. Page 8.

PART II
COLLEGE PLANT
SECTION I

THE SITE

The original site selected by the first Board of Trustees included thirty-three and one-third acres of farm land in the east
ward of the City of Radford on the second of the three terraces
which gives the city the name "City of Terraces." Five additional
acres of land have been purchased (1929) bringing the total acreage
of the campus to about thirty-five acres. The terrace on which the
school is located rises two hundred feet above the main street of
the city. This sloping hill, when the site was purchased was covered with a virgin oak grove. These trees, known as the Heth Grove
was on the outskirts of the city and served as a rendezvous
for the less desirable citizens of the community. The lower part
of the oak grove was a dumping ground for whiskey bottles, empty
cartoons and other debris of the city. The remainder of the plot
was a blue grass pasture. In this pasture lot were two large ponds
formed in sink holes, characteristic of the terrain of Radford.

The pasture and oak grove were separated from Tyler Avenue by
a wire and wooden fence, the only entrance was through a barnyard
gate. Near this gate the cattle were fed fodder, and other litter
were scattered about giving a barnyard effect to what is now the
main triangle of the campus.

Tyler Avenue was a winding dirt road. Across the avenue there
were about one dozen houses. At the time of the establishment of
the school the houses on the section of this street from Grove Avenue to Clement Street were owned by Mr. N. T. Kirtner, Mrs. J. W.
G. McDonald, Mr. Moore, a tenant house owned by the Roberts estate
and Mr. W. E. Bricker on the corner. Across Downey Street there
was the Collins home, three vacant lots of the Roberts estate and
houses owned by Mr. T. J. Northcross, Doctor J. A. Noblin and Mr.
J. T. Beamer.

South of the college grounds bordering on Fairfax Street there
were no houses except the Presbyterian Church, a negro cabin and
rear of these a small home owned by Mr. Sam Worley. The greater
part of this section lay very low and marshy with several ponds.
To the east of the campus there was no street, only a narrow lane
with no houses except the La Belle Inn and three or four houses
east of this building occupied by negroes. The northern boundary
was a winding road "Lover's Lane" leading through the grove, the
Norwood house faced this. In this isolated environment the members
of the board thought that they were locating the college well into

the country. However since the school has been established this section has so built up that the college is now literally in the business heart of the city and is hemmed in by residences except for a small area reserved by the Heth estate.

On the side of Tyler Avenue next to the college site there was a deep gulley, in many places ten feet deep, after storms torrents of water rushed down this gorge seeking an outlet to the river. The street was unpaved and during the winter season the mud was often eight inches deep.

The Board devoted much time to a consideration of the exact spot on the campus to locate the Administration Building. By a survey the building was put on what was geometrically the top of the hill near the former site of a two room tenant house. In order to erect the building several trees were removed, but an effort was made to preserve the original trees of the oak grove. In the excavation for the Administration Building several cannon balls were found. These had been fired at the time of the bombarding of Radford during the War between the States. The depth of the excavation ranged from ten to twenty feet. This dirt was thrown out against the trunks of the trees causing the death of many of them.

SECTION II

IMPROVEMENT OF THE CAMPUS

The first problem for the improvement of the campus was the grading of the section covered by the dirt from the basement of the building. This had smothered the roots of the trees and it became necessary to dig out large areas around them. The first campus job of Paul and Carl McConnell was to brick up these circular spaces around the trees. This early preservation of the trees has probably prolonged their life. For the erection of the Tyler Hall it was necessary to fill in a large sink hole and pond, (jokingly called "Gilbert Lake"). To do this a general fill and grading of the triangle back of the Administration Building was necessary. This entire area of about five hundred square yards was filled in depth ranging from two to five feet. All of this grading was closely supervised and directed by Doctor McConnell.

The development of the campus, especially the propagation of grass, has been a matter of deep concern to Doctor McConnell, under his direction the entire campus has been sown in blue grass which with the natural growth has produced a splendid sod. To thoroughly clean the campus occupied the first three or four years. It was a herculean task to convert the neglected wood and pasture lot into one of the most admired campuses of the State. By 1916 the worst of the debris had been carried away. One warm February day a final clean-up holiday was declared. All the students and faculty devoted themselves for an entire day to cleaning, they literally raked and swept the oak grove. Wagon loads of leaves, bark, sticks and stones were hauled away. This effort with subsequent weeding by the students contributed much to the beautification of the campus.

PATHS AND WALKS

There were no permanent paths or walk ways for the first several years. Doctor McConnell decided to see how people would go about the school and let these paths form the general direction for the permanent paths. There was much debate as to where the main entrance to the grounds should be located. First it was planned at the foot of the hill with the approach direct from Norwood Street to the main entrance of the Administration Building. For the first few weeks of the school this approach was used. Soon, however, those who approached the Administration Building from the city adopted the old wagon gate as the easiest entrance. This later became the main driveway entrance to the campus. A turn stile gate was placed on Tyler Avenue parallel to the entrance of the Administration Building. During these early years the students used "Lover's Lane" as the approach from the business streets to the La Belle Inn. They made a narrow path from La Belle Inn to the rear entrance of the Administration Building. This led through the pasture lot, the barnyard by the power house, hence over a double stile to the main campus.

The Heth house girls made another path by the red barn (now library site) to join this path from the dormitory. This route has since become the graveled driveway from the Administration Building to the heating plant. With the erection of the Tyler Dormitory the routes of travel began to change. In 1916 the concourse back of the Administration Building and a concrete walk way from the Administration Building to the front entrance of the Tyler dormitory was laid. Several years later the concourse was lengthened into a driveway to the main entrance on Tyler Avenue. The fact that nearly all the students entered the Administration Building by the rear entrance tended to direct the traffic across the campus to the rear entrance led to the establishment of a diagonal walk to the turn stile on Tyler Avenue. In 1916 this short cut through the grove was concreted. With the erection of each of the new units of that building the walk way from the Tyler dormitory was extended. For the other buildings gravel walks have been made on the routes most often travelled by students. It was planned to have a driveway enter the campus at the corners of Norwood and Tyler and to wind around the hill to the Administration Building. The class of 1923 named this proposed driveway "Rambler Way" and planted rambler roses over the stone wall and along the route of the driveway. This class gave an iron entrance archway with the name of the State Normal School in brass letter. This archway was erected at the foot of the hill but upon the change of the name of the school it was removed. At this time it was decided to abandon the project of grading the road at the corner and make the main entrance between the Administration Building and Tyler Hall. The idea of having this main entrance at the foot of the hill at Norwood Street was not officially abandoned until 1924.

In 1922 the Legislature made the first appropriation for the erection of the stone wall which has been built in sections around the campus. In 1930 it reaches the front entrance of the training school. The classes of 1922 and 1923 gave the iron entrance gates.

The improvement of Tyler Avenue was started in 1915 when Mr. Fred Cannady gave many Sycamore trees to be planted in the park way of this avenue as a memorial to his wife. Doctor McConnell and Governor J. Hoge Tyler assumed the responsibility for the planting of these trees. The city graded, hard surfaced the avenue in 1923. A six-foot concrete side walk was laid from the upper entrance to the Tyler dormitory to Norwood Street as a joint project of the city and college.

TREES, PLANTS AND SHRUBBERY

The Virgin Oak grove which covers about two acres of the campus of the college gives a natural setting for the institution. In 1915 Mr. Watkins of Midlothian, Virginia, was employed by the college to landscape the campus around the Administration Building and the Tyler Hall. His general design has been followed in the planting of shrubbery around the other buildings.

The campus has been the most productive spot for beauty about the college. Doctor McConnell is personally intensely interested in it. On warm spring days he spends hours digging and raking on the campus. Since 1916 Mrs. McConnell has also spent hours planting seeds and doing much of the cultivation of the plants. Gradually she has become the official gardener in charge of all planting and landscaping. To her should be given the credit for the effective development of plant life on the campus. For the past

fifteen years she has supervised this work. Most of the present
growth is due to her labor and planning. In appreciation of Mrs.
McConnell's untiring efforts the students dedicated the Beehive
of 1926 to her thus:

> To one, who fair the earth would make,
> As fair Elisia's flowering grave,
> To one who makes our lives more bright
> By beauty - the language of our love.
> 'Tis she who tends our campus flowers
> and does to them her sweetness lend,
> She gives a nobleness to each plan
> And to us all- a friend.

CLASS TREES

The first tree planted by man on the campus of the college was
at commencement in 1914 by the first graduating class. A maple tree
was planted as a part of the class day exercise with Superintendent
R. C. Stearnes as the chief orator. This is on the main triangle of
the campus about twenty yards from the Southeast corner of the Administration Building. Mr. Joseph Avent, sponsor of the class, tended
this tree with great care. A small lead standpipe was inserted to
its roots through which he watered the tree throughout the summer.
The class of 1915 planted a poplar tree at the main driveway entrance.
Ex-Governor J. Hoge Tyler made the address upon this occasion, choos-
ing as his theme "The Meaning of a Tree". Two special arbor day celebrations have been held. On one of these occasions a sycamore tree
was planted in the parking of Tyler Avenue to replace a tree which
had died. On the other three, walnut trees, brought by Mrs. McConnell
from Iron Mountain, Missouri, were planted to the east of the Administration Building.

INGLES STUMP

In 1922 a heavy sleet storm caused one of the large oak trees
to fall. This tree was apparently in good condition; the romance
of its tragic end appealed to the students with the result that the
President of the Ingles Society, Miss Gertrude Shumate, requested
Doctor McConnell to give the tree to the society. The tree near
its base was forty inches in diameter and had two hundred and seventy-five growth rings. For two months the students devoted their
spare time to sawing it into log lengths with cross cut saws. Their
fete was so unusual as to win for the society and college much newspaper publicity. After the tree was sawed, Mr. Andrew Ingles had
it hauled to West Radford to a saw mill, where Mr. Coletraine sawed
the logs into lumber. This was stored for use in the Ingles Society
Home. This was the first of the large trees from which any count of

the number of rings as indicative of its age was made. Since then
others have been counted, all indicate that the older oak trees of
the Radford campus had been in existence from two to three hundred
years. A small oak was planted by the society with an impressive
ceremony near the stump as a memorial to its efforts.

MEMORIAL TRIANGLE

In 1918 the French Club sponsored by Mattie C. Denny planted
poplar trees in the form of a triangle as a memorial to the three
young men of Radford who lost their lives in the World War. Alfred
Harvey, Jake Carper and Elliot Howe. These three boys were the only citizens of Radford who were killed in action during the World
War. A patriotic service with songs and sketches about each of the
boys was held by the French Club in the presence of the faculty,
students and family of the honorees and many ex-soldiers from Radford.

The willow tree by the main gate from Tyler Avenue was planted
by Mr. Whitt and was brought from his home at Whitt's Mill. The
tree on the right was brought from William Williams' home on Rock
Road.

THE MOTHER TREE

On Monther's Day, 1924, the students planted a tulip poplar
tree near the entrance from Tyler Avenue to Tyler Hall. The idea
of having a tree as a living tribute for mothers originated with
Doctor McConnell. He chose a tulip poplar, the queen of the forest for this tribute. The service of dedication of this tree was
unique and most impressive. All the students wrote home for a
small quantity of dirt, this was placed at the roots of the tree
so the tree which stands as a living tribute to motherhood grows
from earth from all sections of Virginia and many other States.
Near the tree Mr. Huddle built a concrete box into which each
student of the college placed a tribute to her mother. This is
covered by a marble tablet inscribed:

This tree
A Living Tribute
To
All Mothers
By
The Students
of
State Teachers College
May 12, 1924

"The Perfect Woman, Nobly Planned
To Warn, To Comfort, To Command."

The tablet was unveiled by William Cooper and Elizabeth Gilbert.

LIVING CHRISTMAS TREE

In December 1929 the spruce pine near the Tyler Hall planted by the landscape gardener had grown to such size it was selected for a living Christmas tree. Electric decorations were provided by the Young Women's Christian Association. The tree is lighted each evening during the week prior to the Christmas holidays.

ARBOR VERGILI

As a part of the Vergilian Celebration in 1930 the row of poplar trees near the site of the library building was named "Arbor Vergili." The plans are to plant near this cluster of trees the types of trees mentioned by Vergil. This project is sponsored by the Latin Club.

ORCHARD

In 1916 Doctor McConnell had a small orchard of various fruit trees planted on the slope of the hill between the Heth House and Oak Grove. Maple trees were planted around the entire campus. As the Oak trees have died many beech, maple, pines, oaks have been planted to replace the original grove. Two clumps of native Osage trees and several locust trees have been frequently pruned by Mr. Roop. These form popular shady spots near the tennis court and at the rear of the Administration Building.

FLOWERS

The first shipment of trees received at the college was packed in large quantity of saw dust. Miss Moffett was kicking around in this and unearthed a small rose bush. This she and Mr. Huddle planted in the school garden. This Dorothy Perkins rose bush has grown to immense size and from it many slips have been planted on other parts of the campus. (It was removed January 1932).

The bamboo plant in the corner of the school garden near the Student Activity Building was brought from Doctor McConnell's home on Obeys Creek in Scott County.

The landscape gardner's plans called for the use of large quantities of iris around the flower beds. The senior class of 1921 adopted this as the senior flower. Since it has become the college flower because of the blend of purple and gray in its coloring. In the elaboration of the landscaping of the campus Mrs. McConnell has used many varities of iris in the flower borders and beds.

IVY

The first ivy was brought by Mr. Gilbert from the old Charlton home in Draper's Valley and planted near the Administration Building. The class of 1916 planted ivy at the Tyler Hall. The class of 1926 planted a Virginia Creeper at the Helen Henderson Hall. The class of 1930 planted English Ivy at the Student Activity Building.

FLOWER GARDENS

Miss Mattie C. Denny was the first teacher of Nature Study and School Gardening at the College. Under her direction a small school garden was laid out near the Administration Building. At this time school gardening was a popular fad and fancy in education. A small plot of land three feet by four feet was assigned to each student. These were planted with vegetables of all kinds. The students made a great show of labor in cultivating these miniature gardens. Such play did not appeal to the practical mind of Doctor McConnell and school gardening was soon abandoned. As a border to these vegetable gardens, beds of flowers were planted by the students. When the campus was graded these gardens fell under the surveyors line and were destroyed by the dragging of earth. Miss Flora Bryson who succeeded Miss Denny as teacher of nature study laid out a formal flower garden on the site of the original gardens. This garden was planted and cultivated by the nature study students. This was not satisfactory and the plan for student work in the garden was abandoned. Doctor McConnell appointed a campus committee of faculty members. This group functioned in a superficial fashion and soon became nonexistent and Mrs. McConnell took charge.

THE HOLLYHOCK TRAIL

Mrs. McConnell brought some hollyhock seed from the University of Virginia. These have grown until they dot every section of the college campus giving it a blaze of color and beauty during the summer quarter when the height of its blooming season is reached. In 1928 Doctor McConnell gave hollyhock seeds to the students as a tangible impetus to his plan for a general beautification to Virginia. Through the newspaper publicity given to this idea and the spreading of hollyhock seeds over the State by Radford Students, the idea became known as the "Radford Hollyhock Trail."

Mrs. McConnell brought from Farmville some violet slips. These she put around the flower beds of the campus. In these flower beds she arranges for a rotation of flowers according to the seasons.

In 1927 Casselton, the home of Judge and Mrs. George E. Cassell was purchased by the Norfolk and Western Railroad. This had been one of the old aristocratic homes of Southwestern Virginia. The Cassell family lived there for forty years, Mrs. Cassell had surrounded herself and home with many beautiful plants and shrubbery. When the property was turned over to the railway company much of the old shrubbery was given to the college. The lilac bushes planted by the pergalo and the rock lilies border near the stone wall were transplanted from Casselton.

In 1928 the terraces were built around the Madame Russell Hall. The arrangement of these terraces gave an effect to the campus of a sunken garden. In this section of the campus are two walnut trees of original growth on the campus. The sunken garden is bordered with flower beds of summer flowers. In 1929 Mrs. McConnell planted a rose garden on the site of the original Heth Barn and College chicken house.

ATHLETIC GROUNDS

Across the center of the original pasture lot from which the campus of the college has developed is a row of Osage orange trees. In 1913 this made a natural border line for the outer edge of the campus. It now marks the mid point. On the street side of this row of trees the first tennis courts were laid out. These two courts were used for fifteen years. When the construction of the buildings made them too near the dormitories the tennis courts were changed to the other side of the trees and another court was built near the Arbor Vergili.

In the early years of the school a "track" was laid out in the cow pasture "far away from the building". Where the pergalo is now the first hocky field was marked off in the outer field. A temporary baseball diamond was also in this neighborhood.

In 1918 a model play ground equipped with giant's stride, seesaws, slides, and merry-go-round for children was provided near Tyler Avenue. It was designed for the use of training school children who were permitted to play there under the supervision of student teachers. Later this play ground was moved "far away" to the water tank which was so remote from the usual activities of the college that it was considered safe to have the children play here. However, for the erection of Madame Russell it was necessary to move the play ground again. The equipment was stored until the completion of the training school when it was again established as a recreation center for the children.

OUTDOOR SWIMMING POOL

The outdoor swimming pool was built in 1925. At that time it was considered one of the largest outdoor swimming pools of the colleges of the State. The dimensions are 90X45X10X2. This pool was dedicated as a feature of the Allegaynianna program in 1925. It is one of the most used of the athletic resources of the college especially during the summer quarters. The bath house was erected in 1926.

In 1929 Mr. H. C. Fulcher, Professor of Mathematics, interested Doctor McConnell and several other faculty members in the possibilities of a golf course. He laid off a nine hole golf course on the campus and gave the first instruction in golf. This was enthusiastically taken up by members of the faculty. A golf club was organized and became a self-supporting organization on the campus. The dues paid by the members of this organization are used to improve the greens and provide markers. Paul McConnell and S. L. McConnell have labored to improve the original greens, three mound greens have been built and sown in grass. In 1929 Mr. Roop made tee boxes for each of the greens. These were painted to show the length between greens and the par by Miss Lillian Simmons. Sand tees were installed in 1930.

Mr. Henry Crowgey, who has sponsored athletics for boys at the college during the summer quarters has built several temporary quoits and volley ball courts on the campus. He and Mr. W. D. Smith have had charge of many of the track features and athletic contests of the "Allegayniana".

The main triangle of the campus has been used by the physical directors for outdoor physical education classes, recreation, May festivals, student rallys, pep meetings and campus picnics.

VEGETABLE GARDENS

At the opening of the college in 1913 only a small area of the thirty-three acres was used for school purposes. Two-thirds of the campus was still devoted to pasture and garden use. A wire fence was run across the campus north and south which cut off about ten acres of pasture land between the Administration Building and the La Belle Inn. A double stile was built over this wire fence for the students to use in passing between the buildings. On the south end of the campus bordering Fairfax Street, an east and west wire fence cut off about five acres as a vegetable garden. All of this land was devoted to the production of products, mostly corn, beans, and potatoes, which could be used in the boarding department of the college. The garden was planted under the supervision of Doctor McConnell by day laborers. Later gardners were employed to tend the garden on shares.

LIVE STOCK

In the north end of the pasture lot was a hog pen which covered the entire hill side where the store rooms, museum and tennis courts now stand. Twenty to thirty head of hogs were kept in the hog lot and fed from the waste of the dormitories. These hogs were butchered from time to time for use in the dining room. The hog killing was carried on in typical farm method and usually took place near the boiler house. After the hogs were butchered they were brought to the "little white house" back of the Norwood Dormitory and here they were cut up and salted. Mr. Huddle took charge of cutting up the hogs, and Alva, the head man, took charge of the rest. Butchering was a great occasion for "miration" as Mr. Huddle would say. The "little white house" was originally built for a refrigerator house to cover a large ice box in which milk and other supplies were stored. With the coming of electric refrigeration the ice box was sold and the "little white house" was moved to the pasture lot where it served as a bath house for the outdoor swimming. It was finally torn down when the section of the campus was put into the main campus.

In 1916 Mr. Harden was employed as professor of nature study and agriculture in the college. Mr. Harden was very enthusiastic about poultry. Under his direction a large chicken house was built on the present site of the rose garden. Here he raised over five hundred chickens of different varities. He introduced to Radford and the college the first capon. Even after the chicken business was abandoned this bird lived on the campus for many years.

Upon the resignation of Mr. Harden in 1919, Mr. John Lucas, a cousin of Mrs. McConnell was employed to take charge of the garden and the chicken business. Mr. Lucas planted the garden, cared for the live stock and raised a number of chickens. As the buildings were erected on the campus it became necessary to reduce the area allowed for the garden purposes. In 1925 Mr. Lucas gave up the work as gardner and was succeeded by Mr. Strader, a retired Methodist preacher, interested in agricultural activities. Mr. Strader planted the garden on shares until the plan was abandoned when the erection of Madame Russell Hall took the site. With the departure of Mr. Lucas it was decided to abandon the chicken project. All chickens were used except a small flock which Miss Mary Clark tended. These were more for pets than for utilitarian purposes.

It was one of Doctor McConnell's ideas to keep the campus home
life and to surround the students with those things with which
they were associated at home. For a few years Mrs. McConnell
kept a flock of geese; Miss Clark had some guineas, ducks, and
turkeys. Two pair of peafowls were bought and turned loose on
the campus. These added much to the beauty of the gardens.
However the town environment was not suitable for such fowls.
They were killed. With this tragedy the keeping of all the
kinds of domestic birds was abandoned.

COWS

In the pasture lot several cows were kept. These were the
property of Doctor and Mrs. McConnell. For several years they
served as a chief source of milk for the school. Night and morning the McConnell boys milked these cows, to the sound of milking
many of their early romances with college girls took place.. With
the expansion of the college buildings the cows yielded their pasture lot to swimming pool and campus training school.

In the early days of the college one of the largest problems
of care takers was to keep the city cows off the campus. A cow
law was not effective in Radford until 1923. Up to that time cows
were allowed to run at will. It required constant diligence to
keep them from destroying the flowers and gardens.

On one Halloween the students captured a young steer which
was being raised on the campus and placed in the gymnasium. However the animal was able to walk a plank and was led from the
gymnasium to the slaughter pen. This animal had a beautiful
black and white hide which was tanned for Annie McConnell and is
now used as a rug.

HORSES

At the opening of the school Doctor McConnell bought a horse
for the college, "Old King". He was used for many years for hauling, grading, mowing, plowing and draying around the campus. Old
King also served as a driving horse for Doctor McConnell's buggy.
He finally died and his hide was tanned. He is buried near the
store house. The second horse "Dan" owned by the college was
first hired from the Brown Brothers of Belspring. This horse had
the misfortune to fall into the swimming pool. He came through
his accident unhurt. The college then bought him and he is used
for dray purposes around the institution at the present time.

CAMPUS PETS

Beautiful

During the first week of the school in 1913 a half grown kitten
appeared in the old dormitory. This kitten seemed to be a cross between a tiger cat and a maltease. She soon became a great pet of all
the students. She was adopted by Mrs. Brugh who called her "Beautiful". This cat became the aristocrat of all the campus pets. She
was privileged and allowed to roam at will throughout the buildings
of the college. She lived for fourteen years filled with the vissi-
tudes of the nine-cat-lives. The first tragedy of her life occurred
while she was still a kitten when her tail was amputated by a slam-
ming door at the barn. She went through life with a stub tail. She
next broke her leg which was set by Doctor Noblin. When bobbed hair
became the fad some gentlemen callers assisted by some students
bobbed Beautiful's hair. They clipped the hair from her stub tail,
made a part down her back with bobbed hair fringed off at all angles
on the round part of her stomach. For weeks she was an object of
great distress.

Beautiful was the mother of many many kittens. She and her
kittens were a continual source of entertainment and amusement to
the college. Several times she convulsed the audience during the
solemnity of the assembly hour by moving her family across the
stage from one dressing room to the other. She usually reared her
family in some public place. She was a constant source of embarrassment to Mr. S. L. McConnell as several litters of her kittens
were born in his office.

Beautiful and her families were objects of biological research
by the students of the college. She became so accustomed to this
investigation that she would submit without a whine. Beautiful died
in 1927 and was buried under the large Dorothy Perkins rose bush in
the corner of the garden. The report of her death received national
recognition. The following is copied from the Baltimore Sun:

> "As a lasting tribute to the memory of the oldest attendant
> at the Radford College, students will erect a monument in
> the garden where Beautiful, the pioneer cat of the institu-
> tion has been buried.
>
> Beautiful has been in attendance at the college fourteen
> years since its organization in September 1913.
>
> To the majority of the 11,000 students who have been resi-
> dents of this institution since that time the recent death
> of the pet brought considerable sadness.

Beautiful, Maltease tiger cat, in the period of her
residence had become an institution in herself. Her
constant association with the intellectual life of
the college gave her an air of dignity not exceeded
by a single professor. She played an important part
in the life of the college and made the place home-
like for many a homesick student,

At the same time she served as a subject for many of
the biological and physiological lectures and with
her offspring formed the basis for many extended arguments on heredity."

SQUIRRELS

It is said that the Heth Woods had always been the haunt of
many squirrels, however, as the college buildings were started
the squirrels disappeared. In 1923 Doctor McConnell decided
to propogate the grove with squirrels again. Several pair were
brought to the campus. The first of these were named Maggie and
Jiggs. They were pet squirrels, and received much attention from
the students and particularly from Mrs. Huffard and Miss Clark.
Black walnuts were bought as their food. Through their effort to
provide for themselves the squirrels planted many of the walnut
trees which now dot the campus. The most interesting of these
is the one directly back of the Administration Building which was
planted on a true line to the center of the building.

THE DECORATIVE ARTICLES ON THE CAMPUS

For several years the cleaning up and planting of shrubbery
and flowers consumed the major interest of those in charge of the
beautification of the campus. Mr. Roop, the carpenter, made a
number of benches for use of the students. In 1916 the students
of the summer quarter raised sufficient money to purchase a sun
dial and a gazing globe for the campus. These were selected by
June McConnell. They were located under the direction of Doctor
McConnell. The mathematical placement of the sun dial was determined by Mr. Bowers, Professor of Mathematics.

In 1920 the summer students bought a small bird bath with a
fountain figure. "The Boy and The Goose". This pool was stocked
with gold fish from the fish hatchery at Wytheville and was
planted with water lilies. A large Grecian urn gift of the class
of 1923 was placed nearby.

In 1923 the students of the summer quarter raised money
to erect a pergalo near the memorial triangle. The United States
Government gave the college a machine gun used in the World War.
This was placed in the center of the triangle. Here was placed
the grecian bench gift of the class of 1923. In 1924 the students purchased a drinking fountain for the campus. For two or
three years an effort was made to keep this iced and a large
concrete ice box was built through which the water for the fountain was piped. This cooling arrangement proved impracticable.
The drinking fountain however has been a great asset to the campus.

In 1926 Mr. Phillips gave to the college two mill stones
which were taken from the Tyler Mill on Plum Creek. These were
placed as seats near the pergola. In 1924 Mr. Roop built between
the two oak trees in the oak grove an outlook and a secluded retreat for the students. This was dubbed the Crow's Nest. Its
nearness to the railroad however made it impracticable due to
the train dirt.

A number of bird houses were bought from "The Bird Man" a
whistling artist and nature student who wandered into the school
one day. The Ingles Society placed a Lincoln Log Cabin bird
house in the thicket near the Ingles Stump.

LIGHTING SYSTEM

The campus lighting system was installed in 1921 by Messrs.
Kuhn and Holden Barnett who at this time were engaged in elec-
trical work. The original system included twelve standards on
the campus with lights on the main entrance gates of the college. These two young men dug the ditches, placed the conduits
and installed the entire system. No permanent additions have
been made to this original lighting system, temporary extensions
have been run to Madame Russell Hall, in the sunken garden and
near the Student Activity Building. This work has been done by
Mr. George Mills and Mr. Rusmissell.

SECTION III.

BUILDINGS

The first Board of Trustees at its second formal meeting authorized an advertisement to be run in the leading newspapers of Virginia
addressed to the architects of the State asking for a general plan for
the lay out of the school plant at Radford, and for detail plans for
the erection of the Administration Building of this college. Many
plans were submitted. From these the Board selected the plan proposed
by Charles M. Robinson, Incorporated of Richmond, Virginia. The general
lay out for the school plant proposed by Mr. Robinson was designed in
the form of a flock of geese in flight with the Administration Building
as the leading bird. His plan called for the erection of the Administration Building first, followed by dormitories on either side, a central library building and a row of faculty houses to face Tyler Avenue.
He proposed as the general architectural design, oblong semi-colonial
structures to be built of red brick with a brown stone base, with a
white trim effected by columns at the porch entrances.

ADMINISTRATION BUILDING

In 1911 the Board let the contract for the erection of the Administration Building to Mr. J. C. Curtis. Mr. Curtis employed about fifty
men for the erection of this building. It required fourteen months to
complete it. Mr. Ed Roop, who has been identified with the college
throughout its history, assisted in the staking off of the site for this
building. The building was located near the brow of the hill and close
to the site of a small tenant house, the only building on the original
campus. Mr. Charles M. Robinson as architect directed Mr. Curtis in
the erection of the building. The general plan for the building was
utilitarian rather than for beauty. The plan was a slight modification
of the general school building plan being used in the better school buildings of 1911. The gymnasium and auditorium form the center with wide
corridors surrounding, from these open the class rooms and offices of
the building. It was by far the largest and most elaborate building between Roanoke and Bristol and when dedicated in 1913 it was considered
unusually elegant. Particularly noteworthy in its construction were the
mahogany doors and the terraza floor. Upon arrival in Radford the author
was told of the wonderful floors of the hallways before any of the other
features of the building were described to her. Very few changes have
been made in the building since its erection. Temporary partitions to
provide small offices in the hallway have been placed.

Doctor McConnell has often said if he had listened to all the pro-

posals made to him for the improvement of the Administration Building there would scarcely be a brick of the original building left.

DEDICATION OF THE ADMINISTRATION BUILDING

The Administration Building was formally dedicated on August 9,
1913. This was a gala day in Radford. People came from miles around,
the entire campus was covered with wagons, carriages, buggies, riding
horses and a few automobiles. Picnic dinner was served in the Oak
grove. Mr. Luther Sherer, Vice-Chairman of the Board, came in a private C & O Railroad car. He, Governor Mann, Mr. Johnston of Christiansburg, Captain William Baldwin and Doctor McConnell were the chief speakers. Professor W. E. Gilbert was the only member of the faculty present.
He arrived in Radford the day before. The Grand Master of the Masons
presided at the laying of the corner stone. Into this stone was placed
a Bible, some money, the first catalog of the school, the program of the
day, names of the members of the Board and officers of the school. The
building was gaily decorated with bunting and flags. At this time it
was practically completed although it was many months before the final
finish was made.

At the opening of the school on September 17, 1913, there was
practically no furniture in the building. A few class room chairs had
been purchased from William Hawthorne of Max Meadows, Virginia. The
first Board of Trustees had furnished the Administrative offices very
elaborately. These were equipped with mahogany furniture of good
quality. In the President's office was a large double mahogany desk
with several large rockers and stiff mahogany chairs. A very expen-
sive solid blue rug was placed in the reception room. This rug showed
tracks so badly that it was practically ruined on the opening day. After this it was cleaned and sold, and a figured rug was bought in its
place.

ROOM ASSIGNMENTS IN 1913

When the faculty assembled at the college during the week of September 11 to September 17, 1913, no definite class rooms had been assigned. Soon after his arrival each member of the faculty began to select
the room which he most desired. First come were the first served, so
there was much talk but little conflict.

In 1913-1914 the rooms were used as follows: entering the Administration Building from the front door to the right was a suite of administrative offices, reception room, the President's private office and
his secretary's office. Next to the secretary's office the small room,
now used as the Treasurer's office, was the Young Women's Christian

Association parlor; Room 5, was the Home Economics kitchen; Room 6, Home Economics dining room; Room 7, Home Economics Clothing department. To the left of the front entrance, Room 13, was the College Library; Room 12, the Science Room, Chemistry; Room 11, now the Dean's office, was the book store; Room 10, was the Mathematics class room; Room 9, was the French and German class rooms; Room 8, Public School Music room. Going up the front steps to the right, Rooms 101, 102, were Education class rooms. The present library was the Pocahontas Literary Society Hall in which the private piano lessons were given. Room 106, was the History class room, Professor Gilbert used the small room next to his class room as an office. On the left, Room 112, was used for Physics class room. Room 111, Drawing room; Room 110, Registrar's office; Room 109, now the Pocahontas Literary Hall was the physics laboratory; Room 108 was an office for the English department; Room 107, the English class room. In the basement at the foot of the rear steps where the post office is now, was a vacant room used for dressing for "gym" and as a locker room for the indoor swimming pool. At the rear of the hall was Mr. Roop's carpenter shop. What is now the store room was a large open space next to the gas room. Off the right corridor, a large Chemistry laboratory was located. Two rooms were devoted to Industrial Arts. In the basement were dressing rooms for women and men. The gymnasium formed the center of the basement floor. Above this was the auditorium. In the tower or dome the Ingles Literary Society. The Museum was housed in large cases in the upper hall way.

Major Changes

In 1915 the Pocahontas Literary Society exchanged places with the library and moved down stairs to room 13. Later the Pocahontas Society moved to the physics laboratory Number 109. The book store was moved from Room 11, to Room 13, and later to Room 9, and hence to the Library Building. Room 12, served for many years as the headquarters of the Science Department. Here Chemistry, Nature Study and later Biology were taught. When the Chemistry class room was moved to the basement of the building and Biology to Madame Russell Hall, Room 12, was used as a History class room.

The Home Economics Foods laboratory was moved to Madame Russell Hall in 1927. Room 5, was used as a History class room for one year, then as an Art room.

The Art classes travelled from Room 111, to the basement where for many years Miss Simmons taught drawing and shop work. In 1926 Miss Simmon's shop was moved to the gas room. The carpenter's shop was taken from the building and this room used for two years as a drawing room, later the drawing room was moved to Room 5, and the old carpenter's shop was used as the museum. The basement Art rooms were converted into Chemistry laboratories with the expansion of the Science Department. In 1928 a reading room was established for the library in Room 106. Mr. Gilbert's office and his classes moved to Room 13. In 1929 the library was further extended by the use of Room 102 as a reference library. Mathematics was moved to the Training School Building.

ADMINISTRATIVE OFFICES

The Registrar's office originally located in Room 102, later was moved to Room 110, and then to Room 1, of the administrative suite on the first floor. The Young Women's Christian Association parlor was moved from the Administration Building and the Treasurer's office was moved into that room. The Dean's office was established in 1920 in the Room 11, formerly used by the Bookstore and later as an English class room.

SOME NOOKS

In 1924 an Alumnae office was established in the small office adjacent to room 106, Mr. Gilbert who had used this as a private office moved his office into his class room. Later he located on the hall landing near the gallery entrance of the auditorium. The east landing of the auditorium balcony was furnished as a small social corner called "Wren's Nest". The first degree class (1921) gave a statue of Joan of Arc which was placed in the middle of the landing at the head of the stairs, comfortable chairs were placed nearby. This spot became known as "Joan's Room".

The Tea Room was located in the balcony of the gymnasium. This room was used for the overflow of audience at the basketball games. It was usually cluttered with packing boxes and other plunder.

The first post office was a row of pigeon holes in the corner of the reception room. The mail for the faculty was distributed through these pigeon holes. The student's mail was distributed in the dining room and the main corridors of the dormitories. The class of 1920 gave the first section of post office boxes. These were placed in the front lobby of the Administration Building. A small partitian was made for these boxes adjacent to the Registrar's office. The class of 1923 gave another section of post office boxes. In 1926 the post office boxes were moved across the hall. A small stenographic room was made in the original post office. In December 1929, the post office was moved to the basement of the Administration Building and placed in the rest room which had been used for many years by the day students. The old post office was made into a Bureau of Information.

PICTURES AND OTHER DECORATIVE ARTICLES
IN THE ADMINISTRATION BUILDING

The decorating of the Administration Building started in the early days of the college. Each of the teachers made an effort to beautify his class room by the use of flowers and growing plants. The first permanent decoration consisted of a series of pictures purchased by Doctor and Mrs. McConnell. These were good copies of standard masterpieces of art finished and framed in tones of brown. When this collection arrived each member of the faculty was allowed to select two or three pictures from the group for his class room. Practically all of these pictures still hang in their original locations.

In 1925 Davidson's collection of historic pictures of Virginia was bought by the college. There are fifty-five photographs of historical spots in this collection. They were photographed and tinted by Mr. Davidson, a photographer of Newport News, Virginia. These pictures are hung in the various buildings.

In 1926 five artists reproductions were purchased by Doctor McConnell and Miss Moffett in Washington. Among these is Stuart's Washington which was hung on the landing of the stairway of the Administration Building. Opposite an oil painting of Doctor McConnell which was purchased by the student body and the faculty in 1919. The money ($275.00) was raised by contributions of the students and the faculty. This picture of Doctor McConnell was painted from a photograph. The portrait was never entirely satisfactory as it is not a good likeness of Doctor McConnell. It was first hung in the library of the college but after the purchase of the Washington picture it was hung on the landing to associate the two first Presidents since both have birthdays on February 22.

Each year since the summer session of 1914 a picture has been made of the student body. This is a pictorial review which shows the growth, change of style in dress and keeps alive the memory of the students who have attended the institution. These pictures have been framed and hung in the upper hall of the Administration Building. The class of 1924 gave two wall plaques for the auditorium. The class of 1928 gave two bronzed plaster plaques of Washington for Joan's room.

The class of 1917 gave a painted curtain of the roller type for the front of the auditorium stage. This was replaced in 1927 by a velvet drapery purchased with money given by the various classes. The college at the same time purchased gray and blue stage draperies from The Clifford Devereau Company of New York. The Glee Club gave the numbers for the seats and the book racks of the auditorium.

The majority of the pictures, bric brac and other decorations in the offices are the property of the persons holding the offices. The office furniture in the President's, Secretary's, and Dean's offices is mahogany. That in the Registrar's and Treasurer's offices is Oak. Most of the original furniture of the college, teachers desks, library tables, shelving, cabinets, temporary partitions, and wood work were constructed by Mr. Ed. Roop.

HEATING PLANT

A central heating plant was provided for in the original plans for the college plant. In 1914 the Board of Trustees incurred a personal indebtness to erect this plant. The building was started in 1913 but was not completed until after the new year of 1914. The building was so planned that provision was made for the location of three boilers and a large coal bin in the basement and for laundry space on the second floor. A single boiler was installed in 1914. This was used for heating the entire school plant until 1920 when the second boiler was installed. In 1929 a third boiler of the stoker type was installed. For many years the heating plant was inadequate to meet the needs of the institution. The distance from the power plant to the Administration Building and to the dormitories was so great that the steam pressure was not great enough to bring full heat to the buildings. In 1928 and 1930 the entire heating plant was reconditioned. New steam lines were laid and a general overhauling and improvement of the old equipment was undertaken.

Before the completion of the heating plant in 1913-14 the Administration Building was heated with the city steam roller. This was attached to the steam line at the rear of the building. A high pressure of steam was kept in this boiler constantly. Much good natured humor was poked at this heating devise. On one occasion the students came to classes wrapped in blankets. The good natured shivering of that year forms a rich memory for many students and faculty members.

La Belle Inn was heated with a thrashing machine engine. Both of these crude boilers were fired night and day. Mr. J. A. Huddle who served as head fireman in the early days had charge of these boilers. After the main plant was completed he was assisted by his son Bryan Huddle and John Mills. When Mr. Huddle was made head of the laundry in 1920 John Mills was made head fireman. He with Jim and George Mills have had charge of the firing and heating throughout these years. No more faithful service can be recorded than the work of these men through many long cold winters.

WATER SUPPLY

During the summer of 1913 prior to the opening of the college the water supply of Radford City gave indication of not being adequate to meet the demands of the institution. In view of this the Board decided to drive a well on the campus to provide a private water supply for the school. A well of 517 feet was bored. A storage tank and pumping system were installed. This pump house and water tank have been an outstanding land mark on the campus. However, it has never been necessary in the history of the college to use the storage tank of water. Before the incorporation of the lower part of the pasture lot into the campus of the college the small rooms of the pump house were used as a home for John Mills and his wife. With the erection of Madame Russell Hall and the enlargement of the campus the Mills family moved to a small house erected for them near the boiler house. The rooms under the tank were designated as the Young Women's Christian Association hut. They were furnished by this organization and are used for social purposes during the summer. One room is equipped as a kitchen where the students can make candy and other light refreshments. The other room is furnished as a living room.

In 1922 great class rivalry developed between the classes, each one tried to outdo the other. The climax was reached at midnight on Sophomore day when the class of 1922 painted its numerals on the tank. Two girls, Ella Harvey and Virginia Painter climbed the tank and did the work while their faithful colleagues watched. This venture was so dangerous that the administration threatened expulsion for all tank climbers thereafter. The numerals were preserved for many years.

DORMITORIES
James Hoge Tyler Hall
First Unit - Tyler Hall

The Legislature of 1914 made an appropriation of $35,000.00 for the erection of a dormitory on the campus of the Radford school. Mr. Charles M. Robinson was employed as the architect for this building. He designed the building in three complete units. The general layout for the school plant as had been proposed earlier by Mr. Robinson indicated the location for this building to the right of the rear of the Administration Building.

As this was the first building erected since the opening of the school an elaborate ceremony for the breaking of the ground was held by the students and the faculty. At this time a shovel was purchased which has been used for the breaking of ground for each of the buildings since. After the singing of school songs and an address by Doctor

McConnell, he broke the ground followed by the students and members of the faculty each of whom shoveled away a portion of earth.

The contract for the erection of the building was let to E. M. Tessier and the first unit cost $33,349.05. This unit provided bedroom space for sixty students and a parlor as social unit for the institution. The first and second floors were completed in 1915. The third floor was not completed until 1916. Students were housed here for the first time during the fall quarter of 1915. For many years this unit was known as the "new dormitory" in contrast to the La Belle Inn familiarly called the "old dormitory". On August 9, 1923 at the celebration of the tenth anniversary of the school this building was christened Tyler Hall. Miss Inez Hicks, President of the student body in 1923, accompanied by Miss Elizabeth Gilbert christened this first building. It was named in honor of ex-Governor James Hoge Tyler, the most prominent citizen of Radford. With the completion of the other two units each was given a name Norwood and McGuffey. The official name of the entire building is now James Hoge Tyler Hall. Tyler Hall has always been considered as the main dormitory of the college and for several years was called "Main Dormitory".

As the center of the home life of the college it has been hard usage and has been the scene of many of the outstanding social events and entertainments. The furniture for the parlor was selected by Mrs. J. P. McConnell and was purchased from Thurman and Boone of Roanoke, Virginia. In this room the mahogany furniture from La Belle Inn was placed. In 1920 Miss Moffett purchased a number of decorative articles for the decoration of this room. About twenty sofa pillows were purchased. These however were quickly worn out by the nervous swains who called upon the students. During the administration of Mrs. Kate Huffard the parlor was used for formal purposes only. The formal receptions of the college, and for the entertainment of regular "dates" and the friends of the students.

The wicker furniture of this building was purchased from the Fiber Craft Department of the State Pennitentiary. It was originally in the color of ivory and it was later painted oak and reupholstered.

OTHER UNITS OF TYLER HALL

The Legislature of 1916 made an appropriation for the erection of the second unit of the dormitory. The construction of the building was let to E. M. Tessier. This unit was designed for dormitory rooms only and increased the facilities of the dormitory to such an extent that it was possible to abandon the use of La Belle Inn. On the tenth anniversary this unit was christened "Norwood Hall" by Miss Grace Davis, President of the Pocahontas Literary Society and Miss Eleanor Bowers who broke the bottle of water by the entrance door.

In 1918 Mr. Roop and Mr. Huddle built the long porch on the Norwood Unit. The Junior class of 1919 dedicated this porch and named it "Senior Promenade" in honor of the Senior class of 1919. They removed one brick from the wall of the building and instead placed a box in which each of their names were placed. An inscribed brass tablet was placed over the box. Miss Annie McConnell, daughter of Doctor McConnell, christened the porch and made the dedicatory speech. This was one of the most elaborate social affairs ever held in the institution. The entire lower floor was decorated as a bower of spring flowers.

The Legislature of 1922 made an appropriation for the erection of the third unit to complete this dormitory. This unit provided additional dining room space and increased the bedroom space. The construction contract for this building was let to Mr. W. H. Painter. The building was completed in the summer of 1923 and was named McGuffey Hall in honor of William H. McGuffey. It was christened by Miss Frances Fitzpatrick, President of the Ingles Literary Society and Miss Josephine Noblin broke the bottle of water. With the completion of the McGuffey Unit this dormitory gave accommodations to two hundred and eighty students. As the institution has grown the use of the separate names for the units has been abandoned. From 1927 to 1929 the entire building was called "Main Dormitory". In 1932 it was officially decided to call the entire building Tyler Hall.

USE AND FURNISHING OF THE BUILDING

In this building the Bee Hive has an office on the second floor which was furnished by money raised by the Bee Hive of 1926. An office in McGuffey was set aside as the headquarters for the student executive council. Here the regular meetings have been held and most of the trials of diciplinary cases have taken place. Since the building is centrally located and is the place where all the students assemble for meals many of the meetings of the groups and organizations are held in the rooms of this building.

The original furniture purchased for the La Belle Inn was transferred to the Tyler Unit. Similar furniture was purchased for the Norwood Unit. By the time the McGuffey Hall was completed the style of college furniture had been changed; smaller day beds were purchased instead of the three quarter Murphy beds and chiffoniers were used instead of dressers. The decoration of the building consists of pictures belonging to the original set purchased by Doctor and Mrs. McConnell, two pictures from the Washington purchase and a number of Davidson's historic pictures. In 1928 the Tyler family presented the college a photograph of Governor Tyler, which was hung in the main entrance of Tyler Hall.

The Sophomore class of 1924 gave the lighting fixtures for the halls of the first floor of this building.

MADAME RUSSELL HALL

Madame Russell Hall was built from funds borrowed from the Literary Fund of the State under the Noell Act of 1926. Externally this building is a reproduction of Tyler Hall built according to the three-unit plan. It was built, however, as an entire building at one time. It is two feet narrower and three feet shorter than the Tyler Hall. Inside the dormitory rooms are smaller and are built for the accommodation of two students. A central lounge with small parlors is located in the center of the building. This lounge opens upon the large porch which provides the largest social unit of the college. The remainder of the building follows the Tyler plan and provides bed room accommodations for one hundred and eighty-eight students. This building has many modern improvements which had developed in the fourteen years of the college. It provides a central switch board for the lighting controlled from a board located near the hostesses door, an incinerator, laundry tubs and terraiza floors in the pressing rooms. The electric wiring is so arranged as to provide vacuum outlets and base plugs for lighting fixtures in the building. Mr. James F. Mac-Tier of Roanoke, Virginia was the architect and Mr. J. D. Huffard and Son contractors.

The provisions by the Legislature for the construction of this building made no appropriation for the equipment. The furnishings were acquired by great financial pressure on the revenues of the college. The furnishings of the lounge and the small parlors were purchased with money made by Miss Moffett in the management of the Undertaker's Convention, June 1927.

THE NAME "MADAME RUSSELL"

This building was completed in the summer of 1927. A special feature of the commencement week of 1927 was its dedication. At this time Honorable Robert J. Noell, author of the Noell Act, made the dedicatory address. Miss Nellie Preston of Seven Mile Ford, Virginia the great granddaughter of Madame Russell gave a review of the life and achievements of her ancestor, for whom the building was named. Madame Elizabeth Russell was a sister of Patrick Henry. She was born and brought up in Eastern Virginia and frequently accompanied her brother to the assemblage of the House of Burgesses at Williamsburg, Virginia. On one such occasion she met General William Campbell, whom she later married. General Campbell was a leader in the Battle of King's Mountain. Earlier he had received great distinction at the

Battle of Mount Pleasant where the Indian federation, under the leadership of General Cornstalk, was defeated. After his death she married another general of Kings Mountain fame, General Russell. Madame Russell had only one child, who married William Preston, from her many distinguished citizens of Southwestern Virginia are descended. Madame Russell was widowed for the second time while she was still quite young. From that time forward she spent her life in promoting the cause of christianity in Southwestern Virginia. Through her efforts the Methodist church was greatly augmented in its development. She is described thus by a citizen of Chilhowie, Virginia:

He says, "Just over the hill from the famous cock-pit where in the early days of Southwest Virginia many dollars were wagered on roosters fighting in it, is the location of the famous old Methodist camp ground, scene of some of the greatest preaching and most soul stirring religious experiences that Southwest Virginia has ever known. About a hundred yards from the old cock-pit stood the two stories log house in which Madame Russell spent her declining years having moved there from Abingdon, because of the impious atmosphere pervading the fashionable society of that place. The old lady had this house built according to her own ideas of Christian consistency. It was severely plain and simple, an unadorned barnlike wooden structure, when she might have built an elaborate mansion such as her daughter occupied in Abingdon.

There were two rooms below, large and spacious--the one first entered being her common sitting room. A door from this opened into one much larger which contained a pulpit and seats for a moderate sized congregation. When a preacher visited her she said "Brother, how long will you tarry? There's the pulpit. Shall I send out and call a congregation?" No visitors came to see her and remained an hour without being asked to pray. If they declined, she prayed herself, mentioning everyone for whom she prayed by name.

She dressed in the style of "76-full skirts, with an overgarment, long, flowing, open at front, and confined at the waist by a girdle, and made of a material called bath coating. In this girdle were tucked two or three pocket handkerchiefs. The sleeves of her dress came just below the elbows, the lower part of the arm being covered with long half-handed gloves. She wore a kerchief of linen lawn, white as snow, and sometimes an apron of the same material. On her head a very plain cap, above which was usually placed a broad-brimmed hat, given her by Bishop Asbury in days long gone by, and worn by the old lady with probably the same feeling with which Elisha wore Elijah's mantle. She was erect as in the meridian of

life, though she must have been seventy years old when I
first saw her. A magnificent woman, she walked every inch
a queen, reminding me of one of the old-fashioned pictures
of Van Dyke. She never shook the hand of a poor Methodist
preacher at parting without leaving in it a liberal donation;
she knew that the Gospel was free but she also knew that the
laborer is worthy of his hire."

The Junior class of 1927 requested a section on the second floor of the
West Unit of the building as Senior Hall. The lounge has been very
popular for receptions and other social activities of the students.
An especially attractive feature of the Madame Russell Hall is the
fireplace, the first ever provided in the institution. A fire was
first kindled here for the faculty reception of the students in the
fall of 1929.

CLASS ROOMS

The two wings of the basement of this building have been used for
class room purposes. The Biology Department located in the East wing
is divided into three laboratories and a class room with storage space
for the biology experiments and equipment. The West wing has been used
for the Home Economics Food Department. This unit is arranged to provide for two laboratories and a small apartment which is used as practice house by the students in Home Economics.

STORE ROOMS AND SMALL DWELLING HOUSES

Two store rooms, two dwelling houses, one barn and one garage
have been built. These have been constructed at a minimum cost and
largely by Mr. Roop. One store room housed the museum for several
years. John Mills and his family have always occupied the fireman's
house near the Boiler House. The second dwelling was occupied by
George Mills, later (1932) it was remodeled as a Home Economics Cottage.

STUDENT ACTIVITY BUILDING

In 1929 at the suggestion of Mr. W. E. Gilbert a project was
launched by the Pocahontas and Ingles Literary Society to raise funds
to erect society homes. This project was received with great enthusiasm by students and alumnae. The plans were proposed to the
Alumnae Association at the Richmond meeting at Thanksgiving. Many
pledges were made. The societies started the custom of having an
Annual Roll Call for the Ingles Society and a Pow Wow for the Pocahontas Society. At this time many old members returned to the col-

lege and made pledges to the building fund. In the subsequent development of the idea the original plan of separate society homes was abandoned. Mr. Kearfort of Bristol was employed as architect. He proposed a united society building with two wings, one to be known as Ingles Hall and the other as the Pocahontas Hall. It was decided to accept this plan and locate the building to the south of Tyler Hall on Tyler Avenue. Two foundations were laid during the Fall of 1924. These were built by local labor and were paid for from the first money collected. These foundations were dedicated to the two societies. Each society held a celebration while the concrete was being poured. As a perpetual emblem the Oak leaf was buried in the first foundation by the Ingles and an arrow head was placed in the second by the Pokies.

By thus having the building started it was hoped to secure an appropriation from the 1924 Legislature for its completion. Failing in this the students continued the collection of funds and by the Summer of 1927, $11,000.00 (estimated from records as shown by the Treasurer's book), had been collected by the two literary societies, from the students, alumnae, faculty and special entertainments. The plan had so developed by this time that the erection of a Student Activity Building seemed most feasible. Doctor McConnell, therefore, decided to use the money to erect the first unit of a Student Activity Building. Frye & Stone, architects, drew plans for a small colonial building. A site for this building was chosen near the Administration Building. It was erected during the fall and winter of 1927-28. The building provides a lounge or parlor on the first floor, on the second floor six office rooms. These were assigned by Doctor McConnell to the major organizations of the college, beginning at the head of the stairs on the right the first office was assigned to the Alumnae Association, next the Young Women's Christian Association; next the Ingles Society and across the hall, the Pocahontas Literary Society, the Grapurchat, and the Bee Hive. These various organizations have undertaken the furnishing of their respective offices. At the present time the Alumnae Association has provided a rug, the Young Women's Christian Association a rug and tapestries, draperies, folding chairs; the Ingles a rug, the Pocahontas a rug. Uniform standing furniture cabinet, table, typewriter, desks were purchased by the college from the State Pennitentiary.

Doctor McConnell appointed a committee of the faculty composed of Mrs. J. P. McConnell, Miss Pearl Andrews, Miss Alice Zollman, Doctor Virginia O'Hudson, Miss Marian Williamson, and Mrs. J. P. Whitt to plan the furnishings of the lounge. This committee decided upon walnut furniture upholstered in mohair. This committee presented the building with tapestry, "A Scene in Venice" to be hung over the fireplace. In the Spring of 1930 Doctor Moffett and Mr. McConnell with funds raised from the Alleghanians of 1929 purchased rugs for the lounge. The Radford Alumnae Association presented a radio in 1930. A piano was also bought by the Alumnae Association and placed in the building. A picture of three ships painted by Mrs. J. P. McConnell was presented to the Young Women's Christian Association and hung in the Student Activity Building. The brass candle sticks were pruchased by Doctor Moffett in New York for the Young Women's Christian Association. The lower basement room was completed in the summer of 1930. A contest for a name of this room was held. The name "The Cove" proposed by Miss Beatrice Dickerson was selected. The color scheme of blue and white is being carried out in the decoration of "The Cove".

WILLIAM H. McGUFFEY SCHOOL.

The Legislature of 1928 made an appropriation of $67,500 for the erection of a Campus Training School. The plans for this building were made by Frye & Stone of Roanoke, Virginia. The building was erected during the summer and fall of 1928. The building as erected is the first unit of a three-unit plan. The present unit provides class rooms, activity rooms and teacher's offices for the first six grades of the elementary school. With a library, health office and basement laboratories. The Campus Training School was first used during the summer of 1929 and was formally opened as a training school in September 1929. The general plan for this building from the educational standpoint was worked out with the architects by Doctor Minor Wine Thomas, Miss Flora Dungy, Mr. J. P. Whitt. The equipment for the building was planned by Doctor Winifred Bain, Director of Training School in 1928-29. The furniture was purchased by a special permission of Governor Byrd from the State Pennitentiary where it was made after the designs recommended by a faculty committee, Doctor Bain, Chairman. It was named in honor of William H. McGuffey, a pioneer in elementary education and author of the famous McGuffey readers.

RENTED BUILDINGS

During its history the college has used several rented buildings as dormitories. The original dormitory "La Belle Inn" was rented from Mrs. Stockton Heth and was used as a dormitory, 1913-1919. This building as described elsewhere in this history was originally a hotel. The college made certain improvements to adapt it better for the use as a dormitory. During the first year the college also rented the Norwood Home (Heth House) and leased rooms in the Baldwin Home. During the summer of 1922 the college rented the Briggs Building which is now the Dixie Inn and the Simmons Building on the Main Street of Radford and used these as dormitories for the summer students.

HELEN HENDERSON HALL

Across the street from the college a corporation composed of citi-

zens of Radford erected a hospital in 1925. This hospital was directed by Doctor Harris for one year. In 1926 the building was
rented by the college and used as a dormitory and an infirmary until the fall of 1931. The building was rented for the first time
on a lease of five years at $2500.00 a year with $300.00 improvements. Upon the renewal of the lease in 1930 the rent was reduced
to $1500. This building was named for Mrs. Helen Henderson of
Council, Virginia. Mrs. Henderson was the first woman elected to
the Virginia Legislature and served for one term with great credit
to herself and the women of the State. She died in 1927. The
building provides studies for the Art and Music Departments; a
sorority room for Tri Sigma; Infirmary and diet kitchen for twelve
patients and dormitory rooms for forty students.

PART III
ADMINISTRATION OF THE COLLEGE
SECTION I
STATE BOARDS OF CONTROL

BOARD OF TRUSTEES OF THE STATE NORMAL AND INDUSTRIAL SCHOOL

During the twenty years of its history the Radford College has been administered by three types of State Boards of Control. The first of these, authorized by the Act of Establishment, was incorporated as "The Board of Trustees of the State Normal and Industrial School for White Women at Radford." To this board Governor Mann appointed Captain W. T. Baldwin of Radford, Virginia; W. D. Smith of Gate City, Virginia; L. L. Scherer of Richmond, Virginia, to serve for a term of two years. For four years he appointed: J. P. Jones of Newcastle, Virginia; James White Sheffy, Marion, Virginia; B. T. Wilson, Lebanon, Virginia; R. L. Blanton, Richmond, Virginia; Edward Rodgers, Dendron, Virginia, State Superintendent of Public Instruction; Honorable Joseph Eggleston was an ex-officio member of the Board.[1]

The first meeting of the Board was held upon call of the Governor on July 26, 1910, at the Llewellyn Hotel, East Radford, Virginia. (The Llewellyn Hotel was a large building located on Norwood Street, opposite the station. Many of the original plans for the organization of the college took place in this building. The building is now used as the Alleghany Hotel).

The members of the Board, who had not been previously sworn in were duly sworn by Honorable George E. Cassell, Judge of the Corporation Court of Radford. The organization meeting resulted in the election of Captain W. T. Baldwin of East Radford, as Chairman and George E. Cassell as Secretary of the Board. The first business consisted in the appointment of a committee to draft bylaws and rules for the government of the Board. These bylaws and regulations as presented and adopted at a later meeting give an insight into the early purposes and management of the institution. They provide for the organization of the Board which in addition to a chairman and a Vice-chairman, Treasurer and Secretary, had four standing committees; Executive Committee, Finance Committee, Committee on Buildings and Grounds, and a Committee on Instruction.

The early scheme for the organization of the college provided for the Board of Trustees to elect a president of the school, assistant-president, secretary and treasurer, physician, steward,

---

1. A full list of the personnel as later changes occurred appears in the appendix.

matron, housekeeper, and any other officers or employees it deemed
proper. The duties of each of these major officers of the institution were defined. To the president was entrusted the full management of the school with complete charge of all other officers and
employees with the stipulation that he should submit an annual report of the condition of the school and furnish all other information desired by the Board.

The major part of the time of the first meeting was devoted to
a study of the sites proposed for the institution by the citizens
of the City of Radford. After visiting each of these the Board selected as the site the Heth Grove, a tract of 30.3 acres of land in
the East ward of Radford. Negotiations were begun with Captain Heth
and his family for the purchase of the land with $20,000.00 guaran-
teed by the city of Radford in the Act of Establishment.

Immediately objections were raised by certain citizens of Radford to the Heth site. A general misunderstanding developed in
the city of Radford between the citizens of the two wards. Those
who lived in the west ward wanted the college located on the Adams
Site which had been selected by the original Legislative commission of 1908, nevertheless the governing board, acting upon the
authority given in the Act of Establishment, persisted in its selection of the Heth Site. As a result of this difference of opinion legal injunctions and litigations were started. It required
over a year to perfect a settlement of these matters by the proper
legal authorities.

The Board did not enter into the active organization of the
college until October 3, 1911. At this meeting, held in Radford,
Doctor John Preston McConnell, then Dean of Emory and Henry College, was elected as President. Others elected at the same time
were: Doctor B. E. Copenhaver of Marion, Virginia, as Assistant-
president, (this position never became an active part of the
school and the office was abandoned), Robert J. Noell as Secretary and Treasurer of the College and George E. Cassell was re-
tained as Secretary of the Board.

At the same meeting of the Board a notice to architects calling for plans and specifications for the general layout of the
school and for the proposed administration building was authorized
and such a notice was published in the leading papers of the State.
It was contemplated that the first building would cost between
seventy-five thousand and one hundred thousand dollars. Several
subsequent meetings of the Board were devoted to the study of the
plans, letting of contracts, revising and approving the acts of
the building committee relative to the erection of the Administration Building.

On June 6, 1913, the Board of Trustees, upon the recommendation of Doctor John Preston McConnell, elected the first faculty of the college. Education: Joseph E. Avent; English, Miss Lucy Goode Puryear; Assistant-English, Miss Eleanor Terry; History and Social Sciences, William E. Gilbert; Assistant, Miss Mary Wortley Montague; Household Arts, Miss Mary Ledger Moffett; Director of Music, Miss Florence Baird; Modern Languages, Miss Mattie Denny; Mathematics, Miss Eloise Harrison; Physics and Elective Mathematics, Mr. Ernest P. Lane; Physical Education, Miss Louise Ruggles; Residence Physician, Doctor J. A. Noblin; Piano Teacher, Miss Mary E. Moss. Doctor McConnell was instructed to select his own stenographer, to employ a matron and housekeeper, and a director of the training school. He later selected Miss Blanche Bullifant as Director of the Training School; Mrs. Phoebe Brugh as matron and Mrs. N. P. Walker as housekeeper. Mrs. Walker did not serve in this capacity and this position was filled by Miss Cecil Crockett. Miss Moss did not accept the position as teacher of piano and at a subsequent meeting Miss Lizzie Fay James was appointed. Miss Lillian Simmons was appointed to the first faculty on September 27, 1913. With this group as a nucleus President McConnell began active organization of the instructional policies of the institution. On August 9, 1913, the Administration Building was dedicated. On September 17, 1913 the school opened its first session.

The first Board of Trustees continued in the active administration of the college until July 1914. During the first year of the instructional life of the institution the major business of the Board was the settlement of certain debts which had been incurred for the heating plant. The original appropriation for the Radford School was twenty-five thousand dollars made by the Legislature of 1910. In 1912 Honorable Charles A. Johnson of Christiansburg was defeated for re-election to the State Legislature. Mr. Johnson had been the first patron for the Radford School in the Legislature. His defeat was due largely to local antagonism and misunderstanding relative to the part he had played in the Legislative fight for the establishment of the school in 1908 and to the enmity which had developed as a result of the site selected for the school. The removal of Mr. Johnston left the Radford school without any particular patron in the Legislature of 1912. This influenced the appropriation which the college received and greatly handicapped the activities of the governing board. The total appropriation for 1912 was $25,000.00. In order to build the heating plant the Board borrowed money from various banks and gave their personal notes as security for this debt.

Following the Legislative Act of 1914, abolishing the separate Boards of Control for each of the four Normal Schools of the State, the Radford Board as a unit and as individual members spent several months adjusting the personal indebtness which had been incurred. The interest on this debt was paid from any funds in the Normal School Treasury at the time payments came due.[1]

A total of $29,625.00 with interest remained as the indebtness at the time of the transfer of the control of the Radford School to the Virginia Normal School Board. However at the extra session of the Legislature of 1914 a special appropriation was made to cover this debt.

VIRGINIA NORMAL SCHOOL BOARD
LATER VIRGINIA TEACHERS COLLEGE BOARD

The second board to assume responsibility for the administration of the Radford school was a centralized board established by act of the Legislature in 1914, incorporated as the Virginia Normal School Board. This Board likewise assumed the control of the schools at Farmville, Harrisonburg, and Fredericksburg. The personnel appointed by Governor Stuart consisted of Honorable Otto S. Mears; Merit T. Cooke; W. Clyde Locker, O. M. Shoemaker, Brock T. White, John W. Price, Alfred G. Preston, R. Shakleford, B. Davis, Wyatt King, with Superintendent of Public Instructions, R. C. Sternes, ex-officio member. Both ladies and gentlemen served as trustees. The first woman was Miss Belle Webb appointed in 1916.[2]

This Board held its organization meeting at the call of Governor Stuart in the office of the governor on July 10, 1914. The Board was organized according to a committee system. Committees of the members were appointed to be responsible for the various aspects of the administration of schools. Until this organization could be perfected the presidents of the institutions were authorized to discharge the administrative functions of the institutions. This was the beginning of a policy of freedom for the presidents in the administration of the schools. The Act of Establishment of this Board charged it, as a major responsibility, with a study, with such resulting regulations, as would perfect unnecessary duplications in the offerings of the four schools. Each of the presidents was called upon to make a complete report of the offerings of his respective institution with the number of students enrolled, the relative importance of each of the curricula and other special courses offered. A careful study of these reports was made by the executive committee in frequent meetings with the presidents of the four schools. Much time was spent in the study and discussion of problems relative to the unification of the work of the Normal Schools with the public school system of the State, with the State

1. From a report of John Preston McConnell to State Normal School Board.
2. A full list of the personnel can be found in the appendix.

Board of Education and with each other. One of the major problems
discussed dealt with the entrance requirements particularly to the
admission of the students who had not completed a standard high
school course. Up to this time each of the Normal Schools had maintained a secondary department. From 60 to 70 per cent of the student
bodies of these institutions were registered in secondary courses.
The Harrisonburg School had opened in 1909 with only 38 students who
could be classified as high school graduates; Fredericksburg school
had opened in 1911 with 25 such students and Radford had opened in
1913 with 59. Such a ratio had continued, hence the problem of secondary students was a matter of grave importance.

"After much discussion it was finally resolved that in consideration of the present limited high school facilities
in Virginia the educational needs of the State will be
best served and the purposes of the State Normal Schools
for Women will be best carried out by continuing to meet
the present needs; provided that no pupil shall be admitted
to the high school department in any of the said Normal
Schools until she shall first have exhausted the high school
facilities in her own home community, except upon the recommendation of the Division Superintendent of Schools of her
own county in which recommendation shall be set forth the
peculiar circumstances of her particular case on which such
recommendation is based and then only in the discretion of
the President of the Normal School to which she applies for
admission."[1]

Various committees of the Board investigated the offerings
of the four schools to find evidences of overlapping. It was
agreed that conditions in the States justified the offering of
the courses as they were being given in each of the schools.
Certain changes in curriculum were proposed at the meeting of
the executive board, April 6, 1915. These abolished the Rural
Arts and Manual Arts courses in all the schools and offered in
their places a course in Industrial Arts. Each of the schools
was entitled to offer the same type of courses. The acceptance of students of high school grade for the full four year
course was limited to the school at Harrisonburg and Farmville.
Radford was authorized to admit students of third and fourth
year grade with such others of lower rank as the President considered advisable.

The Normal School Board annually visited the four Normal
Schools and held an executive meeting at each school. The
president of the other schools were always present at these
meetings and studied with the Board the needs of each school.

1. From Minutes of the Board.

The first visit to Radford occurred in September 1915. At this time the Board inspected the new dormitory in process of erection and visited the entire school plant. One of the acts of general interest at this meeting was the acceptance of a proposal of Doctor McConnell relative to a home for the President. He said in his report to the Board: "It has occurred to me that it would be a wise and economical plan for me to build a house that will serve the President of this institution for a number of years, and that you pay me rent for the use of this house at the rate that you are now paying for the use of the house that is so inconvenient and remote. If this arrangement were made any time that you were able to build a house for the President on the Normal School grounds, you would of course, discontinue paying rent for that house and it would not obligate you in any measure other than to pay the rent for such time as you think it well for the President of this institution to occupy the house. This would not cost this institution any more than it now costs for me to occupy the house I now use and it would put me in easy touch with the Normal School and enable my wife and myself to do many things for the school that we cannot well do living where we are now." "Sometime ago I bought a suitable lot adjoining the Normal School ground." This request was granted, Doctor McConnell built his home and has lived in it ever since.

In 1916 the Virginia Normal School Board secured an amendment to the Act of its establishment which allowed the four institutions to confer the Bachelor of Science degree. Under this act the first degrees were conferred at Radford, June 1921.

In 1924 the Board secured the passage of an act to change the name of the four Normal Schools to State Teachers College. This change in name was consistent with the trend in teacher training throughout the United States. The bill in the Virginia Legislature was hotly contested by the liberal arts colleges of the State. It passed, however, with an almost unanimous vote. Doctor McConnell was in Richmond at the time. He sent the following telegram to Miss Moffett:

MISS M'LEDGE MOFFETT
EAST RADFORD, VIRGINIA

MU Richmond, Virginia
318 P M February 8

BILL CHANGING NAME TO TEACHER COLLEGE PASSED BOTH HOUSES
ALMOST UNANIMOUSLY GREAT VICTORY

JPMcCONNELL
357 P M

The school bell was rung, and many students assembled in the auditorium to hear the telegram read. A great demonstration followed. A new era had begun! Songs and emblems were changed; scholarship was more easily emphasized; personal and professional prestige budded which culminated a few years later in full collegiate accredited standing by national accrediting agencies. To attain these distinctions the Board co-operated unfailingly with the presidents and faculties in meeting those standards.

During the administration of the Virginia Teachers College Board the schools at Harrisonburg, Farmville, and Radford were admitted to the Southern Association of Secondary Schools and Colleges and the four schools were placed in Class A by the American Teachers College Association. Based on the report of 1929 the Radford College was admitted to Class A "no conditions noted against it." It was one of the first thirty-six colleges of the United States to win this distinction.

One of the major problems of the boards of control is always how to secure appropriations from the legislature. The members with the co-operation of the presidents and local representatives in the Legislature have been forced to make strenuous fights in the Legislature before the various appropriation committees to secure support.

The budget system (1920) and State control of the finances of the colleges did much to limit the power and management of the Board. The budget commission and appropriation committees of the House and Senate made several visits to the institutions to determine the needs and evaluate the requests of the local schools. These new representatives of the State government assumed much of the former authority of the Boards through its legal control of finance. As a result the Board in its last years devoted its time largely to co-ordinating the policies and work of the institutions, approving the instructional policies as they were developed by the faculties and to legalizing the appointments and policies of the administration of the various schools.

One of the chief advantages of establishment of the centralized board of the four schools was the destruction of the keen competition raised in the Legislature as the result of the appeals of the separate boards of trustees for each of the educational institutions of the State. It became the policy of the centralized board to present the claims of all of the institutions in one report. Each school however had a particular patron on the Board. Through this patron and the influence of the president the claims and requests of the various institutions were made and later unified into one request.

The Board kept in close contact with each of the institutions through its Secretary and Auditor, Mr. A. Stuart Robinson of Orange, 1914-17 and Mr. Robert K. Brock appointed in 1917-29. These kept the full minutes of all actions of the Board, audited the books of the business manager and made frequent visits to each of the institutions. Through this careful supervision and official reports much of the business of the Board was transacted.

A policy of the Board, adopted early in its organization, allowed much freedom to the presidents of the schools. At the same time it required such a unification of purpose that prevented duplication and resulted in a strong spirit of co-operation between the administrators of the four institutions. The presidents of these institutions had many conferences. This mutual co-operation and friendship among the presidents of the schools has done much to unify the entire program of teachers training in Virginia.

The last meeting of this Board was held in Richmond in December 1929 at which time the President, W. C. Locker, was authorized to prepare a summary of the achievements of the Teacher Training Institutions during the administration of the Board. This report as given by Mr. Locker is herein included:

VIRGINIA NORMAL SCHOOL BOARD
1914-1924
BOARD OF VIRGINIA TEACHERS COLLEGES
1924-1929
o

		1914-15	1928-29	Increase
1. Enrollment Regular Session	(Farmville	628	791	343
	(Fredericksburg	222	460	238
	(Harrisonburg	288	875	587
	(E. Radford	211	620	409
2. Enrollment Summer Session (1914 & 1929)	(Farmville	380	339	----
	(Fredericksburg	288	284	---
	(Harrisonburg	592	514	---
	(E. Radford	337	861	524
3. Total Students Enrolled	(Farmville	1008	1310	302
	(Fredericksburg	510	744	234
	(Harrisonburg	775	1300	525
	(E. Radford	548	1481	933
4. Per cent of Students Doing Work of College Grade	(Farmville	60	100	
	(Harrisonburg	50	100	
	(Fredericksburg	10	100	
	(E. Radford	38	100	

5. No. of Teachers employed in Faculty	(Farmville	41	53	22
	(Fredericksburg	23	37	14
	(Harrisonburg	32	61	29
	(E. Radford	16	36	20
6. No. of Teachers holding some degree	(Farmville	19	58	39
	(Fredericksburg	8	32	24
	(Harrisonburg	12	58	46
	(E. Radford	8	33	25
7. Salary of President	(Farmville	4000.00	5500.00	1500.00
	(Fredericksburg	2500.00	4500.00	2000.00
	(Harrisonburg	2500.00	4500.00	2000.00
	(E. Radford	2500.00	4500.00	2000.00
8. Average Salary of Faculty	(Farmville	1192.00	2511.00	1319.00
	(Fredericksburg	978.19	2169.80	1191.61
	(Harrisonburg	1260.00	2700.00	1440.00
	(E. Radford	875.00	2625.00	1750.00
9. Value of Physical Properties	(Farmville	1,110,000.00	1,610,000.00	500,000.00
	(Frederic.	250,000.00	765,000.00	515,000.00
	(Harrison.	500,000.00	1,200,000,00	700,000.00
	(E. Radford	148,800.00	900,000.00	751,200.00
10. College dormitory Capacity	(Farmville	411	800	389
	(Fredericksburg	222	320	98
	(Harrisonburg	150	600	450
	(E. Radford	0	436	436
11. Rented Dormitory Capacity	(Farmville	-	118	118
	(Fredericksburg	-	95	95
	(Harrisonburg	15	100	85
	(E. Radford	175	60	--
12. Total Dormitory Capacity	(Farmville	411	918	507
	(Harrisonburg	165	700	535
	(Fredericksburg	222	415	193
	(E. Radford	175	496	321
13. Amount of Students Loan Fund	(Farmville	4000.00	17,000.00	13,000.00
	(Fredericksburg	820.00	10,441,49	9,621.29
	(Harrisonburg	1500.00	23,000.00	21,500.00
	(E. Radford	230.00	18,693.10	18,463.10
14. No. Volumes in Library	(Farmville	7,833	17,200	9,367
	(Fredericksburg	2,775	11,000	8,225
	(Harrisonburg	3,000	14,000	11,000
	(E. Radford	1,500	14,871	13,371
15. Aggregate Legislative Appropriations from 1914 to 1929	(Farmville	1,668,739.00		
	(Fredericksburg	1,074,178.84		
	(Harrisonburg	1,545,058.00		
	(E. Radford	1,132,102.00		
		5,420,077.84		

16. Amounts Other than	(Farmville	150,000.00	
Legislative Appropriation Expended	(Fredericksburg	72,000.00	
	(Harrisonburg	200,000.00	
for Capital Outlay	(E. Radford	67,325.97	489,325.97

17. Total No. of Students Receiving	(Farmville	405	
	(Fredericksburg	165	
Degree for Four Year	(Harrisonburg	378	
Course 1914-1929	(E. Radford	205	1,153

18. Total No. of Students Receiving	(Farmville	2,639	
	(Fredericksburg	1,055	
Diploma for Two	(Harrisonburg	1,908	
Year Course 1914-1929	(E. Radford	1,155	6,757

Board of the Virginia Teachers Colleges,
by W. C. Locker, President.

STATE BOARD OF EDUCATION

On January 1, 1930 a constitutional amendment placed the four State Teachers Colleges under the administration and control of the State Board of Education. The personnel of this board as appointed by Governor Pollard is: E. Lee Trinkle, Roanoke; Joseph H. Saunders, Newport News; Rose MacDonald, Berryville; Herbert H. Harris, Lynchburg; Robert M. Hughes, Norfolk; R. Walton Moore, Fairfax; Robert W. Daniel, Prince George; Dr. Sidney B. Hall, State Superintendent of Public Instruction, Richmond, Virginia; Dr. Thomas D. Eason, Secretary of State Board of Education, Richmond, Virginia.

Its organization meeting resulted in the election of Honorable E. Lee Trinkle of Roanoke, Virginia, as President of the Board. This Board holds monthly meetings, the problems of the Teacher Training Institutions are considered quarterly. The presidents of the colleges are required to make a monthly report to the State Board.

On July 17, 1930 the State Board of Education paid its first visit to the Radford College. At this time it inspected the entire school plant, studying the needs and present condition of the institution. To date the Board has attended to routine activities relative to the teacher training institutions. Two resolutions have been adopted which affect the policy and activities of

the college. The first resolution requires the Business Manager
of the college to submit a copy of all requisitions for supplies
to the office of the State Superintendent of Public Instructions.
Second resolution reiterates the facts that the four State Teachers
Colleges were established for women and that men are not to be admitted during the regular session.

SECTION II

ADMINISTRATIVE ORGANIZATION ON CAMPUS

THE PRESIDENT

The active administration of the Radford College has centered
around President John Preston McConnell, the only administrative
head the institution has had in the two decades of its history.
From the inception of the idea of the school at Radford it seemed
to be the consensus of public opinion that whenever the school
was established Doctor McConnell would be president. Although he
was aware of this feeling he never became a candidate for the office and was unaware of his appointment until he was called over
the telephone on the evening of October 3, 1911 by a correspondent
of a Radford newspaper requesting information in regard to himself
for publication.

For some time Doctor McConnell debated the wisdom of accepting the new position. He was happily located at Emory and Henry
College and had served for nine years as Dean of the College and
Professor of History and Economics. Through his contacts and position at Emory he was able to reach and influence the educational and religious life of Southwestern Virginia to which cause and
section he had dedicated his life's work.

In 1911 education for women was generally unpopular throughout the State and a man who identified himself with the cause of
"Female Education" was regarded as a lost soul in the educational
world. Doctor McConnell tells with humor of the various bits of
advice given him. One of the most influential educators of the
State approached him on this "delicate" subject, saying he had
great regard for the ability and scholarly mind of Doctor Mc-
Connell and he regretted to see him throwing himself away in the
education of woman, especially in a Normal School where light
method courses would stifle out real scholarship and learning.

However, in spite of such professional protest Doctor Mc-
Connell accepted the presidency of the Radford College. He secured permission from the Board of Trustees of Emory and Henry
College to spend part time, 1911 to 1913, in the organization of
the new school. He identified himself with the Board of Trustees
and gave personal attention to the planning and erection of the
Administration Building. He served two years without compensation.

On June 6, 1913, at the time of the appointment of the first
faculty of the school the salary and active full time service of
Doctor McConnell began. He and his family moved to Radford on
August 8, 1913.

BIOGRAPHICAL SKETCH OF JOHN PRESTON MCCONNELL
A. B., M.A., Ph. D.

Family and Boyhood Home

Doctor John Preston McConnell is of Scotch-Irish extraction.
His ancestors settled at the close of the revolutionary period at
Philadelphia and in the adjacent counties of Pennsylvania. About
1800 they migrated to Virginia and acquired a large tract of land
in Scott County.

Hiram K. McConnell, father of John Preston McConnell was born
at Nickelsville, Virginia, July 10, 1838. His Mother Ginsey E.
Brickey was born at Fort Blackmore in Scott County, Virginia, in
1840. After their marriage his parents settled on the upper waters
of Obey's Creek in Scott County much to the objection of the Senior
Brickey; Mrs. McConnell, however, justified her move to this primitive undeveloped wooden region saying that her children, if any
were born, would not have hurtful influences to mar their lives.
She felt that by going into this community and working with their
neighbors she and her husband would be able to develop an atmosphere helpful and stimulating to children, whereas if they settled
in the more open communities the children would be exposed to influences from which she wished them to be free. Immediately after
making their home in the Obey's Creek community they began to do
everything possible to get good roads, to build churches and school
houses, to encourage education, morality, culture and religion in
every way possible. They enriched the life of the community by
organizing a debating society, singing school and a Sunday School
which met for many years in the log school house located on their
farm. Their home became the headquarters for the school teacher,
the preacher and all outsiders who came to the community with a
message of a larger life.

To this family came John Preston McConnell as the first
child, February 22, 1866. Many of the characteristics of his
personality and philosophy which dominate every phase of his
philanthropic, altruistic and educational work in later life
were embued from the influence of his parents, their mountain
home and an isolated mountain community. His father as chairman or clerk of the district school board visited the schools
in the district regularly and gave ardent support to all their
work. He was for many years one of the best known and one of
the most respected justice of peace in Scott County. He was
firm, fair, and without passion as a magistrate. As long as he
lived he was affectionately known as "Squire McConnell". He
was a democrat although he did not always vote the democratic
ticket, especially in local elections. He was an ardent prohibitionist and as early as 1888 he and his son John Preston
voted the national prohibition ticket. On his mother's side
Doctor McConnell acquired perseverance, in dominant will power
and deliberate judgement. His mother, he says, "was pre-eminent-
ly a mother, a wife, and a home maker. She represents the type
of woman described in the Thirty-first Chapter of Proverbs. She
had a natural aptitude for medicinal arts which she practiced
in the home and community. In disposition she was not demon-
strative. Her judgment was not hasty and her opinion of all
matters and persons was the result of deliberation and good
reason. She was unshaken in her religious affiliations, rev-
erent and devoted to the reading of scripture which she accepted without the slightest doubt in its fullest amplifica-
tions. Both of his parents had very meagre elementary education, however they co-operated in the creation of a cultural
atmosphere in the home. Although isolated and for many months
of the year completely cut off from the rest of the world they
surrounded their children with books of substantial character
and such current literature as local weekly and Philadelphia
newspapers. Book agents frequently passed through this community. Before the children were able to read both parents read
to them constantly. One of the favorite books of Doctor
McConnell in his infancy was "Ten Thousand Wonders of Nature
and Art" which was an immense book with a great number of interesting things about men, personages, things, places, and
events covering the whole world.

EDUCATION

Largely through the influence of the McConnells a teacher
although often poorly qualified, was kept in the community. John
Preston with the other children of the community attended what

was then a typical one room school.[1]

The school buildings were crude and uncomfortable. The school house was built of logs and was set above the ground with no under pinning. The cracks in the walls and floors were from one-half inch to one inch wide. One of the chief events in the life of the school child was the day given to dobbing cracks. The rooms were heated by wide fireplaces or an immense wood stove, for which the boys cut and carried the wood. The county made no provisions for the equipment of the school except a box of crayons of one hundred and forty-four sticks for each year, an ax, water bucket and sometimes a dipper. The school had a crude painted blackboard, long benches, and sloping writing slab for the older children. It was after arduous practicing on this slab that Doctor McConnell one time won a prize in penmanship. The method of instruction was largely individual. Each child advanced at his own speed in learning; there were no uniform textbooks and the children used any book from the almanac to the Bible as a reader. John Preston became an expert at the ciphering and was entrusted with the duty of helping or teaching the less proficient scholars. His success as a tutor aroused his first desire to become a teacher.

After exhausting the resources of the home school he attended the River View Academy, a private school of secondary level. Here he was introduced to the classics and more advanced ciphering. Upon completion of this course he was qualified to teach by the county superintendent and became the master of the home school on his father's farm. Here he taught one year with great personal satisfaction, so much so that he determined to get a higher education. After a summer as a fruit tree salesman he left the "Kingdom of Scott" to seek an education at Milligan College in Tennessee. He was now eighteen years of age. This was his first real journey away from home and opened up a new world to him. On this trip he had his first experience with a railroad train; was introduced to ice cream, was launched upon a successful courting experience; bamboozled flowers from the good women of Johnson City for his lady loves; and formed some of the lasting friendships of his life. The life and education at Milligan removed some of the crudity produced by the isolation of Scott, it awakened and stimulated the intellectual power of the boy to such an extent that he rose to leadership in his class and was graduated with first honors and the Bachelor of Arts degree four years later (1890). He was greatly influenced in his personal and religious life by Doctor and Mrs. Josephus Hopwood. The ideals of the Hopwoods set for him many of the standards which he has attempted to maintain in his philosophy for the guidance of young women of the twentieth century. Doctor

1. See Old Time Schools in Scott County for full description of these schools.

Hopwood became one of the dominant influences in Doctor McConnell's life and to the present day has been a constant source of spiritual and moral inspiration.

Upon the advice of Doctor Hopwood young McConnell was sent to the National Normal University at Lebanon, Ohio for some special training in educational methods. This institution was one of the most prominent so-called professional schools of the early nineties. It had a large enrollment. Doctor McConnell's registration number was 3864. This journey to Ohio was Doctor McConnell's first visit out of the Appalachian Mountain region. His entire experience had been limited to rural life in Scott County, a chance visit to Knoxville, Tennessee, and the environment of Milligan College. He studied less than one year in Lebanon, however this experience, he considers as one of the chief factors of his liberal education. He learned much about the ways and manners of people different from those with whom he had been reared. Many of the ideals, and his unfailing confidence in youth were developed from the observation of the results of the free life lived by the boys and girls in this institution. Here the students life was practically unrestrained and the social intercourse between the boys and girls was unchaperoned. Doctor McConnell, rather enjoyed this new life. From his observation and participation he became convinced that young people were capable of much freedom and judgment in their own moral problems. A room at this school cost forty cents per week and table board for girls was one dollar and for the boys was one dollar and twenty-five cents per week. The religious form was so marked that some of the boys were able to earn their board by saying grace at meals, upon certain occasions however, grace was not said. Upon inquiry one of the "fellows" said "The food was not worth grace on such occasions".

While a student at Lebanon he with some other students took a long trip to Canada and Niagara Falls.

After completing his professional course at Lebanon, Doctor McConnell returned to Milligan College where he had contracted a debt of seventy-five dollars for his earlier education. In those days this was a considerable sum of money and weighed heavily on the conscience of the young student. He therefore took up his work willingly as an instructor in the college in order to pay off his indebtness. During this time he also studied for the Master of Arts degree which he later received from Milligan College.

MARRIAGE

When Doctor McConnell was a senior at Milligan College
there entered that institution as a freshman, Miss Clara Louisa
Lucas of Childress, Montgomery County, Virginia. As soon as
Doctor McConnell saw this young woman he told some of his friends
that he intended to marry her. At this early period he recognized
in the future Mrs. McConnell a real help mate. Her ability, her
sincerity, her pursuit of education, her piety and her optimism
attracted him. These qualities have made her a real companion in
all of his personal and professional advancement.

They were married on May 21, 1891 in the Young Ladies Home
of Milligan College. The president, Doctor Josephus Hopwood performed the ceremony as a part of a double wedding. The other
couple was Mr. Thomas Cox of Washington County, Tennessee and Miss
Betty Lee Matthews of Barbesville, Kentucky. Accompanied by Doctor
and Mrs. Hopwood the newly married Mr. and Mrs. Cox, Mr. McConnell
and his wife spent their honeymoon on Boone Creek. The McConnells
returned to Milligan College where Mrs. McConnell was graduated
with the Bachelor's degree in the spring of 1892 and Doctor Mc-
Connell served as an instructor. Later he was appointed Professor
of Latin and Greek in which capacity he served until 1900.

Doctor and Mrs. McConnell have five children, four of whom
were born at Milligan. June, now Mrs. H. C. Graybeal of Emory,
Virginia; Robert L. McConnell, a dentist in the City of Radford,
Virginia; Hiram McConnell, Doctor of Philosophy of the University
of Virginia, and research worker in Europe and John Paul McConnell
Professor at the Young Men's Christian Association School at Nashville, Tennessee. Their youngest child, Annie Ginsey, now the
wife of Mr. Ernest Grigsby, County Farm Agent of Pulaski County,
was born in Charlottesville. Doctor and Mrs. McConnell have seven
grandchildren: Mac, Charlton, William, Clare, and David, children
of Mr. and Mrs. H. C. Graybeal and Nancye and Robert, children of
Doctor Robert L. McConnell.

THE CHANGING POINT - GRADUATE STUDY

Up to 1900 the education and professional experience of Doctor
McConnell had more or less "just happened". He had not definitely
decided upon his life work. Since early youth he had looked forward to entering the profession of law. In 1900, however, he decided that he would be more useful and happier if he would devote
his life to educational work than to any other field that seemed
to be opened. He had had ten years of successful teaching experience at Milligan. His educational preparation seemed adequate to

the demands of the times, nevertheless, Doctor McConnell sensed
the trend of the educational development which was to come in
the new century and decided he would be ready. Forthwith he
sold his home in Milligan and moved with his family to Charlottesville, Virginia where he entered the University and continued as
a student for four years. He specialized in History, Economics,
and English Literature. His outstanding physical appearance,
strong scholarship and personality made him prominent on the
campus of the University where he became identified with the
leading student organizations. He was President of the Washington Literary Society, as a member he took an active part as a
winner in the inter-society debates between the Jefferson and
Washington Societies. He was secretary, vice-president and president of the Graduate Club. He was a charter member of the "Raven
Society", one of the most distinct honors that could come to a
student at the University.

After his graduation from the University he was elected a
member of the University Chapter of Phi Beta Kappa. In the mean-
time, however, he had been elected and accepted membership in Phi
Betta Kappa Society of William and Mary College.

While in Charlottesville Doctor McConnell and his family became intimately acquainted with the leading authorities and pro-
fessors of the University. With these he established a relationship of equality due to his maturity, scholarship and intellect.
He was appointed instructor at the University and also taught
history at Rawling Institute, a school for girls located in
Charlottesville. History became the major field of his research.
As a dissertation problem he studied and published the treatise
"The Treatment of Negroes in Virginia During the Reconstruction
Period". The requirements for higher degrees were less definite-
ly stated in 1900 than now, so Doctor McConnell stayed at the
University until he was deemed "ripe" for the Ph. D. The com-
mencement exercises of 1904 at the University marked the begin-
ning of an era. Doctor Edwin Alderman had recently been made
President. He instituted the use of academic costume. Doctor
McConnell speaks with pride that he was one of the first to tread
"The Lawn" so splendidly robed. He was one of three to receive the
Doctor of Philosophy degree. Of those who had secured this degree
some had become egotistical with a general loss in efficiency. On
the night of Doctor McConnell's graduation from the University
Dean Page of the School in complimenting him upon winning the
highest place of distinction said; "You have now earned the Doctor
of Philosophy degree, forget it". This advise Doctor McConnell
has transferred to many other potential Doctors of Philosophy, he
himself has never presumed upon his attainment of high scholastic
rank or the unqualified success in scholarship which attended his
entire education.

Following his graduate work at the University of Virginia Doctor McConnell was appointed Professor in History and Economics at Emory and Henry College where he served for nine years. For most of this time as Dean of the College also. Thus he became actively identified with the cause of education in Southwestern Virginia. Through his work as publicity agent for Emory he travelled throughout the entire of Southwestern Virginia, East Tennessee, and North Carolina. This brought him a wide contact and favorable acquaintanceship with all of the types of people of this section.

Although a member of the Christian Church he became actively identified with the interests of the Methodist churches within the Holston Conference and was associated in the training of many of the ministers and lay leaders for this church. He was one of the most popular members of the Emory faculty and was affectionately known a "Ecie". His home on the campus was a mecca for the students. He and Mrs. McConnell roomed and boarded many of the students. The informality of their home made it an easy place for the students to come and go.

From the practical experience as an administrative officer of Emory and Henry College, Doctor McConnell developed his native executive ability and learned the technique and diplomacy of a successful administrator.

POLITICAL AFFILIATIONS

Politically Doctor McConnell is a democrat. Throughout his childhood he was much impressed with the practices, governmental policies and the administration of the law as he saw it carried out under the jurisdiction of his father, a Justice of Peace in Scott County. As a child he made a monthly pilgrimmage on horseback with his father to Gate City to attend the meetings of the county court. In the court room and on the street he heard political issues of the day being debated. From these debates he formed his political convictions. Both of his parents were ardent prohibitionists and instilled in their children a hate of liquor and all other alcoholic beverages. In 1888 at the Peters Creek precinct in Scott County Doctor McConnell (his first vote) and his father voted the National Prohibition Ticket. They were unable to secure a printed ballot with the national prohibition candidates names so they prepared written ballots for themselves and thus voted the straight prohibition ticket. The laws of Virginia at that time did not require uniform tickets. So far as the records show these were the only prohibition tickets voted in the precinct and probably in the whole county. The two

McConnells were branded as "fanatic cranks" and were ridiculed
as having thrown their votes away. This was a challenge to the
younger McConnell and from that day to this he has crusaded
through every avenue and influence which he could muster to defeat the liquor traffic, locally, in the State and in the Nation. He is politically known as one of the dryest men in the
State of Virginia. One of the joys of his life has been that
his father lived long enough to see the ratification of the
eighteenth amendment.

For years Doctor McConnell was President of the Anti-Saloon
League of Virginia. In this organization he has always had great
faith and has supported its work financially and morally.

In the presidential campaign of 1928 his Democratic ideals
for the State Government of Virginia were brought in conflict
with his ardent support of prohibition. After several months
of careful thought and consideration in which he weighed the
ultimate results, as they appeared to him, he decided to support
the straight democratic party in the national election in order
to preserve for the democratic party the control of the moral
and the political life of the State. As a result of this decla-
ration his position as a prohibitionist was challenged by his
political foes. His uncompromising position as prohibitionist
however was unshaken and his influence on the future development of the political life in Virginia passed through this
crisis untarnished. In his support of prohibition he has been
ably assisted by his wife Mrs. Clara McConnell, who is a leader
in the work of the Woman's Christian Temperance Union. Both of
them are actively identified with the state work of this organization.

Doctor McConnell has never been a candidate for public
office although he is recognized as one of the most influential democrats of the state. Frequently he has been approached
as a possible candidate for various offices ranging from those
of minor local importance to the governorship of the State.
All of these he has refused and has devoted himself as a layman
in the political progress of the State.

RELIGIOUS AFFILIATION

Reared in a home where Christian ideals were uppermost in
the minds of his parents and where the Bible was the most familiar book Doctor McConnell approached the problems of life

with a sound foundation of religious ideals and concepts. His father, as a youth, was identified with the Methodist Church but later joined the Freewill Baptist Church. His mother, as her mother and father before her, was a firm believer in the practices and ideals of Primitive Baptist Church. She was a regular attendant at the Christian Irvington Primitive Baptist Church at Mack in Scott County. His parents however kept open house to ministers of all faiths and practices.

In October 1887 while Doctor McConnell was a student at Milligan College he professed faith, was baptized by Doctor Hopwood in the Buffalo Creek at Milligan and became a member of the local Christian or Disciples of Christ Church. For many years he has been a member of the State Mission Board of the Christian Church, Member of the Board of Directors of the Christian Church; Chairman of the Board of Recommendations at the Inter-National Convention; Member of the Commission on Ministry of the Christian Church at Washington, D. C., State Chairman of Pensions and Ministerial Relief, and for many years a member of the International Board of Education of the Church. He is elder in First Christian Church of East Radford, Virginia where he frequently serves in the capacity of religious leader for the congregation or the Sunday School.

Doctor McConnell has always been an effective Sunday School teacher. When he entered school at the University of Virginia he found the student members of the Christian Church had no organization or affiliations with any church in the city of Charlottesville. He, therefore gathered around him such members of the Christian Church as were registered at the University and invited them to join with him in bringing together all of those who had no church affiliations in Charlottesville. He became the leader of this group and for several years held one of the largest and most active Sunday School classes in Charlottesville. Many of the richest friendships of his life developed out of this affiliation, notably that with Doctor John W. Wayland, a dunkard (later a Baptist) from Rockingham County.

Although devoted to the progress and development of the Christian Church Doctor McConnell's religious activities may be truthfully said to be inter-denominational. Through his affiliation with Emory and Henry College he became actively identified and interested in the activities of the Methodist. Frequently he attended the conferences and was cognizant of the inner policies of this denominational organization through his close contact with bishops, ministers, and laymen of the church. Doctor McConnell is a constant reader of religious publications. In this way he keeps himself informed of the religious problems of all of the churches.

CIVIC SERVICE AND AFFILIATIONS

Dr. McConnell is primarily a loyalist to Southwestern Virginia. His wide first hand experience with the primitive and at the same time his contact with the more developed sections of the Appalachian region has made him one of the leading interpreters of the mountain folk. Doctor McConnell is himself an example of the possibilities for the real development of intellect, character, and personality of the sturdy Scotch Irish stock of the Appalachian Mountains. Through his knowledge of of the human and material resources he realizes the possibilities for this section. He therefore has devoted much of his time to its development.

In 1925 he participated in the organization of the nineteen counties and three cities of Southwestern Virginia into a sectional chamber of commerce. He and his colleagues presented this project and enthusiasm resulted in the organization of Southwestern Virginia Incorporated, of which Doctor McConnell has been the only President. This organization has grown rapidly into a civic and industrial agency for the entire development of Southwestern Virginia. Each of the counties in this organization is represented by directors. The Board of Directors with the officers of the organization have advertised the resources of Southwestern Virginia, built an attitude of co-operation in the development of the best spiritual and economical resources of this section and its half-million population.

Doctor McConnell, although he believes in the "Mountain Empire" is not sectional in his civic endeavours. He is a member of the State Chamber of Commerce, as a member of its educational committee he has assisted in campaigns for the betterment of all sections of the state. Through his leadership of Southwestern Virginia Incorporated he had advanced the cause of good roads, better schools, and a greater development of the natural resources throughout the State.

Doctor McConnell was a member of the original group to project the idea for the building of the Lee Highway from Washington, D. C. to San Diego, California.

Locally, he has been a leader in the civic development of Radford. He originated the Radford Forum, where by free discussion a public opinion was created that led to changes in the city form of government, a bond issue for streets, public utilities, schools, and a general civic awakening in Radford. He was a charter member of the Radford Rotary Club. His sponsor-

ship and active leadership is sought in all civic betterment.
He is a frequent speaker, committee member or advisor in all
community projects.

BUSINESS AFFILIATIONS

In his early life in Scott County, Doctor McConnell, had
many opportunities to try his hand at business adventures. When
he reached the age of eighteen his friends tried to induce him
to go into business, to ally himself with the development of
timber land and the railroad which was just then coming into
Southwest Virginia. All of these offered a large financial
harvest to the young man. However, from childhood Doctor Mc-
Connell had dreamed of being the editor of a weekly newspaper
he felt and realized the importance and power of the paper in
the lives of the people of Scott County. To him, editor of
such a paper was a most powerful and successful person. He had
also become interested in the study of law through his association with his father. These two goals became his objectives in
life. However the temptation presented in the elementary school
where he was allowed to serve as a substitute teacher became too
great for him. He decided to teach, at the age of eighteen he
was appointed the teacher of the rural school on his father's
farm. His success in educational work stirred his ambition to
secure a better education. In order to do this he launched upon
his first business adventure, selling of fruit trees for the
Knoxville Nursery of Knoxville, Tennessee. Back and forth over
Hancock, Hawkins, Granger, and Claiborne counties of Tennessee
and Lee County of Virginia he peddled his trees. This first experience in contact with people in a business way proved exceed-
ingly beneficial and led to the development of the most dominant
characteristic of the later life, his study and knowledge of
human nature.

He early recognized that to be a success in life he should not
allow books to absorb his attention, nor should he keep himself
aloof from people with whom he was striving to do business. His
learning and this desire to know human beings, their peculiari-
ties and eccentricities has enabled Doctor McConnell to maintain
the viewpoint of the practical business man as well as the vision of the idealistic educator. Throughout his professional
life he has felt the challenge to prove that school teachers
and so-called educators could also be sane practical business
men. With his professional activities Doctor McConnell has
always carried some business interest. Farming and agricultural development are his hobbies. For many years he has owned

and directed the work of his father's farm in Scott. At Emory he owned his home and devoted much time to its development. Shortly after coming to Radford he purchased a small farm in Pulaski County which he planted as an orchard.

He became the director of many business organizations at Emory and in the City of Radford. The chief of these have been the Radford Sales Corporation, Radford Finance Corporation, Jackson Hardware Company, Radford Hospital Corporation.

The most critical test of his business ability, other than the administration of the Radford College has been as president of the Farmers and Merchants Bank of East Radford. He was elected President of this bank in 1919 and during the eleven years of his administration the revenues of this bank have increased from $200,000 to $1,000,000.00. Through his affiliation with this bank Doctor McConnell has become actively identified with the State Bankers Association. In this organization he is Chairman of the Committee on Education. He frequently attends the meetings of the State organization. In his committee work he has been active in creating an interest in the need for sound education in the principles of banking through the medium of elementary, high schools and colleges of the State.

EDUCATIONAL AFFILIATIONS

For thirty years Doctor McConnell has been identified with the educational development of Virginia, East Tennessee, West Virginia and with certain educational factors operating in the South. He has stamped his influence upon education throughout this entire section. His life has been consecrated to the development of moral, intellectual and natural resources of the State and Nation. He has been identified with the foremost educational agencies of Virginia for the last quarter of a century. He was one of the original members and organizers of the Virginia Cooperative Association organized in 1903. His faith and confidence in this organization has been manifest in many ways. He was a member of the Board of Directors and has served four years as President. He is one of its most active leaders, especially in Southwest Virginia in the May Campaign of 1905, sponsored by this organization. This resulted in the educational renaissance in Virginia.

Doctor McConnell has been actively identified with State Teachers Association as President of this organization in 1911 and 1913, an active speaker and leader in various sections,

President of the Southern Educational Societies, an active organization in the South for many years. In 1922 he was elected president of the Southern Cooperative League for Educational and Social Service. He has served one term as Vice-president of the American Association of Teachers College. His interest in his major academic subject of History and Economics has brought him several appointments from the Virginia Historical Society and a place on the War History Commission.

In 1910 the State Conference of Charities and Corrections became an active organization in Virginia. Doctor McConnell identified himself with this movement and became a leading propagandist in the State for the same and christian treatment of crippled children. He made one of the first public addresses in Virginia in the interest of crippled children's education. His interest in this work augmented the work of Doctor Drewry and Doctor Mastin who were the active leaders and organizers of State Conference of Charities and Corrections, later the Virginia Conference of Social Work and ultimately the State Board of Public Welfare.

Doctor McConnell was President of this association for two or three terms and has always been an active director and member of the Board of Trustees of the Crippled Children's Hospital of Virginia. At one time the Virginia Conference of Charities and Corrections held its regular meeting at the Radford College with Doctor McConnell host of the conference. For many years in every address he delivered, regardless of subject, he made a plea for the crippled and handicapped of the State.

Doctor McConnell has played an active part and has been identified as a member, committee leader, and as an officer in practically every educational organization in the State of Virginia. So strong is his interest and influence in those organizations that he has now reached that point where he is practically "officer emeritus" of every organization in the State. His influence is of first magnitude in the solution of any educational problem of the State, he is regarded in the minds of the general public as above office, hence he is one of the most dominant leaders in educational thought and activities of the Commonwealth. In addition to these major extra professional interests Doctor McConnell has been identified with many other altruistic, humanitarian, educational and industrial organizations.

Since 1913 he has been appointed by the Governors of Virginia to many of the most important commissions of the State. He has likewise been elected member of the leading honorary societies and other organizations of State and National importance.

The objective measures as have been reviewed in this biographical sketch of Doctor John Preston McConnell give some insight into the background, character, personality and spirit of the man who was elected to the presidency of the State Normal and Industrial School at Radford on October 3, 1911. He identified himself for two years with the administrative board of this institution in the development of the preliminary organization of the institution and in the detailed work of the planning and erection of the administration building. In June 1913 his resignation from Emory and Henry College became active and he entered upon full time duty as first president of the Radford College. Practically all of the history of this institution which is to follow in this account is the outgrowth of the ideas and influence of Doctor McConnell.

LIST OF AFFILIATIONS OF JOHN PRESTON MCCONNELL

Appointments by Governor: 1914, Delegate to the Fourth International Congress on Home Education in Philadelphia; 1915, Delegate to the Forty-second Annual Meeting of the National Conference of Charities and Corrections, at Baltimore, Maryland; 1916, Delegate to the National Conference of Charities and Correction, Indianapolis, Indiana; 1916, Delegate to the Eighth Annual Convention of the Southern Commercial Congress, Norfolk, Virginia; 1917, Delegate to the Ninth Annual Convention of the Southern Commercial Congress, New York; 1917, Delegate to the Seventh Annual League of Compulsory Education officials, Chicago, Illinois; 1919, Honorary Delegate to Atlantic Congress, New York City; 1919, Member of the Virginia War History Commission; 1920, Delegate to represent the Commonwealth of Virginia at the Conference on Negro Education to meet in the Senate Chamber of the Capitol at Atlanta, Georgia; 1921, Delegate to represent the Commonwealth of Virginia at the State Conference of Charities and Corrections, Norfolk, Virginia; 1921, Delegate to represent the Commonwealth of Virginia at the Ninth Annual Convention of the United States Good Roads Association, Greensboro, North Carolina; 1922, Delegate to represent the Commonwealth of Virginia at the Tenth Annual Convention of the United States Good Roads Association, Phoenix, Arizona; 1922, Delegate to represent the Commonwealth of Virginia at the International Convention of the World League against Alcoholism, Toronto, Canada; 1923, Delegate to represent the Commonwealth of Virginia at the Centennial Celebration of the Monroe Doctrine under the Auspices of the Southern Commercial Congress to be held in Richmond, Virginia; 1924, Delegate to represent the Commonwealth of Virginia at the Thirty-year Jubilee Convention of the Anti-Saloon League of America, Washington, D. C.; 1924, Delegate to represent the

Commonwealth of Virginia at the Fifty-first Annual Meeting of
the National Conference of Social Work to be held in Toronto,
Canada; 1927, Delegate to represent the Commonwealth of Virgin-
ia at the fifty-fourth Meeting of the National Conference of
Social Work, Des Moines, Iowa; 1927, member of the Advisory
Committee on Historical Markers of the Bureau of Archaeology
and History at the recommendation of the State Commission on
Conservation and Development; 1927, Delegate to represent the
Commonwealth of Virginia at the Institute of Public Affairs,
University of Virginia; 1913, Delegate to the Fourth Interna-
tional Congress on School Hygiene, Buffalo, New York; 1913
Delegate to the International Conference relating to program
for celebration of Centenary signing of Treaty of Ghent, and
one hundredth Anniversary of Peace among English speaking
Nations, Hotel Plaza, New York City; 1913, Member of the Board
of Visitors of the Virginia School for the Deaf and Blind at
Staunton.

MEMBERSHIP IN FOREIGN NATIONAL HONOR SOCIETIES

1919, member of Societe Academique France; 1917, Phi Beta
Kappa of Virginia; 1920, American Association for the Advance-
ment of Science; 1921, Virginia Society of Sons of the American
Revolution; 1922 Lee Highway Association; 1923, the Author's
Club, England; 1924, Historian Virginia Division (Sons of Con-
federate Veterans); 1926, Pi Gamma Mu, Winfield, Kansas; Ground
Hog Club of America, Number one, Roanoke, Virginia.

SECTION III

BUSINESS ADMINISTRATION

The original plans for the teacher training institutions of Virginia provided for the administration of all phases of the institutional life by the President of the College who was in turn directly responsible to the Board of Trustees. The original Board of Trustees for the Radford College recognized this policy in an early ruling which required the President to make an annual report of the financial status of the college—all others therefore who function in the business administration of the college do so under delegated power from the President. The philosophy of the business management of this institution has always been no secret manipulation of funds, good credit with no debt for which the payment is not foreseen and no deficit at the end of the fiscal year.

ROBERT J. NOELL - TREASURER 1911 - 1914

On October 2, 1911, Robert J. Noell was appointed Treasurer of the College. He was intrusted with the financial business and bookkeeping for the original Board. Prior to the opening of the school the financial business of the Board was limited to the costs of construction of the Administration Building and the current expenses for travel, and postage by the Board.

The real business management of the college, therefore, begins with the opening of the college, September 17, 1913. No business office was opened at the college in 1913. Mr. Noell conducted his part of the business management from his local place of business in Radford. He was most meticulous in his bookkeeping. There are deposited in the safe of the treasurer's office of the Radford College the first records and books of the institution. These are all kept in longhand and are most detailed and minute in entry and form. Mr. Noell opened accounts for each of the students. These were kept in ledger books. He also opened separate accounts for the various employees, members of the faculty and the firms with which the college did the greater part of its business. In another book he kept a complete inventory of the first purchases of the college.[1] This recounts in actual items the purchase of all books for the library, all equipment for the Administration Building, complete list of the original purchases for the Home Economics, Industrial Arts, and Chemistry Departments.

1. These lists are interesting and are available to the reader in the Treasurer's office of the College.

A general policy of "pay-as-you-go" was adopted by the college. The expenditures of the college were met in terms of existing revenue. Very little indebtness of any type was incurred. The salaries of the teachers were paid at the first of each month. The method of payment was usually amusing. Mr. Noell would make out the checks and entrust them to his son, John, to deliver personally. Frequently at ten o'clock at night or later this youth would call the teacher to his boarding house porch and solemnly present the check and get a receipt.

MISS WILLIE GRAY ALLEN - TREASURER

With the establishment of the Virginia Normal School Board in 1914 Mr. Noell's services as treasurer were discontinued and these duties were placed upon Miss Willie Gray Allen, then Secretary to the President. Miss Allen assumed the duties of the treasurer and worked most intimately with Dr. McConnell in the administration of the finances of the institution. She kept her books and records in the Secretary's office. In order to relieve her of the laborious task of bookkeeping Mr. J. Harvey Barnett was employed as part time bookkeeper. With the coming of Mr. Barnett the first business office was opened at the school, Room 1, near the main entrance of the Administration Building. Here the books and other business records were filed. Mr. Roop made several desks and cabinets to fit the voucher forms and books in use. Mr. Barnett was so short it was necessary to build a platform for him to stand on to reach the high top desk. He seemed almost like a midget as he labored over the large ledger books spread out on the ill proportioned desk. (This desk is now used for the storage of cuts in the basement of the Administration Building). All money collected and bills paid by Miss Allen from the Secretary's office. During this period the records were kept in ledger books; accounts were opened for each student, a day book for expenditures kept and a separate filing of paid bills with returned checks in voucher envelopes, thousands of these packages are stored in the college basement.

The Board of Trustees employed Honorable Stuart Robinson of Orange, Virginia, 1914-17, and later Robert K. Brock of Farmville, Virginia, 1917-26, as secretary-auditor. Mr. Brock describes his duties thus: "I was required to attend the meetings of the Board, keep a record of the proceedings and furthermore to go around to each of the schools monthly and examine their books and accounts and make report to the Board and also to perform any other duty which the Board requested of me. After three or four years, instead of requiring me to visit the schools every month, the Board directed me to visit the schools every two months and that practice was followed until my duties as auditor ceased. When they ceased, I only attended the meetings of the Board and only went to the schools once a year when the annual meeting was held, the Board visiting the schools successively on these occasions, starting you might say, at Farmville, then to Radford, then to Harrisonburg and then to Fredericksburg."

These monthly audits, a general report once a year to the governing board, and an annual summary of financial status to the State Superintendent of Public Instruction, constituted the procedure for reporting on the financial resources of the institution to off-campus authorities.

APPROPRIATIONS

From 1910 to 1920 it was necessary for the local administrators of the college and its sponsoring Board of Trustees to make a personal appeal to the Legislature for the appropriations necessary for the support of the institution.[1] The appropriations were largely determined by the finance committees of the House and Senate and were usually hotly debated in committees of the House, the Senate, and joint committee meetings of these bodies. The appropriations were recorded in the proceedings of the Legislature and this statement of income, payable from the State Treasury in lump sums, was used as a guide in the expenditures of the institution. The appropriations as made were divided in three categories, appropriations for support; appropriations for capital outlay and occasionally a special appropriation to cover some specific item. No effort was made by the Legislature or the Board of Trustees to itemize the amount of expenditure other than the general division between capital outlay and support. These details were left to the discretion of the local administrators. It was Doctor McConnell's policy to determine the fixed charges as, salaries and general maintenance and set this aside. The balance of the appropriation and revenue from student fees was spent as he saw fit in terms of institutional needs.

STATE BUDGET SYSTEM

In 1918 a State Budget System was started, following a survey of the State government by the Virginia Commission on

1. See Appendix for list and amount of appropriation.

Economy and Efficiency. This movement culminated in Legislative Acts requiring all proposed expenditures of the State to
be budgeted. This scheme was largely initiated and perfected by
Honorable Leroy Hodges, during the administration of Westmoreland Davis as Governor. The plan as developed by Mr. Hodges was
an application of the Belgian System for budgets and was copied
from the general budget system of the Federal Government of the
United States. The introduction of this system brought a radical change in the business administration of all State institutions. Like most new movements it was considered very drastic
and necessitated an unreasonable change. It was widely debated
throughout the State.

For several months the business administrators of the colleges
were in a state of chaotic misunderstanding and apprehension which
culminated in a general meeting in Richmond late in the fall of
1919. At this time the Presidents with their respective bookkeepers or financial assistants went to Richmond and worked under the
direction of Mr. Hodges in the preparation of their respective
budgets. Miss Allen accompanied Doctor McConnell on this trip.
They spent about one week in Richmond. Doctor McConnell tells
with much humor of the development of this first budget. He
says Miss Allen would get so nervous she could neither add nor
subtract and he would get so confused in the subject headings
that it took many hours to adjust the simpliest sort of proposed
expenditure. The State provided these officials with immense
sheets of paper for records. The record required a statement
of past expenditure and a request for appropriation in terms
of specific items grouped in categories which were coded. With
these tentative budgets before them Colonel Hodges and the finance committees of the Senate and House visited each State institution. This visit caused a strenuous day at Radford as it
was the first time the school had been inspected and challenged
to prove its needs to a group of disinterested strangers. However after much debate and revision Virginia produced her first
budget for presentation to the Legislature of 1920.

Following the adoption of the budget plan the method of
keeping the records and accounts in the institution was changed.
Large sheets for loose leaf record books were furnished by the
State Budget Director for the keeping of all accounts. These
sheets were ruled and headed to correspond to the plan for the
budget. Practically all of the vouchers were coded to the same
budget scheme. A printed book of directions for these codes
and use of these forms were supplied with the budget. This became the "Bible" of the business office.

SYLVESTER MCCONNELL - TREASURER AND BUSINESS MANAGER

In the reorganization of 1920 Mr. Sylvester McConnell was appointed Treasurer of the College. For some time Mr. McConnell devoted his attention to the reorganization of the business office which was now formally opened and all business transactions taken from the Secretary's office and centralized in the Treasurer's office. Room 1, of the Administration Building was used for a year or two, later the office moved to the room next to the Secretary's office. As a part of his duties Mr. McConnell was intrusted with the purchasing of all supplies for the college. Doctor Moffett, dean of women, was associated with him in this capacity in so far as the purchasing of food supplies and equipment for the Home Department was concerned. Heretofore the purchasing of supplies had been theoretically confined in the president's office. Certain employees of the college had been intrusted to purchase supplies for their respective departments as: Mr. Huddle, engineering; Mr. Roop, carpenter; Mr. Gilbert, College book store; Food Department, Professors of certain scientific subjects as, Home Economics, Industrial Arts, Chemistry, Biology, would place their own orders for needed supplies. The centralization of all this purchasing power in Mr. McConnell's office was one of the big problems of reorganization made necessary by the establishment of the central business office. At this time an inventory of the physical equipment of the institution was taken. A reorganization of the receiving of goods and supplies was instituted. Prior to this the shipments were delivered to the persons most concerned in their use. The change required the drayman and other persons making deliveries to report all deliveries to the central office. Forms were designed for checking purchases and delivery of supplies. Mr. McConnell[1] gradually was given more and more responsibility until his duties by 1927 had grown into those of local business manager as: officer in charge of all purchases, director of work of campus employees; employer of all servants and general labor of the buildings and campus; director of the physical upkeep of the buildings. All of these duties were delegated by and were under the direct supervision of Doctor McConnell.

CENTRALIZED STATE CONTROL OF FINANCE

With the establishment of the State Purchasing Agent (1920 amended 1924-28) with legal authority[2] requiring all major supplies to be purchased through a central officer of the State the

1. During a three months leave of absence granted Mr. McConnell in 1925, Miss Mary Sandidge acted as Business Manager.
2. See Act of Legislature No. 1920, Page 245, Chapter 172. Section I.

purchase of supplies become a less important function of the business office. The major duty being the preparation of requisitions for these supplies and carrying on correspondence with offices in Richmond relative to the purchases. Mr. McConnell and Doctor Moffett were active in the work of the committee of the State for the standardization of supplies to be used in the institutions under the State Purchasing Act. They paid several visits to Richmond where they met with representatives of other institutions, purchased supplies and assisted in the development of the standards which are now generally used by the Purchasing Department of the State.

Since 1920 Mr. McConnell and Miss Moffett have been largely responsible for the selection and purchase of the college equipment. They have consulted with the manufacturers and selling agents for the kitchen and bedroom equipment, the equipment for the library building and such standard furniture as is purchased from the State penitentiary.

In 1928 an entire reorganization of the State system of financial control was established. All State finances were taken from the local banks and turned over to the comptroller of the State who in turn administered the payment of all indebtness incurred by the institutions. This increased the work of the business office of the college to such an extent that it was necessary to employ a full time Secretary to Mr. McConnell. Miss Gladys Dixon was transferred from the Correspondence Department to the Treasurer's office. It is her duty to keep the books and to assist Mr. McConnell in preparation of the forms relative to all purchases, requisitions, and resources for the Richmond offices. This centralization of the business management of the State necessitated much reorganization in the general policies of the office. These are not unique to this institution and are administered here in the same way as in all other State institutions.

The general procedure now (1931) for the purchase of new supplies consists in the selection of the article to be purchased, sending of a requisition for its purchase to the State Department of Public Instruction for approval, a duplicate to the Comptroller's office, triplicate to the selling agent and a copy kept in the institution. All purchases must have the approval of the purchasing agent or his representatives. These forms are all coded according to uniform standards for the distribution of the money. In Richmond accounts are kept according to the different budget allowances. No change from one allowance to another is permissible without the approval of the governor through State Budget Director.

A petty cash account of $1,000 is allowed the treasurer for use in emergency purchases, payment of day laborers, and other minor expenditures of the institution. This petty cash account is very carefully checked by the State. The centralization of finance under State control relieved the Board of Trustees of direct responsibility and placed the supervision of the business management of the college entirely under the State Comptroller. The auditors representing the central office pay frequent visits to the college and audits all accounts. Other officials approve and check all expenditures, assist in determining budget requests, approve salaries and furnish the institution with comparative data on financial matters.

BUSINESS MANAGEMENT OF THE BOARDING DEPARTMENT

Business management of boarding department, although entirely self supporting, has always been an integral part of the business administration of the college. At first Mr. Noell kept the books for the general administrative expenses and Miss Cecil Crockett, housekeeper, kept the books for the boarding department. Miss Crockett kept an itemized account of all purchases. It is interesting to note that the first purchase made by the Food Department of the college on September 16, 1913, was for a quart of milk. Many of the items in these early books are in such detail as quarts of milk, two or three pounds of butter and other domestic measures of food supplies. Miss Crockett describes the early system thus: "When Mr. Noell was Treasurer he would give me $10.00, $25.00 and $30.00 to pay for vegetables at the door, but the large bills I would send to him to pay. I kept the school bill heads and would make them out. Miss Allen paid them (all bills) after she became Treasurer. Mr. Crockett Brown furnished my milk. I generally got my eggs from Mr. Shelburne, sometimes from Mr. N. B. Harvey and Mr. John Lucas. I would buy a quarter of beef some times, but as I didn't have any place to keep it most of the time I bought from the local dealers. I would buy a hog occasionally. We opened school with just a barrel of glasses and had to borrow every dish to serve the first meal. We borrowed from local merchants, fed eighty persons the first meal."

With the growth of the college and war conditions the purchasing of supplies became so great that Mr. Gilbert was appointed (1919) as assistant purchasing agent to the housekeeper. It was his responsibility to purchase supplies from wholesale firms, mostly represented by travelling salesmen, while the housekeeper purchased supplies from the farmers, local merchants, etc. There was little system for the purchase of supplies. In 1920 the contract system for the purchase of such supplies as meat, flour, milk, butter, was adopted. Most of the food was bought in small

quantities from wholesalers in Roanoke or Radford. With the change
to State Purchasing the local purchasing of supplies was limited to
perishable food stuff which are now purchased by the dietitian. In
1924 the dietitian (Miss Elsie Palmer) under the direction of Doctor
Moffett established a checking system for the use of food supplies.
This system is the first written record of the use of food in the
kitchen. It required a daily requisition from the cook, entry of
the food as used, keeping of a perpetual inventory, and a quarterly
report from the dietitian to the President and Business Manager of
the daily per capita cost for the food department. At present Miss
Martin has transferred these forms to a card system and an accurate
account is kept of all expenses relative to the use of food. These
reports are frequently checked with the records of the Business Manager and give an index as to the status of the management in the
food department.

It is the practice of the State officials to send to the college each quarter data showing a comparative study of the expenditures in the four Teacher Training Institutions of the State.

The revenues of the boarding department are secured from the
board charged the students ($15 for 28 days in 1913, and $25 for
28 days in 1931). These charges include room, heat, light, laundry, food, the proportionate cost of supervision service and sanitary supplies. In 1931 the allowance for each student is budgeted $6.00 for room, $2.00 for laundry and 32 cents per day for food.

STUDENT LOAN FUND

The Act of the Legislature provides that a sum equal to one
per cent of the appropriation may be used as a Student Loan Fund.
The original appropriation of the college therefore provided
$250.00 as a student loan fund. In the early years of the insti-
tution it was practically impossible to find students who were
willing to borrow money to go to school. This condition existed
until the World War. After the War the spread of independence,
the idealization of working your way through college, general
economic condition resulting from the War and reconstruction, encouraged many students to depend upon their own resources for a
college education. This increased the necessity for student loan.
With the result that the legislature has increased the budget allowance for student loans until the present annual allowance from
the State fund is $2,000.00.[1]

1. See Table Appendix for full summary of appropriation.

In 1930 the situation became so acute that the State gave
the college authority to borrow $10,000.00 for the purpose of
student loans. A survey of the financial status of the students
of the college in 1931 reveals that fifty-three per cent are
borrowing or working their way through college. The student loans
have always been administered directly by the President who ap-
proves each loan. To legalize the loan the students of the college are required to give a note at five per cent rate of interest.
One of the major responsibilities of the business manager is the
collection of these notes.

To supplement the student loan, various small funds have been
collected as gifts from the senior classes; the Mrs. Thomas L.
Phelps fund, established by Mrs. Phelps as a special student loan
fund; the various scholarships and loan funds established by the
Daughters of American Revolution, the United Daughters of Confed-
eracy, and the Knights Templar Educational Fund.

Book Store

About thirty days before the first session opened in 1913
Doctor McConnell asked Mr. Gilbert to organize and manage a book
supply department. There was neither capitol nor credit on which
to start. With the college guaranteeing the payment of bills there
was no difficulty as to credit. It was located in the room now occupied by the treasurer, later in what is now the dean's office and
then in Rooms 13 and 11, and finally in the Library Building. At
first only pencils, textbooks, and tablets were stocked but later
fountain pens, tennis rackets, gym shoes, and rings with the college seal on them were sold, and later the stock was increased to
include pictures, art supplies, and picnic goods. At the request of
two of the merchants in town the Commissioner of Revenue and the
Treasurer of the City came to the bookstore and asked the manager
to take out a merchant's license. This was done. However, all
agreed that it was not legally necessary since the bookstore was
operated for the convenience of those connected with the college
and not for profit. Mr. Gilbert was enthusiastic about having in
stock all items called for. He bought and handled second hand
books in large quantities.

In the reorganization of 1920 Mr. Gilbert was relieved of the
book store duties and this business was transferred to the business
manager who very soon reduced the stock to include only the necessary school supplies and textbooks for the students. The bookstore
was then moved to Room 9, where it now remains. In the proposed
Library building the bookstore will have a room on the first floor.
Until the State took control of the finances of the institution the
bookstore funds were kept in a separate account and were independent

of the other financial resources of the institution. Since the
1928 reorganization it has been included in the general business
management of the college. The business manager is responsible
for the purchasing of all supplies for the bookstore and student
clerks are used in its maintenance.

STUDENT BUILDING FUND

The project for the erection of literary society homes undertaken by the Ingles and Pocahontas Literary Societies in 1922 was
carried on for several years independently of the general business
management of the college. Each literary society was responsible
for the collection of its own pledges. This was done by student
treasurers for the Ingles Society and by Professor Gilbert for the
Pocahontas Society. With the appointment of Miss Helen Cook as
Alumnae Secretary the business of the collection of these pledges
and care of the "Home Fund" was turned over to the Alumnae Secretary. A major part of her work was the making of records of the
pledges, collecting pledges, and keeping accounts of the funds.

When Miss Cook resigned her position these funds were turned
over to the college business manager who continued to keep the
money as a separate fund for the students. The funds were combined
into one account and a cooperative plan for collecting the pledges
was organized by the business manager and Miss Allen, Secretary to
the President. Through their efforts the pledges were collected
and the money was used for the payment of the foundations and later
for the erection of the Student Building. Since the completion of
the building the fund has been kept and supplemented by miscellaneous contributions and profits of non-state functions within the institution, such as receipts from tea room, Undertaker's Convention,
Motion Picture Shows, and various gifts from the students to meet
the interest and indebtness on the building.

At the time of the erection of the Student Building $11,040.20
had been collected from the faculty and students for payment on it.
The approximate cost of the building was $22,000.00. Since the
erection the cost has been reduced to $4,000.00 by the paid-up
pledges, special funds, and student-faculty contributions.

SECTION IV.

ORGANIZATION AND ADMINISTRATION OF THE OFFICE FORCE

Rose Stacy, The first staff appointee

On May 21, 1913 Doctor McConnell made his first formal recommendations to the Board of Trustees as to the organization of
the instructional policies of the new school. He requested authority to publish a catalog and other advertising materials.
In order to correspond effectively with students and to carry on
the initial organization of the school he requested the authority
to employ a stenographer, where upon the board authorized him to
employ the first stenographer. Her salary was fixed at forty
dollars per month with board. It was suggested that she be employed for half time as the Board felt there would not be enough
work to keep her busy. This was the first salary authorized in
connection with the school. For this position Doctor McConnell
selected Miss Rose Stacy of Emory, Virginia, a graduate of Davenport College in North Carolina and of the stenographic course at
Martha Washington College of Abingdon, Virginia. She served as
private secretary to Doctor McConnell from 1912 until 1914. She
assisted Doctor McConnell in the preparation of the first catalog
of the institution published in June 1913. They also prepared a
viewbook filled with pictures of the city of Radford and the neighboring country with architect drawings of proposed buildings.

Miss Stacy moved with the McConnell family to Radford. Here
she organized and opened the office of Secretary to the President.
This office was located adjacent to the President's office in the
Northwest corner of the Administration Building on the first floor.
Before the opening of the college in 1913 the Board had these offices furnished with a large double desk of mahogany, mahogany
stenographer's desk, one typewriter and several paste board letter
files. In these were kept the correspondence relative to the institution. Throughout the first year of the college Miss Stacy
was the only stenographer employed. She did all the stenographic
work of the institution. In the Spring of 1914 she resigned her
position to continue her work as a student.

MISS WILLIE GRAY ALLEN, SECRETARY TO THE PRESIDENT

Miss Stacy was succeeded by Miss Willie Gray Allen of Howerton,
Essex County, Virginia. Miss Allen was an experienced stenographer
having previously been employed at the State Hospital at Williamsburg and as Secretary to the President of Blackstone Female Insti-

tute at Blackstone, Virginia. She was employed as Secretary to
the President, however, closely following her arrival at the
college the Legislative Act transferring the Control of the
school from the original board to the centralized board took
place. In this connection the office of Secretary and Treasurer held by Honorable Robert J. Noell was abolished. Miss Allen
was then designated as Secretary and Treasurer and Secretary to
the President of the college. At this time the business management of the institution was largely in the hands of the President
it was therefore of vital importance that the treasurer of the
institution be located in his office and thus of easy access to
the central administration of the school. The chief function of
the treasurer was to look after the local business of the school.
The treasurer drew such checks as were necessary, made payment
for purchase of supplies for the various departments of the institution, paid the salaries of the faculty members and kept the
books of the institution in such a manner that the President could
make a report upon the financial status of the college upon call
from the Board of Trustees. Miss Allen was most conscientious and
careful in her business management. She was soon identified in
the institution as one of the most hard working and persevering
of the employees. She worked untiringly early and late to carry
on the increasing duties of the President's office.

From 1913 to 1920 the entire administration of the college
was centralized in the office of the President. Through this
office all the activities of the institution were directed except
those confined to the Registrar's office and the purely instructional activities of the institution. In this way the Secretary
to the President became identified and played a large part in the
development of all aspects of the college life. Miss Allen was
particularly interested in the securing of students, she devoted
much thought and attention to the preparation of advertising
materials, and to the development of a personal contact through
letters with prospective students. Each correspondent aroused a
keen interest and assumed a personal identity for her.

Miss Allen especially was active in the development of the
summer quarter which in the early history of the institution was
one of the most trying of all of the administrative problems. It
involved the handling of many hundreds of students with a multi-
tude of problems attendant upon the housing and teaching. In
preparation for the opening of the summer quarter Miss Allen
would spend many weeks. It was her practice to inspect the homes
of the city of Radford where the students were to be located. In
this way she became well acquainted with the women who "desired
to keep Normal girls." With her accumulative and intimate acquaintance with the students and with the homes of the city of

Radford she managed to house the great number of students who
entered the college most successfully. In 1918 when the tent
village was established on the campus for the housing of the students of the summer quarter, the section devoted to girls was
named "Willie Gray Allen Village." For sixteen years she was an
outstanding figure in the feverish excitement of the registration
days which opened the summer quarters and the regular sessions in
September.

Under Miss Allen's administration as Secretary to the President the original equipment of the President's office was increased.
She selected and supervised the installation of all the office
equipment including the filing cabinets, storage cabinets, multi-
graph, addressograph, additional stenographer's desks, typewriters
and many of the little conveniences of office equipment. In all of
these she had a pride of possession. She guarded them carefully
and directed their use by others.

In 1916 she combined duties of the two offices which Miss Allen
held became too great. Mr. J. Harvey Barnett at that time the ticket agent for the Norfolk and Western Railroad, East Radford, Virginia was employed as part time bookkeeper. With the coming of Mr.
Barnett the first expansion of the administrative office took place.
The room to the right of the stairs of the front entrance of the
administration building was used as a business office. Mr. Barnett
spent three or four afternoons each week posting the books. This
relieved Miss Allen of the bookkeeping but left her entrusted with
such business management as was directed by the president.

OTHER STENOGRAPHERS

In 1920 in the general reorganization of the administration
of the college, Mr. Sylvester L. McConnell was appointed Treasurer and Business Manager of the College and Miss Allen's connection with the business management ceased. Thereafter her duties
were confined to those as Secretary to the President. These so
rapidly increased that other stenographers were necessary to assist her with the routine work of the office. In 1921 Miss Allen
resigned her position and spent several months working in Richmond. During this time the position as Secretary to the President was filled by Miss Mary Louise Galloway who had entered in
1920 as assistant stenographer and secretary in the Extension
Department. The Extension Department had been organized in 1919.
Miss Galloway was Secretary to the Dean of Women, Secretary in
the Extension Department and assistant-stenographer in the president's office from 1920-1923. Miss Galloway was the daughter of
Mr. and Mrs. W. H. Galloway of Radford. As extra work while in
the employ of the college she copied the Manuscript for Mr. F. B.
Fitzpatrick's book, "Present Day Practices in Education." The

first book to be written and published by a member of the Radford College Faculty. Miss Lottie Roberts, daughter of Mr. and Mrs. Arthur Roberts of Radford, Virginia, was employed as assistant stenographer. The stenographers who have been employed for the Extension Department, as Secretary to the Registrar, and Secretary to the Dean of Women have been: Misses Loretta Grubb, Mary Sandridges, Halley Otey, Elizabeth Breckenridge, Cecil Hazelwood, Gladys Dixon, Ruby Feathers, Cales, Elizabeth Roop, Helen Hall, Beaulah Cox, Zella Blackard, Geneva Taylor, and Ruby Shrader.

In 1924 during the illness of Mr. Sylvester L. McConnell, Miss Mary Sandridges who was then employed by the Farmers and Merchants National Bank returned to the college and acted as Treasurer for three months. Upon the reorganization of the business department under the centralized State control in 1927 it became necessary to transfer Miss Gladys Dixon who had been serving as Secretary in the Extension Department to the business department in which capacity she has served to the present time. Miss Dixon entered the service of the College during the summer of 1926 and served for two years as Secretary to Mr. J. P. Whitt, the Registrar. She was succeeded as Secretary to the Extension Department by Miss Elizabeth Roop who had been acting as assistant-stenographer in the President's office. Miss Roop was later made assistant in the Extension Department when it was transferred from the direction of Professor Fitzpatrick to the Direction of Mr. J. P. Whitt. The correspondence courses of the Extension Department were largely put in shape by Miss Roop. She organized the records, assembled the materials, combined the courses and developed the present system for the management of the mail for the correspondent students. She also did much of the publicity work for the college under the direction of Doctor Moffett. In 1930 whne Miss Allen resigned her position as Secretary to the President Miss Roop was promoted to this position. Throughout her entire association with the college she had been ambitious to complete her education which she felt was limited. In view of her position she was granted a leave of absence effective during the academic year of 1930 and 1931. Associated with Miss Roop as assistant-stenographer was Miss Helen Hall who devoted a large part of her time to assisting Miss Allen and to acting as Secretary to the Dean of Women and in full charge of the stenographic work of the publicity department. Upon the leave of absence of Miss Roop, Miss Hall was promoted to the position as Secretary to the President. Her work in the Extension Department was taken by Miss Beaulah Cox of Lebanon, Virginia, who at present is the Assistant in charge of the Extension De-

partment of the College. Miss Zella Blackard of Groseclose,
Virginia, was employed as stenographer in the summer of 1930.
One of the major pieces of her work since coming to the college
has been the preparation of the manuscript of the history of
the college. From time to time it has been necessary to have
extra helpers in the stenographic work, the chief of these has
been Miss Ruby Feathers and Miss Geneva Taylor. The stenographic work of the college has so grown in the two decades of the
history of the institution that the work formerly done by one
person now requires the full time service of six regular secretaries and stenographers. Various students have served as office assistants and mailing clerks. Chief among these have
been Helen Martin, Maude Payne, Alma Mitchell, Mary Watkins.
At present the mailing of catalogs, bulletins, etc., is done by
students who work in the Information Bureau.

OFFICE NICKNAMES

The humanness and sense of humor of Doctor McConnell is
shown in the nicknames with which he dubs each stenographer
and his more intimate associates. Most of these are chosen
from the "funny" paper or strips. Helen Hall is "Tillie",
Beaulah Cox, "Bubbles", Elizabeth Roop, "Flapper Fanny",
Zella Blackard "Polly", Ruby Shrader, "Dutchman", Geneva
Taylor "Annie", Mr. Whitt "War Horse", "Lord Baltimore", "Jasper"
or "Old Superintendent", Miss Moffett "Old Dean", Professor
Gilbert "The Buck" or "General", Sylvester McConnell "Colonel
Sylvester", Gladys Dixon, "Rosie".

SECTION V.

BOARDING OR HOME DEPARTMENT

HOUSING AND SUPERVISION OF LIVING HALLS

The home department or that department of the institution devoted to the housing and boarding of students has always been an integral part of the administrative activities of the State supported institutions in Virginia. In the development of each of the teacher training institutions the problem of housing and boarding of students has been one of deepest concern to the administrative heads. Until the passage of the Noell Act in 1926 the State made direct appropriations for the erection of dormitories on the campus of all of the State supported institutions. The management of these dormitories devolved upon the President and the Board of Control of the institution.

THE ORIGINAL HOME DEPARTMENT

In the original organization for the administration of the Radford College it was planned by the first Board of Trustees to have a matron as the head of the Home Department. Her chief duties were the direct supervision of the social life of the students and the physical care of the dormitories. In addition a housekeeper was employed to have charge of the purchasing of supplies, the planning and serving of meals. These employees worked under the personal direction of the President.

On June 6, 1913, the Board fixed the student charges for furnished rooms, board, laundry, lights, and heat at fifteen dollars per month. Doctor McConnell was instructed to employ a matron and housekeeper. To this position he appointed as matron Mrs. Phoebe Brugh and as housekeeper Mrs. N. P. Walker. Mrs. Walker did not accept this position and Miss Cecil Crockett of Wytheville, Virginia was appointed.

MRS. PHOEBE BRUGH

Mrs. Brugh is a New Orleans woman. She has the culture, graciousness of manner, beautiful face and good taste in dress characteristic of the better type of Southern gentlewomen. As matron she was an unusually successful leader of girls. She served in this capacity for four years. During this time she stamped her personality indelibly upon the students who came under her supervision.[1] She successfully met many problems of student adjustment and physical inconvenience which

1. See Volume II. Student Personnel and Social Life.

rose from the use of the old "La Belle Inn" as a dormitory.

La BELLE INN

The First Dormitory

The La Belle Inn had been built in the boom days of Radford for a hotel and had been used for this purpose for several years. It was later converted into a hospital for the use of the employees of the Norfolk and Western and Virginian Railroads during the construction of the double track of the Roanoke, Radford and Bluefield Divisions. It belonged to the Heth Estate (Miss Virginia Heth) and was rented by the College for $1200 a year. The building is a large frame structure of the popular architectural design of the late nineties with long rambling porches, dark, crooked halls which become more narrow as they approach the less frequently used parts of the building. At the East end is a large tower in which there are two large circular rooms with many windows and a look-out pergole at the top. The rooms are not uniform in size. Those on the second floor are more spacious and airy, those on the third floor have sloping roofs and dormer windows. No uniformity could be practiced in the rooming of students in this building. In some of the rooms four students were placed, others three, some two and the tower room had six. In all there were about one hundred and twenty-five girls housed in this building during the first session. In addition Mrs. Brugh, Miss Crockett and Miss Simmons of the Faculty had rooms in the "La Belle Inn". The building provided very limited bath rooms and toilet facilities. The furnishings provided for the students included three quarter Murphy beds of good quality, dresser, washstand, student table and a chair for each student. The lower halls were covered with crex runners in green and tan design. The parlor was on the first floor. In this room were the prize possessions of the school, a baby grand piano bought by the Board of Trustees, a large oval mahogany table, a long davenport and three or four mahogany rockers. The furniture from this room is now in the Tyler Parlor of the College. The windows were draped with lace curtains. This parlor was considered a place of great elegance, it was in fact, the best furnished spot, with the exception of the administrative offices, in the institution. In this room much of the early social life of the college took place. The informal social center for the students, however, was in the old hotel lobby where a large counter separated the office from the lobby. Students spent many hours leaning on this counter talking, gossiping and philosophizing upon the problems of life. Mrs. Brugh used the office as headquarters. She took an active part in these discussions and through her wisdom guided the thinking into the most helpful channels.

THE HETH HOUSE

In order to care for the students who could not be housed in La Belle Inn the college rented the Norwood Home, known as the "Heth House", where twenty-five students were housed during the first twelve months of the life of the college. This house was the homestead of the Heth farm on which the college was established. It has been the home of the Hammets and Heths for many years. It is one of the oldest homes in Radford. The original house has been built to and remodeled. It is somewhat Victorian in design. The rooms are very large fully 20X30 feet. These rooms are built around a central hall or a reception room which has a high rotunda ceiling and is circled by a gallery. This room is connected by means of folding doors to a tower library on the left, a drawing room and family liv-rooms on the right. Back of the hall is a large room once used as a dining room, this is connected by a narrow passage to an outdoor kitchen and also to a stairway leading to the basement kitchen of the original house. Upstairs there are spacious bedrooms. The upper tower room is on a higher level than the remainder of the rooms and is reached by several steps. The tower itself has a winding stairway. During the occupancy of the house by the students this room was reserved by the Heths and was kept securely locked. The mystery of "Blue Beards Chamber" could not equal the haunting romance of this forbidden chamber. This "thrill" added to the local stories of "haunts" made living in the Heth House an adventure of great daring. Locally many fascinating yarns and tales are told about this residence. The chief of which is the mysterious maneuvers of a ghost. There is supposed to be a buried fortune in the basement. Many people sought permission to dig for this treasure. From time to time new holes appeared in the basement kitchen showing that some really believed the yarn.

Each of the rooms with the exception of the main hall and dining room were assigned as bed rooms to the students. In most of the rooms there were three or four girls. The Heth family had left some of their very large and massive furniture. This was supplemented by the standard college furniture. Students built their own fires in the open grates and carried the fuel from a central coal box.

Nearby were three disused ramsackled barns or old stables which were popular resorts for loafers. Back of the house was a small tennant cottage which the students dubbed "the bungalow".

The first arrangement made by Doctor McConnell for the administration of this building was for Mr. and Mrs. Avent to live in one of the large downstairs rooms and for Mrs. Avent to act as the matron of this building. This arrangement lasted until the first of November 1913. The ghost tales, frequent alarms from the students, the continual passage through the yard of prowling visitors so unnerved Mrs. Avent that they gave up the Heth House. When the Avents moved out Doctor McConnell put Miss M'Ledge Moffett, the youngest member of the faculty in charge of the house. Miss Moffett with her friend Miss Lucy Puryear moved to the Heth House, took the room vacated by the Avents and there lived the remainder of the first year of school. Miss Puryear had nothing to do with the management or control of the students but lived in the house merely as a companion to Miss Moffett. As a general protector for all these young women, Professor Gilbert then a bachelor, was asked to live in the bungalow. Mr. Gilbert used to whistle the air "I Know a Place Where the Four Leaf Clovers Grow" as a signal when he came into the yard to save himself from the volley of shot which Miss Moffett would peal from her pistol when the prowlers became too aggressive. All of the residents of the Heth House and the Bungalow took their meals at the La Belle dormitory. In addition to these two main dormitories the college authorities rented rooms in the home of Mr. and Mrs. W. T. Baldwin, Jr. Twelve girls lived here and their social life was supervised by Mrs. Baldwin. All of these students likewise took their meals in the dormitory.

EXPANSION OF THE HOME DEPARTMENT

In 1915 the first unit of the dormitory located on the campus was erected. The appropriation made for this building by the Legislature of 1914 was not sufficient to complete more than the first two floors. A large section of the basement and the third floor were left unfinished. During the session of 1916 and 1917 this building was used as a dormitory. Miss Flora Bryson teacher of science at the college was made matron of this building. She and the students who lived here ate at La Belle Inn which now became known as the "old dormitory". The Heth House and the Baldwin House were given up. All the students were roomed in the La Belle Inn, the "new dormitory" and at the home of Mrs. H. P. Anderson. The basement kitchen which afterwards became the main kitchen for the institution, was equipped with a hotel range which was given its first use at a candy stew. Miss Crockett who had been housekeeper in the "old dormitory" moved into the "new dormitory" (1916) and managed the new kitchen. Miss Mary Clark was employed as housekeeper for the old dormitory. In the summer of 1916 the summer students were so crowded that the third floor of the building was partly finished. Floors were laid but no doors were hung, large muslin curtains were hung over the doorways. A large canvass inclosed room was built in the open space on the landing. Miss Moffett acted as matron in this dormitory for the summer.

This was the year that the boys of Radford were sent to the encampment at Anniston, Alabama for preparation and training for the World War. A large encampment of soldiers were stationed at Radford. This increased the problems of the discipline of the school. The whole situation pending the departure of the boys created many humorous as well as pathetic scenes. Miss Crockett and Miss Moffett roomed in the first room to the right of the entrance of the dormitory. This room is now used as the office for the building. Almost hourly in the night or day time a rap would come at the window and some lovesick boy would beg for permission to tell his ladylove goodby. They were so confident they would be sent away within an hour. This sincerity and the emotional strain which was reciprocated by the girls gave many dramatic scenes on the front porch of the dormitory. Finally the boys were sent away and Radford became a drab uninteresting place as far as boys were concerned for the next two years. This dormitory was literally christened in the passion of war time and in the emotional stress of that period.

During 1916 and 1917 while the home of Doctor McConnell was being built the McConnell family lived in an apartment in the La Belle Inn. Mrs. McConnell assumed the supervision and direction of the few students who were still housed in this building.

In 1917 and 1918 the second unit of the dormitory was completed. This enabled the college to discontinue the use of La Belle Inn except during the summer quarters. Mrs. Brugh who had been matron in the La Belle Inn since the establishment of the school resigned her position and was succeeded by Miss Mary Berkeley of Farmville, Virginia. Miss Berkeley was matron for two years in the "new dormitory". Her administration of the home life of the students was one of calmness, gentleness and refinement. She was primarily a teacher. She abhorred cats and during her sojourn in the dormitory "Beautiful" never came about the building but spent two years at the homes of Mrs. McConnell and Brs. Bricker. When Miss Berkeley left the college "Beautiful" returned and stayed until her death ten years later.

During the administration of Miss Berkeley it became necessary to employ a nurse. Mrs. Grace Dobyns was employed as nurse. She opened the first infirmary on the second floor of the dormitory. When Miss Berkeley resigned Mrs. Dobyns became matron and was succeeded as nurse by Miss Edmonia Goode. Miss Goode was nurse for one year and upon resignation Mrs. Dobyns again became nurse. Miss Ella Smith was employed as matron. The latter remained only a short time and resigned on account of her health. She presented to the college the large mirror with the handsome brass frame which hangs in the main office of Tyler Hall.

Miss Smith was succeeded by Mrs. Lulu Lemon of Roanoke. Mrs. Lemon was a different type matron from any the college had had before.

She was conscientious in her work, severe in her discipline. She was matron during the last year that secondary students were admitted to the college. Many problems arose as a result of her adjustment to these students. By this time the college had grown so large and the home life had become such a complex problem that it became obvious that the form of administration must be changed. Up to this time a most intimate relationship had existed between the home department and the administration of the college as a whole. All the problems of the home department of any importance were brought to the President for solution. Doctor McConnell devoted a large part of his time to the consideration of these problems. He gave almost daily attention to the physical appearance of the dormitories and took many meals with the students. This with the manifold duties which came as a result of the increase in the instructional policies and business management of the college culminated in the reorganization of 1920.

REORGANIZATION OF 1920
Appointment of Dean of Women

In 1920 Miss M'Ledge Moffett who had been a member of the faculty and active in the development of the student life on the campus was appointed Dean of Women. The Radford College was the first of the State supported institutions in Virginia to create this position and Miss Moffett was the first woman dean appointed in the State. During the summer of 1916-1919 and 1920, she had been taking the course of Deans of Women and Advisors for girls at Teachers College in New York City, New York. In 1921 she received her Master degree with this work as a part of her major course. To Miss Moffett was entrusted the reorganization of the home department. Her plans for this reorganization are shown in the following outline of duties which she set up for each of the departments. So far as is known this is the first written organization of the home department.

DEAN OF WOMEN

Administrator of the girls and parts of the institution which affects their social life.

I. Students
    a. Discipline - Students Government and Special cases.
    b. Social life - Parties, entertainments, guests, etc.
    c. Co-operate in all other activities of a recreational sort.
    d. Dress and conduct.
    e. All permissions:
        1. Home and trips.
        2. Callers (new person).

      3. Class absences.
      4. Special, if of any importance.

II. Food
    1. Plan with housekeeper menu.
    2. Approve policy for food purchase.
    3. General oversight of kitchen, dining room, storeroom, pantry and meal service.

III. Home
    1. Plan with matron policies for best management and social life.
    2. General oversight and management.
    3. Matron must consult for purchases.

IV. Laundry
    a. General oversight.
    b. Receive and adjust girls complaints.

V. Administration Building
    a. Hostess for guests.
    b. Management of cleaning.

VI. General School Work.
    a. Teach some regular work.
    b. Charge of calendar of events.
    c. Membership on Committees.
    d. Oversight of all teacherages in which girls live.

VII. Try to meet emergencies which arise in any of the above places.

MATRON'S DUTIES

1. Supervise the dormitory above the dining room floor, cleaning, arranging furniture and decoration, inspect girl's rooms twice each week oftener if necessary.

2. Hold office hours for the purpose of conferring with girls about matters of the life within dormitory - such as rooms, laundry, etc.

3. Keep records of girl's town visits.

4. Give special permissions of an emergency character.

5. Give permissions for callers - meet all callers who come to dormitory for social visits.

6. Be hostess for guests at dormitory.

7. Cooperate and confer with student government association upon discipline and routine control of dormitory.

8. Ring bells, lock doors.

9. Supervise and train waitresses and all other dining room conduct.

10. Have frequent conferences with Miss Moffett about general management and policy.

11. Cooperate with housekeeper and nurse in all routine matters.

12. Attend house conferences of housekeeper, nurse and Dean of Women. Member of Home Committee.

13. Be great assistance in social functions.

NURSE'S DUTIES

1. Have entire charge of infirmary, cleaning and management.
2. Care for sick, report same to office.
3. Hold office hours for students, morning and evening.
4. Attend all emergency cases.
5. Visit with school doctor.
6. Have charge of dormitory linen, distribution and keeping records sending to laundry.
7. Member of Home Committee. Conference with Matron, House-keeper and Dean of Women.
8. Assist in Health examinations of all students.
9. Report to Dean of Women all sanitary facts of Administration Building and dormitory.
10. Supervision of pressing room.

HOUSEKEEPER'S DUTIES

1. Supervise the kitchen, dining room and pantry, cleaning.
2. Give out supplies to cooks.
3. Supervise the preparation of meals, assign tasks and order of work chef is first, assistant and acts in her absence.
4. Confer daily with Miss Moffett, plan menu with her, decide with her on market order and other purchases necessary, consult about servants and general management.
5. Confer with business manager and Miss Moffett about purchases.
6. Supervise the serving of meals, table arrangement, kitchen service, cooperate with Matron to make table service and waitress work a success.
7. Member of Home Committee.

KITCHEN FORCE

Waitresses	1.	Set tables
	2.	Place food
	3.	Serve meal
	4.	Clear table
	5.	Keep flowers on table
Chef	1.	Baker
	2.	Dessert Cook
	3.	General oversight over all work of kitchen
	4.	Report to housekeeper any failure at duty
	5.	Clean all baking equipment
	6.	Keep everything going on the right way in kitchen
Vegetable Cook:		
(a woman)	1.	Cook Vegetables
	2.	Prepare salads
	3.	Assist in bread work
	4.	Care for cooks' table
	5.	Assist in service of meals
	6.	Have oversight over cleaning of kitchen
Meat Cook	1.	Cook meat
	2.	Assist with vegetables
	3.	Fire range and water heater
	4.	Have charge of cleaning of pots and pans
	5.	Assist in meal service
	6.	Assist housekeeper in store room
Dish Washer	1.	Wash dishes
	2.	Clean pantry
	3.	Clean dining room
	4.	Help in kitchen when needed
Dish washer	1.	Wash dishes
	2.	Clean pantry
	3.	Clean dining room
	4.	Ring triangle and bells
	5.	Help in kitchen when needed
Forest	1.	Carry coal
	2.	Slop
	3.	General helper
Laundry		
Head Woman	1.	Count clothes

2. Mark clothes
3. Assign work to helpers
4. Sort clothes
5. Check for return
6. Keep records
7. Hear complaints

Helpers, wash and iron according to assignment.

Suggestions for Management of Laundry

1. Have clothes well listed by girls.
2. Limit amount from each girl.
3. Have each bundle checked at time of opening in laundry. Return unlaundered all not properly listed.
4. Use small number, place in uniform position on garment.
5. Sort clothes into kinds and wash, iron and sort accordingly, for instance all waists together, etc.
6. Fasten handkerchiefs together.
7. Check each list as return-package is made.
8. Mistakes must be reported at once by girl in writing.
9. Have very close supervision by a clean person.

At the same time of the reorganization of the home department the business management of the college underwent a change. Mr. S. L. McConnell was appointed treasurer and business manager for the school. A close cooperation was established between the business department and the home department. He and Miss Moffett became the purchasing agents for the institution. Miss Moffett assumed the purchasing of all supplies used in the home department and assisted Mr. McConnell in purchasing supplies for other parts of the institution.

Mrs. Kate Huffard of Bristol, Virginia was appointed matron of the new home department. In this position she served for nine years. Mrs. E. C. Lloyd was appointed nurse and served for eight and one-half years. Under the administration of these ladies, directed by Miss Moffett, many changes were made in the home department. A new system for the care of callers was instituted. Each student was required to get a calling card from the Dean. In this way a number of undesirable young men were eliminated from the social list of the college. Other very desirable young men were admitted. A closer contact for the students of the college was developed with the students of Virginia Polytechnic Institute. In this way the social life in the institution developed a more collegiate atmosphere. Conscious effort was made to develop the personal life of the students. The matron and nurse devoted much time to discussion and in assisting the students in their personal problems. A course, first called "Junior

Special" later "Orientation" was required of all Freshmen. This was taught by Miss Moffett and dealt with such problems as personality, character, personal hygiene, mental hygiene, etiquette and other common social practices as well as a study of the vocations and their opportunities for women. This course became one of the most popular with the students and created much discussion and interest on the campus. The course was enriched by many pieces of illustrated material which were posted on the bulletin boards in the Administration Building.

From time to time formal social gatherings were held in the main parlor of the college. In these the various members of the faculty assisted. Many different plans were tried, under the direction of the home department to perfect a greater cultural development of the students. One year the faculty was divided into groups and each group held a tea in the tea room for the students. In 1926 Doctor McConnell appointed a committee of the members of the faculty composed of Miss Florence Baird, Virginia O'Hudson, and Susan Roberts as a culture committee, to bring before the students and faculty a discussion of as many cultural problems as possible.

THE HOSTESS SYSTEM

The Madame Russell Hall was completed in June 1927 and was used for the first time during the summer term of 1927. With the addition of this building and the general evolution in the problems of social life, campus life became more complex. It was decided therefore to try a new form of administration for this building. The hostess system was originated. Miss Ethel Roberts who had received her Bachelor degree in 1927 was appointed hostess of Madame Russell Hall. Miss Roberts was a young woman of good intellectual ability, quiet, gentle, and usually successful in leading girls. She had been student president during her last year as a student. Her youth brought her in close contact with the students and made it easier to establish a friendship. With her initiative foresight and perseverance she started the hostess system successfully. The hostess plan provides for the supervision of social life of the dormitory by a young teacher who has other interests and yet time to live and work with the students. In such a plan it is of vital importance that the personality, judgment, social background and interest of the hostess be considered. The plan is not workable unless the hostess herself is possessed of these qualities.

Miss Florence Belle Ogg succeeded Miss Roberts as Hostess in Madame Russell Hall for the academic session of 1928-29. During her stay in the dormitory Miss Ogg placed emphasis upon a refine-

ment of the social life of the students. She inaugurated a series
of teas for her students and did much individual work.

The Madame Russell Hall gradually become the headquarters of
the more advanced college students of the institution. The Juniors
of 1927 requested that one floor of the west wing be set aside as
Senior Hall. This was done and almost uniformly the Seniors have
desired to live on this hall. The arrangement of the building with
its large lounge has made it a center for much of the social life
of the institution.

Miss Ercelle Bennett succeeded Miss Ogg as Hostess in 1929 in
which position she has served up to the present day.

DOCTOR VIRGINIA O. HUDSON, ACTING DEAN OF WOMEN 1927-29

In 1927 Miss Moffett was granted a leave of absence to study at
Teachers College, New York City. During her absence Doctor Virginia
O. Hudson acted as Dean of Women. Doctor Hudson had been a professor
of English in the college for one year prior to her appointment as
Dean of Women. She assumed a part of the duties performed by Miss
Moffett, particularly those devoted to the supervision of the social
life and activities of the students. She was not given the responsibility for the food department. This was assumed by Miss Elsie Palmer
and Mr. Sylvester McConnell. Nor was she directly responsible for the
supervision of the nursing and health in the college. Under her direction Mrs. Huffard continued as matron in the Tyler Hall. Miss
Ethel Roberts for one year and Miss Florence Belle Ogg one year, were
hostesses in Madame Russell Hall. During her administration Doctor
Hudson took her meals in the dormitory and gave close supervision to
the life in these buildings. She held the students to high standards
of conduct, was firm and strict in her discipline, devoted much time
to the cultural development of the life of the institution and placed
emphasis upon the more formal group activities. She established a
greater respect for office hours and somewhat systematized the routine
of the Dean's office.

During these two years the "family spirit" largely disappeared,
the student's acquaintance was more or less limited to the building
in which she lived and the administration of the home department became functional and lost the personal unity of the early years. Such
a change is natural and is generally characteristic of large groups
living in separate buildings. Within the building, however, the
groups are more homogenous, although life within each building is
different, it is marked with a unity and loyalty peculiar to itself.

EXTENSION OF HOSTESS SYSTEM - 1929

In 1929 Doctor Moffett returned from Columbia University. She
resumed her former position as Dean of Women. Doctor McConnell then
decided definitely to adopt the hostess system for the administration
of all the dormitories. This new and enlarged system provided for a
division of the work formerly done by the matron.

The supervision of the social and personal life of the students
was separated from the supervision of the physical appearance and
equipment of the buildings. The hostess became the head of the dormitory life, she was charged with the development of social ease and
grace in the students with the guidance and leadership of the group
life and to act as counsellor of the students in the solution of personal problems. Naturally there is a close relation between these
latter factors and the physical environment. Hence the plan provided for the employment of a superintendent, who was responsible
for the physical appearance of all the buildings of the college plant,
the employment of maids and janitors. Miss Helen Martin a graduate
of the Home Economics Department of the College was employed as the
first superintendent of the buildings. She took up her work September 1929. In six months she had brought about a reformation in the
physical appearance of the buildings and in the amount and quality
of work of the maids and janitors. Unfortunately for this phase of
the scheme when Miss Palmer became ill in January 1930 and was forced
to resign her position Miss Helen Martin was appointed dietitian.
Since the position as superintendent of buildings has been vacant
Miss Martin, Miss Moffett, and the hostesses have partly directed
this work.

In the fall of 1929 Miss Mae Kelly, a graduate of the College
and a critic teacher in the City Training School was appointed hostess of the Tyler dormitory. Miss Ercelle Bennett, critic teacher at
Belspring for the Madame Russell dormitory, Miss Ruth Lewis, a critic
teacher of the seventh grade of the city training school hostess of
Helen Henderson Hall. The personality of each of these young women
has been such as to make a success of the hostess system. The sepa-
ration of the drudgery of housekeeping from the social life made it
possible for the supervision of the social life to be part time work.
Each hostess lives in her building. Most of her dormitory work is
done at night and on weekends. The problem of discipline is largely
cared for by the student government. Permission giving, except emergency is centralized in the Dean's office. This frees the hostess
and affords her more time and a better basis for working with the
group or individual students. Each hostess has developed a social
hour program, 6:30 to 7:30 in the evening. Music, games, stunts,
stories, discussions are planned by them and student committees for

116

the entertainment and recreation of the group. The hostess has
a student-assistant, who inspects the student's rooms and attends
to emergencies during the absence of the hostess in the dormitory.
These assistants are chosen with care from the Junior and Senior
classes. The assistants for 1929-30 were: Tyler; Stella Mae Agnew; Madame Russell, Audrea Sharpe. For 1930-31 were: McGuffey,
Maxine Scyphers; Madame Russell, Julia Bryant. The nurse has assisted Miss Lewis in Helen Henderson Hall when such assistance is
necessary. The student executive council has an auxiliary organization in each hall. These provide a house president, floor monitors
and representatives responsible for study hour, minor disciplinary
offenses and general morale of the building.

HOUSING OF STUDENTS DURING THE SUMMER QUARTER

The first summer school was held in the Radford College in
1914 with a total enrollment of 346 students. Each summer there
was an increase in the number of students until 1926 when the enrollment reached the grand total of 1591. This great influx of
students for three months overtaxed all the facilities of the Home
Department. As many as possible were housed in the dormitories,
others were housed in the homes of Radford. For sixteen years
Miss Willie Gray Allen had the responsibility of rooming these students. She spent many months, prior to the opening of summer school,
inspecting and assembling information in regard to the desirable
homes in the city of Radford for students. Practically every home
in East Radford had from one to six or eight students for the summer
session.

THE TENT VILLAGES

In 1923 the desirable facilities for housing students in the
city were exhausted. To meet the emergency it was decided to build
tent villages. Sixty army tents were bought by the college and set
up on the campus in two villages, one for the boys (James Hoge Tyler
Camp) and the other for the girls, (Willie Gray Allen Village). The
villages had a central street with a water spigot, like the town
pump, in the center. The tent house was constructed with a wooden
floor and a thirty inch side wall of wood with canvass sides and top.
Each tent was furnished with a bed, washstand or dresser, a table
and several chairs. Water was piped to the tent villages and toilet
facilities were provided in the nearby dormitories. The adventure
of living like soldiers in tents appealed to the students. It was
not difficult to get them to live in the villages. To save a tent
in a thunderstorm was one of the fascinating sports of the campus.

THE BRIGGS AND SIMON BUILDINGS

In 1923 the college also rented two large buildings on the Main Street of the city of Radford as dormitories for the students. The second and third floors of the Briggs building was used and two floors of the Simon Building were used. The college spent much effort and labor in getting these two buildings into fit condition to be used by the students. Mrs. Winston acted as matron and had general supervision of these houses. The students took their meals in the college dining room. The Briggs' building has since been converted into the Dixie Inn and the Simon building has been used as apartments. This plan did not prove entirely satisfactory and it was abandoned after one year. For several years after the La Belle Inn was abandoned for the regular sessions of the college it was used as a dormitory during the summer quarter. Miss Mattie Weaver was the matron of this building. Since the college has discontinued the use of this building for dormitory purposes groups of students have rented rooms there and done light housekeeping. After three years of hard usage the tents began to wear out, the enrollment of the summer school decreased so that the newly acquired Madame Russell and Helen Henderson Halls made it possible to house the greater percentage of the students in the campus buildings and better homes of the town.

THE FOOD DEPARTMENT

The Food Department was managed by Miss Cecil Crockett, a member of the famous Crockett family of Wythe County. She had had many years of experience as housekeeper on a large farm. She transferred this experience to the management of the Boarding Department of the new school. The first kitchen was located in the South wing of the La Belle Inn. It was equipped with one hotel range with three double eyes, a large kitchen table, several large kettles, frying pans, baking pans and zinc tubs for dish washing. A small room was set aside as a store room for canned goods. Potatoes, apples, and fresh vegetables were stored in the basement. The kitchen was managed in a home fashion. Plain simple country meals were served, beans, cabbage, corn, home killed pork, potatoes and such fresh vegetables as were available from nearby farms or school gardens were used in large quantities. Students were employed as waitresses and were given a part of their board for this service. The kitchen staff included two cooks, Emma and Alec Christian and a dish washer, Sonny Jones. The dining room was furnished with long ten-seat tables made by the school carpenter Mr. Roop. The bent-back chairs, at that time considered the par excellence for college dining rooms were imported, dishes were borrowed for the first meal. China dishes of good quality and designs were used. These were soon broken and heavy hotel crockery was purchased.

FOOD SUPPLIES

The college raised much of the food it used. Across the road from La Belle Inn near the present heating plant twenty to twenty-five hogs were fed from the garbage and waste from the tables. These were butchered as needed, dressed and cut up according to home fashion and served in bountiful plenty to the students.

Monday was "drummer day". At this time representatives of the wholesale supply houses of Roanoke, Radford, and Bluefield consumed hours of Miss Crockett's time discussing their wares. The purchasing of all food supplies was left entirely to the housekeeper. Supplies were not bought on requisition or very far in advance since it was necessary to spend only as the income from the students so justified. The McConnell's kept several cows. From these cows and from other places in the community small quantities of milk was supplied for use in the coffee and over the cereals. Milk was not served to drink. Butter was bought from the farmers. The Boarding Department of the Normal School became the mecca for the farmer and merchants of the community. Competition was keen, often the butchers would call Miss Crockett at five o'clock in the morning in order to get the order for the day. Miss Crockett was a careful buyer, good manager of the food supplies and accurate in her accounts. Much of the early financial success of the institution was due to her economies.

WAR TIME AND THE FOOD DEPARTMENT

The war period complicated the administration of the food department. Miss Crockett resigned her position in 1918. She was succeeded by Mrs. Dobyns who managed the food department throughout the summer quarter and was then succeeded by Mrs. Knight of Emory. Both of these women attempted to manage the larger problems of the food department in the same home fashion which had been the practice throughout the history of the institution. Mrs. Knight remained with the college one year. She then resigned and was succeeded by Miss Mary Clark.

The purchasing of food became an acute problem in 1918 and 1919. It required so much time and skill that Doctor McConnell had Mr. Gilbert (then manager of the book store) to attend to the purchasing of such supplies as had to be bought from wholesale houses and any place other than local firms. Mr. Gilbert continued the same general methods of purchasing supplies as had always been used. The drummers called at his office and orders were given to them. Many of the supplies during the war period had to be bought as "futures" subject to war conditions for delivery. Mr. Gilbert entered into contracts for meat with the local butchers. By this arrangement meat for specific uses was delivered on specified days of the week. By this method the students quickly determined when they would have a roast, beef stew, steak, etc. Throughout this entire period the object of the food department had been to serve as good wholesome and bountiful meals as the resources of the boarding department permitted.

One of the major "goods" that came out of the World War was the emphasis upon scientific feeding. The research and popular publicity given to the importance of food in health and in the general vitality of people made greater progress during this period than it had made in the one hundred years since the French Revolution. The movement for trained dietitians as the heads of the food department of institutions rapidly became popular.

THE NEW FOOD DEPARTMENT STARTED IN 1920.

Miss Moffett as Dean of Women devoted much time and attention to the development of the food department. The kitchen was completely refurnished. The first piece of equipment bought was an electric dish washer. In 1920 a second hand baking equipment was purchased from Mr. C. W. Beard, baker in Radford. This was placed in one corner of the kitchen and Mr. Beard was employed as the college baker. Until this time the college had bought the larger part of its bread and only attempted to make such rolls and biscuits as could be handled by two women cooks. Mr. Beard was responsible for the preparation of all the bread and desserts used in the college. He remained with the college for one year and was succeeded by Frank Campbell, a colored man of wide practical experience as baker and cook. Frank had been employed for eleven years at the Catawba Sanitorium. With his coming the baking of bread, making of ice cream, pastries and cakes became an important function of the kitchen force.

In 1920 the dining room was moved from Tyler unit to the Norwood unit of the dormitory and the Tyler unit was converted into an extra store room, bed rooms for the cooks and a dining room for the servants.

The McGuffey unit of the dormitory was completed in 1923 and the basement was finished in 1924. With the completion of this additional space the dining room was moved into the McGuffey unit. This gave more room and space for the kitchen which was laid off in such a way as to provide a room for baking, a meat and vegetable kitchen, a utensil room, a three-chamber refrigeration plant, a large area for dish pantry with storage space and electric dish washer and an ice cream compartment. At this time it was decided

not to provide rooms for the servants and all of these were required to secure rooms outside of the college. As a special convenience for the colored help a bath room with toilet, tub and
basin was placed in one section of the basement unit. This consideration of the servants was greatly appreciatted by them. Alva
Armstead, the head cook, was charged with the responsibility to
see that each of the servants bathed frequently in the tub. For
several weeks he reported that Sidney refused to take a bath in
the new tub. Sidney in defense of himself stated that "he wasn't
sure that he were going to live and die in the Normal School and
therefore he wasn't going to get used to nothing he wasn't going
to have no place else."

Miss Moffett and Mr. McConnell purchased a quantity of new
equipment for the kitchen. Several thousand dollars was spent for
a Hobart mixer, steam tables, aluminum steam kettles, cast iron
steam roaster, metal kitchen tables. Practically all of this equipment was bought through Knobe of Richmond. An automatic refrigerating plant was installed by the Automatic Refrigerating Company
of Hartford, Connecticut.

In 1926 the large universal bake oven was installed, the port-
able oven which had been purchased from Mr. Beard was sold. In
1928 the fearless dish washer was discarded and a large Colts-
Auto-San was purchased. New zinc covered tables were added to the
pantry equipment and a Van Vaughan electric meat cutter was placed
in the pot room, this cutter will cut a quarter of beef into steaks
in a half hour.

THE DINING ROOM

The cultural program of the college placed special emphasis
on the dining room service. In order to give more detailed and
personal attention to the work of the student waitresses employed
in the dining room Mrs. Lula Coward was employed (1923) as hostess
of the dining room and superintendent of the Administration Building. Mrs. Coward was considered a very beautiful woman, she added
greatly to the tone of the dining room. She paid much attention
to the little nicities of services, to the beautification of the
tables and linens of the dining room.

DIETITIANS

Since the reorganization of the home department Miss Moffett
gave daily supervision to the food department, purchased the supplies, planned the menus and gave general direction to the work of
the servants. Miss Mary Clark was continued as housekeeper until

1924 and was in direct supervision of the kitchen work.

Miss Clark had been employed as housekeeper when the student group was small. She had had hotel experience as a stewardess and was a splendid cook. She is a lover of nature, at all times she is surrounded with pets, cats, squirrels, o'possums, goldfish, and any other chance animal which comes her way. A constant warfare is waged between her and those who would destroy her pets. In all kinds of weather she plods over the campus putting food in some hiding place for her pets. She is a recluse in her personal habits, lives alone with her fancies and her pets. These she shares with those whom she admires. She is most loyal and faithful to any task assigned her. Her advancing age and general health made it impracticable to expect her to assume the full responsibility or to secure the training in scientific feeding required in 1924. She was therefore transferred from the kitchen duties to linen supervisor. She repairs and makes much of the linen used in the college. She spends her days in the pressing room busily sewing and regaling the students with fanciful tales of college lore.

By 1924 the position of Dean of Women had increased the work of Miss Moffett to such an extent that it was decided to employ an assistant dietitian to take direct charge of the kitchen and dining room. Miss Parke Ferguson of Danville, Virginia, a graduate of Home Economics Department of the College in 1920 was employed as dietitian. On the day Miss Ferguson arrived to assume her duties, Mr. Eddie Wilcox, the engineer in charge of the installation of the refrigerating plant, also arrived. As each entered the kitchen they met by the coffee urn. Over a cup of coffee a romance began which after a year of courtship ended in marriage. During the year which Miss Ferguson spent as dietitian at the college she brought about many improvements in the work of the kitchen perfecting a better organization of the help and served scientifically planned meals. Miss Ferguson struggled for cleanliness. During this year white uniforms were purchased by the college for use of the cooks. Uniformed aprons were provided for the waitresses and a larger supply of table linens was purchased. Miss Ferguson stimulated the waitresses to better service.

Miss Ferguson was succeeded by Miss Elsie Palmer of Gate City, Virginia, another graduate. She remained in this position from June 1926 until January 1930. Miss Palmer worked under the direction of Miss Moffett for one year. In 1927-1929 she assumed full charge of the kitchen, purchased perishable supplies and such other commodities as could be bought locally.

Miss Palmer is a student, in spite of her heavy duties as dietitian, she carried one or two courses each quarter. She was a good

manager and cooperated most successfully in the difficult period
of transition from local to State purchasing of supplies. She resigned in 1930 because of ill health and since has started her
professional training as a nurse in Bellevue Hospital, New York
City.

Miss Helen Martin, who had been employed as superintendent of
buildings in September 1929, supplied for Miss Palmer during her
illness and upon her resignation, Miss Martin was appointed dietitian. Miss Martin is the first registered dietitian the college
has had. She graduated in the four year home economics in June
1928 and entered immediately upon a six-months course of special
training as dietitian at the Memorial Hospital in Richmond. Upon
graduation from this course she became dietitian in a hospital in
Wheeling, West Virginia. From this position she accepted the position in her Alma Mater. Miss Martin understands her job, puts
her whole spirit and energy into it and creates more than an institutional life in the dining room. In the short time she has had
the position she has wrought a revolution in the table manners of
the students by a series of impersonal talks on etiquette. She
plans attractive as well as wholesome and economical meals.

STATE PURCHASING OF FOOD SUPPLIES

In 1926 the Legislature established a central purchasing agent
for all the State institutions. This act required the institutions
to purchase all supplies other than perishable foods through the
State Purchasing Agency. Two or three years were spent in organization of this department, to the mutual satisfaction of the State
authorities, the various institutions and the selling public. The
institutions were required to submit requisitions for their supplies
to the State Purchasing Agent who in turn set a day for the representative of the institutions to gather in Richmond to sample the
foods and other commodities offered by the competitors. Miss Moffett
and Mr. S. L. McConnell paid several visits to these State Purchasing orgies. In this way they became well acquainted with the standards and practices of other institutions in the purchasing of foods.
After several such meetings the State Purchasing Commission attempted to standardize on certain supplies. Miss Moffett represented the
Radford College on this committee which spent some time in the study
of the various commodities most suitable for the various types of
institutions. As a result of the work of this committee certain minimum descriptive standards were set up. With these as a basis of the
selection by the State agents better satisfaction has been brought to
the local purchasers so that now most of the supplies are bought on
requisition. From time to time Mr. McConnell attends the Purchasing
"Convention" which is held annually in Richmond. Perishable supplies

are bought by the local dietitian.

Early in her administration of the food department Miss Moffett established a competitive bid basis for the purchasing of perishable supplies from wholesale houses of Roanoke and Bluefield. These firms submit their bids in writing. On each Monday morning the representatives of the firms visit the college and their bids were gone over by the dietitian. In this way the perishable supplies are bought with great economy. The salesman have always been very interested in the life of the campus. One of them dubbed their Monday morning meeting in the College as a "Recess in Heaven". They arrange to arrive at the college shortly before ten o'clock the hour set for purchasing in order to see the students going to assembly.

THE MEALS

Miss Moffett started the system of having the meals planned one week in advance. The menus are posted in the kitchen and the servants adjust their work according to these menus. In 1920 the meals were changed from breakfast, dinner and supper to breakfast, lunch and dinner, the evening meal being the heaviest in the day. The first nutritional change was to provide milk for the students to drink at least once a day.

In the State budget a per capita allowance of thirty to thirty-four cents per day is made for the raw food served in the State Teachers Colleges. From time to time Mr. Bradford, Director of the Budget, makes comparative studies of the food expenditures of the Radford College with other State institutions. The Radford College always uses the maximum allowance for food. However, its total for maintenance is consistently lower therefore the Radford College feels that it can justify its maximum expenditures on food.

In 1922 Doctor Ennion G. Williams, State Health Commissioner made a study of the diet being offered in the various institutions in the State. The report made to him by the school at Radford attracted much publicity. An article appearing in the Roanoke Times, dated August 12, 1922 reads as follows:

In an effort to improve the summer diet offered by the various institutions of the State, Doctor Ennion G. Williams, State Health Commissioner, recently sent out letters to the dietitians and boarding housekeepers of these institutions asking them to submit a record of the food served by them during the summer months in order that any unhealthful menus might be corrected.

Answers were received from several and the State Board of Health

desires that the principles which should govern a proper
hot wather diet be made public.

It is found that many people eat unsuitable food during
the summer months, and it is with the idea of correcting
the diet of such persons that the Board of Health desires
to make public the following facts:

The Radford State Normal School has scientifically worked
out important conclusions concerning the proper arrangement of a summer diet and these have been endorsed by the
State Board of Health.

The average requirement per student is found to be 2,084
calories per day. They need the heaviest meal in the evening, 40 per cent of food requirements being allowed for
dinner, 32 per cent for lunch and 28 per cent for breakfast. About 60 per cent of carbohydrates should be allowed in planning the three meals, these being contained in
bread, cereal, fruit, vegetables and sugar, protein should
be about 33.3 per cent, about 10 per cent of this being
meat, cheese, and beans, while the remaining 23 per cent
is milk, eggs, etc. Fats, such as butter, salad dressing
cooking fats, etc., take up the remaining 7 per cent.
Based on these scientific facts the following meal blocks
should be followed:

Breakfast...Cereal or fruit, light meat, biscuits,
            coffee or cocoa, butter, sugar.
Lunch... ...Salad or meat, croquette, hot bread,
            butter, pudding or fruit, iced tea, milk.
Dinner......Meat, starch vegetable, celulose, rolls,
            vegetable, butter, frozen dessert, milk,
            iced tea.

Starch vegetables include beans, corn, potatoes, rice and peas,
while celery, cabbage, string beans, asparagus, spinnach, onions
and lettuce are cellulose vegetables.

Meals should be planned at least a week ahead, minor changes
being made to suit emergency conditions. This also gives
greater variety in diet, lless work, better marketing, and
also saves time and money, the health authorities assert."

STUDENT WAITRESSES

From the beginning of the institution student waitresses have been used for the serving of meals in the dining room. This has been one of the means provided by the college to help students work their way through school. Many of the students who have assumed these scholarships have been faithful in their work in the institution. A statement of the duties of these girls is described in a letter sent to each of the students who assumed this duty in September 1922.

DUTIES OF GIRLS ON DINING ROOM SCHOLARSHIPS

All girls who have been awarded dining room scholarships accept the scholarship under these conditions.

They will receive $16.00 a month toward their school expenses and will be granted the privileges and opportunities of all the other students in the school. For this compensation they are to render the following services:

First: Serve as waitress at two tables, that is, twenty people in the dining room. The duties of a waitress are: First: to set the table, keep it in good condition, serve the food as directed. The girl who is designated as hostess at the table will make all the requests to the waitresses for additional food service, or whatever may be needed. The waitress is supposed to serve every person at the table in the same way and see to it that every girl gets an equal share of the food provided.

The dining room has been put in first class condition and it must be kept in that way. The waitresses must clean up from the floor anything which she spills, crum her table thoroughly, and wash off spots which are gotten there from carelessness on the part of herself or on the part of the people at the table. Any girl at the table who unduly soils a table linen, abuses the china, etc. must be reported to the Dean at once in order that the waitresses may be relieved of such careless habits.

At the completion of the meal all the dishes must be carried by the waitresses on the trucks to the pantry. They must be stacked in an orderly fashion so that the dish washers may do their work rapidly. All food which is not consumed at the table must be brought in the pantry and placed on the cabinet shelf near the kitchen door. It will be taken up by the cooks and cared for properly.

Before leaving the dining room the waitresses must see
that the chairs are all in position, their aprons neat-
ly folded over the back of the chair, and the window shades
near their table drawn to an equal length. Under no circumstances is anything to be placed in the window sills.
Each waitress is provided with a serving table where she
can keep her water pitcher and any other extra supplies
for each meal. There must be no accumulation of dishes,
sugar bowls, and other things on the serving tables.
Sugar bowls, catchup, syrup and things of that sort are
placed on the table at the meal as it is needed and must
be removed at the completion of the meal the same as any
other unused food.

The food will be served by the cooks and maids and the
waitresses are not to take anything from the serving table,
cooking utensils or anything else until it is indicated
that the food is ready by the servants.

Nothing so marks the refinement and culture of a person
as the table manners he displays. It is absolutely essential that every part of service connected with this
institution be of such high standard of neatness, cleanliness, courtesy of manner, and congeniality of spirit
that no girl will allow any unrefined tendency to come
forward in her table and dining room conduct.

The waitresses must keep fresh flowers on the tables, these
can be gotten in the flower garden until frost and after
that time they will be secured from the green house.

There are a number of girls who are anxious for the privilege of receiving one of these dining room scholarships.
If any girl who has already received these does not feel
that she can comply with the above directions wholeheartily
and good spirited and feels that the dining room is just
as important as anything else that she undertakes and feels
that by doing this work well she can make for herself a
reputation for trustworthiness and general ability, must
forfeit her scholarship at once and allow some other girl
to take up this work.

The same standard of perfection must be maintained throughout the year. The girl who finds that she is unable to
keep up to this standard must notify me at once. I feel
sure that with a spirit of cooperation you will all be
very happy in your work in the dining room.

_____Dean.

As is indicated in this letter the first problem with the student waitresses has been to develop those standards of service most desirable in the dining room. Many of the students who have worked on dining room scholarships have not had the social and home training to qualify them for their work and the pressure of school studies has made it very difficult for them to acquire the skill and technique of the best service. However, the educational benefit to these students by securing an education at a minimum cost has somewhat justified their employment. The allowance for this service has been changed from time to time as the college expense has increased. In 1913 it was $10.00 per month, in 1922 $16.00 per month and in 1930 it is $50.00 per quarter.

BLUE GATE TEA ROOM

In March 1922 the Sixth District Educational Conference met at Radford. In preparation for the entertainment of this group the administration decided to have a special cafeteria for the serving of meals to the visitors. The balcony of the gymnasium which had been used as a storage room was cleaned out and a make shift cafeteria set up. This seemed such a wise use of the balcony, which had always been more or less an eye sore, that Doctor McConnell advised Miss Moffett and Miss Smenner to plan a permanent tea room for the balcony. Their plans resulted in the Blue Gate Tea Room. The furniture and lattice work for this room were made by Mr. Roop. A color scheme of blue and yellow was carried out in the furniture and china. The students of the home decoration classes under the direction of Miss Myrtle Hyer, teacher of clothing, painted japanese motifs on the furniture.

The tea room was managed under the supervision of the Home Economics Department. For several years each student in this department devoted one week to the management of the tea room. The profits were used for the student building fund. In 1927, the use of the tea room as a home economics project was abandoned. Individual students were given the management of the tea room with a share in the profits. The profits made by the college have been used for the replacement and general upkeep of the tea room. Approximately $1000.00 was earned for the building fund. The managers average $50.00 to $75.00 a quarter as their share in profits.

The tea room has formed a social center for the entertainment of small groups for meals. Throughout the history of intercollegiate basketball the visiting teams were always tendered a reception or luncheon in the tea room. From time to time luncheons have been served there for the board members, banquets for the oral English class, Spanish dinners, special luncheons, breakfasts and dinners for distinguished visitors and clubs of women of the city of Radford. The town students are allowed to eat their luncheon in this room. Until 1927 the supplies were purchased for this tea room through the Boarding Department of the College but since that time the students have purchased their supplies as they saw fit from the stores of Radford. The summer quarters have been especially profitable seasons for the managers. Some of the managers have been Maude Eldridge, Ruth Carter, Emma Wall, Oakley Pritchett, Mary Harris, Eleanor Bowers, Louise Mahaney, Vivian Harnsberger, Faye Snider, Edna Penley, Mab Carter and Arlene Williams.

MEAL SERVICE DURING SUMMER QUARTERS

The greatest problems of the heavy enrollment of the summer quarter were in the food department. Seventy-five per cent of the students who attended the college took their meals in the dormitory. The feeding of these students was almost a Herculean task for those in charge of this department. The limited dining room facilities made it necessary to serve double meals. The meals were served to eight or nine hundred students in two groups which reported forty-five minutes a part. This required two sets of waitresses, additional kitchen force and very experienced and rapid dishwashers. Various plans were tried to meet this problem. At first student waitresses were used but the work in the heat of the summer proved to be too great for them so it became impossible to get an adequate number to serve the double meals. Negro waiters were next tried. Twenty-five negro boys were employed. Most of these were students at the Industrial School at Christiansburg. The college housed them in a large frame building erected near the power house and now used as a store room. The problem of discipline and supervision of these boys was very great. So many living together made their work a lark although their service in the dining room was very satisfactory. William Hayden who had been waiter at Mountain Lake Hotel for many sessions was employed as head waiter. He was a "costume" waiter and the burden of his work was changing his costume appropriately for each of the meals. He was very dignified in his manner and added a degree of style and elegance to the dining room service. But neither he nor the boys ever saw any need to hurry in the service especially between meals. Each meal was a hectic time for the manager in charge, probing negroes to hurry, keeping food hot, and encouraging the hungry students who packed impatiently against the entrance doors. The marvel to those who lived through the hectic summers from 1920-1925 is how this problem was ever met with any degree of satisfaction to all concerned.

After the colored boys were used for two summers it was decided to try colored girls. Miss Virginia Allison, a graduate of the Home Economics Department, was employed as superintendent of the dining room and to have charge of these waitresses. This proved the better plan. The colored waitresses were used for two sessions. In 1925 the decrease in enrollment made it possible to go back to the use of student waitresses for both summer and winter sessions. Order had been brought out of chaos and the summer students are now housed and fed with comparative ease with the present facilities.

COLORED PERSONNEL OF THE HOME DEPARTMENT

The work of the home department, its growth, and development has been largely due to the faithful service of the few colored people who have been employed by the college. Their life and service has entered into the very warp and woop of this part of the institution. In the kitchen the first help employed were Emma and Alec Christian who did most of the cooking during the first year of the college. They were unusually fine cooks, hot tempered but faithful in their service.

When the new kitchen on the campus was opened Jim Wade was employed as cook. Jim had worked for a number of years for the Norfolk and Western Railroad. He remained in the college as cook for several years. After a leave of absence to go North he was employed as night janitor in the Administration Building and was employed off and on at the college until his death in 1926.

AUNT MARGARET BRANCH

Aunt Margaret Branch who died July 1930 was identified with the institution throughout its history. She became the bread maker while the old dormitory (La Belle Inn) was still in use. She came with the new force to the new kitchen where she and her niece Halley Bowles were the bread makers for many years. After the establishment of the bakery Aunt Margaret helped with the cooking, picked chickens and was a general substitute cook. Aunt Margaret was the aristocrat of the negroes of the college. She had been born in slavery and was reared by General James Hoge, Grandfather of Ex-Governor James Hoge Tyler. Her ideals were very high and her criticisms of young negroes most severe. She held herself aloof and above those with whom she was associated. When the dining room for the servants was made in the Tyler Hall Aunt Margaret refused to eat at the table with some of the negroes. She preferred to take her plate and eat by the stove in the kitchen. Aunt Margaret was true to her rearing as a real colored gentle woman. In every phase of her work she was faithful and trustworthy. As she grew older she was unable to carry on active service in the school. Until a few weeks before her death, however, she dressed all of the chickens and strung the beans which were served. No special occasion was complete in the college without Aunt Margaret.

HALLIE BOWLES CONNOR

Aunt Margaret had no children but her nephew whom she reared, married Hallie who had been born and reared in Lynchburg. As a girl Hallie had spent much time in service in the North. When Hallie's husband became ill she returned with him to Aunt Margaret and entered the service of the school where she has been in active service for thirteen years. Hallie, like Aunt Margaret, is a superior negress, intelligent, faithful and conscientious in her work. She has devoted herself whole-heartedly to the service of the institution, first as a baker, later as assistant cook and now head woman in the pantry. She is the only woman employed in the kitchen.

ALVAH ARMSTEAD

Alvah Armstead, a nephew of Aunt Margaret, who had been reared by the Tyler family, served as pantry man and cook at the college for ten years. As a boy of twelve he had gone to Richmond and served as door boy for Governor Tyler in the Governor's mansion. Alvah was the best educated of all the negro employees of the institution. Through the influence of Governor Tyler he had been sent to Tuskegee Institute where he was well taught. Alvah was the dominating character in the kitchen throughout his entire affiliation with the school. He was a great debater and general intellectual leader of his group. As long as the Christmas banquets were given at the college for the students, a banquet was also held in the kitchen. Alvah was toastmaster of this affair. He was the chief letter writer for the other negroes. He was a good cook and throughout his entire service in the institution was devoted to his work. He adjusted himself to the reorganization of 1920 and became an active leader in getting the best type of help for the kitchen. These he disciplined and required their subservance to him. For six or eight years his stepdaughter, Jennie Gray, was assistant to Hallie and worked in the pantry.

Jennie is a light negress, neat and clean in her work. She is
very quiet in her manner. She was very much dominated by Alvah.
The most dramatic scene which has ever occurred in the kitchen
was a fight which Jennie had with Dorsie Miller, a negress.
Some moral question was at stake. Dishes flew in all directions,
knives were brandished in the air and words fell thick and fast.
Miss Moffett arrived in the niche of time and ordered calmness.

FRANK CAMPBELL

Alvah was responsible for securing Frank Campbell as baker
for the college. Frank has been baker for eleven years. He is
the most superior of all the help. He is intelligent, courteous,
well trained and dependable. Frank is a master baker and has the
gift of being particularly proud of his success ih this work. Upon the resignation and subsequent death of Alvah Frank was made
head of the kitchen. He is the most effective leader of the entire force. Frank's two sons, George and Emmett, have been tutored
by their father in the college kitchen. George came as a boy of
twelve, grew up in the bake shop where he served as his father's
helper for six years. Emmett is being educated at the Christiansburg Industrial School. He works with his father during the summer.

SIDNEY WALKER

The year that the colored boys were first used as waiters,
Sidney Walker came as an employee in the pantry. Sidney has
since been continually employed by the college and is now serving as cook. During his first year in the institution he fell
desperately in love with Viola Ford, one of the negro waitresses.
Viola is a beautiful negress. Their love affair was waged with
great difficulty due to parental objections. Sidney who is extremely emotional became very much distressed and heartbroken.
Viola went away to teach school. Alvah acted as the intermediary
for the lovers. He wrote letters for them and also talked to
Viola's parents. The ups and downs of this affair kept the kitchen force in an emotional uproar for several weeks. Sidney finally conquered and won the consent of the parents. He and Viola
now have three beautiful children. Sidney was the only employee
of the college kitchen who saw service in France during the war.
The distinction set him apart from the other negroes for several
years. Frequently he refers to what he did in France.

FORREST SAUNDERS

The most unique character ever employed in the kitchen was Forrest Saunders. Forrest was a colored boy of low mentality who served as the slop-boy for the hogs for many years. He with his wheelbarrow trudging across the campus was one of the outstanding pictures of the early college days. He was serenely happy when he had a long black cigar in his mouth. The effect of the picture made by this half crippled boy with a long cigar in his mouth, his baggy trousers, wabbly wheelbarrow, and the slopping garbage placidly strolling across the campus was very amusing. It is frequently described by Doctor McConnell in his talks to the students against the use of tobacco. The use of tobacco has always been forbidden on the campus with the single exception of Forrest.

MURRAY SAUNDERS

Murray Saunders has hauled the coal for the college since the very early day. Each year he has hauled about fifteen hundred tons of coal up the hill from the station to the boiler house. Murray is a highly respected negro of Radford, he preaches sometimes. He has never been employed by the college except by contract for hauling or mowing parts of the campus for hay. When the raising of hogs was abandoned on the campus Murray agreed to haul the garbage of the kitchen away each day for it. In this way he has become definitely identified with the kitchen force. Whenever a deep snow falls Murray takes the students on bob sleigh rides. This treat means much to the Porto Rican students.

OTHER HELP

Others who have served in the kitchen have been William Johnson, George Campbell, Floyd Conner, Amy and Phillip, Herman Hill.

PHYSICAL CARE OF BUILDINGS

In the original plans for the Home Department no definite provision was made for the supervision of the physical appearance of the buildings. One maid, Cytheria Armstead, for the La Belle Inn, and one woman "Bonnie" who gave half-time to the Heth House were employed. These maids worked under the direction of the matron in charge of the building. The housekeeping of these buildings was always an important function of the matron. The physical appearance of the buildings varied in proportion to the standards of cleanliness of the various matrons.

The custom of having three or four big house cleanings each year grew up. This orgy of scrubbing, waxing, and spraying of beds took place at the end of the Spring and Summer quarters and during the Christmas holidays. A large supplementary force of maids was employed for these events. They were very trying to the matrons and all others concerned. Due to the limited funds it was impossible to hire an adequate force of regular full time maids.

In 1920 when Mrs. Huffard assumed charge of the dormitories she had one maid, a white woman, Mrs. Hite. As Mrs. Hite's health became impaired she was assisted by her daughter, Barbara. They cleaned and cared for the buildings for several years.

During the heavy pressure of the summer quarter two very intelligent colored girls, Hortense and Gladys Casey of New River, were employed as waitresses and later became regular maids in the dormitory.

In 1923 when the last unit of Tyler Hall was completed three colored maids were employed, Alice Ramsey, Minnie Frayser, and Ellen Coleman, these with Brownie Hubbard later succeeded by her daughter, Daisy, have been employed for eight years as maids in the dormitories. They have fought bed bugs, cleaned bathrooms, waxed floors, gathered trash, and distributed linens for several thousand students. Minnie Frayser served for five years as maid at Helen Henderson Hall and the Infirmary. Ida Hamilton and her daughter, Sara Jackson, have been the only maids employed at Madame Russell. Martha Johnson has been the only maid employed at the McGuffey School.

JANITORS FOR ADMINISTRATION BUILDING

Mr. Sam Worley was the first janitor employed at the College. He was a factotum in the institution for many years. His chief duties were the cleaning and care of the Administration Building, carrying of the mail, cleaning walks, acting as watchman, and general custodian of the main building of the college. Mr. Worley was a genial old man. He took his work very seriously and was very proud of his connection with the College. One of the standing jokes of the early years of the institution occurred one afternoon when he was busy sweeping the front hall of the Administration Building. A salesman, anxious to impress him with the importance of advo-

cating the purchase of "No-Dust" became too insistent and finally forced Mr. Worley to raise his head from the floor and his
industrious sweeping to reply, "Go see Doctor McConnell, can't
you see that I'm a busy man".

From time to time Mr. Worley was assisted by Sol Jones.
They kept the Administration Building clean except for the "semi-
annual miration" scrubbing and cleaning which were conducted by
Mr. Huddle. Regular "floods" occurred when the Administration
Building became so dirty that a large force of workmen directed
by Mr. Huddle would flood the halls with water and scrub the
various rooms.

As Mr. Worley's work increased maids were employed to do
some of the cleaning in the Administration Building. Cytheria
Armstead, who had been maid at the La Belle Inn served in this
capacity for several years. She was succeeded by Cora Robinson
who was appointed as head maid. Cora was one of the most efficient helpers the college has ever had. She soon tired of
her job, however, and recommended the appointment of Laconia
Buckner. Laconia who is a very intelligent colored woman had
been trained in maid service in the North. She had been a school
teacher and after her marriage to John Buckner made her home at
New River. Laconia was a very efficient maid and was connected
with the college for many many years. She served as head maid
in the Administration Building and later as special maid for
Sunday and Friday afternoons and special occasions in the dormitories. Through her influence the general appearance of the
Administration Building was improved. She identified with her
as other maids, Maggie Day, who has been in the college for
seven years. She is now head maid in the Administration Building. From time to time other maids have been employed to assist
in the cleaning.

In 1923 Jim Wade returned to Radford after several years
of absence to be employed as janitor to work at night. This
scheme did not prove very satisfactory.

It has been the practice to keep two maids and a janitor
in the employment of the school for the janitor service in the
Administration Building. The janitor being responsible for the
carrying of the mail and acting as errand boy. George Mills,
Jim Mills, Booker Frazier, and Robert Whitsey have served as
janitors.

MR. J. E. BAKER

The chief employee of the college for many years was Mr.

J. E. Baker who came to the College from the High School where
he had been janitor. Mr. Baker succeeded Mr. Worley as the head
janitor for the Administration Building. For many years he was
responsible for the cleaning, carrying of the mail, and such outside work as he was assigned by Doctor McConnell. As age crept
on Mr. Baker has been tried in various capacities. Chief of these
was his work as fireman of Helen Henderson Hall, during the years
it was used as a dormitory. Since this building has been given
up he has served as watchman. For many years he was the mail car-
rier.

SUPERINTENDENT OF BUILDINGS

Dirt is almost a mania with Doctor McConnell. He has spent
hours in conference on this subject with various people, chiefly
the matrons, Doctor Moffett, Mr. Whitt and Mr. McConnell. To
these he has outlined volumes of plans for promoting cleanliness.
In later years he has prided himself on his expert knowledge of
janitorship acquired from experience as a student at Milligan.
The location of the college building so near the railroad has increased the cleanliness problem.

In the reorganization of 1920 Miss Moffett assumed a general
supervision of the buildings.

In 1921 Mrs. Lulu Cowherd was employed as dining room hostess and superintendent of the Administration Building. She supervised the work of the maids and conditions improved. She organized a property room for stage fixtures. She married in a
year. She was succeeded by Ethel Mae Duagherty, a student who
did very well but it was soon shown that the position demanded
more than a student could give.

In 1927-1929 Mrs. Rachael Leader of Wytheville was employed
as supervisor of cleaning in Madame Russell and the Administration Building. She organized the janitorial work and supplies.

In 1929 with the extension of the hostess system Miss Helen
Martin was employed as superintendent of all the buildings. She
had just gotten a good system to working well when Miss Palmer
became ill and Miss Martin was forced to become dietitian.

WATCHMAN

The first watchman employed by the college was Mr. Zachariah

136

Taylor Slusher who was employed to watch around the Heth House
and the La Belle Inn, during the first years of the College.
Mr. Slusher saw little importance attached to his job and spent
many hours sleeping under the porch of the Heth House. Throughout the history of the school no real success for watching has
been developed. Doctor McConnell has always held to the position
that there is really no great need for a watchman other than for
the physical care of the school.

From time to time various persons have been employed to pa-
trol the grounds. Mr. W. H. Kinser was the first of these. He
served for several years as watchman. He occupied the greater
part of his time in the entertainment of the girls and in the
acceptance of fudge as bribes. He became a very familiar figure
on the benches and around the buildings of the College. He was
succeeded by Mr. Baker who has served several terms as watchman.

With the development of good roads and the closing in of
the college grounds with residences there was an increase of
traffic and unnecessary visitors. In 1929 Mr. Peterson was appointed as watchman. He was the first watchman of the College
to have policeman's authority given by the city. He served one
year in a most affective manner and did much to straighten up
the unnecessary riding around on Tyler Avenue and the number of
undesirable visitors who came to the campus. Mr. Isaac Edmond-
son served as watchman during the summer of 1931.

CARPENTER

Mr. Ed. Roop has been identified with the College the long-
est of any person now employed. He assisted in the staking off
of the site for the Administration Building. He worked as a
carpenter on this building. With its completion he was employed
as the college carpenter. He has served in this capacity for
twenty years. At first he made furniture, tables, cabinets, teachers' desks, shelving and innumerable pieces of special equipment. In later years he has been kept busy with repair work.
Wherever a hammer, nail or saw is used on the campus, there you
will find Mr. Roop.

THE MILLS BROTHERS

The three Mills brothers, John as fireman, Jim as campus
man and George as general handy man, have been connected with the
school in some capacity most of the time. John assisted from time
to time by his brothers has kept the fires going. Jim will lift
anything and can do any kind of outside work. He is chief grass

mower and hauler of laundry. One year he served as watchman.
George is very mechanical, he has worked as electrician, re-
paired much machinery, directed the laundry, gardened, mowed,
and been a general substitute in all the various campus and
janitorial jobs.

MR. J. H. HUDDLE

Mr. Huddle was blacksmith at the time the college opened.
He was employed in connection with steam roller heating system.
From this contact he grew into the generalissimo of the campus
force. He was fireman, plumber, and general boss of all the
workmen. He was a unique character, an ardent believer in Rus-
selism. Many times he predicted the end of the world and put
himself in readiness. He spent many hours in religious discussion. His death in 1928 removed from the campus a most familiar
figure and worker. He was the first employee of the college to
die. His funeral was conducted in the college auditorium. A
special eulogy was given by Dr. McConnell as a tribute to the
varied forms of service Mr. Huddle had preformed in the trying
pioneer days of the school.

SUPERVISION OF HEALTH AND NURSING

The health record of the Radford College has been unsurpas-
sed by any other institution in a similar period of time. It
is one of the achievements for which the school is justly proud.
During the entire history of the college no resident student or
member of the faculty has died. There have been but few serious
illnesses. The natural location of the school, the climate and
health conditions of Radford, the regular life and the practice
of sane health habits required of all the students, the close
supervision and scientific planning of meals, the corrective physical exercise, the rigid follow up of all students afflicted
with disease, the isolation of ill students in the infirmary, the
educational program for health conducted by the departments of
physical education and home economics and the general sympathetic
and conscientious work of Doctor Noblin and the various nurses of
the college are some of the factors which have contributed to this
health record.

Doctor J. A. Noblin was appointed school physician by the
first Board, he has served continuously for eighteen years in
this capacity. Doctor Noblin makes regular calls at the dormitories at nine o'clock each morning. During the first years
the students who were ill stayed in their rooms and were cared

for by the matron and their roommates. Fortunately there was little illness. In the Spring of 1914 an epidemic of measles developed but this was successfully passed through with no serious after affects. Each year there are slight epidemics of measles, mumps, and colds. None of these have been serious or beyond the facilities of the school to care for the patients.

INFLUENZA EPIDEMIC 1918

The crucial test of all medical science came with the influenza epidemic in 1918. The first case in the college was developed by Miss Louise Ninde, a teacher, who had been exposed to the disease at the Quantico Marine Camp. She was treated but her trouble was not diagnosed as influenza. The first student to have influenza was Hessie Byer who developed it on October 2, 1918. Following these two cases the disease spread rapidly among the students, reaching its peak in the latter part of October when fifty-five students were ill at one time. To meet the emergency of this illness Doctor McConnell decided to relieve all the women teachers who would become nurses from their class room duties. He decided to keep the classes running, the men and such women teachers who were not nursing continued the classes. The students were quarrantined and kept on the campus. Careful supervision was given their diet and regular hours of rest and recreation were enforced. As soon as a student developed any symptoms she was taken to the infirmary. A schedule of hours was worked out for the teachers who had become nurses, several were kept on duty throughout the day and night. The teachers who were acting as nurses met many humorous situations. Miss Elizabeth Allen who was teacher of expression introduced dramatic art into her nursing, particularly in the much-be-masked costume she effected. Most of the teachers seemed fearless of the disease and none of them actively engaged in the nursing contracted it. No cases of pneumonia developed in the college and only one student was forced to withdraw from school because of the seriousness of her illness. The students who were illest were placed in the infirmary under the special care of Mrs. Dobyns and Mrs. Harry Walker. Mrs. Harry Walker, wife of Mr. H. W. Walker, road superintendent of the Norfolk and Western Railroad was boarding in the home of Mr. and Mrs. J. Barnett, became interested in the college and volunteered to nurse. She went in to the infirmary where the students were the most ill and became the head nurse in this part of the infirmary. She devoted two or three weeks both day and night to the care of the students. As the number of ill students increased the negro employees became alarmed and were afraid to wash the dishes or prepare any food for the sick. Miss Moffett and Miss Myrtle Burnett prepared the meals for all of the patients. For one Sunday dinner they sent out fifty-five trays from the home economics kitchen.

During this time the epidemic in the city had become very great. Many of the wives of the professors and Mrs. Moffett devoted their time to the preparation for food for the sick in the school and college neighborhood. Miss Ninde, as she recovered from her illness, became the official hair dresser and spent several hours each day combing the hair of the sick women.

Since no treatment for influenza had been determined by medical science each doctor was put on his own resources to determine how to treat the disease. Doctor Noblin was most successful in the treatment of all the cases in the college as well as in the cases he had in the city. He chose a feeding policy, plenty of well prepared food was given all patients, he gave very little medicine except large doses of calomel. The height of this latter experiment was reached when he administered twenty grains of calomel in one day to Miss Moffett (January, 1919). The success of Doctor Noblin in his treatment of the disease received State wide recognition followed by a request to prepare a special discussion for the Southwest Virginia Medical Society.

A FALSE ALARM OF SMALLPOX

On the registration day for the summer quarter of 1924, a student developed the symptoms of smallpox. After several days her case was diagnosed as such. Since she had been with the other students the college authorities decided to have all the students vaccinated who had not been vaccinated. Vaccine points were secured from the Department of Health in Richmond. Sunday afternoon was set for the wholesale vaccination. Some teachers, nurses, and other physicians of Radford assisted in this performance. About two hundred and fifty students were vaccinated on this day. Some of the students were in a high state of hysterics and excitement, however, since the law of Virginia required all teachers to be vaccinated it was easy to reconcile them to vaccination. The success with which this seige was passed through was almost unbelieveable. There were no additional cases of smallpox and practically no illness from sore arms. For the first three weeks of summer school the campus password was "watch my arm".

In 1928 a second epidemic of influenza passed through Southwestern Virginia. There were a few cases among the college students. Near the time of the Christmas holidays the disease seemed to be increasing so the school was closed one week earlier and opened one week later in January. This prevented an epidemic in the school and allowed the students to return to their homes during the holidays. Very few of them had the disease.

ACCIDENTS

Throughout the history of the college there has been no serious accidents, with the single exception of an explosion in the Biology Department in November 1929. This explosion resulted from a combustion of alcohol being used in an experiment on leaves. Noblin Huddle was seriously burned about the face, neck and hands and Louise Bond was burned slightly about the ear and neck. Miss Huddle was confined to her bed for many weeks, she was attended by the college nurse and physician.

Miss Kate Buchanan in 1918 dislocated her knee in a basket-ball game. These two accidents are the only ones which have occurred in the entire history of the college which have in any degree permanently impaired the physical health of the students.

A COMEDY OF COOTIES

In 1922 the students developed a great deal of gossip. They declared "cooties were in the heads of all the students". To prove this untrue Miss Moffett, Mrs. Lloyd, and Miss Huffard inspected the heads of all the students. This was one of the most ludicrous scenes that has ever occurred in the infirmary. It soon became a comedy as each student attired in a kimono with her tresses of hair draped over her shoulders solemnly knelt and presented herself for inspection. No lice were found. This gossip and excitement among the students was a reaction of the war tales of the "cooties" the boys told to the girls on their return from the war.

From time to time the students get up agitations on the subject of itch. In 1925 this became so exasperating that Dean Moffett quarantined a group of seven girls who insisted that they had itch and kept them in quarantine until the so-called disease vanished.

INFIRMARY FACILITIES

For seven years no special provision was made for the housing of the sick other than in their own bed rooms. Upon the completion of Tyler Hall a room was set aside as an infirmary. This room had been built for the purpose with a private bath and toilet. It provided space for four beds. An office for the Doctor and nurse adjoined this room. This infirmary was furnished with modern hospital beds, tables, and small equipment; medicines and small surgical equipment were kept in a cabinet in the Doctor's office. These supplies formed the dispensary from which the students secured all medicine except that especially prescribed by prescription. Students pay for the medicine as used. The medical fee is used for the nurse's and doctor's salaries whose services are furnished without additional charge to all students.

In 1923 the linen room, second floor of Tyler Hall, was equipped as a diet kitchen, a sink, electric stove (the first owned by the college), an ivory painted breakfast room set, blue japanese china and small cooking utensils were provided. To be sick enough to eat in the diet kitchen became a popular fad.

When the Helen Henderson Hall was rented in 1926 it was decided to move the infirmary to this building. The Helen Henderson Hall had been originally built for a hospital. The former operating room and the adjacent suite of rooms on the second floor were set aside as the college infirmary. The diet kitchen was moved to a small room nearby. During the Christmas holidays the infirmary was moved to the Helen Henderson Hall. This new infirmary provided space for eight beds. Mrs. Lloyd the nurse also became matron of this Hall. The medical office was maintained for one additional year in the Tyler dormitory. In 1927 it was also moved to the Helen Henderson Hall which has since been the medical center of the college.

THE HEALTH POLICY

Since 1922 the students have been given a physical examination and a record made of their general health condition at the time of their entrance in college. These physical examinations have been given by the instructors in the department of health and physical education, the nurse and the college physician. The examination consists of a complete physical examination of the student and the making of a record of her family and personal health history. The form of records are kept in the nurse's office and are frequently referred to in the remedial health program of the college. Very few students have been found suffering from organic diseases which would impair their work or health as college students. The chief negative physical condition is under weight.

DIET TABLES

From time to time those under weight students have been seated at special tables in the dining room and their diet carefully watched. Such changes in food intake and habits are made as will bring about normal development. Practically all of the students who have been given this attention have improved in general physical health and have been brought up to their standard of weight. The diet tables have been a source of continual interest to the students of the college. They have served as admirable examples of the importance of a balanced diet in building up the physical strength of the body. The fad of reducing which swept the country for several years had many followers in the college. A definite educational program was carried on against this. Students have always been required to attend meals three times each day. For several years the fad of cutting breakfast made this a disciplinary problem, however, the majority of the students have found that their own physical condition is much improved by eating regular meals.

RECREATION HOUR

The physical education department has always devoted much time to the discussion of preventive health measures, personal hygiene and corrective recreation. In spite of this many students developed the habit of taking little outdoor exercise. For six years, 1920 to 1926, the students were required to take an hour of recreation on the campus after lunch. For four years this was directed by the Dean of Women and the Physical Education Director. Later certain students were employed as recreational directors. The recreation period was devoted to large group games, pep meetings, and such individual athletics as tennis and games for small groups. This daily hour for physical exercise offered a splendid opportunity for group development in school spirit as manifest in songs and yells. Each spring for several weeks the students spent the recreation period weeding the campus. Contests were held between the classes to see which class could get the highest pile of weeds. This was a very interesting scene and did much to rid the campus of weeds, especially dandelions.

The more extended development of athletic grounds and the increase in number of separate buildings forced the students to walk in order to meet their obligations and made it possible to abolish the required recreation hour. The athletic association now places much emphasis on individual recreation. The students are able to win monograms or numerals by devoting two hundred hours to some form of physical exercise. In warm weather the physical education classes are taught on the outside athletic fields.

CARE OF SICK

All students are required to go to the infirmary if they are indisposed sufficiently to stay in bed. Each day the nurse makes an official report of the condition of the students in the infirmary. This daily report keeps the administration well informed of the physical condition of the students. The policy of the school has been to keep the students and their parents informed in cases of emergencies, epidemics, or other health conditions which would prove unfavorable to the student. Doctor J. A. Noblin has always been the school physician. During his few vacations and leave of absences, Doctor Fuqua, Doctor Harris, Doctor Gieson, and Doctor Early have substituted for him. The nurses have been: Mrs. Grace Dobbins, Miss Edmonia Goode, Mrs. E. C. Lloyd, 1927-28; Miss Mayme Bennett, 1929-30; Miss Margaret King, 1930. For one year, a student, Miss Blanche Davis assisted the matron. Mrs. Lloyd, Miss Bennett and Miss King have taught the course in Home Nursing for the students majoring in Home Economics. The latter has also worked in close cooperation in the health program and work of the Campus Training School.

LAUNDRY

The monthly charges for board provide for the student's personal laundry. Since the establishment of the school in 1913 a laundry has been operated on the campus. During the fall and spring of 1914 the heating plant of the college was completed. The upper floor of this building was designated as the laundry. In the beginning this was a wash house. A number of colored women were employed as washer-women. Washing at the "Normal" was similar to a community gathering for these colored people. Many fat, greasy, cheerful women with numerous children infested the place, carried the water, and kept the open fires under the boilers roaring. This laundry was run with practically no supervision. The colored women were hired and given the job of washing and ironing, this they did according to their own methods and ideas. There was no particular system of marking and caring for the clothes. The students were required to mark their own clothing with indelible ink. In this lack of management and organi-

zation it seems almost impossible to believe a laundry could be
as successful as this slip-shod fashion work proved to be.

After several years Mr. J. A. Huddle, chief engineer of the
college assumed the control and the direction of the laundry.
He brought system out of the chaos. As the school enrollment
increased it became necessary to send the flat work to commercial
laundries, and for many years all of the sheets, towels, table
linens, were sent to the Pulaski Laundry. The colored women continued to do the students'work. Through his contact with the commercial laundry especially with Mr. Sasher of Pulaski, Mr. Huddle
learned many of the modern methods for the management of a laundry. He also studied the equipment which these laundries had.
He was therefore ready to take charge of the college laundry when
it was equipped. In 1921 the room devoted to laundry purposes
was furnished with modern laundry equipment, electric washers,
condensers, one steam presser and a drying room purchased from
the American Laundry Equipment Company, and a mangle bought from
Mr. Sasher. Mr. Roop made a series of pigeon holes for the storage of the students'clothes. Mr. Huddle was placed in entire
charge of the laundry. He devoted two or three days each week
to the supervision of the work. Colored help was discontinued
and white employees who were intelligent enough to learn to run
the machinery were employed.

At the death of Mr. Huddle in 1928 George Mills became the
supervisor of the laundry. Various women have served as the
head woman in charge of marking and distribution of clothes,

The laundry has improved and is now adequately equipped
with electric washers, steam pressers, improved parts to the
mangle, boilers, electric irons, and other equipment necessary
to care for all laundry work of the institutions. The laundry
is operated three days each week. The popular use of silk un-
derwear, silk hose, and fewer garments has reduced the amount
of personal laundry. Although the number of students served
is greater, the proportionate amount of laundry is less. This
fashion however has made it necessary to establish more pressing rooms and to permit more laundry work to be done by the
students in their own rooms. A pressing room is maintained in
each dormitory and is directed and supervised by students who
are working their way through college.

PART IV
INSTRUCTION

SECTION I

THE FACULTY

Appointment of Faculty

The original faculty appointed June 6, 1913, had seventeen members in all departments. The present staff has fifty-four members in all departments. In preparation for the meeting of the Board of Trustees when the first faculty was to be appointed Doctor McConnell as President of the College, prepared a slate of nominees. At the meeting Doctor McConnell maintained that the members of the faculty should be nominated by the President and that the Board of Trustees should approve those nominated. This policy met with decided opposition from some members of the Board who felt that it should be the perrogative of the Board to make the nominations. A heated discussion followed. After considerable negotiations to effect an agreement the faculty, as nominated by the President, was appointed by the Board under the policy that the President thereafter be entrusted with the responsibility of making a thorough investigation of the qualifications of the individual applicant for any specific position to be filled on the staff. This policy inaugurated on June 6, 1913 has continued throughout the entire history of the College. Each teacher who has been appointed to the College has been employed upon the definite recommendation of the President, who acting in the name of the Board has entered into negotiations and made the necessary arrangements with the candidates whom he proposed to nominate. The President is empowered to name the salary. However following the financial reorganization of 1928 no salary can be increased either by the President or by the governing board without the approval of the Governor of the State.

The selection and appoinment of the faculty has been a matter of major consideration by President McConnell. At the time of the establishment of the Radford College it was generally conceded that the teachers who were employed for a Normal School faculty were of lower intellectual and teaching ability than the person employed for College or University work. The popular basic requirement for the teachers of this type was ability to teach methods courses and give reviews in elementary subjects. Such an idea never found favor with Doctor McConnell. From the very beginning he consistently followed the policy of selecting only those who were personally, intellectually and professionally capable of teaching in the best colleges and universities. He maintains that there should be a balanced proportion of men and women on the faculty. He has a high regard for the ability of women. He maintains that women who are qualified to do the same work should be paid the same salary as men doing the same or similar work. These three policies have dominated his hominations and recommendations to the faculty.

Qualifications of Faculty Members

The original faculty of the Radford College represented the standards of educational achievement most common at that time: 6 per cent of the members of the faculty held Doctor's degrees; 17.5 per cent held Master degrees; 23.5 per cent held Bachelor degrees and 52 per cent had no degree. In the present faculty 22.6 per cent hold Doctor of Philosophy degrees; 43.4 per cent hold Master degrees; 24.7 per cent hold Bachelor degrees and 11.3 per cent no degree. Those who hold no degrees in 1930 are special teachers of Music and Art and have had the equivalent of a degree in special training. The difference between the qualifications of the two faculties compared above indicates the growth in development in educational and professional scholarship, not only at Radford but is indicative of the trend throughout the country. In 1924 the President adopted the policy of not recommending for appointment any persons who had less than a Master's degree. In 1927 he raised this to the Doctor's degree for a professor and the Master's degree for the supervisors and assistant professors.

The average salary in 1913 was $700.00; in 1930, $2640.00. The increase in salaries paid is in proportion to the increased appropriation given by the legislature. The increases in salary have been made biennially on an average of two hundred dollars each with the exception of the large increase in salaries made in 1928 to reach the standards of the Southern Association of Secondary Schools and Colleges.

The year 1927 marks a new era in the faculty life of the Radford College. The institution had become a member of the American Teachers College Association in 1924 and was now making application for membership in the Southern Association of Secondary Schools and Colleges. Up to this time the growth and development of the curricula and instructional activities of the College had been largely professional. All progress in academic standards depended upon the growth and development from the ideas of the faculty. The emphasis being placed upon the teachers training institutions by the accrediting agencies for liberal arts colleges stimulated the Radford College to apply for membership in the Southern Association. In order to get such membership it was necessary for the college to make some radical changes in its policies. Upon its first application to the Southern Association the Radford College was turned down on the basis of salaries paid its instructors. In order to meet this standard Doctor McConnell determined upon a policy for improving the academic and professional scholarship of the faculty. In February 1927 he called to his office those members of the faculty who were most permanent and who had the desire to continue in positions of responsibility and leadership in the college. To these he explained the situation and required all members of the faculty who could do so, to begin at once plans to get the doctor's degree or at least to do additional study in some institution. At this time the major professors in the college were holders of master degrees. Doctor McConnell also announced his intention to pay a salary of $3000.00 to all professors who held Doctor of Philosophy degrees and further that no teachers would be employed for the training school who did not hold master degrees. All members of the faculty who were affected by these changes in policy were notified. This was followed by much discussion and readjustment in the lives and plans of the various members of the faculty. It was a hectic spring! Professors Fitzpatrick, Bowers, Gilbert, and Sowder were granted leaves of Absence during the summer quarter of 1927. They studied at Columbia University, Cornell University, and the University of Virginia. Misses M'Ledge Moffett, Susan Roberts, Lillian Simmons and Mr. John Paul McConnell were granted leaves of absence for the academic year of 1927-1928. These three ladies studied at Columbia University and Mr. McConnell studied at the University of North Carolina. Miss Moffett was also granted a leave of absence for 1928 and completed her Doctor's degree in 1929. Miss Mary Eolian Coppedge was granted a leave of absence for 1928-29 and did one year of advanced study towards her Doctor's degree at Columbia University. In 1929-30 Professor J. W. Sowder was granted a leave of absence to study at Cornell University where he completed the requirements for the Doctor's degree.

The absence of so many members of the faculty and the policy to increase the educational opportunities of the institution enabled Doctor McConnell to employ several new members for the faculty. In 1927 he employed four with Doctor of Philosophy degrees, Doctors George Williams, Minor Wine Thomas, C. B. Swaney, Ethel Ne-Smith. In 1928 he employed six more all of whom held Doctor's degrees. Doctors W. S. Long, Jean Taylor, Winifred Bain, Gertrude McCain, John W. Humphreys, Paul R. Burch. These new professors were selected from different sections of the United States. They had completed their graduate study at the University of Missouri, Columbia University, Northwestern, Cincinnati, and the University of Virginia. The original faculty and those who had been added

148

prior to 1927 were in the most part representatives of Virginia
and of the South. They had been educated in southern Universities
Columbia and Chicago Universities. The influx of new professors
on the campus brought to the college an influence which was quite
different to that of former years. The new professors in most cases represented the liberal arts point of view. Each was charged
with the responsibility of developing his respective work, increasing the offerings and raising the standards for the courses in his
field of study. In many respects they were personally different
and their backgrounds had been very different from that of the former local faculty. This called for a period of readjustment which
has had a decided influence upon the faculty life and college organization.

FACULTY FOR THE SUMMER SCHOOLS

The summer quarter has always been organized as an independent unit of the academic year. The formal contracts of the regular faculty are effective from September to June. Each year such
members of the faculty, as are necessary for the carrying on of the
summer quarter courses, have been employed. To these have been added many other instructors. As long as the teaching of review
courses was the main function of the summer faculty those who were
added were successful public school teachers and principals of
high schools. Doctor McConnell felt that such teachers were closely in contact with elementary schools and were capable of carrying
on the review courses for the summer students. Many of those employed were graduates and advanced students of the college. With
the gradual elimination of the review courses the summer faculty
was built of those who were professionally trained and met the academic and professional standards of the regular faculty. Professors from other institutions, graduate students from Columbia University, North Carolina University and University of Virginia, were
employed as summer instructors. Many of these afterwards became
members of the regular faculty.[1]

FACULTY ORGANIZATION

The instructional faculty has never had an organization of
its own independent from the administration. The faculty has met
upon call of the President. He has served as the Chairman and
presiding officer at practically every faculty meeting held throughout the life of the institution.

The original faculty was summoned by letter to come to Radford one week prior to the opening of the College on September 17,

[1] A list of the regular faculty with dates and subjects taught is
shown in the appendix.

1913. Professor William E. Gilbert was the first member of the faculty to arrive in Radford. He came August 8, 1913 the same day that the McConnell family moved to Radford. Mr. Gilbert and Doctor McConnell were the only members of the faculty to attend the dedication of the Administration Building on August 9, 1913. Mr. and Mr. Joseph Avent were the next to arrive in Radford early in September. Miss Moffett arrived on September 11, and the other members of the faculty came within the next few days.

Prior to the opening of the first session each member of the faculty was interviewed by the President. This interview made a lasting impression upon the minds of the faculty members. In these first personal interviews and contacts the spirit of the administration was shown. Doctor McConnell gave the impression of democratic leadership. He was open to suggestions and sought the cooperation and loyal support of each member of the faculty.

The first few days after the faculty arrived in Radford were spent in getting acquainted. Most of the single members of the faculty boarded at the home of Mrs. H. P. Anderson. In this home, around the dinner table, many of the early policies and activities of the Radford College were planned. During this period each member of the faculty selected a class room and started by means of plants and simple decorations to stamp his personality upon the institution.

FACULTY MEETINGS

The first meeting of the faculty as a group took place in September 1913. At this time some of the preliminary plans which had been worked out by President McConnell were announced. These early plans related to the registration procedures, class and room assignments. Frequent meetings of the faculty were held during the early weeks of the school. The first one which makes an indelible impression upon the author, occurred in Room 111 in the Administration Building. At this time the first steps toward student organizations were taken and the committee for organization of the literary societies was appointed.

The first formal records of the faculty meetings begin on November 19, 1913. On this date Mr. Ernest P. Lane was appointed by President McConnell to assume duties as Secretary to the Faculty. Prior to this there were no formal minutes kept although various important committees were appointed, functioned and many controlling policies determined. Among these, the selection of purple and gray as school colors, system of class advisors, determination of assembly procedure.

The meetings throughout the early years of the college were held upon call of the President. They were not held at any regular time or place, and averaged three or four a year. The meetings were held in the President's office and usually occurred at 4:30 or 4:40 in the afternoon. Later the faculty used Room 106, Mr. Gilbert's Class room as a regular meeting place.

In 1914 Mr. Lane resigned from the college and was succeeded as secretary of the faculty by Miss Mary Montague who served as secretary until 1920. She was succeeded by Professor Joseph E. Avent as secretary who served until 1921. He was succeeded by Mrs. Jaynie Whitt, the present secretary. A resume of the minutes kept by these various secretaries show that the faculty meetings have been devoted largely to the discussion of routine activities in the school. The discussions centered around such problems as the general assembly, the cultural development of the students, reports of the course of study committee, explanations of registration and schedules, discussions of physical equipment, holidays, grading, class absences, etc. Doctor McConnell has encouraged much freedom in discussion, but has never been inclined to settle any of the policies of the institution by a vote of the faculty which might result in a division of opinion.

In 1918 the faculty united with the students of the college in raising a $2000.00 war chest. The faculty donated $500.00 of this amount. The motion as proposed by Miss Montague and seconded by Mr. Gilbert provided for a certain per cent to be paid from the salary of each member of the faculty to this fund. In 1922 the faculty made pledges to the literary society home later the Student Activity Building. These are the only financial obligations that the faculty, as a group, has assumed.

In 1920 the faculty devoted itself as a group to the study of the Carnegie report on teacher training. Monthly meetings were held, a chairman was appointed for each meeting, this person prepared the discussion based on the report.

In the fall of 1929 Doctor McConnell instituted a pre-session institution. He called the faculty to the college for a three-day meeting prior to the opening of the fall quarter. At this time the most constructive educational procedures were discussed. The faculty meeting of 1928 was devoted to a discussion of the problems of professionalized subject matter and the extra-curricular activities of the students.

In 1930 the pre-session institute was more elaborate and

better organized. Prior to the opening of this institute Doctor McConnell sent to the members of the faculty a list of committees; each committee was responsible for the preparation of the subjects assigned.

FACULTY COMMITTEES

In 1913 and 1914 Doctor McConnell adopted the policy of having standing committees of the faculty responsible for certain activities of the institution. By these committees many of the policies of the institution have been determined. The actual contributions of these, however, is recorded in other phases of this history. These committees as announced from time to time are indicative of the points of emphasis being stressed by the administration at the time. For a number of years the standing committees were published in the annual catalog. Theoretically this committee organization has been of great importance. Practically, however, some of the committees have been most active while others have been dead. In many cases one individual of the committee has become the only functioning member. In 1924 Doctor Sherrod, a graduate of Peabody College, visited Radford and made an analysis of the work of these committees. His Report of this work shows that the Radford College had more standing committees in proportion to the number of faculty and students enrolled than any other of the forty-three institutions studied. Following the publication of Sherrod's study Doctor McConnell placed more emphasis upon the work of the faculty committee. His instructions to the faculty committees for 1925 were as follows:

"Early in the summer a book dealing with the organization and work of committees in higher educational institutions was bought and placed in the library. I very much desire that every member of the faculty read this book before the 31st of October. It is a small book and it is invaluable to members of College Committees.

Enclosed you will find a list of the committees of which you are a member. The first name in each committee is Chairman. I wish each committee to have monthly meetings and to make a written report for my office the last day of each month containing the report of what has been done by the committee, what matters have been planned and suggested for the functioning of the committee in connection with the college and the other committee. I very earnestly desire to have this prompt and

full report of each committee the last day of
each month. Some committees only have one member.

Such committees will make the same formal report
that other committees make. Each committee will
be called together at the opening of the session
by its chairman and a time and place fixed for the
montly meetings. Special meetings will be held
on the call of the chairman and reports submitted
at such times as may be called for by the President of the institution or at the discretion of the
committee when the committee has anything it wishes
to report.

I am anxious for the committees to function very
actively for the present year for many and obvious
reasons. Each committee will keep a written record
of every meeting and the substance of the matters
discussions and the conclusions and recommendations
reached. At faculty meetings I wish reports of committees to be available for consideration and discussion if called for. Oral reports will not be
accepted except as supplementary to the written report." [1]

PROFESSIONAL ORGANIZATIONS OF FACULTY

The faculty of Radford has always had a local association
of the State Teachers Association. The first of these was organized in the fall of 1913, prior to the meeting of the Educational Association in Lynchburg. Each year prior to the educational conference the local association has been reorganized,
officers elected and delegates named for the conference. This
organization has been largely perfunctory and has functioned
chiefly as the collecting agent of dues for the State Teachers
Association. For a number of years the faculty of the State
Teachers College at Radford was one hundred per cent in its
membership in the State Teachers Association.

AMERICAN ASSOCIATION OF UNIVERSITY WOMEN

In 1928 a branch of the American Association of University
Women was organized by those members of the faculty and such ladies of the town who were eligible for membership. The organi-

[1] Several lists of faculty committees are shown in the Appendix
as illustrative of the type existing at various dates.

zation was perfected by Doctor Virginia O. Hudson who was elected first President.

This organization holds montly meetings and has devoted itself to a study of international relationships, literature and educational problems. In 1928 it was hostess to a joint meeting with the Blacksburg Chapter of the American Association of University Women and also attended the luncheon and meeting of the State Convention of the Association in Roanoke. In 1929-30 Doctor Jean E. Taylor was President. She represented the Radford Branch at the State Meeting held at Williamsburg. Under the auspices of this organization the Ruth St. Dennis Dancers were brought to the college in February 1930. During this year the chapter donated $100.00 to the fellowship fund of the National Association of University Women. In 1930-31 Doctor Ethel Ne-Smith is President. One of the chief acts for the current year was the establishment of two prizes of twenty-five dollars each to be awarded to the sophomore and the junior in college who has high scholarship, professional promise and shows creative ability by some piece of original work in any field of literary, scientific or professional study.

RADFORD CHAPTER OF UNIVERSITY PROFESSORS

In the spring of 1930 Doctor McConnell took steps to have organized within the faculty a chapter of the American Association of University Professors. He selected some professors who were eligible for membership as the charter group. The nominations were signed by Doctor Moffett who was a member of the Columbia University Chapter and by other representatives of the Blacksburg Chapter. This group of nominees were elected to membership in the Association in December 1930. In February 1931 this group perfected a local organization. Doctor Moffett, President.

EXTRA-MURAL ACTIVITIES OF THE FACULTY

A major problem of any new institution is the need for stamping its identity upon the minds and within the interest of the general public. At the opening of the Radford College Doctor McConnell recognized the importance of the personal contacts which he and the members of his faculty could build up with educational, welfare and civic interests of the general public of Virginia and the Nation. For many years it was his policy to seek for the professors and to allow them to accept invitations which would bring them before the public.

Just prior to the opening of the college in 1913 the Appalachian School Improvement Foundation League was organized with J. R. Hunter of Emory as the executive Secretary. A primary purpose of this organization was to furnish speakers to any community or organization interested in advancing the cause of education or other forms of welfare work. All of the members of the faculty of the college who were willing to make addresses were placed on the list of speakers. Many of them won reputations for themselves as speakers. Mr. William E. Gilbert was for many years known as the best speaker in Southwestern Virginia. He was in constant demand and took an active part in the educational work of Southwestern Virginia. He became Secretary of the Appalachian School Improvement League and later was most active in the State and District Community League organizations.

Mr. Avent was frequently a speaker before various educational conferences. He was also active in the religious organizations of the Methodist church. After Mr. Fitzpatrick joined the faculty he was frequently called upon to make educational addresses. He rendered "expert service" in many localities. In addition to his addresses he was instrumental in the organization of community leagues. He conducted educational surveys in Lynchburg, Pulaski, and Page County. Mr. J. R. L. Johnson was frequently sought for the literary addresses for high schools and colleges. Dr. Swaney, Mr. Paul McConnell, Professor Gilbert, Dr. Humphreys have been active as supply ministers. From time to time other members of the faculty have appeared on educational programs or for commencement addresses. Miss Blanche Bulifant was a popular speaker before educational groups. Miss Blanche Daniel, as she matured in educational experience became a popular speaker at County Institutes the college could furnish.

Of the women members of the faculty Miss Moffett is the most active speaker. In 1915 she represented the college on the Norfolk and Western demonstration Train which made a tour over the entire lines of the Norfolk and Western Railroad holding exhibits and giving demonstrations in farming and home making activities. She was also a frequent speaker before the women's clubs, community leagues and acts as a judge in women's departments of County Fairs.

Miss Florence Baird was devoted to all causes for the advancement of music. She was active in all the musical organizations of the State and frequently gave addresses on the value and appreciation of music. Through her activities the Virginia

Music Teachers Association was organized. In addition to their
service as speakers the faculty of the college has been active
leaders as officers or committeemen in community organizations,
Rotary, Kiwanis, American Legion, Women's Clubs, State Federation of Music Club, Woman's Christian Temperance Union, and Sunday Schools and the religious organizations of the various denominations.

SOCIAL LIFE OF THE FACULTY

The underlying policies of the institution; close co-operation, mutual sharing of joys and sorrows, the intimate relationship of students and faculty, the small group of faculty
members, the common purpose of developing a new institution have
dominated the entire life, both social and professional of the
college.

The family spirit made the faculty and students socially
equal. Practically all of the social life of the faculty has
taken place with the students. They have been invited to the
student functions and have participated in all phases of student activities. The Red-letter social days in the student
life were also the red-letter days in the faculty life. In
the early years these were primarily associated with the annual
Christmas party or banquet, celebration of Doctor McConnell's
birthday on February 22, and the annual Thanksgiving dinner for
those members of the faculty and their families who did not
attend the educational conference.

Shortly after the opening of the college members of the
faculty who were married established homes in Radford. Doctor
McConnell's policy to encourage home-building bore fruit in
faculty reactions. Nearly all the married members of the
faculty, own their homes. Since the erection of the Radnor
Apartment house the lady teachers have likewise established
small homes for themselves.

With the growth and development of the institution it became necessary to discontinue many of the celebrations in which
the students and faculty had participated during the early years.
This led to the abandonment of the annual Christmas banquet, the
Thanksgiving dinner and changing of the February 22, dinner to
a party. With the enlargement of the faculty there also came
a divergence of social interest. The faculty broke into smaller
social groups and personal social functions were largely confined to those of the same personal interest and propinquity.

In 1927 a faculty social club was organized. This club
proposed to meet twice a quarter with two or more ladies of the
faculty as hostesses. The organization was self-supporting.
Throughout the years of 1927-28 social meetings of the faculty
were held. At other times in the history of the school the
faculty has held informal social gatherings at which time each
member paid a small fee for refreshments. One of these was held
following the National Educational Association meeting in February 1930 at this time those who had represented the college
at the meeting made reports of the meeting. In October 1930
another such informal social was held. The members of the faculty who had spent the summer in European travel told of their
trip and displayed many of the curios collected.

CONTRIBUTIONS OF THE FACULTY TO EDUCATIONAL LITERATURE

In connection with this history an effort has been made to
compile an accurate bibliography of the personal writings and
literary contributions of the faculty members of the college.
As complete a list as possible of these publications is shown
in the Appendix.

The first book published by the members of the Radford Faculty was from the pen of Mr. F. B. Fitzpatrick who has been one
of the most prolific writers of the faculty. Mr. Avent while
connected with this college prepared the manuscript for the
first series of books which he has published since. Miss Bulifant, since she left the college has become very prolific in
writing for teachers magazines. Doctor Moffett and Doctor Thomas are both liberal contributors to magazines.

In 1931 the Radford branch of the University of Professors
took as a project the collection of copies of the published
work of the present and former faculty members. Those which
were collected are deposited in the library of the college.

THE SERVICE OF THE FACULTY TO EDUCATION IN VIRGINIA

Many members of the faculty have been very active in the
work of the State Teachers Association. Three or four members
of the faculty have appeared on programs of this conference since
the establishment of the school in 1913. Many of them have served as officers of the various sections. Some of these are Professor William E. Gilbert, President of the Virginia Branch of
the American Peace League; President of the Social Science Section; Mr. Bowers, President of the Mathematics Section; Doctor

W. S. Long, State Secretary of the Isaac Walton League and President of the local organization; Mr. Fitzpatrick, President of the Rural Department; Miss Moffett, twice President of the Home Economics Section; Miss Coppedge, Secretary and President and Treasurer of the Grammar Grades Geographical Section; Miss Blanche Daniels, Secretary of the Geographical Section; Miss Florence Baird, President of the Music Section and leader of the Virginia Music Teachers Association; Doctor McConnell and Mr. Fitzpatrick have each served one term as President of the entire association. Miss Moffett, Mr. Gilbert, Mr. Fitzpatrick, and Mr. Bowers have been members of the Board of Directors. Mr. Gilbert and Mr. Bowers have been Vice-Presidents of the association and Presidents of District I.

For many years the District Association held its annual meeting at the Radford College. On these occasions all members of the college actively participated in the local arrangements and on the program. They have visited and spoken before many of the other District Conferences of the State. There is scarcely a Committee, Institute, or District Educational Conference meeting of the Cooperative Educational Association, or meetings of special sections, such as Home Economics, Teacher Training, Science, that some member of the Radford faculty has not participated.

In the two educational surveys which have been made of the State the college has taken an active part in the collection of data, interpretating the findings in the educational re-adjustments which have followed. The Radford college, under the leadership of Dr. McConnell, was especially active in the second May Campaign. The interest of the faculty has extended beyond the boundary of the State and practically all of them are members of the organizations in which their interests lay. They have frequently attended the meetings of these national organizations. The detailed report from those members of the faculty responding to the questionnaire in regard to these activities is shown in the appendix.

THE NON-PROFESSIONAL ACTIVITIES OF THE FACULTY--

Aside from their professional and alturistic services certain members of the faculty have been active in non-professional organizations. The Radford Forum was organized by Doctor McConnell and other forward looking citizens of Radford. This Forum devoted itself to the discussion of the needs of the city of Radford. Professor William E. Gilbert allied himself with the movement to change the form of city government from the councilmatic to the city manager system. After much discussion and a hotly contested election the managerial form was adopted by the city. This system provided for the government of the city by a council elected by popular vote. The council in turn selected a city manager and named one member of the council as mayor. Mr. Gilbert was named as mayor of the city, he served for three terms. He and his colleagues were largely instrumental in the passage of the bond issue for the improvement of the streets and building the high school. During his administration Norwood Street, Tyler Avenue and several other minor streets of the city of Radford were paved with asphalt; sidewalks were laid; the city sewage system was improved and many ordinances providing better sanitary measures as the exclusion of cows and hogs, and chickens from the streets were passed.

Following the World War there was decided boom in real estate. Mr. Gilbert was identified with the Radford Land Company and other smaller reality companies. He invested largely in real estate and is now the owner of many lots and building sites in the city of Radford. He was a charter member of the Kiwanis Club and rapidly rose to positions of importance in this organization. He was the Lieutenant-Governor of the Kiwanis Club for Virginia and in this capacity addressed many of the Kiwanis Clubs of this section of the country.

Mr. Joseph E. Avent was winner in a Car Contest offered by the Household Magazine. The purpose for this contest was to secure subscriptions to the magazine by systematic and extended activities. Mr. Avent won a Dodge touring car. Mr. Fitzpatrick was a charter member of the Kiwanis Club and has been active on the Program Committee and the Educational Committee of this organization. In the summer of 1928 he represented the local club at the National Meeting in Milwaukee, Minnesota.

A great many of the faculty members have identified themselves with the active church work of Radford and many of them have extended it beyond the city of Radford. The personal contributions to this field of service is shown in the report from the individual members shown in the appendix.

The lady members of the faculty have been active in the women's organizations in the city, particularly the Women's Club. Many of them have had active parts as committeemen in this organization. They have also been identified with the

Daughters of American Revolution, Music Club, and the various organizations in the churches. Mrs. Whitt, Dr. Moffett, and Miss Baird have been active in the State Federation of Women's Club. With the organization of the American Association of University Women various Presidents of this organization have attended the State meetings of the American Association of University Women.

COLLEGE PUBLICATIONS

COLLEGE PUBLICITY

No definite program for college publicity or personal responsibility was given for this phase of the college life until 1923. From time to time Doctor McConnell or his Secretary, or some member of the faculty would send what was known as the "normal school notes" to the newspapers of the State. These were not kept and no record is in the institution of the early newspaper publicity.

In 1923 Doctor McConnell appointed a Publicity committee composed of Doctor Moffett, Miss Baird, and Mr. Fitzpatrick. The last two functioned very little in this work and it soon became the full responsibility of Doctor Moffett. Since 1923 with the exception of the years when she was on leave of absence a weekly news letter has been sent to the daily papers of the State and many county papers. Copies of this news as printed in the newspapers have been kept in the historical files of the college. Special feature articles in regard to students and college activities have been sent from time to time to papers for whom the feature had a particular appeal.

Doctor Moffett has attended two of the State Conferences on Publicity called by the Virginia Chamber of Commerce. She has cooperated with Mr. Nelson, the State Publicity Chairman, in the preparation of a booklet on the Colleges of Virginia, special feature articles, and pictures.

In 1927, Mr. Nelson accompanied by a representative of the Paramount News Reel visited the college and took motion pictures of the features of the Alleghanna program (a copy is preserved in the school). In 1928 another News Reel Company took a series of special posed pictures of student life at Radford. These latter pictures have been given great publicity. Although they are not typical of the student life of this college the pictures from this series have been shown on the screens in the larger movie

houses of the United States and have appeared twice in the rota-
gravure sections of the leading newspapers as represented of
student life in America.

ANNUAL CATALOG

Since the summer of 1913 the college has published an annual catalog each spring. Dr. McConnell prepared the first one.
From 1914 to 1920 the catalog was prepared by Mr. Avent in cooperation with Doctor McConnell. Since 1921 it has been prepared by Mr. Whitt and Miss Moffett. Bound copies of all the catalogs are on file in the offices and library of this college.
These serve as the most authentic picture and documented source
of information of the college. It has been the custom to publish
a special bulletin announcing the courses for the summer quarter.

THE RADFORD NORMAL BULLETIN

The first publication from the college after it opened was
issued in January 1914 as the Radford Normal Bulletin. This gives
a review of the first quarter of the college showing the activities and general achievements of the first three months of the
school. This bulletin is a supplement to the preliminary catalog
issued, Summer 1913, and was used for advertising purposes to stimulate students to enter for the winter and spring quarters. From
1915 to 1917 a number of educational bulletins in this series were
published:

The Radford Normal Bulletin - Volume II, Number I - July 1914
"A Plea for the Children"
The Radford Normal Bulletin - Volume II, Number 2 - August 1914.
"The Old-Time School in Scott County"
The Radford Normal Bulletin - Volume II, Number 3 - October 1914
"Special Features"
The Radford Normal Bulletin - Volume II, Number 4 - January 1915
"The Question Box"
The Radford Normal Bulletin - Volume III - Number 1 - July 1915
"The Ethical Function of the College"
The Radford Normal Bulletin - Volume III - Number 2 - September
1915 "Ingles Literary Society Exercises at Unveiling of Ingles
 Memorial Tablet"
The Radford Normal Bulletin - Volume III - Number 3 - November
1915 "A Plea for Improvement in Rural Conditions"
The Radford Normal Bulletin - Volume III - Number 4 - December
1915 "History and Work of the Appalachian School Improvement"

The Radford Normal Bulletin - Volume III, Number 5 - February
1916 "Proceedings of the Second Joint Educational Conferences
for Sixth and Ninth Congressional Districts including Carrol
and Grayson Counties held at Radford State Normal School, March
11-13, 1915"
The Radford Normal Bulletin - Volume III, Number 6 - March 1916
"The Radford Normal Plan Bible Study"
The Radford Normal Bulletin - Volume IV, Number 1 - November 1916
"The Principles of Teaching Practicalized" or "The Question Box"
The Radford Normal Bulletin - Volume IV, Number 2 - March 1917
"Program for the Fourth Educational Conference, Sixth and Ninth
Congressional Districts, March 8, 9, 10, 1917"

Miscellaneous publications

"Recipes" prepared by M'Ledge Moffett for use on the Norfolk and
Western Demonstration Train 1915.
Cook Book - compiled by Home Economics Department, sold by Alum-
nae Association.
Programs of Teachers Institutes
Handbook for May Campaign

THE NORMAL SCHOOL GLIMPSE

In 1923 the college started the publication of the Normal
School Glimpses, a small folder announcing features of the college
designed for advertising purposes. These were continued for several years as a means of reaching the public.

RURAL SCHOOL MESSAGES

In 1919 the publication of the Rural School Messages was
started as one of the features of the newly established Extension
Department. This publication was edited at first by an editorial
committee composed of Miss 'MLedge Moffett, Professors W. E. Gilbert, J. Avent, F. B. Fitzpatrick and Miss Dora States. This
publication was published bimothly, as a one-sheet educational
newspaper with editorial comment. It had a wide circulation in
the State and Nation. In December 1920 Mr. Fitzpatrick became
the director of the Extension Department and assumed the editor-
ship of the Messages. In November 1922 the paper was increased
to four pages. In 1925 the name was changed to Virginia School
Messages. This paper was published and distributed to educational workers free of cost. In 1927 it became too great a financial
strain and was discontinued.

STATE TEACHERS COLLEGE BULLETIN

In 1924 the College Glimpses were changed to the State Teachers College Bulletin and eight or nine times each year thereafter small bulletins dealing with some educational problem and
designed as an advertising feature have been printed and distributed to the high school students and teachers of the State. All
of these bulletins have been prepared by Miss Moffett and circulated under the direction of the Publicity Department.

STUDENT PUBLICATIONS

The students have sponsored the publications of the annual
for four years known as the "Radnor" in the years 1914 to 1917,
the "Beehive" from 1926 to 1929. In 1921 the students started
the publication of the newspaper "The Grapurchat". In 1928 one
issue of the Grapurchat was devoted to literary productions.
These student publications are discussed in full in the section
of this history dealing with student activities.

SECTION II

ORGANIZATION OF THE ACADEMIC YEAR

The academic session of the Radford College has always been
organized upon the quarter system, average length of twelve weeks
per quarter. The courses and activities of the college have been
arranged on this system; the courses evaluated on quarter hours,
three quarter hours equal to one session hour; three quarters
constitute one year of academic work. The academic session opens
in September and closes in August. Since the organization of the
summer quarter in 1914 the advanced courses have been considered
an integral part of the regular academic work. The summer quarter from 1913 to 1924 at Radford was designated as one of the
State Summer Schools or Institutes. It was managed and financed
as a summerschool of the State and not as a part of the State
Normal School. With the abolishment of the review classes the
summer quarter in its entirety became an integral part of the
academic year of the college.

ENTRANCE REQUIREMENTS

A summary of the entrance requirements as announced in the
1913 catalog gives an insight as to the type of student who was
expected to enter the Radford College at the time of its opening. In contrast with the entrance requirements as announced
in the catalog of 1930 it shows the progress and development
which has been made in the seventeen years of instructional
life of the institution.

ENTRANCE REQUIREMENTS IN 1913

1. A graduate of a two-year high school (a third grade
high school) may enter the First Year of the Regular
Normal Course. At the end of the second year's work
she may receive the High School Certificate and by
continuing through the third year she may receive the
Professional Normal Certificate and with a fourth year's
work the full diploma.

2. A graduate of a three-year high school (a second-
grade high school) may enter the second year of the
Regular Normal Course. At the end of one year's work
she may receive the High School Certificate. With one
more year's work she may receive the Professional Cer-

tificate, and with one additional year's work the Full Diploma.

3. A graduate of a four-year high school (a first-grade high school) may enter the two-year Professional Course and at the end of two years receive the Full Diploma.

In certain cases where such students can remain only one year, they may be awarded the Normal Professional Certificate at the end of one year's work.

4. Graduates of four-year high schools may also enter any one of the special courses: Rural Arts, Household Arts, or Manual Arts, and after two years receive a Diploma, which is of the same rank as the Full Diploma.

5. Applicants coming from schools other than public high schools will be given credit for the work they have completed. The faculty deciding the amount of credit to be allowed in each case.

6. Teachers holding certificates from the State Board of Education will be admitted on their certificates.

7. Exceptions to the entrance requirements will be made in the spring and summer quarters in the cases of students preparing for the State Examinations. Any student will then be allowed to enter any class for which she is prepared.

8. Exceptions will also be made in the case of mature persons who have not had the advantages of high school work.[1]

ENTRANCE REQUIREMENTS 1930

1. The standard basis of entrance credit is the "unit" which is the pursuit, for not less than 36 weeks, of a subject coming five times a week in the periods of not less than 40 minutes in length provided the subject be passed and the standard amount of the subject covered. In time, the minimum amount for one unit is 36 (weeks) times five (periods per week) times 40 (Minutes per period). Graduates of four-year accredited high schools having a minimum of sixteen(16) units credit if they have attended high school four years will be admitted without conditions.

1. Entrance Requirements in Radford Normal Bulletin July 1913-May 1914, Pages 21,22,23.

2. In making up the sixteen(16) units for which unconditional admission is given to the First Professional courses, the following eight units are required:

English	4 units
History	1 unit
Mathematics	2 units
Science	1 unit
Total	8 units

The remaining eight units may be made up from Mathematics, Latin, French, German, Spanish, History, Science, and other as given in the standard courses of accredited four-year high schools.

3. An applicant who has had four years of high school time and has earned 16 units of credit is admitted without conditions to her choice of the First Professional curricula and may become candidates for graduation and for the Normal Professional Certificate at the end of two years or for the Bachelor of Science degree in four years.

4. Entrance certificates signed by tutors or others than bonafide principals of schools will not be accepted. Students wishing credit on work under private teachers or tutors may get it by passing our entrance examination on the subjects so covered.

5. No credit is allowed for professional work done at institutions other than Normal Schools or Colleges, except upon examinations here.

6. By a ruling of the State Board of Education a holder of a First Grade Certificate secured by State examinations may enter, take three quarters' work, and receive an elementary certificate. Before graduation or receiving a higher certificate she must complete the requirements as outlined in Number 2, above.[1]

STUDENTS RECORDS AND REGISTRATION

The discussion of a system for grading consumed much discussion time of the first faculty. There was a decided difference of opinion as to the relative value of numerical and

1. Radford Normal Bulletin, 1930-31. Pages 34-35.

letter grading. It was finally decided to adopt the letter
system of grading and the following standards were assigned
to each letter:

A: 92-100	C: 81-86	E: 70-75
B: 86-92	D: 75-81	F: 0-70

According to this system, D was a passing grade. No effort was
made to determine an academic average for the institution and
no quality standards were set up other than the passing grade.
At first grading was regarded as a faculty function. It was
decided to give the students monthly grades. These were to be
read before the faculty as a whole and then recorded by the
Secretary on the students reports.

On the evening of November 15, 1913, the faculty met in
the Sewing Room, Number 7, of the Administration Building and
grouped themselves around one of the sewing tables with Doctor
McConnell as Chairman. The reading of grades started. The
scheme was: as a teacher read his grades they were entered by
some other member of the faculty on the student's report. The
relative merits of each student was discussed in turn. When a
name was called and the grade given all the other teachers
would search through their records to see the grade the student had made for them. This brought on much discussion and
difference of opinion. After several hours of such procedure
the faculty adjourned with the grades still unrecorded. Two
such meetings were held during the Fall of 1913. The impractica-
bility of such a system was evident. For the winter quarter of
1914 it was decided that the reports of the students would be
filed in the Registrar's office and that each teacher would
transfer to the student's record his grade. This was done independently and privately. By this method the teacher spent
many hours entering the grades on the student's reports and
many spent much time studying the grades of the students that
had been entered by other members of the faculty. This system
resulted in many blotted, torn and dirty record sheets. The
task was very boresome to the teacher. It had the advantage
however of keeping the teachers cognizant of the standards of
their colleagues and of the total achievement of individual
students. This system was continued until 1923.

Since 1923 the teachers have been supplied with uniform
record sheets which they file in the Registrar's office and
the grades are recorded by clerks in the Registrar's office.
No comparative studies of student records or grading other
than the informal and heated discussions of the faculty and
the chance perusal of the record of some individual student
were made until 1928. Upon request of the President Doctor

Minor Wine Thomas made a scientific study of the grades as filed in the Registrar's office. He charted his findings by a multiple curve. This chart was discussed before the faculty. A thorough misunderstanding resulted due to the fact that many of the teachers did not understand the Normal curve as a basis for grading. The discussion however has placed greater emphasis on grading practice and has brought about a better continuity in the practice of the individual teacher.

STUDENT REPORTS

For many years the student's reports were sent out once each month. Later they were sent twice each quarter. This system still prevails in a modified form. It is now the practice of the college to send to the guardian or parent of the student one report each quarter. The teachers are required to make a mid term report to the Registrar's office. These reports are carefully gone over and the students who have fallen below "C" on any subject are notified by what is commonly called the "D" slip. It is also an administrative practice for the faculty to report to the Dean of Women any student who is not doing efficient work in class. She follows these up to determine any cause which may explain the deficient scholarship.

The permanent records of the students were originally kept on file in the Registrar's office in a large loose leaf book. Each record was kept on a separate sheet with a very complicated entry space for personal data, courses, grades, and student attendance. The records for all the students were bound together in a doomsday book. This system continued until 1919 when Mr. Avent started a system of individual files. This system has been perfected and developed by Mr. Whitt. Individual folders are provided for each student who registers in the college. These are filed alphabetically and numerically. Each student is given a number. A card index is used for identification of the student by means of numbers. Application blanks for admission are now used. These include certain personal facts as to family, birth, occupation, as well as the high school record of the applicant. The permanent record contains information of the students' achievements, extra-class activities, additional personal data, a record of practice teaching and professional rating by the supervisors. Since 1926 three pictures have been required of each student who graduates. Much of the development in the Registrar's office is due to the faithful service of Mrs. J. P. Whitt, assistant Registrar. Mrs. Whitt has recopied the records of all the early students putting them into neater and more perfect order.

REGISTRATION

Prior to the opening in 1913 Doctor McConnell appointed a Registration Committee, Mr. Joseph E. Avent, Professor of Education, was chairman of this committee. Under his direction the first system of registration was developed. He copied the plan used in similar institutions at that time. Registration was an individual matter. The academic background was evaluated and classification for each candidate was worked out by the registration committee. The student was then assigned the subjects to make up the course she should follow. There were no uniform curricula. The students wrote in duplicate the name of the course and the name of the teachers on small cards for each of her courses. On registration night these were shuffled, sorted and sent to the instructors. At the first meeting of the class the student presented her card which must check with that held by the instructor before the student was admitted to the class. On registration day all members of the faculty assisted in the registration of the students.

With the development of uniform curricula the students courses have become more uniform and the registration simplified. For ten years uniform schedules for the various curricula have been copied on the boards in the registration rooms. These the students copy on their individual schedule cards. Since 1930 several additional copies of these cards are made and a copy is filed in the Bureau of Information. With the development of the standard curricula it has been possible to care for the registration of the students who are taking the regular courses in a comparatively short time. The students who are in the advanced courses have their records checked once or twice each year by the registrar, who then plans with them their future courses.

For the last ten years the registration has followed the same general scheme: upon entrance the student is given a room assignment by the Secretary of the President, (since 1930 by the Dean of Women), she then goes to the office of the President. This personal contact with Doctor McConnell has been one of the outstanding features of registration at the Radford College. His intimate acquaintance with the background environment of the students has been a great help in the adjustment of personal and academic difficulties of the students. Next they visit the Treasurer's office where all fees are paid. With a receipt in hand the student is assigned a seat in the auditorium. General Assembly attendance is a

requirement. The student next goes to the registration rooms
where she is guided in the selection of her course by faculty
committees in charge of the room. The registration is completed by the copying of five copies of the schedule.

THE DAILY SCHEDULE

The daily schedule has been one of the most complex problems
of the institution. The first schedule was written on the blackboard in the front hall. This schedule did not attempt to provide for separate courses. The time assignments were to departments, for instance, Home Economics was scheduled for eleven
o'clock and no attempt was made to divide the various types of
Home Economics work to be given. Such a schedule was impracticable and wild confusion resulted. Doctor McConnell immediately
appointed a schedule committee, Miss Eloise Harrison, Chairman.
She had had some experience in this work at Farmville. She, in
cooperation with Mr. Avent, Registrar, prepared the schedule. A
forty-five minute period was determined upon. The student's
load ranged from twenty-five to forty-five periods per week.
During these early years the members of the faculty spent practically all of their time in their class rooms. The all-day
service in the institution prevailed and any member of the faculty could be found in his class room at any time of the day.
Classes started at eight o'clock and continued until four o'clock.
Assembly period was scheduled at ten o'clock and lasted for thirty minutes.

An attempt to produce a uniformed schedule was made by the
schedule committee and printed in the catalog of 1914. This
schedule shows that all of the classes were offered each day.
The double periods necessary for laboratory was one of the most
complex problems of the schedule committee. The demands upon
the schedule committee were very severe and were met with great
agony and anxiety. Miss Harrison and those associated with her
usually spent several weeks in preparing the schedule.

In September 1921 the administration decided to arrange the
schedule on hour class period basis with the practice of each
class reciting three hours per week. All daily classes were
abandoned and the schedule of 1921 was worked out according to
the new scheme. There was much apprehension on the part of
some members of the faculty as to the amount of work that could
be accomplished in three hours.

At the faculty meeting in September 1921 when the new
schedule was announced Doctor McConnell stressed the impor-

tance of more careful and comprehensive preparation of the assignments and suggested the enlargement and enrichment of the class work by a more extended use of the library and parallel reading. With the coming of the hour period the teachers' average schedule was reduced to eighteen hours. In 1925 this was reduced to a maximum of fifteen hours. The curricula for the students were organized to allow a minimum of fifteen credit hours work. By 1924 when the curricula became more or less fixed the work of making the schedule was greatly reduced and uniform block schedules could be used as the basis for the new programs. Since this time the matter of schedule making of the courses has been more or less routine. Since 1921 the schedule has been made by the registrar.

At the opening of the winter quarter of 1931 the college went on a six-day basis. Classes were scheduled for Saturday morning. The schedules were so made that each member of the faculty and all students were assigned to at least two hours of work on Saturday morning.

ACADEMIC DISTINCTIONS AND HONORS

From the beginning of the school until 1920 no real effort was made to set up academic distinction and honors of any sort. The literary societies carried a clause in their constitutions which limited the membership to students who had an average of "C". This standard was never enforced.

In 1926 the student organization committee made a requirement that any student to be eligible to hold a major office must have an academic average of "B" and no student is allowed to represent the college in any inter-collegiate relation who falls below "C" on any subject.

Honor Students

A faculty committee, Miss Harrison, Miss Moffett, and Mr. Avent was appointed (1915) to determine a basis for the selection of the first and second honor graduates. This committee sent a questionnaire to several other institutions to investigate the practice in other colleges of the same type. It also spent much time in discussion. The records show no official report and the author is under the impression that the final decision of this committee was to wait until the student group had become more stable before conferring honors.

In 1920 the Sophomore Class, who were then called Seniors, requested the privilege of having a valedictorian and a salutatorian on their class day program. This privilege was granted and the students selected the persons by popular vote to serve in these honored positions.

In 1921 first and second honors based on academic attainment were announced for the two-year graduates by the administration.

With the granting of degrees in 1922 the administration announced the selection of honor students in the four-year course.[1] These students were selected according to their academic records, campus activities, and general promise.

For the commencement of 1928 a more elaborate system of classification was introduced. The honor graduates in the four-year class were grouped according to academic standards in three classifications; Summa Cum Laude, Magna Cum Laude and Cum Laude. The standards for the first group are: A to A plus average, Second group B to A minus; third group B to B plus. The system for announcing the first and second honors in the two-year course was continued.

Since December 1929 a scholarship list showing the students who make an academic average of A on all courses taken for the quarter and those students making B, and above is announced and published in the newspaper of the State.

SECTION III
THE DEVELOPMENT OF CURRICULA AND COURSES

The original course of study announced in the catalog for 1913 was compiled by President McConnell to serve as an announcement of the type of course which would be given at the new Normal School. This course of study was based upon general practices being followed in the other three normal schools in Virginia and what in the opinion of the President and Mr. Everett Worrell, then in charge of certification of the State, seemed to be the outstanding need for the people of the section of the country, the school at Radford was intended to serve. No attempt was made to evaluate the courses or to assign class periods. The requirements for admission were based upon two years and four years of high school work, certificates held by teachers, and the maturity of the stu-

1. See appendix for list of honor graduates.

dents. These curricula were never followed literally as the
organization of the school, the schedules, abilities and interests of the faculty, etc. had a decided influence on what was
actually given.

COURSE OF STUDY COMMITTEE

The curricula of the Radford College have been developed
largely through the work of a faculty committee on course of
study. Early after the opening of the school in the fall of
1913, President McConnell appointed the first curriculum committee. Mr. Joseph Avent, Professor of Education, Miss Blanche
Bullifant, Supervisor of training schools, Miss M'Ledge Moffett,
Director of Home Economics, and Miss Eloise Harrison, teacher
of Mathematics. These teachers were chosen not because of their
position on the faculty, because of their training and experience in course of study work.

During the first year this committee had frequent meetings.
Catalogs were collected from practically all the Normal Schools
in the United States. These with the modern educational theories
formed the background for the organization of the course of study
which appeared in the 1914 catalog. At this time there were no
definite standards required by the State or the Board of Trustees
other than to meet the certificate requirements of the State Department of Public Instruction. These were rather vague and in-
definite. The committees therefore worked in a virgin soil. The
courses proposed were adjusted to meet the needs of the school,
they were largely experimental, each succeeding year brought
radical changes in the evolution of the present curricula. This
committee has always worked in conjunction with the president of
the college. From time to time the other members of the faculty
have appeared before the committee to discuss the points to be
brought out in the curricula as they saw the need of emphasis
from their department. In practically every instance any change
in the department of any teacher has been thoroughly discussed
with him before this change has been officially made. If in the
opinion of the course of study committee, a new course has been
thought wise, this matter has been referred to the department in
which it would appear. The selection of the textbooks and the
descriptions of all courses as they appear in the catalog are
prepared by the teachers in the departments offering the course.
The organization of the courses, however, for the curricula is
left to the committee.

The evolution of the curricula of Radford College may be
divided into three main periods, first: the professional high
school period; second: two-year professional courses; third:

the four-year collegiate curricula.

THE PROFESSIONAL HIGH SCHOOL PERIOD

For seven years high school students were admitted to the school. Standard four-year high school courses were offered. These courses were largely academic and were designed to meet the standards of the State for accredited high schools. Over one-half of the faculty devoted their full time to high school instruction. One-half to one-third of the students were of high school classification. This situation and the limited teaching force made the course of study very cumbersome.

In 1916 the Legislature of the State of Virginia passed a law eliminating all high school courses in the four State Normal Schools of the State. At the same time they raised the admission to these institutions to sixteen high school units. An interesting fact in this connection is that the admission for entrance into the Normal Schools was raised higher than that in the other State supported colleges and the State University. Following this act the offering of high school courses was gradually eliminated.

The two-year professional courses offered were largely academic, consisting of a review of elementary school subjects with methods of teaching and practice teaching. Many curricula were offered which differed more in name than in content.

In the early organization of the school no effort was made to number the courses other than 1, 2, and 3, in the departments in which the course was offered. A study of these early curricula show a great number of courses. Practically every type of content offered under a department was grouped as a separate subject and this appeared in the numerous curricula of the early years. There was a consistent effort on the part of the committee to reduce the number of courses and curricula and concentrate on organized subject matter grouped into broader and more extensive courses under one heading or number.

THE INDUSTRIAL COURSES

All of the Normal Schools established 1908 to 1910 were designated as industrial schools. This name influenced the curricula offerings for several years and accounts for the establishment in the original curricula, such courses as Home Economics, Manual Arts and Rural Arts. These were of equal status with the professional curricula offered by the institution. Radford College, however, never placed great emphasis upon its so-called industrial courses. From the very beginning the courses were offered from a professional standpoint leading to the preparation of teachers of vocational subjects. It was necessary, however, to have a more or less elaborated set-up for industrial work. All the students of the college were required to take manual arts. These courses consisted of wood work, furniture making, clay modeling, basketry, and paper work. School gardening was also required. A section of the campus was laid off into miniature gardens which were planted and tended by the students in school gardening. The Home Economics Department placed its major emphasis upon manipulation of food, cookery and clothing. All of the students of the college were given an opportunity to take work in this department. The outward activities of these departments would indicate more vocational stress than was really true of the actual activities within the class room. With the changing of the name of the college in 1914 these courses became even more professionalized. The Home Economics curricula continued leading to a two-year diploma. In 1920 the courses of this department were placed on four-year basis and the diploma was no longer given at the completion of two years of work. The students who studied for two years received a special certificate which was later abolished and the Home Economics work became a standard four-year college course. The Rural Arts curricula was abolished by the Board of Trustees in 1915. The subjects of this department were improved, enlarged, and offered to the students as Nature Study, Science, and later were incorporated in the departments of Biology and General Science. The Manual Arts curricula as such was discontinued in 1918. The emphasis in this department was changed to Industrial Arts, a study of the industrial influence in modern life. Extensive work in wood was abolished and only minor projects in wood making were continued as a part of the Industrial Arts Courses.

TWO-YEAR PROFESSIONAL CURRICULA

With the elimination of the high school students an increased emphasis was placed on the development of the two-year curricula leading to the Normal Professional Diploma. A period of professional awakening, study, and constructive thinking began in the faculty. The influence of this is manifest in the series of changes in the curricula from 1916 to 1922.

In 1919 there was a state wide survey of education in Virginia conducted by Doctor Ingles of Harvard University. This survey revealed many startling facts about the educational conditions of the State. These were challenging to the faculty and provoked much thought as to the professional needs of the teachers which could be met through the teacher training curricula.

On April 28, 1919 Doctor Charles McMurray of Peabody College was the guest of the college. He held two professional conferences with the faculty as well as delivering several addresses before the students and faculty. These were stimulating and had far reaching effect upon the instructional practice in the school.

In 1915 the Carnegie foundation for the advancement of teaching sponsored a survey of the Missouri teacher training institutions. The findings of this survey and the report of the survey committee which was headed by Doctor William C. Bagley opened a new era in teacher training in the United States. The full report "The Professional Preparation of Teachers for American Public Schools" published in 1920, became the "Bible" for teacher training. This with the suggestive curricula prepared by Doctor Bagley charted the way for more scientific study of curriculum construction. During the year 1920-1921 the entire faculty of the Radford College devoted itself to a study of these publications. Round table discussions were conducted by the committee chairman. Out of these grew the general acceptance of the ideals of professionalized subject matter in so far as the individual instructor was able to apply it to his courses; a tendency to avoid many special methods courses as previously offered; a change in terminology to describe courses as academic rather than as methods; a more definite policy to tie up methods with practice teaching. All of this growth is reflected in the curricula of this period.

INFLUENCE OF CERTIFICATION STANDARDS

There has always been a domination of the content of professional curricula by the prevailing regulations and requirements for the certificates issued by the State. The trend in certification has been continually higher. At the time of the opening of the Radford College in 1913 the State authorized the second and first grade certificates based upon the State examination. No academic achievement as measured by elementary or secondary school was required, merely the passing of the examination. Soon the second grade was eliminated and the standards for the first grade were raised to passing the State examination and the completion of two years of high school work.

In 1913 the first professional certificate was based upon the achievement of the first grade certificate and six weeks of professional study. This introduced a series of certificates known as the elementary certificate. The standards for these certificates were gradually raised to twelve weeks, to eighteen weeks, to twenty-four weeks and finally to one year of professional training based upon high school graduation. The present and last elementary certificate is to be abolished September 1, 1931.

Those students who entered the Normal Schools as graduates of standard high schools with sixteen units of credit were given the Normal Professional Certificate upon the completion of two years of work. This certificate was considered of a very high type and was good for ten years and renewable for ten years. It was practically a life certificate. With the abolishment of the elementary certificate September 1, 1931 the Normal Professional Certificate will be the minimum for the teaching profession in Virginia and will be good for five years and renewable for five years.

The evolution of the present certification standards are reflected in the professional curricula of the teacher training institutions. The State Department of Public Instruction had no legal control over these college curricula, however, since certification was the major objective of the students it became expedient for the colleges to have a part in determining the standards. Therefore, in 1922 Miss Rachel E. Gregg, Supervisor of Teacher Training in charge of certification called a meeting of representatives of the teacher training institutions to study her proposed recommendations for the elementary certificate. Mr. J. P. Whitt represented the Radford College. At this conference a set of standards for the distribution of subjects were set up. The influence of these requirements dominate the curricula which follows 1922 for both the winter and summer work. This recommendation was as follows:

REQUIREMENT FOR AN ELEMENTARY CERTIFICATE OR FIRST YEAR
NORMAL COURSE

1. Academic subjects
        English, History, or Science - - - - - 3-4 session hours
2. Educational subjects
    a. General Education   )
        Principles of teaching)
        Educational Psychology)- - - - - - - - 2-3 session hours
        School Management   )
        Rural School Problems)

        b. Health and Physical Education
            1. School Hygiene and Physical Inspection
                of School Children - - - - - - - - - 1 session hour
            2. Physical Education - - - - - - - - - 1 session hour

        3. Elementary Education - - - - - - - - - - 3-5 session hours
            Including special methods of teaching school subjects
        4. Applied Arts - - - - - - - - - - - - - - 2 session hours
            Music
            Manual Training
            Drawing
            Penmanship

Since 1922 the course of study committee has held annual
meetings with representatives of the State Department of Public
Instruction for the discussion of the formation and revision of
the curriculum. Frequently resolutions and acts of the State
Department of Public Instruction are referred to the colleges
and considered by them in the formation of the course of study.

Since 1925 there have been but few changes in the professional curricula of the college. The two-year course meets the
requirements of the State Board of Education for Virginia. The
number of students however who have graduated from the Radford
College and entered the teaching service of West Virginia and
North Carolina has made it necessary to meet the requirements of
those two States. This problem has been met as an individual one
and additional courses in Geography and Education have been required of those students expecting to teach in other States. The
general balance in the elementary curriculum has made it so that
the students who receive the Virginia certificate are qualified
for the certificates of the other States with a slight modification of their course.

The most significant trends in the curricula of the teachers
training institutions in Virginia for the last decade were sum-
marized by Doctor Moffett in an address delivered before the Section of Schools and Colleges of the Virginia Teachers Association,
November 1929. She said in part - "An analysis of the catalogs
of the four Virginia Colleges for 1921-1922 and for the year 1928-
1929 gives some idea of the curriculum trends in this state. In
1922, 28% of the courses offered by the Virginia Teachers Colleges
(determined from catalog descriptions) were methods courses. In
1929, 19% of the courses are methods, a decrease of 10%. During
the same period there has been an increase of 52.4% in academic
subjects. There is a distinct trend in the field of education

away from methods courses and toward professionalized subject
matter; and a general reduction in theory courses with a por-
tionate increase in laboratory courses for observation and
participation in actual school room activities. The major
improvement, she said, is not in content so much as in method
of instruction. The professional treatment of subject matter
she described. The professional treatment of subject matter
is one of the baffling phrases being used in teachers colleges
today. This implies more than the mere accumulation of facts,
it assumes the presentation of subject matter content on the
collegiate level plus an understanding and use of the psychology and history of the subject; the grade placement and method
of teaching on that level, the selection and organization of
instructional illustrative materials and the standard achievement tests of the subject. To successfully teach and to successfully learn by such a method required thinking on the
part of both teachers and student - it requires resourceful-
ness, alert attention to all phases of education and a deeper
and more thorough appreciation of the educational possibilities of every subject and each lesson."

COURSES FOR THE SUMMER QUARTER

The first summer school was held at Radford in 1914 as a
separate unit from the regular session. The course offerings
were determined by the certification standards of the State.
At first, the courses were largely review. The major objective was to prepare students for the State examinations. No
entrance requirements or academic standards were inforced.

Many successful principals and teachers were employed as
instructors to augment the regular staff. The efficiency of
the school was measured by the number of students able to
pass the state examinations. In this the Radford school was
most successful. Although the summer work was of a hetero-
geneous sort it was thorough as far as it went and the
students were required to work hard.

THE STATE EXAMINATIONS

For the first two or three years the examinations were
made out in Richmond and were sent to the college to be given
to the students. Later each local instructor submitted to
the State Department a set of questions based on the work
which he was giving in his courses. From these questions
assembled from the various summer schools a uniform examination was compiled. Finally the State Department merely

approved the local examination. This latter method allowed more leeway and gave the teachers of the review courses a feeling of greater freedom which contributed to a great improvement of the instruction. It somewhat reduced the nervous tension for the students. The examinations were graded by the local instructors and the final record sent by the registrar to the State Director of Certification who issued the certificates.

PROFESSIONAL COURSES IN SUMMER QUARTER

For ten years the administration of the professional courses during the summer quarter was hectic. Each year brought some change in requirement. Since none were retroactive, the problem of course construction became almost an individual matter especially for those students who sought certificates based upon the old first grade certificates. The original elementary certificates required methods courses in the teaching of elementary school subjects. As the length of time of preparation for these certificates was increased the type of course improved until 1922 when the same professional courses were offered in the summer as in the regular session.

Since 1922 the summer quarter has been conducted as an integral part of academic year, with the same courses, credit and same opportunities as in any other quarter.

FOUR-YEAR COLLEGIATE PROFESSIONAL COURSES

In 1916 the Legislature and the Board of Trustees of Virginia Normal Schools authorized the normal schools of the State to offer four-year courses. This fact is announced first in the catalog of 1917 and these courses are announced in the catalog of 1918. The catalog of 1918 beginning with Page 54, contains a very elaborate arrangement of four-year courses. These, however, were never carried out in any definite form.

In 1918 a differentiation of work was ordered by the Normal School Board which gave to each of the four Normal Schools a designated piece of work for its four year course. Radford was designated to do the work of training rural school supervisors, rural teachers, and specialists in rural education.

In 1919 the college announced courses to meet this assignment. Here the first effort is made to organize a course leading to rural supervision and the Bachelor of Science degree.

This course was planned on the basis of graduation from any two
year curriculum offered in this school or any other of the Normal Schools of the State and the additional two years of work
as outlined in the catalog of 1919. A marked tendency is shown
in the curriculum beginning at this period to place more emphasis on rural work. A loosely organized department of rural education was established and a course for rural education required
of all students in the school. This tendency is shown at its
height in the course of study for 1919, 1920, 1921. However the
idea of differentiated curricula was never popular with the students or faculty of the Radford College. The Radford College ap-
preciates very keenly the problems of rural education and emphasis is placed upon this phase of service in Virginia. A general
theory prevails in the institution, however that good teaching
is as applicable in rural schools as in city schools and that
teaching can be good, regardless of the location of the school.
The course for supervisors to receive special emphasis during
the summer quarter. All of the catalogs carry announcements of
courses in supervision during the summer quarter. This meets a
Virginia condition which makes possible summer study for supervisors in service.

The year of 1924 marks the opening of the new period in the
curriculum history of this institution. At that time the name
of the school was changed from State Normal School to State
Teachers College. The motion adopted in 1918 differentiating
the activities of the various schools was abolished, allowing
the privilege of straight four-year courses in any line of work
to each of the colleges. The catalog of 1924-25 shows a very
definite effort on the part of the course of study committee to
meet this new requirement. During this year there was also
abolished the two-year course in Home Economics and training
for Junior High School teaching. No longer in Virginia are
diplomas given for two-year work in either of these curricula.
The two-year work is confined to those desiring to teach in the
primary and grammar grades. For high school teaching and the
teaching of special subjects it is confined to four year courses.

With the introduction of these four-year courses the State
offered Collegiate Professional Certificates and raised the
standards for teaching in the high schools of the State to the
Collegiate Professional Certificate as a minimum. The course
of study for 1924-25 shows the organization into major and
minor system. Several meetings were held with the officials of
the State Department of Public Instruction and representatives
of the other teachers colleges. The standards for constant
subjects were determined and have been followed as the basis

of all four year curricula since 1925. The original major was nine hours respectively.

In 1930 the requirement for the degrees are:

Total quarter hours required - - - - - - - - - - - 186
Distribution:

      Constant or required course for all
      candidates

English - - - - - - - - - - - - - - 18
Education and Supervised
Teaching - - - - - - - - - - - - - 36
Social Sciences - - - - - - - - - 18
Physical or Natural Sciences - - - 9
Health & Physical Education - - - 9
Psychology (including Logic) - - - 9
             Total Constants 99

Majors and Minors:

One major selected by candidate - - 36
Two minors selected by candidate - 27 ea.

Candidates may major in Biology, Chemistry, Education, English, History and Social Sciences, Home Economics, French, Mathematics. Candidates may select two minors from the above subjects, and in addition they may select Latin, Geography, and Sociology, Health and Physical Education, and specialized fields of Education.

    Electives:

      After the constant and the major and minor requirements are met candidates may elect courses from any related field as are being offered during a quarter.

      Languages and Mathematics are not required for the degree, however, candidates are strongly advised to select Languages as a major or minor. These are also adjusted to meet the requirements of the professional field or graduate school the candidates expect to enter. For instance--Science, and Mathematics, History and English, English and Languages are types of combinations commonly made. The constant subjects and the careful advisory system we use in the selection of major and minors usually makes it possible for each graduate to meet the State requirement for teaching in at least three fields.

In 1930 Doctor Moffett made an analysis of the election of majors and minors by the students who received the degrees in that year. This table shows the influence of the enlarged departmental offerings:

Percentage.
Distribution of major and minor subjects by subject courses of the Bachelor of Science graduates for 1930.

Subjects	Percent Selected as Majors	Percent Selected as Minors
English	61%	27%
History	18%	16%
Home Economics	11%	2%
Mathematics	11%	2%
French	8%	8%
Biology	1%	24%
Chemistry	0%	2%
Education	0%	2%
Physical Education	0%	1%

SPECIAL COURSES

PHYSICAL EDUCATION

Physical Education and Athletics were given an important place in the original plans for the development of the courses at Radford. Unlike most of the educational institutions which had been planned prior to this time a gymnasium and swimming pool was designed and included in the first building erected on the campus. The large area under the auditorium was built as a gymnasium. The place that Physical Education was to have was indicated in the tentative courses of study proposed by Doctor McConnell in the first catalog. Class instruction in Physical Education was justified by stating that the purpose of the college was not only to train the minds of the students but also to develop their bodies to the highest degree of efficiency. The courses aimed to increase muscular control, to develop poise and disciplinary powers. "Gym" classes met twice each week throughout the year and the work consisted of plays, games, gymnastic exercises, training in the use of dumb-bells, clubs, corrective exercises for faulty posture, folk dancing, hygiene, with such extra-class activities as swimming, basketball, baseball, and track.

In the original faculty Miss Louise K. Ruggles was named as instructor of Physical Education. She devoted full time to this work. This was unusual as the other educational institutions at this time employed only part time or no instructor of Physical Education. All students were required to take some form of Physical Education.

Play and corrective physical exercises have been emphasized in the instruction rather than the formal drill work of the Swedish type. A standard gymnasium uniform of blue or black bloomers with white middy blouse has been required throughout the entire history of the college.

The local emphasis on Physical Education grew and developed as this subject gained popular recognition in the State. At first it was conceived as supplementary to the everyday life of the student in the college and was not recognized as definitely preparing them for any professional activity. Beginning in 1916 there was a general movement throughout Virginia to encourage supervised play and to have directed playground and athletic activities in the public schools. This movement culminated in the employment of State Supervisors of Physical Education. Much of the impetus to this movement was given by Mr. Thomas H. Settle of the National Playground Association. He made many speeches throughout Virginia to interest the people in the development of the physical life and recreation of their children. Physical Education, ability to direct games, and the conservation of health of the children through body control became an important item in the professional training of teachers. Thus the aims of the department became more extended. As stated in succeeding catalogs the aims show the increasing importance of Physical Education; in 1915 the aims were to develop body harmony, to improve the functions of the body, to correct physical defects and to develop coordination and self-control. In 1930 "The aims are to develop a wholesome attitude toward physical education, to foster social mindedness and to teach the student how to carry these aims into her teaching. The unity of mind and body is an accepted scientific fact--the aim in modern physical education goes far beyond mere physical development, it is socially minded and develops mental stimulation."

The courses offered provide natural and formal exercises, tactics, games, folk dances, natural dancing, singing, athletic games, and major sports, administration of playgrounds.

THE WEST LAW

The Legislature of 1920 passed what is popularly known as the "West Law". This law made it necessary that all the pupils of elementary and high schools in the State receive as a part of educational program such physical examinations, health instruction, and physical training as shall be prescribed by the State Board of Education with the approval of the State Board of Health. This law included the requirement that the State Teacher Training Institutions should provide such courses as would meet the needs of the teachers in giving the courses required in the elementary and high schools of the State. The West Law placed emphasis on health education and directed the education to the study of disease, preventive medicine, personal hygiene, first aid, community health, and the general health of the teachers with such physical exercises as would develop proper body functions and give wholesome physical recreation.

Following the passage of this law the Radford College extended and elaborated its course in hygiene which had been formerly given as a part of the Physical Education and Home Economics work into a formal course in health education, designated as Science 11.

For some time the instruction of this course was given by the instructor of Physical Education. In this connection Doctor Mary Evelyn Bryden of the State Department of Public Health paid many visits to the college. She frequently addressed the students in the general assembly and lectured to the students in Science 11. She was employed by Doctor McConnell for one summer (1920) to have charge of the Health Education work. During this time she taught Science 11. Under her direction, Miss Flora Bryson, Science teacher in the college, became interested in Health Education. Miss Bryson's work attracted the attention of the State Health Department, who employed her for three months to work in Richmond under its direction in organizing the content of the State's required courses in Health Education. Miss Bryson returned to the college and was made teacher of Health Education and continued this work until she resigned in 1928. She was succeeded by Miss Wanda Ellis who had become Director of Physical Education.

The State requirement of the completion of the West Law Course for all the certificates made this one of the most frequently demanded courses both in residence and by correspondence. Miss Bryson prepared a correspondence course. Several hundred students have taken this course by correspondence from the Radford College. A similar course was also given by Miss Mary I. Bell of the Public Board of Health for several years, however, after the development of the correspondence course at Radford the students were directed by the State Board of Education to complete the West Law requirements here.

During the summer Miss Ellis was assisted by Mr. Kuhn Barnett, as teacher of Health Education. Under his direction of the Department of Physical Education the students were trained in the physical inspection of children. Skill in this course was required as a part of work in practice teaching. For many years the students assisted the city nurse in the inspection of the children of the Radford Schools.

The major supplementary factors for Health Education at the Radford College has been the everyday living of the student, the use of diet tables, the practice of prevention of illness, the care of the sick, the general supervision and oversight of the sick, physical examinations, and required physical recreation. These practices give objective evidence of the value of the principles of Health Education as being taught in the Department of Health Education, Biology, and Home Economics.

SEX EDUCATION

The national movement for sex education for all the children in the public schools received favorable recognition from the State authorities in Virginia. This movement received great impetus from the results of the medical examinations of the soldiers during the World War. At first the emphasis was upon the prevalence of social disease. Numbers of pictures showing the ravages of syphilis, gonorrhoea, prostitution and like social evils were spread throughout the country. Many of these pictures were shown under the auspices of the State Health Officials in the Radford College. Although the pictures were presented under normal conditions and students prepared for the content, the result is debatable. The general reaction of the students was an abnormal fear and suspicion of their associates.

During the later years of the War a very fine woman physician, Doctor Noble was sent to the College under the auspices of the Social Hygiene Department of the American Red

Cross. Doctor Noble gave a series of talks on the social and medical aspects of sex. This series of talks was the first to swing the emphasis from the negative fear complex to an intelligent appreciation of the social evil in its personal application.

The State Board of Health under the direction of Doctor Mary Evelyn Bryden was given the responsibility for sex education in the State. Doctor Bryden was a sensible woman physician and approached the problem in a sane manner. She traveled about the State giving lectures to mothers and to teachers, training them in the principles of sex instruction. In this capacity she made frequent visits to the Radford College. She soon combined general health education with her courses in sex education and child welfare and thus paved the way for the more extensive health education program launched a few years later throughout the State. As her work increased other women were employed by the State Health Department and the Red Cross to assume some of her duties. Chief among these was Mrs. Freba Croxton who became director of sex education. Her theory was to teach sex in connection with the other courses of the school curriculum. A state committee worked for several months to develop the outlines for such correlation.

In 1928 the State was instrumental in bringing to Virginia for a series of lectures in the institutions of the State Doctor Galloway of the American Society of Social Hygiene. Doctor Galloway stayed in the Radford College for two weeks and gave a series of most impressive lectures. His influence was the most constructive of any of the people in the field of social hygiene who ever visited the college. His lectures were so deeply appreciated by the students that they presented him with a gift (a gold fountain pen), the only gift ever presented to a visitor by the students. The gracious kiss which he gave Miss Anna DeHart who presented the pen seemed to win the full confidence of the entire student group.

EXPRESSION

In 1918 Miss Elizabeth Sheffield Allen was employed as teacher of Expression and Oral English. The courses given in this department were designed to meet the needs of students for training in oral reading, Oral English, Public Speaking with less emphasis upon the usual elocution, recitation and dramatic expression. The courses were required for all Sophomores.

Miss Allen proved to be a teacher of Expression, she placed emphasis upon dramatic reading, extemporaneous speeches and training for dramatic performances. During her instruction the halls echoed with the practice of "ah, ah, ahh" and other exercises in voice placement. "The leading hand" as a gesture became a campus joke.

Miss Allen was personally a most gifted reader. It was her custom each year to give public recitals. "Esmeralda" was one of her favorite programs. From time to time she gave this program in other communities. She was especially effective in her production of plays. During the time she was at the college she coached all of the plays sponsored by the various classes.

Miss Allen was succeeded by Miss Elizabeth Brown one of her students who proved to be quite gifted in Expression. Miss Brown taught the courses for several years while she was a student at the college. Other students who have taught courses in Expression were Annie Sue Anderson, Ina Addington, Helen "Bill" Brown, Kathleen Henessay.

In 1927 Miss Florence Belle Ogg, a graduate of the Emerson School of Oratory, Boston, Massachusetts, was employed in the English Department with special responsibilities to teach Oral English and coach all dramatic performances.

With the emphasis placed upon Forensics and Public Speaking under the direction of Doctor Long started in 1929, three courses in Public Speaking were offered. Two of these deal with the problems of organization and presentation of debates and orations taught by Doctor Long and one with the Technique of Public Speaking, taught by Doctor NeSmith.

SPECIAL MUSIC

In the original faculty Miss Lizzie Faye James was appointed as instructor of Piano. A Piano Department has been maintained in the College since this date. Fourteen pianos were purchased in the first few years of the life of the college for practice and instruction purposes. Great emphasis has been placed upon the importance of music in the institution.

In 1916 Miss Alice Jones was employed as Voice Instructor. Since then Voice instruction has been given.

In 1915 Mrs. W. C. McCarthy started Violin instruction in the college. She had this for several years and was succeeded by Miss Grace Jewett who came to the college as instructor in Piano and Voice.

In 1922 Miss Alice Gleaves became the teacher of Violin. Under her direction the number of students in this department greatly increased. Children other than college students were admitted to her classes. About the same time there was an increase in the number of young town students who took voice and piano at the college. All of this special instruction is conducted on private basis and the fees are paid to the teacher.[1]

FINE ARTS

Special instruction in Fine Arts was started in 1924 by Mrs. John Hopkins in a studio provided by the college. Since that time she has taught courses in China Painting, Oil Painting, Water Color, and Charcoal. All of this work is private nature.

ORGANIZATION OF CONTENT MATERIAL

There has never been a departmental system of organization at the Radford College. Officially the professors are of equal rank. Upon employment each has been given the opportunity to develop his respective work, organize the subject matter and teach his subject as he saw fit. The curriculum committee has worked with the faculty as a whole and not with department heads. Each individual has had the opportunity to propose such courses as he felt necessary for the best development of his field of work. The catalog statements of these courses have been prepared by the professors. The curriculum committee has put into uniform shape and grouped them according to the major fields of instruction.

Textbooks as the basic guide for organization of subject matter have been rigidly adhered to. The use of a good text is practically the only requirement Doctor McConnell, as President of the institution has been insistent upon. "Each course must have a textbook and the textbook must be used by the students" has frequently been stated by him as a fundamental principle of good teaching. As a result of this requirement some courses especially in the early years were designed in terms of a specific textbook rather than as an original organization of material. In the advanced courses however there has been more freedom in the use of texts and supplementary material.

EVALUATION AND NUMBERING OF COURSES

The original curriculum committee determined upon the term-

1. A fuller account of the activities of these music teachers is given in a discussion of musical organizations in Volume II.

inology of A, B, and C for the quarter. With the development later of the summer quarter this terminology was changed to Fall, Winter, Spring, and Summer quarters.

The courses were originally indicated numerically for each of the departments as Education I, II, and III. In 1920 this plan was changed and the courses were numbered numerically by departments according to the year and quarter in which they came, for instance Education II, which is the first course in Education, is offered in the Fall quarter of the freshman year. The first numeral of the course classification indicates the year, the second, the quarter of all required courses. Elective courses are numbered in sequence above the numbers necessary for required courses, for instance, Biology 31 is a required course in the third year, first quarter, while Science 37 is an elective course for Juniors or Seniors.

Since the organization of the school the courses have been evaluated by the standard session hour. For a number of years the periods were forty-five minues long, five recitations a week, however the final record the "points" were recorded in terms of session hours. In 1920 the class periods were lengthened to one hour, three times per week. Since that time the terminology used has been session hour as a basic of credit. A total of sixty-two session hours is required for the Bachelor of Science Degree from this institution.

METHODS OF INSTRUCTION

The presence of so many high school students in the early years forced the instructional practices to be largely on a secondary level. The teachers although well qualified for higher work confined their efforts largely to the methods commonly used in high school; namely, questions and answers with a strict adherence to the textbook content.

With the gradual professional development greater emphasis was laid on professional courses, methods of instruction were somewhat modified by the prospective use of the content by the student. The persistent requirement of Doctor McConnell, however, that each course should have a textbook tends to place a great emphasis on the content of the text with little use of supplementary or enrichment material. The question-answer and lecture method with an extensive making of notebooks seem to have been the most common methods of the majority of the faculty, with the exception of those teaching laboratory courses. The laboratory work has usually been one of student activities with demonstrations from the teachers.

In 1920 the theory of professionalized subject matter began to bear some fruit. Some departments, particularly those in education, tied their work very definitely to the training school. Many formal demonstrations were given to illustrate the types of lessons and educational theories being taught in these courses.

There have always been some members of the faculty who have fought against the extensive use of the textbook. However, so far as the author knows no full outlines or syllabi have been prepared for the content of courses except in the department of Home Economics. Since 1924 there have been more extended outlines made, bibliographies prepared and a gradual growth in the use of reference and supplementary material in all departments. There has been a rapid growth and extension of the library facilities in both books and service areas. In some departments especially History, Home Economics, Journalism and Science emphasis has been placed upon individual problems, projects and group activities.

TESTS AND EXAMINATIONS

Formal long term examinations have never been the practice in the college. Testing has been limited to class periods and one hour in length. Tests were scheduled monthly at first, later the practice of giving a report semi-quarterly reduced the number of required tests to twice a quarter. Written lessons are given at the discretion of the instructors.

Objective tests as opposed to essay type has been the subject of much discussion. Upon the first extensive introduction of these in 1927 the students became very much dissatisfied because they were not used to them. The discussions were rabid and faculty judgment so divided that Doctor McConnell forbade the use of such tests to determine final grades. As the use of objective tests has become more common and the practice better understood there seems to be less objection to their use.

Standard classification tests have been given to all
freshmen since 1925. At first these were limited to English.
Since 1927 these entrance tests have included a battery of
psychological tests and various college entrance examinations.
In 1931 the Greeley Colorado tests for teachers college students were used.

The degree classes of 1921, 1922, and 1923 were required
to prepare a thesis as an individual piece of work based on
the major field of the students interest. These thesis were
in reality good term papers which showed the ability of the
students to organize and present material in an original
fashion.

The improvement of instruction was announced as the
major project for the improvement of the college by President McConnell in 1929. Persistent emphasis is now being
placed upon this problem as is indicated by the program of
the 1930 pre-session institute of the faculty.[1]

1. See Appendix-faculty committees.

SECTION IV.
TRAINING SCHOOLS

THE TRAINING SCHOOL FACILITIES

The first instructional problem of the Radford College recorded in any of the official records of the institution is a statement made by Doctor McConnell at a meeting of the Board of Trustees
in May 1913 when he requested that a committee be appointed with
authority to enter into an agreement with the Public School Board
of Radford for the use of the city schools as training schools.
This committee was empowered to make whatever financial arrangements
necessary. Fortunately no difficulty arose in this connection and
an affiliation was established with the school board of Radford to
use the East ward school as a training school for the college. To
date, 1930, this affiliation exists. There has never been any fric-
tion, misunderstanding, or lack of cooperation. The seven grades
of the East ward school form the nucleus of the training school facilities of the Radford College. These were used first in 1913
when practice teaching was started by Miss Blanche Bulifant, Director of Training. The affiliation provided for a small subsidy
to be paid the teachers by the college. These teachers who were
already in the service of the city schools were employed as the
first critic teachers.

The Fall of 1914 the Teachers of the West ward requested the
college to do some form of practice work in the Central school.
They particularly desired Home Economics and Manual Arts. Accordingly these subjects were offered for several years in the Central
school. The equipment for these departments was furnished by the
School Board and the teaching was done by the student teachers under the direction of the teachers of the college.

RURAL SCHOOLS

In 1916 the first extension course of the college was undertaken. An agreement was made with Superintendent Hagan of Montgomery County Schools to offer Home Economics and Industrial Arts
in the Simpkins and Hill Top Schools. Both were one-room rural
schools, seven and three miles respectively from Radford. The college hired from C. C. Brown's Livery Stable a horse and a buggy.
With this outfit Miss Moffett and the Practice Teachers in Home
Economics would drive to the country once a week and the student
teachers would teach Home Economics in each of the schools. Large
cabinets were constructed by Mr. Roop in which the entire equipment

could be kept and safely locked up. The equipment consisted of
an oil stove and the necessary cooking utensils for classes of
six or eight children. The work was primarily cooking and sewing.
The work in these two schools was continued for one year. The expense and difficulty in transportation of the college people caused
it to be abandoned.

ROCKFORD SCHOOL

In the Fall of 1917 the College entered into a contract with
the Superintendent of schools of Pulaski County, Mr. Darst, to use
as a one room demonstration school the Rockford School. Rockford
is about two miles from Radford and is reached by ferry across New
River. The Rockford School was a typical one-room school admirably
suited for demonstration purposes. Miss Ethel Garrett, graduate of
the class of 1916 was employed as teacher. She and Mr. Coggin, Professor of Rural Education organized the work, interested the people
of the community and during the first year got the project started.
For the second year Miss Blanche Daniels was employed as the demonstration teacher. The old school house in the same school lot was
converted into a teachers home and equipped for housekeeping. Miss
Daniels with one or two student teachers lived in this house. The
platform was used as a bedroom and the remainder of the house was
furnished as a living room with a corner screened off as the kitchen. The home economics work was taught in the teachers home.
This was the first teachers home in this section of the country.
It was very successfully managed by Miss Daniels.

Miss Daniels and her student teachers devoted themselves enthusiastically to the development of a community interest centering in the school. The school garden, home economics, and industrial arts were introduced into the curriculum. These were taught
from the rural standpoint. Various experiments in the organization of the teachers schedule and unified activities for the un-
graded classes were worked out by Miss Daniels in cooperation with
Mr. Avent who was at this time director of the training schools.
A two-room rural school in Montgomery County taught by Misses Elrica Shelbourne and Ruby Graham were also used by Mr. Avent for
experimental purposes for one year. No practice teaching was done
in this latter school.

NEW RIVER AND BELSPRING SCHOOLS

The Rockford School was run with creditable success for three
years. It proved so successful that the college and School Board
of Pulaski County enlarged the facilities for practice purposes in

the rural schools of Pulaski by opening the three-room school at
New River and the Belspring consolidated school for demonstration
purposes. Miss Nell Hayter, Miss Sena Kirby and Miss Pearl Stone,
graduates of the College were employed as teachers for the New
River School. The practice work in this school was conducted in
the same way as for Radford in the city schools under the direction
of Mr. Joseph Avent.

A house located about one-half mile from the school house on
the Lee Highway was rented by the college, renovated and used as
a teachers home. Student teachers were assigned to the New River
School and lived in the teacherage with the teachers. Those students who were assigned to the teachers home paid their board to
the college and the college in turn made a food allowance to the
teachers for the students who were living with them. Much of the
food was bought at wholesale through the college. Miss Sena Kirby was head of the home and under her direction the house work
was done. The system of teacherage in connection with the demonstration school attracted great attention. Mrs. Henrietta Calvin, Director of Home Economics in the National Bureau of Education visited the school and the teachers home. The Radford plan
for housing teachers was described by Doctor Moffett in an article
which appeared in "School Life" April 1924. This article describes
the practice houses as they were conducted at that time in the two
demonstration schools at New River and Belspring.

"Teacher's homes are provided in connection with the two
practice schools which the Normal School maintains in rural communities, one a rural Junior high school with elementary grades, the other a typical two-room country school.
The practice teaching period for the normal student is 12
weeks; six spent in one of these rural schools, and during
this time the student lives in the teachers home and participates in the housekeeping for the group besides carrying on her school and community activities. The manager of
the teachers home is the home economics critic teacher; all
members of the group are responsible to her and do their
housekeeping under her supervision. When a new group of
pupil teachers arrive at the home they are divided into
housekeeping units of three or four members. To each unit
is assigned a working day or week, at which time it takes
charge of all the duties of the home. One member plans the
meals, does the marketing, and directs the preparation of
the food; another has charge of cleaning and others do the
cooking, take care of any one who may be sick, and meet
the emergencies which arise as in any home. By rotation
of work all the pupil teachers are given experience in the
various phases of home making. Frequently the unit plans

the recreation and social life for the group, great
interest and rivalry are shown in this phase of the
life. The noon lunch is another feature which stimu-
lates interest and ingenuity; it must be prepared
during the recess periods because housekeeping reson-
sibilities do not excuse a student from her practice
teaching activities."

The school at New River was used continually as a demonstration school until 1924.

In 1919 the Belspring Public School was also taken over as a
demonstration school by the college. At this time there were seven
grades being taught at Belspring. All of these grades were used
for demonstration purposes. The teachers employed for this school
were Miss Ethel Garrett, as Principal; Miss Frances Long, Miss
Elizabeth Painter, and Miss Ada Lou Hurley. The organization of
the school made it possible to offer practice teaching for the
students who were taking the Junior high school curriculum. An
effort was made by Mr. Avent to organize the Belspring school according to the educational theories for a rural junior high school.

A house near Buckton's Store in Belspring was rented as a
teacherage and here the same kind of life was carried on as has been
explained above. The time for practice teaching was divided so that
students were given experience under both rural and city conditions.
In 1925 a new school building was erected at Belsprings and the old
school building was converted into a teachers home. The furniture
and equipment for all of the teachers homes was supplied by the college.

In 1926 the College purchased a bus for the transportation of
the students from the college and the plan of having students board
with the teachers in the teachers home was abandoned. This was
made necessary by the complications which resulted from the college
schedule and the campus activities of the students. In the judgment of the administration it was felt that the students lost too
much of college life while forced to live in the country. All the
rural practice schools except Belspring were abandoned. By this
time the Belsprings school had so grown that additional teachers
were employed and a four-year high school course was given. This
with the city schools provided sufficient practice facilities.

WILLIAM H. McGUFFEY SCHOOL

In 1928 the Legislature made an appropriation for a campus training school. This building was carefully planned by the architects

with the close cooperation of Mr. J. P. Whitt, Misses Flora Dungy
and Hermine Menzie as advisors. This building is the only one
connected with the college built definitely for practice teaching
purposes. The building is built to provide a class room, an activity room and an office for each grade. The equipment for this
building was planned by Doctor Winifred E. Bain, Director of Training 1928 and 1929. In these plans she used the most modern ideas
for educational equipment; movable tables and chairs adjusted to
the size and activities of the children were planned for the lower
grades. Most of the equipment was made to order by the Industrial
Department of the State Pennitentiary. The building was opened
for use during the summer of 1929. Doctor Minor Wine Thomas held
demonstration classes of Individual Instruction according to the
Montgomery plan then beginning to develop. The remained of the
building was used as class rooms for college courses.

The building, as a training school, was formally opened in
September 1929 with a kindergarten and three grades. Miss Christine Wright was principal of the building and Critic of the first
grade, Miss Kathryn Fritz the second grade, and Miss Lillian Mc-
Clanahan the third grade. Miss Ethel McLeod was in charge of the
kindergarten. In 1930 a fourth grade with Miss Jonnie Gore as
Critic teacher was added. Miss Wright resigned in 1930. She was
succeeded by Mrs. Mildred Kocher. All of these teachers are holders
of Master degrees. A policy controlling the McGuffey school placed
emphasis upon the academic training of the teachers and no person
has been employed as critic teacher who did not hold the Master's
degree. The campus training school is entirely under the administration of the college and is supported by the college funds.
The children for this school were secured by announcing in the
papers that parents who wished to send their children to the college training school should make applications to the college. A
number of applications were received. These with a few transfers
from the East ward school gave a total of one hundred and twelve
for the first year's enrollment.

In 1930 the Simpkins School which had been used by the school
in 1917 was again affiliated with the institution as a demonstration school for the Montgomery plan of instruction under the direction of Doctor Minor Wine Thomas. Miss Thelma Price is the
teacher. Her salary is supplemented by the college. No practice
teaching is done here but the students who are interested in the
theory of individual instruction and who are enrolled in a course
on this subject taught by Doctor Minor Wine Thomas have observation
in the school.

The Fall of 1930 an affiliation was made with Superintendent
Barnett for the introduction of home economics in the high school.

This is the first practice work to be done in the City High School. The organization of the department, the planning of its equipment, and supervision of practice teaching has been done by Miss Luna Lewis of the Department of Foods and Cookery of the College. Mathematics was added for practice purpose in 1931 under the supervision of Mr. Alfred Eagle.

INSTRUCTIONAL WORK OF THE TRAINING SCHOOLS

Directors of Training and Their Major Contributions

Supervised teaching for one quarter has been required in all two and four-year curricula. The content, administration and technique of the course has been left to the judgment of the director of the training school and critic teachers. To date there have been five directors of training, one assistant director and for this year 1930-31 the work is being directed by a committee. Each of the directors has stamped his identity upon the training school and made a definite contribution to the general scheme of today.

MISS BLANCHE BULIFANT - 1913-1917

The first director, Miss Blanche Bulifant, 1913 to 1917, had the hard problem of initial organization. Miss Bulifant was an experienced elementary school teacher. She had had no experience or training as a director, however, her experience, keen intellect, and good judgment made her a successful leader in this department. Associated with her were good teachers. Some of the most effective teaching of children ever done in the practice schools was done by these teachers. They were limited in training and experience for critic work. The methods for the induction and development of student teachers was largely the result of the thinking and experiments of Miss Bulifant. She placed emphasis upon lesson plans. These were very extensive and took much time to prepare.

In 1913 a transition in educational theory, teaching methods and lesson plans was sweeping the teacher training institutions of the country. The five formal steps which are so effectively described in the Methods of Recitation by the McMurrays were generally used as the pattern for the lesson plans. Miss Bulifant became quite skilled and efficient in this method. The plans she required were an elaborate adaptation of the McMurray formal steps.

During this period much observation of the formal type was carried on by the subject matter and methods teachers. The critic teachers gave many demonstration lessons. The activities of the school were such as were typical in a good elementary school of that period. Practice teaching was one of the most awe inspiring experiences of the students' life. There was much talk about it and there was a general fear and dread for the course.

The equipment of the training schools during this period was limited to the necessities for formal class instruction. The college supplied certain drawing materials, Industrial Arts equipment, supplementary books and standard devices for motivation. The students made flash cards and many devices. Gradually a small library of reference material was accumulated for the grades.

The most helpful experience of the first five years of the college in this connection was a visit made by Doctor Charles McMurray, then Professor of Education at Peabody College. Doctor McMurray spent several days at Radford, had several conferences with members of the faculty and gave demonstration lessons on teaching by the unit plan. He stressed the importance of effective teaching by the supervisors and gave the first professional direction to the work of the training.

Miss Bulifant resigned her position in 1917 to be married. She married Mr. C. A. McFarland. With her husband she moved to Colorado where she became identified in educational work. She has been a frequent contributor to the Normal Instructor and Primary Plans and other educational journals. Her work at Radford and her subsequent carreer have been a credit to this institution. Under her influence her husband has also become an educator. In 1928 he was the only Democrat elected as Superintendent or any political office in his district of Colorado.

MR. JOSEPH E. AVENT 1917 - 1921

The second director of training, Professor Joseph E. Avent, had been identified with the college since 1913 as head of the Department of Education. Upon the resignation of Miss Blanche Bulifant, Professor W. B. Coggin was employed as Professor of Education with special work in rural education. This relieved Mr. Avent of some of the work in the teaching of education classes and enabled him to assume the duties as director of the training schools. He served in this capacity until 1921 when he resigned to continue graduate work at Teachers College and Columbia University towards his Ph. D. degree. Mr. Avent had been Superintendent of schools in several North Carolina cities prior to his connection with the Radford College. In this connection he worked out an administrative scheme for the routine and formal class room activities. He was gifted in the technique of inducting student teachers into the class room situation. He was systematic and given to great detail in all directions. This enabled the students to understand what was expected to do. He developed a lesson plan form which modified the scheme previously followed and greatly reduced the problem of lesson planning. This plan was printed, and sold to students who filled out one for each lesson to be taught. It was used as the basis for all lesson plans in the training schools until 1928. Mr. Avent worked for definiteness and concreteness in all of his practice work with students. In this connection he developed a number signal system for use by the children. These signals indicated all desires of the children and were also used by the teachers for direction. Such as "42, put books in desk"; "10 leave the room" etc. This system was learned by all of the children and is still practiced in some of the more formal grades of the training school.

One of the early publications of the Radford College was a Question Box, prepared by Mr. Avent. This was a series of questions with the appropriate answers for the guidance of teachers in the most common problems in class room technique. In connection with the Rockford School Mr. Avent worked out a daily schedule for a one room school. This was widely circulated and became standard in many of the one room schools of the State.

The system of having the director of the training school as a head of the Department of Education has some advantages. It provides for a closer integration of theory and practice. In this connection Mr. Avent developed and enlarged the scheme of observation. Education 13, School Management was taught by Professor Avent to the college students. In connection with this course there was detailed observation by the group in each of the grades. There was some development in the professional attitude of the critic teachers. He inaugurated a system of general conferences for all the student teachers. From time to time during the quarter the entire group came together to discuss the individual practices as being illustrated in the training schools.

The Avent Administration of the training schools was marked by a careful administration of details and systematic procedures in each of the rooms.

MR. JEREMY PATE WHITT 1921-1928

Upon the resignation of Mr. Avent in 1921 Mr. J. P. Whitt was appointed Registrar and Director of the training schools. Mr. Whitt was Superintendent of the City Schools in Radford from 1910 to 1920. With him the affiliation for the use of the public schools of Radford for training schools had been effected. He was in deep sympathy with the educational program of the college, had taught during the summer quarter at the college and as a part time teacher since 1914. In 1920 Superintendent Whitt was given a leave of absence from the college and city to spend one year in graduate work at George Peabody College for Teachers at Nashville, Tennessee. At Peabody he made a study of teacher training and the problems of elementary education. Mr. Avent resigned at the opening of the summer quarter of 1921.

The versatility of Mr. Whitt, his genial disposition and his willingness to work had won for him the nickname "War Horse" or the "Old Superintendent". This characteristic of his personality made it very easy for him to gradually assume many more duties than he was physically able to carry on in connection with the college work. The general reorganization of the administration of the college which took place in 1920 gave to the positions which he occupied much responsibility in determining the policies of the college. In assuming the position Mr. Whitt did not take any of the instructional work which Mr. Avent had been doing in the college, instead he devoted full time to the Registrar's office and the Training Schools. The chief mark of the Whitt Administration of the Training Schools was the development of a spirit of cooperation, easy running administration, and a better liking of practice teaching by the students than had characterized the work before. The thorough understanding that Mr. Whitt had of the City of Radford assisted him greatly in interpreting the work of the Training School to the parents of the children "practiced upon".

In 1922 the American Teachers College Association became active. Throughout the next eight years emphasis was placed upon the development of the Training Schools to meet the standards of this organization. Mr. Whitt regularly attended the National Conferences on Teacher Training and visited a number of the training schools of the United States for the local improvement of the training facilities.

This period 1921-1928 also marks the rapid growth and development of the entire college, especially in the enrollment of the summer quarter. Gradually the work of the Registrar's office con-

sumed more and more time. This made it necessary to reduce the
amount of personal attention given to the training schools by
Mr. Whitt. Much of the class work of the training schools was
left to the direction of the critic teachers.

Mr. Whitt devoted himself to the general administration of
the schools, the placement of student teachers and group conferences. Being a practical minded Superintendent much of the value
of Mr. Whitt's work as director of training school centered a-
round his analysis and interpretation of the everyday problems
of a teacher. He closed each quarter's work with a three-day
teachers' institute. At these times each student teacher gave
a report and discussed some professional problem. These proved
very effective as a summary. He placed emphasis upon the school
laws, preparation of reports and records by the teachers.

MISS FLORA DUNGY, ASSISTANT DIRECTOR 1927-1928

In 1927 the growth of the college made it essential that
some one be appointed to assist Mr. Whitt. Miss Flora Dungy,
who had come to college in 1925 as Professor of Elementary Education was appointed assistant director of the training schools.
Miss Dungy had been a critic teacher in a Nebraska Normal School.
She was well prepared by professional study at Chicago University
and by practical experience in the problems of the elementary
schools. She devoted her time and attention to the work of the
class room. She definitely worked with the critic teachers in
improving the technique of teaching of both critic and student
teacher. Under her direction the first comparative testing
program which compared the East ward training school with the
other schools of Radford was made. This was the first effort
made by the college or the city authorities to study objective-
ly the work of the training school. Through her personal influence and foresight a greater professional spirit was developed among the critic teachers. There was a rapid growth
in professional interest. The student teachers developed a
keener appreciation of the technique of teaching. Miss Dungy
with Mr. Whitt conducted the group conferences. She worked
out a systematic schedule for observation, which placed less
emphasis on the demonstration lesson as a show and more upon
the learning process carried out in each of the lessons. Miss
Dungy resigned her position in 1928 to be married. At this
time Doctor McConnell decided to relieve Mr. Whitt of the directorship of the training school and instead to appoint him director
of the Extension Department.   Heretofore this department had
been separate, gradually the dependency of the Extension Department upon the Registrar's office became apparent. Mr. Whitt
assumed directorship of the Extension Department in 1928.

DOCTOR WINIFRED BAIN 1928-1929

These changes made it necessary to employ a new person as
director of training schools. In this connection Doctor McConnell made a thorough search through the graduate institutions
for a desirable person. The standard for Doctor of Philosophy
degree for heads of departments had become a policy in the college. It was some time before a suitable person could be found,
however, the college was most fortunate to secure the services
of Doctor Winifred E. Bain who had just received her Doctor's
degree from Columbia University in New York City. Prior to her
graduate work Doctor Bain had been connected with the Milwaukee
Teachers College. She had specialized in Primary Kindergarten
work and her practical experience had been largely in this field.
However, she had been trained at Both Columbia University and the
University of Chicago in all phases of elementary education. She
assumed the directorship of the training school in September
1928.

In 1927 the college administrators started a definite effort to raise the standards of the critics in the training schools
to meet the academic standards of the American Teachers College
Association. Miss Ida Einstein and Miss Blanche Daniels, two
critic teachers who had been connected with the college for some
time were given leaves of absence to continue their work for the
Bachelor of Science degree. Conscious emphasis was placed upon
academic preparation. All of the critic teachers were made to
feel the challenge and need of a better preparation for their
work. Doctor Bain herself was professionally and academically
sound in her educational preparation. Her spirit and enthusiasm
were caught by the critic teachers. Her administration of one
year is marked with great professional growth on the part of individual critics. It became necessary to employ two critic teachers during the time that she was director. Miss Ruth Borders
who had critic work in Bowling Green, Kentucky, and Miss Ruth
Lewis, Master of Arts of the University of Virginia who had had
experience as a critic at the State Teachers College at Harrisonburg were employed. Miss Lewis was the first critic teacher to
hold the Master degree in the training schools of Radford. With
her coming the intention of the administration to employ as new
critics only persons qualified with Master degrees became more
evident.

Doctor Bain largely devoted her work to a stimulation and direction of the work of the critics, through them she directed the student teaching. She devoted much time and attention to the planning of the equipment of the campus training school. She became very much interested in the proposed plans for the development of this school. During the Spring of 1928 Doctor Bain conducted a testing program for all of the city schools of Radford. This program which was an enlargement and extension of the work done in the previous year by Miss Dungy included a thorough testing of all the children by standard achievement tests. In connection with the testing program she secured the cooperation of Doctor Minor Wine Thomas and his class in educational testing. This group with the critic teachers tabulated and put into permanent form the records of all children in the training school. These were filed in the administrative offices of the college and have been used by the critic teachers in such remedial programs as they have instituted since 1928-1929.

In the Spring of 1929, Doctor Bain was offered a position as Associate in the Department of Kindergarten Education, Teachers College, Columbia University in New York City. Since this position was a promotion Doctor Bain accepted. Her resignation at Radford became effective June 1928. She has paid several visits to the college in her capacity as field supervisor from Columbia University.

MISS ADA VEILE

Doctor Bain was succeeded as director of the training school by Miss Ada Veile, graduate of the Teachers College, New York and an experienced elementary school principal of various schools in North Carolina. Miss Veile had not any experience as director of training schools. She was employed by the college for one year. During this time she assisted in the organization of the three grades of the Campus Training School. She devoted much time to the higher grade work particularly the practice teaching on secondary level being done at Belsprings. She placed much emphasis upon the group conference. She enlarged the activities of the group work and required much supplementary reading and preparation of the unit plans.

COMMITTEE DIRECTORSHIP

During the current year 1930-31 a committee composed of Registrar Whitt, Doctor Moffett, and the critic teachers are directing the work of the training school. A plan for the general

conferences has been worked out whereby each critic discusses
some problem with the students. The various committees of the
critic group have worked out patterns for the practice teaching work of each student under her respective critic and the
group as a whole have organized the examinations for the general conferences. This conducting of the training school by
the committee is experimental and to date has proven very satisfactory. It has been marked by a greater professional growth on
the part of the critics. They have devoted much time to the
preparation of their material for the conferences. Their responsibility for the college students has been greatly increased.
This has been challenging and stimulating to each of the critics.
Monthly conferences devoted to a discussion of the current problems of all the critics are held. At the end of the Fall quarter each critic prepared an extended resume of the work she had
done. These reports are being read by all the other critics,
out of this it is planned to develop a more uniform procedure for
the work.

SUPERVISING TEACHERS

The backbone and strength of any training school system is
dependent upon the critics or supervisors in charge of each grade.
The Radford organization provides for a critic teacher for each
grade. The student teachers are assigned to these critics in
groups of two, three, and seldom more than five student teachers.

In the organization of the training school (1913) only those
teachers who were then employed in the public schools were used
as critics. Most of these teachers were holders of the elementary certificate. None of them were Normal School Graduates.
All of them had had successful teaching experience and were, according to the standards of 1913, considered good teachers. With
the realization of the full meaning of training school work many
of them eliminated themselves from the system. Their positions
were filled by Normal School graduates. As is characteristic of
many teachers colleges a professional in-breeding started. Most
of those appointed to positions as critic teachers were graduates
of the local school. This system has many advantages in that the
critic teachers understand the philosophy, policy, and routine
procedures of the institution. It has the disadvantage, however,
of maintaining between the training school and the college faculties a teacher-student attitude which tends to prevent a close
inter-relation on an equal basis of the work of the two departments.

Following the adoption of the standards of the American Teachers College Association (1926) all critic teachers were notified

that after two years only those holding Bachelor of Science degrees would be continued as critic teachers; all new teachers who were employed must be holders of Master of Arts degree and after 1932 all critic teachers must hold a Master's degree. Since this announcement there has been a gradual improvement in the preparations of teachers. Several eliminated themselves as unwilling or unable to devote the time and money to the academic study necessary to raise their qualification to those of the standard. Misses Mae Kelly, Ida Einstein, and Blanche Daniel were granted leaves of absence to continue their work upon their Bachelor of Science degree and later for graduate study for the Master of Arts Degree. With the appointment of Miss Ruth Lewis in 1928 the emphasis upon Master degrees became active and since this time no teacher has been employed in the training school system who did not hold a Master degree. The teachers employed in the campus training school hold this degree.

In 1930 Misses Ida Einstein and Lillian McClanahan attended the National Conference of Supervisors of Student Teaching as the first critic teachers to represent this college.

In the Summer of 1930 Miss Mae Kelly entered Teachers College, New York City as a student in the experimental group directed by Doctor Thomas Alexander in the training of supervisors for training schools. During the current year Miss Kelly has worked under the supervision of this department and is carrying out an experiment in student-teaching and third grade work in the East ward school. Her work has been visited and supervised by Doctor Florence Stratemeyer and Doctor Winifred E. Bain. During 1930-1931 Misses Ida Einstein and Blanche Daniel are on a leave of absence. They are members of the experimental group at the Teachers College.

ASSISTING DEPARTMENTS IN THE TRAINING SCHOOL

Since the early organization of the training school the special departments of the college have been responsible for the supervision of the work of their respective departments in the training schools.

Public School Music was originally conducted by Miss Florence Baird who was succeeded by Miss Grace Jewett and Miss Edmee Smith. These ladies have made weekly visits to each of the grades of the city and the campus school conducting public school music for the children and planning with the critic teachers all the music in schools. Their plans have been supplemented by some particular student teacher in ratio to the musical ability of the teachers.

Miss McLeod of the Campus Training School (1929) assumed charge
of the rhythmetic orchestra for the third grade and kindergarten.

From 1913 to 1928 Miss Lillian Simmons supervised the work
in drawing and Industrial Arts in the training school. She planned a monthly program in art for each grade. In the early days
this was followed in detail by the critics. In the later years
her work was largely advisory and suggestive. In her work she
cooperated with each of the critic teachers and for many years
the borders, calenders, and patterns for decoration in the school
rooms   were prepared by Miss Simmons or the students of Industrial Art. As the critic teachers became better trained in
this work they have originated the art program for their respective grades.

Physical Education work has been conducted in the same manner as the music. The physical education directors, Misses
Louise Ruggles, Ninde, Foswick, McMurran, Clark, and Ellis supervised the games and recreation of the training school. Until
the last year or two these instructors gave short classes in
each of the class rooms. Now their work is largely advisory.

The Home Economics work in the training schools has always
been under the supervision of the Home Economics Department.
For a number of years Miss Moffett supervised this work in the
training school. Home Economics was taught in the Sixth and
Seventh grades of the East ward school, in the Sixth and Seventh
grades of the Central School where laboratories were provided
by the city and furnished by the College and Woman's Club and
in connection with the teachers'home in New River, Belspring,,
and Rockford. In 1927 Miss Marian Williamson and Miss Alice
Zollman assumed the supervision of the Home Economics. The laboratory work was stopped and the work centered around health projects and clothing in the Sixth and Seventh grades of the East
ward school. The teaching of these courses has always been done
by students. In 1930 a project was started for Home Economics
in Radford City in the high school. Under the direct supervision
of Miss Luna Lewis, Professor of Foods and Cookery at the College. Miss Lewis has planned the equipment, directed the organization of the foods and clothing department in the high school
and supervised the work of the student teachers. With the establishment of this new department the Home Economics work in the
grades was discontinued.

In 1916 the Board of Trustees designated the Radford College
to train rural school supervisors as a special function. At this
time Mr. W. B. Coggin was employed in the Department of Education

and as Director of Rural Education. Under his supervision the
Rockford School was started. He devoted much time to the development of this school. He was connected with the college
for one year, then resigned to become director of the Vocational Agricultural Teachers Training at Virginia Polytechnic
Institute. He was succeeded by Miss Dora States, graduate in
Rural Education of Teachers College at Columbia University.
Miss States continued the work of Mr. Coggin, gave courses in
rural education and cooperated with Mr. Avent in the supervision
of the rural schools at Rockford, New River, and Belspring. Miss
States became ill and was forced to resign her position at the
end of one year. Mr. F. B. Fitzpatrick was employed in the Department of Education in 1919, and was teacher of Rural Education and Supervision. He did not, however, have any responsibility for the Supervision of the Training Schools.

Other departments of the College have used the training
schools for demonstration lessons and observation. From time
to time some of the professors have taught lessons, planned u-
nits of work with the supervisors and assisted student teachers.
However apart from required observation the contact with the
training school has been limited.

In 1929 Doctor McConnell made visiting and observation in
the training schools a requirement for all members of the faculty. This created a training school consciousness which has resulted in a closer integration of work for some departments. At
this time the critic teachers were required to attend all faculty meetings, to be members of general faculty committees and
to assume the privileges of full faculty membership on equal
rank with the other members. In theory this relationship had
always existed, in practice it had not. The change has been
most effective in producing a spirit of "oneness" in the institution.

DISTINGUISHED VISITORS OF THE TRAINING SCHOOLS

The Radford Training Schools have frequently been visited
by superintendents, supervisors and other teachers. The first
distinguished visitor was Doctor Charles McMurray of Peabody College who spent several days visiting the Radford College observing the work of the training schools and holding discussions with
the faculty of the college. In 1918 Mrs. Henrietta Calvin of the
Bureau of Education of Washington visited the training schools
and devoted much time to the rural practice and the teachers home.
In 1925 the Supervisors from the Training School of the Concord

208

Normal School at Athens, West Virginia, spent a day in observing the work of the various grades of the East ward training schools of Radford. From time to time the district supervisors of Southwest Virginia have held a conference at the college. The schools have been open for demonstration lessons and general observation during the various district educational conferences held in Radford.

SECTION V

THE LIBRARY

The library of the Radford College was organized in the
Fall of 1913. There were about five hundred volumes in the
original collection located in Room 13, of the Administration
Building.[1] The first official communication received by the
author after her appointment to the Radford Faculty was a request made August 1913 for a suggestive list of books for the
proposed library.

The library was administered by a library committee from
the faculty, Mr. Gilbert, chairman, assisted by students who
kept the library open throughout the school hours. The books
were placed on open shelves, grouped by departments, they were
cataloged. A very simple card system for checking those using
the books constituted the library system.

At a formal board meeting in 1914 Doctor McConnell requested permission to spend $500.00 for the purchase of books.
Upon his request one of the members of the Board said, "Well,
Doctor you are certainly cutting it fat." This expression in
opposition to the expenditure of "so much" money was characteristic of the attitude of many intelligent people of this
period toward the accumulation of supplementary material, especially libraries in educational institutions. Many of the
older institutions of the State had very small collections of
books. These were kept in musty dusty rooms, open one or two
hours each week. Even these few were seldom used by either
student or faculty. Generally the books in such libraries
were antiquated. Many institutions prided themselves on having books of such ancient style of printing, and obsolete
language that they could not be read. Doctor McConnell did
not believe in this library practice. He, therefore, started
the library at Radford on the principle that it should always
be a store house of supplementary and valuable material for
actual class work and the general education of the students.
He determined to keep the contents of the library modern and
contemporary with the educational thought and development of
the school. He refused to have the college library made a
mere depository for antiquated books which could not be justified in the actual use of the college. The present library is therefore representative of the best literature,
modern educational books, and the standard publications in

1. A complete list of these books is shown in the inventory
   taken by Mr. Noell in 1914.

the major fields of thought. The students have constantly
been urged to make the library the headquarters for their intellectual life. Human interest and close contact with current conditions has been kept by means of the County papers
of the State and Nation and standard periodicals. Each year
Doctor McConnell has secured an increased appropriation for
the support of the library, with the result that to date
there is a total of 15,546 volumes. Of this number 1703 are
duplicates; 18.7% of these are in the Juvenile Library for
the use of the Training Schools.

LIBRARIANS

In the first group of faculty committees Doctor McConnell
appointed a committee on library composed of Professor Gilbert
Misses Simmons, and Baird. It was the duty of this committee
to have general oversight of the library, to suggest, and to
approve the purchase of all books. Each member of the faculty
recommended the books he desired for use in his department.

The students acted as librarians for two years and were
paid a small wage for their work. In 1915 Miss Carrie Green,
a graduate of the college who had been acting as student assistant, was appointed as the first full time librarian.
Miss Green had had no training as librarian other than her
experience as a student librarian. She was industrious, very
methodical and systematic in her work, and was most careful
in keeping up with the books.

Miss Margaret Godby was appointed librarian in the Fall
of 1917. She was the first person to work in the library who
had any training in the library science. She had had the summer courses in the University of Virginia. She was a graduate of Milligan College. She adopted the Dewey System of
classification and started the endless job of classifying and
cataloging the library. Following her marriage she resigned
and was succeeded by Miss Pearl Andrews, 1919, who came from
Sullins College where she had been Librarian. Miss Andrews
had had a number of courses in Library Science. She had
studied in the University of Virginia, Peabody College in
Nashville, Tennessee, and at Columbia University, New York
City. She is personally very neat and systematic in her
work. Under her direction the library had been one of the
best managed departments of the college. She brought order
out of chaos, classified the greater part of the library,

supervised by careful selection of books and periodicals the gradual development of the present collection of books. Miss Andrews is artistic and most successful in the production of flowers and has always kept the library filled with beautiful plants and artistically arranged flower decorations.

Each of the librarians have been assisted by a group of students selected from the student body. The number has ranged from four to ten or twelve assistants. These are paid by the hour for their work and have charge of the distribution of books to the students.

In 1927 Miss Lula Reynolds, a graduate of the college was employed as full time assistant to Miss Andrews. She worked in this capacity for two years and assisted in the classification and cataloging of many new books.

In 1930 Miss Florence Belle Ogg, formerly employed in the Department of English was transferred to the library as assistant librarian to Miss Andrews.

From time to time there has been an advisory library committee from the faculty. The original committee was succeeded by a committee with Mr. J. R. L. Johnson as chairman. The present committee is composed of Miss Andrews, Professor Whitt, Miss Moffett and Miss McLeod.

LIBRARY ROOMS

From 1914 to 1927 the library was confined to the one large room on the second floor of the Administration Building. In 1927 the class room, number 106, formerly used by Professor Gilbert as History Class Room, was taken over and converted into a reading room where the periodicals, newspapers, and general reference books were placed. In 1928 Room 101 was added as a reference room. Special reference material required for special class use by the various members of the faculty was placed here. Each member of the faculty is given a shelf on which his reference material is placed. The Legislature of 1930 made a conditional appropriation for a library building. This building is under process of construction and will be available for use early in 1932. The Board has approved its name "John Preston McConnell Library."

SPECIAL BOOK COLLECTIONS

In 1913 the college established an affiliation with the State Library in Richmond whereby many books and materials have been loaned by the State Library for use in the college. This affiliation has enabled the school to have available much valuable reference material which in the early days it was unable to purchase for itself. Since the beginning an effort has been made to assemble in the Radford Library a complete collection of Virginia Literature and History. So far as possible all publications dealing with Virginia have been assembled in one collection.

In 1931 the Association of University Professors started the collection of publications of the former and present members of the faculty of the Radford College which is to be placed in a special section of the library.

About two dozen old books (account, record, early textbooks, etc.) have been presented to the college as historic relics. These are stored in the college museum.

At the time of the discontinuance of the Conference of Education in the South (commonly called Ogden Movement) and the Southern Educational Society a number of the volumes of the proceedings of these associations were sent to the college for safe keeping. A complete set of these publications with many other documents have been stored in the storage houses on the campus. One complete set was placed in the library. This is the only collection the college has of distinct research value, it is probably not duplicated in any other library of the State or in the South.

Following the naming of the McGuffey Hall after William H. McGuffey the public was requested to donate copies of Old McGuffey Readers to the College. Many people responded. Several interesting letters of reminiscent type on the use of the McGuffey Readers were received by the college. Several copies of the older series of the McGuffey Readers were received. This collection was placed in the Juvenile Library at McGuffey School.

These few collections with the bound volumes of the publications of the Radford College complete the unique features in the library.

A more complete analysis of the contents of the library was prepared by Miss Andrews in the Fall of 1930, in preparation for the annual report to the American Teachers College Association. According to the Dewey System of classification the following table is indicative of the possessions of the Radford College at this time. (1930)

CLASSIFICATION OF BOOKS, RADFORD LIBRARY 1930

Classification	No. of Books	Duplicates	Percentages
General	1068	20	7.5
100	551	16	3.5
200	329	27	2.1
300	3675	687	23.5
400	435	53	2.8
500	1232	314	7.7
600	1161	165	7.5
700	477	47	3.0
800	3520	290	22.6
900	3080	144	19.8
	15,546	1703	10.9

Total in Juvenile Library 2894 or 18.7%

SECTION VI
EXTENSION SERVICE
___

COLLEGE USED AS HEADQUARTERS

The Radford College has considered its function to be
much wider than the activities of its own campus.

Prior to the opening of the College in 1912 the Appalachian School Improvement Foundation was organized at Emory
largely through the efforts of Professor J. R. Hunter and
Doctor McConnell. Mr. Hunter was secretary of the Foundation
until his death when he was succeeded by Mr. W. E. Gilbert.
Doctor McConnell was President throughout the life of the organization. In 1913 Miss Virginia Owens of Shawsville was
active executive secretary of the Foundation. She maintained
a headquarter office in the College at Radford. Through this
organization the faculty had many opportunities for speaking
and coming in personal contact with education in Southwest
Virginia. The purposes of the Foundation are described in an
early college bulletin.

The Appalachian School ImprovementFoundation, incorporated
under the laws of Virginia in 1912 has its headquarters at
the State Normal School for Women at Radford. The Board of
Trustees include many of the most prominent men in public
and business life in Virginia. The President of the Board
of Trustees is Doctor J. P. McConnell, President of the
Normal School at Radford, Virginia; Secretary of the Appalachian School Improvement Foundation is Professor William
E. Gilbert. This Foundation invites the cooperation of all
public-spirited citizens. Its activities are many and varied. It distributes bulletins and all kinds of printed
matter on the improvement of schools, particularly Rural
and Village Schools; Sanitation, both personal and community Hygiene, Health, Agriculture, Good roads, Sunday School
Work, and on practically every phase of human need and interest. It has enlisted a large number of lecturers and
entertainers, who go to the communities wherever they are
needed without charge, except mere traveling expenses and
entertainment. It provides scholarships in a number of
educational institutions and maintains a number of young
women and men in our higher educational institutions. It
is supported altogether by voluntary contributions of
public-spirited citizens. Professor William E. Gilbert,
Secretary of the Foundation will be glad to give full

information and to supply any community with suitable speakers, lecturers, or entertainers on request."[1]

In 1917 Miss Edna Cox, county home demonstration agent had headquarters in the College. From this center she directed the 4-H Club Work and home demonstration clubs in Montgomery County. Many food specialists made the college their headquarters while they demonstrated food preservation and other measures of national defense during the war period.

In 1914 the Young Men's Christian Association of Southwest Virginia designated Radford as its headquarters. Mr. W. C. McCarthy was the district secretary for this organization and conducted his work from the school at Radford. From time to time the college has served as headquarters for the representatives of the Virginia Co-operative Educational Association. Each year Miss Freeda Koontz, Executive Secretary for this organization spends some time at the college while she works in Southwest Virginia. This contact was particularly strong during the years when Doctor McConnell was President of the Co-operative Educational Association.

ORGANIZATION OF THE EXTENSION DEPARTMENT

The formal organization of the Extension Department of the College was effected in 1919. Miss Moffett was put on half-time teaching and charged with the responsibility of organizing and directing the Extension Work of the College. She spent the greater part of the year in acquainting the people with the opportunities of the college and the help which this new department offered to the teachers in the field. Under her direction the Rural School Messages was organized and its publication started by the college.

In the reorganization of 1920 Mr. Fitzpatrick was made Director of the Extension Department. Under his supervision the first courses by correspondence were organized. These courses were written and prepared by the various members of the faculty. The first bulletin announcing such courses appeared in 1921 (October). The majority of these courses were designed for high school students who were trying to qualify for the first grade and elementary certificates. A bulletin has been issued each year announcing new courses offered by the Correspondence Department. All the high

1. Radford Normal Bulletin. Volume IV, No. V.

school courses have been eliminated. All Correspondence
Courses are now of full collegiate value. The courses are
prepared and supervised by the professors. The papers, in
the most part, are graded by advanced students. A student
may earn fifteen session hours of the professional credits
for a diploma of the college by correspondence. The enrollment is now over 600.

Mr. Fitzpatrick continued as director of the Extension
Department until 1928 when he was succeeded by Mr. J. P. Whitt.
By this time so many students had registered in the Correspondence Department that the transfer of credits to the regular
courses and records was one of the major technical problems
of the Registrar's office. Mr. Whitt has continued to en-
large and increase the offerings of this department. For four
years Mr. Fitzpatrick and Mr. Whitt were assisted by Miss Elizabeth Roop. She developed the present system for keeping the
records in the department.

In 1927 Extension courses were started in the Radford
Public Schools and the Buena Vista Schools. From these a
series of study centers have been developed. These courses
have been taught by Professors W. E. Gilbert, R. O. Bagby,
F. B. Fitzpatrick, Flora Dungy, and W. S. Long. Wherever
a group of teachers can organize a class of eight or more
students the college sends a teacher. The expenses of the
instructor and a fee for each student is charged. This is
paid the instructor. These courses carry full college
credit.

SECTION VII

ACCREDITING AND STANDARDIZATION OF RADFORD COLLEGE

State Standards

The acts of establishment of Teacher Training Institutions of Virginia passed by the Legislatures of 1908 and 1910
gave full power to the institutions to offer such courses as
would prepare the students to meet the standards for certification in Virginia. These same acts empowered the Boards of
Trustees to set up the entrance requirements. The requirements were therefore largely determined by the educational
conditions of Virginia at the time of the opening of the respective institutions.

Secondary education was very low in Virginia at the time of the opening of the College in 1913. It was necessary therefore for the College to permit secondary students to enter and as has been described in another section of this history, a large percentage of the students of this College were of secondary level for many years. In 1916 the power to grant the Bachelor of Science degree was given to the four teachers colleges by the State Legislature. Beginning at this time the standards for entrance were gradually raised to sixteen units of high school work from an accredited high school.

The State standards for accrediting high school were the first standards applied to anything in connection with the college. These were confined entirely to the entering student and had nothing to do with the quality or standard of work given within the college. Graduation from an accredited high school with two years of work led to the Normal Professional Certificate. There was no effort to standardize the content of the curricula leading to this certificate until 1922 when a general committee representing the Teacher Training Agencies of Virginia was called by Miss Rachael E. Gregg, Director of Teacher Training and Certification in the Department of Public Instruction. This committee determined the standards for elementary certificates.

In 1924 the Legislature changed the name of the Teacher Training Institution from Normal School to State Teachers College. This change by an Act of the Legislature raised the standards of the institution to that of collegiate level and placed the institutions in competition with the liberal arts colleges of the State. Up to this time the liberal arts colleges of the State had supplied the greater percentage of the high school teachers for the high schools of the State because they conferred a Bachelor of Arts degree. The Bachelor of Arts degree was the standard for teaching in secondary schools which were accredited by the Southern Association of Secondary Schools and Colleges. With the development of the four-year curricula in the teachers college designed to prepare teachers of regular and special high school subjects forced the teachers colleges to become conscious of a need to standardize their institutions in such a way that the graduates of the four-year course with the Bachelor of Science degree would not suffer any embarrassment in securing positions in the better high schools of Virginia.

SOUTHERN ASSOCIATION OF COLLEGES AND SECONDARY SCHOOLS

In 1926 the Radford College made its first formal application for membership in the Southern Association of Secondary Schools and Colleges. To receive recognition by this organization it was necessary for the college to prepare elaborate reports setting forth an inventory of its equipment, the professional standards for its faculty, salary scale, type, and quality of curricula, general academic and professional ideals and philosophy of the institution. This report was presented to the Southern Association and was received favorably. However the report of the college was placed on the waiting list pending the adoption of the resolutions by the Association to admit Teachers Colleges. Up to this time practically no teachers college had been admitted to full standing in the Southern Association. Through the strenuous efforts of the Representatives of the Texas Teacher College these institutions had succeeded in securing recognition and had precipitated a fight in the Association between the more conservative liberal arts faction and those who were willing to recognize the teachers colleges. The Association sent Doctor Bond of the University of Tennessee to inspect the institution. In 1927 the Radford College presented its second request for membership. The institution was represented by Mr. J. P. Whitt. Mr. Whitt was received courteously by the committee on memberships and was told that the only standard the Radford College was unable to meet was in the scale for teachers salary. This report from the Southern Association precipitated the crisis in the instructional life of the institution in 1927 which has been described elsewhere in this history. This standard forced the payment of three thousand dollars as a minimum salary to the heads of the departments. This requirement was used by Doctor McConnell as a basis for his efforts to increase the professional and academic standards of the faculty members.

In the fall of 1928 Doctor William Moseley Brown, then of Washington and Lee University, inspected the College and made a most favorable report of the academic and professional standards of the institution. At the 1928 meeting of the Southern Association at Fort Worth, Texas, the College was represented by Doctor and Mrs. J. P. McConnell. At this time the application for membership was accepted and the college was given advanced standing in the Association. Membership in the Southern Association had a great significance in the life of the institution. It stimulated a consciousness of outside standards and broadened the horizon for the service of the institution. The faculty and the students were made conscious of the necessity for high standards of scholarship and personal and professional attainment. For each year a report is made to the Southern Association from the institution. Mr. Whitt is largely responsible for the preparation of these reports. He has represented the College at the meeting of the Association in Jackson, Mississippi; Jacksonville, Florida; Lexington, Kentucky; and Atlanta, Georgia.

AMERICAN TEACHERS COLLEGE ASSOCIATION

In 1916 a group of Teacher College Presidents from the middle West organized a conference of presidents of teacher training institutions to meet annually in connection with the Departments of Superintendents of the National Educational Association. This group of College presidents devoted themselves to a discussion of their problems of teacher training. Early in the history of the organization Doctor McConnell became identified with it and attended several of these group conferences. In 1922 this conference with several affiliated organizations became the American Teachers College Association. For several years the Association conducted its early policy of holding annual meetings and devoted itself to the study of problems of teacher training. Doctor McConnell was elected Vice-President of this organization at the Atlantic City meeting. He spoke frequently from the floor and in the Chicago meeting won quite a recognition in his retort to a previous speaker on education of negroes in the South. Parallel with the meetings of this association there was the pressure being brought upon the individual members by the accrediting agencies. Many of the Teachers Colleges were being turned down by regional associations. The North Central group were having a particularly hard time. It was therefore decided that the Teachers College Association should set up standards for itself by which the teacher training institutions should be accredited. A committee on standards was appointed. This committee made a survey of the existing conditions in teacher training institutions and with this objective data as a basis set up a series of standards. These standards were adopted at the meeting of the American Teachers College Association in Washington in 1926 and have been revised, strengthened and raised at each subsequent meeting. The standards provide for the classification of teacher training institutions into

three classes A, B, and C. By 1929 a large number of the
teacher training institutions had reached the standards of
Class A, which permits a ranking in this class if the institution was deficient in not more than three of the standards.
The Radford College was admitted to this group in the first
classification of "A" Colleges. In 1929 only twelve teachers
colleges had achieved all of the standards. Radford College
was minus three. Those applied to the size of the library,
training of critic teachers, and the ratio of class size to
faculty members. By 1930 these three deficiencies had been
completely eradicated from the Radford College and the institution was admitted to Class "A" with no deficiencies against
it. In 1930 only thirty-six of the one hundred and seventy-
nine institutions accredited by the American Teachers Colleges
were in Class "A" with no deficiencies noted against them. In
1931 this number is fifty-one institutions with no deficiencies.
In addition to the annual reports from the local institutions
the Association appointed a committee of representatives to
visit each of the training schools of the country and get a
first hand impression of the quality of instruction and of
the achievements of the institution. Radford College was inspected in 1927 by Doctor Charles McKenny, President of
Teachers College, Ypsilanti, Michigan and in 1928 by Dean
Minnick of Ohio University, Athens, Ohio.

All annual reports are made to the executive committee
of the Teachers College Association. These are prepared with
great care by Professor Whitt, Doctor McConnell, Doctor Moffett
The institution is represented at the annual meeting by some
member of this administrative group. Doctor McConnell has attended the meetings at Atlantic City, Chicago, Washington,
Cleveland, and Detroit. Doctor Moffett has attended the meetings at Cincinnati, Washington, Atlantic City, and Detroit.
Mr. Whitt has attended the meetings at Cincinnati, Washington,
Cleveland, Atlantic City, and Detroit. The standards as laid
down by this Association have been carefully studied by the
faculty of the college. In the Fall of 1930 Doctor McConnell
secured copies of the standards for the members of the faculty
and each was required to read and study them. From time to
time these have been explained in detail to the faculty and
the general rating and classification of the college has been
announced to the students each year. Doctor McConnell, in
the administration of the college, has consistently adhered
to the standards and has notified all members of the faculty
who would be affected by new standards.

SIGNIFICANCE OF THE OUTSTANDING ACCREDITING AGENCIES

The establishment of a relationship with the outstanding accrediting associations such as the Southern Association and the American Teachers College Association, has a vital significance in the development of teacher training institutions and brings to the institutions national, as well as, a State recognition. The first advantage occurs to the graduate who as graduates from institutions of such high standards receive unquestioned recognition in their profession. This makes it possible for a graduate to secure positions in accredited schools and insures entrance to graduate schools. In the second place it brings to the institution itself a certain prestige which makes the institution eligible to National organizations. Since the Radford College has been recognized by these accrediting agencies it has been invited to become an active member of the American Council on Education, which is devoted to research and study of problems of higher education. It has brought to the professors the privilege of recognition and membership in the American Association of University Professors and the American Association of University Women. It has opened to the students of the institution, the doors of the Kappa Delta Pi Fraternity, an honor society in Education. A chapter of this organization was installed February 7, 1931. Third, the emphasis upon standards broadens the horizon of the institution, makes better professional service within the college. The salary standard makes it possible to attract to the faculty people of higher academic and professional preparation and through the application of standards to the quality of work and achievement of these people the entire tone of the institution is raised. The standards to date have been largely of an objective and material nature. It is obvious that the trend is towards the setting-up of standards for the measurement of the more intangible qualities of the institution such as instruction, personality, development, and student and faculty adjustment.

THE NATIONAL SURVEY OF TEACHER TRAINING

In 1930 the United States Government made an appropriation of two hundred thousand dollars for a National Survey in Teacher Training. This survey is being conducted by the Department of Education by the United States Government under the leadership of Doctor E. S. Evensden of Teachers College, New York City. Doctor McConnell has appointed Miss Moffett responsible for the reports of this institution to the Na-

tional Survey Committee. To date a report of the research
and a bibliography of the publications of the faculty of
this institution have been submitted along with certain
fundamental questions which the administration of this institution considers vital in the study of teacher training
in the United States.

VOLUME II
PART I
STUDENT AND CAMPUS LIFE

SECTION I
STUDENT PERSONNEL

Miss Ara Lee Hicks of Shawver Mill, Virginia was the first student to arrive on the campus of the Radford College. Her father brought her late in the afternoon September 15, 1913. The news of her arrival spread rapidly among the faculty. All were anxious to see the first student. Miss Lena Stafford of Mechanicsburg, Virginia, was the first student to register. These two started a long line of students into the portals of the college. In 1929 by actual count of registration records there had been 10,498 different students registered at the Radford College during its history; 1155 of these had completed the two-year professional course; 205 had completed the four-year professional course. In the same year 2,220 of the active teachers of Virginia had secured their certificates on work done at this college.

The student population of the Radford College has been affected by the organization of the academic year on the quarter basis and the standards for certification. The quarter organization makes it possible for students to enter the college at the opening of any quarter, in September, January, March, or June. Any three quarters constitute an academic year of work.

For many years the minimum standards for certification ranged from one to three quarters of academic work. This made it possible for a student to stay a comparatively short time on the campus and receive recognition for her work. Many students entered the institution in September and completed their work the following June. The quarter organization however made it very tempting for students working for short term certificates to enter in the Spring or Summer quarters. To offset this disadvantage of a shifting population there has been a decided tendency for students to re-enter the institution, to return after intervals or several quarters and even years, to continue their work. In the year 1929-1930, there were students in the college who had also been students in the first year. Therefore, although the population changes frequently the student personnel has been largely confined to the same students, who though they have not remained for a long period of time at any one time, have averaged two years on the campus.

DISTRIBUTION OF STUDENTS

The Radford College is located in Southwestern Virginia and has largely served this geographical area of the State. Seventy-five per cent of the students have been recruited from the counties of Southwestern Virginia, however, throughout the history of the college other sections have been well represented notably, Eastern Virginia, Southside Virginia, and the Piedmont section West of Lynchburg. In 1913 there were two other States, North Carolina and Tennessee represented. The college has always had a large number of students from North Carolina, Tennessee, and West Virginia. At one time there were eleven different States represented in the student body. Students have been registered from Washington, Illinois, Louisiana, Florida, New York, New Jersey, Ohio, Kentucky, Iowa, Montana, California, and Texas.

INDIAN STUDENTS

In 1923 Chief Cook of the Pamunkey Indians from the reservation at Lester Manor, Virginia, visited the college. He made the chief address at the Pow Wow of the Pocahontas Society. He became interested in the Radford College and in the summer of 1926 sent his daughter and two of her cousins to the summer school. These students boarded in the home of Doctor McConnell. During the next summer three other Indians from the reservation attended the college. On July 21, 1923, Misses Cook, Bradley, and Page assisted Chief Cook in an Indian program given as a feature of Virginia Folklore Week.

FOREIGN STUDENTS

In 1923 the American Red Cross requested Doctor McConnell to award two scholarships to students from Porto Rico who should be selected by the Red Cross for education in the United States. Under this arrangement Miss Rosa Carlo and Miss Pura Pastrana were sent to Radford College in the summer of 1923. These students were typical Spanish beauties, they charmed the faculty, students, and young men of the town. They created much interest in the Radford community and paved the way for a long line of Porto Rican students who have followed them.

Each year the college gives two scholarships to these students who in turn teach Spanish. Each year, in addition to the scholarship students, two or three other Porto Rican students have enrolled in the college. These students are high in scholarship and outstanding in personality. Today twelve of our graduates are teaching in Porto Rico, three in the University and the remainder in the larger high schools of the Island.

In 1927 Miss Maria Odulio of the Philippine Islands entered the college. She came upon the recommendation of Mrs. Marianna Rainey, a graduate of the college who with her husband taught English in a high school in the Philippines. Miss Odulio stayed in the college for three years and made a good record. She is now teaching English in a Normal School in the Islands.

In 1930 Cholie MacNair, a Mexican entered the college. These students have been known as the "foreign" students in the college and have done much to educate and emphasize the international point of view in the entire student group.

TYPE OF STUDENT

For many years no definite effort was made to determine the personal background of the student entering college. The usual questions about: parental occupation, age, religious affiliation, and professional experience were asked and the answers filed as a part of the registration of the student.

In 1928-1929 Doctor Moffett in preparation of her dissertation "Social Background and Activities of Teachers College Students" made a study of the social background of three hundred and ninety students of the Radford College. Her study which is the most exhaustive study ever made of the background of Teacher College Students, presents a summary of the findings from 1,080 students in fifteen teachers colleges in the United States. The data she collected shows that the "average" student of the Radford College is nineteen years of age, is the daughter of a farm home. The student describes her home as moderate in size, and comfortably furnished with little emphasis upon the artistic or luxurious. The sewing machine and the automobile are the chief modern pieces of equipment. (Fifty per cent do not have inside toilets, bathrooms, and modern improvements, such as central heating plants, refrigerators, etc.) (Fifty-nine per cent of the homes have two hundred or more books). She has attended a small church. (Forty-two per cent of the students are Methodist; twenty-seven per cent, Baptist; eight per cent Christian; seven per cent Presbyterian; three per cent Lutheran; three per cent Episcopalian; two per cent Catholic. Practically all the students are communicants of some church). She was educated in the one and two-room elementary rural schools, graduated from consolidated or small country high schools. Her entire life has been spent in one community. The community did not have distinct social classes, there was much informal social life, such as neighborhood visiting, small parties, annual county or community fairs. The community however furnished none of the enrichments which come from a public library or art museum. The recreation was largely of self creation. There was not more than twenty-five young people of her own age. Participation in group organizations is largely confined to the college experience with the single exception of church and young people's religious organizations."

The students are of moderate circumstances. Their fathers own their own farms, their spending resources have been largely affected by agricultural conditions and prices.

In the beginning 1913 to 1917, the need for student loan and assistance was practically unknown. All of the students kept their accounts paid up to date. It was difficult to find students who would borrow enough from the loan fund to keep it alive. As the number of students increased, the war came on with its market fluctuations and as the general agricultural depression developed the use of the student loan fund became very extensive.

Next to the daughters of farmers the students have been recruited from the homes of mechanics associated in some way with the Norfolk and Western Railroad, merchants, ministers, teachers, and business men of Roanoke, Pulaski, Radford, Wytheville, Gate City, and the other small towns of Southwestern Virginia.

The students of the Radford College have been marked by the characteristics of the mountain folk. As described by Doctor McConnell, "the people who live in the mountain are individualistic in their thinking and habits of life. The high peaks of mountain ranges, separating the sweeps of the valleys also separate the vision and opportunity of social contact for these people, even with each other." "This isolation" he says, "develops the individualistic type characteristic of mountain people, independent, silent, undemonstrated, stalwart, upright, determined, tenacious, and loyal in the friendships and allegiances which he makes; aggressive to the point of fight for what he considers his rights; possessed of keen intellect, independent of tradition, slow to accept unproven truth, religious, a lover of nature, persevering and hard working."

To a large extent the Radford students have been of Scotch-Irish stock, uncontaminated by Southern European races or the mingling of any other stock. This has left in them the freshness and durability of the pure Anglo-Saxon, Scotch-Irish, and German people who settled Southwestern Virginia. It is natural, therefore, with such a student background that the campus life of the Radford College should be somewhat unique and distinct from that of the usual college.

SECTION II

ATMOSPHERE OF THE INSTITUTION

The attention of the Board, the faculty, and the administration of the college was centered first upon the physical and instructional life of the institution. Little attention was given to the development of the early traditional student life on the campus. The intangible atmosphere which grew and developed of its own accord is largely the outgrowth of the daily living of the students and the faculty and the inter play of the environmental influences upon these personalities and activities.

THE FAMILY SPIRIT

The first students were housed in the La Belle Inn. All of the students ate together and lived in this building or in the Heth House. Mrs. Brugh familiarly called "Muddy Brugh" by the students, was the center of the social life, around her rotated the activities of the students. She was like the hub to the wheel as she sat in her open office by the counter in the lobby. All the students passed by many times each day and exchanged with her greetings and the gossip of the hour. There were always groups of students gathered in the lobby or in her office, practically every student of the institution was drawn into one of these groups, they chatted, sang, laughed, and cried together in a great communal relationship.

Miss Crockett, Miss Simmons, Mr. Gilbert, Miss Moffett, and Miss Puryear ate with the students in the main dining room, they too were an integral part of the group life.

When the students came to the Administration Building they met the other members of the faculty. The entire group was so small that both students and faculty were well acquainted with each other. The students were called by their first names, it was very seldom that the surnames were used. A really affectionate fellowship grew up between the students and their "professors." All felt a personal responsibility to make a success of the Radford Normal. They were challenged by the progress of the other Normal Schools of the State. They sensed the unspoken resentment held for the people "West of the Mountains" by Eastern Virginians. They wanted to show them!

The necessity for self-creation of all recreation and social life led to a centralization of personal interests and social activities on the campus of the school. The idea of oneness prevailed with the faculty and students. There were few clashes of personality. Little jealousy, practically no personal rivalry and a wholehearted support of the projects of the institution. This sense of loyalty and unity was characterized by the students and faculty as the "family spirit". This spirit was enhanced by the democratic administration and sympathetic understanding of Doctor McConnell. The life of the institution was permeated by his spirit. To the students he was nearly a God. They had been reared to revere his name and respect his word. He knew practically all of their parents and spent many hours discussing with them family traditions, telling them anecdotes and describing the characteristics of their family or some ancestor and challenging them to be like the stock from which they came. This humanness appealed greatly to the students and stimulated an undying love and loyalty. Doctor McConnell was approachable on all subjects. The doors of his office were open to students and the faculty at all times. There was little formality in this intercourse. The faculty, likewise,

was at the college at all hours during the day. They put in
full time duty and were constantly accessible to the students.
Practically all the members of the faculty were interested in
one or more student organizations. These informalities in the
early life of the college made it easier to stand the hardships
of the unheated Administration Building, the unpaved muddy paths,
lack of equipment, and other appointments which mark the modern
institution of today.

SECTION III

INFORMAL SOCIAL EXPERIENCES

The students have had their fullest social experience in
the dormitories. This social life is difficult to describe in
detail. It has been customary to observe birthdays, to provide
programs for the social hours, to allow dancing, to encourage
freedom of visiting, to provide attractive nooks and corners
where a quiet conversation could be enjoyed and to stimulate a
social spirit among all the students. The campus itself has
been a continual source for social outlet; walks, athletics,
recreations of all types. Music has played an active part in
the institutional life. Pianos have been provided in all the
buildings and students have been encouraged to sing and play
and to carry on such informal social programs as appeal to
their taste and the popular style of the period.

GENTLEMEN CALLERS

Although the acts of establishment decree that the school
should be strictly for "White women only", no effort has ever
been made to keep the students from having young men as company.
On Thanksgiving Day in 1913 the first reception was held. At
this time many of the young men of Radford were invited to the
college to meet the students. This started a long series of
courtships in Radford. In this first group of callers were:
Mr. Henry Roberts, who met and afterwards married Miss Mary
Pope, Mr. Tom Jones, Mr. John Turner, Mr. Harry Moorehead, Mr.
Sidney Johnson, Mr. Gene Kirby, Mr. William Bond, and many
other of the present group of young business men of the city
of Radford. These all became the "regular dates" and "heavy
suitors" at the Normal. Some of them became serious in their
attentions. In order to help the cause along Mrs. Brugh extended "courting privileges" to the halls. Each year since
there have been college-town romances to absorb the interest

of the gossips. In the early days strolling through "Lovers Lane" or stealing a church date was the chief diversion of the lovesick. Later when the new dormitories were built the six o'clock strollers became racers with time to reach the hill-top before or as the whistle blew. In this group are Mr. Clarence Hall and Miss Mildred Elgin, later his wife; Mr. Alfred Goodykoontz and his wife Claudine Noell, Charlie Mottesheard, and his wife Virginia Allison; Frank Caldwell and his wife Pauline Perfater; Gene Grayson and his innumerable girl companions, Holden Barnett and Kuhn Barnett; Artie Roberts and the Caldwell brothers.

The girls who had "regulars" in town organized the Radford Club. This organization survived for many years, in its aroma of romance clung Easter flowers, moonlight picnics, stolen sweets in the city drug stores, forbidden car rides, long campus sentences, black lists, and ex-campus agonies all mingled to make membership in the Radford Club most desirable. Many of these romances have ended in marriage, at least forty such couples now make their homes in Radford.

Radford as the source of supply of gentlemen companions for the students began to weaken during the war period when most of the eligible young men of the city were in France. About this time a closer association with the Virginia Polytechnic Institute was established. The students of this institution became more frequent callers at the college. With the completion in 1926 of the good road between Radford and Blacksburg this affiliation became very close with the result that practically all of the "Callers" now came from Virginia Polytechnic Institute with the exception of the few friends who come from the home communities of the students.

SOME CAMPUS BEAU BRUMMELS

For the first four years of the college Mr. Gilbert was the "beau brummel" of the campus. He was a bachelor and was most zealous in his attention to the ladies. It was a campus joke that Mr. Gilbert would "fall" for any girl who was a blonde. Each blonde was primed for good grades in History and an easy time with the professor. Such romances both imagined and real furnished unending conversation, conjecture and gossip for the romantic. The climax was reached when Mr. Gilbert purchased a large lot. He immediately became very active in his efforts to build a foundation on this lot. After school hours he worked strenuously digging and throwing dirt. A very droll and interesting student who had paid very little attention to Mr. Gilbert's romances and the campus gossip suddenly took interest

and remarked she reckoned he really meant something this time
as he "never flung dirt before". The flinging of dirt by Mr.
Gilbert became a campus slogan. It was used thereafter to indicate the degree of ardor with which he paid court to his various girls. In spite of all of this romance he did not marry
a student but married Miss Harriett Cooper of West Chester,
Pennsylvania, a teacher in the High School of Radford.

Doctor McConnell had three half-grown sons at the time of
the opening of the college. These grew up and each in turn became a suitor for the college girls. His eldest "Doctor Bob"
married Jeff Neidermeyer, a popular student of the college.
After her untimely death he married as his second wife, Miss
Martha Townsend, a graduate of the college. His second son,
Carl, never paid much attention to the college girls. The
third son, Paul, popularly known on the campus as "John Paul"
attended the college for two years as a student. Being the"only
boy" in school the girls beseiged him and lent much romance to
his milking by twilight in the pasture lot. After his graduation from Lynchburg College he became a teacher in the high
school at Radford. He lived with his parents. During this
time he was quite active in his attentions to the college
girls. Later he became a member of the faculty and replaced
Mr. Gilbert as the "beau brummel" of the campus in both fact
and fiction. Always on the verge of marriage, his real marriage
in the fall of 1930, came as a thunderbolt to those who still
had hopes. John Lee Johnson, the only other boy to attend the
college during the regular session was always "girl shy".

When Mr. S. L. McConnell first became identified with the
college in 1920 he was a prince charming, well dressed, and
handsome. To catch him became a campus contest. At first he
paid attention to several of the students, however, as the
other single men married off he seemed to become immune to
the attractions of the college girls and devoted his whole
attention to one, Miss "Cass" Copper.

In 1920 a more rigid supervision of the gentlemen who
were allowed to call at the college was instituted; the gentlemen who desired to call made application for a "caller's
card" through the girl upon whom he wished to call. These
gentlemen were carefully investigated, the callers card when
given was an official approval of the gentleman. The adjustment of this list was one of the most difficult of the Dean's
office when it was first established. It resulted, however,
in a general toning up of the social life especially between
the students and the young men of Radford.

For many years the social life was confined entirely to
the campus. After the war, however, the development of the
drug stores became an acute problem; the glamour of the street,
the "jazz" crowd, movies, stimulation of the soft drink, the
music of the radio, the ever passing of crowds, the romantic
chance acquaintance, have all aided to induce certain types of
irresponsible students to loaf on the streets. This has created one of the acute social and disciplinary problems of the
campus and has contributed much to the break down of the family
spirit during the latter years.

SECTION IV

ORGANIZED SOCIAL EXPERIENCES

RECEPTIONS

The first formal reception was held at Thanksgiving (1913)
when Doctor and Mrs. McConnell, Mrs. Brugh, and Miss Crockett entertained in honor of the students. This reception was a great
success. It was held in the parlor of La Belle Inn and was the
first dress-up occasion in the life of the college. For several
years a Thanksgiving reception was an annual event. Gradually
it was replaced by the intersociety reception.

INTER-SOCIETY RECEPTIONS

Early in their history the societies established the custom
of holding receptions in honor of the new students during the
fall quarter. At first each society held a reception soon after
the initiation of new members. In 1916 the two organizations decided to combine resources and give an elegant inter-society reception. This reception was such a success it has been repeated
each fall since and is the outstanding social event sponsored by
the students during the Fall quarter. It usually occurs near
Halloween. For many years it was a costume affair. For days
students would labor to decorate the gymnasium. Wagon loads of
leaves, trees, pumpkins, and fodder would be hauled in for these
decorations, fancy costumed ladies, ghosts, and fairies added
the human touch to the decorations. The thrills from fortune
tellers, devil's den, apple bobs, and many secluded nooks where
romance budded and blossomed all in one evening made this a gala
event in the life of the students.

In 1925 the students changed the general scheme for the inter-society reception to a more formal one. The scene changed to one of simple dignity with the splendor of evening dresses as the chief decoration. The gymnasium has been used for this reception each year except in 1930 when the Madame Russell Lounge was used. The young men of Radford and Virginia Polytechnic Institute and other friends of the new students are invited by means of formal invitation to these receptions. Each society tries to have its President appear to the best advantage. Usually the Presidents are given corsages and wear the best new dresses the campus can muster. During the first part of the reception a dramatic skit (many of them original) or musical program is given. Following this formal entertainment, music and informal conversation fills the evening. Refreshments for these affairs are both artistic and elaborate and test the culinary art of the students of Home Economics.

CLASS RECEPTIONS

The members of the Junior Class of 1914-15 gave the first formal banquet. In the spring of this year they held a banquet in the La Belle Inn in honor of the Seniors of 1915 and the faculty. The Juniors prepared all the food, arranged the tables, and did the serving. They were directed by their class advisor, Miss Baird. The tower dining room was decorated in the class colors. The class President, Miss Irene Allison, was toastmistress. This was the first effort of the students to have after dinner speeches or to carry through a formal dinner program.

This banquet started the tradition for class receptions to be given by the Junior Class in honor of the graduates.

During the first years the "Junior Class" corresponded to the present Freshman Class or those students who were in the first year in the two-year professional course. Graduates of the two-year course were called "Seniors" until 1924 when the name of this group was changed to "Sophomores" and the fourth year students were called Seniors. Until this change took place the receptions were given in honor of the two-year graduates. With the change to the standard four-year Teachers College, the receptions were confined to the Junior and Senior Classes or third and fourth year students. The nature of these receptions has varied from time to time. Most of them have been held in the Spring of the year. Dogwood, Red Bud, and Rhodendrum have been the most favored as floral decorations. The receptions have been held in the Tyler parlor,

Madame Russell Hall and on the Senior Promenade. These receptions are very "exclusive" and are the most nearly "a couple affair" of any socials given on the campus. A gentleman is invited for each Senior.

As has been described (Section on Buildings) the Senior Promenade was dedicated by the Class of 1919 as a feature of the reception in honor of the Seniors of that year. This porch was dedicated as the Senior Promenade and has been used for many receptions.

CLASS GARDEN PARTIES

The first class to receive degrees (1921) started the custom of having an annual garden party as a feature of the commencement activities. The first garden party was held in the oak grove in front of the Administration Building. In the open spaces suites of furniture were arranged to represent outdoor sitting rooms. Punch was served from a large stump in the center of the grove and an ice course from a shady bower made of spring flowers. Each senior had an honor maid selected from the student body. These honor maids were dressed in organdie dresses, wore large picture hats and carried baskets of flowers. Each Senior invited her commencement guests and the members of the faculty. These were received with great formality. This started a tradition of an annual Senior garden party.

The second garden party given by the Class of 1922 was very elaborately arranged; the decorations centered around many varied colored parasols which had been most artistically made from crepe paper. Just before the time for the party which had been planned for the section of campus near the fountain a shower came up and it was necessary to hold the party in the Tyler Hall, but it passed off with great credit to the class. Since these first two most elaborate parties, the plan has been somewhat simplified but the idea has been preserved and an outdoor party held each year by the Seniors.

In June 1930 the garden party was held in the sunken garden near Madame Russell Hall.

For the last five years the Seniors have had the custom of selecting "little sisters" from the Freshman Class. Once during the year the Seniors entertain their "little sisters" usually with a theater party down town and with a drug store party following. The "little sisters" in turn give a party of some sort.

From time to time they have had sunrise breakfast parties and
have gone to Plum Creek or Sunset Hill to cook breakfast out-
of-doors.

FACULTY RECEPTIONS

In 1914 the formal commencement exercises were held in the
morning at 11:00 o'clock. After the program was changed to the
evening (1915) it became customary for the college to tender a
reception in honor of the graduates and their friends in the
gymnasium immediately following the graduating exercises. These
receptions were usually "jams" and gave very little satisfaction
to the college. It was customary "to attempt" to serve ice cream
and cake. The small area in which to entertain the guests and
the lateness of the hour led to the abandonment of the custom in
1920. In its place a Sunday afternoon tea was held at the college in honor of the visiting parents. These informal receptions
have been held on the Tyler porch. They afford a good opportunity for the parents to meet the members of the faculty, and officials of the College.

In 1929 the faculty club gave a very formal reception in
honor of the Seniors. This reception was one of the first social gatherings held in the Student Activity Building. Evening
clothes for both men and women were stressed in preparation for
this reception. Formal invitations were sent and the reception
was carried out in a very formal fashion. So much discussion
arose in the faculty over the receiving line for this occasion
that Doctor McConnell has dubbed it the Radford edition of the
"Gann-Longworth Social War".

It has been customary for the faculty to hold some sort of
opening reception or tea for the students in the Fall and frequently during the Summer quarter. The fall receptions have usually taken place on the first Saturday after the opening of the
season.

In 1925 Miss Moffett started the custom of having these receptions preceded by an "At Home" with the students as hostesses
in each of their bed rooms. She required the students to have
their rooms ready for inspection and each group of room mates to
be at home to receive the faculty who passed through the dormitory and looked at the rooms and visited with the students.
After this the faculty gathered in the Tyler parlor where they
received the students. This activity took the whole afternoon

but served the purpose of stimulating the students to get their rooms in good order early in the season.

THE FIRST OPEN FIRE

In 1929 the feature of the faculty reception was the lighting of the fire in the Madame Russell Lounge. Although this building had been completed in 1927 the fireplace had not been used. It had been planned to purchase electric fire fixtures and the degree class of 1927 gave the money for these fixtures. However this proved impossible because of the size of the fireplace. The faculty reception of 1929 came on a cold, damp afternoon. It was therefore decided to have a wood fire in the fireplace. This was laid by George Mills and was lighted by several members of the faculty. The success of this first open fire started the custom of using the open fire for many of the receptions.

A fire in the fireplace of the Student Activity Building was lighted in the same fall. A very attractive house warming service was held by the Young Women's Christian Association, at this time many legends connected with the fire were told, home making songs sung, and the fire was lighted by the officers of the Association.

CHRISTMAS PARTIES AND BANQUETS

On the last Friday night of the quarter in December 1913, the faculty gave the first Christmas party. This first party is an outstanding event in the memory of all those who attended and dates one of the most successful entertainments ever given in the college. It was a family party. Each member of the faculty represented some "grown-up" in a family group. Miss Baird and Mr. Avent were the Grandmother and Grandfather; Doctor McConnell and Miss Moffett were the mother and father; Miss Denny, a widowed daughter and Misses Simmons, Montague, Harrison, were grown up daughters and other members of the faculty were aunts and uncles. All the students were dressed as children. In the center of the gymnasium was a large Christmas tree and the family party took place around this. Mr. Lane was Santa Claus, from his pack he drew appropriate gifts for each one. This party was one of the best illustrations of the spirit which was being developed on the campus at that time.

For several years a Christmas party was held. The second one was a Mother Goose party in which members of the faculty played the part of Mother Goose characters. A large Jack Horner pie formed the central motif. Out of this came gifts for all of the students.

The third party was developed around the theme of a toy shop. By the fourth year the student body had grown so large it was decided to abandon the Christmas parties and instead to hold a Christmas banquet. Three or four of these were held in subsequent years. They were served in the main dining room on the last evening before the students left for their homes for the Christmas holidays. These banquets were very elaborate and were great occasions with tables laden with turkey, and other Christmas foods; negro waiters to serve the meal, music and festive clothes. Christmas greens and colors were used for decorations. One year Mr. Avent sent to North Carolina for long leaf pine, very few of the students had ever seen this. Each year barrels of holly were gotten from Potts Valley. Hand painted place cards were made by Misses Simmons and Montague. Some members of the faculty acted as toastmaster, speeches were made by the student officers, Doctor McConnell and various members of the faculty. It was customary for the college to give each student a favor. On one occasion they were presented with a photograph of Doctor McConnell, on another time they received copies of the college song book. Candy boxes and small place favors gradually replaced the more elaborate gifts. With the growth of the school it was finally decided it would be impracticable to hold the banquets and they were abandoned.

PRESIDENT'S DAY

The twenty-second of February, President's Day, became a festive day in the school. This is the birthday of Doctor McConnell as well as of George Washington, hence the name "President's Day". For five years a family birthday dinner was held in honor of Doctor McConnell as the chief feature of the celebration for this day. The faculty and students joined with the students of Scott County in the celebration. All the pride of an artist went into a large birthday cake (27 X 22 X 6) inches in size which Frank baked each year. This was decorated with birthday candles to represent each year of Doctor McConnell's life. The climax of the evening was reached when this lighted cake was rolled into the dining room by the students of Scott County to be cut by Doctor McConnell. Each student got a piece, the candles were the most prized possession. Those who were fortunate enough to get a candle treasured it very much. Apples, the favorite fruit of Doctor McConnell was always featured in the birthday dinner. The McConnell family with the students of Scott County were seated in the center of the dining room. Often the faculty or the students would present Doctor McConnell with some birthday gift, on one occasion the faculty gave him a leather traveling bag, on another an umbrella, and on another a toilet set. The first gift by the students to Doctor McConnell was a brass lamp presented Christmas 1913.

On February 22, 1917 the Pocahontas Society presented the College with its first large American flag. With an impressive patriotic service this was raised on the flag pole at the center of the campus.

In 1926 the student body had grown so large it was impossible to seat all the students and faculty in one dining room. It was therefore decided to abandon the birthday dinner and hold a party in the gymnasium instead. The cake was reserved, as the main feature all the students and faculty joined in cutting it after an evening of stunts in the gymnasium. It is still the custom to hold such birthday celebrations when Doctor McConnell is on the campus, unfortunately on several occasions recently he has been absent attending the National Educational Association Meeting.

A portrait of Doctor McConnell is hung opposite the portrait of George Washington on the landing of the stairway in the front entrance of the Administration Building as symbolic of the common birthday of the first President of the College and the first President of the country.

THANKSGIVING

There has never been a uniform practice for the holidays at Thanksgiving time. The length of holiday has been controlled largely by the State Educational Conference and the number of the members of the faculty who planned to attend. From time to time the conference has made it favorable to give two days, on other occasions only one day has been given.

In 1922 the custom of having the members of the faculty and their families who did not attend the conference to eat Thanksgiving dinner with the students at the college was started. For many years this practice was continued. This

Thanksgiving dinner is one of the feature meals of the year,
it has become more and more the "big meal" since the abandonment of the Christmas dinner. Since 1929 the meal has been
limited to the students. The growth of the faculty and the
large number who remained on the campus during Thanksgiving
recess made it impossible to continue the meal for all.

PICNICS

In 1921 Doctor McConnell decided to declare a surprise
spring holiday of one day. At this time all the members of
the faculty and students forsook the campus for a day in the
country. All the students were required to go and the day was
spent in some natural beauty spot. A large picnic luncheon
was provided by the dietitian and was shared in true community
fashion on the picnic grounds. The first of these picnics was
held at Cowan's. A special train was charted from the Norfolk
and Western Railroad and the students and faculty went to this
beautiful spot on New River where they spent the entire day
fishing, rowing, and playing games. The second was held at
Little River. A train was again charted and the students were
taken to the Little River Dam. The third was held on Plum
Creek. On this occasion all of them walked. This was one of
the most delightful picnics as it gave a wonderful opportunity
to study nature. Many ferns and wild flowers were collected
and many enjoyed wading in the branch. This was the last time
that a large group had a picnic by the old mill. The next year
it was completely destroyed by a storm. The mill stones were
brought from the site of the old mill to the campus of the college. Plum Creek has always been one of the favorite haunts
of the students. The walk to it is filled with many natural
interests. The fourth picnic was held at Natural Bridge. The
Norfolk and Western provided special rates and many of the
students went. It was not compulsory to attend this picnic
as the railroad fare was higher than on the previous excur-
sions. On this occasion the students got off at Natural
Bridge Station and walked the three miles to the bridge where
they spent the day. This trip introduced the element of sight
seeing into the psychology of the picnic and tended to destroy
the simple pleasure of a day in the woods. The fifth picnic
was held at the Dixie Caverns. The chief feature of this
picnic was the trip through the cave followed by wading and
swimming in the Roanoke River.

Informal picnics have been one of the most popular social activities for small groups of students or faculty throughout the entire history of the college.

In 1913 some members of the faculty discovered the high hill back of the cemetary on the Roberts Estate in Radford. This they dubbed "Sunset Hill" and here they held many bacon bats, and informal picnics. From this spot a magnificent view of New River and surrounding mountains of Giles, Pulaski, and Montgomery Counties may be seen. One of the features of the picnics, when Mr. Gilbert was present, was for him to explain the local historical events, the sites of which can be seen from this point. The students soon followed the faculty to Sunset Hill. For sixteen years on any holiday or Sunday students could be found carrying their "bags" to Sunset Hill. It is a favorite resort for Science groups. Several times the Young Women's Christian Association and Literary Societies have held picnic suppers there.

BARBECUE

In 1924 the Athletic Association held a barbecue as its annual money-making activity. A bed for the barbecue roast was dug near the present site of the swimming pool. George Hall of New River, an expert barbecue cook, was employed. For two days he roasted a pig, a couple dozen chickens and several large roasts of beef. This process was watched with interest and excitement by all the students. When the day of the barbecue came practically all the students, the faculty, and many people from outside shared in the sumptuous feast.

SOUTHWESTERN VIRGINIA RALLYS

In 1927 Southwestern Virginia Incorporated established an annual spring rally day for Southwestern Virginia. The students were expected to take an active part in this celebration. The first of these celebrations was held in Christiansburg in 1927 when the last link of the Lee Highway was completed and Southwestern Virginia was connected with Washington City by one continuous hard surfaced road. All the Radford students attended the celebration and took part in the pageant showing the development of Southwestern Virginia.

The college provided several floats for the parade. The most spectacular of these was an immense white one upon which

Education sat enthroned. From the hands of this beautiful figure were streamers to other figures symbolic of the opportunities in Virginia for educated women.

Each of the literary societies provided a float to typify some feature of the pioneer and Indian history of Southwestern Virginia. Miss Charlsie Camper was the herald for the College. She, attired in a costume of purple and gray, headed the procession of college students on horseback. Behind the banners and flags of the college came the marching students arranged in groups of four. Each wore a head band of purple and gray to give a uniform effect. The students of Radford were followed by the students of Virginia Polytechnic Institute. This long line of young men and women gave a beautiful effect and typified the youth of today. They were followed by the floats and certain historic characters from the towns of Southwestern Virginia, to show the development of this section from the Indian Trail to the modern road represented by the various civic groups. The Christiansburg celebration was the first of several sponsored by the Southwestern Virginia Incorporated.

One hundred of the students represented the college at the opening of the highway at Fancy Gap in October 1928. In the Spring of 1928 a large group of the students gave the dances of the college May Day at the Southwestern Virginia celebration in Wytheville, Virginia. In 1929 they gave a similar program at Blacksburg.

TRAINING IN SOCIAL USAGES

The number and type of entertainments as described above have been stressed by the administration of the College for educational purposes. The philosophy of education "learn by experiencing" has been stressed in the social program of the college.

In 1927 Doctor McConnell appointed a "culture committee" composed of Doctor Virginia Hudson, Miss Florence Baird, and Miss Susan Roberts. He has appointed such committees each year. These committees have devoted themselves to a study of the needs of the students and from time to time have sponsored talks, a number of teas, socials, etc. in order to give the students first hand experience in the practice of the principles of etiquette.

In 1926 the faculty was divided into committees and each committee received a small number of students in the Tea Room. In 1927-1928 Miss Florence Belle Ogg held frequent teas for the students in Madame Russell Hall.

ORIENTATION

Probably the most successful educational experience in this field has been given through the courses in Orientation, especially during the years of 1929, 1930, 1931. During the second quarter of this course "Social Conventions " are stressed. The students are divided into committees and work out various types of etiquette situations. A chief feature of this program is the freshman banquet held on Valentine Day. This banquet is furnished by the College but the students working through committees are in charge of all the arrangements, planning and carrying through a formal program with toastmistress, after dinner speeches, and toasts. The freshmen had the faculty as their guests in 1931. Miss Caroline Honts was the toastmistress for 1930, and Miss Mary Lucas for 1931. In 1931 this class also gave three afternoon teas in honor of the faculty and seniors.

SECTION V.

RELIGIOUS LIFE AND ORGANIZATIONS

Doctor McConnell has summed up his religious philosophy thus: "I have an ambition to impress our students that a religious, Christian life is the normal life of the human being, we try to impress them that any person failing to keep in touch with God and failing to live a religious life is an unnatural person. We strive constantly, in a wise and prudent manner, to leave the impression that God and Righteousness have more to offer to a human being, can do more for him and bring him more satisfaction, pleasure, comfort, and recreation than the devil and his influences in the world can offer; in other words, that God made the world and put us here. Any one wishing to get the most out of life will live with this understanding; God is his friend and will be a daily companion and a comrade of all of us from the greatest to the least."[1]

The entire program of Radford College has been controlled and guided by this philosophy of religion expressed in Christian living. Doctor McConnell has been guided in his administration by his close and intimate relationship with God. Frequently, he says, in meeting the critical problems of the institution he has left everything to God, awaited a solution, when it came he acted upon it and has never had an occasion to regret it. This same simple faith has been exemplified in the personal life of Doctor McConnell. He has made an effort in the selection of his faculty to employ only those whom he felt were Christians in their ideals and practices. He has insisted upon a hearty cooperation and identification with some Christian church and its work from each member of his staff. The students have been taught by example to put faith in God. The religious teachings of the institution have been through direct practice and example rather than word of mouth and preaching.

DAILY ASSEMBLY

The College was opened with the General Assembly exercise on September 18, 1913. At this time Reverend W. H. Rader of the Grove Avenue Methodist Church conducted the devotional exercises and presented the College with its first Bible.

Beginning with this service a daily assembly of students and faculty has been held each school day at ten o'clock. In the

[1] Letter written by Doctor McConnell to Doctor Minor C. Miller, September 30, 1930.

devotional period hymns are sung, the Bible is read, and prayer is offered. The members of the Faculty, Doctor McConnell, Ministers of the City, officers of the Young Women's Christian Association and the students themselves conduct these services. A Bible has always been kept on the rostrum of the auditorium. Doctor McConnell has insisted upon the use of the St. James version. The first Bible presented by Mr. Rader was used for a year, then placed in the Library. The second, a larger book, was purchased from the American Bible Society. This was used for fifteen years, when practically worn out it was replaced by a very handsome Bible, gift of the Cabinet of the Young Women's Christian Association for the summer of 1928.

For seventeen years Mr. Gilbert was Chairman of the Assembly committee and had charge of the devotional period. For the present year 1930-1931 the faculty decided to administer the Assembly through committees composed of various members of the faculty. These committees in turn plan the programs for the Assembly for a week at a time. Each member of the faculty has had this responsibility three or four times during the year. In this way the students have a contact with the religious thinking of the entire faculty.

The General Assembly program has furnished an outlet for all of the distinguished visitors to all the various churches of Radford. The platform of the College has been open to them and the ministers feel free to bring to the college any visitor they may have. In this way practically all of the denominations have been represented by outstanding speakers at the Radford College.

FORM OF SERVICE

The devotional program as now followed opens with a hymn followed by a scripture reading and prayer. The scripture lesson selected from the Bible is read by the presiding officer. The present hymnal has a number of responsive readings which have been used extensively during the past three years. A second hymn divides the devotional program from the secular activities of the General Assembly. The latter activities include speeches, music, announcements, or the presentation of some educational feature of general interest or entertainment.

AFFILIATION WITH THE RADFORD CHURCHES

The affiliation with the Radford Churches started on the first Friday of the academic year in 1913. At this time the min-

isters of the city invited the students to attend the Sunday
service in their respective churches. Ever since on the first
Friday of the summer and fall quarters all the ministers of the
City attend the General Assembly. They are presented to the
students and extend invitations to them to participate in the
church and religious activities of the community. Each church
maintains a special Sunday School Class for the students of the
College. These classes are taught by superior teachers, many
of whom are professors of the College. Miss Bryson, Mr. Fitzpatrick, Mr. Sowder, Doctor McCain, the Pastors, Mrs. M. M.
Jackson, Mrs. W. E. Bricker, Mr. J. P. Whitt, Mrs. Harvey Barnett, and Mrs. Fred Bullard have been most active as the Sunday
School teachers of the College students.

CHURCH ATTENDANCE

The students have been urged to attend church regularly.
Although no ironclad rule has been enforced the students have
been so stimulated by Doctor McConnell and other members of the
faculty that church attendance is almost obligatory. For many
years a weekly report of the students' church attendance was
taken. These were checked by Miss Allen, Secretary to the President, who frequently made reports to parents, the students themselves, and the ministers of the church. Likewise the Dean of
Women has had the students make statements as to their church
attendance. She also sends letters to the students who fail to
tend reminding them of their religious obligations. A summary
of these reports indicate that about eighty per cent of the students attend one church service each Sunday.

The students have been urged to attend the church of their
personal or family affiliation. In 1930, one hundred and eighty-
four of the students were Methodist; one hundred and eight Baptist; forty-nine Presbyterians; twenty-eight Christian; eight
Catholics; five Lutherans; three Moravians; two Bretherns; one
Quaker, the religious affiliation of twenty-two was unknown.

Many churches have established affiliated membership for
students. By this arrangement the ministers have been instrumental in having many of the students join the local churches
for the time they are college residents. The students have
been allowed to affiliate and participate in all church activities.

In the early years of the college revivals were very popular. Each year a revival was held in the Grove Avenue Methodist

Church, the Baptist Church and from time to time in the Presbyterian and Christian Churches. The students have attended these meetings. As a result many have been converted, made a profession of faith, and joined the church. The evangelists have made many talks at Assembly. On one occasion Doctor McConnell invited all of the ministers to join with him in a general revival at the college. Each minister spoke to the entire group and special prayers and work was done with the non-church members of the student group. Each year the ministers have made definite efforts to interest the non-church members in joining the church.

TEACHER TRAINING FOR SUNDAY SCHOOL WORKERS

In 1914 Inter-denominational classes for the training of Sunday School teachers were introduced as a feature of the religious program of the college. In each of the churches a class was organized. An inter-denominational course was planned. By completing the course and passing the examination a student could win the diploma of her respective denomination. For several years these diplomas were delivered by Mr. Avent at the Baccalaureate Service. As the years have passed this course has been concentrated in one or two of the churches. The largest number has been enrolled at the Methodist church where the class is taught by Professor F. B. Fitzpatrick.

YOUNG PEOPLES ORGANIZATIONS

Some of the students have been active in the Young Peoples Organizations in the various churches. Particularly in the B. Y. P. U. and Epworth League. The Baptist Student Association on the campus has been associated with the Southern Baptist Student Association on the campus for many years. Through this affiliation contests in church attendance and programs have been held between the Radford church and the churches of other sections of the country.

In 1930 Mr. Dickerson reported that the Radford College group in the Baptist Church was the leader for the entire Southern Baptist Church in participation in Young People's work. During the year of 1929-30 this group has maintained a student secretary, Elizabeth Einstein, on the campus. This person has been charged with the responsibility of keeping the Baptist Student group functioning in its activities.

BAPTIST STUDENT UNION CONVENTION

November 1, 3, 1930 the Baptist Student Union of the Radford College was hostess to the Baptist Student Unions of Virginia and Maryland. This brought to the campus about two hundred delegates. The conferences were conducted by William Hall Preston, Southern Baptist Student Secretary. Some of the speakers who were featured on the program were: Honorable Pat Neff, Ex-Governor of Texas, Doctor Cecil B. Cook, of Farmville; Mr. E. H. Potts of Lexington; Doctor John L. Hill of Nashville, Tennessee; Doctor J. H. Ceiger of William and Mary College. Miss Lucille Christian, local president of the Baptist Union acted as hostess.

METHODIST CLUB

Mr. Natt E. Long, representative of the Board of Religious Education of the Methodist Church, Nashville, Tennessee in 1929 organized a Methodist Club of the students of this denomination on the College Campus. This group has functioned during the past two years, and has brought about a closer affiliation of the students with the members of the Grove Avenue Church. Each group of ten students has a big sister or sponser in the church.

CHURCH SOCIALS

It has been customary for the churches to hold receptions in honor of the students near the opening of the fall and frequently during the summer quarters. These social entertainments have taken various forms, but have usually been held in the church basements where games, programs, and social intercourse brought the students and members of the congregation together.

From time to time the students have been entertained in the homes of the members of the churches, taken on automobile trips, given picnics, made welcome at church nights and socials and shared in the church life of the various denominations.

RELIGIOUS EDUCATION ON THE CAMPUS

The religious experiences of the students has not been limited to church activities. Since 1925 the ministers of the major denominations of Radford (Methodist, Baptist, Christian and Presbyterian), have conducted a series of non-credit lectures at the

college on church history, and the denominational and doctrinal
basis for the faith of the respective church. In 1927 and 1930
on each Tuesday during the winter quarter at the General Assembly
period, the students of the various denominations have met in
separate rooms of the college and have been taught by the ministers. The type of work of the groups has varied somewhat but
all have been given an insight to the deeper and more fundamental
principles of their respective denomination. The students have
been required to attend these meetings. This has been one of
the most successful and interesting experiments in religious education tried in the college.

CREDIT COURSES IN BIBLE

In February 1916 the college issued a bulletin "The Radford
Normal Plan for Bible Study". The bulletin is a summary of a
plan, Doctor McConnell, Mr. Avent, and Miss Byrson proposed for
Bible Study to be offered for credit in the high schools and State
institutions of Virginia. It includes an outline for the course
offered at the Radford College beginning in 1915-1916. To promote these courses at the Radford College Doctor McConnell appointed a Council on Bible study consisting of the local pastors, Sunday School Superintendents, President of the Normal School and
representatives of the Young Women's Christian Association. This
council prepared a syllabus of thirty-two lessons to cover the
Old Testament and a similar syllabus was later worked out for the
New Testament. The plans for this course included different topics to be taught by well qualified teachers who would require
real study, examinations, and place the study of Bible on an equal
degree of difficulty with the work of other regular courses of the
curriculum. Credit was given for this course towards the diplomas
issued by the institution.

For many years these courses in Bible were taught by Mr. Avent,
Miss Flora Byrson, Mr. F. B. Fitzpatrick, at the college at regular class hours. Many students selected these courses and earned
units for their denominational diplomas and academic credit in
the college. Teaching of these courses was voluntary on the part
of the faculty and was in addition to their academic load.

PROFESSORS OF BIBLICAL LITERATURE

In 1929 Doctor McConnell employed Doctor John Lee Allison,
an outstanding Presbyterian Minister of Southwestern Virginia, as
Professor of Biblical Literature. Doctor Allison had been identified for many years with the leading Presbyterian Churches of Wash-

ington, Baltimore, and had been supply pastor of the Radford (Central) Presbyterian Church for two years. Owing to physical weakness, Doctor Allison was unable to continue as an active pastor of a church. He had the vigor, personality, keen knowledge of the Bible necessary for teaching as a part time instructor in the college. He organized courses in Biblical Literature which were given for credit under the English Department of the College. Many students elected these courses which were successfully taught by Doctor Allison for two years until the breakdown of his health in the Fall of 1930.

VIRGINIA COUNCIL OF RELIGIOUS EDUCATION

From time to time the college has cooperated with the various churches in bringing to the city leaders in religious education who have conducted courses in religious education. The first of these, a week's conference began February 22, 1924 in the Methodist Church. These classes met for two hour periods each day and were taught by Doctor J. N. Hillman of Emory and Henry College, Doctor Eugene Blake, President of the Holston Orphanage of Greenville, Tennessee, Doctor J. S. Schesler, Chairman of Instructional Board, Nashville, Tennessee, and Professor F. B. Fitzpatrick. These gentlemen offered courses in organization and administration in the Sunday School, Principles of Religious Teaching, Bible Study, and Pupil Study. The students were enrolled in one course for ten hours, took an examination and received one unit of credit toward the church certificates. Four of these units entitled the student to the Sunday School Teachers Diploma. The Methodists have held several such study groups.

A more extended effort for religious education of this type was held in January 1930 under the auspices of the Virginia Council of Religious Education. This course was conducted by the Reverend Minor C. Miller, Secretary of the Religious Council of Education. The teachers were: Reverend John F. Lock, Secretary of the Virginia Council, Reverend F. C. Longaker, Professor of Philosophy, Roanoke College; and Mrs. Edgar Smith, Superintendent of the Junior Department of the Melrose Church of Roanoke, Virginia. The teachers and Sunday School leaders of the various churches and the students of the college were enrolled in these courses which were conducted for two hours each day for one week in the college administration building and led to inter-denominational credit on diplomas.

Reverend F. B. Shelton, educational director of the Holston

Conference of M. E. Church, South was Dean of the School. In addition to his official duties he taught a class on the "Life of Christ". Reverend J. J. Fix taught "The Message and Program of the Christian Religion". Reverend H. G. Williamson taught "Training in Worship and the Devotional Life". Dramatization and Pageantry was discussed in the class led by Mr. J. M. Garrison.

YOUNG WOMEN'S CHRISTIAN ASSOCIATION

The Young Women's Christian Association was organized in the Fall of 1913, under the auspices of the National Board of the Young Women's Christian Association. This organization has as its three-fold purpose; First: Bringing Young Women to Christ; Second: Bringing them up in Christ; Third: of sending them out for Christ, and seeks to develop the student physically, mentally, socially, and spiritually.

For many years the association was controlled and closely affiliated with the National Board. Its work was guided through suggestions, proposed activities, and programs. The Regional Secretaries were frequent visitors to the campus. They linked the school with many other colleges by the transfer of ideas and problems. State and inter-school conferences were held for student officers and advisors at which Radford was always represented.

By the administration of the college the Young Women's Christian Association has been designed and guided so that is it primarily a Christian association devoted to religious principles and living. It has been discouraged from any efforts to become a social club or to devote itself to the more worldly forms of service sometimes sponsored and approved by the national organization through its various associations.

With the growth of the student body and the development of more initiative and assurance in meeting local problems the Young Women's Christian Association has become more independent and able to meet the local campus problems of spiritual life.

The formal routine activities of the Association include weekly vesper services, and daily prayer meetings held in each of the dormitories.

WEEKLY VESPERS

The Weekly Vesper Services were held for many years in the Tyler Parlor. They have been held in the Student Activity Building since 1929. The programs for these services are developed by the students as an expression of their idea of the religious topics and experiences of most vital importance to students.

From time to time the members of the faculty, ministers of the town, leaders of the Young Peoples Society Work in the churches, visiting secretaries and missionaries have addressed the students. Special music features have been given. For the most part the students have conducted these services. Students who have been timid in all other public performances have been developed through the opportunity to participate in the programs of the Y. W.

In 1929-1930 the Association conducted a series of informal round table discussions on contemporary religions. The material for these discussions was assembled on a special table in the library by the program committee of the Young Women's Christian Association. In 1931 a similar round table discussion and study of historic churches was sponsored by the Association.

SPECIAL PROGRAMS

Since 1922 the Young Women's Christian Association has sponsored a special Christmas Carol Service. This service of Christmas Carols, music, pageants, is held on the Sunday night previous to the close of the Fall quarter. The churches of Radford have cooperated in making the program a success and usually a large audience from the city attends this service.

The first of these programs made a lasting impression. The stage was decorated in evergreen and arranged to represent an altar. The lighted candles in five seven branch candles shed a glow of light on the mass of red and green decorations and the chorus dressed in white. All of the students entered the auditorium singing Christmas Carols which was followed by a simple yet most sincere song service. Such has been the general type of programs since. Mr. E. S. Jones and his daughter, Mrs. Sublett cooperated with the students in making this first Christmas Carol a success. From time to time pageants and dramatizations based on Christmas stories have been given.

THE LIVING CHRISTMAS TREE

In 1929, as a feature of the Christmas celebration, the Young Women's Christian Association purchased fixtures for the lighting of an outdoor Christmas Tree. The Norway Spruce located near the entrance of the Tyler Hall was selected as the Christmas tree. This was strung with electric lights which were lighted as a part of the Christmas Carol service. In 1930 the Young Women's Christian Association purchased additional lights and the tree was again used. Its beauty was greatly enhanced when a snow fall covered the tree with a blanket of snow which with the colored lights gave a fairy touch to the tree and landscape.

At some of the Christmas Carol services special silver offerings have been taken from the congregation. In 1925 this offering was used to purchase Christmas toys, candies, and fruits for some poor children of Radford. In 1929 the contribution was used to buy health material, wash basins, buckets, towels, soap, etc. for a one-room school in a neglected part of Montgomery County which was being taught by one of the former students of the college. In 1919 the Young Women's Christian Association packed a box of books and clothing for children of a school in Pulaski County.

EASTER SERVICE

In 1923 the Young Women's Christian Association held its first Sunrise service. This was held in the Tyler Parlor and was most impressive. All the students arose early, dressed in white and assembled on the third floor of the dormitory. From here they marched down stairs singing anthems. The choir carried Easter lilies and assembled at an improvised altar in the parlor. Thus the Easter Service became a tradition. From time to time these services have been held on the Senior Promenade which faces the East. On the morning when the weather has been pleasant this has been one of the most beautiful scenes as the rising of the sun shone on the band of youthful worshippers. In 1930 the service was held at the Pargalo; 1931 in the Student Activity Building.

COLLEGE DAY IN THE CHURCHES

From time to time the Young Women's Christian Association has sponsored college night in the various churches of the city. Each of the ministers have been requested to preach a special sermon to the students of a particular class. The members of these classes have marched to the church in a body, contributed music, and listened to the sermon in their honor.

NIGHTLY PRAYER MEETING

Probably the richest religious experience in the memory of the students who have attended the college has been the nightly prayer meeting held in each of the dormitories. This has been entirely directed by the students themselves and is sponsored by the Young Women's Christian Association. Each night at the end of the study hour just before the students go to bed they assemble for ten or fifteen minutes in the student parlor where they sing hymns, conduct informal prayer meeting, read the Bible and hold a religious discussion. These prayer services are usually well attended by the students of the college. No records have been kept of what has happened in these services yet practically any student who has attended one will mention it as one of her richest religious experiences, the informal group clad in night clothes, sitting on the floor seems to bring them closer to God and real religious feeling than the more formal services. Many students have actively participated here who were never brought into any other form of student activities.

SOCIAL LIFE IN THE Y. W. C. A.

The Young Women's Christian Association has sponsored the first social activities of each of the Fall quarters since 1914. These parties have served to bring the old and new students together at an informal gathering. For many years they centered around a bonfire on the campus near the present site of the outdoor swimming pool or on Sunset Hill. Tacky parties, "Kid" parties, and informal stunt programs have also served to break the ice for the new students. During the fall the Young Women's Christian Association sponsors the annual stunt night. Through this performance it has been able to raise much of its money which it has used for the various campus activities.

From time to time during the year the organization holds informal parties for all the students in the Gymnasium. During the past two years the teas it has sponsored on Sunday afternoon have been very popular. Members of the Cabinet have taken turns in presiding at the tea table and arranging for these informal social gatherings.

For many years it was a custom of the Young Women's Christian Association to celebrate once a month the birthdays of those students having a birthday in that month.

The Y. W. has always been generous in its social service
programs. In a quiet manner it brightens the lives of the more
homesick and diffident students of the college with flowers here,
a note there, with helping hands it has stood ready to serve.

Y. W. C. A. HANDBOOKS

The Young Women's Christian Association is one of the richest student organizations. It has been uniformly successful in
collecting its membership fee of $1.00. For many years this fee
was shared with the National Board. However, with less close affiliation the Young Women's Christian Association has been able
to keep most of its money for its own use. It has also been assisted from the Student Activity Fund of the College.

Since 1915 the Young Women's Christian Association has published each biennial a student handbook and this is designed to
meet the needs of the incoming students. It includes directions
for the general routine life of the campus and describes in detail the opportunities for religious life through church affiliations and the Young Women's Christian Association.

Y. W. C. A. ROOMS

The first permanent headquarters for this organization was
in the room in the Administration Building now occupied by the
Treasurer's office. Mr. Roop built a suite of mission oak furniture finished in black and upholstered in green and black tapestry for this room. Although it was painfully uncomfortable the
students were very proud of this furniture. The room was used
for cabinet meetings and as a storage place for the records, membership cards, handbooks, and publications of the association.
With the growth and expansion of the school this room was taken
as an office by the college. The Young Women's Christian Association was then given a room on the second floor of the Tyler Dormitory.

In 1926 the two rooms under the water tank was fitted up as
a Y. W. C. A. hut. This is used during the Summer quarter and
the warmer weather of the fall and spring as a gathering place
for the students. The Y. W. C. A. has furnished and equipped a
kitchenette where the students can make candy and have a living
room for informal gatherings.

The Young Women's Christian Association was given an office
in the Student Activity Building. This the cabinet has more completely furnished than any office in this building.

In 1916 a Y. W. C. A. bulletin board with a glass door was
placed in the main hall of the Administration Building. This is
used for the announcements of the programs and the posting of
special clippings of interest to the members.

BLUE RIDGE CONFERENCE

The Radford College annually sends two to eight delegates
to the Southern Student Conference held by the National Board
at Blue Ridge, North Carolina. The College has been represented
each year since 1919. This conference is a Red Letter experience
in the life of all those who have attended. It brings to these
students a rich religious experience which they seem to be unable to get under any other association. The natural location
of this conference in the mountains of North Carolina brings one
nearer to God. There has never been a student so responsible
who has not been given a new insight and religious experience
here which has made an everlasting impression upon her character.

On three occasions these students have been accompanied by
faculty members. Miss Andrews in 1919, Miss Moffett in 1921,
Miss Bryson. The delegates to these conferences have been financed partly by the Young Women's Christian Association, the
College, and the students themselves.

THE NATIONAL WORLD FELLOWSHIP CONFERENCE

For the last two years Miss Carrie Mears, Student Secretary
for the National Board in this division with the Young Men's
Christian Association has sponsored a series of conferences on
World Fellowship. Two of these conferences have been held at the
Radford College. By this plan instead of having a State Conference to which the delegates of the College go the speakers are
brought to the College and the entire student body is given the
opportunity of sharing in the conference. With the close affiliation between the Radford College and the Virginia Polytechnic
Institute, these conferences have been held jointly on the two
campuses. The speakers migrate between the two institutions.
The last of these conferences was held in February 1931.

STUDENT VOLUNTEERS

The first Student Volunteer group was organized in the College in 1922. This group is composed of those students who have dedicated their lives to foreign or home missionary service. There have usually been from two to six members of this group on the campus of this college. Although few in number the group has been faithful to its vows, held frequent meetings, and advanced the cause of missions on the campus. Each year they have attended the State meeting of the Student Volunteer Association. Some of the outstanding Student Volunteer leaders representing the College have been Misses Mab Carter, Leona Giles, Lula Reynolds, Louise Scott, and Mary Carpenter.

STUDENT VOLUNTEER CONVENTIONS

Two Student Volunteer Conventions have been held at the Radford College. On February 24-25, 1923, the College was hostess to the Eighth Annual Conference of the Student Volunteer Union of Virginia. Delegates were present from practically all the colleges and Universities of the State. Many distinguished speakers were brought to the campus under the auspices of this organization. The delegates and visitors were entertained in the homes of the people of Radford. Some of the chief speakers were: Doctor J. F. Williams, Doctor Flemming of New York City, former Missionary to India. The conference was presided over by H. E. Warnom of Randolph Macon College. This convention was one of the first student conventions held at the College.

The second of these conventions was held February 22, 1929. About one hundred and fifty delegates were in attendance representing Bridgewater, Hampton Sidney, Farmville, Harrisonburg, West Hampton, William and Mary, and Virginia Polytechnic Institute, and Radford College. The conference was led by Richard Gaffin of Hampton Sidney College. Chief addresses were delivered by Milton Stauffer, representing the National Movement and Colonel Joseph H. Cudlipp, representing the Maryland and Delaware Sunday School Association, Doctor Fletcher Brockman, Doctor Donald W. Richardson of the Union Theological Seminary of Richmond, Virginia.

Radford has been represented at the various State conferences held in other colleges of the State.

SECTION VI.

DISCIPLINE

All group living needs some kind of organized control. This popularly called discipline implies the maintenance of certain standards of behavior by some recognized authority. What these standards of conduct shall be, how they are to be developed, how and by whom they shall be enforced have been some of the baffling problems for educational thought for the last two decades. The Normal School as developed in the South provides for group living in dormitories. For many years these dormitories were conducted after the pattern of boarding schools for young women. The victorian standards of propriety of the cloistered life of the Southern gentle woman were stressed.

Paralleling this personal life was the strenuous effort of the faculty to develop a professional attitude of mind and to create personal and individual independence in the students. This two-fold philosophy functioning in the normal school brought about a hodgepodge in student life which was questionable in its ultimate effect upon the individual and institutional life.

A third group of factors entered into the conduct problems of Radford College, namely, a perplexing local situation resulting from the location of the college plant in the heart of the town, the type of people who constitute the community, and the rural background of the students.

The discipline or control of the students at the Radford College has passed through three distinct stages in its development. In the first place all discipline was centralized in the matron of the dormitories. She determined the rules and regulations, set up the routine regulations for group living and disciplined those who violated these requirements.

The faculty has never had any part in the discipline of the personal conduct of the students. In the entire history of the college no case of discipline has been referred to the faculty for action or judgment. There has been an understanding that the faculty would uphold the highest personal standards of conduct and would cooperate with those having direct supervision of the students by reporting any violation of the proper standards of conduct which they observed. Doctor McConnell has always felt that the faculty had too much to do with the instructional and professional activities of the students to spend their time as disciplinary agents. The faculty on the whole, therefore, has directed its attention to education and the

development of the proper personal standards rather than to
the punishment for violations of such standards as might be
written into the regulations of the school.

THE MATRON SYSTEM

Mrs. Brugh in cooperation with Doctor McConnell set up the
first regulations for the students. These were patterned very
closely after those practiced in the girls colleges of this
section of the State. These rules and regulations were announced to the students in house meetings or at meals. They
were formulated as the necessity for a regulation arose.

SOME EARLY REGULATIONS

The minor violations of these regulations were remedied by
talking to the individual student. Discipline was maintained
by the force of the personality of the matron. Personal appeals
were strongly made; no set forms of punishment were mated out to
the students for minor violations. Where real character was involved as in stealing, lying, or personal delinquency, Doctor
McConnell added his personal persuasion to that of the matron
for right living. No students were expelled from the institution during the first three years of its history. So far as
the author is able to recall no student was expelled until the
Student Government expelled one or two for cheating in 1917.
It has never been a policy of the school to insist upon student
withdrawal from the institution when their conduct became ob-
jectionable. Doctor McConnell maintains that more can be done
for the student on the campus than can be done by sending her
out into the world under the stigma of expulsion. Very few
students have been expelled from the institution and these only
after most careful consideration of the case, its effect on the
other students, the institution, and its ultimate effect upon
the character development of the individual.

SOME EARLY CASES OF DISCIPLINE

The first real case of discipline in the college which the
author recalls occurred in the early fall of 1913 when one of
the students living in the Heth House attempted to run away to
be married. The whole circumstances of this affair are very
amusing. One afternoon when Miss Moffett and Miss Puryear came
into the Heth House they were met by students who were agog to
tell of the whisperings they had overheard between one of the

students and her so-called cousin. The family spirit was so
strong that the students felt no hesitancy in relating some
of the thrilling plans of this intended elopement. Miss Moffett
and Miss Puryear were appalled. This was their first case for
discipline. Not knowing what to do they rushed in a suppressed
state of excitement to Doctor McConnell's home at the top of
the hill to tell him of the impending calamity. Doctor Mc-
Connell was amused and at the same time very much distressed.
It was also his first case of dealing with girl students. He
sent the two teachers home and said that he would come in a
short time to deal with the case. When they returned to the
House it was as still as death not a student could be located.
In her search for the lost Miss Moffett saw a foot protruding
from the gallery which surrounds the reception hall. Here she
found all the inmates of the house flat on their stomachs with
their ears cocked to hear everything the lovers were saying in
the reception room below. With much excitement the students
crawled out from the room on their hands and knees after having
this romantic experience of eavesdropping. The tales which
they related were marvelous indeed. "The lover was supposed to
have a pistol and knives with which he was to cut his way out
of the college with his ladylove."

Finally Doctor McConnell arrived with Mr. Pat Bowren, Chief
of Police of Radford. The tales of the students were related.
The man, when brought before Doctor McConnell and the policeman,
confessed that he was not the cousin of the girl as he had
stated upon his arrival, but denied all intentions to elope with
the girl. The man was escorted away by Mr. Bowren and Doctor Mc-
Connell and put on the Train Number 30, and sent from the town.
Miss Moffett and Miss Puryear were left to settle the hysterical
girls. The heroine was weeping violently, threatening suicide.
This dramatic flourish alarmed her room mates who became afraid
to stay with her. Miss Moffett took her into her room where upon Miss Puryear became excited and hid all the scissors, finger-
nail files, and other potential weapons under the mattresses. A
pallet was made for the girl on the floor where she slept sound-
ly all night while the teachers watched her and the students
hovered by in a state of hysterical expectancy. Thus the first
case of discipline passed into history. It afforded gossip and
excitement for the students for many days. The girl became a
heroine. The teachers and Doctor McConnell learned much from
this first experience to guide them in later discipline of
students.

CREATING SPIRIT

In fact the students were so "good" during the first year that on one occasion Miss Baird and Miss Moffett decided they were not getting out of college life what they should. So these two ladies called together a group of the students and suggested the need for greater school spirit, more life and activities. The motive of these two teachers was very high and the principles which they stated to the students were sound and would stand the test of sound educational philosophy. Alas the student's interpretation was quite different. They returned to the dormitory and immediately organized a mid-night serenade or a general rough house. They threw trash cans, slammed doors, banged the water buckets and paraded in a rude fashion throughout the La Belle Inn. This was a shock to Mrs. Brugh, her girls had never behaved like this before. Having a quick temper she let it fly and challenged the entire group as they swarmed down the main stairway. Her outburst of temper rather nonplussed the more timid students, the "dare-devils" however, created spirit. The report of this "uprising" astonished Miss Moffett and Miss Baird. They were powerless to do anything. After much investigation, talk, and argument, Mrs. Brugh by some process of elimination decided on seventy-nine girls as the real leaders of this party, where upon she put them "on campus" took away all their privileges and confined them to the campus for a month. For one month they paraded the campus and made martyrs and heroines of themselves. The campus period ended on the first day of March and although this was a cold snowy day the seventy-nine students dressed themselves in spring clothes, straw hats, and carrying sun shades paraded through the main street of the city. This was a big event and was the talk of the town.

THE PROBLEM OF DRESS

The emphasis on uniform dress for formal occasion reached its climax at commencement 1915. For graduation a faculty committee decided that the students should wear a simple white dress, made from cotton material. The students were forbidden to use silk or any material which would border on extravagance or tend to embarrass any student in the group who might not be able to afford a dress as fine as her classmate. When the night arrived one of the graduates came attired in a white net dress. This disobedience scandalized the committee members. They immediately decided that the student would change her dress or not graduate. The student persisted in her determination to wear the net dress. The line of march was held up for three quarters of an hour while this matter was debated. Finally the committee requested that Miss James, one of the teachers who had a new white organdie dress to change with the girl. Thus discipline was maintained.

THE FLAPPER PERIOD

Bobbed hair and short skirts brought a wail of complaint and upset the ideals of proper dress on the campus. When short skirts became the style the students proceeded to tie strings around their waists and roll the top of their skirts up until the dress barely covered the knee. This was considered most shocking! Particularly were the men members of the faculty strongly opposed to the short skirts. Where upon the lady teachers gave many talks trying to discourage the extremely short skirt. Regulations required the skirt to be at least four inches below the knee.

Bobbed hair also received its due opposition. The bobbing of hair swept like wild fire through the college. On one Sunday eighteen heads were bobbed. At this rate the style swept through the student body until there were very few girls left with long hair. This so impressed Doctor McConnell that he ordered a picture taken of the students who had long hair before they became "extinct".

Hair rats, huge pompadors, many curls, excessive use of rouge, bandeaux of narrow ribbon with long streamers hanging down the back, knickers, use of men's clothing as costumes have all received due consideration, each has been considered as an evil with which the students have been beset.

In 1915-1916 a regulation was made requiring all students taking the part of male characters in plays to wear men's coats, shirts, and collars but black skirts. Trousers were not allowed. The students have not yet been allowed to wear knickers except on very unusual occasions and then only with special permission from the Dean.

For years students were not allowed to appear on the campus in their "gym" suits, these must be hidden by a coat or skirt over their bloomers. Those students who lived in Helen Henderson Hall or boarded in town were required to dress for "gym" at the college. Gradually the skirts and coats were eliminated and then the war centered on stockings. As the warmer days came on some of the students insisted upon rolling down their stockings. Many students were punished by the student council and the matrons for this indiscretion.

The middy blouse was the most troublesome garment ever worn by the students. The middy blouses when well made were generally accepted but many of the home made ones did not fit and were used as an excuse for sloppy dressing.

Breakfast has always been served at seven o'clock. This early hour has been a great temptation for students to be careless in their dress for breakfast. This has caused endless reproofs and regulations.

A simple white dress has been used for all uniform purposes. While the hat was being stressed as a necessity for the well dressed woman the students were required to purchase a simple white duck hat to wear on commencement Sunday.

The borrowing of garments was forbidden. This regulation prevented many students from abusing other students' clothing but was practically impossible to enforce.

HONOR SYSTEM

Practically none of the students who entered for the first session of the Radford College had had any experience with self-government. They were used to close supervision by their high school teachers. Early in 1913 the faculty of the Radford College decided to develop an Honor System for the control of the class room activities and examinations of the students. It was soon discovered that in order to make such a system effective there would have to be a gradual education of the students before they would be willing to accept personal responsibility for their own conduct and for the conduct of other students.

Doctor McConnell appointed a committee of the faculty on honor system and self-government composed of Misses Harrison, Moffett, and Terry to investigate methods and honor systems in other Normal Schools and Teachers Colleges. This investigation showed that such a system was highly desirable but it was evident that it must be developed slowly and in such a way that nothing

would have to be retracked. Accordingly the student government
association was organized March 1, 1914, and became active in
September 1914. The first officers were: Carrie Green, President; Ada Jennings, Vice-President; Gay Hudson, Secretary. This
group of students devoted themselves to the development of an
honor code to apply principles of honor to independent work on
class assignments, examinations, and study hour. There was some
hesitancy on the part of some of the faculty to leave the students
to conduct the examinations, and some were willing to leave the
room and allow the students to work without supervision; others
required a pledge declaring upon honor that all work had been
done without aid and assistance from others. Professor Gilbert
who had been convinced of the value of the honor system at the
University of Virginia was enthusiastic and explained in much detail to the students and faculty the work of this system at the
University. His ideal was to have the same kind of honor system
developed at Radford. He has held throughout the years to the
signing of a pledge. Doctor McConnell maintains that it is the
duty of the faculty to create an environment to prevent the
students from being tempted to cheat or to do dishonest work.
Other members of the faculty have believed in absolute freedom
with no supervision and allowed the students to conduct their
problems of examination according to their own ideas. For three
years the student government devoted itself to these class room
activities, the education of the students in favor of self-government and development of the best form of honor system. The
original organization as set up called for a President, Vice-
President, Secretary, and a student government committee consisting of nine members to represent the various classes of the
school. This group of students constituted the student government board and were charged with the administration of the honor
system, to try and to punish any violator of these standards.

Early in its life the student government was told that as
rapidly as it showed itself ready and capable of dealing with
student problems it would be given more and more the responsibility for all phases of student conduct. Its growth and development in this responsibility is shown by the change in
rules and regulations and points of emphasis stressed by the
organization. With the acceptance of the responsibility for
the conduct of the students during the study hour the organization gradually extended its province to punishment of students who violated the honor code in personal conduct, in the
dormitories or any who brought reflection upon the student
body by personal conduct on the street or outside the school.

STUDENT GOVERNMENT ASSOCIATION

The first recorded constitution of the Student Government was adopted in 1917-1918. The purpose of the organization as stated by this constitution is:

The purpose of this organization shall be to preserve the student honor and to further the interests of the students of the school; to protect the student body from criticism caused by thoughtless and indiscreet conduct of individual members of the student body; the enforcement of such regulations of the institution as are not reserved to the jurisdiction of the faculty.

From this the organization has developed to the present which states the purpose in the preamble in the Constitution and By-laws as:

Whereas we believe that the greatest personal liberty lies in self-government; that the basic principle of self-government is character, that character is founded on honor; and whereas we believe that democratic student government, emphasizing and based upon personal honor, is both possible and desirable, its successful operation requires both individual and group honor of the students so governed; it must be guarded by wise selection of its officers and by the education of the students in the principles of student honor; therefore, we the Student Association of the State Teachers College of East Radford, Virginia, in order to form a more perfect student association, do ordain and establish this constitution for the reorganization and enforcement of student government.

The purpose of this organization shall be:
(1) The preservation of the Honor System.
(2) The promotion of college spirit.
(3) The promotion of a more sisterly feeling and a greater love for the college.
(4) The settlement of affairs which concern the best interest of the student body.
(5) The attainment of those things which tend to make the college greater in every way and which will develop character in every student.

With the adoption of the constitution in 1918 the student
government association became one of the most important student
organizations on the campus with an elaborate organization of
far reaching effect. This constitution gives the best statement of the honor system as it had been developed to this time.
It also indicated the methods of procedure for the trials which
followed for many years by the council.

1. The Honor System included as a part of these By-laws,
requires absolute honesty in all oral and written class
work, in all examinations and in such other work as the
instructors shall assign to be done without assistance.
This honesty applies as fully to the giving as to the
receiving of illegitimate help. It shall be understood
as applying to honesty in all the affairs and relations
of student life.

2. It shall be the duty of any one believing that a breach
of the honor system has been committed, to have a personal
conference with the offender. If the student who makes
the accusation is satisfied with the result of the conference there shall be no further investigation of this particular offense. If the conference is not satisfactory to
the student upholding the Honor System or if in the first
place she has not felt able to bring herself to the interview urged above, she shall report the offender to the
President of the Student Association, who shall report
the offender to the President of the Student Association,
who shall investigate the matter as quietly and as speedily
as possible, or refer it to the Executive Board.

3. After a thorough investigation has been made, two members of the Board shall be appointed by the President to
go to the accused student and demand of her an explanation of her conduct. If convinced of guilt, they shall
warn her as to future consequences should she again be
guilty of any act of dishonesty.

4. The accused shall have the privilege of demanding a
hearing before the Executive Board at any time.

5. If the offense is repeated, or any other breach of the
Honor System is committed by the same student and is reported to the Executive Board, they shall summon her to
appear before the Executive Board by serving a written
notice in the ordinary letter form.

6. If after hearing her explanation and all available evidences or after her refusal to give an explanation, if three-fourths of those composing the Executive Board are convinced of the guilt of the accused, and shall so cast their vote in secret ballot, this shall mean that the decision of the Board is for asking the student to withdraw from school. Before any announcement of this decision is made, the Executive Board shall report the case in full to the President and Faculty Committee. If the President and Faculty Committee meeting independently shall come to the same decision as the Board the student shall be asked to leave school at once. If the President and Faculty Committee do not come to the same decision as the Board the Board shall meet with the Faculty and these two bodies conferring together shall reach an agreement.

7. In the trial before the Executive Board if necessary both the accuser and the accused shall appear. If the accused refuses to appear before the Board without valid excuse to the President the Board shall meet them and render its decision without trial.

Each year the by-laws of the constitution are modified to include the regulations which are to be enforced by the council. A study of these shows the trend of social thinking. In 1918 the rules were specific and attempted to define in detail the "thou shalts and thou shaltnots" of campus life.

The major emphasis was placed on the honor system, dress regulations which forbade the borrowing of clothing; the wearing of middy blouses at public exercises and on more formal occasions. The middy blouse was still a most popular form of dress in 1918. Hats were required on the street. Students were allowed to go to town twice a week, Tuesday and Saturday afternoons, by signing in the matron's office before leaving. Boisterous laughing, lingering in drug stores, flirting, waving at trains (except troop trains), hanging over the fence talking to boys were not allowed. All girls with escorts had to sit in front of the balcony in the auditorium. Students were allowed one visit during study hour not to extend over ten minutes. The study hall was conducted by monitors who sat at a table in each hall. Here the students desiring to pass from one room to another or to use their visit time received permission and signed up. The monitor's table was a

fine place to gossip. Many regulations were necessary to
control the monitors. In 1918 a Sunday afternoon "quiet hour"
was started. This required the students to spend two hours
quietly in their rooms.

The enforcement of these regulations made it necessary to
grant Senior privileges. These allowed the Seniors to go to
town three times a week; an additional half-hour of study; to
chaperon other students to the picture show, station, and
walking; to have callers from out of town any time provided
the matron was notified before their arrival. Other students
were allowed to have callers once every two weeks. Town boys
were received on Friday evening and out-of-town boys on Sunday.

MINOR AND MAJOR CALLS

The Student Government Association of 1918-1919 was the first
to state a definite punishment in terms of a specific offense.
This council set up an elaborate system of minor and major calls.
Three minor calls constituted a major and a major call carried
with it a definite campusing. One page of the record of the
council for this year shows calls issued to seventeen students
for violations of dress regulations which probably meant down
the street without a hat or wearing a middy blouse; four for
flirting from the dormitory windows; five for walking or talking
with a boy on the street; two for talking with boys over the
campus fence and one for sitting under the balcony at a public
performance; one for handling the truth lightly. The record
shows that nine days on the campus was the punishment administered for three minor calls. Car riding was the most serious
offense of the students of this period. Several received six
weeks on the campus for car riding with boys.

This system of minor and major calls multiplied problems
for the council. In order to stimulate better conduct the
council decided to charge the offense against the class to
which the students belonged. It was "Each class is responsible for the conduct of its members. Although each girl as
usual suffers from her own punishment yet on the dishonor
roll in the front hall of the Administration Building, the
name of the girl and the offense she has committed with be
written up under her respective class. If a girl receives
a major call then a major call is put on the dishonor roll
under the name of her respective class. Three minor calls
count as one major call against the class, but the individual is punished only when she receives three minor calls
which constitutes a major call."

A bulletin board with a glass door was placed in the front hall of the Administration Building as an official board for the student council. Here the "Dishonor" roll was posted. It caused great excitement. The friends of those whose names appeared finally slipped into the college, broke the glass and stole the roll, thus the board has remained ever since without a glass and the dishonored roll was discontinued.

The constitution of the student government has been revised from time to time. In 1920 the council became more lenient and allowed many privileges heretofore not granted to the students. These are:

1. The girls may go to the post office to attend to business matters whenever necessary, on down town days.

2. The girls may go through Main Street to the Methodist or any other church in that direction if they wish.

3. Every girl may go down town twice a week by signing up in the matron's office before leaving, on Tuesday and Saturday afternoons.

4. Girls may go to the picture show on Friday night when properly chaperoned, provided no other entertainment is scheduled at the Normal that night.

5. Girls may be allowed to go down town without hats in the evening after six o'clock.

6. Girls having company on Sunday afternoon may be allowed to walk with them on the campus, that is walking within sight of the dormitory.

7. Boys may be allowed to escort girls to the dormitory from public entertainments without dates.

8. Any propaganda against the student government will be investigated and if found to be guilty the result will mean severe punishment.

BLACK LIST

During this year the council originated the "black list" which includes the names of the men who are involved in any

case which necessitates the punishment of a student. There
had grown up a custom for the boys to cause or to be a party
in some misdemeanor of the girls, the girls in turn received
punishment while the boys made new friendships and continued
their enjoyment of the society and activities of the college.
The ex-campusing, popularly known as the "black list" excluded
the boys from the college for the same length of time as the
girls were campused. If he did not respect this campusing
during this period he was placed on a permanent list to be excluded from the college for all time.

FORMS OF TRIAL

The student executive council is the trial jury for all
students who violated the regulations. At first it was customary for them to call the offender before them and question
her. This questioning and ultimate discussion consumed hours
and hours of time. For a big trial the council frequently
sat in session from seven o'clock in the evening to two and
three o'clock in the morning. Gradually the officers adopted
the policy of approaching the student who was under suspicion
and have her write a full statement of what she did. In case
she made a full confession and did not argue any technicality
in her case the council rendered a decision without an elaborate personal trial before the board. This same method is
followed at the present time and as far as possible the case
is kept impersonal. The President reports the case to the
council, in this way it is felt that the student received
great justice, since the council is not influenced by personal prejudice or the likes and dislikes of the students. The
most serious cases which have come before the council have
been recorded by the secretary.

THE SUMMER COUNCILS

Since 1923 the student government has been active during
the summer quarter. The summer council is made up of representatives from each of the classes and officers of the association. While so many students lived in the city during the
summer the council zoned the city and a representative was
elected from each zone to serve on the main council. The auxiliary council is composed of the house president and representatives elected by the students living in each hall. It
is the duty of this organization to take care of the minor and

routine duties of the student council in its respective building. The president represents her building on the general
council.

THE STUDENT ASSOCIATION

In 1920 the function of the student government was changed
to include not only the disciplinary activities on the campus
but to serve as a general student organization to represent the
interests of the students in all college relationships. The office of student president was assigned ten honor points, as the
highest honor within the power of the student body to confer.

INSTALLATION SERVICE

In order to impress the students with the dignity and importance of the student association an elaborate inaugural service
was planned for the incoming president. Louise Graham, the retiring President, and the student executive council planned an
impressive ceremony which all the students attended dressed in
white. The president and the retiring president, members of
the executive council and the president of the classes occupied
the stage. Addresses were made by the old and new presidents.
When the new president took the oath of office she was presented
with a mallet, to this each class president tied the ribbons of
her class as the members of her class stood and pledged allegiance to the student body by repeating the pledge "As a student
of Radford College I hereby pledge upon my honor to uphold the
ideals for which this college stands." On two occasions representatives from other colleges were invited to deliver the main
address at the installation. In 1921 Miss Marian Wells of Randolph Macon Woman's College, delivered this address. In 1923
Mr. George Stejes, Senior of Roanoke College, made the chief
address. In 1925 the installation of the Young Women's Christian Association was combined with the inauguration of the
student president.

The student council conducts the installation of all other
student officers. The president of the student body adminis-
ters the oath of office to the other officers who in turn sign
their names in the official record book of the student council.

THE SYSTEM IN VOGUE - 1930

The third level in the development of the government of the
students is not so marked by a difference in the form of govern-

ment as by a difference in the philosophy or attitude of those
administering the conduct standards of the students. The gradual evolution reached in 1929 a growth in group and social consciousness which justified a breaking away from the boarding
school idea with its close supervision of individual students
to a more constructive group life which allowed more freedom,
offered a greater challenge for self-control and placed less
emphasis on punishment and more on preventive government.

The present system of government provides for an organization known as the "Student Executive Council" composed of a
president, vice-president, secretary, and three representatives
of the Senior class, three of the Junior class, three of the
Sophomore class and three of the Freshman class and the presidents of the auxiliary councils. This council is responsible
for the general administration of the student life on the campus.

OPEN FORUM

Once each month it holds an open forum for the discussion
of the problems of the student body. This forum is attended
by all the students. It is never attended by the faculty members or the administrative officers. On these occasions the
students discuss the problems of the campus, make requests for
privileges and attempt to develop a campus public opinion. The
forum was established as an active part of the student work in
1924.

ELECTORAL BOARD

The student president appoints an electoral board composed
of four members, a representative of each class, with the approval of the student council. This board has control and supervision of student elections, keeps the polls, count the
ballots, and posts the results of the elections.

RULES AND REGULATIONS

The Student Executive Council as a whole is responsible for
the regulations which are made for the student body. These are
approved by the administration of the college. The standards
are stated as principles of conduct rather than as rules to
control specific forms of behavior. The council investigates
and handles all problems of discipline covered by these principles.

The council holds a weekly meeting at which time it discusses the problems of the campus or hold trials of the offenders of the rules and regulations. The powers of the present student government are very extensive. They have full power to punish a student as long as they keep her within the institution. In case they vote to expel the student their action is subject to the approval of the Dean of Women and the President of the college. So far, in the history of the institution, neither the Dean nor the President has seen fit to reverse the council's decision. They have from time to time advised less hasty judgment and more deliberation but when the case has been finally decided the council action has been agreeable to the administration of the college. The council has been supported by the college in all of its activities. An effort is made by the college administration, particularly by the Dean of Women, to train the council to be objective in its judgment, fair to the student concerned, to study the personality and development of the individual in such a way that the punishment will really be of worth in the character development of the student, hence the council's motto, "We are working for character not for fame." Very few students have been expelled. Those who have been expelled have been guilty of stealing, cheating, and of extreme violation of the automobiling privilege of the college. Strict probation is the favorite form of punishment for students who violate to any serious extent the regulations of the council. This prohibits the student from leaving the institution for any cause except illness and death and confines her activities to the campus life of the institution.

STUDENT COUNCIL ROOM

Since 1923 the headquarters of the Student Council have been in a council room on the first floor of Tyler Hall. Here the regular meetings are held. The room is furnished with a director's table and chairs. Each year a picture of the council is left for the room.

PUBLICATIONS

The first printed rules were issued in 1921. These were printed on cards which were tacked on each closet door in the student's room. Later the regulations were included in the student's handbook. For the summer quarter the rules are included in a bulletin of general information given the students at registration. It is customary to hold a mass meeting of the students soon after the opening of the new quarters and

explain the principles of conduct expected to be applied by
Radford students.

SOUTHERN INTER-COLLEGIATE STUDENT GOVERNMENT
ASSOCIATION

In 1925 the Student Government Association of the Radford
College became a member of the Southern Inter-Collegiate Association which is an organization of the Student Government Associations in the larger women's colleges of the South. This
association holds an annual meeting. Since 1925 the Radford
College has been represented by the active president and usually the retiring president at these conventions. Students have
attended the convention at Tallahassee, Florida; Montevallo,
Alabama; Macon, Georgia; Randolph Macon College; Greensboro,
North Carolina, and Atlanta, Georgia.

In 1925 the local association cooperated in a State program of the S. I. S. G. to establish student government in
the high schools of the State. Radford was sponser for the
high school in its study of student government.

PART II

STUDENT ORGANIZATIONS

———

SECTION I

CONTROL OF THE STUDENT ORGANIZATIONS

In the fall of 1913 Doctor McConnell appointed a committee of the faculty to have supervision and to set the standards for the student organizations which were beginning to be perfected on the campus. This committee composed of Miss Moffett as Chairman, Miss Terry, Miss Denny, Mr. Lane and Mr. Gilbert with Miss Puryear as Secretary, held its first meeting on December 12, 1913. From this date a written record has been kept of the standards controlling the student organizations of the college and the acts of this committee.

Early in 1914 the committee set up a Point System to control the number of offices a student could hold: ten points was the maximum. A record of these points was posted in the front hall of the Administration Building, published in the Radnor and filed in the Committee records.

No organizations were allowed to exist upon the campus which were not approved by this committee. On January 22, 1914, the committee approved the following organizations: A class organization of the Junior, Senior, Sophomore, and Freshman and Preparatory classes, the Young Women's Christian Association, Ingles and Pocahontas Literary Societies, the B. B. Dramatic Club, Richard's Fireside Club, the Athletic Association.

This committee also acted as umpire to settle matters of controversy between the organizations. Two of its chief activities of the early years was (1) The controlling of the methods of raising money for support of the annual; (2) Determining upon the length of time a member of the faculty could serve as an advisor for an organization. By 1915 the competition and rivalry between the literary societies had become so acute that the committee decided it would be advisable to change the advisors. It, therefore, recommended to Doctor McConnell that the advisors for the Literary Societies should be appointed by himself and that the advisors be changed each year. All other advisors were elected by the students.

The committee at this time (1915) was composed of Miss Moffett, Chairman; Miss Baird, and Mr. Gilbert. These three acted as student organization committee until 1922 when Miss Baird resigned and was replaced by Mr. John Paul McConnell. This committee served until 1927 when Miss Moffett and Mr. McConnell were granted leaves of absence from the College.

By 1926 the committee perfected a very definite set of standards to control the organized activities. This system adopted has been generally accepted as the law controlling all organizations. The rulings of the committee have been final in all matters pertaining to the organizations.

The greatest student opposition was met when the scholarship standard was first enforced. A test case was made in the election 1927, of student president. A popular nominee was debarred because of scholarship from the race, pandemonium reigned, many students became indignant. The committee remained firm, the storm passed and scholarship was accepted as a standard by the students. The application of this standard to the "varsity" basketball players was most difficult. The desire for victory some times almost won a concession but none was ever given. Several times potential players were kept busy pulling up low grades to meet the standard until almost time for the whistle to open game.

PRESENT (1930) REGULATIONS FOR CONTROL OF STUDENT ACTIVITIES

The college recognizes the importance of student activities in all the all-round development of the students. It holds, however, that the primary purpose of the student in college is to secure the best academic education possible. In order to maintain the highest standards of scholarship and at the same time afford the greatest opportunity for student participation is the extra class activities of the college the Faculty Committee on Student Organizations have set up the following standards to be followed in the election of officers:

1. A student is not allowed to be president of more than one organization at a time.
2. She may hold at one time two offices which carry as many as four points or three if the points are less than four.
3. After once accepting a position or nomination the student is not allowed to resign from a position in order

270

to accept another office or nomination, except in the
case of the student government and the Y. W. C. A.
election which come in the third quarter, and, further,
in special cases approved by the Faculty Committee.
The points for these offices do not count until the
following year.

4. A student is allowed to carry at one time only two
outside activities in addition to her school work. For
instance, if she is a member of the Glee Club and the
officer of a society she is not to take any active part
other than membership in any other student activity.

STUDENT ELECTION DAY

The second Tuesday of October is Student Election Day,
at which time all student officers are elected. Previous to this, nominating conventions are held, platform speeches made, and a study made of pre-election
methods in national and State elections.

STANDARDS FOR STUDENT OFFICERS

1. All offices which carry four points or more are known
as major offices.

2. All offices which carry three points or less are
known as minor offices.

3. Academic standards herein stated are based on the
last three quarter's work of the student with the exception of freshmen who are entering college for the
first time. In this case freshmen are not eligible
for major offices until they have been a resident of
the college for one-half year or three terms which records are used in determining their eligibility.

4. The above regulation in regard to freshmen does not
apply to the election of freshmen class officers.

5. A student to be elected to a major office must have
a scholarship record of an average of B or above for
each of the three quarters determining her eligibility.
The B average is reckoned from all the courses and all
the grades completed by the student and recorded in the
Registrar's office.

6. A student to be elected to a minor office must not have fallen below C on more than one subject.

7. Students who represent the college in any inter-collegiate relationship must have attained the scholarship record required for minor offices, based on the last quarter's work. During the period while the student is representing the college they must not fall below their original scholarship record.

8. No student is allowed to run for office who has broken the trust of the Student Council within two quarters of the time she seeks office.

9. The record of all nominees must be examined in the Registrar's office by the student Nominating Committee, approved by the organization committee and the President of the Student Council before they are posted.

10. The same recognition as a basis of grading as followed in the Registrar's office must be considered in determining the eligibility of the student.

NOMINATIONS

1. In floor nominations the person placing a candidate in nomination must give the qualifications of her nominee for the office for which she is being nominated.

2. As far as possible floor or written nominations by all members of the organizations affected by the election has to be followed.

STUDENT NOMINATION COMMITTEE

In some organizations it seems advisable to use a Nominating Committee to make the first nominations for office. Therefore each class shall elect one representative to the Student Nominating Committee. These four members and the President of the Student Body are to act as a Nominating Committee for all student organizations desiring nomination by a committee.

The duties of this committee are:
1. To look after all nominations and to conduct all nominating conventions.

2. They shall nominate two persons for each office to be filled.

3. These nominations must be approved by the Faculty Committee of Student Organizations.

4. They will then be posted.

5. If any student does not care for the nominations thus made she has the privilege of nominating some one else for the office, providing she can secure the signature of 5% of the student body, or member of the respective organizations affected by the nominations made by the committee. Such additional nominations must be made within forty-eight hours after the posting of the report of the nominating committee. In case more than two are nominated for an office a primary election will be held to determine who shall be the final cnadidate nominated for the office.

6. The above method of changing nominations made by the Nominating Committee does not apply to the floor or written nominations which are made by the membership of the organization present.

7. Prior to the election all major candidates shall appear before the organization and make known her policy as to the carrying out of the office for which she is a candidate.

VOTING

1. In case a primary election is necessary this shall be held by the organization affected at a call meeting. The majority of votes cast by the group attending the meeting to be considered the decision of the election.

2. All final elections for major offices shall be held in the following manner: A voting precinct shall be established in the lobby of the Administration Building.

3. An Electoral Board composed of one representative of each class appointed by the Student Nominating Committee shall act as the judges of all elections. These shall preside at the voting booth, have ready a complete registration of all people eligible to vote and check off all names of the voters when they have voted.

4. The organization holding the election shall provide uniform ballots. A definite hour shall be set
for the election during which time all ballots must
be cast.

5. No candidate is to be declared elected until she
has received a majority of the votes cast. If a
majority is not determined after three balloting of
votes the candidates shall be dropped and new nominations made, in which the same candidates do not
appear for the same office. Returns of all major
elections shall be posted on the Student Organization.
Bulletin Board in the main lobby and read at the General Assembly hour.

SECTION II

LITERARY SOCIETIES

ORGANIZATION OF INGLES AND POCAHONTAS SOCIETIES

At one of the first faculty meetings held either on September 17th or 18th in 1913 Doctor McConnell appointed a committee composed of Misses Moffett, Denny, Puryear and Professor Gilbert to perfect the organization of two literary societies. From Doctor McConnell's experience with the student life at Emory and Henry College he was much impressed with the importance of the literary societies as the nucleus around which the organized activities of the students should center. Miss Moffett had been a charter member of the Lee Literary Society at Harrisonburg Normal School. Mr. Gilbert had been active in the literary societies at Virginia Christian College and the University of Virginia. The committee therefore entered upon the organization of literary societies with great enthusiasm. This faculty enthusiasm permeated the life of the literary societies as organized and largely accounts for the outstanding position the Ingles and the Pocahontas Societies have had in the student life of the Radford College.

The faculty committee held its first meeting at the home of Mr. and Mrs. H. P. Anderson where all were boarding and discussed the form of organization. It was decided to organize two societies and to name them for outstanding women. No record of this meeting was kept but as the author remembers it Mr. Gilbert proposed the name of Pocahontas. Miss Moffett then asked Mr. H. P. Anderson who was a well read and intelligent man who was the most outstanding woman in the history of Southwestern Virginia. He replied, "Mary Draper Ingles" and gave the committee a copy of a book entitled "The Trans-Alleghany Pioneers". This book gives an interesting account of the life and trying experience of Mary Ingles. The committee decided therefore to name on society "Pocahontas" in honor of the Virginia Princess and the other "Ingles" in honor of Mary Draper Ingles, the heroine of Southwestern Virginia.

The names of forty students were selected from the student roll. These were arranged in two lists of twenty each. These twenty students thereby became the charter members of the two societies. The committee decided that they would become advisors of the two organizations. The name Pocahontas and Ingles was written on two slips of paper which were drawn and resulted in Mr. Gilbert and Miss Denny becoming advisors of the Pocahontas Society and Miss Moffett and Miss Puryear advisors of the Ingles.

The lists of students were then placed on the table and drawn.
In this way the charter members of the respective societies were
selected.

On September 20, 1913 the faculty committee Miss Moffett,
acting as chairman, held a meeting of the student body in the
auditorium of the college. It presented the plans for the or-
ganization of the two societies. The charter and first members
were: for the Pocahontas; Ethel Garrett, Maude Goodwin, Mosby
Charlton, Ruth Halsey, Sena Jones, Anne Muse, Virginia Pugh,
Carrie Bagwell, Blanche Graybeal, Clara Stone, Lula Mae King,
Ida M. Shaffer, Rubye Akers, Susie Higgins, Mary Pope, Lena
Andis, Bertie Fisher, Grace Deaton, Ada Jennings, Beulah Top-
per, Eva Deaton, Osa Graham, Grayce Graham, Florence Jackson,
Flora Atwell, Nina Miller, Lillian Wolfe, Eulalie Gardner,
Eula Cundiff, India Covey, Emma Einstein, Nina Einstein, Burr
Wolfe, Eugenia Wolfe, Virginia Brown, Lois Showalter, Mayme
Boyer. For the Ingles; Addie Allen, Nancy Allen, Mary Bishop,
Annie Roper Brown, Jessie Calfey, Julia Cook, Mary Davis, Ellen
Dailey, Ruth Davis, Sara Davis, Pearl Daniels, Clara Delp, Ruth
Dobyns, Nancy Daughtery, Ethel Fisher, Violet Fleenor, Jessie
Falls, Bess Gilespie, Bill Gaines, Winnie Hurt, Mary Hicks, Ara
Hicks, Helen Huddle, Gay Hudson, Sallie Mae Hurley, Benona Heath,
Rebec Kearsley, Maxie King, Elizabeth Kelley, Ada Kyle, Ella
Kelley, June McConnell, Lois McConnell, Mary Morgan, Mona My-
ers, Ethel Myers, Elizabeth Moran, Rachael Oglesby, Lucille
Phipps, Bernice Phillips, Nell Painter, Bertha Richardson, Vir-
gie Rhudy, Carrie Snyder, Lena Stafford, Elrica Shelbourne,
Gertrude Shumate, Evelyn Shumate, Sarah Sowder, Beverley Taylor,
Marie Walker, Ruth Welsh, Ethel Bernard, Carolla Crockett, Lu-
cille Gilber, Bess Lucas.

The charter members immediately perfected a temporary organization. The temporary chairman for the Ingles Society was
Elizabeth Moran with Margaret Rogers for the Pocahontas. The
most important event of this temporary organization was the
selection of rooms to serve as society halls. In the original
plans for the Administration Building the "Tower Room" was
written on a slip of paper and a blank slip was used to indicate the other room. The temporary chairman with great solemnity drew for these rooms which resulted in the Ingles Society
getting the "Tower Room" where they have been to the present
time. The Pocahontas Society not so successful were assigned
to the large double room, however, with the growth of the school
it soon became necessary to use this room as a library. The
Pocahontas Society was then moved downstairs to Room 13. In
1915 it moved to the physics laboratory on the second floor,
this room it has used to the present time.

Immediately after the temporary organizations the societies
set about to perfect permanent organizations. Working with their
advisors they wrote their constitutions. At first an effort was
made to keep the organizations identical in purpose and activities, this soon became impossible and each developed a peculiar
personality of its own.

Since these societies were the first student organizations
perfected on the campus they were given a clean sweep to embrace
everything as their function. For this reason they have never
been strictly literary as the name would imply. Their various
purposes are implied in the constitutions as originally drafted:

"The purpose of Pocahontas Society shall be to strengthen
the ties of life among its members:
First: To strengthen the ties of friendship.
Second: To develop power of self-expression.
Third: An Appreciation of Literature."[1]

The Ingles Society stated its purpose in the preamble to the
constitution as:

"Prompted by a laudible desire to cultivate our intellectual moral and social endowments to virtue and to
promote friendship and patriotism we hereby pledge our-
selves to support this constitution and by-laws."

THE INGLES CREED - ADAPTED 1920

I believe in the Ingles Literary Society as an organization for the promotion and development of literary,
social and political life.

I believe in the traditions of pioneer life preserved
by it.

I believe in the idealization of the life of Mary Draper
Ingles.

I believe in the perpetuation of her characteristics of
courage, loyalty, sacrifice, endurance, kindliness, and
love as living monuments to the heroism of the past.

I believe through these the future is made more glorious
and in truth if we give to the world the best we have the
best will come back to us.

[1]From the Constitution. Minute book of the Society.

The Faculty likewise recognized the various functions of the literary societies. In a survey of student organizations of 1921 the committee on literary societies stated the purposes of the literary societies:

The aims and purposes of the literary societies as they have been organized in this institution should be:

1. To develop ability to think and speak correctly and effectively before an audience.

2. To develop ability to express one's self forcibly and clearly in both oral and written productions.

3. To give training in parliamentary procedure and usage in conventions.

4. To give practice in dramatization and to develop appreciation of and skill in music and other arts, such as drawing, decoration, etc.

5. To give training and experience in social conventions of today, and to develop the spirit of fellowship and good will toward one another regardless of society affiliation or personal attainments.[1]

MEMBERSHIP

Membership in the two societies was open to all students of the college. The Ingles attempted to limit active membership by including a clause in its constitution "That active membership in the society is open to any student after one quarter of residence, provided she has received a grade of eighty-five on nine-tenths of her courses during the said quarter". The faculty committee on student organizations also ruled that a student must have at least a C average before she was eligible for membership.[2] These rulings were never actively enforced.

Honorary membership in each society was extended to all members of the faculty and any other whom the society might select by a two-thirds or majority vote.

Many distinguished persons have identified themselves with the two societies. Some honorary members of the Pocahontas are: Mrs. Woodrow Wilson, Miss Zeda Craft, an actress, Strongheart,

[1] From minutes of the Faculty.
[2] Minutes of Organization Committee, Puryear Secretary. (History File.)

Indian Chief of Ya Kiana Indians, Chief Cook of the Pamukey
Indians, Mr. Harry F. Byrd, Judge and Mrs. George Cassell,
F. Blanco, Chief of Insular Police, San Juan, Porto Rico.

Some honorary members of the Ingles Are: Ex-Governor J.
Hoge Tyler, Miss Cornelia Adair, President of National Educational Association, Honorable E. Lee Trinkle, Mr. J. Bas-
com Slemp, Mr. David Anderson, an author; Mr. John S. Draper
of Pulaski, and Captain William Ingles.

SPECIAL PATRONS OF THE SOCIETY

For many years the Ingles Society made a strong appeal to
the citizens of Radford since it was named for Mary Draper Ingles,
the pioneer heroine of Southwestern Virginia who had spent the
latter years of her life near Ingles Ferry at the West End of the
present site of Radford. In this neighborhood there are many members of the Ingles family still living. There are also many de-
cendants of the Draper family living near Pulaski. All of these
were honored by the naming of the society for their progenitor.
In the early years of the society they contributed much to the
development of the ideals and the preservation of the history of
Mary Draper Ingles.

On May 15, 1915, the descendants of Mary Draper Ingles presented to the society a tablet setting forth the chief events of
the life of Mary Ingles. The presentation and unveiling of this
tablet was the first formal and outstanding event in the history
of the college. So much importance was attached to it that the
college printed a report of the entire program as one of its bulletins.[1]

On this occasion Honorable I. T. Eskridge of Pulaski sketched
in detail the life of Mary Ingles and other historic characters
and events of Southwestern Virginia. This story as he gave it
and as it is printed in the "Trans-Alleghaney Pioneers" became
the accepted story of Mary Draper Ingles. Around it the society
has built many of its programs and activities. A bronze tablet
was presented by Captain William Ingles the oldest descendant of
Mary Ingles, living in Radford. The Ingles family have further
shown their interest in the society by a number of socials given
in the home of Captain Ingles on New River. This home is erected
almost on the site of the home of Mary Ingles after her tragic
escape from the Indians. Upon the death of Captain William Ingles,
his portrait was presented to the society by his widow. The intimate interest and relationship with the society has been continued by Mr. William Ingles, Jr., nephew of Captain William Ingles

[1]Radford Normal Bulletin, Vol. III, No. 2.

who is at present cashier of the First National Bank of Radford, Virginia.

INGLES MOTHER - MRS. MARY S. MOFFETT

On February 14th, Mrs. M. S. Moffett found a Valentine at her door containing the following message:

"The members of the Ingles Literary Society have
chosen you as a permanent mother of the society.
Every girl feels that you are one to whom she may
go for motherly advice. By doing this we wish to
show you how much we feel what you and Miss Moffett
have done in making our society what it is today.
We wish you happiness and success in fulfilling the
duties that may be encumbered upon you in the future."

In electing Mrs. Moffett as mother of the Society
the Ingles girls have bestowed on her the greatest
honor they could bestow on any one in connection
with the society. They will ever look to her for
wisdom and superior judgment in matters pertaining
to the society."[1]

In this she has not failed.

"GRANDPA" CASSELL

Early in its history the Pocahontas Society elected Judge and Mrs. George Cassell as honorary members of the organization. Judge Cassell was identified with the early organization of the college as secretary to the first board of trustees. He has always felt a keen and personal interest in the development of the college and calls himself "Grandpap" to the college students. He has been a loyal supporter of the Pocahontas Society and has played an active part in its development. He has not only contributed greatly by speeches and discussions of points of local history but has frequently appeared before the society and entertained them with music on his mouth harp.

Judge Cassell believes there is sufficient historic evidence to sustain the story that the Shawnee Indians had a trail which passed through the campus of the college to a large camping ground near the spring on his farm, Cassleton. Around this spring many arrow heads and other relics have been found. As long as the Judge lived at Cassleton he made it an annual practice to entertain the

[1]Grapurchat March 2, 1922, Vol. 2, No. 4.

Pokies. On November 14, 1913 he gave the first of these entertainments. Each of the students robed herself in a blanket and
in true Indian fashion went to Cassleton. When the tribe had
gathered a rousing war whoop brought Judge Cassell and his family
rushing from their home to invite their guests into the house
decorated in Indian fashion, to a lavish Indian feast. Each
spring when the cherries were ripe he entertained the society
by the big spring. Here he told them many stories and legends
of the Indian trail and life in this great Alleghaney region
which the Indians reserved as their hunting ground.

INDIAN ALLIES

From time to time the Pocahontas members have invited Indian
chiefs to become honorary members of the society. The first of
these was Chief Cook of the Pamunkey Indians, a direct descendant
of Powhatan, the father of Pocahontas. Chief Cook has visited the
society several times. He made the chief address at the Pow Wow
on February 20, 1924.

On February 2, 1928 Chief Nipo Strongheart of the Yakinan
tribe of Washington delivered an address before the student of the
college. "From Peace Pipe to War Trail". Chief Strongheart was
the orginator of the American Indian Citizens Bill passed in Congress in 1924 and has since devoted himself to an interpretation
of Indian life in an effort to bring about a better understanding
between the white and red races. He was invited to become an
honorary member of the Pocahontas Society. He was very much honored by this courtesy and has kept in close touch with this society.
He frequently sends them postcards, pictures, clippings, etc. to
interest them in the development of Indian life.

SOCIETY EMBLEMS

The societies adopted the historic period of their respective
heroine as the central motif for the decoration of the society halls
and the dramatic activities of the two societies. The Pocahontas
Society idealized Pocahontas, the Indian Princess, and her contribution to early Virginia life. Episodes of her life became vivid
through frequent dramatizations. Her spirit, personality and life
were glorified through songs of praise. Many stirring addresses
typified Pocahontas as the first Virginia Lady and the Savior of
the Commonwealth.

This society adopted as its motto "Fortune favors the brave".
At first the tomahawk was selected as the emblem, however, this was

soon abandoned and the pine became the emblem. Copper and green were adopted as the colors for the organization.

The society did not have a popular society song until 1921.

Miss Mamie McLees became the advisor of the society in 1921. She was especially talented in the writing of songs. She wrote several for the Pokies, from these the official song of the society "Red Skin Maid" was selected.

RED SKIN MAID

Pocahontas of Indian Story
  Pocahontas of Virginia's glory!
Pokies love you, heap much too,
  Just like you our redskin maid,
Pocahontas, our tribal queen.

Pocahontas, we heap much love
  You like star that shines above;
Make us see the victory.
  Pocahontas in copper and green,
Like forest tree with autumn sheen--
  Pocahontas, our tribal queen.

Miss McLees also started the custom for those who studied art to present to the society a picture of some Indian maid or scene which they had painted. Several such pictures were presented by Miss McLees, Ada Lee Cannady, Ruth Bricker, and other members of the society. These were hung in the society hall.

Thermutus Parrack and Elizabeth Brown designed an Indian border of a quiver, arrows, and deer. This border was stenciled around the society hall and was preserved for many years as the chief decoration of the hall.

Mr. Gilbert purchased for the society a handsome vase of rich brown color with the head of an Indian Chieftain as the central figure of the design. He also selected five copies of famous Indian pictures, these are now the chief decorations of the hall. Judge Cassell presented the society with photographic copies of the monuments to Pocahontas and Captain John Smith at Jamestown. The photographs of Mrs. Woodrow Wilson, Zeda Craft, and Storngheart, honorary members of the society were presented by these persons to the society.

Through its members and interested friends the society has collected a number of real Indian trophies. In this collection there

are stone tomahawks, Indian moccasins, Peace pipes, etc. These
have been stored in the college museum in Pocahontas collection.

In 1915 the Pocahontas Society adopted mahogany as the finish for furniture of the hall. The college equipped the hall
with one hundred mahogany chairs and four tables. In 1914 Mr.
Roop made for each of the societies a cabinet on the top of which
he built a glass case in which the debate cup was stored during
the time it was held by the society.

INGLES EMBLEMS

The Ingles Society adopted the colonial as its central theme
in the decoration of its hall. The oak leaf was selected as the
emblem of the society because the acorn had served as food for
Mrs. Ingles on her journey from Ohio. The colors maroon and tan
typified autumn, the season of her hardship. The central object
in the decoration of the Ingles hall is the bronze tablet presented by the Ingles family on April 15, 1915. Above this has always hung the banner of the organization. In 1915 one hundred oak
chairs and two oak tables were provided for the hall. For many
years two rocking chairs were used in the Ingles Hall which had
been used in the Heth House. An imitation colonial fireplace was
built by Mr. Roop. Around this the students assembled a number of
old spinning wheels, guns, pioneer cooking utensils, kettles, and
other colonial relics. One of the most valued possessions is a
small piece of silk taken from a dress owned by the daughter of
Mary Ingles, presented to the society by a descendant of the Ingles;
The society had the original dress reproduced in red silk, as a
costume to be worn by the girl who acted the part of Mary Ingles
in the pageants and skits which the society has given.

The motto of the society "Give to the world the best you
have and the best will come back to you" was selected from   the
poem by Madeline Bridge:

> There are loyal hearts, there are spirits brave,
>   There are souls that are pure and true,
>   Then give to the world the best you have,
>   And the best shall come back to you.
>
> Give love, and love to your heart will flow
>   A strength in your utmost need;
>   Have faith and a score of hearts will show,
>   Their faith in your word and deed.

For life is the mirror of king and slave,
'Tis just what you are and do!
Then give to the world the best you have,
And the best will come back to you.

In 1921-1922 Grace Tietje and Gertrude Shumate set the motto
to a chant rhythm. This has been used as the concluding feature
of the programs ever since.

The Ingles adopted a popular pep song of 1913 as the society
song. This has been sung throughout the history of the organization.

INGLES PEP SONG

Maroon and tan will wave on high,
The Ingles spirit will never die,
Rah, rah, oh, Ingles, Ingles,
Rah, rah, oh, Ingles, Ingles,
Rah, rah, oh, Ingles,
Rah, rah, Rah!

Chorus:

We're Ingles born, we're Ingles bred,
And when we die we're Ingles dead,
Rah, rah, oh, Ingles, Ingles,
Rah, rah, oh, Ingles, Ingles,
Rah, rah, oh, Ingles,
Rah, rah, rah!

Where'er we stay, where'er we roam,
The Ingles Hall is always my home,
Rah, rah, oh, Ingles, Ingles,
Rah, rah, oh, Ingles, Ingles,
Rah, rah, oh, Ingles,
Rah, rah, rah!

Mrs. Lois Bertling a loyal member of the society wrote a ballad based on the history of Mary Draper Ingles which has become one
of the traditional pieces of literature of the society. This was
published in the Grapurchat.

In 1928 Miss Lillian Smith wrote "The Ingles Maid".

THE INGLES GIRL

She's an old-fashioned dear of a quaint, bygone year,
That Ingles Girl of whom we always dream,

With her sweet smiling face and her old-fashioned grace,
As she holds in her glances that dear Old Ingles gleam.

Chorus:

It seems the years have missed her,
For time has gently kissed her,
Her silken tresses, sweet carresses,
The same old smile so true.

In all our dreams we're hearing
Her gentle voice endearing,
"Give to the world the best you have
and the best will come back to you".

In her old-fashioned way of a lost yesterday
Our Ingles Girl is always ling'ring near;
Bless her dear gentle heart, may the years that depart
Always greet her and keep her, our quaint, old-
fashioned dear.

THE INGLES TREE

In February 1921 a large oak tree in the grove fell in a sleet
storm. The President of the Ingles Society, Gertrude Shumate, asked
Doctor McConnell to give this tree to the Ingles. This he did. No
one really expected the society to do anything with the immense tree
as it lay sprawled over the campus. However, the girls gave all
their spare moments to a strenuous effort to saw the tree up. They
borrowed cross-cut saws from the hardware stores and from neighbors
of the college. For six weeks they sawed incessantly and finally
succeeded in cutting the tree into four sections. This activity
attracted a great deal of newspaper publicity and many people became
interested in the sawing activity of the students. The tree was a-
bout thirty inches in diameter. The rings of the stump were counted
and indicated two hundred and thirty-six years of growth. When the
tree was finally sawed Mr. Andrew Ingles brought a team of horses
and hauled the logs to West Radford where Mr. R. M. Coltrane had a
sawmill. Mr. Coltrane was interested in the organization and offered
to saw the logs into lumber. This was done and the lumber was moved
to the college where it has been stored for future use in the society
hall. When the job was finished at the sawmill all the members of
the society hiked to West End. Mr. Coltrane sawed canes for each
of them. Two large strips showing the entire width of the tree are
preserved in the society hall.

A small oak tree was planted by the stump of this famous tree
with an elaborate ceremony. At the base of this tree a tin box was

placed with a list of the members and advisors of the society and a story of the parent tree. For several years a feature of the society program was reading of the "Ingles Log" named for this e-vent.

SOCIETY BULLETINS

Two bulletin boards were placed in a conspicuous place in the main hall of the Administration Building, one on either side of the Tea Room door. These have played an active part in the publicity of the societies. On them have been displayed society announcements, posters, and programs. At the time of the fall rushing season, debate and other contests they are covered with messages from loyal members, endless chains of oak leaves, historic relics, welcome signs, in fact everything that can be stuck to a board to arouse curiosity, stir envy or stimulate interest has found a place here.

TIME OF MEETING

The societies held weekly meetings. Saturday evening was turned over to their activities. Practically nothing was allowed to interfere with the programs. In 1930 the students decided to hold the society meetings on alternate Saturday nightx.

SOME TYPICAL PROGRAMS

The chief emphasis in the programs of the first few years of the Ingles Society was on literary topics. Very little attention was given to debating, while music and literature became a major interest. A typical program of this period was:

History of Short Story - - - - -Faith Camden
A Story as a factor of
Literature - - - - - - - - -Lute Finley
A Short Story - - - - - - - - - Virginia Rudy
Recitation - - - - - - - - - -Chloe Carson

Following the opening of the World War in 1914 the societies spent much time on a discussion of the European countries involved in the war. In this connection the Ingles held one of its first debates, Resolved, "That Germany was not justified in declaring war on other countries". The debaters were: Negative, Addi Allen and Gay Hudson; Affirmative, Violet Fleenor and Carrie Green.

The faculty regarded the literary societies as a place for education. Much discussion was held by the faculty as to how to make the societies most worthwhile. In accordance with this idea Dr. McConnell suggested to the societies on January 8, 1915, that some definite attention should be given to the use of parliamentary rules, at the same time he presented each society with a copy of the Roberts' Rules of Order. The societies followed this request by a definite effort to improve on parliamentary procedures.

THE FIRST DEBATE

During the first few years the Pocahontas Society placed much emphasis on debate. The first debate in the history of the college occurred in this society on November 1, 1913. The question Resolved; "That Radford Normal School should not have been opened until the fall of 1914" was debated by Burr Wolfe and Ada Jennings on the Affirmative, and Mary Pope and Ocie Graham on the Negative. The negative won.

The early debate subjects show the interests of the students in these early days. Some of these questions debated: Resolved, "That students receive more benefit from each other than from the faculty"; Resolved, "That women should be given the right to vote"; Resolved, "That the fear of punishment has greater influence on conduct than hope of reward"; Resolved, "That elementary curriculum should be reorganized to make a storng vocation"; Resolved, "That girls are more deceitful than boys".

Some typical programs are quoted from the minutes of the societies to show some interests and activities of the societies at different periods of their history. On December 6, 1913 the first open program of the Pocahontas Society was held in the College Auditorium and visitors were present. The program consisted of:

```
        Piano Solo - - - - - - - - - -Grace Graham
        Roll Call - - - - - - - - - -Secretary
        Original Story - - - - - - - -Rubye  Akers
        Faculty Journal - - - - - - -Nina Einstein
        Vocal Solo - - - - - - - - - -Georgia Morris
                                      (Anne Muse
        Dialogue - - - - - - - - - - -(Ada Jennings
                                      (Eula Cundiff

        Chorus (Roses Everywhere).
```

On October 3, 1925 the Ingles Literary Society held its regular meeting in the Ingles Hall. A very interesting program was given. The house was called to order by the President after the minutes and roll call the following program was rendered:

Maroon and Tan - - - - - - - - - Society
Devotional Exercises - - - - - -Chaplain
Scene (Four Ages of Friendship) Group
That Old Gang of Mine- - - - - -Quartette
Associations tend to make us what we are:
   1. In the Student Council - - -Hattie Ogburn
   2. In the Y. W. C. A. - - - - -Margaret Black
   3. In the Literary Societies -(Crizell Holland
                               (Annie Obenshain
Chant - - - - - - - - - - - - - Society

"We were very fortunate in having Doctor Allison, one of our honorary members, present. He led us in prayer and gave a short but helpful talk. The Society adjourned to meet the following Saturday in the Gymnasium for the joint society reception."[1]

INGLES PILGRIMAGE
May 27, 1927

The Ingles girls made their annual pilgrimage to the Mary Draper Ingles Monument Friday afternoon, May 27. The girls left the college at four-forty and walked to West End. A short program was held at the monument. Our President made a short speech followed by "Maroon and Tan" and the devotional. Miss Eleanor Bryant then played a violin solo, "Somewhere a Voice is Calling". Her encore was "The Rosary". Miss Anna Lee Bonham made a very sincere talk on "What the Ingles Society has meant to me". Following the program we built a fire and roasted weiners and ate the rest of our lunch, after which we started for home. This pilgrimage was in honor of our debaters who are working hard on the debate.[2]

Annie Mae Harrington was in charge of a musical program which was held in the Ingles Hall:

1. Maroon and Tan
2. Devotional
3. Violin Solo - - - - - - - - - - Eleanor Bryant
4. Vocal Solo - - - - - - - - - - Sadie Miller
5. Dance - - - - - - - - - - - - - Miss Wanda Ellis
6. Harp Selection - - - - - - - - Lillian Smith
7. Chant - - - - - - - - - - - - - Society

This program was short but unusually interesting. Several new

[1]From Minutes of the Societies - Minute Books.
[2]Society Minutes.

members were initiated during the business meeting. The President
commended the custodians for the attractive appearance of the hall.
Many of the girls expressed their ideas about the hall being more
like home than any other meeting place of the society.

The Ingles Literary Society gave a Minstrel in the Auditorium
in honor of the Pocahontas Literary Society on February 8, 1930.
It was one of the best programs of the entire season, very clever,
well acted, and very entertaining.

1. Song. (Painting the Clouds with Sunshine).
2. Jokes and Dialogue - - - - - - - - - -Wilson, Morgan
                                   Honts, & Snead
3. Music and "Swing Low Sweet Chariot".
4. Negro love scenes - - - - - - - -Hardwicke & Hubbard
5. Song (Am I Blue) - - - - - - - -Hubbard
6. Jokes
7. Song (Sympathy)

The Pocahontas Literary Society chose as a setting for its
meeting on Saturday evening, October 3, 1925 the lovely fish fountain.
Under the beautiful moon, by the wigwam and campfire the maidens
realized what was truly their heritage. As soft music was played
and the winds gently rippled the water of the fountain the following program was rendered before an audience of more than two hundred:

Red Skin Maid - - - - - - - - - - -Society
Devotional - - - - - - - - - - - -Chaplain
Indian Love Song - - - - - - - - - -Ruth Briker
Piano Duet - - - - - - - - - - - -Rhee Graybeal
                                   Mary Snavely
Humorous Reading - - - - - - - - -Ina Addington
Hiawatha's Melody of Love - - - - - Group
    From the shadows of the wigwam came
    Minnehaha in the arms of her lover,
    Hiawatha. Pocahontas appears with
    Powhatan telling him of her society.
Our Vision (Talk) - - - - - - - - - -Mr. Gilbert
War Dance - - - - - - - - - - - - -Group

Ice cream and cake were served. Genevieve Geisen convulsed
the audience with her reading "Sis Hopkins" and the famous "Duck".
After the program a very important business meeting was held. A
letter from the Calliopean Literary Society of Emory and Henry College was read asking that the "Pokies" become their sisters. It
was voted that we do this. Amid shouts and great enthusiasm a
large number of girls joined the Pokies making a total of fifty-two

new girls.

On October 20, 1928 the regular meeting of the Pocahontas
Literary Society was held in the Society Hall. Our first debate
of the quarter was given and it was definitely decided once and
forever that the girl of 1860 was neither more beautiful nor
more attractive than the girl of today. The affirmative, Ruth
Stoke and Eva Mears; Negative, Trula Roberts and Lucy Beahm.

The varied and interesting program included music, readings,
and dance. The following was presented:

Song - - - - - - - - - - - - - - - Society
Devotional - - - - - - - - - - - - Chaplain
Piano Solo - - - - - - - - - - - - Rosella Sayers
Reading - - - - - - - - - - - - - Flora Fannon
Debate:
Clog Dance - - - - - - - - - - - - Colleen Seagle
Talk - - - - - - - - - - - - - - - Paul McConnell

The talk by Mr. McConnell was enjoyed by all as he is an old
Pokie. He received a hearty welcome.

November 23, 1929
o
—————

Society Song - - - - - - - - - - Society
Devotional - - - - - - - - - - - Chaplain
Piano Solo - - - - - - - - - - - Lucille Christian
Debate:
     Resolved: "That Co-education should be
           adopted by Radford College."
   Affirmative   Negative
  Catherine Riggle   Louise Forbes

The decision was unanimous for the negative. There was a
surprise Yo-Yo contest in which Doctor Humphreys, Doctor Thomas,
and Mr. Bowers participated. They were as much surprised as any-
body else. Doctor Humphreys received a Yo-Yo for being best,
Doctor Thomas a stick of chewing gum for second and Mr. Bowers
half a stick of gum as third. Judge Cassell talked and played
his harp. A business meeting followed the program.

OPEN PROGRAMS

In the beginning the programs and other activities of the
societies were kept secret from each other and the programs were

closed to all except the members and especially invited guests.
The faculty committee for the literary societies decided it would
be stimulating to the societies for each to hold at least one open
program a quarter to which the members of the other society and
the public would be invited.

The first of these open programs was held by the Ingles Society on October 18, 1913 when the society was formally opened
by Honorable John S. Draper of Pulaski, Virginia, a collateral
descendant of Mary Draper Ingles. On this occasion the descendants of Mary Ingles presented to the society a framed photograph
of the monument which they had erected in her honor. Mr. Draper
reviewed the life and achievements of Mary Draper Ingles.

The Pocahontas Society held its first open program on December 6, 1913. These early open programs were designed to represent the real work of the society and were typical of the programs which the societies were holding each week in the society
hall. For several years these quarterly open programs were continued. They were held in the auditorium. Gradually the students
adopted the policy of allowing visitors to attend any of their
programs. This tended to reduce the interest in the open program
as all were welcome and often visited back and forth at the regular weekly meetings of the societies.

SOCIETY PLAYS[1]

By 1920 the societies were placing much emphasis on dramatic
presentations. This form of program had become so popular it was
destroying interest in all other types. In order to better balance
the society the faculty committee decided to allow each literary
society to hold one play during the year. This play to represent
the dramatic efforts of the societies. Accordingly the Pocahontas
Society started the custom of presenting a play on the last Friday night of the Fall quarter. The Ingles in turn presented its
play on the last Friday night of the winter quarter. These plays
for many years were the outstanding dramatic productions of the
year.

The first of the Pocahontas plays was a dramatization of
Dickens' Christmas Carol, arranged by Miss Elizabeth Brown. Her
interpretation of the Christmas spirit as portrayed in this mas-
terpiece of literature was most effectively presented by the members of the society with herself in the leading role as Scrouge.

In 1922 the Ingles Society dramatized the life of Mary Draper
Ingles.[2] This play was written by Miss Moffett, Gertrude Shumate,

[1]See list of plays in appendix for names and dates of other Society plays.
[2]Grapurchat March 16, 1922. Copy of play on file in Moffett's personal
file.

and Grace Tietje. It was presented with unusual skill. At this
time the society planned to repeat the play once every ten years
and to make it an epoch in the life of the society. The leading
character, Mary Draper Ingles, was taken by Annie Sue Anderson.
Sketches from this play have been given from time to time as features for the programs to acquaint the new students with the heroine and ideals of the society.

INTER-SOCIETY BASKETBALL GAMES

While the spirit of rivalry and competition was keen between
the two societies basketball contests arose to major importance on
the campus. Immediately the societies started having inter-society
basketball games. The first of these was held on April 15, 1916.
Frequently thereafter the inter-society games opened the basketball season. On these occasions the gymnasium was decorated in
the colors and emblems of the two societies. The bleachers are
divided equally. Each society team loyally supported, society
songs, cheering, yelling, parades, private arguments and closely
fought games marked the occasion. Such contests have been held
nearly every year from 1916 to 1931.

SOCIETY SPIRIT

The real life or spirit of the two societies is not reflected
in the programs. These programs were merely incidental to the real
activities of the members. The real society was in the spirit de
corp that developed within the society and between the members of
the two organizations. The societies in the early years absorbed
the entire interest and affiliations of the students and supplied
the chief outlet for their social contacts. Each society developed
a unique type almost impossible to describe, its ideals, activities,
former members, type of program, decoration of hall, faculty advisors all contributed to the atmosphere which the new students soon
felt. This attracted into the membership different types of students. Their interests were different, their ideas were less unified and the rivalry between the two groups was keen and many times
hostile to each other.

In the early days you could almost predict which society a
student would join from her general manner. In later years the
types have become less distinct and the membership less distinctive.
in type.

The loyalty and allegiance to the two literary societies dominated the social life of the college until about 1928. During
the Fall quarter a rushing season by the members of the societies

of the new students took place. There was much rivalry. New
students were met at the train by loyal supporters of each society. Their bags and suitcases became light as feathers for
the royal boosters to carry up the hill to the college if the
owner bore the ear marks of an Ingles or Pokie. Pep meetings,
stump rallys were held by the Ingles, Pow Wow's by the Pokies.
Elaborate and enthusiastic announcements of the meetings in
the general assembly, singing of society songs, elaborate decorations of bulletin boards, thorough house cleaning of society
halls, many trips with new students to the halls marked the
opening days of each academic session. Much labor attended
the programs for the first Saturday nights while the new girls
were making a choice. The Pocahontas extended an invitation
of membership at the first meeting of the fall quarter. For
many years the Ingles did not extend an invitation for membership until the students had had an opportunity to attend both
societies. This difference in policy caused endless discussion.

Enthusiasm and popularity have varied. For many years the
Ingles had the largest enrollment then the Pocahontas was in
ascendency. The membership, however, of the two societies has
averaged about the same throughout the years of their history
with the Pocahontas having a slight advantage in numbers.

The height of society enthusiasm and rivalry was reached
in the years from 1920 to 1925. The home building project, the
keen competition of the inter-society debates, the hotly contested inter-society basketball games and the general jazz age
of this period gave an extreme tempo to the society life. The
faculty had a large part in this enthusiasm. The original faculty was practically divided in its affiliations with the two
societies. Much of the spirit of these organizations centered
around the devotion and service of the respective advisory groups:
for the Pocahontas, Mr. Gilbert, Miss Denny, Mr. Avent, Mr. Bowers,
Miss Coppedge, and Miss McLees. For the Ingles, Miss Moffett,
Miss Baird, Miss Bowen, Miss Puryear, Mr. J. R. L. Johnson, Mr.
Swaney, and Mr. Fitzpatrick. Especially was the faculty competition keen in connection with the inter-society debate.

Beginning in 1926 society spirit of the old type as has
been described above began to wane. Many new faculty members
came into the school in 1927. They knew nothing of the old
temposity or the early allegiances. Their interest in the literary societies was primarily in the quality of work. Other
student organizations came. With the result that the societies
lost much of the prestige and dominance over the student life.
So marked was this decline of interest that by the spring of
1930 students decided of their own accord to give up the inter-

society debate. To those students who lived through the hectic years of 1920-1925 such an action was almost unbelievable yet to those on the campus it was a sincere reaction to a series of natural causes.

SOCIETY HOME PROJECT

In the fall of 1921 Mr. Gilbert suggested to the Pocahontas Society that it invite the Ingles Society to join with it in a project to erect society homes for each of the organizations on the campus of the college. This suggestion (Mr. Gilbert's) was enthusiastically received by the members of both societies. At once an active campaign was started to raise money and perfect plans for these homes. The original idea as proposed by Mr. Gilbert was to erect on the campus a log cabin for the Ingles and an Indian hut or wigwam for the Pocahontas Society.[1]

This building was to serve as a social hall for the members of the organizations and as far as possible as a meeting place for the formal programs. Doctor McConnell and the faculty advisors united with the students in planning the details of the project. Elaborate plans were made for the presentation of this idea to the Alumnae at the Annual Thanksgiving Dinner of the Alumnae Association in Richmond. This meeting proved to be one of the most enthusiastic and successful alumnae celebrations ever held. It was held in the Murphy Hotel. Over one hundred and fifty alumnae, faculty, and friends of the college were present. Irene Allison of the Class of 1916 was toastmistress. Each Literary Society was represented by a representative, Blanche Daniels, Pocahontas, Virginia Harwood, Ingles. These explained the plans for the erection of the homes. The Alumnae accepted the idea and immediately joined with the students in perfecting plans to raise the money.

Mr. Kuhn Barnett standing in the lobby of Murphy's Hotel following this meeting made the first donation to the Ingles Society Fund.

The Ingles soon perfected an official organization of its members to act for the Society on the building project. Stella Mae Agnew of Floyd was appointed Treasurer, Annie McConnell, Chairman of the building committee. Miss Moffett, faculty advisor. The Pocahontas appointed Mr. Gilbert as the treasurer and so far as is known they had no official committee of members other than the officers who met and discussed with the Ingles Committee architectural designs and represented the society in joint planning. The committees decided to raise the money as far as possible by personal contributions.

[1]Grapurchat, November 24, 1921.

ROLL CALL AND POW WOW

The Ingles Society held a Roll Call in January 1922. In preparation for this occasion all former members of this society were invited to the college and were urged to send pledges to the building fund. Many Ingles returned for the reception which culminated in the Roll Call of all active members and those former members who were present. The pledges were written on oak leaves made of tan paper printed in maroon. As the name was called the pledge was dropped into a miniature log cabin. This cabin was the central feature in the decoration of the hall. Gertrude Shumate, Grace Tietje, Natalie and Ella Harvey were active in perfecting the plans for the first Roll Call. Eight or ten former presidents were present. These formed the receiving line for the reception of the guests.

The Pocahontas Society held a Pow Wow on March 18, 1922. At this time they had back many of their former members all of whom made pledges to the building fund. A feature of the program was a dramatization of the life of Pocahontas written by Elizabeth Brown. Into this skit was woven the ideas and purpose of the society and introduced to the audience a vision of the home to be built by the money collected through the pledges made by the members of the society. Members of the society dressed in an Indian costume danced an Indian march around the fire as they presented their pledges. This entertainment and pledge service was held in the auditorium followed by a reception in the "Pokie" Hall.

These two receptions started the custom of holding an annual Roll Call and Pow Wow. These were features of the winter quarter each year until 1930 when they replaced the debate and were held on Saturday evening during commencement. Most of the money for the Society Homes was pledged at these annual celebrations.

In February 1923 the faculty held a call meeting at which time Doctor McConnell explained the purpose of the student building and requested pledges from the faculty for the benefit of this building.

In 1923 upon the suggestion of Doctor McConnell Mr. Kearfoot of Bristol, Virginia was employed as architect for the building. By this time the idea of having separate buildings had somewhat evaporated. Mr. Kearfoot acting upon the suggestions and ideas which he could gather at the college designed one building of two distinct parts connected by a colonnade. The two units were each complete within itself. Although identical in external appearance the internal arrangement and finish was according to the ideas and motif of the two societies. Behind the building he proposed to build an open air theater. The architect's drawing was unveiled before the students amidst much applause. Postcard reproductions of this drawing were distributed to the alumnae. Many former students commenced the payments of their pledges. Doctor McConnell decided to start work on the building according to the Kearfoot plan. He therefore used this money to start the foundations of the two buildings. He thought after the buildings were started it would be easier to secure an appropriation from the State Legislature for their completion. In order to interest the legislature, dormitory rooms to be used by Alumnae were planned for the third floor of each of the buildings. The site selected for this building faced Tyler Avenue to the rear of Tyler Hall.

In the late fall of 1923 the two literary societies broke the ground for the foundations to their buildings. The Ingles Soceity was to have the North wing and the Pocahontas Society the South Wing. With appropriate ceremony of songs and speeches the foundations while being laid were dedicated to the societies. The Ingles dropped oak leaves into the soft concrete which were embedded and hardened into the foundation. The Pocahontas dropped an arrow head at the spot which was to mark the main entrance into the building.

The excavation, building of the frame for the foundations, and the pouring of concrete was done by local laborers under the direction of Doctor McConnell.

The money on hand was used to complete the foundations and a small tool house was erected nearby. The building project was in this state when the request for the appropriation was made to the 1924 Legislature. No money however was appropriated to complete the building. The foundations were left. The students and alumnae bravely began again to collect pledges and to continue their project. Interest waned and for some months the project seemed doomed.

In 1925 Miss Helen Cook was appointed as Alumnae Secretary; one of the chief duties of her office was to further the interest and plans for the society homes and to collect the pledges which had been made. The money collected and the records of the two societies relative to this building program were turned over to Miss Cook. Through continuous efforts Miss Cook assisted by the alumnae had collected a total of $6,930.91 of the pledges by February 25, 1926. The Ingles Society had $5,834.92 in unpaid pledges and the Pocahontas had $11,323.10. The Class of 1922 which had been responsible for the launching of the project made the most complete payment of its pledges. Miss Cook resigned her position in 1926 and the business management of the project was taken over by Mr. Sylvester McConnell. He with the cooperation of Miss Allen, Secretary to Doctor McConnell, collected a large number of the funds.

By the fall of 1927, $11,000.00 was in hands. It seemed impossible to raise sufficient money from the alumnae or an appropriation from the State to justify the building of the original building as planned by Mr. Kearfoot, the architect. Doctor McConnell therefore decided to use the money which he had and erect a smaller building. During the summer of 1927 he and Mrs. McConnell spent much time in locating this building. Mrs. McConnell was finally responsible for its location near the Administration Building on line with the Heth House. By this time students had given up their idea and enthusiasm for separate society homes. Doctor McConnell was left to his own ideas for the smaller building.

Frye and Stone of Roanoke, Virginia, were building the Campus Training School at this time. They made the plans and designs for the Activity Building according to the ideas of Doctor McConnell. This Building was erected by T. G. Moore, of Christiansburg. It was open for use by the students in the spring of 1929. The building is so designed that it can be built to. When sufficient money is raised two units are planned for either end to follow the general architectural scheme of the other buildings on the campus. In this building the societies were given offices. Since the completion of the building they have shown some interest in furnishing it. Each purchased a rug. From the general equipment appropriation for the college oak furniture of uniform style was bought from the State Penitentiary for use in the offices on the second floor of this building. The Literary Society offices are used as a storage and office for the records and activities of the executive officers of the organizations.

SECTION III

FORENSICS

INTER-SOCIETY DEBATES

In the Spring of 1914 when the plans for the commencement
season were being perfected the faculty and representatives
of the two literary societies decided to establish as one of
the chief features of the commencement an inter-society debate
between the societies. The first of these debates was held
June 1914. Such debates were held continuously, thereafter,
until June 1930, when the two literary societies decided to
discontinue them.

In 1914 a faculty committee was appointed by President
McConnell to purchase a silver trophy cup to be held by the
winners of debate. Miss Blanche Bulifant selected this cup.
It was held by the Pocahontas Society for the years of 1914,
1915, 1916, 1918, 1921, 1922, 1924, 1926, 1927, 1928, 1929;
the Ingles for the years of 1917, 1919, 1920, 1923, 1925.

The method for conducting these debates varied from time
to time. In the beginning the advisors and representatives
of each of the societies agreed upon a question. It usually took several weeks to perfect an agreement since each debate was attended with great rivalry, suspicion, and animos-
ity on both sides. However, in spite of this feeling the
debates were conducted with dignity and for many years justified their existence by the keen society spirit which developed.

As this spirit grew more undesirable and amicable agreement more difficult to reach, the two societies agreed upon
a plan whereby each society submitted a question. These were
placed in uniform envelopes; at the General Assembly period
the Presidents of the two societies drew for the question.
The ceremony was conducted by the President of the College
or some neutral faculty representative. A coin was usually
flipped to decide which should draw first. The question
was thus selected. In like manner the two presidents drew
for sides.

There was no uniform practice in the societies for the
selection of debaters, however, it was customary to hold preliminary debates and from these the representatives were

chosen. There were no standards other than ability to debate
to control who should represent the societies. Because of
this several times the societies were represented by the same
students for two or three successive years.

Much time was devoted by the debaters and the advisors of
the societies in the preparation of the debates. The debates
were always carefully prepared and delivered. The main speech
of the debates ranged from twelve to twenty minutes with re-
buttals from three to eight minutes. The questions which have
been debated are:

1914 - Resolved: That Education Contributes more to Success
       than any other Factor.
1915 - Resolved: That the future welfare of the United States
       has more to fear from internal forces than from external
       forces.
1916 - Resolved: That country life offers more opportunities
       than does city life.
1917 - Resolved: That the United States after the War should
       join with other nations of the world in formation of a
       league to enforce peace.
1918 - Resolved: That teachers should form a nation wide feder-
       aration and thus by force of organization develop pro-
       fessional attitude and secure proper appreciation of
       service.
1919 - Resolved: That during the next five years there will be
       a greater need in the State of Virginia for building
       and improving public roads, for building and improving
       elementary and high schools.
1920 - Resolved: That the present Congress should prohibit
       foreign immigration into the United States during the
       next five years of the reconstruction period.
1921 - Resolved: That after 1925 two years normal or college
       training should be a prerequisite for teaching in the
       public schools of Virginia.
1922 - Resolved: That the promotion and free exercise of a
       true democratic citizenship for the United States
       depends upon the organization and development of a
       new political party.
1923 - Resolved: That a system of compulsory voting should be
       adopted in the United States.
1924 - Resolved: That during the next four years the one-room
       school of Virginia should receive more support and at-
       tention toward its improvement than any other type of
       public school.

1925 - Resolved: That the organization of Virginia into sec-
    tions for the purpose of exploiting economic, social,
    and historic advantages will lessen interest and united
    support of the State program of advancement.

1926 - Resolved: Virginia should develop an adequate school
    system before developing an adequate road system.

1927 - Resolved: That all foreign indebtedness to the United
    States made in connection with the World War should be
    conciled.

1928 - Resolved: That Congress should have the power to over ride
    by a two-third vote decision of the Supreme Court.

1929 - Resolved: That the publication and broadcasting of crime
    news should be restricted.

THE DEBATERS

Ingles	Pocahontas
1914 Estelle Grear	Anne Muse
Ada Kyle	Susie Higgins
1915 Carrie Green	Anne Muse
Clara Delp	Ethel Garrett
1916 Mary Davis	Bonnie Alderson
Josephine Pratt	Ethel Garrett
1917 Stella Muncy	Mary Hohn
Bess Lucas	Evelyn Lavinder
1918 Lucille Blackard	Josephine Wassum
Margaret Watson	Marie Carter
1919 Kate Repass	Emma Quessenberry
Thelma Atkinson	Maude Parks
1920 Evelyn Shumate	Emma Quessenberry
Ada Lou Hurley	Willie Lee Stowers
1921 Mary George Hedrick	Elizabeth Brown
Virginia Porter	Clara McCauley
1922 Mary George Hedrick	Elizabeth Brown
Grace Tietje	Ina Addington

306

1923	Helen Cook	Myrtle Dobbins
	Gertrude Brophy	Elizabeth Brown
1924	Elsie Tompkins	Virginia Peery
	Charlotte Caldwell	Genevieve Giesen
1925	Charlotte Caldwell	Sallie Vaughn Turner
	Maude Rimmer	Genevieve Giesen
1926	Audry Authur	Eulalia Gompton
	Dorothy Sharitz	Esther Kilgore
1927	Lourine Holstead	Sallie Vaughn Turner
	Helen Chumbley	Genevieve Giesen
1928	Hildred Wessel	Rosalie Blanton
	Pauline Osborne	Genevieve Giesen
1929	Addie Johnson	Ann Jennings
	Pauline Osborne	Helen Einstein

The inter-society debate was held always on the Saturday night of the commencement season. The members of the societies attended as a body. The two sides of the auditorium were reserved for the societies. Frequently these were decorated in oak leaves, and maroon and tan colors, for the Ingles and with pine; copper and green colors for the Pocahontas. The banners of the two societies were displayed. The processional of members was a spectacular feature of the program. Some times the Pokies wore Indian costumes. The Ingles featured children in colonial costumes as flower carriers. Much enthusiasm, pep songs, cheers accompanied the arrival of the debaters. It was the custom for each society to shower its debaters with flowers and gifts. The Ingles gave the debaters pins while the Pocahontas gave the society pin. For some years the presentation of these trophies was a feature of the program. Each society trying to outdo the other in its method of presentation.

The question of judges was always an acute one. Many hours of discussion and investigation were spent in determining qualifications and in the selection of suitable judges. The judges were usually approved and invited by Doctor McConnell. Upon arrival they were met and entertained by a committee of the faculty representing the interest of both societies.

In many respects the inter-society debates were contests between the faculty members who were advisors of the organization. They worked very actively with the representatives of the societies in collecting material and in some instances in actual preparation of the debate. The entire populus of Radford was more or less divided in its affiliation with the societies. All of this feeling was emphasized in the ceremonies attendant upon the debates. The President of the two societies presided at the debate on alternate years. The representatives of each of the societies kept time. This reached its climax in the years of 1918 and 1919 when the advisors of the societies were very solemnly marched to the stage of the auditorium and received the decisions of the judges. Later the decision of the judges, taken secretly, was presented to and read by the presiding officer. The rendering of the decision of the judges was always a tense moment; as soon as the decision was announced pandemonium reigned.

Aside from the inter-society debates each of the societies placed emphasis upon public speaking and debating. For a number of years the program of the literary societies was more or less literary. Into these programs were introduced a number of debates. Most of these debates were impromptu or did not require much preparation. At the same time they had sufficient depth to test the ability of the speaker to present and organize material for debate and rebuttal. Many of those who were chosen as final debaters for their society were introduced to the societies and made a reputation for themselves at these less formal debates. Debating however, as a real art has never been emphasized in either society. The debaters who participated in the final debates were especially coached and thus gave a creditable performance.

In the early years of their organization the literary societies just grew. Little effort was made to define or limit the scope of their activities. In November 1922 Doctor McConnell appointed several faculty committees to study, evaluate, and state the purpose of the various organizations on the campus at that time. The preliminary report on the place and activities of the literary societies was presented by Miss Moffett and Mr. Gilbert. This report provoked much discussion and was finally referred to another committee who brought in recommendations relative to the opportunities of the literary societies. Both of the committees stated as the major objective of the society the ability to think and speak clearly and effectively before an audience. Second, to develop ability to express oneself forcibly and clearly in both oral and

written productions. The same committee attacked the problems
of the society debates and recommended that the final debate
between them should not receive aid from the advisors, except
first: that the advisors only give assistance in criticizing
outlines of the questions to be debated: Second, that they must
give information as to sources of material on the subject to be
debated; third: they may offer suggestions as to the relative
value of arguments proposed and submitted by the debaters;
fourth, may give training in the delivery and presentation of
the debates prepared by the contestant. To a certain extent
these recommendations were followed in the latter years of
inter-society debating.

INTER-COLLEGIATE FORENSICS

Under the date of October 12, 1925, the President of State
Teachers College, East Radford, Virginia, received a letter
from Miss Martha Willis a student of the State Teachers College
at Farmville, Virginia, asking for the co-operation of the students at Radford in forming a league of the four State Teachers
Colleges for the purpose of carrying on inter-collegiate debates.
This letter was referred to the student organization committee.
The committee replied favorably to the proposal and after considerable correspondence a triangular debate was organized between the State Teachers Colleges at Harrisonburg, Radford, and
Farmville. Fredericksburg refused to join the league. The
agreements reached in the preliminary correspondence was summed
up in an inter-collegiate debate contract:[1]

SELECTION OF INTER-COLLEGIATE DEBATERS

The domination of the literary societies over the forensics
of the college is shown in the method used in selection of the
debaters to represent the Radford College. The faculty committee on student organizations was the representative officer for
the debate. Miss Moffett conducted the correspondence and perfected the arrangements with the other schools. Miss Ethel
Roberts, President of the Pocahontas Society and Miss Anna Lee
Bonham, President of the Ingles Society co-operated. The following regulations for the selection of the debaters were set
up as follows:

1. See Appendix for Contract.

HOW RADFORD DEBATERS WILL BE SELECTED

1. Each Literary Society shall select four representatives making eight in all.

2. These representatives shall be divided into two negative and two affirmative teams with an Ingles and a Pokie on each team.

3. The last week in February these teams will meet and hold a preliminary debate before the faculty, the representatives of the student body and Literary Societies. From the number four will be selected, two who are members of the Ingles and two who are members of the Pocahontas, as the final debaters to represent the college in the Inter-collegiate debate.

4. An Ingles and a Pocahontas member will be on the affirmative team, which will meet the negative Farmville team for debate in this college, April 15. The other two members will form the negative team which will meet the Harrisonburg affirmative team in Harrisonburg, April 15.

5. The Inter-Collegiate Debate as outlined in the contract and the above scheme for administration in our local college, gives promise of being one of the outstanding student activities between the Teachers Colleges of Virginia. It is hoped that every student in this college will become intensely interested in these debates and will put forth a special effort to assist the debating teams.

6. The question is alive and full of interest to Virginians. Practically every community is interested in one side or the other. Every student should make an effort to collect material, opinions, and ideas on this question, from the representative citizens of her home community and give this material to the debaters. Watch the newspapers and magazines for anything that relates directly or indirectly to the question. Two months is a short time in which to work up such an extensive debate and we cannot hope to win without the help and cooperation of the students and faculty members in this college.

SIGNED BY COMMITTEE

The societies selected their representatives for the preliminary debate from which the debaters who represented the college were selected.

In November 1926 the Farmville debating club took the initiative in reestablishing the Inter-collegiate Debate. After some correspondence with Miss Evelyn Beckam, Chairman of the Debate Club of Farmville and Miss Mary McNeil of Harrisonburg, the debate was finally held on May 5, 1927 under the same contract as for 1926. The question debated was, "Resolved That the Virginia Municipalities should be financially independent." The Radford College was represented at Farmville by Miss Helen Chumbley and Miss Edna Haines; at home by Miss Pauline Osborne and Miss Elsie Brogan. Both teams won. The same method for the selection of the debaters was used in 1927 as had been used in 1926. The faculty organization committee, Miss Moffett, Mr. Paul McConnell and Mr. Gilbert with the addition of Doctor Hudson supervised the selection of the debaters in the preliminaries.

The success of the Radford teams in Inter-collegiate Debate had greatly increased the interest in this activity in the college. All of the debates which were held at Radford were attended by large representative audiences of the students who showed much enthusiasm and interest. This interest tended to weaken the interest in the inter-society debates.

In the fall of 1927 the personnel of the student organization committee was changed due to the absence of Miss Moffett and Mr. Paul McConnell. Doctor McConnell appointed a debate committee composed of Professor Gilbert, Doctor Swanpy, and Doctor NeSmith as committee on Inter-collegiate Debate. This committee continued the plans and policies of the organization committee. The third triangular debate was held with Harrisonburg, Farmville, and Radford on May 12, 1928, after the same manner as the previous ones. The question debated was, "Resolved That the Nicaraguan Policy of the United States should be approved." The Radford College was represented by, the affirmative, Misses Genevieve Giesen, and Addie Johnson; the negative, Misses Pauline Osborne and Elizabeth Jackson. Through a misunderstanding as to the wording of the question both Radford and Farmville were prepared to debate the affirmative on the Radford floor. The judges were asked to base their decision on the general merits of the debaters. For the third consecutive time the Radford College won a double victory. This was the last triangular debate between the three State Teachers Colleges.

CHANGE IN POLICY FOR INTER-COLLEGIATE DEBATES

The seasons of 1928 and 1929 mark a change in the Inter-
collegiate Forensics in the College. The plan of having the
representatives of the college selected from the Literary Societies was abandoned and any student who was interested could
enter the debates. The representatives of the college were
chosen from the standpoint of merit. Neither Farmville nor
Harrisonburg seemed willing to continue the triangular debate.
Therefore, the Radford College entered into negotiations with
other institutions. During the season the question discussed
was "Resolved That the System of Trial by Jury should be abolished." The debaters who represented the College were Misses
Addie Johnson, Pauline Osborne, Elizabeth Jackson, and Ollie
Wilson.

On March 30, 1928 the Radford College had its first inter-
collegiate debate with men. Radford was challenged by the
College at Waynesburg, Pennsylvania. The gentlemen representing this institution were met by Misses Pauline Osborne and
Addie Johnson at Radford who defeated them in a discussion of
the Jury System.

During this season inter-collegiate debates were held with
Hampden Sidney, Milligan, and Waynesburg Colleges. The Hampden Sidney team visited the Radford College and were defeated
by Misses Addie Johnson and Pauline Osborne. A dual debate was
held with Milligan College in which Radford lost on both sides.
Emory and Henry forfeited one debate to Radford.

The faculty committee appointed the previous year continued the work of coaching the debates. The members divided
the responsibilities; Doctor Swaney and Mr. Gilbert supervised
the argument and Doctor Hudson and Doctor Long, and Doctor
NeSmith supervised the English and delivery. From the experience of this year there seemed to be a concensus of opinion
that a single coach from the faculty would be a more advisable
system for the management of the inter-collegiate debate.

THE FORENSIC COUNCIL

Early in the fall of 1930 the students interested in debating organized a debating club "The Question Mark," Addie
Johnson, President and Violet Lewis, Business Manager. This
club was the first formal organization for inter-collegiate
forensics. This club selected as their advisor Doctor W.
S. Long. Heretofore the selection of the debaters, the

policies and coaching for the debates had been controlled by
a faculty committee and the literary societies. This club
very soon became the forensic council. All former methods of
management were abolished so that the council might set up its
own policies and regulations. Membership in the Forensic Council was open to all students interested in debates. The organization holds regular monthly meetings. The preliminary debates are open to any student of the college. Doctor Long
conducted the preliminary debates and selected as representatives for the college for the 1930 season Misses Addie Johnson,
Elizabeth Jackson, Freda Harmon, and Jean Taylor. The question
was, "Resolved, Installment Buying of Personal Property is Socially and Economically Desirable." Dual debates were held with
Milligan College, Hampden Sidney, and Waynesburg College, single
debate with Emory and Henry College. Bridgewater College forfeited one debate to Radford. During this season various systems for judging the debates were used. Mr. Prufer, coach of
debating at Roanoke College, was invited as a critic judge for
the Waynesburg debate. Following the debate and the decision
of the judges he gave an analysis and criticism of the debate
which was constructive and helpful to the Forensic Council.

In order to stimulate greater interest in the inter-collegiate debates, Doctor McConnell offered two prizes of five dollars
in gold for the best old debater and the best new debater. At
the close of the debate season Doctor Long announced to President
McConnell as winners, old debater, Miss Addie Johnson and new debater, Miss Jean Taylor. These young ladies were presented with
the gold by Doctor McConnell with an effective speech setting
forth the value of debate.

Upon recommendations of several members of the Tau Kappa
Alpha Fraternity Doctor Long wrote the Secretary of this organization for an estimate of the eligibility of the members
of the Radford Forensic Club becoming a chapter of the fraternity. In reply the Secretary indicated the only shortage
of Radford to meet the requirements of the fraternity was the
lack of a class in public speaking. A class was organized in
the opening of the fall quarter in 1930 and is now being
taught by Doctor Long.

The organization for 1930 and 1931 of the Forensic Council
places membership on a class representative basis. The President, Miss Rosalie Blanton, requested all students interested
in debate to indicate their interest to the business manager,
Miss Violet Lewis. These were then elected as members of the

Forensic Council on the following basis: six from the Seniors, four from the Juniors, six from the sophomores, and four from the Freshmen and any others who made the debating team by means of the preliminary debates.

The full expense of the inter-collegiate forensic activities have been borne by the college from the student activity fees.

SECTION IV

CLASS ORGANIZATIONS

<u>NOMENCLATURE</u>

Since the first month of the history of the college the classes have been organized. The names used for the designation for these class units have been changed according to the type of courses and classification of the students in the institution. In the beginning the most advanced students completed the two-year course, therefore they were called Seniors. Those who had four years of high school work were called Juniors, fourth year high school students, Sophomores, third year high school students, Freshmen, and all other students, preparatory. This terminology was used until 1920 when secondary students were eliminated from the college. The terminology of Juniors and Seniors for the two-year course was continued and Unclassified was used to designate all students having less than sixteen units of high school credit. With the establishment of the four-year course the question of nomenclature came up again. The two-year students were very reluctant to give up the name of Juniors and Seniors, therefore, for three years, from 1921 to 1925 the upper classmen, those completing the four-year course and receiving the Bachelor of Science degree were called "Degrees." The third year students who had completed the two-year course and were working towards degrees were called "Postgraduates" and the second-year students "Seniors", the first year students "Juniors". In 1924 the name of the school was changed to College. This change in name made the students more willing to be classified according to the usual academic classification. Since this time freshmen has been used to indicate those students who are starting on their course, Sophomore for the second year students (those completing the Normal Professional Course), Juniors for the third year students, and Seniors for those who are candidates for the Bachelor of Science degree.

CLASSIFICATION

The quarter organization has made it very difficult to classify the individual student. The student organization committee adopted the policy of allowing those students who were within four quarters of the achievement of a degree to be classed as "Seniors" and those within the four quarters of the achievement of a two-year diploma as sophomores, thus the classes are graduated as members of the class of a given year whether their course is completed in June or August.

The greatest controversy of this classification has arisen during the course of the year when a student comes within four quarters of graduation at some other time than September and desires to have the Senior privileges. This problem, however, has been met without real difficulty and the system of classification seems to be the most reasonable under the unusual organization of the academic year.

CLASS SPIRIT

For many years the entire student life was dominated by the literary societies. For this reason it was practically impossible to stimulate class rivalry or to develop a spirit which would color the life of the group. Until 1924 the class organizations were of a routine type responsible for the activities of the respective groups, however, practically none of the student life of the institution originated and developed from these class organizations with the single exception of the spirit which animated the preparation of the annual stunt.

From time to time the classes have rallied around their respective basketball teams and supported them in class competition. The Freshmen and Sophomore Classes have always been able to maintain a good basketball team. The upper classes however have been forced to combine with sister classes, the Freshmen and Juniors and the Sophomores and Seniors for these basketball contests.

In the "collegiate" changes of 1924 the Sophomores assumed the role of hazers of the Freshmen whom they dubbed "rats" in imitation of the Virginia Polytechnic Institute. It presented a difficult problem to the administration which of course was opposed to any such drastic measures being applied to the young

women students of the college. In order to offset any continual
program of "rating" the college officials allowed one day to be
designated as "Rat Day". At this time the Sophomores were allowed to impose comic requirements upon the Freshmen. "Rat Day"
was held for four years. It was customary for the Sophomores to
require the Freshmen to dress in ridiculous fashion. A typical
picture of a "Rat Day" procedure is taken from the Grapurchat,
October 29, 1925, as written by one of the Freshmen.

"THE FRESHEST DAY OF THE YEAR"

The wee small hours of Tuesday morning found each Rat in
the hall--some tying her green bows on her shoes, others
trying in despair to button a coat or sweater backwards.
Finally, each Rat was dressed, if you could call it dressed.
Their heads looked like a garden patch of spinach, and you
couldn't tell if they were going or coming. With their
dresses and coats wrong side out and backwards. To look
at their feet and legs one might get dizzy, green hose,
red hose, and green bows in galore, oh! Such a green crowd
of Freshies.

They started chasing up and down the hall, showing the
ability of their lungs, until there wasn't a wise old
Soph in the hall who wasn't glad at the chance to crawl
out and defend herself.

Promptly at six-thirty o'clock the priestess of the Holy
Owl and President of the Sophomore Class, by a blast of
the sacred trumpet, declared each Rat under the control
of their Superiors, the Sophomores. If some one, not
knowing it was Rat Day should have walked in they would
certainly think they were in "Buddahland" by the way the
humble little Rats were bowing to their Superiors.

Rats were sternly ordered to go on the campus where they
did a snake dance and sang praises to the Holy Owl.

The Sophs preceded the Rats into the dining room where
they stood on each side of the steps holding their rose
and silver triumphantly for the Rats to march under.
Each hungry little Rat had to bow separately to each one
of the Sophomores. They had to eat with their chairs
backwards and use only a knife for everything. This
wasn't so bad for some of them as they have had quite a
bit of practice with the knife. Each Rat had to count

twenty before taking a bite. At lunch each Freshie
carried her umbrella, and at dinner they looked like
the eye of departure carrying their handbags.

The Rats were certainly in demand all the morning,
making beds, washing clothes, sweeping and dusting
for the Sophs some of them were very popular. They
also had to use the back entrance to go to all their
classes, this was quite uncomfortable, especially
walking so far on one high and one low one.

In General Assembly the Rats preceded their Superiors
into the auditorium backwards and stood at attention
while each Soph was seated. After lunch the Rats
congregated on the campus to watch a little bird come
out of the photographer's machine. Then they went into the gym where they were ordered to seat themselves
on the floor and pitch both shoes into a pile in the
middle of the floor. Ruth Hubbard was called by the
Holy Owl to the middle of the floor to make a talk on
the "Benefits of Rat Day". Mildred Dayis was asked to
discuss "Which took more space up or down". This was a
very inspiring talk and was enjoyed by every one.
Mildred Baylor walked out in her barefeet and made a
very wonderful and interesting talk on "The Whichness
of What". The Holy Owl then demanded Miss Virginia
Mae Roberts to make an interesting address on "Which
is the Mightier, the Needle or the Sword". The Rat
speeches were all very good and indeed helpful. They
were then told to scramble for their shoes, each Rat
went at one time, and it looked more like a massacre
than anything else. A shoe this way--a boot that way!
Such a fight and only a few came out looking the same.

All the afternoon the poor Rats labored until dinner
time, each Rat was very fatigued. And was a very piti-
ful looking piece of humanity. Poor Rats! When dinner
was nearly over, the Holy Owl perched in the middle of
the dining room and with a great air of superiority demanded quiet, while she read the names of the fresh
Rats that had disobeyed in any way their superiors and
who were thus sentenced to Kangaroo Kourt. Every Rat
was very still and frightened for fear her name should
be called to go to this dreadful Kourt. They were
quickly ushered out of the dining room by the Sophs to
this horrible place. Its mysteries are yet to be unfolded, but I'm sure there is not a Rat who would go

through those terrible things again.

While these unruly Rats were getting their punishment, the others were made to stay in the dining room until 7:30.

When the seven-thirty bell rang a very successful Rat Day was over--and I'm sure there wasn't a Rat who wasn't glad to crawl into their beds. But Rat Day of '25 will be something that will long be remembered by every one at S. T. C.[1]

CLASS PRIVILEGES

The granting of certain class privileges started in 1918 when the student council accorded certain exceptions to its rules and regulations for the Seniors. These privileges have been a source of annual discussion and have varied in terms of the general regulations placed upon all students. The most frequent request from the Seniors is to go down town at night. From 1921 to 1924 this was granted as a Senior privilege, three seniors in a group were allowed to go to town one night each week. Local conditions in the town and the size of the classes made it necessary to revoke the privilege. Night privileges are now accorded with special permission from the Dean. The usual senior privileges have allowed the seniors to accompany other students as a chaperon, wearing hats in the dining room, additional half-hour for study, lights out at eleven o'clock and half anhour extension of calling hours with the privilege of using the small parlors in the Madame Russell Dormitory.

In 1921 the inauguration of the Student President was preceded by class week. Each class was given a day. On this day the class had charge of the General Assembly for that day and was allowed to have some form of social activity. It was a hilarious week. So hilarious that it was never repeated. Outstanding was the contest between the Juniors (Freshmen), Seniors (Sophomore), classes. During this week each class sprung some stunt to outdo the other classes. The Juniors reached the climax when in the middle of the night two of the students climbed to the top of the water tank and painted '22 on the tank. For several nights it was necessary to keep a class guard around the tank. Where upon the students were forbidden by the college authorities to climb the tank. For several years the tank

1. Grapurchat Issue, October 29, 1925. (By "Rat" Sis Murray).

flaunted this triumph of the Class of 1922. During the class week each faculty advisor entertained his class and the class held picnics, egg hunts, and gave special programs in the General Assembly. They placed placards around the building telling of the exploits of the class, and had pep meetings during all intermissions.

SENIOR WEEK

Beginning in 1921 a week was set aside as "Senior Week". The members of the first degree class established a camp near Ripplemead, Virginia, where they were given the use of the log cabin on Clare Wood Farm, the home of Mr. and Mrs. William Crowgy. Here they spent the entire week fishing, swimming, hiking, cooking their own meals before the open fire, feasting under the trees, playing musical instruments and having a jolly good time. During this week they caught up with back work, did parallel reading and made an educational tour in observation in the Pearisburg High School. The Juniors, chaperoned by Miss Moffett, the Senior advisors joined them for the weekend.[1]

The two-year graduates were also given a Senior week with all rules removed. During this week they were entertained extensively by class advisors, the four class sponsors, and various clubs of the college. They spent their spare time preparing for the class programs and having a last good time together. Similar senior weeks were held for two or three years. The dissipation and hilarity of so many idle students about the college became too great so the holiday week was cancelled. Now the senior examinations are held one week before the end of the term, but the students are required to attend classes until the end of the quarter.

SENIOR CLASS ACTIVITIES

The students who completed the two-year and later those who completed the four-year course as senior classes have actively functioned during the commencement week.

The Class of 1914 held the first class day program. This program which was simple in its nature preceded the general graduating exercises. At this time the class presented the first manplanted tree on the campus, a maple located on the driveway about seventy-five feet to the left of the Administration Building. This class numbered five students and ad-

1. Grapurchat, May, 1921.

visor, Mr. Joseph E. Avent. They presented the first class
play "Bibi" as a feature of the commencement. These activities
as started by the Class of 1914 have continued as the major
class features of the commencement activities to the present
time. It has been customary for the two-year graduates to present a class play on Friday night of commencement week. After
the organization of the degree or four-year class it became
customary for this group to give a class play in the early
spring. In 1930 the two classes combined and presented the
commencement play.

Class Day for the two-year students has been held on Monday
morning of the commencement. The four-year students since 1921
have held a garden party on Saturday or Monday afternoon.

CLASS GIFTS

Each graduating class has given a gift to the college. The
first of these were drinking fountains in 1915, In 1916, Student
Loan Fund; 1917, Roller curtain for the front of the auditorium
stage; 1918, Liberty bonds for Student Loans; 1919, Contribution
to the portrait of Doctor McConnell; 1920, First section of the
Post Office; 1921, (Degree Class) Statue of Joan D'Arc; 1921,
(Two-year Class) Post office and white caps and gowns; 1922,
(Degree Class) Grecian Flower urn; 1922, (Two-year Class) Iron
entrance gate on Tyler Avenue; 1923, (Degree Class) Stone Grecian
Bench; 1923, (Two-year Class) Rambler Way, Arch and entrance
gates; 1924, Electric light fixtures for Tyler Hall; 1924, Money
for stage properties; 1925, $250.00 for use in Society homes;
1926, (Sophomores) Money for stage properties; 1926, (Seniors)
Plaques for auditorium; 1927, Fireplace fixtures and tapestry
in Madame Russell Hall; 1928, Plaques in the lobby of the Administration Building; 1930, Money for Post Office boxes.

SECTION V

COMMENCEMENT

The pattern for the commencement season of the college was planned by the faculty on May 8, 1914. After an extended discussion as to what should constitute a well balanced program the following general pattern was adopted:

Saturday Night   June 6, Joint program of Literary Societies

Sunday Morning   June 7, Baccalaureate Sermon

Sunday Evening   June 7, Vesper Service

Monday Morning   June 8, Class Day Exercise

Monday Afternoon   June 8, Field Day

Monday Evening   June 8, Pageant

Monday Evening   June 8, Reception to graduates and Visitors

Tuesday Morning   June 9, Graduating Exercises

The following committees were appointed:

To prepare Vesper Service: Miss Terry, Miss Puryear, Miss Baird and Mr. Avent

To Decide on dress and regalia for students and faculty: Miss Moffett, Miss Simmons, Mrs. Brugh

To Supervise Class Day Exercises: Mr. Avent

To have charge of the reception: Miss Bulifant, Miss Harrison, and Miss Denny.[1]

This program was followed as an outline for the first two commencements. After this the graduating exercises were changed from Tuesday morning to Monday evening. The regulations for the commencement as announced for 1925 give a very definite picture of the way in which the commencement season has been conducted at the Radford College for many years.

REGULATIONS FOR COMMENCEMENT

Friday   8:00 P. M. Senior Play. All students expected to attend. Admission 50¢.

Saturday   2:00 to 5:00 P. M. Exhibits: Home Economics, Manual Arts, Fine Arts, Invite everyone to attend these exhibits. All students expected to attend.

1. Faculty Minute Book, Page #5.

Saturday 2:30 P. M. Swimming Meet.

Saturday 3:00 P. M. Alumnae Business Meeting. All second, third, fourth year students must attend.

Saturday 4:00 P. M. Alumnae Reception to graduates. Tyler Hall. All Seniors, second and fourth year must attend.

Saturday 5:00 P. M. Alumnae Reunion. Third and fourth year girls expected to attend.

Saturday 7:30 P. M. Members of the Pocahontas and Ingles Literary Societies meet in their respective halls. Dress, march, and otherwise conduct themselves according to regulations of the society.

Saturday 8:00 P. M. Inter-Society Debate. No student is expected to have company, dates, or any engagement of any kind on Saturday evening longer than one-half hour after the conclusion of the debate program.

Sunday 10:45 A. M. All students meet at Tennis Court for academic procession. All undergraduates wear white dress, white hose, dark shoes, no flowers or colored ribbons.

Sunday 11:00 A. M. Baccalaureate sermon. Every student is required to attend this service.

Sunady 5:00 P. M. Reception to guests of seniors and second year students, Tyler porch. All seniors and second year students are invited and urged to bring their guests to this informal reception given by the college in their honor.

Sunday 7:00 P. M. Vesper service, Y. W. C. A., Oak Grove. This is one of the most impressive and sweetest of all the commencement exercises. Students should make avery effort to be present.

Monday 10:30 A. M. Class Day exercises of second year class. All students of the college should consider it their privilege to honor the second year class by their presence at this program.

Monday 4:00 to
6:00 P. M. Senior Garden Party. Invitations.

Monday 7:30 P. M. All students meet in the Gym for procession.

Monday 8:00 P. M. Graduation exercises. The conclusion of the exercises of the commencement does not end the responsibility of the students to the college. All students are expected to abide by the usual regulations during the commencement and after the commencement is over until they return to their respective homes.

On one occasion in August 1926 the commencement exercise was planned for the evening. Early in the morning Doctor McConnell received a message of the illness of his father which made it imperative for him to leave for Gate City. The students were hurriedly called together. The graduates assembled as many of their friends and parents as they could and the exercises were held at twelve o'clock in the auditorium. With this single exception the commencement exercises have been carried out as indicated in the pattern.

The quarter system makes it possible for a student to complete her course at the end of any quarter. In the beginning the commencement was held whenever a student graduated. Only two commencements were held in March. The numbers graduating at the end of quarters soon centered around December, June, and August. When degrees were conferred it was decided not to confer any until the June commencement. However, all these irregularities have been adjusted so that now only two commencements are held, one in June and one in August. The students who complete courses at the end of the other quarters return for graduation at one of these exercises. The student however is allowed the right to her certificate and the privileges of a graduate as soon as she has completed her course.

ACADEMIC COSTUME AND GOWNING SERVICES

Until 1917 the students wore white dresses for graduation. Beginning at this time the academic costume was adopted as the official dress for the graduates. From 1917 to 1921 all those completing the two-year course wore the black cap and gown. When the degrees were conferred in 1921, the two-year graduates were attired in white caps and gowns; the postgraduate students in gray with purple cords and purple tassels on their caps; the fourth year graduates in the black cap and gown. The Class of 1921 used hoods after the graduation as a feature of their ceremony. The gray gowns were discontinued in 1926. The present custom is for the two-year graduates to wear white caps and gowns and the four-year graduates to wear black caps and gowns. Since 1917 the faculty have worn academic costume which has added greatly to the spectacular effect of the commencement activities.

The first gowning service was held by the Class of 1923. This class adopted the custom of wearing the gown during the last week of one quarter. Practically all of the Senior

Classes have worn the gown at some time during the year to the General Assembly to distinguish them from the other students.

In 1930 the gowning service was instituted as a feature of the campus night program. Following the garden party by the Seniors they were escorted by their "Little Sisters" to the Senior Prominade where they formed a line of march. Miss Elizabeth Jackson as spokesman of the class gave a brief outline of the origin of the academic costume. She then called the name of each Senior who was gowned by her Little Sister; as each knelt for her cap to be placed a suitable remark was made about her personally or her academic achievement. This service was impressive. The class of 1931 held a gowning service similar to that for the Class of 1930 in the auditorium. This service is now held twice a year for the Seniors who are candidates for degrees in August as well as for those who finish in June.

In 1924 with the change of the name of the college and the growth in the number of four-year graduates there was much discussion as to whether the public graduation of two-year students should be continued. However due to the fundamental purpose of the institution to train teachers for the elementary schools the four Presidents of the Teachers Colleges of Virginia decided to continue to emphasize graduation from the two-year course. This necessitated a combination commencement for the two-year and four-year graduates. The invitations have been issued in the name of the faculty and the graduating classes. The features of the program have given equal recognition to the graduates in the two courses. The chief distinction being in academic costume.

COMMENCEMENT CEREMONIALS

An effort has been made to make all of the commencement exercises impressive and through them to stimulate the students toward the higher goals of education.

Since 1914 all of the students have been required to participate in the academic procession. The undergraduates, dressed in white, lead the student group into the auditorium. The line of march forms in the gymnasium. The students march around the Administration Building to enter through the front door. The Presidents of the Student Council, Y. W. C. A., and the two Literary Societies act as the official student marshalls.

In the procession of graduates the two-year graduates entered the auditorium first followed by the four-year graduates followed by the faculty. Since 1928 the faculty have been seated on the stage. The reverse order is used for the recessional. The auditorium is divided into sections and the classes seated in groups, freshmen on the sides and in the balcony, members of the upper three classes who are not graduating, and friends of the graduates and faculty in the middle section. The formal exercises of graduation open with the singing of the Motto and close with the Alma Mater. On several occasions musical programs have been given by the special music department one-half hour before the opening of the formal exercises.

DELIVERY OF DIPLOMAS

Marjorie Combs was the first student to receive a diploma. Until the classes became too large in number Doctor McConnell introduced a unique feature into the delivery of diplomas. As each girl was presented for graduation it was his custom to relate some anecdote of her own or ancestral history; to trace her relationship or to give some analysis of her college achievements. The witticism and humanness of these remarks were looked forward to from one commencement to another. Many a girl as her college life would develop would punctuate it by saying, she hoped that Doctor McConnell would not tell that about her when she graduated.

Until 1928 the graduating exercises were kept as individual and personal for the students as possible. Since then they have been graduated in groups. The classes have been seated in the middle section of the auditorium and the faculty occupied the stage. It is customary for Registrar Whitt to read the list of names at which time the students come to the platform and the diploma is delivered by Doctor McConnell assisted by Dean Moffett.

CONFERRING OF DEGREES

Miss Lorena Caldwell was the first student to receive a degree from the college. From 1921 to 1928 a kneeling service was used as a feature of the graduation exercises at the time the degree was conferred by the President of the College. A pillow, made of grey satin with a band of purple satin, was brought in and placed in front of the Dean. As each student

was presented for graduation she knelt on the cushion facing the
President of the College, as he conferred the degree the hood was
put over the student's head by the Dean of Women and the tassel
was turned.

Since 1928 the classes have been so large that the kneeling
ceremony has been discontinued and the students have been presented in a group for the conferring of the degree. In this service the students turned their own tassel when the degrees are
conferred and the hood is not used.

DIPLOMAS

The diplomas awarded by the institution have been very
simple in design. Until 1930 Miss Simmons, printed the names
of the four-year graduates on their diplomas. The names of
the two-year graduates were written by the teacher of penmanship. A large diploma was used until 1930 when the style was
changed to the folder type. Purple leather covers lined with
grey silk were purchased from the E. A. Wright Company of Philadelphia. Two types of diplomas were designed for the two
classes. The diplomas have always been signed by Doctor Mc-
Connell, the President of the Board, and the State Superintendent of Public Instruction. To date no student has been
graduated who has not had her diploma handed to her by Doctor
McConnell.

PROGRAMS

A printed program, showing the names of the graduates,
honor students and on three occasions a summary of achievement
have been prepared for the exercises.[1]

COMMENCEMENT SPEAKERS

Many distinguished men and some women have delivered the
literary addresses and the baccalaureate sermons at the commencement of the Radford College.[2] On two occasions Doctor
McConnell has conducted what he calls a "home-made" commencement. On one of these he had a series of five-minute talks
made by himself, Paul McConnell, F. B. Fitzpatrick, Mr.
Gilbert, and Doctor Moffett. Only two women other than Doctor
Moffett have delivered commencement addresses, Mrs. John Vines
of Roanoke, Virginia, and Mrs. M. M. Caldwell of Roanoke, Virginia.

1. A complete file of these programs from 1917 are on file in
   the Dean's office.
2. A list of these is shown in the Appendix.

BACCALAUREATE SERVICE

The same line of march as described above has been used for the baccalaureate service with the exception   that all had been seated in the main auditorium with the ministers, President McConnell and the choir on the stage. Until 1929 it was customary for the churches of Radford to join with the college in the baccalaureate service and not hold the regular morning service in the respective churches. A vesper service has been conducted by the Young Women's Christian Association on the portico of the Administration Building. This service is conducted entirely by the students and is devoted to a song service, special pageants and special music. In the early years some local minister was invited to make a short address. In the later years the students have had one of their number to make this address or have presented pageants.

In 1930 the Young Women's Christian Association discontinued the Vesper Service and substituted an afternoon tea in honor of the commencement guest.

SECTION VI

ATHLETICS

The original plan for the Athletic Association organized in 1915 provided for a number of recreational activities through tennis, basketball, swimming, hiking, track, and supervised games under the Department of Physical Education.

The element of competition was confined to inter-mural contests between the various teams which developed in these forms of activities.

INTER-COLLEGIATE ATHLETICS

In 1916 and 1917 Miss Louise Ruggles, then the Director of Physical Education allowed some of her better basketball players to organize a school team. This team in turn played a number of basketball games in competition with some of the high schools of Southwestern Virginia.

With the discontinuance of high school students all such secondary contests were abandoned. Although these games never dominated the athletic interest of the college they did however place emphasis upon basketball as the only inter-school athletic sport. It was easy therefore to build the inter-collegiate spirit around this game.

Basketball reigned supreme on the Radford Campus from 1920 to 1929. To become a member of the Varsity team became the major ambition of the athletically minded students of the college. The entire college community was an enthusiastic supporter of the six or eight students who represented the school in these inter-collegiate contests. Games were held each year with Harrisonburg, Farmville, Sullins, Concord, (Athens, West Virginia), and East Tennessee Normal, Johnson City, Tennessee, and various other organizations and schools. The greatest rivalry, however, existed between the schools at Harrisonburg and Radford. Both of these schools developed very strong and capable teams. The games between the two colleges were hotly contested. The Radford team for many years was unusually successful in all of its contests, as it is shown by the athletic record.[1]

Some of the outstanding basketball players in the history of the Radford College have been: Mary Hayter, Willie Shumate, Lucinda Thomas, Charlsie Camper, Ann Gimbert, Evelyn Shumate, Audrey Baylor, Jeannette Mears, Virginia Perry, Ruby Showalter, Carmen Showalter, Ruth Jenkins, Esther Gobble, Angie Fugate, Ina Russell.

In 1921-1922 Mr. Holden Barnett became very much interested in the Varsity team. He was employed as a referee and accompanied the team on several trips. Later he assisted Miss Fosdick in the coaching. To him and the players the game was so serious that it became their custom to hold prayer before entering a contest.

As the approach of the Harrisonburg game in 1922 the enthusiasm of the students resulted in a gift by them of the bleachers for the gymnasium. These were built by Mr. Roop. They became the scene for gayly bedecked and wildly cheering supporters of the teams. The first cheer leader was Miss Grace Tietje of Roanoke, Louisiana. Miss Tietje was very peppy and under her leadership and with the work of Miss Ella Bishop many songs and cheers were developed and sung by the students.

THE IMPORTANCE OF THE VARSITY

Every member of the Varsity was known on the campus. The pride of the entire institution was centered in these girls. They were the wearers of the purple and gray. Like the gladiators of old they went forth to give all for the sake of their institution. In 1923 the student body united to raise a fund sufficient to purchase purple and gray uniforms for the Varsity.

1. See Appendix.

These consisted of very full pleated gray bloomers worn with
a gray sweater on which was a purple "R". These were the pride
and joy of every student in the college and were worn with great
pride by the members of the Varsity. In 1927 they were replaced
by tight pants style bloomers with a sleeveless gray sweater worn
over a white blouse.

Whenever the team would leave to visit another school its
members had at their disposal all the finery of the institution.
Each student felt it her duty to help "dress up" the team. All
the new clothes, baggage, and other personal paraphenalia were
showered upon the departing warriors. The team was accompanied
to the train by hundreds of students and was sped on its way amid
the din of lusty cheers and songs. As soon as it was out of
sight the students began to pepper the absent team with telegrams
and special delivery letters. Many times the team would receive
dozens of such messages in a single day. It was customary when
the team was visiting another college for the captain or business manager of the team to telephone the score home. For hours
the students would wait this call huddled together as near the
telephone as possible. In case Radford was victorious pandemonium reigned on the campus. Frequently at midnight snake dances
would be held around the dormitories and on the campus.

When teams from other colleges came to Radford the "cutest"
rooms in the dormitory were selected for the guests. Into these
were poured the best sofa pillows, dolls, pennants, couch covers,
etc., of the other girls. Programs were carefully worked out for
for the entertainment of the visitors and the facilities of the
college were taxed to give them a royal reception. Following the
game it was customary for the local association to hold a reception for the visitors. For many years these took the form of an
elaborate meal served in the tea room or a reception to which
the students of Virginia Polytechnic Institute or the young men
of the city were invited.

Around the basketball games many of the most bitter contro-
versies of the institution developed. The remarks, discourtesies,
rash speeches of hot competition and rivalry punctuated all the
visits of the teams from other schools and of the Radford team
when it was visiting. One of the most heated of these came up
between Radford and Farmville over some decision in a game. The
question of referees was always hotly contested. Many of the
referees were brought from Washington and other cities to serve
as officers in the games.

FINANCING THE GAMES

At Radford the Athletic Association was supported through the sale of season tickets to the games. The annual cost for the season for basketball was $500 to $700. Until 1926 it was unnecessary for the school to subsidize from the campus fee any of the athletic activities.

THE WANE OF INTER-COLLEGIATE ATHLETICS

In 1927 the interest in inter-collegiate athletics began to wane. The popular movement to discontinue or prohibit inter-collegiate contests between women students gained impetus in the United States through the influence of the Association of Physical Directors. For some time it had been the opinion of some of the administrators of the Radford College that too much of the interest and enthusiasm of the students was going into these contests and too few girls were receiving the benefit, therefore, in 1929 Doctor Moffett and Miss Ellis proposed to Doctor McConnell the discontinuance of inter-collegiate athletics. No contests of this kind have been held since the season of 1929. The abandonment of this interest has taken out of the institution a certain hilarity of school spirit. The old days of cheering, yelling, and singing of school songs, seems to have passed. From the newspaper reports of other institutions the ballyhoo of athletics is also passing in similar institutions.

INTER-MURAL ATHLETIC PROGRAM

As a substitute for the inter-collegiate program of athletics an inter-mural program was developed in 1929, 1930, and 1931. This program was planned by Miss Wanda Ellis and the officers of the Athletic Association. It places emphasis upon athletic achievement and gives credit towards the numerals and monograms of the college to any student who participates to the extent of two hundred hours in any or many forms of athletic recreation. The students, who through a system of careful checking report this achievement are given the numerals of their respective class. Those who achieved more than the minimum and have an outstanding record as winners of tournaments of basketball games, tennis, golf, swimming, etc. are awarded the monogram of the college.

Tournaments are held each year in swimming and tennis. Neither of these activities have centered around any particular organization or team, the work in both sports being largely individual.

In the early days two tennis clubs were organized, the Avent and the Lovers. These clubs were primarily organizations for representation in the annual and did not function in the athletic program of the college. All contests, except in basketball, have been largely confined to the classes and not to clubs and organizations of the sport.

INTER-HIGH SCHOOL CONTEST

In October 1924 Doctor McConnell appointed a committee composed of Professors William E. Gilbert, chairman, Miss Moffett, Mr. Whitt, and Miss Bryson to study the problems of Inter-high school contests to be held at the Radford College.

The purpose of this contest as conceived by Doctor McConnell was to stimulate interest in certain activities of the students of the high schools and to bring these students to the campus of the Radford College where they in turn might become interested in the activities and opportunities afforded by the college.

In 1909 there was organized in Southwestern Virginia a Southwest Virginia Association of Secondary Schools and Colleges. Mr. Fitzpatrick as principal of a high school in Roanoke was active in this organization. The State organization, now centered at the University, was an outgrowth of this regional movement which originated in Southwestern Virginia. One of the major actions of this organization was an inter-county contest in certain literary and athletic fields.

It was Doctor McConnell's idea to revive to a certain extent an interest in this form of competition in the high schools of Southwest Virginia. He, therefore, proposed to the committee to study the best type of contest to conduct and to set up certain standards and regulations for the contest, determine the prizes, make announcements and give publicity to the proposal. Plans for this contest were carefully developed by the committee under the leadership of Professor Gilbert. A bulletin was issued by the Extension Department announcing the contest. This bulletin set forth the rules for each of the groups of contests. These were representatives of the major interests of the Radford College. The original committee was enlarged to include the Professors of the various departments having an interest in the subjects of the competitions.

THE PROGRAM

April 17-18, 1925

11:00 A. M. Recitation
    Group 1. Ingles Society Hall
    Group 2. Pocahontas Society Hall

12:40 P. M. Luncheon
1:30 P. M. 1. Reading................ Pocahontas Hall
           2. Oration....................Ingles Hall
           3. Essay....................... Room 106
           4. Poster Making.....Manual Arts Room A
2:30 P. M. 5. Swimming................ College Pool
3:00 P. M. Automobile Ride, Courtesy of Members of
           Kiwanis and Rotary Clubs of Radford
5:00 P. M. Reception to all contestants, Tyler Hall
           Parlors
6:00 P. M. Dinner, College dining room
7:00 P. M. Picture Show. "When a Man's a Man". College
           Auditorium
8:30 P. M. Physical Education Demonstration, College
           Gymnasium

Saturday, April 18.

8:30 A. M. (Contests continued)
           1. Bread Making.....Home Economics Dining
                        Room
           2. Meal Planning....Home Economics Dining
                        Room
           3. Dress Selection................ Room 6
           4. Piano...............College Auditorium
           5. Violin........................Room 111
           6. Voice............Miss Baird's Studio
    11:00 A. M. Final Contest in College Auditorium
    12:00 A. M. Awarding of Gold Medals
    12:30 P. M. Luncheon

All contestants and chaperons will be entertained free
by the State Teachers College.

o

CONTEST

Eighty-two students, representatives of the high schools
of Southwest Virginia, competed in twelve activities. The

winners in the contests were, Essay: Hazel Crawford of Bristol,
Virginia; Dress Selection: Frances Vernon of Blacksburg, Virginia;
Piano:Hazel Crawford, Bristol, Virginia; Voice: Florence Price of
Blacksburg, Virginia; Swimming: Margaret Sherwood of Bristol, Vir-
ginia; Recitation: Jeannette Cross of Bristol, Virginia; Oration:
Hilda Davis of Buena Vista, Virginia; Bread Making: Hattie Wall
of Blacksburg, Virginia; Meal Planning: Phoebe Wall, Blacksburg,
Virginia; Violin: Susie Cutherell of Blacksburg, Virginia; Poster
Making: Elsie Calhoun, Belspring, Virginia; Reading, Helen Brown,
East Radford, Virginia.

Nearly all the contestants were accompanied by their teachers. Gold medals made according to original designs by the
Robbins Company were delivered to the winners. Most of these
were presented as a part of the commencement exercises of the
local schools from which the students came.

SECTION VIII

MUSIC

INSTRUCTORS

The musical activities of the College have been largely a
reflection of the personalities, talents, and leadership of the
various instructors of music.

Miss Florence C. Baird was appointed the first professor of
Public School Music at the Radford College. She was one of the
outstanding personalities of the first faculty. She is a woman
of striking personal appearance and was long known as the most
stylish person on the faculty. Her poise, social technique, and
temperament gave her great influence on the early student life.
Music was her major interest and hobby. She was enthusiastic,
persevering and untiring in her efforts to advance the cause of
music.

Public School Music was a requirement in all the curricula
of the college. As teacher of these courses Miss Baird was able
to impress her personality on all the students. This contact
gave her far reaching influence in their various extra class activities. The interest in music grew so rapidly that it has been
necessary throughout the history of the school to have a teacher
of Public School Music, a teacher of piano, and for several
years assistants in the Piano Department and a teacher of Voice.

The teachers have been: Miss Florence C. Baird, Public School
Music, 1913-1922; in 1922 Miss Baird resigned her position in
Public School Music and became teacher of Voice and Piano. At
that time she opened a studio in Roanoke and spent only one day
at the college. Miss Lizzie Faye James, Piano, 1913-1916; Miss
Grace Jewett, Piano, 1917-1919; Miss Edith Ashworth, Piano, 1919;
Miss Alice S. Jones, Voice, 1918; Miss Dorothy Rich, Piano, 1919-
1921; Miss Anna N. Jett, Voice, 1921; Miss Bruna Sprole, Piano,
1921; Miss Grace A. Jewett, Public School Music, 1923-1926; Mrs.
Henry Stone, Assistant in Piano, 1923; Miss Frances Kittrell,
Public School Music, 1922; Miss Alice Gleaves, Violin, 1920-1927;
Miss Florence C. Baird, Piano and Voice, 1922-1928; Miss Madeline
Guthrie, Piano, 1925; Miss Edmee Smith, Public School Music, 1927-
1931; Miss Harriett C. Perkins, Piano, 1928; Mrs. John Einstein,
Voice, 1918; Miss Ruhama Clem, Piano, 1930.

MUSIC IN COLLEGE ACTIVITIES

The musical history of the college opens with a faculty recital given in the Fall of 1913. This is the first and only recital ever given by the faculty. The report of this occasion is
taken from the first annual. The recital was, in a way, an illustrated lecture on the appreciation and history of music. The
numbers on the program represented different types of music,
from rote songs to classical, involving all the basic principles
of vocalization. Miss Baird had previously given the students a
talk as to the purpose and scope of the selections rendered, thus
preparing them for a more thorough and critical appreciation of
the program.

PROGRAM

Row us Swiftly - Vocal Trio ....Campana
Misses Baird, James, Terry
Impromptu in A Flat, Piano Solo ....Shubert
Miss James
Aria and Cavitina, Vocal Solo..................Shubert
Miss Baird
Selected, Violin Solo............................
Mr. E. S. Jones
Go, Pretty Rose, Vocal Duet...................Marzials
Misses Baird and James
Wouldn't you Like to Know? - Vocal Solo...... Linding
Miss James
Fruhlingarauschen, Piano Solo................. Linding
Air de Ballet, No. 2 - Piano Solo..........Chaminade
Miss Darst

Rote Song
No Sir - Vocal Solo........................ Old English
Miss Baird
Danza.. Chadwick
Sognoi...Schira
Holy Night......................................Adam
Selected, Vocal Solo...........................
Mr. E. S. Jones
Rest Thee, Vocal Trio.........................Smart
Misses Baird, James and Terry

ASSEMBLY SINGING

The conducting of the Assembly singing has been the duty of
the teachers of Public School Music. It has been customary to
have much singing as a part of the program of the Assembly. The
type and quality of this singing has varied with the interest
and abilities of the times and attention to the singing of heart
songs and old melodies. During her leadership of the Assembly
singing the "Golden Book of Songs" and "Twice Fifty-Five" song
books were most commonly used. The first book purchased for use
in the Auditorium was "The School and Assembly Book". In this
book on Page six, "All is Good, Great, and True" became the
popular and traditional song for use when nothing else could be
produced in Assembly. Miss Jewett's favorite song was "Onward
Christian Soldiers" and this became a traditional song in Assembly. Through the efforts of Miss Edmee Smith a new book on "The
Assembly Hymnal and Song Book" has been purchased. This book is
now in use. The Assembly is always opened with a hymn. The religious and secular parts of the program are divided by another
hymn or classical song. Frequently the entire program is devoted
to group singing of popular, classical and "pep" songs.

Miss Jewett organized a choir for the General Assembly. This
group of students opened the Assembly by a processional through
the auditorium to the stage. Here they were seated in a group
and led the hymns and the group singing of the Assembly. The
choir was used for one year. Although it added greatly and improved the music it delayed the Assembly by the inability of the
students to gather promptly at ten o'clock.

GLEE CLUBS

Miss Baird organized a Glee Club composed of the students of
special musical talent at the opening of the first year of the

College. Under her leadership it was one of the most active
student organizations on the campus. Miss Baird was exacting
in her standards for membership, attention to practice, loyalty and quality of program. The public programs of this club
were "red letter" occasions.

Miss Baird was quite adaptable in the use of dance steps
and costuming to add to the effectiveness of these programs.
Her originality, ability to write words, and compose music
was shown in all of her programs. She wrote a "Hello Song"
for one of her programs which became very popular. Each
program worked up to a dramatic or spectacular climax. The
Gypsy was a favorite theme.

Miss Kittrell emphasized group singing and popular music in
the Glee Club. She was a different type of person from any
other teacher of music who has been associated with the college. She had unusual vivacity of spirit. She came to the
college at the time that jazz and popular music was at its
height. She was an effective leader of this popular music.
Miss Jewett who succeeded Miss Kittrell was particularly fond
of weird, soft, and sonata music. She was fond of moonlight
effects and dreamy music. This she emphasized very much in
the type of songs selected for the Glee Club. One of her
favorite numbers was a Balcony Scene with moonlight, softly
sung accompanied with string instruments. Her sister from
California was a most able assistant to Miss Jewett in the
Glee Club Work. The younger Miss Jewett contributed a number
of solos. Her most popular was "Out Where the West Begins".
While Miss Jewett was director of the Glee Club it was affiliated with the State Federation of Music Clubs.

With the coming of Miss Edmee Smith in 1927 the students
of musical talent of the college were divided into two groups.
She had the advanced club composed of Sophomores, Seniors, and
Juniors federated with the State and named for John Powell. A
freshman Glee Club was named for Mrs. Stillman Kelly, President
of the National Federation of Music Clubs.

In later years the Glee Clubs have been open to any student
of the college who wished to join. The better voices are
grouped and trained for the special programs by the organization.

CHORAL CLUB

The students of special music under the direction of Miss Florence C. Baird first, later by Mrs. John Einstein are organized into the college choral club. This club is used for very special musical productions. This organization is usually featured at the annual spring recital of the music departments and the commencement season. Many of the talented women of the city of Radford have contributed to the success of this organization. Among these are Miss Alice Jones, Miss Elsie Jones, Mrs. Lillian Staunton Waldrige, Mrs. Kirkwood, Mrs. Sophie Jones Sublett, Miss Alma Smith, Mrs. Walter Roberts, Mrs. Hattie Linkous. The Glee Clubs and the Choral Club have frequently been the representatives of the Radford College at the Educational and Community League Meetings held in the neighboring communities. Each year representatives of these organizations make trips to Riner, Floyd, Narrows, Pearisburg, or other nearby places with Professors Fitzpatrick and Gilbert to give special musical programs and features for the teachers and community leagues of these localities.

The Choral Club has participated in two State contests sponsored by the State Federation at Roanoke in 1930, and at Charlottesville in 1931. In 1927 the Glee Club broadcast from the Roanoke Broadcasting Station in connection with a program by Southwestern Virginia Incorporated.

PUBLIC RECITALS

It is a custom for the special teachers of voice, piano, and violin to hold annual recitals.[1] During the years when Miss Guthrie and Miss Gleaves worked together they held a series of Chamber Recitals, one a month, for the younger piano students. One year Miss Baird offered a prize to the student making the most improvement in piano. This prize was won by Miss Elsie Jones.

VIOLIN AND ORCHESTRA

Mrs. W. C. McCarthy, wife of the Executive Secretary of the Young Men's Christian Association of Southwestern Virginia, was a talented violinist. She gave instruction in violin and organized the first college orchestra in 1914.

Mrs. McCarthy was succeeded by Miss Alice Gleaves as teacher of violin. Miss Gleaves came from her home in Wytheville and spent two or three days each week at the college. Through her

1. Several typical programs are shown in the Appendix.

efforts the small orchestra which had been organized by Mrs. McCarthy was developed and the violin department became very large and active. Miss Gleaves was most generous with her music. The orchestra played for many of the public exercises at the college. Once each year she gave a recital. These recitals were outstanding for the artistic presentation of music.

Miss Gleaves is a lover of flowers. Her studio, located in Room 108 of the Administration Building for many years was later moved to the Helen Henderson Hall. This was always filled with beautiful flowers. For her special recitals she brought many plants and cut flowers from her home in Wytheville. Each fall she contributed much to the pleasure of the college students by her generosity in supplying the college with beautiful dahlias.

THE CASSELL HARP

To encourage talent in violin, Mrs. George Cassell, wife of Judge Cassell, offered a prize known as the "Cassell Harp". This harp was given to the student making the most progress in violin during the year. It was awarded by Judge Cassell at the commencement exercises. The winners of the harp have been James Cord, Lorene Caldwell, Alma Smith, Billy Burton, Gertrude Shumate, Elinor Bryant; other talented violinists in the student group have been Eugenia Patterson, Isabelle Hoge, and Jakie Lepchitz.

Mr. J. W. Comstock who was employed in 1929 gives instruction in all the orchestral instruments and mandolin and guitar. He has a small orchestra. The spring of 1931 Mr. Comstock is projecting the organization of a brass band. In 1924 the college purchased a number of brass instruments for band and orchestral purposes. These have been loaned to the students and many of them have learned to play. Mr. Comstock's present effort is to organize a band. In 1929-1930 he organized a mandolin and guitar club.

From time to time throughout the history of the college the Radford band, directed by Mr. Sembler, has given concerts on the campus of the College.

Mr. E. S. Jones

No history of the musical activities of the Radford College would be complete without some record and tribute to the loyalty and work of Mr. E. S. Jones, popularly known as "Singing

Bill Jones of Southwestern Virginia." Until his death in
1929 he was unfailing in his musical contributions to the
life of the college. Soon after the opening of each fall
and summer quarters he would sing in the General Assembly
period. No voice ever filled the auditorium and his hear-
ers with such pleasure and satisfaction as did Mr. Jones.
On the occasion of Warrenrath's visit to Radford many people
remarked they would rather hear Mr. Jones. He was a natural
musician. He never received any training except from his
daughter Miss Alice Jones. He was generous with his music
and had a keen sense in the selection of appropriate music
for all occasions. Since his death his daughter Mrs. Sophia
Sublett has come to us in the same capacity as her father as
one of the chief Assembly singers.

COLLEGE SONGS

ALMA MATER

Hail, all hail, to our Alma Mater!
Bare our heads, make the welkin ring;
Here's our hearts and our fond allegiance,
Honors to her we bring.
Praise her broad and her lofty aim,
Her purpose ne'er will fail.
Hail to thee, our Alma Mater,
Hail, all hail!

Hail, all hail, to our Alma Mater!
Let this slogan be heard for aye;
May her name with immortal names
Be blazened across the sky.
Year by year shall her power increase,
Her splendor ne'er will pale,
Hail to thee, our Alma Mater,
Hail, all Hail!

Hail, all hail, to the Radford Normal!
Give three cheers, and then one cheer more;
Let the praise of our Alma Mater
Echo from shore to shore;
She is ours and our loyalty
Will never, never fail.
Hail to thee, our Alma Mater,
Hail, all hail!

In 1913 Miss Baird wrote the Alma Mater. This was adopted by the students and faculty as the official song of the college. It has been sung on all formal and many informal occasions since 1913.

The class song of 1922, written by Annie McConnell, Mrs. June McConnell Graybeal, and Mrs. Clara Carner, was an adaptation of the Motto set to the tune of Sol Mio.

> If we work on marble, it will perish;
> If we work on brass, time will efface it;
> But if we work on immortal minds,
> We engrave something that will shine always.
>
> Chorus:
> Oh, Radford College,
> We dearly prize
> The precepts you've set
> Before our eyes.
> All hail, our Alma Mater,
> We'll loyal be--
> Your daughters.

This motto was so popular and favorably received by the college that it was soon adopted as another one of the official songs and has been used for the opening number at many formal convocations. The motto is usually sung, then hummed through, and sung again in dimuendo fashion.

In 1930 Miss Lillian Smith, a graduate of the College, wrote the toast to the college. She set it to the tune of Yale Boola Song.

> Among the hills in the great Southwest
> Is the college we'll always love the best
> She spares not time nor effort small
> To be faithful to us when'ere we call.
> We'll sing her praises ever more
> From mountain top to shore.
> Let us drink her health with hearts sincere
> And her honor hold always very dear.
>
> Chorus:
> Radford College! Radford College!
> We are singing, praises ringing.
> Hail the pride of Old Virginia;
> Radford College, here's to you!

This song is very popular at the present time but it has not lived long enough for it to be given a permanent place.

The Ingles Society song "Ingles Born and Ingles Bred," was an adaptation of a popular song of 1913.

> Maroon and tan will wave on high,
> The Ingles spirit will never die.
> Rah, rah, oh, Ingles, Ingles,
> Rah, rah, oh, Ingles, Ingles,
> Rah, rah, oh, Ingles,
> Rah, rah, rah!
>
> We're Ingles born, we're Ingles bred,
> And when we die we're Ingles dead,
> Rah, rah, oh, Ingles, Ingles,
> Rah, rah, oh, Ingles, Ingles,
> Rah, rah, oh, Ingles,
> Rah, rah, rah!
>
> Where'er we stay, where'er we roam,
> The Ingles Hall is always home,
> Rah, rah, oh, Ingles, Ingles,
> Rah, rah, oh, Ingles, Ingles,
> Rah, rah, oh, Ingles,
> Rah, rah, rah!

In 1921 Gertrude Shumate and Grace Tietje set the Motto, "Give to the World the best you have and the best will come back to you", to a chant rhythm.

The Pocahontas Society had no definite society song until 1923 when Miss Mamie McLees wrote "Our Redskin Maid" which has been the official song of the society since:

> Pocahontas of Indian Story,
> Pocahontas, Virginia's glory!
> Pokies love you, heap much too,
> Pocahontas, we are not afraid,
> Just like you our redskin maid,
> Pocahontas, our tribal queen.
>
> Pocahontas, we heap much love
> You, like stars that shine above;
> Make us see the victory.
> Pocahontas in copper and green
> Like forest tree with autumn sheen--
> Pocahontas, our tribal queen.

The National Association of the Young Women's Christian Association adopted "Follow the Gleam" as the official song of the "Y.W." Since this song has been used very extensively by the Young Women's Christian Association and other religious organizations on the campus.

> To the knights in the days of old,
> Keeping watch on the mountain heights,
> Came the vision of Holy Grail,
> And a voice through the waiting night--
>
> Follow, follow, follow the gleam,
> Banners unfurled o're all the world,
> Follow, follow, follow the gleam,
> Of the chalice that is the grail.
>
> And we who would serve the King,
> And loyally him obey,
> In the consecrated silence know
> That the challenge still holds today.
>
> Follow, follow, follow the gleam,
> Standards of worth o're all the earth,
> Follow, follow, follow the gleam
> Of the light that shall bring the dawn.

PEP OR ATHLETIC SONGS

The inter-collegiate basketball reached its height in 1921-1922. Up to this time there has been no particular effort made to organize cheering and grandstand support of the teams. During this year under the direction of Grace Tietje, many pep songs and yells were developed. She was assisted in this development of pep and spirit by the Shumate girls, Miss Moffett, Miss Ellis, Elsie Tompkins, Ella Bishop, and Holden Barnett. During the daily recreation period these songs were taught to the students. They were lustily sung on all occasions. The jazz age as a reaction to the World War made boisterous, loud singing popular. Under the leadership of the group named above the students were taught to snake dance. Many times the recreation period would be given over to snake dancing or pep meetings on the campus. At ball games, the gymnasium would ring with the cheering and songs of the routers. Each game was opened with a snake dance. On several occasions the entire student body danced into the gymnasium. Between halves they would form R. N. S. or R. T. C. on the floor

with their bodies swaying and bending in unison to the rhythm
of the songs.

The athletic association published the first yell and song
book for the college in 1920-1921. This book contains the words
of the more popular songs at that time. During this year some of
these songs were:

ATHLETIC SONG

Radford! Radford! Show the world how to play.
We are here to win this game today.
So show your might, girls!
FIGHT girls!
Roll up the score today
And bring victory to the
Purple and the Gray!

Radford! Radford! Keep your eye on the ball.
We are here to back you one and all.
So show your PEP, girls,
STEP girls.
Take all the goals today
And bring victory to the PURPLE and the GRAY.

---Florence C. Baird.

Oh! Radford they say "She ain't got
No speed!" Ain't got no speed?
Got speed all the while
Got speed all the while
Oh! Radford they say "Ain't got no speed
Got speed all the while
All the while, all the while.

Oh! Radford they say "She ain't got no
Pep." Ain't got no pep?
Got pep all the while!
Got pep all the while!
Oh! Radford they say she ain't got no pep!
Got pep all the while!
All the while all the while.

Oh! Radford they think "She ain't got the
ball!" Ain't got the ball?

Got the ball all the while!
Got the ball all the while!
Oh! Radford they think "She ain't got the ball!"
Got the ball all the while!
All the while, all the while!

———————

Stand'em on their heads!
Stand'em on their feet!
Radford! Radford!
Can't be beat!

Many yells were developed.   One of the most popular yells at
that time was:

Two, four, six, eight
Who do we appreciate?

For the Alumnae luncheon June 5, 1922, Miss McLees prepared a
number of songs of local hits.   These proved so successful that
during the next year these songs with many other popular college
songs were combined by a committee, Miss McLees, Chairman, into
a Radford Songbook.   This book has been on sale in the college
book store since and is used for assemblies and rallies of the
students and the graduates of the college.

STATE MUSIC ASSOCIATIONS

From 1913 to 1928 Miss Baird was a dominant figure in the
musical life of the State.   During the first years of the college she was active in her efforts to have music made a requirement with credit in the secondary schools of the State.   Miss
Baird was most active in the organization of the music section
of the State Educational Conference, later the Virginia Music
Teachers Association.   Through her efforts private and public
music teachers were brought together in the common cause "to
get recognition for music."   With this as the motive the standards and quality of musical instruction was raised.   Many people
joined the Association.   Miss Baird was the dominant force in
the entire group.   She served as President and in various other
offices.   She wrote many articles, made many speeches, and attended many conventions in her untiring efforts to advance
music.   Much of the present status of music is due to this initial work.

In April 1924 the Virginia Music Teachers State Association held its annual convention at the Radford College. Miss Baird was the hostess for the College for the entertainment of the convention.[1]

Mr. Ernest Cosby of Richmond was President of the organization. Many of the leading musicians of Virginia visited the college at this time. John Powell, Virginia's greatest pianist gave a piano recital and addressed the convention.

The chief feature of the program was a recital by Reginald Warrenrath. This was the most pretentious performance ever undertaken by the College and Radford community. The Radford Music Club, State Association and the College guaranteed $1,000.00 for the recital. Strenuous and successful efforts were made to sell the high priced tickets. The young men of the city of Radford were the ushers, this was the first time that full evening dress was worn by men in the college auditorium. For years all musical programs were compared to this great gala event.

FOLKLORE SOCIETY

In 1913 a Folklore Society was organized by Professor William E. Gilbert. The purpose of this organization was to "discover, collect, and publish certain traditional customs, beliefs, ideals, coloquialism, ballads, folk songs, and other historic and traditional matter.[2] The society devoted its time first to collecting English and Scotch ballads, and folk songs. Many of these songs are still sung in Southwest Virginia. A special effort was made by Professor Gilbert, Miss Baird, and Doctor McConnell to interest students in the ballads. The students collected some very old ballads from their home communities. "Sourwood Mountain" supposed to have originated in Russell County near the home of Professor Gilbert, became very popular in the school. Words of this song were taught to the students by Miss Baird and as long as she was identified with the college it was sung frequently. In the last few years Mr. Whitt has adopted this song as a solo and entertains the students of the college once or twice each year with his rendition of the ballad.

One of the most enthusiastic workers in the collecting of those ballads is Miss Alfreda Peal of Salem, Virginia. She has been a student at the Radford College during many summer quarters. Each summer she gives a program of the ballads she has collected. She has contributed a number of collections to the Virginia Collection of Ballads by Doctor Alfonso C. Smith. Doctor Smith once

1. News Notes, April 5, 1924.
2. Organization Number. Volume I, Number 2.

told Doctor McConnell that Miss Peal was the best ballad singer
in the English speaking world.

The Literary Societies have also devoted some attention to
the study of ballads.

SECTION VIII.

DRAMATICS

During 1913-1914 the B B Dramatic Club was organized by a group of students interested in dramatic art who were gathered together and coached for several plays by Miss Blanche Bulifant. This club is the only so-called dramatic club the college has ever had. It was abolished in 1915 and dramatics were included as an integral part of the work of the Literary Societies. Through its efforts, however, the first scenery for use in presentation of plays was made. Mr. Roop made an indoor set on a heavy wooden frame and covered it with white duck. This was used for many years for all interior scenes. It required about one-half day for a man to put it in place. Miss Bulifant and Miss Baird were the chief coaches of dramatics in the early years.

CLASS PLAYS

Mr. Avent sponsor of the Senior Class coached the first class play "Bibi". With this play it became the custom for the graduating class to present a play as a feature of the commencement exercises. This practice has been continued to the present time. These plays usually have been coached by the class advisor. For many years the play was given without admission and was offered as an entertainment feature for commencement guests. Later an admission fee was charged for the benefit of the senior class, the proceeds were used for a class gift.

COURSES IN EXPRESSION

In 1918 Miss Elizabeth Sheffield Allen was employed as teacher of Expression and Dramatic Art. This was the first effort to give formal instruction in dramatic expression. All of the students were required to take courses in Expression. These courses were designed to train students in reading and to help them to arrange recital programs, plays, festivals and to develop a naturalness of expression through the presentation of readings, essays, and orations. This course proved very popular and the halls of the dormitories echoed the expressive "ah's, ah's, ah's" of the would-be actresses. The students entertained their friends by giving demonstrations of a "leading-hand" on exaggerated posture of the hand which they were being taught in class.

Miss Allen became the official dramatic coach. She was quite talented in this work and developed the talents of the students.

She presented a series of well given plays. She made an outstanding contribution to the college through her own dramatic
work. Each year she gave a recital. "Esmeralda" was one of
her favorite presentations. She gave this on several occasions.
She was both a reader of tragedies and comedy. She was exacting
in her standards of stage presentation and costuming. She also
gave courses in public speaking. From time to time she would
present her students in addresses at the General Assembly.

With the crowding of the curriculum to meet the standard
requirements of the State it became necessary to discontinue
this department. Miss Allen resigned in 1922. Courses in Oral
English were incorporated in the offerings of the English Department. These courses were taught by advanced students who
had studied courses in Expression. Some of these were Misses
Elizabeth Brown, Annie Sue Anderson, Helen Smith, Genevieve Giesen
and Catherine Hensley.

In 1927 Miss Florence Belle Ogg, who had received training
in the Emerson School of Expression in Boston, was employed as
a teacher in the English Department. She became responsible for
the courses in Oral English.

As long as Miss Baird was with the college she was one of
the most active dramatic coaches especially of musical comedies
and operettas. In 1915 she presented a Gypsy Operetta. This
was an original production written by herself. This operetta
was based on a visit of some American girls to Japan which gave
an opportunity for an effective stage setting. One of the chief
stars was Miss Ada Jennings, a very fine and striking young woman
who in the play acted the part as chaperon for the American girls.
(Miss Jennings gave promise of a very fine and successful career
but unfortunately in a year or two after she left the college
she died with typhoid fever. She was the first student to die
who had ever attended the college. The operetta in which she
made her debut at Radford was also given at Blacksburg.

In 1916 Miss Moffett coached the presentation of Tennyson's
"The Princess". In the last few years Mrs. Whitt and Dr. Hudson
have coached most of the class and society plays.

PAGEANTS

From time to time the faculty advisors and students have attempted original plays and pageants. In the spring of 1915 Miss
Baird wrote a very elaborate pageant based on the theme of education. This pageant was given on the campus near the tennis
court. Each department of the college gave dramatic demonstrations

of the work of the department. Music appropriate to these activities was written by Miss Baird. Marches and rhymetic movements were taught each group. The queen of Education sat enthroned throughout the performance. This part was taken by
Miss Georgia Morris, a beautiful young woman. This was one of
the outstanding early productions of the students and faculty.
It was well attended by the public and gave a splendid summary
of the opportunities of education.

In 1922 another pageant based on the history and develop-
ment of Southwestern Virginia was presented as a May Day feature.
This pageant introduced the historical characters of Southwestern
Virginia and laid special emphasis upon the history of the edu-
cational institutions of this state introducing the characters
who were instrumental in the founding of these various colleges.
The pageant reached its climax in the establishment of Radford
College.

In 1928 Miss Moffett wrote a pageant "Call of Virginia"
which was given as a feature of the Allegaynianna program. This
pageant brought in the various counties of the State and the
contributions of each county to the economic and social development of the State. As a feature of the program each county
brought some trophy to the college. The character, Virginia,
was taken by Miss Blanche Daniels. The dances worked out by
Miss Wanda Ellis were appropriate for the activities and resources of the State.

A pageant to commemorate the Bi Millennium of Vergil was
one of the outstanding achievements of the Latin Club, 1930.

SOME RADFORD STARS

Miss Elizabeth Brown was one of the most talented student
in dramatic art. Throughout her entire four years as a student
she made a large contribution to the dramatic life of the college. She dramatized Dickens' Christmas Carol as the first play
given by the Pocahontas Literary Society. She also dramatized
many Indian sketches for use by the society at Pow Wow's and
special programs. She was a successful actress and director
of plays. She took all the courses in Expression given by Miss
Allen. Upon Miss Allen's resignation she continued the department of Expression and she was followed by Miss Genevieve Giesen
a very good student of dramatics. Miss Giesen also had the power
and gift to dramatize. She devoted her talent and attention to
the Pocahontas Society. Miss Ruth Bricker was a very gifted
actress. She took an active part in the plays of the college

during her four years of work. It is said she could die more gracefully than any student in the college. She starred as the heroine in "Smiling Through".

Some of the other students who may be classified as college stars are: Misses Louise Steele, Vera Harmon, Louise Hartsel, Annie Sue Anderson, Virginia Porter, Dorrence Smith. No effort was made to keep the programs as they were given in the college until 1920. From that time on a record of the dramatic presentations has been preserved.

LYCEUM

Mr. Gilbert was appointed chairman of public exercises in the first committee appointments made by Doctor McConnell. He has served in this capacity to the present time. The first duty of this committee was to organize and select the programs for the Lyceum course. During the first several years five or six lyceum numbers were given each year. Season tickets for these numbers were sold to the students and faculty. Practically all the students bought tickets and attended all of the programs. These included speakers, musicians, and plays. During the first year of 1913-1914 the Lyceum course consisted of: The Euclid Male Quartet; The Hoosier Schoolmaster, by Mr. Noah Beilbarz; Simon Says Wig Wig, by Mr. Booth Lowry; the Boston Lyrics; Beaulah Buch Quartette. This list is typical of those given for several years. Some of the most popular lyceum numbers brought by Mr. Gilbert to the college are: The Orpheus Four, The Harp Trio, Seven Engagements by the Clifford Devereux actors, Swiss Bell Ringers, David Honey, Jitney Players, Hinshaw Opera Company.

CHAUTAUQUA ASSOCIATION

In 1914 the College cooperated with many citizens of the city of Radford in establishing a Chautauqua Association. Under the auspices of the Chautauqua Association of Swarthmore, Pennsylvania this organization presented a Chautauqua in Radford for the years of 1914, 1915, 1916, 1917, 1918, 1919, 1921, 1924, 1925. These were held during the summer and were well attended by the students, faculty, and citizens of Radford. A Chautauqua tent was located on the present site of the American Legion Hut midway between East and West wards at Connelly's Run. Under the auspices of the organization many prominent speakers were brought to Radford. A junior Chautauqua was conducted for the benefit of the children of the town.

The Chautauqua flourished until after the war, then interest waved. In 1924 the Chautauqua affiliation was revived but the program did not pass off successfully. In 1925 Doctor McConnell again entered into an agreement with the Association to support the Chautauqua to the extent of $600.00 provided the programs were given on the College campus. This was accepted by the association and the guarantors of Radford. The tent was pitched between Tyler Hall and the foundations of the society homes. This was one of the most interesting Chautauquas ever given. Particularly noteworthy performances were given by Miss Clemens, (a cousin of Mark Twain) and a magician. This Chautauqua since it was brought to the campus of the College attracted more of the students and the College had no difficulty in raising the $600.00 guarantee, however, the interest of the city guarantors had completely waned so the Chautauquas were discontinued after 1925.

With the development of the motion picture, amateur shows and recreation the general interest in the lyceum course died. Mr. Gilbert discontinued his contract with a Lyceum Bureau. Since then he has employed such speakers and performers as the resources of the College permitted.

The early appropriations made by the State Legislature provided for lyceum courses and part payment of the course from school funds. This fund was discontinued in the reorganization of 1926.

Since the lyceum numbers must be entirely self-supporting Mr. Gilbert has been very successful in the business arrangements which he has made. After a few years he ceased giving a guarantee, only those who will come on a percentage basis have been allowed to come to the college. Under this arrangement he has brought the Stratford Players during the summer of 1929-1930, the Jitney Players in 1929-30; The Devereux Players have been at the college so many times that they are almost a part of the institution. Mr. Clifford Devereux with Miss Zeda Graft have appeared in many different plays. One of their favorite presentations was "Ibsen's Rosmersholm","Romeo and Juliet", "The Rivals" "Twelfth Night", and many other of Shakespeare's plays.   Mr. Devereux was responsible for the designing and sale to the institution of the present stage curtains. Miss Graft became an honorary member of the Pocahontas Society. Whenever the Devereux Company performs in Radford the Pocahontas Literary Society gives a reception in honor of Miss Graft. Their last Radford performance was in 1928.

MOTION PICTURES

The college installed a motion picture machine in the auditorium in 1921. An arrangement on the percentage basis was made with Mr. Walter Roberts then owner of the Dreamland Theater to furnish the college with films. A show was given once a week. For many years these were very popular, the students attended in great crowds. Mr. Gilbert managed this project for one year and was succeeded by Mr. W. R. Bowers who has carried this responsibility as his major extra class activity for many years. Tom Gravatt has been the chief operator.

With the development of the "talkie" the silent picture has lost its appeal so that now the machine is seldom used except for educational reels.

A reel of college life at Radford was made in the summer of 1927. This reel is kept as a historic record.

STUNT NIGHT

In 1916 the Young Women's Christian Association started the custom of having an annual stunt night. On this occasion each of the classes give a stunt in competition for a prize. The first of these prizes was a banner which was held by the winning class until the next year. Later a money prize for the best stunt was offered.

An original stunt is presented by each of the classes. For many years the stunts were designed to provoke laughter through comic situations. Then came the World War, during this period the stunts were mostly patriotic. Following the war the reaction was again to humor. For the last seven years they have been designed to show artistic features. Some of the outstanding stunts given by the classes were "I dreamed I dwelt in marble halls" played by the degree class in 1923. Probably this is the most artistic stunt that has ever been given. A "Here and There" patriotic stunt given during the war by two of the classes showed the life in the trenches by the soldiers on one side of the stage and on the other scenes in college life. This was very touching and contrasted the agony of war with the frivolity of girls left at home.

For a number of years the faculty joined with the students on this occasion by presenting a stunt. The faculty stunt was given while the judges were preparing their decision as to the best of the class stunts. The students looked forward to these

stunts with a great deal of interest and the faculty worked
whole heartedly in the the presentation of some ridiculous scene.
On one occasion they gave a return to childhood: the scene presented a one room school in which all the faculty were supposed
to be students and played the part of some typical school child.
Doctor McConnell, the dull boy, Miss Moffett and Mr. Avent twins;
Mr. Avent was a small man and Miss Moffett a very large woman;
girls with curls, bad boys, smart children in reading, writing,
and arithmetic, were all shown off by the teacher (Miss Baird)
for the benefit of proud parents. On another occasion the faculty presented a stunt representing an "Old Maids' Meeting and a
Bachelor's Convention."

Stunt night has been one of the best money making schemes
of the students. It was so successful for this purpose and as
an entertainment feature that for many years it has been given
during the summer quarter as well as during the fall. For many
years the stunts for the summer quarter were given by various
county clubs. On one fourth of July these stunts started at ten
o'clock in the morning and continued throughout the day with one
hour intermission for lunch. Each county represented in the
student body gave a stunt. An entire day, July 4th, was consumed
in the program. After this trying experience the summer stunts
were given by the four classes.

CARNIVALS AND BAZAARS

Carnivals and bazaars were two of the most effective ways
of raising money in the early days of the college. The first
big carnival was staged by the freshman class of 1915. It converted the Gymnasium into a carnival grounds with booths, fortune
tellers, and many devices of entertainment. The adjacent class
rooms were converted into side shows, strong men, snake eaters,
and other types of tricks and devices were displayed. Home Economics Department sold hot cakes and syrup, pop corn, apples,
candy, flowers were peddled through the audience. Hundreds of
people attended the carnival, two hundred dollars was realized
as the result.

In 1915 the Young Women's Christian Association sponsored
a Christimas Bazaar. Many students made Christmas gifts, fancy
work and novelties of all kinds to sell. Similar carnivals and
bazaars have been held many times throughout the history of the
college but none has been so successful as the first one.

DANCING

Physical Education was introduced as a requirement in the curriculum at the opening of the college in 1913. Dancing on the other hand was a forbidden activity and at no time has dancing with men been allowed on the campus. This regulation is consistent with the ideals and beliefs of the majority of the parents of the students who have attended this institution. The students, however, have been allowed to dance informally with each other in the dormitories.

In 1915 some students organized an Imps' German Club. Its activities were confined to dormitory groups and "girl dances" in the gymnasium.

The first dancing "shock" in the institution fell on the night of December 4, 1916 when Miss Ninde, Director of Physical education attired in a beautiful black silk ballet costume, black silk scarf, black silk hose, and a red rose in her hair gave a solo dance as a feature of the Christmas party. This dance by Miss Ninde was literally a sensation. The skill and grace with which she danced was appreciated by those who were not opposed to dancing, for those who were it became a subject of great discussion. This episode however broke the ice and started aesthetic dancing in the institution. Miss Ninde was gifted in this art and developed and trained a number of girls to be good dancers. Under her direction many beautiful pantomines were worked out with the stunt programs and in the annual demonstrations by the Physical Education class.

Miss Ninde was succeeded as director of Physical Education by Miss Fosdick who paid very little attention to aesthetic dancing. She was succeeded by Miss McMurran and Miss Clark both of whom were talented dancers. They introduced dancing as a feature of the May Day festivals. The greatest development of dancing on the campus however is due to Miss Wanda Ellis, present director of Physical Education. Miss Ellis has developed a number of talented dancers and introduced them as features of the May Day festival and in the Allegaynianna programs given under her direction. In 1929 she presented the first dance recital in the college auditorium.

In the Spring of 1930 the Radford Chapter of the American Association of University Women brought the Ruth St. Dennis dancers as a feature program. These were most enthusiastically received and with their reception aesthetic dancing won a whole hearted acceptance as an activity in the College.

Since the beginning of dancing the problem of costuming
has been one of acute interest. The Grecian costume has been
used more than any other although Miss Ellis is particularly
fond of the ballet costume. Some of the outstanding student
dancers have been: Misses Kathryn Smith, Genevieve Giesen,
Eleanor Bowers, David Hurley, Coleen Seagle, Lorraine Copen-
havor.

MAY FESTIVALS

Miss Ninde, director of Physical Education conducted the
first May Day festival in 1919. Miss Mamie Lush of Burksville,
Virginia was the first May Queen. The queen dressed in a white
dress with a royal purple train was crowned with a gold pointed
crown in the Oak Grove directly in front of the Administration
Building. She was attended by a group of students as honor
maids. From her throne she presided at the festival of folk
dances, drills, and gymnastic exhibitions by the students of
Physical Education.

From this simple beginning the May festivals have become
very elaborate and beautiful. It is customary to select the
May Queen by popular vote of the students. The student receiving the highest number of votes as the most queenly, beautiful, and gracious, is declared the Queen. She is then attended by the students receiving the next highest votes as
maids of honor.

For several years the program included marches and drills
by all the students enrolled in physical education courses.
Miss Ellis has made it her practice to choose some central theme
as the motif for the festival. Around this she has woven group
and individual dances. Some of these themes have been: "Pan",
"The Japanese Sun God", "Spring", "Health", "Robin Hood", "The
Circus", Grecian Games, "Nations of the Earth", "Southwest Virginia".

The crowning of the queen is the climax of the festival.
For many years the queen was crowned on a throne erected in
front of Tyler Hall. The queen and her attendants approached
the throne from the Administration Building. Many children
of the city have participated as flower girls and train bearers
in the processional. Some of these are Josephine Noblin,
Eleanor Bowers, Warren Bowers, Chandler Noblin, Dorothy Smith,
Betty R. Roberts, Rob Roy Thomas, Elizabeth and William Cooper
Gilbert, Lois Miller, Nancy and Robin McConnell.

Until 1926 the costuming of the May Queen and her attendants was very simple. Beginning at this time the students
decided on a more elaborate costumes. For the last several
years the queen has been attired in a beautiful white robe.
The college owns a train and a crown embroidered in pearls and
rhinestones. This forms the nucleus around which the costuming
for the pageant is centered. Organdie and taffeta dresses have
been used by the maids.

MAY QUEENS

1919 - Mamie Lush
1920 - No Queen
1921 - Exhibition held May 13, in Gymnasium. No Queen.
1922 - Exhibition held May 10, in Gymnasium. No Queen.
1923 - Willie Shumate. Played the part of Peraphone in Spring
       festival.
1924 - Florence Kipps
1925 - Alice Wolferaberger.
1926 - Helen Snider
1927 - Gladys Smith
1928 - Mabelle Durham
1929 - Virginia Snider
1930 - Mrs. Hamilton
1931 - Effie Crews
1932 - Gladys Dunn

ALLEGAYNIANNA

In 1924 the students and faculty decided to have an all-day
festival on the last Saturday of the summer quarter. Mr. Sowder
named this day "Allegaynianna" meaning day of all joy. This festival was designed for two purposes, educational and recreational.
It included a large number of educational exhibits from the Department of Geography, Nature Study, Agricultural, Industrial Arts, and
Home Economics, and such recreational features as athletic contests,
swimming, races. The educational features in the exhibit were more
helpful. Mr. W. D. Smith and Mr. Sowder and their students collected and mounted a large number of plants typical of this section
of the State. The Home Economics Department gave a fashion show
and the Manual Arts Department had three rooms filled with drawing,
furniture, baskets, and industrial projects worked out under the
direction of Miss Simmons, Miss Howard, and Miss Driver. Local
history stories were told by the students of the History Department
under the direction of Professor Gilbert.

The chief feature of the entire program was the crowning
of the summer queen. The first queen was selected as a result
of a beauty contest. The students nominated sixteen young
ladies as the most beautiful in their number. Votes were sold
to select the two most beautiful of these girls. On Saturday
afternoon a week before the festival the students were posed
in the store windows of the stores on Main Street. This created
great interest, much rivalry and speculation as to who would be
the queen. The young men of the town became especially interested in the contest and for many days "Who would be the
queen?" hung in the balance. The contest was narrowed down to
Miss Elizabeth Goodwin, of Newport News, and Miss Janie James
of Rural Retreat, Virginia. Miss Goodwin finally won the place
as queen. She was attended by the other contestants in the
contest. A large number of floats were decorated in honor of
the queen and the winners. These champions were carried through
the main street of the town back to Tyler Hall where the queen
was crowned. Merchants of the city gave prizes to the winners
of the various contests. These were awarded by the queen during
the intermission of the evening program when a play "The Voice
of Authority" was presented by the two Literary Societies, followed by community singing and a glee club concert directed by
Miss Grace Jewett.

This all day festival was one of the most interesting celebrations of the college history. The entire campus and Administration Building was filled with a carnival spirit. Humor was
added by a large group of Spanish Gypsies, clowns, and comedy
characters. The proceeds from the Allegayniannas were used for
the Student Activity Building. Five such festivals have been
held. Selling votes to select the queen was abandoned after two
years. Since the queen has been selected by popular vote by the
students and the public is not allowed to vote for the queen.
The same general program although less elaborate, has characterized each Allegaynianna.

Miss Genevieve Geisen was queen in 1925, Miss Charlsie Camper in 1926, Miss Bess Hillman in 1927, Miss Helen Einstein in
1928, Miss Velma Cash, in 1929.

A special feature of the program for 1926 was the taking
of motion pictures of the Allegaynianna celebration by the Paramount News Reel Company. This photographer was interested in
the Allegaynianna through the influence of Mr. Nelson, Publicity
Chairman of the State Chamber of Commerce. These two gentlemen
spent the entire day at the college and took many pictures of
the activities. A reel of these pictures was purchased by Doctor
McConnell for the College. It shows the crowning of the queen,
several of the dancers, and a special stunt picture in which most
of the students of the college participated. This picture was taken

from the top of the Tyler Hall and shows the students in a typical snake dance and with some leg exercises. A comedy feature was introduced by the photographer in the use of the feet and legs and other exercises by the students. It shows Doctor McConnell, Miss Moffett, Miss Ellis, and other members of the College faculty in action. This film is preserved at the Radford College.

SECTION IX.

STUDENT PUBLICATIONS
_____

RADNOR
_____

In January 1914 the students decided to publish an annual. A contest was held to determine a name for this publication. Many names were submitted by the students. "The Radnor" submitted by Professor Avent was chosen. Miss Eleanor Terry acted as advisor of content for the first annual staff. The general oversight of the business management was assumed by the committee on Student Organizations.

The minutes of this committee show that much time was devoted to the discussion of "how to finance the annual". It soon became necessary to limit the number of entertainments that the various organizations could give. The regulations formulated by the committee provided for one entertainment each to be given by the Seniors, Juniors, Sophomores, and Freshmen and one to be given by the Dramatic Club. All other money to be raised by some other means than by public entertainment. It was raised by individual contributions and advertisements.

The contract for the publishing of the first Radnor was let to J. P. Bell and Company of Lynchburg, Virginia. The total cost was $1500. This Company furnished the photographer who spent several days at Radford taking the pictures. These were taken during a very cold and snowy season, this weather however did not dampen the ardor of students to wear summer clothing for the pictures.

The Radnor was published for four years in 1914, 1915, 1916, 1917. In 1917 the students decided to abandon the publication of the annual and to make an average contribution of $10.00 to a Student's War Chest.

As a substitute for the annual the Class of 1919 secured a velour covered memory book. Into this book they put kodak pictures of each member of the class, copies of programs and accounts of the activities of the group.

The classes of 1922 combined in the first commencement issue of the Grapurchat. In this they placed their pictures and write-ups about each of the graduates.

THE BEEHIVE

Each year (1920-1926) the question of an annual was debated; student meetings rampart with discussion were held. Usually the student opinion was divided. The majority vote was negative.

In 1925 the students voted to sponsor the publication of the annual. During the interim since the publication of the last Radnor the name of the School had been changed; Radnor therefore was no longer an appropriate name for the yearbook. The staff offered a copy of the annual to the person proposing the best name for the new publication. "The Beehive" was chosen as symbolic of the life of the institution and the central figure of the school seal.

Five Beehives were published in 1925, 1926, 1927, 1928, 1929. These publications are the typical school annual and speak for themselves. They have furnished a permanent record for the student life of the years when they were published. The Beehives were published under a new era in the printing world. The first Beehive cost $2,400.00 and the last one about $3,300.00. In comparison with the Radnor this tremendous increase in cost does not seem justified. In the first books practically all the art work was done by the students. In the latter books the engravers and printers stressed with the students the importance of an artistic book. The object of these gentlemen was to sell commercial art, inserts, plates, etc. They stimulated the students to a desire to have their book win in some commercial intercollegiate annual contest. For each of the Beehives a central theme was selected and this idea predominated in the development of the book.

The staff of 1926 was most successful in the business management of the publication. It was the only staff to make a profit from the book. At the end of the year they had about $200.00 over and above the cost of the publication. This was used to purchase the furniture for the Beehive office which was at this time in the old diet kitchen in Tyler Hall. They purchased two tables, a writing desk, and a filing cabinet, and placed the balance of the money to the credit of the incoming staff of the Beehive.

All of the annuals have been published by an editorial
staff selected by the student body. The Radnors were advised
by Miss Terry, Mr. Avent, and Miss Bulifant, Miss Montague and
Miss Moffett. The Beehives were advised by Doctor Moffett in
1925-1926-1927. Doctor Hudson was selected as literary advisor
in 1927, advised by Doctor Virginia O. Hudson in 1928-1929. Professor Gilbert acted as financial advisor in the publication of
the books for 1928. A complete list of the Staff members is
shown in the Appendix.

In 1929 Beehive was awarded second prize for its class in
a State contest by the Virginia Inter-Collegiate Press Association.
The students voted to discontinue the publication of a yearbook in
1930.

GRAPURCHAT

In 1921 Doctor McConnell suggested to a group of students
and members of the faculty the idea of publishing a school paper.
This suggestion was quickly adopted and plans were set on foot
for the organization of an editorial staff for the college paper.
The students were invited to suggest names for this newspaper.
The committee of which Mr. Sowder and Doctor Moffett were members,
selected the name proposed by Miss Virginia Harwood "Grapurchat".
This name is a composite name made up from the school colors,
purple and gray and the word chat.

Miss Harwood as the first editor-in-chief became intensely
interested in the publication and devoted untiring efforts to
making it a success. The paper was printed locally by Mr. Glenn
Minor of the Radford Journal. Miss Harwood and others of her
staff spent many hours in the Journal Printing Office working
over the details of the paper.

The first Grapurchat was issued on January 26, 1921. For
several years an annual birthday party was held on this date as
a feature of the General Assembly period. A large cake with birthday candles representing the years of the paper occupied the center of the stage. This was cut and each subscriber received a
piece. The first editors of the Grapurchat were mature capable
students and were able to carry on the work of the organization
without much advice. They sought help and aid from all members
of the faculty. No one was designated as advisor, but the work
of the editorial staff was supervised by Miss Moffett. This policy
was continued until 1927 when Doctor Hudson became the advisor of
the literary part of the newspaper. She continued as advisor until

the summer of 1928 when Doctor Ethel NeSmith was appointed as advisor. She served twelve months. Doctor Jean Taylor became the advisor in 1929 and continues in this capacity. Under her direction the Grapurchat is used as an outlet and technical laboratory for the students in journalism courses. Doctor Long substituted for her in the summer of 1930.

The Grapurchat is published once each two weeks throughout the entire year. The staff is elected in the Spring of the year and serves for four quarters with a special staff filling in such vacancies as may occur during the summer quarter.

Two complete sets of all issues of the Grapurchat have been bound and preserved in the library and one in the Dean's office with the other historical records of the institution.

At first the subscription rate was $1.50 per year or fifty cents a quarter. Practically all of the students and many alumnae became subscribers. These fees and the revenue from advertisements supported the paper. In 1927 the advertisements were sufficient to support the paper and the college started buying the Grapurchat in large numbers as advertising material for the school. This enabled the staff to give the paper free to all of the resident students.

The size of the paper has been changed twice, first it was increased to eight pages with an occasional twelve page issue. In 1928 it was increased in size of sheet and reduced to four pages.

In 1929 the last issue of the quarter was designated as a literary issue. This reduced the tendency to use so many literary contributions in the regular issues. A definite effort has been made to keep the paper a newspaper and mirror of the college life.

From time to time special issues are circulated. These usually include material of special interest to alumnae, prospective students or for outstanding events.

In 1929 and again in 1931 the Grapurchat has won the silver trophy cup as best newspaper in Class B (bimonthly papers) in the contest sponsored by Virginia Inter-Collegiate Press Association.

SECTION X.

HONOR FRATERNITIES AND SORORITIES

SIGMA, SIGMA, SIGMA

After the World War the tendency to have sororities on Teachers College Campus became more pronounced throughout the United States. Many requests to establish chapters of these organizations came to the student organization committee. On one or two occasions this committee made an investigation of the success with which the other Teachers Colleges were meeting the problem of sororities. The original faculty committee which had organized practically all of the student organizations was consistently opposed to sororities.

In 1927 the entire personnel of this committee changed. The new committee looked with favor upon such organizations and decided to accept the request of Miss Mable Lee Walden of the Sigma Sigma Sigma, an educational sorority for Teachers Colleges, to organize such a chapter on the campus. Doctor McConnell appointed a committee composed of Miss Susan Roberts, Doctor Virginia O. Hudson and Miss Hermine Menzie to select a group of students as the petitioners for this sorority. These students were required to submit a complete description of themselves, their home background, parents, with pictures of themselves. From the group the following students were selected as charter members of the Alpha Theta Chapter of Sigma Sigma Sigma: Mary Anderson, Virginia Deal Lawrence, Addie Johnson, Eleanor Jones, Lucille Christian, Kathleen Jennings, Elizabeth Hardwicke, Susan Roberts, Isabelle Richards, Emma Hurt, Elizabeth Wray, Virginia Snider, Helen Einstein, Ada Goodpasture, Viola Ehtridge, Cecil Shepherd, Izola Akers, Anne Miller, Gladys White, Anne Jennings, Ida Einstein, Marie Deyerle, Mildred Hale, Annie Jones, Virginia Mullan.

The students were initiated and the chapter organized in the Spring of 1929 by Miss Mabel Lee Walden. The chapter selected Miss Susan Roberts as its Counselor. Doctor McConnell gave them a chapter room in the basement of the Helen Henderson Hall which the chapter furnished during the year of 1929-1930.

This organization seems to be supplying the need for social life for the type of students on the campus who would enjoy sorority life. From time to time it holds receptions and teas in honor of the faculty and the students who are being considered for membership. It is customary to pledge members two or three times each year. The chapter is guided in its work by Mrs. Wil-

liam Kersley of Roanoke, Virginia, who visits it once or twice
each year. Annually the chapter unites with the other chapters
of the sorority in the observance of "Founders Day" on April 20.
The "Founders Day" dinner is the climax of the social programs
of the sorority. In 1930 this banquet was held in the Dixie Inn
at Radford, Virginia. In 1931 it was held at the Patrick Henry
Hotel, Roanoke, Virginia.

PI GAMMA MU

In the spring of 1927 the student organization committee decided to place great emphasis upon scholarship as a basis for
student participation and office holding in the student organizations on the campus. This was the first effort of the college
to place scholarship as a controlling factor in the student life.

To further increase this emphasis upon scholarship the administration of the college decided to organize one or two honor
fraternities. Therefore, in 1928 the Virginia Epsilom Chapter
of the Pi Gamma Mu Honor Fraternity in Social Science was organized...   At the time of its organization Doctor McConnell,
Mr. Whitt, Miss Moffett, Mr. Gilbert, and Mr. Fitzpatrick were
invited to become members at large. Some of these accepted membership in the fraternity.

The membership in the local organization is controlled by
the standards of the National Organization and is based on outstanding scholarship in the Social Science field. The students
and faculty members who were selected as charter members of the
chapter are: Doctor John Preston McConnell, Mary Eolian Coppedge,
Francis Burke Fitzpatrick, Virginia O'Rear Hudson, William E. Gilbert, Hermine Menzi, Charles B. Swaney, Jeremy Pate Whitt, Elizabeth Wilson, Ruth Leonard Bricker, Nannie Hardy Clark, Annie Belle
DeHart, Frances Katherine Edwards, Myrtle Elvira Ellis, Cassie
Keturah Gardner, Nora Garrett, Genevieve Geison, Mildred Roberta
McCrary, Nora Morris, Elizabeth Mica Robinette, Concepcion Santos,
Ethel Siner Shockey, Irma Frances Shufflebarger, Garnette Eliza-
beth Shufflebarger, Lillian Smith, Narcissa Eleanor Thompson,
Sally Vaughn Turner, Hildred Wessel.

Miss Coppedge, Doctor Hudson, and Miss Hermine Menzi were active in the organization of the chapter. Miss Coppedge wrote the
ceremonial for the initiation. This organization holds monthly
meetings and each year devotes itself to a study of some outstanding social science problem. In 1929-1930 the programs centered a-
round Russia and its Relationship to the rest of the world. For
1930-1931 the chapter is devoting itself to a study of the New South.

Each year the chapter holds a banquet or reception. In 1930 it was hostess to the Phi Kappa Phi Chapter of the Virginia Polytechnic Institute. Miss Hermine Menzi has been the counselor for the chapter since its organization.

In 1931 Mrs. Ruth Bricker Painter represented the chapter at the annual meeting of the National Council in Detroit, Michigan. She was elected National Recording Secretary.

KAPPA DELTA PI

The Gamma Alpha Chapter of the Kappa Delta Pi (National Honor Fraternity in Education) was installed at the Radford College on February 7, 1931. The installation was conducted by Doctor Florence Stratemeyer the first Vice-President of the National Fraternity assisted by Doctor Moffett, Miss Coppedge, and Doctor Ethel NeSmith, all of whom were members in other chapters. The petitioners and charter members were: Agnes Abernathy, Frances Boothe, Julia Bryant, Elsie Calhoun, Estelle Carmack, Elizabeth Einstein, Monnie Ellis, Myra Greiner, Anna Ruth Gardner, America Gonzalez, Nina Jewell, Mae Kelly, Mildred Logan, Myrtle Logan, Ruth Bricker Painter, Jean Taylor, Marie Updyke.

On February 7, 1931 a luncheon was held at the Patrick Henry Hotel in Roanoke, Virginia, by the petitioners. The guests for this occasion included the installing officers, Doctor and Mrs. Humphreys, and Doctor Thomas. This luncheon was very elaborate. The table was beautifully decorated in snapdragon, calendula, and yellow roses. Following the luncheon the pledging service of the ceremony of initiation was conducted by Doctor Florence Stratemeyer and her assistants.

The formal installation of the chapter and the initiation of the members took place in the Student Activity Building at 7:30 in the evening. It was followed at 9:30 by a formal reception to which the members of the faculty and the students on the scholarship list for the second quarter of the academic year were invited. This was a very elaborate reception. The guests were received by all the petitioners of the chapter and Doctor Stratemeyer. The building was decorated in the same flowers which had been used at the luncheon. New evening dresses, "especially long" made their debut upon the campus for this occasion.

Doctor McConnell has granted the chapter the privilege of using the old Beehive Office in the McGuffey dormitory as the chapter room. The charter has been framed and hung in this room. The

chapter holds two meetings each month. A program for the first
year study has been planned and is centering around the study
of comparative education and the contemporary educational leaders
of the United States.

TAU KAPPA ALPHA

A petition is now pending before the national council of the
Tau Kappa Alpha fraternity for a chapter to be established in the
Radford College. This chapter is to be composed of those students
who have been outstanding in debate and have met the requirements
of the National chapter.

On April 1, 1931, the Forensic Council was investigated by
Doctor C. P. Layman of the Western College at Kalamazoo, Michigan
and favorable reports have been received of the results of his
visit. The chapter is to be installed May 14, 1932.

SECTION XI.

DEPARTMENTAL CLUBS

RICHARDS FIRESIDE CLUB

The first departmental club perfected on the campus of the
Radford College was composed of students majoring in Home Economics.
This club was organized by Miss Moffett and was very active in the
early life of the institution. It was named for Mrs. Ellen H. Richards, the founder of the Home Economics Movement in the United States.
The club held frequent meetings in the Heth House during the first
years of the college. It was customary for the members to hold their
meetings around the grate in the library room of this building. The
club was primarily intended to emphasize the social life of this
group of students. From time to time formal programs on contemporary
Home Economics subjects have been held. After several years active
interest in the club lapsed. It was revived in 1925 and the club
was reorganized and sponsored by the teachers in Home Economics. It
has not been active since 1929.

LANGUAGE CLUBS

Miss Mattie C. Denny organized the students of her French and German classes into French and German Clubs. The meetings of these clubs were largely devoted to social gatherings which afforded an opportunity for the conversational use of the language. The French Club sponsored a special memorial service on the campus in 1918 and planted the memorial triangle dedicated to three young men of Radford who lost their lives in the World War in France.

SODALITAS LATINA

The Sodalitas Latina Club was organized by Miss Gladys Tapley in 1930. This club sponsored the presentation of the Vergil Bimillennium Pageant and later presented a bust of Vergil for the new library. This club is one of the most active departmental clubs on the campus at the present.

ART CLUBS

In 1914 the students majoring in Industrial Arts organized the "Daubers Art Club" sponsored by Miss Simmons. This club was largely for annual purposes to show the loyalty and spirit of these students.

RADFORD CHAPTER OF AMERICAN FEDERATION OF ART

In 1929 Miss Simmons sponsored the organization of the Radford Branch of the American Federation of Art. This organization in the three years of its existence has been a most valuable asset to the campus life of the institution. Membership is open to the students, members of the faculty, and citizens of the town who are interested in the artistic development of themselves and the community. Through the American Federation of Arts a number of exhibits have been brought to the college. These have been open to the public and have stimulated a deeper appreciation and an interest in the finer things. Each year the club has sponsored several exhibits of local articles of art interest. Chief among these have been an exhibit of antiques including many coverlets, old dresses, embroideries, and decorative articles for the home. In the summer of 1929 the club sponsored an exhibit of interesting objects, souvenirs which had been gathered by local people on their various trips and travels. In 1931 it sponsored an exhibit of hand woven coverlets, towels, shawls, and spreads from the mountain women near Berea, Kentucky.

The clubs hold monthly programs for the study of some particular phases in art. Mrs. McConnell recently gave an interesting talk on the designs and weaving of old coverlets. Miss Zollman discussed the appropriate framing of pictures, and Miss Moffett gave a discussion of bric-brac and other articles in the home. Miss Simmons gave a discussion of the manufacture of pottery accompanied by an exhibit of pottery loaned by the members of the club.

From time to time Mrs. John Hopkins, teacher of special art, china painting and water colors holds an exhibit of the work of her students.

MATHEMATICS

In 1919 Mr. Bowers organized a Mathematics Club of the students majoring in Mathematics. This group held meetings from time to time for the discussion of mathematical problems. In 1927 the club was reorganized by Doctor Gertrude McCain.

In 1930-31 this club devotes itself to the study of higher mathematics in its more popular application. The membership has been confined to those students majoring in mathematics and to the professors of mathematics; Professor Bowers, Doctor McCain, and Doctor Richard Smith. Occasionally the club holds a social meeting at the home of one of the Professors or town students.

SCIENCE CLUBS

A Science Club was organized by Miss Flora Bryson in 1915. The purpose of this club was to continue the interest of the students of Science in nature study, field trips, and collecting of science materials. The nature study group of this club continued the organization for many years.

ALICE EVANS BIOLOGY CLUB

In 1929 Doctor Paul R. Burch organized the Alice Evans Biology Club. This is an organization of the students primarily interested in biological science. The membership is based on scholarship and the members are formally initiated and required to attend the meetings. The meetings are devoted to a study of scientific biological material. In 1930 it sponsored an address by Doctor Kepner of the University of Virginia.

CHEMISTRY

In the same year Doctor Williams organized a Chemistry Club. Both Doctor Williams and his wife were interested in this organization and held many meetings of the club in their home. Doctor Williams took the club on picnics, bacon bats. The programs taught the application of chemistry to everyday living.

WRITERS AND ENGLISH CLUBS

In 1927 Doctor Ethel NeSmith organized the Writers Club. This was an organization of those students particularly interested in creative writing. From this organization there grew up an English Club which was subdivided according to the major interest of its members. This club was conducted by the professors of English and existed on the campus from 1928-29.

SECTION XII.

SOCIAL CLUBS

The original committee on student organizations set up a policy of no-secret organizations on the campus. It is natural that in any student group that certain individual will be more congenial and will group themselves together into various types of organizations. There have always been such groups on this campus. None of these, however, were secret in their purposes or activities from the general committee on student organizations. It is a policy to require a statement of all aims, purposes, membership, explanation of mottos, secret codes, and all plans for initiation and activities to be explained in the petition for recognition by the student organization committee. From time to time such organizations have sprung up. Practically none have continued from one year to the next.

Probably the most outstanding in this type of organization was the "Rinktum Ditty Club" of 1917. This was a club of congenial friends who found pleasure in the manufacture of a chafing dish food called "Rinktum Ditty". This dish was composed of tomato soup, cheese, onions, and eggs well cooked and blended in a chafing dish. It was much better if concocted secretly from the eyes and nose of the matron. The group of girls who constituted this club were known all over this campus. They were popular, peppy, and vivacious. The

climax of its activities was a "Rinktum Ditty" party held in
the Home Economics Department when a number of the young men of
the town were invited to help in the concocting of the dish.
This was a big and also a very happy occasion for all who attended.
The club existed for two years. Miss Mattie Clark was president
and Miss Ruth Jenkins the secretary and treasurer.

IMP GERMAN CLUB

In 1913-1914 a group of students organized the Imp German
Club. The membership of this club was confined to those who were
considered good dancers and to those who were interested in social
dancing in the dormitories.

The "Raggs" Club was popularly known in the social group on
the campus. The object of this club was to make the members appear
ridiculous in their ragged clothes.

Many small groups of students have organized themselves each
year as the annual was being published and buy one-half or a full
page and thus perpetuate their friendship by some fancy or "cute"
name.

COUNTY CLUBS

Among the first spontaneous student organizations to grow up
on the campus were the county clubs. These were organizations of
the students from a particular county. The Grayson-Carrol Club
was the first of these organizations to be recognized. Students
of Bland, Scott, Lee, Roanoke, and Wise Counties have been the
most loyal in the preservation of their county organizations. These
clubs are largely social and are designed to bring together the
students of the same home community.

COUNTY CLUBS IN THE SUMMER TERM

The county club has done its most effective work during the
summer quarter. For many years these organizations were sponsored
by Mr. F. B. Fitzpatrick. During the first week of the summer
quarter an assembly period was given over to the organization of
these clubs. Each county was assigned a special place for meeting
and each of the counties perfected an organization, small groups
formed sectional clubs as the Eastern Virginia and Valley Clubs.
Each of these clubs selects some member of the faculty as its advisor. A member of the faculty who hailed from a county automatic-

ally became the advisor, as Mr. Gilbert from Russell County, Doctor McConnell from Scott County, and Mr. Whitt from Montgomery County, etc. These clubs formed the nucleus for the student organizations and social life on the summer campus. They sponsored stunts, picnics, hikes, moonlight hayrides, watermelon feasts, and trips to Mountain Lake, Ingles Ferry, and Sunset Hill.

The County organization was featured in the pageant given at the Allegaynianna in 1927. At this time each presented tropies to "Virginia" symbolic of local, economic, or historic interest. These gifts were later presented to the college. Among them was a dresser given by the students of Franklin County and made in the furniture factor at Rocky Mount, Virginia. This was placed in the guest room of the College.

As the summer quarter became less congested in enrollment and was made a more integral part of the academic year the policy of urging all the counties to organize a club was abandoned. Only those who wish to preserve county organizations have been continued.

PART III.

DISTINCTIVE PERIODS AND EVENTS

SECTION I

THE WORLD WAR PERIOD

The city of Radford began to assume a military spirit during the Spring of 1916 when Company M of the second infantry of Virginia Volunteers was ordered to the Mexican Border. This company of sixty-one members was organized in Radford, February 1913 with Doctor G. A. Bowman as Captain and Wisa Worrell, Lieutenant. Several weeks prior to the departure for the Border the Company was very busy with active drilling and preparing war equipment. Their new khaki uniforms brought to the streets of Radford a military air. The boys left home in June and were stationed at Brownsville, Texas, from June 1916 to February 1917.

As the war clouds approached thirty-six of the younger men of the city of Radford organized a hospital corp. This was the only organization of its kind in the State. It was organized under the auspices of the Medical Corp of Virginia and was commissioned by the United States Army. It was fully equipped with hospital and pharmaceutical stores. These were brought to Radford for a training period of several months. Later the Hospital Corp was sent to Anniston, Alabama. These two companies, Company M, and the Hospital Corp, included practically all of the young men of military age in the city of Radford.

The interest of the students of the College was very great in the maneuvers and activities of these two organizations. They sympathized with and felt the heart throbs of the community as the boys departed for the Border and later for the World War. As described before the Tyler Hall was literally christened with the tears and agony of these separations. Many friendships developed between the students and these soldier boys of Radford. Throughout their absence the girls wrote many letters and sent college pictures to them, thus a touch with the home town college life was maintained. At Christmas time the students prepared many boxes to send to the soldiers abroad.

In 1918 the French Club, under the auspices of Miss Mattie Denny, planted three Lombardy Poplar trees as a memorial triangle to the three young men of Radford who lost their lives in the war, Elliot Howe, Alfred Harvey, and Jake Carper.

The college had its first active participation in the war activities of Radford when a Union Service for the members of Company M was held in the auditorium on July 22, 1917. The auditorium was packed with friends of the soldiers so soon to leave for active military service. Reverend Frank Y. Jackson of Marion, Virginia, preached the sermon. The ministers of the town were seated on the platform. Reverend Harry Whitmore on behalf of the ministers presented a testament to each soldier. This was the first of many community services and activities in the college auditorium in behalf of the soldiers and war activities.

No active professor or employee of the college saw service in the war. Doctor McConnell had three sons and one son-in-law who enlisted. One of them, Carl (Hospital Corp, later the artillery), saw service over seas. All the other men identified with the College were married and had family responsibility. This, however, did not relieve them of a conscious determination to do all they could at home. Practically no local committee appointed for real service during the war period failed to carry the name of one or more faculty representatives.

WAR TIME SERVICE OF DOCTOR McCONNELL

Doctor McConnell, as President of the Institution, stimulated his faculty to give all their spare time, strength, and money for the support of war causes. Doctor McConnell himself has a splendid record for Civil Service during this period of history. He was appointed Director of the Junior Red Cross of Virginia. In this capacity he was charged to enlist the cooperation of the young people of the State in carrying forward the general plan of the government to mobilize all the resources by conservation and economy in the use of food and clothing; to assemble such materials as could be used for the various war and relief purposes. In addition to this responsibility for all the Junior Red Cross Work in the State he was District Director for the Adult Red Cross Chapters for the City of Radford and the fourteen nearby counties. His duty was to encourage the greatest possible activities in the Red Cross. He delivered a number of addresses throughout the State and in practically every community in Southwestern Virginia. He was appointed Director of the sale of War Saving Stamps and assisted in the sale of Liberty Bonds.

In addition to this active war time service Doctor McConnell never lost sight of the responsibility for the relief of those

who were placed in destitute circumstances by the ravages of war
and the economic inflatation following the war period. He was
appointed Director of the Near East Relief Campaign in Virginia
and remained an active member on this Board for ten years. In
this connection he was vice-chairman of the Near East Relief
Campaign in Virginia to raise money to establish a college in
Athens, Greece, and to promote education in the Oriental Countries devastated by the war.

The large salaries and the attractive employment offered by
the government and the war manufacturing plants attracted many
young women from the service of teaching. This presented a
challenge for those who believed in public education to encourage
and bring into the teacher training institutions as many young
people as could be interested in furthering the cause of education.

Doctor McConnell directed himself very definitely to this
challenge. He says "believing in education, morality, and religion, as a safeguard to a country I felt that the Presidents
of our teacher training and higher educational institutions had
a unique opportunity to serve our country by constantly calling
attention to the educational and spiritual needs of our people
and the opportunity men and women have to render a real service
to their country by promoting education, morality, and education in the school room and otherwise."

Following the War in 1919 Doctor McConnell was appointed by
Governor Westmoreland Davis as one of a group of distinguished
Virginians to gather material and write a History of the World
War, its activities and achievements in the State of Virginia.
In this connection Doctor McConnell was responsible for assem-
bling from the various Red Cross Chapters of the State full and
accurate reports of their activities for the permanent records
of the Virginia War History Commission.

Mr. Gilbert who was an outstanding speaker in Southwestern
Virginia at this time actively identified himself with the
Young Men's Christian Association and with the other welfare
activities sponsored by the various organizations of the war
period. He spoke to many audiences in Southwestern Virginia
in behalf of various war relief measures. He was also Chairman of the Montgomery Agricultural Council of Safety. Through
his influence a car load of tin containers were secured for
use in the counties for the preservation of food.

JUNIOR RED CROSS

Mr. Whitt was chairman of the organization of the Junior
Red Cross and was actively identified in the organization of
the Junior Red Cross Chapters throughout the State. Such a
chapter was chartered at the Radford College. This organization became the active working unit for the war activities of
the student body. It was sponsored by Miss Mary Montague and
later by Miss Eolian Coppedge who interested the students in
the making of many garments for the Armenians and other Near
East refugees. Hundreds of pairs of socks, dozens of sweaters,
several rag rugs, hundreds of scrap books, and dozens of lay-
ettes were made by the students. On one occasion the Red Cross
held an exhibit of these materials as they were prepared for
shipment to the Red Cross Headquarters in Washington. The exhibit filled the entire stage of the auditorium. In its midst
was hung a beautiful silk banner of the Junior Red Cross which
had been made by Elizabeth Ward, a student of the Home Economics Department of the College. This flag, the Junior Red
Cross charter, and several of the sweaters knitted by the students are preserved in the museum of the College.

RED CROSS WORK

Miss Mary Montague was the College leader for the Radford
Chapter of the Red Cross. Under her direction a room (108 of
of the Administration Building) was set aside for the making of
surgical dressing. Mr. Roop made several dust proof boxes.
The Red Cross furnished the women with the material for surgical dressings; hundreds of bandages, wound wipes, surgical
gowns were made in this room. A number of the women of the
city of Radford and ladies of the faculty of the college belonged to this unit. They spent many hours each week making
bandages. Other ladies of the faculty were members of knitting units. The knitting bag became the most fashionable ac-
cessory around the college. Many of the students knitted continually during Assembly and classes.

COURSES IN FIRST AID

Under the direction of Miss Montague several courses in
first aid were organized for students. These courses were
taught by Doctor J. A. Noblin as the chief instructor assisted by Miss Montague and Miss Moffett. Many of the students secured certificates for such first aid and relief work

from the National Red Cross Association. Doctor Noblin offered courses in first aid to the ladies of the town. A large group was taught in the city high school. Each of the candidates for certificates were examined and officially approved by Doctor Noblin. Health courses were also conducted in the college. All of the students who were graduated were trained in the techniques of the organization of a Junior Red Cross Chapter, first aid courses, and were encouraged to cooperate in all the civic activities in the communities to which they went.

During the Influenza epidemic which swept through Radford the members of the faculty assisted in the nursing and care of many of the citizens of the town. Mrs. Moffett in her home on Fairfax Street opened a diet kitchen. Here she prepared large quantities of food which was carried to the sick by members of the faculty, Miss Burnette, Miss Ninde, and Miss Moffett. Other members of the faculty nursed in the City hospital and gave voluntarily of their strength, time and service in the care of children, old people, as well as those who were suffering from Influenza.

FOOD ADMINISTRATION

The Home Economics Department under the direction of Miss Moffett assisted by Miss Burnett, teacher of Cookery, was active in carrying forward the food conservation program as outlined by Herbert Hoover. The College was supplied with the recipes and official communications on food conservation and the use of substitute foods. The students of the College were acquainted with all of these measures. Many experiments and lessons in cooking were devoted to war time foods. The students of the Home Economics Department adopted the Hoover Apron as a uniform. These were made up in white for the advanced students and in blue with white collars and cuffs for the freshmen, emblems of the United State Food Administration were placed on the caps. During the summer demonstrations were given in the use of home products, as canning and preserving of food, the use of milk and cheese products. Government experts gave several series of demonstrations on canning and food preservation for the students of the college and the town people.

Mrs. M. S. Moffett was appointed Chairman of Food Conservation for the City of Radford by Herbert Hoover. Her Committee was composed of representative women of the town. As a result of their activities eighty per cent of the housewives of Radford pledged themselves to obey government regulations in the matter of food conservation. The committee distributed much information on food and food substitutes. The Home Economics Laboratory of the College and private homes of the members of this committee became the testing laboratories for the use of substitutes. The students as well as the citizens of the community observed meatless and wheatless days.

FINANCES

The platform of the Radford College was an open forum for all speakers on war relief and war activities. Scarcely a week went by without some representative of some organization being presented to the students. The students were approached by speakers in all the Liberty Loan Campaigns. The Class of 1918 gave $350.00 in liberty bonds as a student loan fund of the college. From various sources the college accumulated about $1,000.00 in liberty bonds for use in the student loan.

Miss Eloise Harrison, Mrs. J. P. Whitt, and Mrs. McConnell were actively identified on the Woman's Committee for the sale of Liberty and Victory Loan Bonds.

CELEBRATIONS

Frequently during the war period patriotic celebrations were held in Radford. Miss Baird was a prominent figure at all of these. She conducted many community Sings. On all occasions the students of the College took an active part. On many occasions they paraded in these celebrations. Mr. Avent was chairman of the Red Cross and the War Chest Drive. The successful work of this organization was culminated by a gigantic parade through the streets of Radford in May 1918. On false Armistice Day, November 10, 1911, the students joined with the citizens of Radford in the celebration. When the Armistice was really confirmed on November 11, 1918 the students held a campus rally around the flag pole with an impressive service by Doctor McConnell and Mr. Avent. The students then joined with the citizens of Radford in their celebration at the Norfolk and Western Station. For several years after this the students united with the citizens of the town in the observance of Armistice Day.

POST WAR RED CROSS

Since the war Mr. Fitzpatrick who came to the college in 1919 has been most active in continuing the work of the Red Cross. Under his direction the Radford Red Cross has taken up peace time activities. He was instrumental in bringing to Radford a Public Health Nurse who is paid in part by the Red

Cross. Each year he conducts the annual Red Cross Drive and cooperates with the citizens committee in the Community Chest Drive. He serves on city committees for the public welfare and economic needs of the poor.

SECTION II

SPECIAL CELEBRATIONS AND ANNIVERSARIES

The end of the first decade of the history of the Radford College was observed at the commencement for June, 1923. At this time a resume of the first decade of the Radford State Normal School was prepared by Miss Moffett. This was distributed to the commencement visitors and newspapers of the State. This resume received extended editorial comment in the leading newspapers of the State.

August 9, 1923 was observed as the Tenth Anniversary of the dedication of the Administration Building which marked the formal opening of the instructional life of the College. The celebration was the first effort of the college to mark in a formal way one of its milestones. The last unit of the first dormitory was practically completed. The christening of the three units of this building was the main feature of the program. For this occasion an effort was made to bring to the college campus all of the Governors who had been the Executive head of the State during the history of the College. Governor E. Lee Trinkle was the chief speaker. The news report as prepared for the newspaper follows:

"At 10:30 o'clock the entire student body passed in review before Governor Trinkle, Ex-Governor J. Hoge Tyler, Colonel and Mrs. Sinclair Brown, Colonel Moore and Colonel Leroy Hodges of the Governor's Staff and the faculty of the Normal School. This review and inspection of the student body was held in front of the Administration Building. The line of march was attractively decorated with United States flags and pennants of the Normal School. Through a formation of the student officers the entire student body passed in review. Assemblying in the oak grove after the review the students gave enthusiastic songs and cheers for the visitors and the institution.

Many interesting facts about the ten years of the school were displayed on attractive posters. During the ten

years of the life of the institution over eight thousand
students have studied in this school.

Immediately following the review an informal reception
was held for the visitors and faculty in the Blue Gate
Tea Room. This was followed by the formal exercises of
the day in the Normal School Auditorium. Here Governor
E. Lee Trinkle spoke most eloquently. He outlined the
value of education and the large sum of money which is
being spent for the promotion of better citizenship
through the schools in the State of Virginia. He touched
most feelingly upon the present crisis in the national
history and emphasized the importance of loyalty to the
Flag and the Country which it represents. Governor Trinkle
who is a powerful speaker, expressed the deep appreciation
on the part of the State for this institution and for
Doctor John Preston McConnell, President of the School, and
the members of the faculty and students who have so loyally
supported this, the youngest of Virginia Educational Institutions. Governor Trinkle was followed by Mrs. Trinkle who
gave a most delightful violin solo and played the accompan-
iment for solo dances by little Eleanor Sue Trinkle. These
two features of the program by the members of the Governor's
family added greatly to the enjoyment of the occasion.

Colonel Brown, Colonel Moore, and Colonel Hodges of the
Governor's Staff were presented and spoke briefly on the
phases of the life of the school and its contribution to
the State. Ex-Governor J. Hoge Tyler, who has been an
invalid for the past twenty-seven months, visited the
Normal School for the first time in that period and delivered a most interesting talk to the student body.
Governor Tyler has been a frequent visitor at the Normal
School and has been a source of much pleasure and inspiration to the students and faculty. He has the most charming manner of a gentleman and is able through simple
stories and illustrations to teach great truths of
Christianity and upright living.

A surprise feature of the program was the presentation
of a handsome watch by Dean Moffett on behalf of the
student body and faculty of the Normal School to Doctor
John Preston McConnell, President. "To you, Doctor John
Preston McConnell, President, Radford State Normal School,
this watch is presented as a token of respect, esteem, and
love felt for you by the Faculty and one thousand students

on the 10th Anniversary of the Dedication of the first
building of this institution."

Immediately following the exercises in the auditorium the
Governor and his party proceeded to the dormitory where
they were again greeted by the entire student body. The
dormitory, which is practically completed, was decorated
and ready for the christening ceremony. President McConnell
outlined briefly the building program of the Normal School
and in a word picture contrasted the campus as a briar patch
and wild oak grove ten years ago with the beautiful, classic
campus of today.

Miss Inez Hicks, President of the Student body, accompanied
by little Elizabeth Gilbert, christened the first unit of
the dormitory. The name of this unit is Tyler Hall in honor
of Ex-Governor James Hoge Tyler, the most prominent citizen
of Radford. The middle unit was christened Norwood Hall by
Miss Grace Davis, President of the Pocahontas Literary Society and Miss Eleanor Bowers. The Normal School is located on
the Hammit property, the name of the estate being "Norwood".
This estate was one of the landmarks of Southwest Virginia
in the early years, therefore, the purpose of the Normal
School to preserve in one of the buildings, the original
name of the estate. The third unit was named McGuffey Hall
by Miss Frances Fitzpatrick, President of the Ingles Literary Society and little Josephine Noblin. McGuffey is more
widely known as the author of the McGuffey Reader and
speller which were studied by many of the older people of
the present generation, but he was also one of the greatest
leaders of education in the State of Virginia and elsewhere.

The three children who assisted in the christening were most
attractively dressed in white and seemed to be fairies of
prophecy of what the future years would hold for the institution during its life, the foundation of which has been so
ably laid in the past decade.

The Governor, his staff, President and Mrs. McConnell, Mayor
Gilbert, Dean Moffett, and Registrar Whitt were entertained
at a beautiful dinner given by the students of the Home Economics Department following the exercises of the morning.
Mrs. Trinkle, Mrs. Tyler, and Mrs. McConnell were presented
with corsages of roses by the students of the Ninth District.
These were presented by Mr. Spivey of Norton, who is President of the Ninth District Organization in the school. These

token of appreciation and esteem were most graciously
received by the ladies.

Following the formal exercises of the day Governor Trinkle
and his Staff made an inspection of the Normal School and
went over the business and the tentative budget with President McConnell. The Normal School has so rapidly out-
grown the accommodations provided for it by the buildings
that during the summer tent cities have been provided for
the rooming of students and for class room purposes. The
Governor and visitors were very much impressed with this
unique way of handling the over-crowded conditions at the
institution.

After the very full day at the Normal School Governor
Trinkle was the guest of the Rotary Club of Radford at
a six-o'clock banquet. At this time he expressed himself
as being impressed with the development and growth of the
city of Radford, the extensive street paving and improvements made by the city and the various organizations of
the town which are most creditable.[1]

FIFTEENTH ANNIVERSARY

The Fifteenth Anniversary of the instructional life of the
college was observed on May 5, 1928. This day was designated
as Founder's Day. It was arbitrarily chosen as a suitable time
for the celebration, the date May 5, has no significance in the
college history. The report for this celebration as prepared by
Doctor Virginia O. Hudson for distribution to the newspapers is
as follows:

FOUNDER'S DAY CELEBRATED AT RADFORD STATE TEACHERS COLLEGE

About one thousand people including students, alumnae, fac-
ulty and guests celebrated the Fifteenth Anniversary of Radford
State Teachers College with a Founder's Day program on Saturday,
May 5, 1928.

The celebration opened at nine-thirty with a pageant on the
campus. The students assembled in a wheel formation. The hub
of the wheel was a large "Bee Hive", the college symbol.

1. From News Release for August 9, 1923.

Students representing various classes in the history of the school were arranged in formations radiating from the center, or the "Bee Hive". Then the doors of the "Bee Hive" opened and girls dressed to represent bees set forth the many activities of the school such as music, athletics, classics, dramatics, debating, arts-craft, social life, and the different organizations.

The representative of the Class of 1913 presented to the President of the Senior Class the mantle of 1913 on which were indicated the activities and responsibilities of the Class of 1913. This was to symbolize that the present class has the privilege of "carrying on the work" initiated by the first class.

CELEBRATION PROGRAM WAS OF A REMINICENT NATURE

Immediately following the pageant the faculty, alumnae, and students filed into the auditorium for the celebration program which began at ten o'clock. Professor William E. Gilbert presided. After the invocation by Professor W. J. Sowder the student body sang the Motto which was followed by a pageant "The Roll Call of the Years". The leader for each of the years stood and told of the activities of her particular class emphasizing the number enrolled, athletics, debating, dramatics, gifts to the college, and the like. At the close of each speech the student body sang the chant "Hail, All Hail to our Sister Class". The difference in the number of graduates in 1914 and 1927, five and one hundred forty-three, respectively was significant of the growth of the school.

The music was furnished by the Glee Club under the direction of Miss Edmee Smith.

Judge G. E. Cassell told in his inimitable way of the first Board of Trustees.

Professor W. E. Gilbert, in his usual forceful manner, spoke very interestingly of the first faculty of which five still remain connected with the college, Doctor J. P. McConnell, Professor W. E. Gilbert, Miss M'Ledge Moffett, Miss Florence Baird, and Miss Lillian Simmons.

Miss Florence Baird told of the first student activities. Her address was made more impressive by the use of the birthday cake with fifteen candles which were lighted by fifteen young ladies representing the following organizations; two Literary Societies, Y. W. C. A., Athletic Association, Music, and Student Government.

The main part of the program was a speech by President J. P. McConnell who told in a happy reminiscent way of the founding of the school and of his early dreams of the mission of Radford State Teachers College.

This program was concluded with the singing of the Alma Mater.

INSPECTION OF BUILDING AND GROUNDS

At two o'clock in the afternoon the alumnae inspected the points of interest on the campus under the direction of Professor W. J. Sowder, Professor F. B. Fitzpatrick, Doctor M. W. Thomas, and a number of students.

ALUMNAE RECEPTION

The Alumnae Association held its reception in the lounge of Madame Russell Hall from three to five o'clock. The lounge was artistically decorated with candles, ferns, and cut flowers which carried out the color scheme of green, pink, and white.

The guests were met at the door by Mrs. George A. Williams and Miss Ethel Roberts who introduced them to the receiving line which was composed of Mrs. L. F. Windle, Miss Blanche Daniel, Doctor and Mrs. J. P. McConnell, Doctor Edgar W. Knight, Miss Florence Baird, Professor and Mrs. W. E. Gilbert, Doctor Virginia O. Hudson, Miss Ida Einstein, Miss Anna Lee Bonham, and Mrs. Clarence Hall.

Those who assisted in the entertainment of the guests were Doctor Ethel NeSmith, Miss Edmee Smith, Miss Wanda Ellis, Miss Hermine Menzi, Doctor George A. Williams, and Professor W. J. Sowder. Delicious refreshments were served and the occasion proved very enjoyable and served to recall many a memory of "Auld Lang Syne."

FOUNDER'S PROGRAM, THE CHIEF EVENT

The Founder's Program at eight o'clock in the evening in the College Auditorium was a fitting culmination of the day's exercises. Doctor J. P. McConnell presided and the program opened with an impressive processional of the student body. After the invocation pronounced by Reverend A. E. Simerly and the singing of the College Motto by the student body, Doctor Edgar Knight of the University of North Carolina delivered a most interesting address.

This address stressed the educational status of the Southern States and was a challenge to all thinkers on the problems of Education in this section of the country. Doctor Knight spoke to a Southern audience challenging the apathy of the typical Southerner in regard to present conditions in the South saying: "We rank low in education not because we were once devastated by war nor because we are too poor to support better schools. The war is sixty-odd years in the past and the South is now strong and prosperous in economic wealth. We cannot any longer point to war or poverty in explanation or defense of our educational shortcomings. The South ranks low in education, when measured by national standards, largely because we have here a distaste for sustained educational effort", he said. "Our aversion to hard work is reflected in the large number of poorly trained unproductive school and college teachers and low standards of scholarship permitted. Too few of our students have respect for thoroughness and excellence of study chiefly because the standards of their teachers are low. They can be given increased respect for higher standard only by teachers who themselves do thorough and excellent work."[1]

The music for the evening was provided by the choral club directed by Miss Florence C. Baird. The program concluded with the Alma Mater.

All present during the exercises were greatly impressed with the growth and progress of Radford College and saw on every hand indications of a promising future as it shall minister to thousands of students who will enter its portals.

TWENTIETH ANNIVERSARY OF THE ESTABLISHMENT

The Act of Establishment of the State Normal and Industrial School at Radford was signed by the Governor in March 1910. This Act was observed by a celebration of the Twentieth Anniversary on August 8, 1930. The program for this Anniversary was held in the Auditorium of the college. The chief feature was an ad-

1. Grapurchat, Volume VIII. No. 8.

dress by President D. R. Anderson of the Randolph Macon College
in which he reviewed the history of higher education for women
in Virginia. In justifying the existence of these colleges he
stressed many of their contributions to the cultural and social
life of Virginia.

On the stage was seated the faculty of the college, repre-
sentatives of the first Board of Trustees and the speakers.
Judge George E. Cassell, Secretary of the First Board presided.
He presented Robert L. Noell, and W. T. Baldwin, son of the
Captain Baldwin, Chairman of the first Board of Trustees. Doctor
McConnell delivered an address on "Policies and Philosophies of
the Radford College.[1]

Doctor M'Ledge Moffett, member of the first faculty gave a
brief summary of the achievements of the college in which she
gave a comparative study of the conditions as they existed twenty years ago with those existing in August 1930:

From a dumping ground and cornfield to a college plant
of six modern, fireproof buildings valued at $900,000.00.

From a Legislative support of $25,000.00 to an annual
appropriation of $88.045.00.

From no students to an annual enrollment of 2,425 in all
departments and a grand total enrollment for its seventeen
years of instructional service of 10,499 students.

From no graduates to 1,229.

From the twelve members of a newly appointed faculty to
an instructional staff of 54.

From a proposed average salary of faculty of $875.00 to
an average salary of $2,625.00.

From a faculty of which no one except the President
hold the Doctor's degree to a faculty of which 22% hold
Doctor's degrees; 43% hold Master's degree; and 27%
hold Bachelor's degree.

From no campus employees to a staff of 30 who daily
prepare meals, care for the campus, and buildings, and
run the laundry.

1. A complete copy of this address is filed in the historical
   files of the college.

From a per capita cost of the first year for the instruction of the students of $80.79 to a per capita cost of $160.31.

From a total proposed Student Loan Fund of $250.00 to $18,693.00 which is expended annually in assisting students to receive their education.

From a college with no Practice Teaching facilities to a self-owned campus training school and affiliated practice facilities in city schools and consolidated rural schools with an enrollment of 518 children.

From no books to a library of 15,000 bound volumes.

From a rented dormitory capacity of 175 to an owned dormitory capacity of 436.

From no furnishings or equipment to such equipment as meets the standard of the most exacting accrediting agencies.

From an institution unknown except to a few Legislators and interested citizens to a college with national recognition; Member of the Southern Association of Secondary Schools and Colleges; with highest rank in the American Teachers College Association, member of the American Council on Education; with students enrolled from eleven different States and three foreign countries, with graduates and former students teaching in twenty-four States of the Union and three foreign countries.

From an institution of no service to one which in 1929 has 2002 of its former students teaching in the State of Virginia, each teaching on the average of thirty children, thus the total approximate annual service in the form of education reaches over 60,000 children.

From a campus bound by a broken down wire fence to a campus which not only includes the students who study locally but also has an Extension Service that reaches through the Correspondence Courses, Study Centers 604 off-campus students.

Following this formal program the visitors were entertained at luncheon in the Tea Room. In the evening the student body, visitors, and members of the faculty were received by Doctor and Mrs. McConnell at a reception on the lawn of the Student Activity Building.

TWENTIETH ANNIVERSARY OF THE PRESIDENCY OF
DOCTOR JOHN PRESTON MCCONNELL

The Twentieth Anniversary of the presidency of Doctor John Preston McConnell was recognized with a special program on June 3, 1931. This celebration opened with a testimonial dinner in the Tyler dining room which many of the citizens of Radford, Southwest Virginia, and the Faculty attended. Each of these guests paid for his plate. This was the first dinner ever given at the college for which the guests paid for their plates. This was considered an additional courtesy to Doctor McConnell.

Following the dinner the guests with all of the students and many hundreds of citizens of the town and community assembled in the auditorium for a formal program. Mr. J. P. Whitt presided at this program. The speakers, all of whom paid tribute to the honoree were: Mayor Robert S. Hopkins, William E. Gilbert, Ethel Bartlett, M'Ledge Moffett.

On this occasion Doctor McConnell was presented with a handsome gold headed cane by Mr. W. T. Baldwin on behalf of a group of professional and personal friends. Mrs. McConnell was presented with a handsome cameo pin as a gift from the students of the College.

In July 1930 Doctor Moffett had started a campaign to raise funds from the students, Alumnae, and faculty of the College to have a portrait of Doctor McConnell painted. In May 1931 Mrs. Sally Mahood of Lynchburg, Virginia, was employed as the artist. She worked for several weeks painting the portrait. As Doctor McConnell posed for this painting the manuscript of this history of the school was read to him for his approval.

The portrait was completed in time for the Anniversary program. As the main feature of this program the portrait was presented by Doctor M'Ledge Moffett on behalf of those who had contributed to its purchase. It was unveiled by Mac Graybeal and Nancy McConnell, the eldest grandchildren of Doctor

386

and Mrs. McConnell. The portrait was hung in the auditorium
until the John Preston McConnell Library was completed. It
was then moved to the main Lobby of this building.

Following the Anniversary program a reception was held on
the lawn in honor of Doctor and Mrs. McConnell.

SECTION III

CONFERENCES AND CONVENTIONS

"From the earliest days of its history the college has pro-
claimed an invitation to all persons engaged in any kind of educational work to make all of the agencies and instrumentalities
of the college a sort of Mecca or Delos for the exchange of holy
ideas on a common ground for all of those engaged in seeing the
invisible and knowing and loving the noble aspirations of man-
kind," thus Doctor McConnell has expressed his policy in making
the Radford College a center for the educational and other alturistic agencies of the State and Nation to meet. As a result
of this open house policy many conventions of various kinds
have been held.

Most frequent among these have been the Educational Conferences for the Sixth and Ninth Congressional Districts and later
for District "I" of the Virginia Educational Association. Five
such conferences have been held. The first of these conventions
was held March 11 to the 13th, 1915. For several years thereafter the conventions were held regularly at Radford. It then
became the policy to meet in various centers throughout this
section of the State, it returned to Radford in 1931 for the annual meeting. In each of these conventions the Faculty of the
College has participated largely in the entertainment of the
guests. They have served on the programs, arranged meetings,
served the luncheons and assisted in the housing of the guests.

STATE CONFERENCE OF CHARITIES AND CORRECTIONS

The first convention held at Radford other than one of
purely educational nature was a meeting of the State Conference of Charities and Corrections, September 2 to 4, 1917.
Honorable Hatcher Seward was the presiding officer. It was
attended by many of the leaders in this movement and other
distinguished visitors, among these were: Doctor Mastin, Mrs.
Kate Waller Barrett, President of the National Florence Crit-
tiden Mission, Alexandria, Virginia; Doctor Hasting Hart of

the Russell Sage Foundation, New York City, and J. W. Magruder, General Secretary of the Baltimore Federated Charities. Doctor McConnell spoke on Crippled and Deformed Children. He was very proud of being host to this organization, the work of which is one of the things dearest to his heart.

HEALTH COMMITTEE OF LEAGUE OF NATIONS

On October 18, 1923 thirty representatives of the Health Committee of the League of Nations visited the college in connection with a tour of Virginia studying the Health Program of this State as one of the constructive pieces of work for the League. The party was directed by E. C. Stoy, scientific assistant of the United States Public Health Service. The countries represented by these visitors included Belgium, Canada, England, France, Italy, Norway, Spain, Switzerland, and health leaders of this nation. The guests were received and shown over the college plant. They were particularly interested in the health program of the college. They were supplied with a complete statement of the health policy as described in another section of this history.

FIFTH DISTRICT BANKERS

On October 20, 1923 the annual banquet and convention of the Fifth District Bankers was held at the College. This meeting took the form of a banquet held in the Tyler dining room. Several hundred bankers representing the Fifth District Bankers of this State heard an address by Mr. Charles N. Evans of Cincinnati. The students gave a music and dance program.

VIRGINIA PRESS ASSOCIATION

The Virginia Press Association, an organization composed of the editors and publishers of the newspapers of Virginia were entertained at the College on August 20, 1926. Their visit of short duration consisted in a campus tour. A rousing welcome with many songs and yells from the students, and an informal reception extended by the College and attended by the administrative officers, faculty and guests.

WOMAN'S CHRISTIAN TEMPERANCE UNION ANNUAL MEETING

The Woman's Christian Temperance Union held its annual State meeting at Radford August 24, 1926. During this conven-

tion the women were housed in the Tyler Hall. Miss Bryson of
the Faculty acted as the official hostess. The convention was
held during the interim between the summer and fall quarters and
was not largely attended by the members of the faculty. Doctor
and Mrs. McConnell were most active in the entertainment of the
convention. Mrs. Howard Hoge of Lincoln, presided at the meeting as President of the State Association.

MEETINGS OF SCIENTISTS

On October 6, 1926 a group of geologists who were touring
Virginia studying the geological formations of the State visited
the College. The group was composed of many outstanding geologists of the American Universities. Their trip was sponsored by
the Virginia State Chamber of Commerce and they stopped at Radford enroute to Southwestern Virginia. The usual reception and
student welcome was given.

On May 7, 1927 the Virginia Academy of Science held its annual meeting jointly at Radford and Blacksburg. While at Radford
they had one of their evening programs and in the afternoon were
tendered a reception by the college.

STATE ASSOCIATION OF FUNERAL DIRECTORS

The most unique meeting ever held on the campus of the College was that of the State Association of Funeral Directors from
June 8th to the 10th in 1927. This was the only group which has
ever been entertained at the college primarily for commercial
purposes. The Tyler Dormitory was organized as a hotel, rooms
were rented to the guests of this convention at $2.00 and $2.50
per day, meals were served hotel style in the dining room. The
North dining room of Tyler Hall was converted into an exhibit
room. Hundreds of caskets, various types of embalming materials,
and other supplies for funerals were displayed. Meetings of the
convention were held in the College Auditorium. A special feature of the entertainment was a barbeque held on the campus of
the college. The management of the entertainment for this convention was carried out by Doctor M'Ledge Moffett and Miss Elsie
Palmer. It was entirely self-supported and the profits were donated to the student fund of the College. The servants of the
college were employed during this period. Many amusing and interesting episodes occurred in connection with the display of
caskets on the ground floor of the dormitory. The fearlessness
of the negroes in moving around in such a ghostly atmosphere was
an outstanding reflection upon the theory of the superstition of

negroes, ghosts, etc., when a quarter tip could be earned by
handling of the most ghostly objects.

PUBLIC HEALTH NURSES

On December 10, 1927 the Public Health Nurses of District
Number 7, including the Counties and Cities from Danville to
Wythe County met in a quarterly regional convention at Radford.
Miss Irma Fortune, a former Public Health Nurse at Radford and
now Assistant Public Health Nurse of the State presided.   The
convention devoted itself to a discussion of the health program
in the public schools.

VIRGINIA FEDERATION OF WOMEN'S CLUBS

On October 15, 1928 the District Meeting of the Virginia
Federation of Women's Clubs was held at the Radford College.
This brought to the campus many of the club women of Southwestern Virginia. A luncheon was held and a reception tendered the
guests.

As has been described under the section devoted to Music,
the Virginia State Music Teachers Association held its annual
conference at Radford on April 5, 1924.

STUDENT CONVENTIONS

From November 1 to 3, 1929, the Baptist Student Union held
its annual meeting for the Virginia and Maryland Schools at Radford. Miss Lucille Christian, President of the Radford Baptist
Student Union was hostess. This conference brought to the campus many outstanding speakers and leaders of the Baptist Churches
in the South. The chief features of entertainment were a banquet
and reception.

The Virginia Inter-Collegiate Press Association met on the
College campus November 23, 1929 at which time the representatives of the student publications of the various colleges of Virginia were the guests of the Beehive and Grapurchat of the Radford
College. The girl representatives were entertained in the College
and the boy representatives were entertained at Blacksburg. The
program for this conference consisted of group discussions on
various problems of student publications. Receptions were held
in honor of the guests.

Other Student Associations which have met on this campus include the Student Volunteer Association meetings which were held
at the College in 1923 and 1927. (Described under religious life).

MOTORCADES

With the development of an interest in the building of good roads and cooperation of the various sections of the country it became a popular stunt to organize motorcades in various sections of the country to pay booster and good will visits to other localities. The location of the Radford College on the Lee Highway made this a convenient place to stop.

STATE CHAMBER OF COMMERCE GOOD WILL TOUR

Chief of these motorcades was an All-State visit sponsored by the Virginia State Chamber of Commerce led by Governor Harry Byrd, May 21, 1926. This party composed of business men of the various sections of the State travelled by motor bus over the main highways of the State. They were received at Radford with rousing cheers and songs by the hundreds of students arranged on the main triangle of the campus to form "VA" Virginia. Governor Byrd addressed this audience and the representative business men of the city from the front steps of the Tyler Hall.

ATLANTA DELEGATION

On September 6, 1927 a motorcade from Atlanta, Georgia made an afternoon stop on the campus of the Radford College. This motorcade of sixty-nine autos was sponsored by the Atlanta Journal. Many distinguished Atlantians were in the party. Chief among these was Bobby Jones who unfortunately had ear trouble just before reaching Radford and did not stop at the College. Long after the motorcade had departed Mrs. Cobb, mother of Ty Cobb, and her daughter who had been delayed at Marion, Virginia, by car trouble reached the college campus. Their visit was most interesting and enjoyable. They spent some time resting and relaxing after their experiences before proceeding to Roanoke to join the other Atlantians.

BOOSTERS FROM OTHER SECTIONS OF VIRGINIA

Local State motorcades have passed through Radford. Among these, a motorcade from Clifton Forge on August 12, 1927. The Roanoke Boosters have paid two visits to the college. These trips have been made by railroad. The boosters have paraded to the College or given talks and distributed souvenirs on the plaza of the Norfolk and Western station.

Various smaller groups sponsoring the Dixie Highway, Lee Highway, Blue Grass Trail, the Shenandoah National Park, the Broadway of America, etc., have stopped at the college when passing through on good will tours.

All of these motorcades have been received graciously by the students of the college. The usual greeting from the students of songs and yells followed by formal greetings from the mayor, Doctor McConnell, and other citizens of the city. Usually they were served light refreshments, mingled with the crowd and hurried away with floating banners and honking horns.

DISTINGUISHED VISITORS

The Radford College has been hostess to a number of distinguished visitors. In addition to those who have visited the college in connections with some of the conventions or motorcades described above, the General Assembly platform has served as the rostrum for many addresses.

NATIONAL POLITICAL LEADERS

The best known national figure ever to visit the Radford College was William Jennings Bryan who as a personal friend of Ex-Governor James Hoge Tyler spent several days visiting in this community. While here he delivered a public address at the college.

Other national figures of the political world who have visited the college are:

Honorable William C. Redfield, July 10, 1924.
Richard Pearson Hobson, who has visited the college
on several occasions, the last of which was November 17, 1927.
Congressman W. D. Upshaw of Georgia, November 9, 1924.
Honorable Patt Neff, Ex-Governor of Texas, November 2, 1929.
Congressman Clifton Woodrum of the Sixth District of
Virginia, several times.

DISTINGUISHED MINISTERS

When Billy Sunday was conducting a revival in Roanoke he spent one day as guest of the Radford College. In the afternoon he delivered a sermon in the auditorium. This sermon attracted the largest audience that has ever been assembled in the auditorium for any kind of religious service. Mr. Sunday was greeted by the ministers of the town. He was accompanied by Mrs. Sunday, Mr. Homer Rodehavor and his sister, Mrs. Thomas who gave a musical program as a feature of the service.

Rabbi Edward N. Calisch gave an outstanding address on July 16, 1930.

Reverend Van Kirk, originator of the Leag   of Nations Flag or the World Peace Ensign, and a delegate to the Edinberg Peace Conference was a speaker at the college on November 18, 1927.

In addition to these should be listed the ministers who have delivered baccalaureate sermons, among them are:

June 7, 1914 - Doctor Winn, Richmond, Virginia
June 6, 1917 - Doctor R. M. Standimer.
1918 - Dr. W. S. Neighbors
June, 1922 - Dr. J. Stuart French
September 1, 1922 - Honorable Hal Tyler
June 3, 1923 - Reverend Z. B. Randall and Doctor
           Ritchie Ware
1924 - Doctor George P. Rutledge
June 7, 1925 - Reverend Thomas K. Young, D.D.
June 6, 1926 - Doctor R. H. Crossfield.
June 5, 1927 - Doctor A. B. Conrad.
June 3, 1928 - Doctor Fred R. Chenault.
June 2, 1929 - Doctor S. M. Bedford.
June 8, 1930 - Doctor H. J. Derthick (twice).

COMMENCEMENT ADDRESS SPEAKERS

June 5, 1916 - Doctor John A. Morehead.
June 3, 1918 - Reverend J. W. Hill.
June 5, 1922 - Albert Pike Bourland, Ph. D.
June 9, 1924 - Doctor Sidney G. Gilbraith.
June 4, 1923 - Honorable Harris Hart.
December 19, 1924 - Doctor J. N. Hillman.
June 8, 1925 - Doctor John Calvin Metcalf.
August 27, 1925 - Doctor Horwix Harlan.
December 17, 1925 - Doctor Charles R. Brown.
June 7, 1926 - Honorable J. P. Fishburn.
August 26, 1926 - Doctor McKensey Folger.
December 21, 1926 - Doctor J. W. Smith
June 7, 1927 - Lieutenant Governor Frank B. Buchanan.
December 20, 1927 - Doctor John R. Hutcheson.

June 4, 1928 - Doctor Richard S. Owens.
June 3, 1929 - Honorable C. H. Morrissette.
August 22, 1929 - Doctor M. L. Moffett.
June 9, 1920 - Doctor Richard S. Owens.
August 28, 1930 - Doctor Sherrod.

Many outstanding evangelists who have conducted meetings
in the churches of Radford have spoken at the Assemblies.

DISTINGUISHED OUT-OF-STATE EDUCATORS

Many out-of-state educators have come to Radford.   Some of
the better known ones are:

From Columbia University:
Miss Mabel Carney, April 23, 1923
Miss Emma Gunther, December 6, 1925
Doctor Thomas Alexander
Doctor Gerald Craig

Doctor Josephus Hopwood and his wife, founders of Milligan
and Lynchburg Colleges and the Southeastern College, have made
frequent visits to the Radford College.

E. A. Winship, Editor of the New England Journal has visited
the College several times.

Richard T. Wyche, widely known story teller and educator
spent several weeks at the College on different occasions conducting Story Telling hours.

Doctor W. A. Kepner, Professor of Zoology at the University
of Virginia was a speaker before the Biology group on May 22,
1930.

Doctor C. C. Sherrod, President of the East Tennessee State
Teachers College, Johnson City, Tennessee, visited the College
on August 4, 1929.

Dean Minnix of Miami University inspected the College for
the American Teachers College Association.

Doctor Charles McKinney, President of the Ypsilanti State
Teachers College, Ypsilanti, Michigan, inspected the College for
the Virginia Educational Survey in 1927.

Doctor McBride, Specialist in Rural Education of the United States Department of Education, March 24, 1921.

President Henry Dirthick, President of Milligan College addressed the student body on February 14, 1924 and also delivered the Baccalaureate Sermon on June 8, 1930.

Doctor Edward T. Devine discussed three modern revolution leaders on February 24, 1925.

Mr. E. C. Wade, Superintendent of Bluefield Public Schools, November 2, 1925.

Doctor Emily D. Jamison, University of California, July 12, 1927.

Doctor Edward Knight, University of North Carolina delivered the Founders Day Address on May 8, 1928.

Mr. Eldridge of the American Education Press, June 21, 1928.

E..Ruth Pyrtle, President of the National Education Association.

GOVERNORS AS VISITORS

The Governors of Virginia who have visited the college are: Governors J. Hodges Mann, Westmoreland Davis, E. Lee Trinkle, Harry Flood Byrd, and John Garland Pollard.

Candidates for the governorship of Virginia who have spoken to the Radford College Students during their campaigns are: Doctor Rosewell Page, July 16, 1929; Senator Walter Mapp, July 23, 1925, and again in July 1929; William Mosby Brown, and John Garland Pollard, July 27, 1929.

OTHER STATE OFFICIALS

All the State Superintendents who have served the State since the establishment of the Radford College have paid frequent visits. Superintendent R. C. Stearnes was the first commencement orator; Superintendent Harris Hart came many times during his long administration; Doctor Sidney B. Hall has been most actively identified with the College since his appointment January 1, 1931. Other heads of the State offices who have visited the college include: Doctor Ennion Williams, State Board of Health; Honorable

Charles A. Osborne, State Purchasing Commission; Honorable Leroy Hodges, State Director of Budget; Honorable John A. Bradford, State Director of Budget; Sinclair Brown and Senator W. E. Garrett, Chairmen of the Finance Committees of the Virginia House and Senate.

LITERARY AUTHORS AND POETS

Writers who have visited the Radford College are:

David Anderson, Author of "Blue Moon" and "Red Law".
Tom Skeyhill, An Australian poet and orator, March 20, 1928.
Mr. James McChesney Prickett of Rural Retreat, Virginia, The Southwest Poet.
Doctor Lyons Tyler, grandson of the former Tyler of the United States and a great historian addressed the students of the college on January 28, 1929.
Colonel James Speed of Louisville, Kentucky, addressed the students on December 13, 1927. He is Editor of the Southern Agriculturist.
George Russell "AE" an Irish Poet, February 20, 1931.
H. Powell Chapman, Editor of the Roanoke Times, April 21, 1929.
Riley Scott, Vagabond Poet, January 29, 1930.

It is impossible to list all of the distinguished visitors who have frequented the Radford College. Scarcely a week passes without one or two State officials, representatives of prohibition causes, Welfare work, religious organizations or the business world speaking to the students and faculty of the college. All are urged to address the students in the : effort to "expose" them to all causes that are receiving human thought.

PART IV

ALUMNAE

SECTION I

ALUMNAE REUNIONS

The Class of 1914 started the long line of alumnae of the institution which in 1930 totals 1347 graduates.

The first formal alumnae reunion was held at the 1917 commencement when many members of the three previous classes returned to their Alma Mater. On this occasion a luncheon was served in honor of the alumnae in the new dining room recently opened in the Tyler Hall. The Faculty members and the wives of the gentlemen of the Faculty were guests of the College for this occasion.

Similar luncheons were conducted for several years. It was customary for some member of the Faculty to act as toastmaster, with Doctor McConnell as chief speaker to review the growth of the College.

FIRST ALUMNAE ASSOCIATION

In 1920 the alumnae group had grown to such proportions that it was decided to perfect a permanent organization of the alumnae association. A simple constitution was drawn up. Membership was extended to all graduates and former students of the College. This organization made no progress other than to establish itself in the minds of the students and to prepare for the 1921 Commencement reunion.

On June 5, 1922 the alumnae association held its first formal meeting. The opening feature of this program was the alumnae breakfast held in the dining room. Miss Mamie McLees had worked with Miss Lorene Caldwell, President of the Association, in the development of the program for this occasion. It was attractively worked out. The main three courses were described in satire on the curriculum then offered in the College. The chief feature of this program was an address by Mrs. Archer Phlegar Montague, Educational Secretary of the Virginia Farmers Union.

LOCAL ALUMNAE CHAPTERS

This meeting was followed by a more complete organization of the alumnae association. Under this plan alumnae chapters were proposed for organization in any community wherever there was a nucleus of the graduates of the college. The plans for the Alumnae Association were first announced in the catalog of 1922 and with this the official records of the organization were put in permanent form.

VIRGINIA INTER-COLLEGIATE ALUMNAE ASSOCIATION

In 1923 the Radford College united with the other Colleges of Virginia in the formation of inter-collegiate association of the alumnae of the higher educational institutions of Virginia. Miss Annie Sue Anderson, Secretary of the Radford association represented the Alumnae at a meeting of this new organization in Richmond. This organization united with a central committee representing the administrative officers of the higher educational institutions of Virginia in a concerted effort to acquaint Virginia with the needs of the various institutions of the State.

In 1924 the local alumnae united with the alumnae of the other teachers colleges in active effort to influence the passage of a bill leading to the change in name of the four State Normal Schools of the State Teachers Colleges.

NATIONAL INTER-COLLEGIATE ASSOCIATION

In 1924 Radford College also accepted membership in the National Inter-Collegiate Alumnae Association. Blanche Daniel and Ercelle Bennett attended the National meeting of this association in Toronto, Canada in 1927. In 1930 Mrs. Nina Helvy Salmons represented the Radford College in the Southern region of this association at Birmingham, Alabama; and at Hollins College, Winter Park, Florida, in 1932.

FULL TIME ALUMNAE SECRETARY

The building of the Student Activity Building increased interest in the Alumnae Association and resulted in the employment of Miss Helen Cook as Alumnae Secretary in 1924. The chief purpose of the Alumnae Secretary's office was to further the plans

for the Student Activity Building and at the same time to keep
the alumnae in closer touch with their Alma Mater. This work
she did most effectively, sending out frequent letters to all
subscribers of the association, collecting the annual dues of
$1.00. She also prepared cards for the alumnae members to keep
a record of their changes in professional positions, marriage,
and personal history.

To further the work of the Alumnae Secretary Doctor McConnell appointed a Faculty committee to work with her in the details of the organization in her office and in carrying forward the plans which were made by the committee. This committee,
composed of Professor William E. Gilbert, Chairman, Miss Moffett,
Mr. Whitt and Miss Cook. At their initial meeting on March 8, 1925,
they drew up an outline of the work which was to be carried on by
the Alumnae Secretary. This decoration of purpose became the
guide for the activities of Miss Cook.

ALUMNAE ASSOCIATION COMMITTEE OF
RADFORD STATE TEACHERS COLLEGE
January 8, 1925

SUGGESTIONS:

1. The office of Alumnae Secretary is one of dignity, development,
    opportunity, and systematic work.

2. The first duty of the Alumnae Secretary is to become so well
    acquainted with the students while in College; be so tied up
    with their work, both class room and extra curricula, that it
    will be impossible for them to disassociate her from any
    thought they may have of the College.

    We suggest as a means to realize the above aim the following:

    (a) An acquaintanceship to the point of name, local and home
    address, society affiliation, chief school interest, dominating
    personal traits, i.e. whether quiet, aggressive, executive abil-
    ity.

    (b) The Secretary should keep "personal" cards of each indi-
    vidual student on which should be noted from time to time such
    points of information as might develop as would at the time
    of graduation make a complete record of the student's life in
    the institution. The Secretary should visit each student in

her room, should freely associate with them on the campus, attend their society and Y. W. C. A. meeting, athletics, and the preliminary activities as in the preparation of plays, annual work, Grapurchat, etc., and at all times gain the confidence of the students to the degree that they will seek her advice and cooperation.

(c) Above all else avoid clanish association with one or only a few students, or taking sides in matter of controversy.

(d) Must hold herself on a democratic level with students, and at the same time possess such dignity and self-respect that the students will not associate her in their mind and actions in the same way they would students.

(e) At present a chasm exists between teaching seniors and the current life of the institution. This condition could well be corrected by the Secretary and would also serve as an ideal practice field for her alumnae activities. She should meet these students at their lunch and tell them of what is going on about the college in general, the announcements of the General Assembly, etc. Get their opinions, etc., report these back to the various organizations as nature of the matter may invite.

(f) Arrange for these teaching students to attend Assembly when big events are on schedule.

(g) She should frequently go to the training schools, go several times to Belspring for weekends.

(h) Keep a list of counties and cities of former students. These should be furnished to faculty members before leaving on trips to these respective localities. Some times letters should be written in advance of visits by members of the Faculty, etc.

(i) Furnish interesting talking points to "going out" Faculty members so that they may easily enter upon conversation with former students.

(j) Report on anything of unusual interest in connection with the life of students who have gone out in the world, as weddings, hospital experiences, achievements, keep a cradle roll, etc.

OUT OF SCHOOL ACTIVITIES FOR SECRETARY

1. The second duty of the Secretary is to work up and preserve
   a closer affiliation with the College of all graduates and
   former students. We suggest as a means to realizing this
   aim the following:

   (a) Acquaintanceship with former students may be got and
   kept up to date.
   (b) Questionnaires, list of teachers from the administrative
   offices of the college.
   (c) Daily reading of the newspapers in fields where many of
   our people are located.
   (d) Conference with members of faculty after they return
   from places where they have made addresses, attended conferences, etc., regarding students whom they have met.
   (e) From time to time consult various members of faculty for
   information they may have received through letters and in
   other ways about students. This should be so constant that
   the faculty would form a sort of habit of looking for and
   reporting such information to the Secretary.
   (f) Edit an "Alumnae Achievement" column in Rural Messages.
   (g) Edit Alumnae notes in the Grapurchat.
   (h) Attend Assembly with promptness and regularity and act
   as though she enjoyed it.
   (i) From time to time she should read letters from former
   students.
   (j) She should have several well prepared educational addresses which could be delivered at teachers institutes, etc.
   (k) Carry on the organization of Alumnae Chapters wherever
   feasible and supply such organizations with outlines of constitution and bylaws. Send out suggestive programs to these
   organizations with topics to be discussed. Send circular
   reports of activity carried on by several chapters.

ACTIVITIES IN CONNECTION WITH LITERARY SOCIETIES
HOME BUILDING PROJECT

1. Keep records of pledges and do any and all other kinds of
work connected with the collecting of same. Make reports to
societies of funds, etc. and confer with society officers and
secure when necessary the aid of these persons in helping to
collect pledges, etc.

2. Cooperate with active members in Annual Roll-Call and Pow Wow.

3. Stimulate as large pledges as possible from resident students.

4. Work definitely on all programs for raising of funds.

5. To work with the Faculty in keeping before the student the solemn fact that the one biggest job for all of the next few years is the erection of the Society homes.

DUTIES OF THE FACULTY ADVISORY COMMITTEE

1. To have a sense of sympathy and appreciation of the activities of the alumnae Secretary and her work.

2. To make her feel this spirit as actuating the work of the Committee at all times.

3. To hold weekly conferences to consider the work of the office and to hold themselves ready at all times to be consulted by the Secretary.

4. To be ready to help the Secretary carry out any and all the foregoing suggestions and especially to pay upon the heart of us all the matter of pushing forward constantly every possible step looking toward the early erection of the society homes.

5. By their actions, thoughts, and manner create in the mind of the student body and faculty the importance of the work of the Alumnae Secretary.

6. This committee should try at as early a date as possible to bring about the affiliation of the secretaryship of this College with the national organization fostering similar work in other Colleges.

COOPERATION WITH ADMINISTRATIVE OFFICES

The committee feels that there is possibly some overlaping of work now being done or may be done by the Alumnae Secretary and some of the administrative workers. In order that this may be cleared up and the greatest economy practiced we recommend that a conference be held soon by the administrative officers and this committee.

This decoration of purpose and outline of work for the Alumnae Secretary gives the most objective picture recorded in the institution of the work of the Alumnae Association. Miss Cook remained in the College for two years.

Upon her resignation the responsibility for the collection of the funds of the Student Activity Building was given to the Business Manager of the College. The Alumnae activities were continued by Miss Blanche Daniel who was elected President of the Association in 1927. Under the leadership of Miss Daniel the Alumnae Association was very active. Through her efforts many local chapters were organized in various parts of the State. A charter was planned for these Alumnae Chapters. This plan was explained in detail to the students of the summer quarter and a temporary chairman was elected to organize each county. This resulted in local Radford meetings and in the complete organization of a chapter in Roanoke, Bristol, Pocahontas, Radford, Bluefield, Wise, Clifton Forge, Franklin, and Pulaski. These organizations held group meetings several times during the year and sponsored activities to raise money for the Student Activity Building and to acquaint the students of their respective communities with the opportunities and work of the Radford College.

The Radford local chapter of the alumnae association naturally has been most active in its support of the College activities. The chapter holds monthly meetings and each year for the past four years has sponsored an entertainment, the procedures of which they have donated to the Student Activity Building Fund or to some gift to the College. In 1929 they presented the Student Building with a radio. The Radford Chapter has taken part in the annual city stunt night and on three occasions has been winner of the prize for the best stunt presented.

THANKSGIVING MEETING

At the Lynchburg meeting of the Virginia Educational Association, November 1913, a joint banquet was held by the representatives of the four Normal schools. This was Radford's first meeting away from home. Faculty members were the only representatives.

In the Fall of 1921 the custom of having an annual alumnae banquet in connection with the meeting of the State Teachers Association in Richmond was started. A faculty committee was appointed to perfect the arrangements for this. The arrangements for these annual reunions were conducted in the President's office of the College. Letters were written to all of the graduates and many of the former students urging them to attend the reunions.

Mr. Bowers was the active manager of the dinners in Richmond. These were held at the Murphey's Hotel. Members of the faculty sold tickets to as many of the former students who could be induced to attend. The first two or three dinners were attended by an average of one hundred or more including friends of the institution who were invited to attend by Doctor McConnell. The most successful of these dinners was held in November 1922 when the project for the building of the Society homes was launched. At this time the alumnae announced the Alumnae Song which had been written by Miss Gertrude Shumate.

In the fall of 1926 the Roanoke Chapter sponsored and made complete arrangements for the annual alumnae dinner in connection with the meeting of the State Educational Conference in Roanoke. This dinner was held in the large ball room of the Patrick Henry Hotel. Many distinguished guests were present. Chief among these was Doctor Benjamin Andrews of Teachers College, New York City.

The local chapter has assumed the responsibility for the commencement reunion of the alumnae association and have perfected the plans for the annual meeting. Their programs have included the luncheons and receptions which have been given in honor of the visiting alumnae. Another courtesy which this chapter has extended has been a reception in honor of the Seniors and the two-year graduates in May of each year. At this time the graduates are received into the Alumnae Association. A very interesting link ceremony has been worked out by Miss Daniel by which the students put their personal link to the endless chain of the alumnae. Those completing the two-year course use gray links and those of the four-year class the purple link. In 1930 (June) this ceremony was carried on as a part of the gowning program preceding the supper on the campus. The old students were grouped according to classes, and representatives of each class since 1914. The Class of 1928 had the largest number present.

The administration of the College keeps in close touch with the alumnae. A letter is sent out to each graduate of the institution two or three times each year. The Grapurchat issues a special Alumnae issue at Thanksgiving time each year. Two local Alumnae usually act as Alumnae Editors of the Grapurchat and each issue gives some news of the achievements of the Alumnae. The College makes an effort to record the personal and professional achievements of the Alumnae. Miss Allen and Mr. Whitt have preserved an almost accurate record of the marriages of the students. Many wedding invitations and announcements are on file in the Alumnae office of the Student Activity Building.

AN ANALYTICAL STUDY OF THE "AFTER COLLEGE LIFE" OF 970
GRADUATES OF THE STATE TEACHERS COLLEGE, EAST RADFORD, VIRGINIA
BY
M'LEDGE MOFFETT, DEAN OF WOMEN
State Teachers College, East Radford, Virginia

On June 4, 1914 the State Teachers College at Radford, Virginia
(then called Normal School) opened its doors to allow its first group
of graduates to pass out into the service of the State. This group
of five fledglings was followed in 1915 by thirty more graduates and
so increasingly each year the line has lengthened until in 1930 there
is a total of 1194 graduates* from the two-year course, a total of
253 from the four-year course, or a grand total of 1347 graduates.
Wither have they gone? What service have they rendered? How has
life unfolded for them? These are questions which surge through the
minds of those who wish them well.

In order to answer these questions in part, a study has been
made of the after-college life of the graduates of the Radford College. This study is another phase of a more extensive study by the
same author "The Social Background and Activities of Teachers College Students", published by the Bureau of Publications, Teachers
College, New York City, 1929. These two studies of the "Before"
and "After College life" of teachers college students are designed
to show some aspects of the type of education the teacher college
should give.

A questionnaire was circulated to the members of the Radford
classes of 1914 to 1930 inclusive. Of these 970 replied, about
200 letters were returned unclaimed from the last known address.
The data compiled from these replies form the basis of this analytical study of "After College Life".

PROFESSIONAL SERVICE

Teaching Experience

Since the Radford College is primarily a teacher training institution and all who attend it pledge themselves to teach, the
first problem of the study was directed to determine the professional status of the graduates. Seven hundred and seventy or eighty per
cent of the entire group report some teaching experience since
graduation. Five hundred and fifty-two or seventy per cent have

*This report was prepared and read June 4, 1932 at the Alumnae
Conovocation by Doctor M'Ledge Moffett.

taught as many as three years; three hundred and fifty-five or
forty-six per cent have taught five years, and fifty-eight or
eight per cent have taught ten years.

TYPE OF SERVICE

The average graduate has held one position. She teaches
in a five to ten teacher school. The entire group has held 1089
positions or an average of 1.4 each. Twelve per cent of these
positions are in one-teacher schools; thirteen per cent in two-
teacher schools; eighteen per cent in three-to five-teacher schools;
twenty-one per cent in five to ten-teacher school; twelve per cent
in ten to fifteen-teacher school; and twenty-three per cent teach
in schools with sixteen or more teachers. Practically all of the
two-year graduates are teachers in the elementary schools.   The
four-year graduates are mostly located in high schools and   are
teaching two or more subjects.

PLACE OF SERVICE

Seventy-three per cent of the graduates found positions in
Virginia; the majority of these within a radius of seventy-five
miles of their homes. Twenty-seven per cent of the teaching positions held by Radford graduates are in other States. Of these
West Virginia and North Carolina tie with thirty-five per cent
each, while the remainder are distributed in fifteen States, two
insular possessions, and one foreign country. These states are:
Maryland, Tennessee, Kentucky, Ohio, New York, New Jersey, Connecticut, Florida, Texas, South Carolina, Georgia, Arizona, Michigan, Colorado, and the possessions and foreign country are: Porto
Rico, Phillipines, and Canada.

SALARY OF TWO-YEAR GRADUATES

For those who completed the two-year course the initial median salary was $75.13 per month with a range of from $50.00 to
$190.00. After three years the median salary increased to
$81.78 with a range of $50.00 to $180.00. For the fifth year
the median salary is $87.40 with an increasing number at the up-
per end of the range, $40.00 to $200.00. For those of ten years
experience the median salary is $108.14 while three of the fifty-
eight find themselves in the $250.00 class and only one is earn-
ing as low as $70.00 per month.

SALARY OF FOUR-YEAR GRADUATES

The initial median salary for those completing the four-year
courses with the Bachelor's degree is $111.36 with a range from
$80.00 to $250.00. For the third year of teaching experience the
median is $125.56 and after five years the median salary is $151.25.
Only two of this group have taught ten years.

ADDITIONAL PROFESSIONAL EDUCATION

Two hundred and seventy Radford graduates report some form of
study in forty-nine other colleges and universities; of these two
hundred and four or eighty per cent have confined this study to
summer courses, thirty-eight or fourteen per cent have attended
regular sessions (September to June) and twenty-eight or ten per
cent have had extension courses.

For summer study forty-three per cent have attended the University of Virginia; seventeen per cent, Columbia University; eight
per cent, Roanoke College; eleven or five per cent, Virginia Polytechnic Institute; nine or four per cent at Peabody College. Columbia University has attracted twenty-nine per cent for full session
study; Peabody College, sixteen per cent; University of Virginia,
sixteen per cent. The extension courses of the University of Virginia and William and Mary College have led in attendance by Radford graduates.

DEGREES EARNED

Eighty-nine per cent of those doing full time study have received degrees from other institutions; of this number fifty-three
per cent received Master of Arts degree, eighty-five per cent of
which were conferred by Columbia University; twenty-five per cent
received the Bachelors degree, six of these were conferred by other
teachers colleges of the State, two by Columbia, and one each by
Roanoke College and Emory and Henry College.

TYPES OF ADDITIONAL STUDY

Of the sixty-two subjects listed as indicative of the type
of work taken in these other institutions, twenty-four per cent
of the four hundred forty-eight courses taken were in Education;
seventeen per cent in History and Sociology; seventeen per cent
in English, while Art, Music, Physical Education, Home Economics
and Mathematics received frequent mention. Since these same fields

constitute the major elections of the students at Radford, it may be concluded that additional study is continued in the same area of interest.

PROFESSIONAL AFFILIATIONS

Five hundred and eighty-eight or ninety per cent of these engaged in teaching report membership in one or more of forty-eight professional organizations. (Total number of memberships, 835). Naturally the Virginia Educational Association and Association and the local county associations enlist the largest membership. Exclusive of these the National Educational Association has twenty-six of the memberships, while more specialized organizations as Science Clubs, National Physical Educational Association, Poetry Society, Childhood Education Association, Home Economics Associations, etc. have fourteen per cent of the remaining memberships.

TRAVEL

The automobile has made possible some expansion of vision by travel. Practically all of the group report one "big" trip, most of these are limited to sight-seeing in Virginia and neighboring states, short visits to Washington, D. C., New York, while several report tours across the continent and to Europe.

FORMS OF ECONOMIC EMPLOYMENT
OTHER THAN TEACHING FOLLOWED BY RADFORD GRADUATES

The versality of the graduates and the adaptability of their education is shown in the fact that Radford Graduates have found forty-eight other occupations than teaching. Two hundred and nineteen or twelve per cent of the entire group have been so engaged. Some of these have preceded or followed this other form of employment by teaching experience.

The forty-eight occupations are classified as follows:

1. Educational work other than teaching, such as Home Demonstration Agents, Librarians, Councilors, Playground and Recreational Directors. In this class fourteen per cent found employment.

2. Clerical and office work, such as Bookkeepers, Stenographers,

Filing Clerks, Deputy clerk, etc. In this class eighteen per cent found employment.

3. Business--Store and Tea Room Managers, Beauty Specialists, Agriculture, Agents, Bankers, etc. In this class fourteen per cent found employment.

4. Religious and Social Service--Deaconess, Y. W. C. A., Sunday School, and other Church assistants, and Settlement Work. In this class four per cent found employment.

5. Other professions: Nurses, Dietitians, Linotype operators, Telegraph Operators, and Journalists. In this class six per cent are engaged.

6. Miscellaneous: Seamstress, Model in Garment Shop, Post Office, Housekeeping, paid employment in the miscellaneous group forty-four per cent distributed over ten or more different types of work found employment.

MARRIED ALUMNAE

Of the nine hundred and seventy alumnae replying to the questionnaire, three hundred and fifty-or thirty-six per cent are married. The median graduate married two years after graduation while eighty-five per cent are married within six years. Therefore, by dropping the last six classes the percentage of married graduates is increased to forty per cent which shows marriage and the resultant home making a major profession of Radford graduates. The median marriage at the time of the report had occurred of one and nine-tenths years before while twenty per cent had been married five years or more.

FAMILY OF MARRIED ALUMNAE

Husbands

The average married graduate either knew the man she afterwards married at the time of graduation or met him within the next twelve months. No insight is given as to the type of man selected by these graduates except his vocational interest. These include (based on a random sample of the married group) twenty-one per cent farmers, eighteen per cent office clerks and bookkeepers; thirteen per cent teachers, and other educational workers; ten per cent merchants; eighteen per cent railroad men or mechanics; eight per cent ministers, doctors, chemists.

Ambition and economic stability is shown by the great number of graduates who report home ownership as already accomplished or as one of their major projects at present. Only two report marriage broken by divorce, several are widowed.

Children

These homse have been blessed with three hundred and thirty-six (163 girls, and 173 boys) children. One hundred and fifty-six of the graduates have no children, ninety-two have one child, sixty-one have two children, twenty-eight have three children, seven have four children, and two have five children. The median age of the children is three and nine-tenths years.

Interests

Husbands, children, and homes have become the absorbing interest of the married alumnae. In reply to the question, "What are your major interests or ambition now?" these always come first, some apologetically qualify the statement as due to the age of the babies and faithfully add Church and Sunday School work. Significant is the lack of educational and school activity.

Professional Work

The large number (131) who have been married less than two years and those who do not have any children (156) may account for the rather high percentage of fifty-one per cent of married alumnae who have continued teaching. Significant is the fact that these are teaching at a somewhat reduced salary. The last median salary prior to marriage was $88.26 and the first median salary after marriage $86.38.

The other data from the professional life of this group were reported in combination with the entire group in the previous section.

Other Employment Outside the Home

Some form of economic work has been continued by many of these married alumnae after marriage. In many cases they have been assistants, partners, or employees in the husband's business while others have worked in the various occupational groups as reported above. The greater part of this employment was for part time or of short duration, average about one year after marriage.

Subjective Reactions

The most interesting part of the entire inquiry was the subjective reactions to those questions for which objective facts are impossible. These were directed to determine growth, maturity, ambition, memory, inspirations, and habits of behavior. In the most part these responses ring with frankness and sincerity. A random grouping of these replies are included as direct quotations from the questionnaires--

"I have become more broad minded since leaving the College, developed an entirely different attitude towards life, a more optimistic one."

"European travel, tutoring of Japanese Naval Officers sent to Princeton University, helped them learn English and make some worthwhile friends is a very interesting experience."

"My first work as a teacher was to open and organize the Home Economics Courses in a Second Rural Unit where I had to teach grils from the grades of five to eight. At first I had no room to work in and I taught in a coffee warehouse. I had to manage a school lunch room for one hundred and forty-four pupils."

"I have had some rich experiences in two mountain schools teaching cleanliness, morals, and honesty along with the regular school work. Comments from the patrons and pupils are proof of the success. I have a broader vision now and realize my place is to give service rather than to tell others to give."

"Teaching in a mining town and association with people who could not speak the English Language."

"My outlook on life is broader an my interests in social problems are much more extensive."

"A visit to the Island of Haiti, Cooking supper in the interior of Panama on a gasoline stove with thirty-two natives looking on. Since leaving school I have learned to live and let live. An interesting experience also was digging Indian graves for pottery."

"One of my most interesting experiences was visiting the Do X-German Flying Boat, it was quite interesting and so different

from anything I had ever seen before. Since leaving college
I have learned to be more self-dependent, and feel that I can
meet the daily obligations more strongly."

"Living one year and working among the Kentucky Mountain
people afforded some of the most interesting experiences for
me."

"The influence and friendship of Dr. McConnell has helped
me to realize my ambition and to make a worthwhile teacher of
myself by telling me how I could make my way by going in the
summer when my parents who owned a farm that then produced an
income of four thousand a year and was free from debt made me
do without a college education or make by own way except for
the last two terms."

"Attending the committee meeting of the House of Delegates
when they were discussing the Senate Bill No. 70."

"I spent the summer as a counsilor in a girls' camp near
Philadelphia, Pennsylvania, and it was a very valuable experience."

"My superintendent asked me to take a class of pupils in
the Beginners Class and keep them for one year and see what
the record would be. I did and as a result they obtained one
achievement score of third grade pupils in reading, two pupils
won a prize over the whole school in their rating. This year
the same pupils scored fifth grade work. They are just about
seven and a few months old."

"My husband and I keep house but I still teach. I have a
maid and my time during the day is taken up with my work at
school. After I meet my husband at the close of his work I
devote that time to my home and him. We have no children but
we claim the neighbors' children and we always have a house
full."

"I teach public school during the week, Sunday School on
Sunday, and keep house between acts. I have been married nearly
seven years and taught school five of that time."

"Perfect happiness reigns in our home. We have many friends
with whom we spend many enjoyable hours. I am keeping up with
my Latin and French. My husband is a writer and I do everything
to encourage it, sometimes I think up plots for stories. He
also gives drawing. I pride myself in being a good housekeeper
and my greatest aim is to always keep the home a place in which

412

both of us are happier than anywhere else."

"Since leaving the college I am more Catholic and tolerant and more efficient professionally."

"My husband and I taught our first school together. I can better appreciate the value of an education now than when in Radford."

College Colors:

        Purple and Gray - Adopted by the Faculty and
        Students in 1913.

School Seal

Adopted by the First Board of Trustees and Modified
as the name of the school was changed.

- MOTTO -

"If we work upon marble, it will perish;
if we work upon brass, time will ef-
face it; if we rear temples, they
will crumble into dust; but if
we work upon immortal minds
and imbue them with prin-
ciples and with a just
fear of God and love of
their fellowmen, we en-
grave on those tablets
something that will
brighten to all
eternity."

                       -- Webster.

Selected by Dr. John Preston McConnell before 1913

APPENDIX

MEMBERS OF THE VARIOUS BOARDS OF TRUSTEES

W. W. Baker, Manchester, Virginia--1913, 1914.
Richard Lee Beale, Bowling Green, Virginia--1924, 1927.
Mr. J. S. Bourne, Independence, Virginia--1925, 1930.
Dr. J. D. Buchanan, Marion, Virginia--1914, 1915.
Honorable T. G. Burch, Martinsville, Virginia--1930, 1931.
Honorable Harry Flood Byrd, Winchester, Virginia--1926, 1930.
Honorable R. L. Chamberlayne, Phenix, Virginia--1919, 1923.
Honorable Cecil Connor, Leesburg, Virginia--1927, 1930.
Honorable George N. Conrad, Harrisonburg, Virginia--1923, 1930.
Miss Kathryn Cook, Roanoke, Virginia--1922, 1925.
*Honorable Merritt T. Cooke, Norfolk, Virginia--1914, 1923.
Honorable Robert W. Daniel, Prince George, Virginia--1930
Honorable Westmoreland Davis, Leesburg, Virginia--1916, 1922.
W. L. Davidson, Jonesville, Virginia--1922, 1924.
Dr. H. M. Dejarnette, Fredericksburg, Virginia--1919, 1930.
*Honorable J. H. Gose, Bristol, Virginia--1914, 1915.
Honorable Norman R. Hamilton, Portsmouth Star, Portsmouth,
      Virginia, 1923, 1930.
Honorable Herbert H. Harris, Lynchburg, Virginia--1930, 1932.
Honorable Harris Hart, Richmond, Virginia--1916, 1930.
Honorable H. L. Hooker, Stuart, Virginia--1923, 1925.
Honorable Robert M. Hughes, Norfolk, Virginia, 1930.
Honorable D. D. Hull, Roanoke, Virginia--1914-1922.
Miss Jemina C. Hurt, Roanoke, Virginia--1925, 1928.
Mr. J. P. Jones, New Castle, Virginia--1913, 1914.
Honorable W. W. King, Mary Baldwin College, Staunton,
      Virginia--1914, 1919.
Honorable E. O. Larrick, Middletown, Virginia--1919, 1923.
Senator George W. Layman, New Castle, Virginia--1925, 1930.
Honorable Robert McIntyre, Warrenton, Virginia--1924, 1930.
Benjamin Mears, Eastville, Virginia--1922, 1928.
Otho F. Mears, Eastville, Virginia--1914, 1920.
Rose MacDonald, Berryville, Virginia--1930.
Mrs. P. W. Miller, Pearisburg, Virginia--1927, 1930.
Honorable R. Walton Moore, Fairfax, Virginia--1931.
W. O. Moore, Wytheville, Virginia--1913, 1914.
Senator R. J. Noell, East Radford, Virginia--1913, 1914.
Mrs. D. W. Persinger, Roanoke, Virginia--1928, 1930.
Honorable Alfred G. Preston, Amsterdam, Virginia--1914, 1925.
George B. Russell, Charlotte, Virginia--1914, 1919.
Superintendent Joseph H. Saunders, Newport News, Virginia, 1930.
*Honorable J. W. Sheffey, Marion, Virginia--1913, 1914.
Honorable O. L. Shewmake, Richmond, Virginia--1915, 1919.

Note: *Deceased.

Miss Frances Shumate, Glen Lyn, Virginia--1923, 1927.
Superintendent W. D. Smith, Gate City, Virginia--1913, 1914.
Honorable. R. C. Stearnes, Richmond, Virginia--1913, 1914.
*Honorable Henry C. Stuart, Richmond, Virginia--1914, 1917.
*Honorable Frank Talbott, Danville, Virginia--1913, 1914.
Honorable George L. Taylor, Big Stone Gap, Virginia--1919, 1923.
Honorable C. S. Towes, Reedville, Virginia--1928, 1930.
Honorable E. Lee Trinkle, Roanoke, Virginia--1922, 1926, 1930.
*Doctor P. E. Tucker, Buckingham, Virginia--1913, 1914.
Honorable S. J. Turlington, Accomac, Virginia--1921, 1922.
Honorable George M. Warren, Bristol, Virginia--1920, 1923.
Miss Belle Webb, Petersburg, Virginia--1919, 1930.
*Honorable Brock T. White, Keezletown, Virginia--1914, 1919.
Honorable B. T. Wilson, Lebanon, Virginia--1913, 1914.

Chairmen of the Board

W. T. Baldwin, East Radford, Virginia--1913, 1914.
Richard B. Davis, Petersburg, Virginia--1914, 1917.
Honorable W. Clyde Locker, Richmond, Virginia--1914, 1930.
Judge John W. Price, Washington, D. C.--1914, 1919.
Honorable V. R. Shackleford, Orange, Virginia--1914, 1924; 1933.
L. L. Scherer, Richmond, Virginia--1913, 1914.

Secretaries of the Board

Judge G. E. Cassell, East Radford, Virginia--1913, 1914.
Dr. Thomas D. Eason, Richmond, Virginia--1931, 1932.
D. Sidney B. Hall, Richmond, Virginia--1931.
Honorable A. Stuart Robertson, Orange, Virginia--1915, 1920.
Honorable V. R. Shackleford, Orange, Virginia--1914, 1924, 1933.
Honorable Robert K. Brock, Farmville, Virginia--1920, 1930.

APPROPRIATIONS BY LEGISLATURE FOR SUPPORT
of
RADFORD COLLEGE
1911 - 1912

For the establishment of the State Normal and Industrial
School for White Women, at Radford, the sum of twenty-five
thousand dollars; for the purpose of the said school there
shall be paid out of the public treasury, from time to time,
such sums as shall be appropriated to incidental expenses,
erection of necessary buildings, the salaries of officers
and teachers, and to maintain the efficiency of said school;
provided, that the Commonwealth shall not in any instance be
responsible for any debts contracted or expenditure made by
the said institution in excess of the appropriation made,
which shall not be available prior to January first, nineteen
hundred and twelve.[1]

For improvement, twenty-five thousand dollars...$25,000.00
For support, ten thousand dollars.............. 10,000.00[2]

State Normal and Industrial School
for Women at Radford:

For improvement, twenty-five thousand dollars...$25,000.00
For support, fifteen thousand dollars........... 15,000.00[3]

State normal and industrial school for women at Radford:

For support, twenty-three thousand dollars.........$23,000.00
For building dormitory, thirty-five thousand
dollars... 35,000.00
For equipment of Administration building, six
thousand dollars...................................... 6,000.00
For laundry building, two thousand dollars.......... 2,000.00
University of Virginia, for support, eighty
thousand dollars, which shall include the ten thousand
dollars provided for by an act approved January twenty-
third, eighteen hundred and ninety-six, chapter one
hundred and thirty-six, acts eighteen hundred and ninety-
five, ninety-six, upon condition that the University of
Virginia shall give instructions to properly prepare white
students from Virginia without charge for tuition or uni-

1. Acts of Assembly, 1910. pp 417-418.
2. Acts of Assembly, 1912. p 253.
3. Acts of Assembly, 1912. p 270.

versity fee in the academic department of more than ten dollars,
which ten dollars shall cover all the items covered by the former university fee of forty dollars, but shall not interfere
with the ten dollars contingent deposit. For support of hospital twenty-two thousand five hundred dollars, for the free
treatment, care, and maintenance of Virginia patients, one
hundred and two thousand five hundred dollars....$102,500.00
For repairs and painting buildings, fifteen
thousand dollars..................................... 15,000.00
For sewerage system, seven thousand five
hundred dollars......................................   7,500.00[1]

State normal and industrial school for women at
Radford:

For support, twenty-eight thousand dollars........$28,000.00
Power house, six thousand dollars.................. 6,000.00
For laundry building, two thousand dollars........ 2,000.00
Furniture for dormitory, three thousand dollars... 3,000.00
Water works, improvement, four thousand dollars... 4,000.00[2]

Chap. 52--An act to appropriate the sum of twenty-one thousand
dollars to the State Normal and Industrial School for women at
Radford.
Approved February 15, 1915

Be it enacted by the general assembly of Virginia, that the
sum of twenty-one thousand dollars, or so much thereof, as may
be necessary, be and the same is hereby appropriated out of any
funds in the treasury not otherwise appropriated to the State
normal and industrial school for women at Radford, said sum to
be used and applied in the payment of debts now due and owing
by said State normal and industrial school for women at Radford.

Provided, however, that no part of this money shall be paid
until the State accountant shall have made a thorough examination of the said debt and approved the items, as having been
expended for the benefit of the above mentioned school.[3]

State Normal School for Women at Radford:

For support, thirty thousand dollars..............$30,000.00
To complete first unit of dormitory and to build
one additional unit, twenty-three thousand
dollars.. 23,000.00

1. Acts of Assembly, 1914. p 333.
2. Acts of Assembly, 1914. p 357.
3. Acts of Assembly, 1915. p 79.

To equip the same, one thousand five hundred dollars.. $1,500.00[1]

Students' Loan Fund

The State normal at Farmville, the State normal and industrial schools for women at Harrisonburg, Fredericksburg, and Radford, the Virginia agricultural and mechanical college and polytechnic institute, the University of Virginia, and William and Mary College, may each draw from the treasury of the State from funds not otherwise appropriated, in addition to the sum appropriated to the support of these institutions, annually, a sum not to exceed one per centum for each year's appropriation to said institutes, for support, which sums shall be used for the establishment of the State Students' loan fund at each of the several institutions, respectively, three thousand eight hundred dollars.... $3,800.00

Each of the said institutions shall, upon such terms and according to such rules as may be prescribed by the respective boards of Trustees or visitors, make loans from the said State Students' loan funds to needy and deserving students of talent and character from Virginia in the academic departments in said institutions, for the purpose of aiding these to obtain an education at such institutions, who might not be able otherwise to do so, the said loan shall not exceed one hundred dollars, in any one session to same student, and shall be made to said student upon such terms as to time and security as the authorities of the respective institutions shall determine in each case; provided, that the rate of interest charged students on such loans shall be four per centum per annum.

The said State students' loan fund shall be preserved from depletion by the said institutions, and, together with the repayment and accretions thereto, shall be held and used for the purpose specified in this act and no other; and each of the said institutions shall annually, not later than July in each year thereafter file in the office of the State superintendent of public instruction a statement in detail, showing for the year past the amounts received by said funds, or the loans made, to whom made, and upon what terms, the amount of the corpus of said fund, the amounts repaid to said funds, and from whom, and any other information deemed pertinent by the institution so reporting, or which may have been requested by the superintendent of public instruction.[2]

State Normal School for Women at Radford:

For support, forty-five thousand dollars.......... $45,000.00

1. Acts of Assembly, 1916. p 930.
2. Acts of Assembly, 1916. p 933.

For completion of second unit of dormitory, seven
thousand five hundred dollars........................ $7,500.00
For boiler and steam connection for power house,
three thousand dollars............................... 3,000.00
For laundry equipment, one thousand five
hundred dollars...................................... 1,500.00[1]

State Normal School for Women at Radford:

For support, forty-five thousand dollars............$45,000.00
For repairs and general equipment, eight
thousand dollars..................................... 8,000.00[2]

State Normal School for Women at Radford:

For maintenance and operation of the State normal school
for women at East Radford..........................$75,450.00
It is provided that out of this appropriation of
seventy-five thousand four hundred and fifty dollars
there shall be expended not exceeding:
For equipment of use in education in professional and
collegiate courses................................... 2,000.00
For equipment for library............................ 1,000.00
For equipment for use in maintenance of students
and employees.. 2,500.00
For making loans to students......................... 600.00
For equipment for use in operation of laundry....... 1,500.00
For equipment for use in connection with the
construction and maintenance of buildings and
grounds.. 500.00
For grading and fencing of grounds................... 4,500.00[3]

The maintenance and operation of the State normal
school for women at East Radford....................$72,830.00
It is provided that out of this appropriation of
seventy-two thousand eight hundred and thirty dollars
there shall be expended, not exceeding:
For equipment for use in education in professional
and collegiate courses............................... 1,500.00
For equipment for library............................ 1,000.00
For equipment for use in maintenance of
students and employees............................... 2,500.00
For making loans to students......................... 600.00[4]
For equipment for use in operation of laundry....... 1,500.00

1. Acts of Assembly 1918, pp 709;
2. Acts of Assembly 1918, p 741.
3. Acts of Assembly 1920, p 144.
4. Acts of Assembly 1920, p 184.

For equipment for use in connection with the construction and maintenance of buildings and grounds........... $1,300.00

It is further provided, however, that no part of this appropriation of seventy-two thousand eight hundred dollars shall be used for board, lodging, tuition or care of students taking high school courses at this school.

For maintenance and operation of the State Normal School for women at East Radford............................... 78,705.00
It is provided that out of this appropriation of
seventy-eight thousand seven hundred and five dollars
there is hereby appropriated for additional equipment.. 3,400.00
For making loans to students.......................... 800.00[1]

For maintenance and operation of the state normal school for women at East Radford............................... $137,447.00
It is provided that out of this appropriation of one
hundred and thirty-seven thousand four hundred and
forty-seven dollars there is hereby appropriated:
For additional equipment.............................. $5,200.00
For equipment for new dormitory....................... 5,000.00
For additional equipment for kitchen.................. 2,500.00
For completion of third unit of dormitory............. 50,000.00
For making loans to students.......................... 0,800.00[2]

For maintenance and operation of the State Teachers College at Radford.................................... $68,055.00
It is provided that out of this appropriation there is
hereby appropriated for:
Additional equipment.................................. 1,250.00
Making loans to students.............................. 800.00[3]

For maintenance and operation of the State Teachers College at Radford................................... $85,130.00
It is provided that out of this appropriation there is
hereby appropriated:
For additional equipment.............................. 19,100.00
For improvement to walks and roofs.................... 800.00
For making loans to students.......................... 800.00 [4]

For maintenance and operation of the State Teachers College at Radford.
It is provided that out of this appropriation there is
hereby appropriated:

1. Acts of Assembly, 1922. p 274.
2. Acts of Assembly, 1922. p 327.
3. Acts of Assembly, 1924. p 171.
4. Acts of Assembly, 1924. p 215.

For additional equipment............................ $7,900.00
For replacing steam line............................ 1,500.00
For sidewalks....................................... 500.00
For making loans to students........................ 1,500.00[1]

For maintenance and operation of the State
Teachers College at Radford........................$87,510.00
It is provided that out of this appropriation
there is hereby appropriated:
For additional equipment............................ 6,800.00
For stone fence..................................... 1,000.00
For making loans to students........................ 1,500.00[2]

For maintenance and operation of the State
Teachers College at Radford........................118,835.00
It is provided that out of this appropriation there
is hereby appropriated:
For additional equipment............................ 9,950.00
For extended steam lines............................ 12,000.00
For making loans to students........................ 2,000.00
For building for training school, teaching and
lecture room purposes only, plans and construction to be approved by the State Board of Education.. 10,000.00
For maintenance and operation of the State
Teachers College at Radford, to be paid only
from the special revenues collected or received
for the use of the said college, and paid into
the State treasury.................................184,425.00
Out of this appropriation it is provided that
there shall be set aside a sum sufficient to
pay the interest accruing on the certificates
of indebtness issued by the aforesaid college,
and to constitute the sinking fund, in accordance with the provision of sections 8, 9, and
10, of chapter 489 of an act of assembly approved March 25, 1926, (Acts of Assembly, 1926,
p 289)... 8,525.00[3]

For building for training school, teaching and
lecture room purposes only, plans and construction to be approved by the State Board of Education.. $57,500.00
For improvement to dormitory........................ 2,500.00
                                                    _____
                                                    $60,600.00[4]

1.Acts of Assembly, 1926. p 158
2.Acts of Assembly, 1926. p 209
3. Acts of Assembly,1928. p 406
4. Acts of Assembly,1928. p 502

For maintenance and operation of the State Teachers
College at Radford.. $86,045.00
It is provided that out of this appropriation there
is hereby appropriated:
For making loans to students............................ 2,600.00
For maintenance and operation of the State Teachers
College at Radford to be paid only from the special
revenues collected or received for the use of the
said college, and paid to the State treasury, and
not out of the general fund of the State treasury.. 224,250.00
Out of this appropriation there is provided that
there shall be set aside a sum sufficient to pay
the interest accruing on the certificates of indebtness issued by the aforesaid college and to
constitute the sinking fund in accordance with the
provisions of sections 8, 9, and 10, of chapter 489
of an act of assembly, approved March 25, 1926. (Act
of Assembly, 1926. p 829)................................ 8,525.00[1]

For maintenance and operation of the State Teachers
College at Radford.. 88,045.00
It is provided that out of this appropriation there
is hereby appropriated:
For making loans to students............................ 2,000.00
For maintenance and operation of the State Teachers
College at Radford, to be paid only from the special
revenue collected or received for the use of said
college and paid into the State treasury, and not
out of the general fund of the State treasury..... 222,250.00
Out of this appropriation there is provided that
there shall be set aside a sum sufficient to pay
the interest accruing on the certificates of indebtness issued by the aforesaid college and to
constitute the sinking fund in accordance with the
provisions of sections 8, 9, and 10, of chapter
489 of an act of assembly approved March 25, 1926.
(Acts of Assembly, 1926. p 829)........................ 8,525.00[2]

1. Acts of Assembly 1930. p 222.
2. Acts of Assembly 1930. p 285.

FACULTY

FALL, WINTER, and SPRING QUARTERS

Name	Years of Service	Subject or position
Addington, Ina	1924-1926	Critic Teacher
Akers, Ethel	1921-1923	Critic Teacher
Alderson, Bonnie	1918-1920	Critic Teacher
Allen, Elizabeth Sheffield	1918-1924	Expression
Allen, Willie G.	1914-1930	Secretary to President
Allison, Irene	1918-1919	Critic Teacher
Allison, John Lee	1930-	Biblical Literature
Allison, Mary	1927-1928	Industrial Arts
Anderson, Daisy	1931-	Librarian
Andrews, Florence	1921-1923	Clothing
Andrews, Pearl	1919-	Librarian
Arnold, Martha Virginia	1931-	Physical Education
Ashworth, Edith Margaret	1918-1919	Piano
Askew, Madeline	1915-1917	Critic Teacher
Avent, Joseph E.	1913-1920	Education
Bain, Winifred	1928-1929	Director of Training School
Baird, Florence	1913-1921	Music
Barnett, J. H.	1915	Bookkeeper
Bennett, Blanche	1929-1932	Critic Teacher
Bennett, Ercelle	1929-	Critic Teacher
Bennett, Mamie	1930-1931	Nurse and Health
Berkeley, Mary	1917-1918	Matron
Blackard, Zella	1930-	Secretary to Dean of Women
Black, Margaret	1926-	Critic Teacher
Borders, Ruth	1928-	Critic Teacher
Bowen, Mary K.	1914-1917	Mathematics and Latin
Boyd, Minnie Claire	1932	History
Bowers, Wilson R.	1919-	Mathematics
Breckinridge, Elizabeth	1923-1925	Stenographer
Bricker, Ruth	1928-	Critic Teacher
Brown, Bessie	1915-1919	Critic Teacher
Brown, Hattie Edna	1924-1925	English and History
Brown, Irene	1931	Physical Education
Brugh, Phebe	1913-1916	Matron
Bryant, Julia	1928-	Critic Teacher
Bryson, Flora	1914-1928	Science

Bulifant, Blanche	1913-1918	Director of Training School
Burch, Paul R.	1928-	Science
Burnett, Myrtle C.	1918-1921	Foods
Caldwell, Catherine	1922-1923	Critic Teacher
Caldwell, Charlotte	1928-1929	Critic Teacher
Caldwell, Grace	1914-1929	Critic Teacher
Caldwell, Nellie	1914-1929	Critic Teacher
Carter, Robert	1932-	Piano
Chapin, Mary W.	1923-1925	Clothing
Clarke, Mabel Doris	1922-1923	Physical Education
Clark, Mary B.	1919-1931	Housekeeper
Clem, Mary Ruhama	1930-1931	Piano
Clements, Anne W.	1923	French
Cluck, Thelma	1920-1921	Clothing
Cocke, Elton	1928-1930	Science
Coggin, Benjamin William	1918-1919	Rural Education
Coleman, Frances	1921-1926	Critic Teacher
Comstock, J. W.	1929-	Music
Coppedge, Mary Eolian	1917-	Geography and Education
Cowherd, Mrs. Lulu	1924-1925	Dining Room Hostess
Cox, Beaulah	1930	Assistant Director of Extension Department
Cox, Edna	1916-1917	Household Arts
Crockett, Mrs. Cecil	1913-1918	Housekeeper
Dabbs, Sophia M.	1925-1926	History
Daniel, Blanche	1919-	Critic Teacher
Darst, Maud	1914-1915	Assistant in Piano
Denny, Mattie C.	1913-1920	French and German
Dixon, Gladys	1926-	Stenographer
Dobyns, Mrs. Grace	1917-1919	Nurse and Matron
Duncan, Emma	1915-1918	Critic Teacher
Dungy, Flora	1926-1931	Education
Ebenholtz, Edith	1931-	Public School Music
Einstein, Helen	1929-1930, 1932-1933	Critic Teacher
Einstein, Ida	1923-	Critic Teacher
Einstein, Mrs. John	1928-	Voice
Ellis, Wanda	1923-1931	Physical Education
Epling, Louise	1919-	Stenographer
Epperly, Camm	1920	Stenographer

Felty, Lola	1928-1929	Critic Teacher
Ferguson, Park	1925-1926	Dietitian
Fitzpatrick, Francis B.	1919-	Education
Fosdick, Euphemia	1919-1922	Physical Education
Fritz, Kathryn	1929-	Principal of Training School
Gallaway, Mary Louise	1920-1922	Stenographer
Garrett, Ethel	1918-1923	Critic Teacher
Giesen, Genevieve	1925-1926	Critic Teacher
Gilbert, William E.	1913-	Social Science
Gleaves, Alice	1922-1928	Violin
Godbey, Margaret	1917-1920	Librarian
Goode, Edmonia		Nurse
Gore, Jonnie	1930-	Critic Teacher
Graybeal, H. C.	1918-1920	English
Green, Carrie	1915-1916	Librarian
Grubb, Loretta	1921-1923	Stenographer
Guthrie, Madeline	1924-1927	Piano
Hall, Helen Hunt	1927-	Stenographer and Secretary to President
Hardin, J. L.	1918-1919	Science
Harrison, Eloise	1913-1919	Mathematics
Harvey, Edna	1926-1927	English
Hickok, Emma	1925	Stenographer
Hopkins, Mrs. John	1922-	Art
Howe, Gladys	1920-1921	Chemistry
Hoy, Helen	1918	Critic Teacher
Hudson, Virginia O'Rear	1926-	English
Huffard, Mrs. Kate	1920-1927	Matron
Huffard, Gladys	1920-1923	French and History
Humphreys, John W.	1928-1933	Education
Hyre, Myrtle	1925-1926	Clothing
Ingles, Julia	1913-1918	Critic Teacher
James, Elizabeth Faye	1913-1917	Piano and Voice
Jeter, Carrie	1921-1923	Foods
Jett, Anne Newton	1920-1922	Voice
Jewett, Grace	1921-1925	Music
Johnson, J. R. L.	1926-1928	English
Jones, Alice Sanford	1918-1919	Voice
Jones, Elsie Hartwell	1922-1929	Critic Teacher
Jones, Georgia	1925-1926	Critic Teacher
Kelly, Mae	1926-	Critic Teacher

Kent, Charlotte	1915	Stenographer
King, Margaret	1930-	Nurse
Kirby, Sena	1920-1923	Critic Teacher
Kittrell, Frances	1921-1922	Music
Knight, Mrs. M. L.	1918-1919	Housekeeper
Kocher, Mrs. Mildred	1930-	Critic Teacher
Lane, Ernest P.	1913-1914	Mathematics
Leader, Mrs. Rachel	1927-1929	Housekeeper
Lemmon, Mrs. Lulu	1917-1918	Matron
Lewis, Luna M.	1930-	Foods and Nutrition
Lewis, Ruth	1929-	Critic Teacher
Littlepage, Caroline	1914-1915	Critic Teacher
Lloyd, Mrs. Elizabeth	1920-1929	Nurse
Long, Frances	1921-1923	Critic Teacher
Long, William S.	1928-	English
Lowman, Ruby	1924-1925	Critic Teacher
Marshall, Annie	1918	Stenographer
Martin, Helen	1929-	Dietitian
Martin, Lucille	1925-1926	English
Martz, Grace	1929-1931	Geography
Mayo, Daisy	1921-1922	Critic Teacher
McCain, Gertrude	1928-1930	Mathematics
McCauley, Clara	1920-1927	Music and Critic
McCarty, Mrs. W. C.	1914-1916	Piano
McClanahan, Lillian	1920-1931	Critic Teacher
McConnell, John Paul	1923-1927	Education
McConnell, John Preston	1913-	President
McConnell, Sylvester L.	1920-	Business Manager
McLees, Mamie	1921-1924	Education
McLeod, Ethel	1929-	Supervisor of Kindergarten
McMurran, Elizabeth	1922-1923	Physical Education
Menzie, Hermine	1927-1931	History and Education
Moffett, M'Ledge	1913-	Dean of Women and Home Economics
Montague, Mary Wortley	1913-1920	English
Motley, Mae	1914-1915	Stenographer
NeSmith, Mary Ethel	1927-	English
Ninde, Louise	1916-1919	Physical Education
Noblin, J. A.	1913-	School physician
Obenshain, Annie	1927-	Critic Teacher

Ogg, Florence Belle	1928-	English
Otey, Hallie Mae	1923-1925	Stenographer
Painter, Elizabeth	1920-1922	Dritic Teacher
Palmer, Elsie	1926-1929	Dietitian
Perfator, Pauline	1922-1925	Critic Teacher
Perkins, Harriet	1929-1930	Piano
Reed, LaVada	1921-1922	Penmanship
Rich, Dorothy	1919-1921	Piano
Roberts, Alta	1919-1921	Clothing
Roberts, Ethel	1929-	Science 11
Roberts, Susan	1924-	Latin and French
Robinson, Daisy	1923-1930	Critic Teacher
Roop, Elizabeth	1926-1931	Stenographer
Ross, Blanche	1921-1926	Critic Teacher
Ruggles, Louise	1913-1915	Physical Education
Sandridge, Mary	1922-1925	Stenographer
Scruggs, Mary	1931-	Critic Teacher
Shrader, Ruby Allen	1931-	Secretary to Registrar
Slusher, Nannie	1926-1927	Critic Teacher
Simmons, Lillian	1913-	Industrial
Smenner, Bess	1923-1926	Foods
Smith, Edmee	1927-1931	Public School Music
Smith, Richard H.	1930-	Chemistry
Sowder, J. W.	1921-	Science
Sproles, Bruna	1922-1923	Piano
Stacy, Rose	1913-1915	Stenographer
Stafford, Lena	1918-1919	Critic Teacher
States, Dora	1919-1920	Rural Education
Stone, Pearl	1920-1923	Critic Teacher
Stone, Mrs. Henry	1922-1924	Piano
Strouth, Mary Ann	1928-1929	Critic Teacher
Swaney, C. B.	1927-	History
Tapley, Gladys	1930	Latin and French
Taylor, Geneva	1930-	Stenographer
Taylor, Katherine	1913	Critic Teacher
Taylor, Jean E.	1928-	English
Terry, Eleanor	1914-1916	English
Thomas, Minor Wine	1927-	Education
Vaughan, Eva	1928-1931	Critic Teacher and Hostess
Viele, Ada	1930-1931	Director of Training School

Ward, Aleen	1921-1922	Critic Teacher
Wassum, Josephine	1921-1924	Critic and Geography
West, Joe Young	1932-	Biology
Whitt, Jaynie	1914-	English and Algebra
Whitt, Jeremy Pate	1914-	Registrar; Director of Training School; Director of Extension Department
Williamson, Marion	1926-1930	Foods
Wilkins, Claudia	1928-1930	Physical Education
Wilson, Elizabeth	1927-1928	French and Latin
Williams, George	1927-1930	Chemistry
Windle, Emilie	1927-1928	Critic Teacher
Wise, Annie	1919-1920	Critic Teacher
Wright, Christine	1929-1930	Critic Teacher
Yeatts, Edna	1930-	Critic Teacher
Zollman, Alice	1927-	Clothing

SUMMER QUARTER

Many of the regular faculty as listed below taught during the summer quarters. This is a list of names of persons who have no connection with the college except during the summer.

Name	Term	Position
Allison, Virginia	1923	Supervisor of Dining Room
Anderson, William	1917	Civics and History
Bomar, Willie	1926	Home Economics
Bagby, Richard O.	1924-1930	Education and History
Barnette, Kuhn	1925	Health Education
Beebe, Mary Elder	1923-1926	Manual Arts
Bell, Walter Herman	1925	Foreign Language
Bell, Leon E.	1921	Education
Bradbury, William Delp	1926	History
Brydon, Mary Evelyn	1921	Health Education
Bower, Mabel	1922-1931	Education
Brierbower, Ada	1919	Primary Methods
Broadwater, Earl B.	1920-1922	Mathematics and History

Brown, Guy H.	1922-1928	Mathematics
Brittingham, Audrey	1917	Critic Teacher
Burt, Mrs. Dorothy Stone	1914-1916	Drawing and Manual Arts
Caldwell, C. C.	1915-1917	Agriculture and Physical Geography
Caldwell, Virginia	1914-1924	Home Economics and Manual Arts
Cannaday, D. A.	1922-1927	English and History
Carner, Mrs. Clara	1922	History
Carter, Cornelia	1917-1923	English
Clark, Joseph	1923	English
Cole, Glenn Gates	1924	Science
Crawford, Sadie B.	1924	Education
Crowgey, H. L.	1916-1931	History and Geography
Dinwiddie, Mary	1932	Education
Dobbins, Myrtle	1922	Arithmetic
Driver, Jane	1924-1928	Manual Arts
Eagle, Alfred K.	1930-	Education and Mathematics
Easley, Gilbert H.	1918	History
Elliott, R. M.	1920	Education
Evans, Ada V.	1918-1927	Reading
Evans, Lottie M.	1918-1931	Education
Farnham, Myrtle	1925	Primary Methods
Fitzgerald, Geraldine	1916-1920	Primary Methods
Fortune, Erma	1923	Science 11
Fuller, Lande	1926	English
Fulcher, Henry Emmett	1931	Mathematics
Garrison, W. A.	1924	Mathematics
Giles, Effie G.	1916-1920	Virginia and General History
Godbey, Stanley	1925-1926	History and Social Science
Graybeal, June McConnell	1918-1920	Physiology, History
Graybeal, H. C.	1918-1920	English
Greene, Lucy	1918	Grammar
Gresham, W. D.	1920	Virginia History and Civics

Harrison, Theta	1924-1925	Education
Hardy, Ellen Irby	1917	Grammar Grade Method
Hayter, Nell	1920-1929	Critic Teacher
Hill, J. W.	1931	History and Sociology
Hoey, Julia	1926	Physical Education
Hedrick, I. M.	1927	History
Huffman, Charles Herbert	1914-1924	English
Ingram, Florence L.	1914-1924	Methods
Johnson, O. W.	1931	Education
Jacobson, Elsie	1929	Home Economics
Jackson, D. A.	1932	Biology 34
Kegley, Frederick Bittle	1914-1916	Agriculture and Rural Life
Kelly, Ida F.	1924-1926	Penmanship
Kimball, Mary L.	1916-1919	Manual Arts
King, Jr., Joseph Leonard	1925-1928	English
Langvick, Clara Georgine	1925-1929	Primary Methods
Lawrence, Mrs. Virginia P.	1931	Critic And Education
Lawrence, N. P. Jr.	1925	English
Lincoln, J. J.	1916-1919	Geography
Lloyd, Lillian	1923	Home Economics
Lucas, Annie	1915-1925	High School Subjects
Martin, Leta Louise	1923	Hygiene
McConnell, Carla	1920, 1921, 1925	History and Hygiene
McConnell, Mary	1918	Household Arts
McGill, L. C.	1928	Home Economics
McWhorter, Elizabeth	1931	Physical Education
Mays, Herman P.	1926	English
Mason, Frances	1929	English
McCarty, Louellen	1925	English
Meadows, Thomas Burton	1928	Education
Meredith, Ann	1927	Mathematics
Moloy, Flora	1925	Clothing
Morgan, Sara	1916	Physiology
Miller, Sadie E.	1929	Piano
Olson, Beatrice	1927	Home Economics
Pamplin, Maude	1914-1921	Writing and Spelling
Pangle, Mrs. M. G.	1930	Mathematics
Pastrana, Pura	1923	Spanish
Pettit, Emma	1923	Physical Education
Potter, Belva	1919	Civics
Pugh, Myrtle H.	1925	Hygiene

Rex, Evelyn I.	1923	Music
Rhenke, Rosetta	1927	Critic
Riddle, Nell	1929	High School Subjects
Rittase, Stanley	1925	Art
Seaton, Mary	1924	English
Shelton, Mary Sue	1926	English
Skinner, Mary C.	1925	Physical Education
Smith, F. Osgood	1917-1919	Education
Smith, J. E. B.	1917-1924	Education and Mathematics
Smith, William Day	1923-1927	Nature Study and Agriculture
Spivey, Gaynelle C.	1928	English
Stevenson, R. T.	1918-1920	Mathematics
Struthers, Marion	1923-1924	English
Sulfridge, H. L.	1918	Civics
Sutton, Margaret	1926	Manual Arts
Thomas, Mary	1921	Ancient History
Vaught I. B.	1926	Education
Walker, Mattie	1926	Home Economics
Ward, Gladys	1925	Home Economics
Waring, Emma Lawson	1914-1916	Physiology
Watts, Joseph	1925	Special Sunday School work
Wheeler, Kate	1918	Primary Methods
Williams, H. C.	1914	Review Subjects
Wright, B. M.	1923	History
Welch, Dorothy	1929	I. A. (Dennison)
Young, G. A.	1918-1919	Education
Young, H. W.	1931	Latin and French

ADVANCED STUDENTS WHO TAUGHT ONE OR MORE CLASSES IN THE SCHOOL

(Several graduates are listed with the regular faculty or on Summer Faculty. This work was done after graduation).

Anderson, Annie Sue	1924	Reading
Blanco, Marida	1927	Spanish
Bohn, Mary	1921	History

Bishop, Ella M.	1924	Virginia History
Bonham, Anna Lee	1926	Virginia History
Boatwright, S. Jean	1923	Manual Arts
Brown, Elizabeth	1921-1925	Expression
Burton, Ada M.	1923-1926	Geography
Byer, Hessie	1920	Home Economics
Carlo, Rosa	1923	Spanish
Carner, Mrs. Clara	1922	History
Carter, Mary	1919-1920	English
Cabanilas, Berta	1924	Spanish
Chandler, Mamie	1929	History
Chapman, Mrs. Bertha	1929	Industrial Arts
Chumley, Elizabeth	1929	Writing
Colberg, Sara	1932	Spanish
Covey, India	1919	Physiology
Cox, Kate	1925	Hygiene
Cromer, Mrs. M. B.	1925	Virginia History
Dobbins, Enola	1924	Drawing
DeHart, Annie	1927	Writing
Douthat, C. C.	1928	Mathematics
Elliott, Mae W.	1924	
Gonzalez, America	1931	Spanish
Funtane, Theresa	1924-1925	Spanish
Gofourth, Virginia	1932	I. A. 13
Gwynn, Ila	1918	Home Economics
Gladstone, Grace	1921	Hygiene
Godsey, Fannie Kate	1921	Reading
Gwynn, Oca M.	1920	Home Economics
Haight, Helen	1923	Geography
Harwood, Virginia	1920-1923	English and History
Howard, Vashti	1921	Drawing
Hobbs, Annie Mae	1925	Writing
Huddle, Helena	1920	Manual Arts
Huddle, Lelia	1924	English History
Huddle, Hilda	1922	Drawing
Hillman, Bessie	1926	Science
Hurley, Blanche	1914	Music and Manual Arts
Hurley, Ada Lou	1920	Critic
Lugo, Luisa	1929	Spanish
Parrack, Evelyn	1930	I. A. 13
Richmond, Elizabeth	1925	Drawing
Roberts, Annie Kuhn	1920-1923	Drawing
Simpson, Hattie	1924	Hygiene
Showalter, Lois	1923	Reading
Simmerman, Sidney	1919	Drawing

Shumate, Willie Marie	1922	Physical Education
Thornton, Evelyn	1929	Physical Education
Vaughan, Mildred	1931	I. A. 13
Williams, Bertha	1924	Hygiene
Wynn, Hazel	1926	Manual Arts
Witt, Mary	1929	Physical Education

FACULTY COMMITTEES
1913-1914
(The President is ex-officio Chairman of the Committees)

COMMITTEE ON STUDENT ORGANIZATION
Miss Moffett, Chairman

| Miss Puryear | | Miss Denny |
| Mr. Gilbert | Mr. Lane | Miss Terry |

SECRETARY TO THE FACULTY
E. P. Lane

REGISTRAR
Joseph E. Avent

CLASSIFICATION AND STUDENT RECORDS

| Mr. Avent | Miss Bulifant | Miss Moffett |

LIBRARY COMMITTEE

| Mr. Gilbert | Miss Baird | Miss Simmons |

HONOR SYSTEM AND SELF GOVERNMENT

| Miss Harrison | Miss Moffett | Miss Terry |

DECORATIONS

| Miss Denny | | Miss Ruggles |
| Miss James | | Miss Montague |

ATHLETICS

| Miss Ruggles | Miss Bulifant | Mr. Lane |

SCHEDULE COMMITTEE

| Miss Harrison | Miss Montague | Mr. Lane |

MUSIC FOR PUBLIC EXERCISE

| Miss Baird | Miss James | Mr. Lane |

MUSEUM

| Mr. Gilbert | Miss Simmons | Miss Moffett |

STUDENT ANNUAL

| Miss Terry | Mr. Lane | Miss Baird |

PUBLICATIONS

| Mr. Gilbert | Miss Puryear | Mr. Avent |

FACULTY COMMITTEES
Session 1921-22

ATHLETICS

Miss Moffett
Miss Fosdick

CLASSIFICATION-REGISTRATION

Mr. Whitt
Mr. Bowers
Miss Coppedge
Miss Moffett

COURSE OF STUDY

Mr. Whitt
Miss Moffett
Mr. Fitzpatrick

DECORATION

Miss Simmons
Miss Coppedge
Miss Reid
Miss Pearl Andrews
Mr. Sowder

EXTENSION AND RURAL
WORK

Mr. Fitzpatrick
Miss Moffett
Mr. Whitt
Mr. Gilbert
Miss McLees

SUPPLIES

Mr. S. L. McConnell

TRAINING SCHOOLS

Mr. Whitt
Miss Moffett

HEALTH

Miss Fosdick
Dr. Noblin
Mrs. Lloyd

HONOR SYSTEM

Miss Moffett
Mrs. Huffard

MUSIC FOR PUBLIC
EXERCISE

Miss Kittrell
Miss Gleaves

MUSEUM

Mr. Gilbert

ORGANIZATION AND
STUDENT ACTIVITIES

Miss Moffett
Mr. Gilbert

PUBLICATIONS

Mr. Fitzpatrick
Miss McLees
Mr. Sowder
Mr. Johnson

PUBLIC ENTERTAINMENT

Mr. Gilbert

CHAPEL

Mr. Gilbert
Miss E. S. Allen
Miss Kittrell

Y. W. C. A.

Miss Andrews
Miss Bryson

SOCIAL COMMITTEE

Miss Moffett
Miss Jeter
Miss Maude Andrews

VISUAL EDUCATION

Mr. Bowers

BIBLE STUDY AND SUNDAY
SCHOOL TEACHER TRAINING

Miss Bryson
Mr. Fitzpatrick

All committees must hold regular meetings
and keep a record of their proceedings which
can be filed in the office

o

FACULTY COMMITTEES
Session 1925-26

CLASSIFICATION-REGISTRATION

Mr. Whitt
Mr. Sowder
Mr. Bowers

COURSES OF STUDY

Mr. Whitt
Miss Moffett
Mr. Fitzpatrick

ORGANIZATION AND STUDENT
ACTIVITIES

Miss Moffett
Mr. Gilbert
Mr. McConnell

TRAINING SCHOOLS

Mr. Whitt
Miss Moffett

LECTURE AND LYCEUM

Mr. Gilbert

ALUMNAE

Miss Moffett
Mr. Whitt
Mr. McConnell

PUBLICITY

Miss Moffett
Mr. Whitt

ASSEMBLY

Mr. Gilbert
Miss Jewett

VISUAL EDUCATION

Mr. Bowers

RELIGIOUS EDUCATION

Miss Bryson
Mr. Fitzpatrick
Miss Andrews
Mr. Sowder

EXTENSION AND RURAL
WORK

Mr. Fitzpatrick
Miss Moffett
Mr. Whitt
Mr. Gilbert

SPECIAL COMMITTEES

Miss Moffett
Miss Hyre
Miss Smenner
Mrs. Huffard

ATHLETICS

Miss Ellis
Miss Moffett

MUSIC FOR PUBLIC
EXERCISE

Miss Jewett
Miss Gleaves
Miss Baird

MUSEUM

Mr. Gilbert

FACULTY COMMITTEE
January 5, 1930

MUSEUM

William Jacob Sowder

Y. W. C. A.

Ethel NeSmith

FORENSICS

William Stapleton Long

INTERCOLLEGIATE PRESS
ASSOCIATION

Jean Taylor
William Stapleton Long

LIBRARY

Pearl Andrews
Mary Ledger Moffett
Jeremy Pate Whitt
Ethel McLeod

ADVISORS TO STUDENTS ON
PROFESSIONAL LITERATURE

CULTURE

Ethel NeSmith
Luna Lewis
Jaynie Whitt
Susan Roberts
Mae Kelly
Ercelle Bennett
Ruth Lewis

STUDENT HEALTH

Wanda Ellis
Margaret King
Virginia Arnold
Mildred Kocher
J. A. Noblin

GOOD SPEECH AND USE
OF ENGLISH

Virginia O'Rear Hudson
Jean Taylor
Jonnie Gore
Florence Belle Ogg
Margaret Black
John Humphreys

Francis Burke Fitzpatrick

PRESIDENT OF LOCAL TEACHERS

Jeremy Pate Whitt, Chairman
Wanda Ellis, Secretary

ADVISORS TO THE INGLES AND
POCAHONTAS SOCIETIES

William Elbert Gilbert
Annie McConnell Grigsby
Helen Einstein

FRATERNITIES, SORORITIES,
AND SOCIAL ORGANIZATIONS

Susan Roberts
Mary Ledger Moffett
William Stapleton Long

COURSE OF STUDY

Jeremy Pate Whitt, Chairman
Mary Ledger Moffett
Ruth Lewis
Mae Kelly

ASSEMBLY

Mary Ledger Moffett
Lillian McClanahan
Charles B. Swaney
Susan Roberts
William Elbert Gilbert

HEALTH

Miss Ellis
Mrs. Lloyd
Dr. Noblin
Miss Bryson

ANNUAL SUPPLIES

Mr. S. L. McConnell

SCIENCE

Paul R. Burch
William Jacob Sowder
H. R. Smith

COUNCIL ON FINE ARTS

Ruhama Clem
Edmee Smith
Mrs. John Hopkins
Mrs. John Einstein
Lillian Simmons

RELIGIOUS EDUCATION

John Lee Allison
Mary Eolian Coppedge
John W. Humphreys
Alice Zollman
Charles B. Swaney

TRAINING SCHOOL

Mary Ledger Moffett, Chairman
Kathryn Fritz
Daisy Robinson
Ruth Borders

COOPERATION WITH ALUMNAE

Charles B. Swaney
Minor Wine Thomas
Mary Ledger Moffett
Annie Obenshain
Blanche Bennett
Ruth Bricker Painter
Annie McConnell Grigsby

LIBRARY

Mr. Whitt
Miss Moffett
Mr. Johnson
Mr. Fitzpatrick

ACADEMIC AND PROFESSIONAL PREPARATION OF
THE RADFORD COLLEGE FACULTY*1

Addington(Cox), Ina
    Honaker High School, 1918-1919; Radford High School, 1919-1920;
    High School diploma; Radford College, 1920-1922.

Akers(Coleman), Ethel
    Dublin High School, 1913-1915, High School Diploma; Radford
    College, 1921-1922.

Alderson, Bonnie Jean
    Lebanon State High School, Diploma; Radford College, Diploma.

Allen, Elizabeth Sheffield
    Private Schools, Curry School of Expression, Boston, Massa-
    chusetts; Leland Powers School of Spoken Word, Boston, Massa-
    chusetts; Summer term at Peabody College, Nashville, Tennessee;
    Summer term at University of Tennessee, Knoxville, Tennessee;
    Ward-Belmont College, Nashville, Tennessee; Summer and winter
    terms in Chicago Conservatory of Fine Arts; Summer term at
    Horner-Redpath School, Kansas City, Missouri; Columbia Uni-
    versity, Radford College.

Allison, John Lee
    High School diploma 1880; Union Theological Seminary, 1886-
    1889, B. D. degree; D. D. honors.

Allison, Mary
    William and Mary College, 1922-1925; Art Institute, Chicago,
    1925, 1926, 1927; Radford College 1915-1919, diploma.

Anderson, Daisy L.
    Mars Hill High School, 1914-1917, diploma; North Carolina
    College, A. B. degree, 1919; Atlanta Library School, A. B.
    degree in L. S., Graduate work at University of North
    Carolina, 1925; Columbia University, 1926, 1931.

Andrews, Pearl
    Lafayette High School, Alabama, 1897, diploma; Carnegie
    Library College, Nashville, Tennessee; Columbia University
    1929.

Arnold, Martha Virginia
    Monroe High School, Alabama, 1918-1922, diploma; Georgia

*Note: The name in parenthesis indicate the present married name.
1. Record based on catalogs and individual replies to question-
    naire, information not available for all of the faculty.

State Teachers College for Women, 1924-1928, Normal Diploma,
B. S. degree; Peabody College 1930-1931, M. A. degree.

Askew, Madeline
Pulaski High School, 1907-1911, diploma; Farmville Normal
School, 1911-1913, Regular diploma; Salutatorian of High
School Class.

Atlee, Sister Maria
High School, Washington, D. C. 1886, diploma; George Washington University; New York University, New York.

Avent, Joseph Emory
Male Academy, Raleigh, North Carolina, 1896-1897; University
of North Carolina, 1897-1901, A. B. degree, Cum laude; Columbia, 1912-1913, M. A. degree.

Bagby, Richard O.
High School, Durham, North Carolina, 1906, diploma; Iowa
University, 1908-1911, B. A. degree; Columbia University,
New York City, 1921-1922, M. A. degree and Diploma as
Superintendent of Schools; Radford State Teachers College,
1925.

Bain, Winifred E.
Portage, Wisconsin Public High School, 1904-07, diploma;
Milwaukee State Teachers College, 1910-1912, diploma;
University of Chicago, 1924-1925, Ph. B. degree with honors;
Columbia University, 1925-1928, Ph. D. National Resident
Council Fellow; Honorary Fraternities, Pi Lambda Theta,
Kappa Delta Pi.

Beebe, Mary Elder Harwood
Private Schools in Christiansburg and Roanoke, Virginia,
1894-1896; Girls Latin School, Baltimore, Maryland; Goucher
College, Baltimore, Maryland, 1896-1900, diploma, A. B. degree; Maryland Institute 1900-1904, diploma; School of Art
and Design.

Bell, Walter Herman
High School, Berryville, Virginia, 1914-1918, diploma; received medal for best average; Randolph-Macon College, 1918-
1922, A. B. degree; received H. W. Murray Medal for Proficiency; John Hopkins University, 1922-1923, Ph. D. degree.

Bennett(Crawford), Blanche
Blacksburg High School, 1916-1920, Diploma; Virginia College,

1920-1921; University of Virginia; Virginia Polytechnic
Institute.

Bennett, Ercelle
Linden High School, Linden, Missouri, 1913-1914; Central
High School, Kansas City, Missouri, 1914-1917, diploma;
Radford College, 1929, B. S. degree; Pi Gamma Mu honors.

Black, Margaret Fisher
Max Meadows High School, 1917-1921, Diploma; Radford College,
1921-1923; 1924-1926, B. S. degree; University of Cincinnati,
1928; University of Virginia, 1930-1931.

Blackard, Zella
Graduate of the High School Department of Marion Junior
College, Marion, Virginia, 1928, Diploma; National Business
College, Roanoke, Virginia, 1930, Secretarial Diploma.

Borders, Ruth M.
Western Kentucky State Normal School, 1920-1923; High School
Diploma, Officer in Literary Society; Western Kentucky
Teachers College, 1923-1927, A. B. degree; Peabody College,
1930; Western Kentucky Teachers College, 1931.

Bowen, Mary K.
Union Town, Kentucky High School; Academy of Rollins College,
Winter Park, Florida, 1905-1907, Diploma; Randolph Macon
Woman's College, Lynchburg, Virginia, 1907-1910, A. B. degree,
Certificate of Proficiency in Mathematics, History, and Psy-
chology, and Education; University of Chicago, 1915.

Bower, Mabel
Hollins College, 1905, A. B. degree; Columbia, 1927-1928,
A. M. degree.

Bowers, Wilson R.
Woodlawn High School, 1891-1895, Stuart High School, Commercial diploma, University of Virginia, 1901-1903; Columbia University, 1918-1919; B. S., A. B., M. A. degrees,
Special Diploma in Mathematics.

Bricker(Painter), Ruth
Radford High School, 1920-1924, Diploma, Valedictorian of
Class; Radford State Teachers College, 1924-1928, Diploma,
B. S. degree, Summa Cum Laude.

Broadwater, Earl B.
    Shoemaker High School, 1910-1914, Diploma; William and
    Mary College, 1914-1918, B. A. degree, Valedictorian;
    Columbia University, 1924-1927, M. A. degree; Universi-
    ty of Virginia, 1929.

Brown, Bessie M.
    High School 1897-1901, Diploma; Norfolk Kindergarten
    Training School, 1901-1903; University of Virginia, 1909-
    1910; Extension work with University of Chicago, 1917-1919.

Brown, Elizabeth
    High School, 1915-1919, Diploma; Medals (first honor) in
    Latin, History, and Mathematics; Scholarship; Radford Col-
    lege, 1919-1920; Normal Professional diploma; Radford Col-
    lege, 1922-1923, B. S. degree.

Brown, Guy H.
    Belspring High School, Belspring, Virginia; Roanoke College,
    Salem, Virginia, B. A. degree.

Brown, Hattie Edna
    High School; Elon College, 1915-1919, B. A. degree; Univer-
    sity of Virginia, 1923, M. A. degree.

Brown(Weaver), Irene
    San Marcede Academy, 1919-1923; Baylor University, 1923-1927,
    A. B. degree; Peabody College, 1930-1931, M. A. degree.

Brugh, Phebe
    New Orleans High School, Louisiana; Peabody College, Tennessee.

Bryant, Julia
    Critz High School, 1918-1922, Diploma; Radford Colege, 1926,
    1931, Diploma, B. S. degree, Summa Cum Laude honors.

Bryson, Olive Flora
    High School Presbyterian Academy, Clinton, South Carolina;
    Holbrook Junior College, B. S. degree; University of Chicago,
    1916, Diploma, S. B. degree; 1918-1921, A. M. degree.

Bulifant(McFarland), Blanche
    Hampton High School, Virginia, 1893-1897, Diploma, honor
    student, scholarship medal, valedictorian; State Normal
    School, Farmville, Virginia, 1897-1898; University of Vir-
    ginia; George Washington University; Cornell University;
    University of Chicago; George Peabody College, 1916.

Burch, Paul Rudolph
Greenwood High School; Mineral High School; Randolph Macon
College, 1915-1920, B. S. degree, Chi Beta Phi honors; Carnegie Institute, 1919-1920; University of Virginia, 1924-
1930, M. S. and Ph. D. degrees, Sigma XI honors.

Burnett, Myrtle
High School, 1911-1915, Classical Course diploma; Pratt Institute, 1920-1923, diploma of School of Household Science
and Arts; Columbia University, Teachers College, Diploma,
B. S. degree.

Caldwell, Grace
High School, 1885, 1886, 1887, Diploma; Peabody College,
1916.

Caldwell, Nellie
Finished High School at Radford before diplomas were issued;
Harrisonburg College; University of Virginia; Peabody Col-
lege, 1916.

Caldwell, Virginia
Roanoke High School, 1907-1909, Diploma; Pratt Institute,
1910-1912, diploma; Columbia, 1919; Roanoke College, 1923-
1924; Columbia, 1924-1925; Teachers diploma, B. S. degree.

Cannaday, D. A.
Radford High School, 1911-15, Diploma, Valedictorian; Roanoke College, 1915-1919, Diploma, B. A. degree; M. A. degree,
first honors;Harvard University, 1920-1921, Diploma.

Carter, Cornelia A.
Asheville Normal School.

Carter(Broadwater), Mary
Shoemaker High School, 1914, Diploma; Radford College, 1918,
Diploma.

Chapin, Mary W.
High School, 1910-1914; University of Minnesota, 1918; B.
S. degree; Teachers College, Columbia University, 1922-1923,
M. A. degree.

Clem, Mary Ruhama
Covington High School, Covington, Indiana, 1925, Diploma;
Cincinnati Conservatory of Music, Cincinnati, Ohio, Col-
legiate Diploma in Piano, Certificate in Voice.

Clark, Mabel Doris
    Graduate of American College of Physical Education, Chicago,
    Illinois, Director of South Park Playgrounds, Chicago, Illi-
    nois, 1922; South Bend, Indiana, 1923; Physical Director,
    Public Schools, Sewickley, Pennsylvania; Warren, Ohio, 1923-
    1924; Physical Director State Teachers College, 1924.

Cluck(Martin), Thelma
    High School, Marlin, Texas, 1912-1916; State College for
    Women, Denton, Texas, Diploma; New York School, 1916-1918,
    Fine and Applied Art, 1918; Columbia University, New York
    City, 1919-1920; B. S. degree.

Cocke, Elton C.
    High School, 1916-1920, Diploma; Richmond College, 1920-1921;
    University of Virginia, 1923-1928, B. S., M. S. degrees.

Coggin, William Benjamin
    High School, 1897-1900, Diploma; William and Mary College,
    1900-1904, Diploma, B. A. degree, Phi Betta Kappa Honor;
    George Peabody College for Teachers, 1915-1916, Diploma,
    M. A. degree; President of Graduate Club.

Comstock, John W.
    High School, 1885-1889, Hudson, Michigan, Diploma; honors
    in music; New England Conservatory of Music, 1894-1900;
    Detroit Conservatory, 1891-1892.

Coppedge, Mary Eolian
    Bedford High School and Belmont Seminary; University of
    Oklahoma, A. B. degree, 1917; M. A., 1919; Honor student of
    Kappa Delta Pi; Teachers College, Columbia University, 1928-
    1929.

Cox, Beaulah
    High School Diploma, 1927; National Business College, 1930,
    Diploma.

Cox(Wolfe), Edna
    Radford Normal School, 1914-1915, Diploma in General Pro-
    fession and Home Economics.

Crockett, Mrs. Cecil
    Plumma College.

Dabbs, Sophia
    Winthrop College, 1916-1920, A. B. degree; University of
    Virginia, 1923-1925, History, M. A. degrees; P. B. K. honors.

Daniel, Blanche Wilson
    King's Grove High School, 1914-1917, Diploma; Radford State
    Teachers College, 1917-1919, 1928-1929, Normal Professional
    Certificate and B. S. degree; Columbia University, New York
    City, M. A. degree, 1930-1931.

Denny, Mattie C.
    Salem Seminary, German-French Diploma, Scholarship medal;
    Columbia; Woman's College, 1910-11; Cornell; University of
    Virginia.

Dixon, Gladys Virginia
    Buena Vista High School, 1920-1924, Diploma; National Busi-
    ness College, Roanoke, Virginia, 1925.

Dobyns(Jennings), Enola
    Woodlawn High School, 1915-1916; Dublin High School, 1916,
    1918, 1919; Radford State Teachers College, 1921-1924,
    Professional Certificate, Collegiate Certificate, B. S. de-
    gree.

Driver, Jane Blanchly
    Private Schools; Temple University; New York University;
    Columbia Teachers College; University of Pennsylvania.

Golding, Mrs. Flora Dungy
    High School work in State Teachers College, Maryville,
    Missouri, 1914, Diploma; University of Missouri, 1920, B.
    S. degree in Education; University of Chicago, 1925, M. S.
    degree.

Eagle, Alfred K.
    Monterey High School, 1913-1917, Diploma; University of
    Virginia, 1919-1923, B. S. degree, Alpha Chi Sigma honors,
    Columbia University, 1926-1929, M. A. degree.

Easley, Gilbert H.
    Milligan College, B. S. degree, Transylvania College, Uni-
    versity of Tennessee.

Einstein, Mrs. Edythe
    High School diploma, 1902; Cornell College, 1903-1904,

Diploma; Special work at the University of Wisconsin; Graduate of the American Conservatory of Music.

Einstein, Ida Warren
Radford High School, 1918, Diploma; State Teachers College,
East Radford, Virginia, 1918-1920, Normal Professional Di-
ploma; State Teachers College, East Radford, Virginia, B.
S. degree; Columbia University, New York City, M. A. degree.

Ellis, Wanda
High School, 1914-1918, Diploma; Valedictorian; Columbia,
1920-1923, Teachers' Diploma, B. S. degree.

Evans, Lottie M.
High School, Richmond, Virginia, Diploma, highest honors;
University of Virginia; Jarvard, Sorbonne, Paris; Univer-
sity of Richmond; William and Mary College.

Ferguson(Wilcox), Park
Chatham High School, Chatham, Virginia, 1914-1916; State
Teachers College, Radford, Virginia, 1917-1920, Diploma.

Fitzpatrick, Francis Burke
Randolph Macon Academy, 1890-1894, Diploma; 1896-1898,
A. B. degree; University of Chicago, 1918-1919, M. A. de-
gree; Teachers College, Columbia University, 1928-1929.

Fitzgerald(Hagan),Geraldine
Danville High School; Farmville State Teachers College, Diploma; Northern Normal and Industrial School, 1917.

Fritz, Kathryn
Covington High School, Ohio, 1919-1923; Wittenberg College,
Springfield, Ohio, 1923-1927; Ohio State University, Colum-
bus, Ohio, 1928-1929, B. A. and M. A. degrees; President of
the Pan-Hellenic Council, Sigma Phi Beta, Social group,
Girls' Athletic Association; Held offices in Literary group,
gave the oration for commencement in Dramatics, Student Assistant in Education, 1926-1927 as honors.

Fosdick, Euphemia
Graduate in Gymnastics, North American Gymnastic College,
Indianapolis; Physical Director and Athletic Coach, Bethany
College, Bethany, West Virginia, 1918-1919; Physical Direc-
tor, Athletic Coach, Swimming Instructor, Radford Normal,
1919.

Fulcher, Henry Emmett
Amherst High School, 1915, Diploma; William and Mary College, 1915-1917, Teachers diploma, B. S. degree; University of Virginia, M. S. degree, 1922-1925; O. D. K. honors; University of Chicago, 1928-1930.

Fultane(de Colon), Teresa
University of Porto Rico, 1919-1921; Radford College, 1924-1925, B. S. degree in Education.

Garrett(Robinson), Ethel
Radford College, 1913-1916, Professional diploma.

Giesen, Genevieve Gertrude
New Castle High School, 1918-1922, Diploma.

Gilbert, William E.
University of Virginia, 1911-1913, M. A. degree; President of Washington Society; Lynchburg College, 1903-1907, B. A. degree; Cornell University, 1928; University of Virginia, 1929.

Gleaves, Alice M.
Plummer College, Wytheville, Virginia; Visitation Convent; Woman's College, Richmond, Virginia; Special work with Miss A. L. Reinhardt, Richmond, Virginia.

Godbey(Smith), Margaret
Dublin High School, 1907, 1908, 1911, Diploma. Class prophet; Farmville State Teachers College, 1911-1913, Diploma; Milligan College, 1915-1917, A. B. degree; Editor-in-chief of College annual.

Godbey, Stanley T.
Christiansburg High School, 1912-1915, Diploma; Roanoke College, 1917-1921; University of Virginia, 1921-1924; New York University, 1931; B. A. and M. A. degrees; Phi Beta Kappa.

Gore, Johnnie
High School, 1912; Lynchburg College, 1917; Two-year diploma; Peabody College, 1920-1924, B. S. degree; Teachers College, Columbia University, 1928-1929, M. A. degree.

Graybeal, H. C.
Emory and Henry College, diploma, A. B. degree; Cornell University.

Green, Carrie Helen
        Petersburg High School, 1910; Radford Normal School, 1915,
        Diploma.

Grubb(Carper), Loretta
        Radford High School, 1918; National Business College, Roan-
        oke, Virginia, 1919-1920, Diploma.

Guthrie(Phlegar), Madeline
        Dublin High School, 1911-1915, Diploma; Music Medal; Stone-
        wall Jackson College, 1915-1917, Diploma; College of Music
        in Cincinnati, 1923.

Hall, Helen Hunt
        Attended Radford High School, 1922-1925; National Business
        College, Roanoke, Virginia, 1925-1926, Stenographic diploma;
        one quarter of work at Radford State Teachers College, 1928.

Hardin, J. L.
        High School, 1891-1895; Emory and Henry College, B. A. de-
        gree; Graduate Student at University of Virginia.

Harrison, Eloise Ambler
        Peabody College, 1903; Student University of Nashville,
        Tennessee, 1903-1904; Summer Student Cornell University,
        1908-1910; Summer Student Teachers College, Columbia Uni-
        versity, 1911; Instructor in Mathematics, State Normal
        School, Farmville, Virginia, 1904-1913; Radford Normal
        School, 1913.

Harvey(Bagwell), Edna
        Grifton High School, Diploma; University of North Carolina,
        1921-1925, A. B. degree; College for Women, Columbia Univer-
        sity; Graduate work in History.

Hayter, Nell
        High School, 1914-1918, Diploma; Radford College, 1918-1920,
        Diploma.

Hickok(Sessoms), Emma
        Christiansburg High School, 1920-1924, Diploma; National Bus-
        iness College, Roanoke, Virginia, 1924-1925.

Howe(Chamberlin), Gladys
        Hampton High School, 1912-1916, Diploma; Lynchburg College,
        1916-1918, Normal Professional Diploma.

Hudson, Virginia O'Rear
Missouri Valley Academy; Missouri Valley College, A. B. degree; Summa Cum laude honors; Missouri State University, 1921-1922, A. M. degree; University of Chicago, 1924-1926, Ph. D. degree, Cum laude.

Huffard(Fillinger), Gladys
Bristol High School; Virginia Intermont College, 1917, Collegiate diploma, A. B. degree; Radford College, 1921-1922, B. S. degree, honor student.

Hyre, Myrtle
Lawrence High School, 1904-1908, Diploma; University of Kansas, 1908-1912, A. B. degree, Columbia University, 1924-1925, M. A. degree; Special student in Home Economics Work.

Humphreys, John W.
Dayton High School, Kentucky; Y. M. C. A. Commercial School, Cincinnati, 1904-1905; Transylvania, 1921; University of North Carolina, 1924, A. B. degree; Loving Cup two years in succession for best scholarship as honors. Ph. D. University of Cincinnati.

James(Carr), Lizzie Faye
High School, 1906, diploma; Cincinnati Conservatory, 1910; Martha Washington College, 1906, 1907, 1908, 1909, Diploma, Piano and Voice; Cornell University, 1914.

Johnson, John Rochelle Lee
Public School, 1879-1880; Academy, 1880-1884; William and Mary College 1890-1894, B. A. degree; University of Chicago, 1919-1921, M. A. degree.

Jewett, Grace Anna
Public School Music Graduate, Crane Normal Institute of Music, Potsdam, New York; Student in Piano, Voice, and Violin, New York City; Violin, Chicago Conservatory; Piano and Harmony, Hill Piano School; Piano and Voice, Buffalo, New York; Public School and Orchestral Music Chautauqua, New York; Supervisor of Music, Ravenswood, West Virginia; Limeston, New York; Clarion, Pennsylvania; Bluefield, West Virginia; Conductor of Music in Institutes in West Virginia; Teacher in Piano, Voice, and Chorus. Blackstone College; Piano and Voice, Radford Normal, 1916; Supervisor of Music in Richmond City Schools; New York University, Summer 1923; Chautauqua, New York; University Summer 1925; Supervisor of Music, Radford State Teachers College.

Johnson, Obed Wilbur
High School work at Elon College; Elon College, 1900-1904,
A. B. degree, Cum Laude; University of Virginia, 1922-1923,
M. A. degree; George Peabody College, five quarters work on
Ph. D. degree.

Jones, Elsie Hartwell
Radford High School, 1918-1921, Salutatorian, Second honors;
Radford College, 1921-1923, 1925-1926, B. S. degree; Columbia
University, New York City, 1929-1930.

Kelly, Ida F.
Stonewall Jackson Institute, 1897-1901; Marion College; University of Virginia, 1902; Columbia University, 1913; Penmanship Colleges, 1921-1923; Penmanship Diplomas and Certificates.

Kelly, Mae
Greensville County High School, 1914-1917; William and Mary
College, 1923; Farmville, 1922; Teachers College, Columbia
University, 1930-1931, M. A. degree; Radford State Teachers
College, B. S. degree.

King,Jr.,Joseph Leonard
Fork High School, Diploma; Richmond College, A. B. degree;
Columbia University, A. M. and Ph. D. degrees; University
of Bordeau, France, Certificate.

King, Margaret Frances
Dublin High School, 1927; Lewis-Gale Hospital, June 1927,
July 1930.

Kirby, Sena (Lineberry)
High School, 1914-1918; Radford State Teachers College, Two
years; Home Economics and Elementary Course, 1920; Peabody
College, 1922.

Knight, Mrs. M. L.
High School, Franklin, North Carolina; A. F. College, Ash-
ville, North Carolina, 1886-1887.

Kittrell, Frances
Public School Music, Student Middle Tennessee State Normal,
two years; Candidate for B. S. degree, Peabody College;
Graduate in Piano, Harmony and Composition, Conservatory of
Tennessee College; Graduate in Public School Music; Thomas

Normal School, Detroit, Michigan; Student of Eleanor Smith, Chicago; Student of American Conservatory, Chicago; one summer term; Student in Music Department of Columbia University, 1920; Supervisor of Public School Music, Palm Beach, Florida, 1917-1918; Supervisor of Music, St. Petersburg, Florida, 1918-1920; Director of Music Department, University of Florida Summer School; 1918-1919; Director of Public School Music, Radford State Normal, 1921.

Kocher, Mrs. Mildred H.
　　Mansfield State Normal, 1911-1913; Columbia University, 1929, B. S. degree, Columbia University, 1930, M. A. degree.

Langvick, Clara Georgine
　　State Teachers College, St. Cloud, Minnesota, 1909; University of Minnesota, 1921, B. S. degree, Teachers College, Columbia University, 1926, A. M. degree.

Lewis, Luna M.
　　High School, 1916-1920, Diploma; State Teachers College; Wilmington College, 1920-1924, B. S. degree; Columbia University, 1927-1928, M. A. degree.

Lewis, Ruth
　　High School, 1920, diploma; State Teachers College, Harrisonburg, Virginia, 1927, B. S. degree; University of Virginia, 1928, M. S. degree; Correspondence courses from Peabody College, Nashville, Tennessee.

Littlepage(Dunn), Caroline
　　State Teachers College, Farmville, Virginia, Diploma.

Lloyd, Elizabeth
　　Woodlawn Normal Institute, Woodlawn, Virginia; Roanoke Training School, Roanoke, Virginia.

Long, Frances W.
　　Big Stone Gap High School, 1918, Diploma; Radford State Teachers College, Normal Professional Certificate.

Long, William Stapleton
　　Private instruction; Randolph Macon College, 1909-1911, A. B. degree, Salem College, 1915-1916; University of Virginia, 1922-1923, 1924-1925, 1925-1928, M. A. degree and Ph. D. degree in English.

Lucas (Kennedy), Annie
    High School work taken at Milligan College; Milligan College
    1897, B. S. degree, 1917, A. B. degree.

Martin, Helen
    R. M. I., Blackstone, 1920-1924; State Teachers College,
    East Radford, Virginia, 1924-1929, B. S. degree; Richmond
    Medical College, 1928-1929.

Martin, Lucille
    English, A. B., Martha Washington College; Columbia Universi-
    ty, A. M. degree; Teacher of English, Marth Washington College
    in 1923-1924; Teacher of English, Radford State Teachers Col-
    lege, 1925.

Martz, Grace Susan
    High School, 1902-1906, Diploma; Hood College, 1916-1920,
    A. B. degree; Hopkins University, 1915, 1917, 1924; Univer-
    sity of Maryland, 1919, 1922, 1925; Columbia University,
    1924-1928, M. A. degree.

McCain, Gertrude
    High School, 1892-1896, Diploma; State Normal, 1897-1898;
    Indiana University, 1908, A. B. degree, 1911, A. M. degree;
    1918, Ph. D. degree; Bryn Mawr College, 1911-1912.

McCarty, Mrs. W. C.
    High School, Athens, Tennessee; Grant University, 1909.

McCauley, Clara J.
    High School, Chapel Hill, North Carolina, 1912-1914; Elon
    College, North Carolina, 1916-1917; Radford Normal, 1919-
    1921, Diploma.

McClanahan, Lillian Sue
    Lawrence High School, 1916-1920; Peabody College, B. S. de-
    gree; Teachers College, Columbia University, M. A. degree.

McConnell, John Paul
    Radford High School, 1913-1917, Diploma; Radford Normal,
    1917-1918, Lynchburg College, 1918-1921; A. B. degree;
    William and Mary, 1922-1923, M. A. degree; University of
    North Carolina, 1927-1930, Ph. D. degree.

McConnell, John Preston
    A. B. Milligan College; Ph. D. University of Virginia.

McLees, Mary H.
    Greenwood High School, 1900-1903; Lander College, 1903-1906,
    A. B. degree; Teachers College, 1920-1921.

McLeod, Ethel
    Davenport Preparatory School for Girls, 1914-1916; Flora Mac-
    donald College for Young Women; George Peabody College for
    Teachers.

McMurran(Nelson), Elizabeth
    Portsmouth High School, 1919; William and Mary College, 1919-
    1920; Columbia Normal School of Physical Education, Chicago,
    1920-1922, B. P. E. degree.

McWhorter, Elizabeth
    High School, Atlanta, Georgia, 1922-1926, Diploma; Randolph
    Macon Woman's College, 1926-1930, A. B. degree; Peabody Col-
    lege, 1930-1931, M. A. degree.

Meadows, Thomas Burton
    Blountsville District Agricultural School, 1903-1907; Alabama
    Polytechnic Institute, Auburn, 1911-1913, B. S., M. S. degrees;
    Peabody College, 1916-1923, M. A., Ph. D. degrees; Columbia
    University, 1928, M. A. degree; Two semesters of graduate work
    at the University of California.

Menzie, Hermine
    High School, 1914-1918, Diploma; University of Chicago, 1922,
    Ph. B. degree; 1926, M. A. degree.

Miller, Sadie E.
    Elizabeth College, Certificate in Music; Hollins College; Pre-
    paratory and Special in College.

Moffett, M'Ledge
    High School, 1906-1909, credits; Harrisonburg Normal, 1909-
    1911, Diploma; 1911-13, B. S. degree; high rank; Teachers
    College, Columbia University, 1916, 1919, 1920, 1921, M. A.
    degree; 1927-1929, Ph. D. degree; Kappa Delta Pi, Scholar-
    ship and Assistant instructor.

Moloy, Flora
    High School, 1911-1914; University of Oklahoma, 1914-1918,
    B. A. degree; University of Columbia, Supervisor's diploma,

M. A. degree.

Montague, Mary Wortley
High School diploma, 1901-1905; B. A. degree in 1910; Peabody College, 1915.

Ninde(Fisher), Louise
Private Schools, Washington, D. C., High Schools; Sargent
School of Physical Education, 1913-1916, Diploma.

Noblin, Joseph Alexander
Shoemaker College, Gate City, Virginia, 1904, B. S. degree;
Medical Department of Central University of Kentucky, 1907;
Hospital College of Medicine, Louisville, Kentucky.

Obenshain, Annie
Buchanan High School, 1919-1923, Academic diploma; Radford
College, 1923-1927, B. S. degree in Education; University
of Virginia, 1930.

Ogg, Florence Belle
W. M. Preparatory College; School of Expression, G. C. D.
Diploma; University of Virginia; Columbia, Summer School;
University of Tennessee, Summer School, B. S., M. S. degrees.

Otey, Hollie Mae
High School, 1918-1920; National Business College, Roanoke,
1922-1923, Diploma.

Painter, Elizabeth
Private Schools; Farmville Normal, 1910-1913; Farmville
State Teachers College, 1913-1915, Normal Professional
Certificate; Summer School at Columbia University, 1913-
1915; 1917, 1919; Summer School at V. P. I.

Pangle, Loula McNeer
Alleghany Coll. Institute, 1902-1905, Diploma; Randolph
Macon Woman's College, A. B. degree, 1905-1909; Columbia
University, 1914-1915; M. A. degree, University of North
Carolina, 1928-1929.

Perkins(Danbury), Harriette
Rising Sun High School, Maryland, 1920-1924, Diploma;
Cincinnati Conservatory, 1924-1928, Diploma in Piano,
B. M.

42-A

Reed, LaVada
High School, 1905-1907.

Rehnke(Gibbs), Rosetta
High School Diploma; Two years Miss Woods' Kindergarten and
Primary Normal School.

Rittase, Stanley
High School, 1911; Pennsylvania School of Industrial Art,
Philadelphia; Thomas Normal Training School, Detroit, Michi-
gan; Detroit School of Design, Detroit; Columbia University;
New York School of Fine and Applied Art; Parsons, New York,
New York.

Roberts, Susan
Asheville High School, North Carolina, 1908-1912, Diploma,
Historian of Class, Scholarship to U. T., Columbia University, 1923; University of Tennessee, 1912-1916, A. B. degree in Latin; Columbia University, 1927-1928, Graduate
student in French and Latin.

Robinson, Daisy
Woodlawn High School, 1915-1919; Radford College, 1919-1921;
Normal Professional diploma; University of Virginia, 1930-
1931.

Ruggles, Louise K.
Graduate Posse Normal School of Gymnastics, Boston, Massa-
chusetts; Summer term at Harvard; Ingleside School, New
Milford, Connecticut; Belmont College, Nashville, Tennes-
see; Akeley Hall, Grand Haven, Michigan; Radford Normal
School, 1913.

Roop, Marian Elizabeth
High School Diploma, 1931; National Business College, Roanoke, 1925-1926, Diploma.

Ross(Scott), Blanche
Draper High School, 1912-1916, Diploma; Radford College,
1916-1918, Diploma.

Sandridge(Blankenbeckler), Mary
High School, 1916-1919; National Business College, 1920-
1921, Diploma from Secretarial Course.

Shrader, Ruby A.
Narrows High School, 1924-1928, Diploma; National Business
College, Roanoke, Virginia, 1929-1930, Stenographic Diploma.

Simmons, Lillian
High School work done at Farmville State Teachers College;
Harrisonburg State Teachers College, 1910-1911; Peabody Col-
lege, 1915, 1924, B. S. degree; Teachers College, 1927-1928,
M. A. degree.

Smenner, Bess
Industrial High School, Alleghany County Academy, 1912-1914;
Georgia Normal and Industrial College, Diploma; West Virginia
University, 1916-1918, B. S. degree; Teachers College, Colum-
bia University, 1921-1923, M. A. degree.

Smith, C. Edmee
Holly Hill High School, Holly Hill, South Carolina, 1909-
1912, Diploma; Winthrop College, Rock Hill, South Carolina,
A. B. and B. M., 1917-1918; Cornell University, Ithaca, New
York, 1918.

Smith, Richard Holladay
Fincastle High School, 1914-1918; Mississippi A. & M. Col-
lege, 1918-1922, B. S. degree; John Hopkins, 1927-1930, Ph.
D. degree.

Smith, William Day
Amherst High School, Mass., 1878; Amherst College, 1882-1886,
A. B. and A. M. degrees, P. B. K. honors.

Spivey, Gaynell Galloway
High School Diploma, 1908-1911; Greensboro College, 1913-
1917, A. B. degree, Magna Cum Laude honors; Columbia University, 1926; University of North Carolina, 1923-1924, M. A.
degree, 1925; Ph. D. degrees in 1928. Phi Beta Kappa honors.

States, Dora A.
High School, 1894-1898, College, 1902-1906, Diploma in Elementary Education, B. S. in Education, 1917; M. A., 1918, Diploma
in Supervision.

Struthers, Marion
Oak Hill High School, West Virginia, 1909-1913, Diploma;
Northwestern University, 1913-1916, B. A. degree; Univer-
sity of Virginia, 1921-1923; M. A. degree.

Swaney, C. B.
    Marengo, Iowa High School, 1904-1908, Diploma, first honors;
    Iowa Wesleyan College, 1909-1912, Ph. B. degree; Garrett Bib-
    lical Institute, 1912-1915, S. T. B. degree; Northwestern
    University, 1914-1917, M. A. and Ph. D. degree.

Tapley, Gladys
    High School diploma, 1916; Lafayette College, 1918; George
    Washington University, B. A., and M. A. degrees; Peabody
    College, 1917; Berlitz School of Languages, Washington, D. C.

Taylor, Geneva Denton
    Radford High School, 1926-1930, Diploma; Piedmont Business Col-
    lege.

Taylor, Jean E.
    Ridgeway High School, Missouri, 1901-1903, Diploma; Missouri
    University, 1903-1907, 1914-1915; 1919, 1928, A. B., B. S.,
    A. M., Ph. D. degrees.

Terry(Noell), Eleanor
    Wytheville High School, 1905-1907, Diploma; Randolph Macon
    Woman's College, 1907-1911, Diploma, A. B. degree; Columbia
    University, Summer, 1915.

Thomas, Minor Wine
    Preparatory High School, 1912; Bridgewater College, 1916, B.
    S. degree;Harrisonburg Normal, 1910-1912; University of Vir-
    ginia, 1913-1914; George Peabody College, 1917, M. A. degree;
    William and Mary College, 1924; Columbia, 1925-1926, 1926-
    1927, Ph. D. degree; Phi Delta Kappa Honors.

Vaughan, Eva
    High School, 1909-1913, Diploma; Radford College, 1914, 1928,
    1931.

Veile, Ada
    North Carolina College for Women; Columbia University; Uni-
    versity of North Carolina; Teachers College, Columbia Uni-
    versity; A. B., A. M., M. A. degrees.

Ward, Gladys, J.
    Toronto University, 1914-1915; Teachers College, New York
    City, B. S., and A. M. degrees, 1916-1918, 1924-1925.

Whitt, Mrs. Jaynie S.
    Bell Seminary; Morrison Seminary, B. S. degree; University
    of Tennessee.

Whitt, Jeremy Pate
Milligan College, A. B. and M. A. degrees; Graduate Student
Peabody College.

Williams, George Albert
Pottstown High School, Pennsylvania, 1906-1909; Lebanon
Valley Academy, 1910; Lebanon Valley College, 1910-1913,
A. B. degree; first honors; Iowa State College, 1913-1915,
M. S. degree, Phi Kappa Phi honors; Yale University, 1923-
1925, Ph. D. degree.

Williamson, Marian
Drexel Institute, Philadelphia, Pennsylvania, Foods and
Cookery Diploma; Student Teachers College, Columbia Univer-
sity, 1923-1924, B. S. degree, 1925.

Windle, Mrs. Mary Emile
High School, 1910-1914, Diploma; Radford College, 1916-1929,
B. S. degree; Pi Gamma Mu, Summa Cum Laude honors.

Wright, Christine
High School, 1918-1922, Diploma; Central State Teachers College, Ada, Oklahoma; Southwestern State Teachers College, A.
B. degree; Peabody College, Nashville, Tennessee, 1928, M. A.
degree.

Yeatts, Edna
Gretna High School, 1921-1925, Diploma; Radford College, 1925-
1931, B. S. degree, Pi Gamma Mu honors.

Young, Henry Wilson
Jena High School, Louisiana, 1916-1920, Diploma; University
of Colorado, 1927-1929, M. A. degree.

Zollman, Alice Mary
Elmira College, B. S. degree; University of Rochester, New
York; Columbia University, M. A. degree.

BIBLIOGRAPHIES OF BOOKS AND ARTICLES BY
MEMBERS OF THE RADFORD FACULTY

————

Allen, Elizabeth Sheffield
    1. Expression, its Cause and Purposes, etc., Daily or weekly paper in Trenton, Tennessee.

Allison, John Lee
    1. Vital Truths, Richmond, Virginia, 1916.

Arnold, Martha Virginia
    1. Present Day Trends in Physical Education as Shown in Educational Periodicals, Peabody College Press, 1931.

Avent, Joseph Emory
    1. Summer Sessions in State Teachers Colleges (399 page-book), 1925.
    2. Beginning Teaching, (599 page-book), 1926.
    3. The Excellent Teacher, (576 page-book), 1931.
    4. Excellences and Errors in Teaching Methods, (577 page-book), 1931.

Bagby, Richard O.
    1. Articles for the Virginia Journal.

Bain, Winifred E.
    1. Practical Handbook for Students, University of Chicago, 1924.
    2. Practice Teaching, International Kindergarten Union, 1926.
    3. Analytical Study of Teaching, Teachers College Bureau of Publication, Columbia University, 1928.
    4. Is Rating of Teachers Possible and Desirable, Virginia Teacher, 1929.
    5. Service Studies as a Means of Helping Students, T. C. Record, November, 1930.
    6. Studying Teaching Problems, Childhood Education, September, 1931.
    7. Classroom Procedures, in Activity Curriculums at Work, National Educational Association, 1930.

Beebe, Mary Elder Harwood
    1. Paragraph and illustration in Ladies Home Journal.

Bell, Walter Herman
    1. A Source For Some Lines of Tartuffe. Modern Language Notes, June, 1926.

Bowen, Mary K.
    1. Loci Connected with a Range of Conics, University of
       Chicago; Thesis, 1922.

Bowers, Wilson R.
    1. Discontentment of America, (never published), 1900.
    2. Martin Luther's "Contribution to Modern Education", (never
       published), 1918.
    3. Cultural value of Mathematics, (never published), 1928.
    4. Several Articles in "Teaching of Mathematics", 1925-26.

Broadwater, Earl B.
    1. Utilization of the Sixty-Minute Period, University of
       Virginia Record, 1929.
    2. Limitations of the Unit Plan of Teaching, Extension Series
       of Volume XIII, Number 11, 1931.

Brown, Elizabeth
    1. Articles on Professional Services in the field of Religious
       Education rather than Secular Education.

Brown, Irene
    1. Play Activity for Children with Impaired Vision, Peabody
       Press, 1931. (Thesis).

Bryson, Olive Flora
    1. The Extent to Which Diagrammatic Drawings Aid in the Under-
       standing of Scientific Facts, Masters Thesis, University of
       Chicago, 1921.
    2. Nature Study Leaflets, Virginia School Messages and the
       Southern Agriculturist.
    3. The Irresistible Undertow, Methodist Herald, June 4, 1929.

Bulifant (McFarland), Blanche
    1. Rocky Ford as the School Children See it, Local Historical
       and Industrial Study Booklet.
    2. Wrote for years for various educational journals, including
       the Normal Instructor, Primary Education, Popular Educator,
       Kindergarten and First Grade; School Board Journal, Journal
       of Educational Method, Virginia School Journal, Colorado
       School Journal, Colorado Parent-Teacher, local and State
       papers, etc.

Burch, Paul Randolph
    1. Endodermal Flagella of Hydra, Biological Bulletin, Woods Hole,
       Massachusetts, 1928.
    2. Effect on Division Rates of Arcella rotundata and A. uulgaris,
       etc. Archiv fur Protistenkunde, Jena, Germany, 1930.

Carter, Cornelia
    1. Language Work Book, Third Grade, Smith, Hammond & Company, Atlanta, Georgia, 1930.

Cocke, Elton C.
    1. Pollen Analysis of Duncal Swamp Peat, Journal of Eli Mitchell, Science Sociology, Chapel Hill, North Carolina, 1929.

Coggin, William Benjamin
    1. The Larger Profect, V. P. I. Blacksburg, 1919.

Coppedge, Mary Eolian
    1. Studies in Geography, Rural School Messages.
    2. Studies in Geography, Virginia School Journal.

Driver, Jane Blachly
    1. Art in a Progressive Education Program, Everyday Art, January, 1930.
    2. Art in the Primary Grade, Sign Posts (Del. State Magazine), January, 1932.

Dungy (Golding), Flora
    1. History of the Certification of the Teachers of the State of Missouri Master Theses, University of Chicago.

Fitzpatrick, Frances Burke
    1. Present Day Standards for Teaching, 1925.
    2. Elementary Supervision, 1930.

Fritz, Kathryn
    1. Primary Arithmetic, Virginia Journal of Education, October, 1931.

Giesen, Genevieve
    1. Pageant, written for the Playground Association of Roanoke in 1930, "Roanoke, Magic Gateway of the Southwest"; has not been published but has been put in the Roanoke Library for local history reference.

Hudson, Virginia O.
    1. "Charles Dickens and the American Theater", Doctor's Dissertaion, University of Chicago.
    2. Browning's "La Saisiaz", Master's Thesis, University of Missouri.
    3. Religious Poetry of the Nineteenth Century.
    4. Alcott in Concord.
    5. Did Emerson Influence Carlyle?
    6. Spenser's Political Philosophy.

7. Better American Speech.
8. A Curriculum for Literature in Grades and Secondary Schools.
9. Numerous Newspaper Articles.

King, Jr., Joseph Leonard
1. The Life of George Bagby, Columbia Press.
2. Edited "Walden", Modern Readers Series.

Lane, Ernest P.
1. "Conjugate Systems with Indeterminate Axis Curves", Thesis, American Journal of Mathematics, Volume 43, 1921.
2. A General Theory of Conjugate Nets, Transactions of the American Mathematical Society, Volume 23, 1922.
3. Ruled Surfaces with Generators in One-to-One Correspondence, Transactions of the American Mathematical Society, Volume 25, 1923.
4. A Characterization of Surfaces of Translation, Bulletin of the American Mathematical Society, Volume 30, 1924.
5. Bundles and Pencils of Nets on a Surface, Transactions of American Mathematical Society, Volume 28, 1926.
6. Wilczynski's and Fubini's Canonical Systems of Differential Equations, Bulletin of the American Mathematical Society, Volume 32, 1926.
7. The Correspondence between the Tangent Plane of a Surface and its Point of Contact, American Journal of Mathematics, Volume 48, 1926.
8. Le direttrici di Sullivan, Bulletin dell'unione matematica Italiana, Amo V, 1926.
9. Quadriche avente per generatrici le tangenti asintotiche in un punto di una superficie, Rendiconti della R. Accademia Nazionale dai Lincei, Classe di Scienze Fissiche Mathematiche e naturali, Volume V, serie 6, 1927.
10. Tubini and Cech, Projective Differential Geometry, Volume I (Review), Bulletin American Mathematical Society, Volume 33, 1927.
11. "The Asymptotic Osculating Quadrics of a Curve on a Surface", Bulletin American Mathematical Society, Volume 33, 1927.
12. The Contact of a Cubic Surface with an Analytic Surface, Transactions of the American Mathematical Society, Volume 29, 1927.
13. Contributions to the Theory of Conjugate Nets, American Journal of Mathematics, Volume 49, 1927.
14. Power Series Expansions in the Neighborhood of a Point on a Surface, Proceedings of the National Academy of Sciences, Volume 13, 1927.
15. Fubini and Cech, Volume II (Review), Bulletin American Mathematical Society, Volume 34, 1928.

16. Joint-Axis Congruences with Indeterminate Developables, The Tohoku Mathematical Journal, Volume 29, 1928.
17. Recent Developments in Projective Differential Geometry, Part B, Bulletin of the American Mathematical Society, Volume 34, 1928.
18. Cononical Configurations Associated with a Surface, Bulletin of the American Mathematical Society, Volume 34, 1928.
19. The Projective Differential Geometry of Systems of Linear Homogenous Differential Equations of the First Order, Transactions American Mathematical Society, Volume 30, 1928.
20. On the Contact of a Quartic Surface with an Analytic Surface, American Journal of Mathematics, Volume 51, 1929.
21. On the Fundamental Transformation of Surfaces, annals of Mathematics, Series 2, Volume 30, 1929.
22. Definition and Classification of Geometries, School Science and Mathematics, Volume 30, 1930.
23. Present Tendencies in Projective Geometry, Mathematical Monthly, Volume 37, 1930.
24. Hypergeodesic Mapping of a Surface on a Plane, Transactions of American Mathematical Society, Volume 32, 1930.
25. Integral Surfaces of Triads of Portial Differential Equations of the Third Order, Transactions of the American Mathematical Society, Volume 32, 1930.
26. Integral Surfaces of Pairs of Partial Differential Equations of the Third Order, Transactions of the American Mathematical Society, Volume 32, 1930.
27. Weatherburn, Differential Geometry of Three Dimensions, Volume II, (Review), American Mathematical Monthly, Volume 38, 1931.

Langvick, Clara Georgine
1. Teacher Growth in Service, 500 copies distributed to Colleges, Universities and State Departments in U. S. A., of 1921.
2. Article on "Teacher Growth in Service", published by National Education Association Journal, 1922.
3. Teacher Rating by Florence Kimball, Clara Langvick, published by Classroom Teachers Association, Minneapolis, Minnesota, 1923.

Lewis, Ruth
1. Lesson Plan, Unit plan on Shakespeare, Virginia Teacher, October, 1928.

Long, William Stapleton
1. Governor James Barbour, a biographical menograph in the J. P. Branch Historical papers of Randolph Macon College, 1914.
2. Voices of the Silent Things, a book of verse, The Corham Press, Boston, 1915.
3. Various Fugitive Verse.

4. Two one-act plays, "That Chicken Debate (1915)" "Ghoses or no Ghoses (1916)"; "The Eldridge Entertainment House", Franklin, Ohio.
5. Survey of Courses of Study in Schools for the Blind, minutes of the Proceedings of the Convention of the National Association of Instructors of the Blind, 1924.
6. A Doctor's Dissertation.
7. The Novels of Charles James to be published soon.

McConnell John Paul
1. After-Prison Life of Released white criminals in North Carolina; Dissertation, 1931.

McLees, Mary
1. The Elementary Teaching Personnel of Hunderton, Morris, Sussex, and Warren Counties, New Jersey, in Relationship to the Teacher Training Program. Dissertation, 1931.

Meadows, Thomas Burton
1. Methods of Teaching, Bulletin published by Miss. Agri. Col,, 1920.

McLeod, Ethel
1. The effect of Summer Vacation on Achievement in Arithmetic, Composition and Reading over a period of Three years.

Menzie, Hermine
1. The Balkans and European Imperialism, University of Chicago, 1926.
2. Extension Course in American History, State Department, Alabama, 1922.
3. Extension Course in High School History Methods, State Department, Alabama, 1923.

Moffett, M'Ledge
1. Social Background and Activities of Teachers College Students, Ph. D. Dissertation, published by the Bureau of Publication, Teachers College, Columbia University, New York City, 1929.
2. An Interpretative Study of the Personal Background of Teachers College Students as a Basis for Determining Factors for Institutional life, National Education Association Yearbook, 1928, Cleveland Meeting, Yearbook for National Association of Deans of Women, 1928-1929.
3. Review of the Sociological Philosophy of Education by Finney, Administration and Supervision, 1928.
4. Participation in the Training of Supervisors, Administration and Supervision, 1920.

5. The Teachers Home as a Practice House for Home Economics Students, School Life, 1922.
6. Weekly educational and publicity articles published in the daily papers of the State of Virginia.

Unpublished research: Significance of the College Catalog; A Psychological Definition of Cooperation of Children; Publicity for State Teachers Colleges; the Relation of Mail Order Houses to the Standard of Living in Rural Communities; How Teachers Live-Economic Study; The Social Conduct of Teachers; Problems in Orientation for College Freshmen.

NeSmith, Mary Ethel
1. An Objective Determination of Stories and Poems for the Primary Grades, 1927.
2. A Professionalized Course in Children's Literature for the Primary Grades, 1931-32.

Ogg, Florence Belle
1. Newspaper reviews on Prominent lecturers and lecture courses in Asheville Summer School. (Lectures by Dr. C. Alfonso Smith, Dr. Edwin Mimos), An Asheville Daily.

Roberts, Susan
1. Research: The Private Life of the Romans as seen in the works of Ausonius" Master's Dissertation, University of Chicago, 1924.

Smith, Richard Holladay
1. Thermal Energy Studies I, Phemyl Derivation of Methane, Ethane, and some Related Compounds, Journal of the American Chemical Society, Volume 53, 3664-3667, October 1931.
2. Thermal Energy Studies II, Thermal Energy Studies, Phemyl Derivation of Metal.

Smith, William Day
1. Various articles in the Virginia Journal of Education and Virginia Teachers (Harrisonburg).

States, Dora
1. An account of County Normal School work in Ohio, Ohio State Journal, 1923.

Swaney, C. B.
1. Episcopal Methodian and Slavery, The Gorham Press, Boston, 1926.
2. Contemporary Public Opinion on Lincoln's Emancipation Proclamation and Methodism and Temperance, in process of preparation.

Taylor, Jean
    1. Social Drama of 1600 and 1900. Main Currents of Regionalistic
       Literature in the Lower Middle West.

Thomas, Minor Wine
    1. Individual Instruction, Virginia Education Supply Company,
       1931.
    2. Montgomery County Plan, Unit Assignments, Virginia Education
       Supply Company, 1930-31.
    3. Public School Plumbing Equipment, T. C. Columbia, (dissertation)
       1928.
    4. How School Buildings Effect School Program, Virginia Journal
       of Education, 1929.
    5. Plumbing Equipment for Schools, American School and University,
       1929.
    6. Plumbing Fixtures too high, American School Board Journal, 1930.
    7. Plumbing Standards, Architectural Forum, 1931.
    8. Individualizing Instruction, Modern Education, 1929.

Ward, Gladys J.
    1. The Field of Research in Family Relations, Journal of Home
       Economics, September 1929, pp. 660-662.
    2. Economic Changes and the Cost of Food, Journal of Home Eco-
       nomics, July 1930, pp. 552-557.
    3. The Cost of Installment Credit to Consumers, Journal of
       Home Economics, January, 1932, pp. 25-26.

Williams, George Albert
    1. A Chemical Study of Laxative Action of Wheat Bran, American
       Journal of Physiology, December, 1927.
    2. A Chemical Study of Laxative Action of Wheat Bran, Proceedings
       of Society for Experimental Biology and Medicine, May 1926.

Wright, Christine
    1. Critical Analysis of Children's Reading in Okmulgee County,
       Oklahoma.

LIST OF MAJOR PROFESSIONAL ORGANIZATIONS TO
WHICH MEMBERS OF THE RADFORD FACULTY BELONGED

National Education Association
Virginia Education Association
American Association of University Women
American Association of Physics Teachers
American Association of University Professors
American Association for the Advancement of Science
American Library Association
American Genetic Association
American Meteor Association
American Medical Society
Council of Administrative Women
Virginia Classical Association
Southern Medical Association
National Council of Geography Teachers
National Council of Teachers of English
National Council of Teachers of Mathematics
National Federation of Music Clubs
Virginia State Teachers Association
Virginia Academy of Science
Virginia Folklore Society
Virginia Music Teachers State Association
National Geography Society
Geographical Association
City Teachers Association
Parent Teachers League
Society of Virginia Biologists
Home Economics Association
State Physical and Health Association
North Carolina Academy of Science
State Board of Examiners
Association for childhood Education
Modern Language Association
Mississippi State Teachers Association
Senior League of America
State Dietetic Association
Montgomery County Association
A. A. A. S.

OFFICERS OF YOUNG WOMEN'S CHRISTIAN
ASSOCIATION 1913-1932

1913

President ....Nell Painter
Vice-President.......................Faith Camden
Recording Secretary..............Florence Jackson
Corresponding Secretary............Carrie Greene
Treasurer................................Clara Delp

1914

President............................Ethel Garrett
Vice-President....................... India Covey
Recording Secretary..................Grace Graham
Corresponding Secretary.............. Ruth Dobyns
Treasurer............................. Ola Graham

1915

President................................Mona Meyer
Vice-President.........................Nancy Allen
Recording Secretary.............Annie Roper Brown
Corresponding Secretary............Ethel Garrett
Treasurer.............................Irene Allison

1916

President.........................Florence Bayless
Vice-President....................Elizabeth Ward
Recording Secretary....................Susie Hurt
Corresponding Secretary........... Willie Preston
Treasurer...........................Ola Graham
Advisory Committee:................(Miss Moffett
                                   (Miss Bryson
                                    Mr. Avent

1917

President ....Clifford Dutton
Vice-President.....................Mary McConnell

Recording Secretary.............Ola Graham
Corresponding Secretary......Blanche Ross
Treasurer...................Mary Page Brown

1918

President..................Margaret Allison
Vice-President ....Christine McCormick
Recording Secretary...... Mary Lucy Bowman
Treasurer................... Kathryn Taylor
Corresponding Secretary...... Eloise Brown

1919

President....................Ruth Jewel
Vice-President.................. Ila Gwynn
Recording Secretary........ Clara Persinger
Corresponding Secretary... Maggie Marshall
Treasurer.................. Kate Henderson

1920

President................. Clara McCauley
Vice-President.............. Margaret Kelly
Recording Secretary....... Josephine Wyatt
Treasurer.................. Natalie Harvey
Undergraduate Reporter..... Willie Shumate

1921

President............... Frankie Lou Farris
Vice-President........ Mary George Hedrick
Secretary...................Nora Lee Billips
Treasurer....................Natalie Harvey
Reporter of Under-
    classmen................ Margaret Sansilo
Advisors: Pearl Andrews, Willie Allen, Flora
    Bryson, Myrtle Burnette, Lillian
            Simmons

1922

President.................. Willie Shumate
Vice-President............. Rowena Stickley
Secretary.................... Leona Stiles
Treasurer.................... Dora Hubbard
Under Classman Reporter....... Reva Turner

1923

```
President...................... Margaret Martin
Treasurer......................Claudine Lane
Secretary...................... Hazel Redfern
Vice-President ................Virginia Allison
Undergraduate Reporter.........Virginia Porter
```

1924

```
President...................... Mabelle Durham
Vice-President................. Violet Snead
Secretary.....................Clarice Clark
Treasurer...................... Mamie Hewry
Undergraduate Reporter.........Margaret Martin
```

1925

```
President...................... Violet Snead
Vice-President.................Louise Martin
Secretary.....................Clarice Clark
Treasurer.....................Susie Wyatt
Undergraduate Reporter.............India Covey
```

1926

```
President...................... Margaret Black
Vice-President................. Sally Turner
Secretary...................... Mattie Richards
Treasurer...................... Janice Blackwell
Undergraduate Reporter......... Annie Obenshain
```

1927

```
President...................... Sallie Stevens
```

58-A

Vice-President.....................Helen Martin
Secretary...........................Myrtle Ellis
Treasurer....................... Kathleen Shumate
Undergraduate Reporter..... Elizabeth Robinette

1928

President....................... Pauline Osborne
Vice-President..................... Frances White
Secretary....................Vivian Harnesberger
Treasurer....................... Effie Obenshain
Undergraduate Reporter...............Ruth Young

1929

President.......................Cecil Sheppard
Vice-President..................... Hattie Tarter
Secretary......................... Frances White
Treasurer.................... Mary Leigh Hubbard
Undergraduate Reporter............ Marie Updyke
Advisor............................. Wanda Ellis

1930

President..................... Louise Scott
Vice-President.................Mary Leigh Hubbard
Secretary.............................Mab Carter
Treasurer............................Jean Taylor

1931

President.............................Emma Creecy
Vice-President..............Annie Ruth Gardner
Secretary........................Agnes Abernathy
Treasurer....................Elizabeth Hardwicke

1932

President...................... Arline Williams
Secretary....................... Pearl Kirkwood
Treasurer...................... Elsie Calhoun

Summer 1928

President.....................Ercelle Bennett
Vice-President................Berta Hartman
Secretary.....................Frances White
Treasurer.....................Irene Caldwell
Reporter......................Nell Dickerson

Summer 1929

President..................... Edna Yeatts
Vice-President................ Ellen Cundiff
Secretary & Treasurer.......... Mary Witt
Freshman Representative...... Marie Deyerle

Summer 1930

President.....................Clara Scott
Vice-President........ Elizabeth C. Minter
Secretary & Treasurer....... Sally Lumsden
Reporter......................Edna Yeatts
Sponsor.......................Alice Zollman

PRESIDENTS OF STUDENT GOVERNMENT

Carrie Green.........................1913-15
Ethel Garrett........................1915-16
Bess Lucas...........................1916-17
Aria Hicks...........................1917-18
Hessye Byer..........................1918-19
Louise Graham........................1919-20
Myrtle Boaz..........................1920-21
Stella Barnett.......................1921-22
Lucinda Thomas.......................1922-23
Frances Herrick......................1923-24
Alice Wolfersberger..................1924-25
Hattie Ogburn........................1925-26
Ethel Roberts........................1926-27
Jeanette Mears.......................1927-28
Anne Jennings........................1928-29
Elizabeth Jackson....................1929-30
Nina Jewell..........................1930-31

CLASS OFFICERS

Senior	1914-1915		
	President	-	Margaret Rogers
	Vice-President	-	Sarah Doak
	Secretary	-	Marjorie Combs
	Treasurer	-	Ida Schaffer
	Historian	-	Susie Higgins
Sophomore	President	-	India Covey
	Vice-President	-	Beaulah Topper
	Secretary	-	Ada Jennings
	Treasurer	-	Eva Parn
	Historian	-	Ethel Garrett
	Adviser	-	Miss Lillian Simmons
Junior	President	-	Anne Muse
Freshmen	President	-	Sina Jones
	1915-1916		
Senior	President	-	Carrie Greene
	Vice-President	-	Rose Stacy
	Secretary	-	Dora Mitchell
	Treasurer	-	Burr Wolfe
	Prophet	-	Margaret Wygal
	Orator	-	Edna Cox
	Historian	-	Anne Muse
	Statistician	-	Grayce Graham
	Poet	-	Ada Kyle
	News Reporter	-	Addie B. Allen
Sophomore	President	-	Sallie Mae Hurley
	Vice-President	-	Elizabeth Richmond
	Secretary	-	Ellen Dailey
	Treasurer	-	Grace Deaton
	Humorist	-	Winnie Hurt
	Adviser	-	Miss Terry
Junior	President	-	Irene Allison
Freshman	President	-	Vergie Rudy
	1916-1917		
Senior	President	-	Bonnie Alderson
	Vice-President	-	Mattie Lou Slemp
	Secretary	-	Mary Strader

	Treasurer	-	India Covey
	Historian	-	Beulah Easterly
	Poet	-	Mary Davis
	Statistician	-	Violet Fleenor
	Prophet	-	Nellie Brown Easton
	Lawyer	-	Irene Allison
	Adviser	-	Miss Bulifant
Sophomore	President	-	Ona Hicks
	Vice-President	-	Ruth Davis
	Secretary	-	Elizabeth Ward
	Treasurer	-	Willie Preston
	Adviser	-	Miss Harrison
Junior	President	-	Lois Showalter
Freshman	President	-	Mae Boothe

1917-1918

Senior	President	-	Emily Grove
	Vice-President	-	Mary Bohn
	Secretary	-	Kate Buchanan
	Treasurer	-	Evelyn Lavinder
	Prophet	-	Helen Albert
	Poet	-	Lelia Stump
	Historian	-	Rachel Oglesby
	Giftorian	-	Annis Ford
Sophomore	President	-	Lois McConnell
	Vice-President	-	Fay Roberts
	Secretary	-	Katherine Repass
	Treasurer	-	Ruth Jenkins
Junior	President	-	Ruth Davis
Freshman	President	-	Elizabeth Bonsack

1918-1919

Senior	President	-	Eugenia Jones
	Vice-President	-	Mattie Clark
	Secretary	-	Ellen Margaret Shannon
	Treasurer	-	Anne Preston Davis
	Historian	-	Sallie Mae Hurley
	Poet	-	Baney Pearl Lewis
	Orator	-	Sarah Elizabeth Ward
	Statistician	-	Mary Hester McConnell
	Adviser	-	Miss Bulifant

Sophomore	President	-	Mable Penn
	Vice-President	-	Elizabeth Bonsack
	Secretary	-	Helen Dewey
	Treasurer	-	Christine McCormick
	Adviser	-	Miss Baird
Junior	President	-	Anabella Goad
Freshman	President	-	Elizabeth Hicks

1919-1920

Senior	President	-	Lorena Caldwell
	Vice-President	-	Annie Mae Tickle
	Secretary	-	Pearl Stone
	Treasurer	-	Lena Hash
	Historian	-	Mary Allison
	Poet	-	Gertrude Friend
	Prophet	-	Sara Allison
	Salutatorian	-	Vashti Howard
	Giftorian	-	Gertrude Shumate
	Valedictorian	-	Effie Jackson
	Adviser	-	Miss Baird
Junior	President	-	Annie McConnell
Sophomore	President	-	Willie Shumate
	Vice-President	-	Margaret Kelly
	Secretary	-	Sallie Oglesby
	Adviser	-	Miss Coppedge
	Treasurer	-	Elizabeth Hawthorne
Freshman	President	-	Laura Pratt

1920-1921

Degree	President	-	Grace Gladstone
Senior	Two-Year		
	President	-	Annie Kuhn Roberts
	Vice-President	-	Eloise Brown
	Secretary	-	Frances W. Long
	Treasurer	-	Mable Grissom
	Historian	-	Nannie Jones
	Poet	-	Blanche Hurley
	Prophet	-	Marie Louise Graham
	Giftorian	-	Gladys Hayter
	Adviser	-	Miss Alice S. Jones
Sophomore	President	-	Robbie Webb
	Vice-President	-	Stella Barnette

	Secretary	-	Josephine Craft
	Treasurer	-	Ella Harvey
	Adviser	-	Miss Harrison
Junior	President	-	Clara McCauley
Freshman	President	-	Martha Wright

1921-1922

Senior	President	-	Annie McConnell
	Vice-President	-	Willie Shumate
	Secretary	-	Gertrude Shumate
	Treasurer	-	Sallie Oglesby
	Student Council		
	Representative	-	Myrtle Dobbins
	Adviser	-	W. R. Bowers
Sophomore	President	-	Grace Tietje
	Vice-President	-	Grace Topper
	Secretary	-	Margaret Sanislo
	Treasurer	-	Maggie Quesenberry
	Reporter	-	Bessie Millen
	Adviser	-	Elizabeth S. Allen
Junior	President	-	Martha Wright
Freshman	President	-	Evelyn Vaden

1922-1923

Senior	President	-	Gertrude Shumate
	Vice-President	-	Mr. Boatwright
	Secretary and		
	Treasurer	-	Elsie Stone
Sophomore	President	-	Elsie Jones
	Vice-President	-	Nancy Allison
	Secretary	-	Helen Hughes
	Treasurer	-	Helen Haight
Junior	President	-	Enola Dobbins
Freshman	President	-	Josephine Cord

1923-1924

Senior	President	-	Annie Sue Anderson
	Vice-President	-	Lelia Huddle
	Secretary and		
	Treasurer	-	Florence Kipp

64-A

Sophomore	President	-	David Hurley
	Vice-President	-	Naomi Brooks
	Secretary	-	Myrtle Bryson
	Treasurer	-	Margaret Sutton
Junior	President	-	Lucinda Thomas
Freshman	President	-	

1924-1925

Senior	President	-	Ada Lee Cannady
	Vice-President	-	Lettie Harding
	Secretary	-	Berta Cabanillas
	Treasurer	-	Annie Mae Hobbs
	Student Council Representative	-	Maude Paine
	Reporter	-	Zella Nunn
Junior	President	-	India Covey
Sophomore	President	-	Georgia Clark
	Vice-President	-	Marie Rickey
	Secretary	-	Garland Poindexter
	Treasurer	-	Carrie Rhodes
	Student Council	-	Susie Cawood
	Representative	-	Carmen Showalter
	Jeanette Anderson,	Emma Hayth	
Freshman	President	-	Grace Robertson

1925-1926

Senior	President	-	Ruby Dobyns
	Vice-President	-	Nina Garrett
	Secretary and Treasurer	-	India Covey
	Reporter	-	Rosa Torres
Sophomore	President	-	Dorrance Smith
	Vice-President	-	Helen Martin
	Secretary	-	Louise Mullen
	Treasurer	-	Virginia Coltrane
Junior	President	-	Frances Coleman
Freshman	President	-	Ellen Chamberlaye

1926-1927

Senior	President	-	Anna Lee Bonham

	Vice-President	-	Susie Wyatt
	Secretary	-	Frances Coleman
	Treasurer	-	Laura Wine
	Reporter	-	Annie Obenshain
Sophomore	President	-	Blanche Obenshain
	Vice-President	-	Audrey Arthur
	Secretary	-	Hattie Tarter
	Treasurer	-	Lourine Halstead
	Reporter	-	Olive Porter Scott
Junior	President	-	Iris Ritenour
Freshman	President	-	Elizabeth Templeton

1927-1928

Senior	President	-	Myrtle Ellis
	Vice-President	-	Helen Smith
	Secretary	-	Sallie Vaughn Turner
	Treasurer	-	Ethel Shockey
	Reporter	-	Cassie Gardner
Sophomore	President	-	Vivian Harnsberger
	Vice-President	-	Eleanor Scyne
	Secretary	-	Lucille Christian
	Treasurer	-	Effie Obenshain
	Reporter	-	Helen Wright
Junior	President	-	Ann Gimbert
Freshman	President	-	India DeHart

1928-1929

Senior	President	-	Louise Mahaney
	Vice-President	-	Hattie Tarter
	Secretary	-	Elizabeth Chumbly
	Reporter	-	Mrs. Mary Windle
Sophomore	President	-	Mildred Hale
	Vice-President	-	Monnie Ellis
	Secretary	-	Myrtle Perry
	Treasurer	-	Marguerite Dotson
	Reporter	-	Geneva Taylor
Junior	President	-	Louise Scott
Freshman	President	-	Tommy Shepherd

	1929-1930		
Senior	President	-	Kathleen Jennings
	Vice-President	-	Isabelle Richards
	Secretary	-	Catherine Abernathy
	Treasurer	-	Anna Maddy
	Reporter	-	Virginia Aldridge

Student Council Representatives - Bertha Harding, Jennie Wood Mead, Eugenia Harris

Sophomore	President	-	Colleen Seagle
	Vice-President	-	Cora Osborne
	Treasurer	-	Ruth Stoke
	Secretary	-	Elizabeth Wray

Student Council Representatives: Margie Mc-Carson, Frances Boothe, Inez Shields

Junior	President	-	Audrey Sharp
Freshman	President	-	Wally Sholz
	1930-1931		
Senior.	President	-	Myrtle Logan
	Vice-President	-	Callie Brown
	Secretary	-	Reba Grim
	Treasurer	-	Nora Gardner
Sophomore	President	-	Mildred Charlton
	Vice-President	-	Maxie Scyphers
	Secretary	-	Hazel Bennett
	Treasurer	-	Mildred Vaughan
Junior.	President	-	Frances Boothe
Freshman	President	-	Emily Taylor

POCAHONTAS OFFICERS
1913 to 1931
o

September 1913.

President - Ethel Garrett
Vice-Pres.- Clara Stone
Secretary - Maude Goodwin
Treasurer - Georgia Morris
Chaplain - Mr. Gilbert
Historian - Lena Walters
Critic - Florence Jackson

January 1914.

President - Rubye Akers
Vice-Pres.- Mosby Charlton
Secretary - Ruth Holsey
Treasurer - Grace Deaton
Reporter - Anne Muse
Critic - Susie Higgins

March 1914.

President - Burr Wolfe
Vice-Pres.- India Covey
Secretary - Grace Deaton
Treasurer - Nina Miller
Critic - Osa Graham
Reporter - Carrie Bagwell

September 1914.

President - Anne Muse
Vice-Pres.- Grayce Graham
Secretary - Mosby Charlton
Treasurer - Bertie Fisher
Reporter - Ethel Garrett
Critic - Burr Wolfe

January 1915.

President - Anne Muse
Vice-Pres.- Mary Strader
Secretary - Carrie Bagwell
Treasurer - Elizabeth Richmond

Critic - Mosby Charlton
Historian - Burr Wolfe
Sgt. at Arms - Ada Jennings
Reporter - Mattie Lou Slemp

March 1915.

President - Bonnie Alderman
Vice-Pres.- Mattie Lou Slemp
Secretary - Elizabeth Richmond
Reporter - Burr Wolfe
Chaplain - Ethel Garrett
Sgt. at Arms - Bess Oglesby

September 1915.

President - Irene Allison
Vice-Pres.- Ethel Garrett
Secretary - India Covey
Treasurer - Florence Bayless
Critic - Lois Showalter
Historian - Lila Stump
Reporter - Ada Jennings

January 1916.

President - Beulah Easterly
Vice-Pres.- Daphne Showalter
Secretary - Mary Strader
Treasurer - Grace Deaton
Critic - Irene Allison
Chaplain - Sadie Johnston
Reporter - Gladys Gollehorn

March 1916.

President - Mattie Lou Slemp
Vice-Pres.- Mary Bohn
Secretary - Julia Keyes
Treasurer - Lucia Showalter
Chaplain - Willie Preston

Critic   - Florence Bayless
Reporter   - Clifford Dutton

September 1916.

President - Thermutis Parrack
Vice-Pres.- Maude Long
Treasurer - Sarah Jackson
Secretary - Helen Albert
Chaplain - Ola Graham
Critic   - Mary Bohn

January 1917.

President - Mary Bohn
Vice-Pres.-Mary Allison
Secretary - Lillian Wolfe
Treasurer - Maude Long
Critic   - Florence Bayless
Chaplain - Baney Lewis
Sgt. at Arms - Rachel Rector

March 1917.

President - Evelyn Lavinder
Vice-Pres.- Ola Graham
Secretary - Sarah Jackson
Treasurer - Tempa Slemp
Critic   - Clifford Dutton
Chaplain - Thelma Cooney
Sgt. at Arms - Josephine Miller
Reporter - Katherine La Fon

September 1917.

President - Mary Allison
Vice-Pres.- Maude Duncan
Secretary - Mabel Young
Treasurer - Madge Howard
Reporter - Maude Parks
Chaplain - Virginia Price
Critic   - Helen Albert
Sgt. at Arms - Tempa Slemp

January 1918.

President - Josephine Wassum
Vice-Pres.- Katherine La Fon

Secretary - Edna Osborne
Treasurer - Emily Topper
Critic   - Blanche Daniel
Chaplain - Margaret Jennings
Reporter - Violet Hurd
Sgt. at Arms - Mattie Kimberlin

March 1918.

President - Maude Duncan
Vice-Pres.- Beulah Grubb
Secretary - Carrie Cox
Treasurer - Daisy Mayo
Chaplain - Fannie B. Davis
Pianist   - Lois Hasselvander
Sgt. at Arms - Etta Spivey

September 1918.

President - Clifford Dutton
Vice-Pres.- Sarah Allison
Secretary - Grace Bevins
Treasurer - Marie Kennedy
Chaplain - Cecile Albertson
Sgt. at Arms - Eliza Slemp

January 1919.

President - Eliza Stickley
Vice-Pres.- Gertrude Friend
Secretary - Annie Kuhn Roberts
Treasurer - Viola Jackson
Sgt. at Arms - Artie Rector
Pianist   - Clara McCauley

March 1919.

President - Janie Broadwater
Vice-Pres.- Lavonia Widener
Secretary - Blanche Killinger
Treasurer - Ona Kirby
Chaplain - Nellie Barnes
Pianist   - Opal Quessenberry
Sgt. at Arms - Christine Hutton

.September 1919.

President - Ola Graham

Vice-Pres.- Sina Kirby
Secretary - Mae Calhoun
Treasurer - Stella Barnette
Critic   - Emma Quessenberry
Sgt. at Arms - Nellie Barnes
Pianist   - Thelma Martin

January 1920.

President - Ella Bishop
Vice-Pres.- Nellie Barnes
Secretary - Clara McCauley
Treasurer - Sarah Price
Chaplain - Josephine Craft
Pianist   - Elizabeth Brown
Sgt. at Arms - Pauline Perfater

March 1920.

President - Nannie Jones
Vice-Pres.- Ruby Graham
Secretary - Maggie Marshall
Treasurer - Nancy Allison
Chaplain - Annie Kuhn Roberts
Pianist   - Clara McCauley
Sgt. at Arms - Jessie Coates

September 1920.

President - Elizabeth Brown
Vice-Pres.- Frances Coleman
Secretary - Lucie Richardson
Treasurer - Maggie Quesenberry
Critic   - Florence Jackson
Chaplain - Mary Louise Carr
Pianist   - Anne Jennings
Sgt. at Arms - Jessie Coates

January 1921.

President - Anne Jennings
Vice-Pres.- Opal Quesenberry
Secretary - Stella Barnett
Critic   - Ella Bishop
Chaplain -
Treasurer - Ina Addington
Pianist   - Agnes Robinson
Sgt. at Arms - Margaret Sanislo

March 1921.

President - Willie May Moore
Vice-Pres.- Roxie Phlegar
Treasurer - Sarah Price
Secretary - Janie Chaffin
Pianist   - Myrtle Pugh
Chaplain - Nannie Taylor
Custodian - Eloise Young
Sgt. at Arms - Barbara Strader

September 1921.

President - Nancy Allison
Vice-Pres.- Jessie Coates
Secretary - Maude Graham
Treasurer - Tinifair Stallard
Chaplain - Eloise Young
Sgt. at Arms - Mae Elliot
Pianist   - Dorothy Mann
Custodian - Chloetta Groseclose

January 1922.

President - Ina Addington
Vice-Pres.- Carolee Noe
Secretary - Alesta Whitaker
Treasurer - Kate Franklin
Pianist   - Nina Williams
Chaplain - Nannie Stone
Sgt. at Arms - Nora Bilips

March 1922.

President - Margaret Sanislo
Vice-Pres.- Nancy Catron
Secretary - Anna Bishop
Treasurer - Margaret Lawrence
Chaplain - Elsie Benson
Custodian - Cleo Parsons
Pianist   - Wilma Dickerson
Sgt. at Arms - Sadie Gilbert

September 1922.

President - Mrs. McGee
Secretary - Rowena Stickley
Treasurer - Lora Jackson
Pianist   - Naomi Brooks

January 1923.

President - Myrtle Dobbins
Vice-Pres.- Eva Pinkard
Secretary - Willie Kelly
Treasurer - Tinifair Stallard
Chaplain - Inez Hicks
Pianist - Margaret Jewett
Sgt. at Arms - Florence Linthicum

March 1923.

President - Audrey Fleenor
Vice-Pres.- Carrie Brown
Secretary - Lillian Swank
Treasurer - Stacey Jennings
Custodian - Vada Reasor
Sgt. at Arms - Bill Brown

June 1923.

President - Bernice Black
Vice-Pres.- Fannie Cox
Secretary - Lotus Barton
Treasurer - Amanda Myers
Chaplain - Eliza Stickley

September 1923.

President - Bernice Black
Vice-Pres.- Virginia Perry
Secretary - Willie Kelly
Treasurer - Kate Cox
Chaplain - Mamie Roberts

January 1924.

President - Ada Lee Canady
Vice-Pres.- Virginia Allison
Secretary - Helen Einstein
Treasurer - Ethel Roberts
Chaplain - Mildred Cawood

March 1924.

President - Roche Alliston
Vice-Pres.-Cecile Simpson
Secretary - Gladys White
Secretary - Jenette Anderson

Treasurer - Cumbia Hicks
Chaplain - Lizzie Robinette

January 1924

President - Emma Cooley
Vice-Pres.- Polly Donaldson
Secretary - Mab Carter
Treasurer - Amanda Hicks
Chaplain - Annie Morgan

September 1924.

President - Genevieve Giesen
Vice-Pres.- Maude Paine
Secretary - Elizabeth Law
Treasurer - Clara Beard
Chaplain - Mildred Elgin

January 1925

President - Helen Einstein
Vice-Pres.- Rebie Hines
Treasurer - Susie Cawood
Secretary - Elsie Palmer
Chaplain - Clara Beard

March 1925.

President - Clara Beard
Vice-Pres.- Mary Ellen Craft
Secretary - Rebie Hines
Treasurer - Maude Paine
Chaplain - Garnett Shufflebarger

June 1925.

President - Rebie Hines
Secretary - Doris Tinsley

September 1925.

President - India Covey
Vice-Pres.- Alleen Carper
Secretary - Mattie Richard
Treasurer - Irma Shufflebarger
Chaplain - Ethel Roberts

January 1926.

President - Ethel Roberts
Vice-Pres.- Jeanette Mears
Secretary - Virginia Dare Davis
Treasurer - Edith Cherry
Chaplain - Virginia Brockman

March 1926.

President - Mattie Richard
Vice-Pres.- Louise Mullan
Secretary - Hazel Jeter
Treasurer - Trula Roberts
Chaplain - Iva Fairfield

June 1926.

President - Bess Hillman
Vice-Pres.- Rosa Torres
Secretary - Margaret Bailey
Treasurer - Eulalia Compton

September 1926.

President - Irma Shufflebarger
Vice-Pres.- Hattie Tarter
Secretary - Lucille Lancaster
Treasurer - Lohren Davenport
Chaplain - Olive Porter Scott

January 1927.

President - Sallie Vaughn Turner
Vice-Pres.- Narcissa Thompson
Secretary - Jessie Britt
Treasurer - Alice Hylton
Chaplain - Louise Hartsell

March 1927.

President - Ruth Bricker
Vice-Pres.- Elizabeth Tyler
Secretary - Louise Mullan
Treasurer - Anna Belle DeHart
Chaplain - Virginia Revere

June 1927.

President - Louise Hartsell
Vice-Pres.- Margaret Bunn
Secretary - Bettie Stafford
Treasurer - Merida Blanco
Chaplain - Mary Sue Davis

September 1927.

President - Anna Belle DeHart
Vice-Pres.- Mary Snavely
Secretary - Garnett Shufflebarger
Treasurer - Reba Grim
Chaplain - Mary Sue Davis

January 1928.

President - Garnett Shufflebarger
Vice-Pres.- Maude Munsey
Secretary - Helen Newell
Treasurer - Lucy Beahm
Chaplain - Frances White

March 1928.

President - Helen Smith
Vice-Pres.- Mary Muse
Secretary - Isabelle Richard
Treasurer - Ethelene Foster
Chaplain - Irene Corbin

June 1928.

President - Blanche Sowder
Vice-Pres.- Virginia Dare Davis
Secretary - Kathleen Wilson
Treasurer - Ruby Hash
Chaplain - Frances White

September 1928.

President - Jeanette Mears
Vice-Pres.- Emma Hurt
Secretary - Elizabeth Jackson
Treasurer - Violet Lewis
Chaplain - Marie Deyerle

January 1929.

President - Emma Hurt
Vice-Pres.- Lucille Christian
Secretary - Ada Blanco
Chaplain - Monnie Ellis

March 1929.

President - Blanche Daniel
Vice-Pres.- Lucille Christian
Secretary - Mary Alma Weaver
Chaplain - Ruth Stoke

September 1929.

President - Violet Lewis
Vice-Pres.- Thomasine Shepherd
Secretary - Monnie Ellis
Treasurer - Lucille Christian

January 1930.

President - Isabelle Richard
Vice-Pres.- Racella Sayers
Secretary - Ruth Stoke
Chaplain - Ruth Painter

March 1930.

President - Evelyn Parrack
Vice-Pres.- Monnie Ellis
Secretary - Eleanor Bowers
Chaplain - Andrea Lane

June 1930.

President - Leona Giles
Vice-Pres.- Pearl Kirkwood
Secretary - Mary White
Treasurer - Claribel Pettyjohn
Chaplain - Maude Nixon

September 1930.

President - Monnie Ellis
Vice-Pres.- America Gonzalez
Secretary - Agnes Abernathy
Treasurer - Andrea Lane
Chaplain - Elizabeth Tinnell

January 1931.

President - Pearl Kirkwood
Vice-Pres.- Claribel Pettyjohn
Secretary - Louise Brower
Treasurer - Andrea Lane
Chaplain - Nellie Parker

March 1931.

President - America Gonzalez
Vice-Pres.- Pauline Fore
Secretary - Mary Lucas
Treasurer - Andrea Lane
Chaplain - Mary McDowell

INGLES OFFICERS
1913 to 1931
———o———

September 1913.

President - Marjorie Combs
Secretary - Nell Painter
Vice Pres.- Faith Camden
Treasurer - Alberta Crockett
Sgt. at Arms - Clara Delp
Critic   - Elizabeth Moran

January 1914.

President - Carrie Greene
Vice Pres.- Ruth Dobyns
Secretary - Sarah Doak
Treasurer - Gay Hudson
Sgt. at Arms - Ellen Daily
Critic   - Estelle Green

March 1914.

President - Lillian Howard
Vice Pres.- Kate Dunn
Secretary - Sara Saunders
Treasurer - Carrie Synder
Sgt. at Arms - Sallie Mae Hurley
Critic   - Bernice Phipps

September 1914.

President - Ruth Dobyns
Vice Pres.- Julia Cook
Secretary - Clara Delp
Treasurer - Rachael Oglesby
Sgt. at Arms - Gene Stafford
Critic   - Nell Painter

January 1915.

President - Winnie Hurt
Secretary - Mona Myer

March 1915.

President - Mary Davis
Vice-Pres.- Maxie King
Treasurer - Elizabeth Kelly
Sgt. at Arms - Bessie Lucas
Critic   - June McConnell

September 1915.

President - Annie Roper Brown
Vice Pres.- Violet Fleenor
Secretary - Bess Lucas
Treasurer - Helen Huddle
Critic   - Mona Myer
Sgt. at Arms - Ara Hicks

January 1916.

President - Rachael Givens
Vice Pres.- Elrika Shelbourne
Secretary - Erma Hubbard
Treasurer - Margaret Spring
Sgt. at Arms - Stella Repass
Critic   - Anita Clark

April 1916.

President - Helen Huddle
Secretary - Ellen Daily

September 1916.

President - Ara Hicks
Secretary - Irene Gary

December 1917.

President - Annis Ford
Secretary - Kate Buchanan

Vice-Pres.- Elizabeth Kelly
Treasurer - Mary McConnell
Critic   - Fannie Kate Godsey
Reporter - Ellen Shannon
Sgt. at Arms - Mary Hayter

March 1917.

President - Fannie Kate Godsey
Secretary - Lelia Fay Huddle

September 1917.

President - Ruth Davis
Vice-Pres.- Elrica Shelbourne
Secretary - Mary McConnell
Treasurer - Mary Hayter
Critic   - Margaret Watson
Sgt. at Arms - Marjorie Allen
Reporter - Marie Hayman
Chaplain - Elizabeth Ward
Pianist   - Gertrude Shumate

December 1918.

President - Margaret Watson
Vice-Pres.- Mattie Clark
Secretary - Blanch Corvin
Treasurer - Margaret Taylor
Critic   - Lucille Blackard
Sgt. at Arms - Willie Shumate
Reporter - Elizabeth Coleman
Pianist   - 'Liz Dubb

March 1918.

President - Mattie Clark
Vice-Pres.- Margaret Allison
Secretary - Dorothy Moir
Treasurer - Elizabeth Bonsack
Reporter - Lena Lowman
Pianist   - Kate Repass
Sgt. at Arms - Carrie Morris
Critic   - Anne Davis

September 1918.

President - Josephine Pratt
Secretary - Virginia Johnson

January 1919.

President - Hilda Huddle
Vice-Pres.- Effie Jackson
Secretary - Mary Gray Ross
Treasurer - Laura Rutherford
Sgt. at Arms - Ella Harvey
Critic   - Jeff Nidemaier
Censor   - Margaret Kelly
Chaplain - Carrie Morris

March 1919.

President - Alice Dunn
Vice-Pres.- Thelma Atkinson
Secretary - Katherine Buford
Treasurer - Myrtle Boaz
Sgt. at Arms - Dorris Moore
Critic   - Effie Jackson
Censor   - Virginia Penn
Chaplain - Parke Ferguson
Reporter - Mary Elinor Lush
Pianist   - Gertrude Shumate

September 1919.

President - Willie Shumate
Vice-Pres.- Sallie Couch
Secretary - Dora Kendrick
Treasurer - Park Ferguson
Chaplain - Nell Hayter
Critic   - Finley Sutherland
Censor   - Merle Kyle
Sgt. at Arms - Virginia Painter
Reporter - Ada Lou Hurley
Pianist   - Katherine Buford

January 1920.

President - Merle Kyle
Vice-Pres.- Ethel Strong
Secretary - Rachael Clark
Treasurer - Jessie Muncy
Chaplain - Gladys Hayter
Censor   - Ella Jackson
Sgt. at Arms - Nannie Buchanan
Pianist   - Ruth Bird

March 1920.

President - Grace Gladstone
Secretary - Kathryn Taylor

September 1920.

President - Hessie Byer
Vice-Pres.- Daisy Robinson
Secretary - Kathryn Caldwell
Treasurer - Kate Henderson
Censor   - Jessie Muncy
Sgt. at Arms - Dora Hubbard
Chaplain - Ella Jackson
Pianist   - Blannie Clark
Reporter - Annie McConnell
Critic   - Lorena Caldwell
Custodian - Neta Tarter

January 1921.

President - Annie Mae Broyles
Vice-Pres.- Virginia Porter
Secretary - Bill Wood
Treasurer - Luninda Thomas
Custodian - Mary George Hedrick
Critic   - Reva Turner
Pianist   - Kathleen Cord
Chaplain - Nell Kabrick
Censor   - Susie Wyatt
Reporter - Virginia Painter
Sgt. at Arms - Vera Harmon

March 1921.

President - Christine Tyree
Vice-Pres.- Sallie Oglesby
Secretary - Lou Elva Dougherty
Treasurer - Ella Harvey
Chaplain - Gladys Cook
Reporter - Mary Greever
Critic   - Grace Tietje
Custodian - Evelyn Vaden
Censor   - Martha Wright
Pianist   - Marie Davis
Sgt. at Arms- Lou Ellen Fugate

September 1921.

President - Rova Turner
Secretary - Nell Kabrick

Winter 1922.

President - Gertrude Shumate
Vice-Pres.- Lois Giles
Secretary - Marie Davis
Treasurer - Natalie Harvey

Chaplain - Sallie Turner
Censor   - Dora Hubbard
Reporter - Margaret Cage
Pianist   - Eugenia Patterson
Critic   - Josephine Wyatt
Custodian - Mattie Brugh
Sgt. at Arms - Edna Lyon, Lois Jamerson
Editor, Ingles Evening Star-Grace Tietje

March 1922.

President - Annie Sue Anderson
Vice-Pres.- Ella Harvey
Secretary - Edna Naff
Treasurer - Martha Wright
Chaplain - Belle Wooding
Critic   - Annie McConnell
Reporter - Gladys Cook
Pianist   - Elsie Jones
Custodian - Helen Buchanan
Censor   - Lucy Porter
Sge. at Arms - Margaret Black, Emily
                                    Hager
June 1922.

President - Mrs. Clara Conner
Vice-Pres.- Mae Shirley
Secretary - Grace East
Treasurer - Belle Wooding
Editor   - Edith Naff
Reporter -- Nina Pettit
Custodian - Edith Shufflebarger
Chaplain - Nola Burkey
Pianist   - Louise Blackwell
Sgt. at Arms - Margaret Wright
                                Mary Johnson

September 1922.

President - Virginia Porter
Vice-Pres.- Margaret Cage
Secretary - Carrie Blackwell
Treasurer - Ora Jones
Chaplain - Stella Mae Agnew
Reporter - Ruth Shumate
Editor   - Helen Buchanan

Sgt. at Arms - Elsie Williams
                Ethel Smith
Critic   - Annie Sue Anderson
Censor   - Ruth Jonas
Custodian - Nina Pettit
Pianist   - Neta Tarter

January 1923.

President - Jane Tyler
Vice-Pres.- Frances Herrick
Secretary - Alta Strickler
Treasurer - Nelle Blackwell
Chaplain - Claudine Lane
Reporter - Minta Davenport
Critic   - Gertrude Shumate
Censor   - Virginia Cornette
Editor   - Elsie Tompkins
Sgt. at Arms - Ruth Carter
                Ruth Culpepper
Custodians - Drucilla McConnell
                Lois Perry
Pianist   - Mae Kipps

March 1923.

President - Nola Burkey
Vice-Pres.- Helen Buchanan
Secretary - Stella Mae Agnew
Custodian - Lois Giles
Critic   - Helen Haight
Censor   - Mamie Daniels
Reporter - Helen Cooke
Sgt. at Arms - Elsie Stone
                Ruth Lloyd
Pianist   - David Hurley
Treasurer - Mollie Smith
Chaplain - Gladys Newberry

September 1923.

President - Elsie Tompkins
Vice-Pres.- Mae Kipps
Secretary - Nancy Barksdale
Treasurer - Mamie Daniel
Custodian - Thelma Mays
Critic   - Oakie Angle

Chaplain - Lucille Deaton
Pianist - Virginia Cornett
Censor   - Mary Sue Dungan
Sgt. at Arms - Dora Hubbard
                Katie Graham
Reporter - Lois Perry
Cheer Leader - David Hurley

January 1924.

President - Elizabeth Hicks
Vice-Pres.- Dora Hubbard
Secretary - Garland Poindexter
Treasurer - Eula Porter
Custodian - Mae Phipps,
                Alice Blackwell
Sgt. at Arms - Katie Carter
                Carrie Rhodes
Pianist - Maybelle Durham
Chaplain - Ercelle Giles
Censor   - Bess Daughtery
Critic   - Annie Sue Anderson
Reporter - Marie Knox

March 1924.

President - Mary Kilgore
Vice-Pres.- Katherine Yeatts
Secretary - Bonnie Lyon
Treasurer - Frances Bragg
Custodian - Ercelle Giles
                Elizabeth Carter
Sgt. at Arms - Dorothy Carter
                Anne Rysler
Pianist - Dorothy Bryant
Chaplain - Clarice Clark
Critic   - Margaret Sutton
Reporter - Violet Snead
Censor   - Thelma Field

June 1924.

President - Kathryn Yates
Vice-Pres.- Blanche Worley
Secretary - Ruby Shreeves
Treasurer - Willie Cornett
Critic   - Elsie Tompkins

Chaplain   - Georgia Repass
Pianist   - Mae Brooks
Censor   - Anna Woodcock
Reporter   - Nannie McConnell
Sgt. at Arms - Ruth Sawyer
              Myrtle Gilbert
Custodian   - Bertha Caldwell

September 1924.

President   - Charlotte Caldwell
Vice-Pres. - Emma Hayth
Secretary   - Lora Hubbard
Treasurer   - Helen Musser
Reporter   - Kathryn Yates
Critic   - Ruby Mann
Chaplain   - Annie Obenshain
Pianist   - Ruth Lloyd
Custodian   - Joy Bakes
              Flora Black
Sgt. at Arms - Marie Rickey
              Carmen Showalter
Censor   - Stella Lea

January 1925.

President   - Helen Jones
Vice-Pres. - Susie Wyatt
Secretary   - Bessie Allison
Treasurer   - Carrie Rhodes
Chaplain   - Lettie Harding
Reporter   - Maude Rimmer
Critic   - Charlotte Caldwell
Pianist   - Billy Robertson
Custodian   - Lelia Jones,
              Hattie Ogburn
              Annie Byrd White
              Nannie Hardy Clark
Censor   - Delhia Hines
Sgt. at Arms - Ruth Spring
              Lillian Johnson
March 1925.
President   - Alta Strickler
Vice-Pres. - Nannie H. Clark
Secretary   - Julia Smithson
Treasurer   - Louise Wright
Chaplain   - Eula Porter
Reporter   - Alice Pierceson

Critic   - Helen Jones
Pianist   - Dorothy Bryant
Custodian   - Mary Jordan
              Louise Scott
              Magdalene Scott
              Elizabeth Kell
Censor   - Annie Snidow
Sgt. at Arms - Susie Wyatt

June 1925.

President   - Ruby Shreeves
Vice-Pres   - Letty Harding
Secretary   - Ruth Spring
Reporter   - Helen Jones
Treasurer   - Charlsie Camper
Chaplain   - Julia Gunn
Critic   - Hazel Redfearee
Custodian   - Ethel Ayers
              Virginia Coltraine

September 1925.

President   - Emma Gregory
Vice-Pres. - Dalphene Burnett
Secretary   - Anna Lee Bonham
Treasurer   - Mildred McCrory
Pianist   - Josephine Lucas
Chaplain   - Anna Byrd White
Censor   - Elsie Jones
Custodian   - Eula Porter
              Mary Beamer
              Etta Kate Charlton
              J.R.L. Johnson, Jr.
Sgt. at Arms - Louise Scott
              Lelia Jones

January 1926.

President   - Anna Lee Bonham
Secretary   - Helen Martin
Treasurer   - Elizabeth Simms
Pianist   - Dorothy Sharitz
Sgt. at Arms - Margaret Rambo
              Blanche Obenshain

March 1926.

President - Margaret Black
Vice-Pres.- Lorinne Holsted
Secretary - Blanche Obenshain
Treasurer - Frances Kremming
Chaplain - Emma Gregory
Critic - Hattie Ogburn
Reporter - Dorothy Sharitz
Pianist - Eleanor Bryant
Censor - Mamie Hardy Claw
Custodians- Marion Jett, Mildred
        McCrory, Kathleen Shumate
Sgt. at Arms - Annie Obenshain
        Mattie Simms

June 1926.

President - Mae Kelly
Vice-Pres.- Annie Rhodes
Secretary - Luch Lockhart
Treasurer - Alice Lowe
Chaplain - Margaret LaRue
Reporter - Virginia Cornett
Pianist - Dorothy Sharitz
Censor - Carrie Green
Custodians - Louise Foutz, C. Lee
  Spencer, Thelma Rosenberry, Mrs.
        Peasley
Sgt. at Arms - Flora Black, Anna
        Agnes, Winnie Agnew

September 1926.

President - Elsie Jones
Vice-Pres.- Iris Kenhover
Secretary - Lelia Jones
Treasurer - Louise Zimmerman
Chaplain - Myra Odue
Critic - Sallie Copenhaver
Censor - Marion Jett
Pianist - Evelyn Epperley
Custodian - Margaret Ross, Hazel
King, Martha Hickman, Eleanor Bryant
Sgt. at Arms-Florence Powell, Helen
        Martin

January 1927.

President - Susie Wyatt
Vice-Pres.- Charlsie Camper
Secretary - Margaret Rawls
Reporter - Louise Mahaney
Critic - Mrs. Chapman

Ushers - Mary Etheridge, Ruth Hayter
Custodians - Sallie Copenhaver, Mary
        Keister, Mattie Turner, Annis
        Crabtree
Pianist - Zollie Cox
Censor - Martha Hickman

March 1927.

President - Annie Obenshain
Vice-Pres.- Elinor Bryant
Secretary - Maxine Cole
Sgt. at Arms - Mary Beasley, Annie
        Daugherty
Critic - Helen Martin
Custodians - Jonnie Jills, Roberta Turner
  Effie Obenshain, Blanche Beamer
Chaplain - Bessie Proffitt
Historian - Mrs. Bertha Chapman
Reporter - Ruby Mann
Pianist - Zollie Cox

June 1927.

President - Ruby Mann
Vice-Pres.- Flora Black
Secretary - Evelyn Gravett
Treasurer - Kathleen Ageon
Chaplain - Mrs. Bertha Chapman
Critic - Josephine Wyatt
Historian - Bessie Payne
Sgt. at arms - Marie Rickey, Nora
        Morris
Custodian - Christine Jessee, Mabel
  Crowe, Glenna Johnson
Reporter - Mrs. St. Clair

September 1927.

President - Iris Ritenour
Vice-Pres.- Nannie Daugherty
Secretary - Elizabeth Templeton
Treasurer - Nannie Hardy Clark
Reporter - Lucille Authur
Critic - Pauline Osborne
Ushers - Vivian Harnesbarger
        Mildred Vaughan

March 1926.

President - Margaret Black
Vice-Pres.- Lorinne Holsted
Secretary - Blanche Obenshain
Treasurer - Frances Kremming
Chaplain - Emma Gregory
Critic - Hattie Ogburn
Reporter - Dorothy Sharitz
Pianist - Eleanor Bryant
Censor - Mamie Hardy Claw
Custodian - Marion Jett
         Mildred McCrory
         Kathleen Shumate
Sgt. at Arms - Annie Obenshain
         Mattie Simms

June 1926

President - Mae Kelly
Vice-Pres.- Annie Rhodes
Secretary - Luch Lockhart
Treasurer - Alice Lowe
Chaplain - Margaret LaRue
Reporter - Virginia Cornett
Pianist - Dorothy Sharitz
Censor - Carrie Green
Custodian - Louise Foutz
         C. Lee Spencer
         Thelma Rosenberry
         Mrs. Peasley
Sgt. at Arms - Flora Black
         Anna Agnew
         Winnie Agnew

September 1926.

President - Elsie Jones
Vice-Pres.- Iris Kenhover
Secretary - Lelia Jones
Treasurer - Louise Zimmerman
Chaplain - Myra Odue
Critic - Sallie Copenhaver
Censor - Marion Jett
Pianist - Evelyn Epperley
Custodian - Margaret Ross
         Hazel King
         Martha Hickman
         Eleanor Bryant

Sgt. at Arms - Florence Powell
         Helen Martin

January 1927.

President - Susie Wyatt
Vice-Pres.- Charlsie Camper
Secretary - Margaret Rawls
Reporter - Louise Mahaney
Critic - Mrs. Chapman
Ushers - Mary Etheridge
         Ruth Hayter
Custodian - Sallie Copenhaver
         Mary Keister
         Mattie Turner
         Annis Crabtree
Pianist - Zollie Cox

June 1927.

President - Ruby Mann
Vice-Pres.- Flora Black
Secretary - Evelyn Gravett
Treasurer - Katheleen Ageon
Chaplain - Mrs. Bertha Chapman
Critic - Josephine Wyatt
Historian - Bessie Payne
Sgt. at Arms - Marie Rickey
         Nora Morris
Custodian - Christine Jessee
         Mabel Crowe
         Glenna Johnson
Reporter - Mrs. St. Clair

September 1927.

President - Iris Ritenour
Vice-President - Nannie Daugherty
Secretary - Elizabeth Templeton
Treasurer - Nannie Hardy Clark
Reporter - Lucille Arthur
Critic - Pauline Osborne
Ushers - Vivian Hornsluger
         Mildred Vaughan

January 1928.

President - Lillian Smith
Vice-Pres.- Eva Vaughn
Secretary - Anna Agnew
Treasurer - Nannie H. Clark
Chaplain - Effie Obenshain
Reporter - Dora Belle Mitchell
Critic - Pauline Osborne
Sgt. at Arms - Rose Helen Duffy
Tillie Hale.

March 1928.

President - Mabelle Durham
Vice-Pres.- Pauline Osborne
Secretary - M. Doris Bell
Treasurer - Nannie Hardy Clark
Chaplain - Mary Leigh Hubbard
Critic - Hildred Wessel
Censor - Anne Gimbert
Reporter - Lillian Smith
Pianist - Elinor Bryant
Sgt. at Arms - Charlsie Camper
Elizabeth Templeton
Custodian - Virginia Hale
Margaret Smith

June 1928.

President - Edna Harman
Vice-Pres.- Hildred Wessell
Secretary - Nora Morris
Elinor Bryant
Treasurer - Ercelle Bennett
Critic - Eva Vaughn
Reporter - Edna Yeatts
Chaplain - Mrs. Mary Snyder
Pianist - Glenna Williams
Sgt. at Arms - Eva Clulen
Anna Agnew
Gasie Updike
Evelyn Thornton
Custodian - Rebecca Kindley
Virginia Clements
Virginia Hale
Annie Mae Harrington

September 1928.

President - Pauline Osborne
Vice-Pres.- Louise Mahaney
Treasurer - Margaret Smith
Secretary - Vivian Hornsberger
Chaplain - Irene Cardwell
Reporter - Kathleen Hines
Pianist - Annie Mae Harrington
Critic - Ercelle Bennett
Historian - Vola Wohlford
Ushers - Naomi Guinn
Mabel Cape
Edna Penley
Rosa Penley

January 1929.

President - Anna Agnew
Vice-Pres.- Fay Snidow
Secretary - Vola Wohlford
Treasurer - Margaret Smith
Custodian - Mary Martin
Virginia Grayson
Martha Garret
Critic - Ercelle Bennett
Ushers - Ollie Wilson
Rosa Penley

March 1929.

President - Elizabeth Harwell
Vice-Pres.- Mab Carter
Secretary - Virginia Snider
Reporter - Martha Garret
Sgt. at Arms - Mary Witt
Custodian - Cora Osborne
Elsie Calhoun
Lorraine Updyke
Lillian Carvion
Chaplain - Ruth Ferguson
Pianist - Myrtle Winston

June 1929.

President - Elinor Bryant
Vice-Pres.- Ercelle Bennett

Secretary - Mae Kelly
Treasurer - Ada Burton
Reporter - Mary Houston
Chaplain - Clara Scott
Pianist - Glenna Williams
Sgt. at Arms - Cora Osborne
     Gladys Mills
     Irene Cardwell
     Blanche Jones
Custodian - Bertha Harding
     Lelia Robertson
     Verdna Crabtree
Historian -Lucille Dudley

September 1929.

President - Vivian Harnesbarger
Vice-Pres. - Elizabeth Hardwicke
Secretary - Mary Witt
Treasurer - Cora Osborne
Reporter - Margaret Savage
Chairman of Program Committee
     Mab Carter

January 1930.

President - Fay Snider
Vice-Pres.-Stella Mae Agnew
Secretary - Elizabeth Hardwicke
Treasurer - Cora Osborne
Ushers - Emily Jones
     Lola Jenkins
Chaplain - Ada Ball
Historian - Ruth Cooper

March 1930.

President - Roberta Turner
Vice-Pres. - Frances Fitzpatrick
Secretary - Blanche Tiller
Chaplain - Dolly Ball
Ushers - Mary Davis
     Keith Goodwin
Historian - Mary Leigh Hubbard
Custodian - Caroline Honts
     Leola Hileman
     Mary Conner

June 1930.

President - Jean Taylor
Vice-Pres. - Freeda Harman
Secretary - Pearl McMurray
Treasurer - Lelia Robertson
Custodian - Claire Tipton
     Helen Brugh
     Mamie Yeatts
     Nell McMurray

September 1930.

President - Annie Ruth Gardner
Vice-Pres. - Lucy Williams
Secretary -- Maxie Scyphers
Treasurer - Myrtle Perry
Reporter - Jean Taylor
Custodian - Alice Miller
     Marjorie Burnette
     Cora Osborne
     Elizabeth Hardwicke

January 1931.

President - Maxie Scyphers
Vice-Pres. - Elsie Calhoun
Secretary - Cora Osborne
Chaplain - Josephine Osborne
Usher - Margaret Pratt
Custodian - Dorothy Clark
     Hazel Bennett
     Mava Hickman

March 1931.

President - Lucy Williams
Vice-Pres. - Helen Rice
Secretary - Naomi Myers
Chaplain - Orpha Pedneau
Custodian - Kathryn Craft
     Fanny Quillen
Usher - Dutch Warren

EDITORIAL STAFF

of

THE RADNOR AND THE BEEHIVE

1914

Editor-in-Chief	- Marjorie Combs
Business Manager	- Maude Goodwin
Literary Editor	- Susie Higgins
Art Editor	- Burr Wolfe
Assistant Editor	- Faith Camden
Assistant Editor	- Rubye Akers
Club Editor	- Sina Jones
Social Editor	- Eva Duping
Assistant Editor	- Stella Greer
Senior Editor	- Margaret Rogers
Junior Editor	- Lillian Howard
Sophomore Editor	- Ethel Garrett
Freshman Class Editor	- Winifred Hurt
Preparatory Class Editor	- Carrie Snyder
Organization Committee	- Miss Eleanor Terry

1914-1915

Editor-in-Chief	- Addie Allen
Assistant Editor	- Mary Strader
Business Manager	- Irene Allison
Assistant Manager	- Elizabeth Moran
Literary Editor	- Edna Cox
Assistant Editor	- Maxie King
Art Editor	- Ada Kyle
Assistant Editors	- Venus Franklin & Burr Wolfe
Club Editor	- Mattie Lou Slemp

1916

Editor-in-Chief	- Mary Strader
Assistant	- Gustave Parsons
Business Manager	- Ina Russell
Assistant	- Mary Goodykoontz
Club Editor	- Carrie Snyder
Assistants	- Josephine Wassum & Bess Gillespie
Literary Editor	- Sarah Saunders
Art Editor	- Venus Franklin
Assistant	- Bonnie Alderson
Assistant Art Editors	- Effie Jackson, Lena Horton M'Ledge Moffett

1917

Editor-in-Chief	- Thermutis Parrack
Assistant	- Elizabeth Ward
Business Manager	- Susie Hurt
Assistant	- Loretta Cooper
Organizations	- Mary Allison
Humorist	- Emily Grove
Literary Editor	- Bess Lucas
Art Editor	- Mollie Myers
Assistant	- Mary Bohn
Chairman	- Miss Montague
Committee	- Miss Ninde & Mr. Gilbert

THE BEEHIVE

1925

Editor-in-Chief	- Ella Bishop
Assistant	- Alta Strickler
Business Manager	- Genevieve Giesen
Assistant	- Charlsie Camper
Alumnae Editor	- Helen Cooke
Literary Editor	- Mary Skiles
Organization Editor	- Helen King
Art Editor	- Ada Lee Canaday
Diarist	- Mattie Richard
Advisor	- Miss M'Ledge Moffett

1926

Editor-in-Chief	- Annie Obenshain
Assistant	- Aleen Carper
Business Manager	- Beryl Echols
Assistant	- Sarah Noffsinger
Organization Editor	- Ruth Bricker
Literary Editor	- Esther Kilgore
Art Editor	- Katherine Harwell
Assistant	- Laura McDonald
Diarist	- Eulalia Matney
Advisor	- Miss M'Ledge Moffett

1927

Editor-in-Chief	- Genevieve Giesen
Business Manager	- Martha Townsend
Assistant	- Lorene Davenport
Assistant Editor	- Narcissa Thompson
Art Editors	- Katherine Harwell, Olive Scott, Katherine Smith
Literary Editor	- Ruby Mann
Organization Editor	- Louise Hartsell
Detourist	- Eleanor Robertson
Detourist	- Louise Mahaney
Advisor	- Miss M'Ledge Moffett

1928

Editor-in-Chief	- Louise Mahaney
Business Manager	- Marie Updyke
Assistant	- Vivian Harnsberger
Literary Editors	- Helen Wright, Lillian Smith
Art Editors	- Katherine Smith, Ella Kate Charlton
Organization Editor	- Irma Shufflebarger
Typist	- Izola Akers
Faculty Committee	- Mr. Gilbert, Dr. Hudson

1929

Editor-in-Chief	- Blanche Daniel
Literary Editors	- Helen Einstein, Rosalie Blanton
Art Editors	- Coleen Seagle, Margaret Smith
Business Manager	- Lucile Arthur
Assistant	- Mary Leigh Hubbard
Photographic Editor	- Jeanette Mears
Organization Editor	- Evelyn Fitzpatrick
Literary Advisor	- Dr. Virginia O. Hudson
Typist	- Jeanette Mears
Financial Advisor	- Professor William E. Gilbert

ALUMNAE OFFICERS

1922

President.....................Miss Lorena Caldwell
Secretary.....................Evelyn Shumate
Treasurer.....................Blanche Daniel

1923-1924

President.....................Annie McConnell
Vice-President................Stella Barnett
Secretary.....................Annie Sue Anderson

1925-1926

President.....................Annie Kuhn Roberts
Vice-President................Reba Price
Secretary.....................Helen Cook

1927

President.....................Blanche Daniel
Secretary-Treasurer..........Elise Jones

1928-1930

President.....................Blanche Daniel
Secretary-Treasurer..........Mrs. Lena Stafford Williams

1930-1932

President.....................Mrs. Lena Stafford Williams
Vice-President................Maude Payne Cory
Secretary.....................Annie Lee Bonham

RADFORD'S RECORD
IN
INTER-COLLEGIATE BASKETBALL, 1921-1929

January 29, 1921.

The first inter-collegiate game of basket ball was with Sullins College, Bristol, Virginia. The team had a very enthusiastic send-off by the school but in spite of all this "pep" that was instilled in them, Radford was unable to win the game as their opponents were superior in speedy playing. The line-up was:

Sullins		Radford
Luna	RF	Bird
Sterchi	LF	Mellon
Thomas	C	Hayter
Carner	SC	Oglesby
Rogers	RG	W. Shumate
Exline	LG	Thomas
Referee		Holden Barnett
Umpire		George King

February 12, 1921.

This was a Red Letter Day for Radford. One of the fastest and most exciting basketball games in history was pulled off in the Normal Gymnasium at Sullins College, noted for its undefeated record of the season met its waterloo at the hands of the speedy Normal Sextette. The final score of this game was Sullins, 15, Radford, 16. The line‑up was:

Sullins		Radford
Bird	RF	Bird
Sterchi	LF	Mellon
Thomas	JC	Shumate
Garner	SC	Oglesby
Exline	RG	Hayter
Rogers	LG	B. Shumate
Referee		Artie Roberts of V. P. I.

The first big Normal School Clash in Radford's basketball history took place Saturday, March 5, when Radford's strong sex-

tette met the Harrisonburg squad on the Harrisonburg Court.
It was another big victory for the Radford Normal. The line-up
was:

Harrisonburg		Radford
Mcgaha	C	E. Shumate
Ward	SG	Oglesby
Steele (Captain)	F	Bird
Faulkner	F	Mellon
Bonney	G	C. Hayter
Upshur	G	Shumate
Houston	Sub.	Coates
	"	Bishop
	"	Thomas
Johnson	Coach	Fosdick
Referee		Holden Barnett
Umpire		Mr. Staples
Timekeepers		Misses Lancaster
		and Moffett

Harrisonburg played Radford the return game March 25, in the
local gymnasium. This final clash ended in Radford's favor
in a score of 21 to 9. This victory which establishes Radford
Normal as the State Normal champions closed the basketball season. The line-ups of Harrisonburg and the local team were as
follows:

Harrisonburg		Radford
R. Mcgaha	C	E. Shumate
E. Ward	SC	S. Oglesby
J. Steele	RF	N. Mellon
Upshur	LF	R. Bird
V. Faulkner	RG	C. Hayter
D. Downey	LG	B. Shumate
Johnston	Coach	E. Fosdick
Referee		Shorts
Umpire		Barnett
Timekeepers		Seagle and Moffett

The Radford Varsity met Sullins on their home court November 19,
and met her first defeat. The line-up was:

Radford		Sullins
C. Noe	C	Thomason
S. Oglesby	SC	Carner

Young	F	Stirkey
Gimbert	F	Luna
G. Noe		
B. Shumate	G	Exline
Thomas	G	Munroe
Hughes		
E. Fosdick	Coach	V. Haile
Barnett	Referee	

February 10, 1922.

Radford met Harrisonburg on the local basketball court and for the third time was victorious. The final score was Radford 23 and Harrisonburg 12. The line-up was:

Harrisonburg		Radford
A. Long	F	Coates
Brooks	F	Thomas
Z. Wagstaff		
Bell	C	C. Noe
C. Rodes	G	Gimbert
H. Wagstaff	C	Baylor
B. Bonney	G	W. Shumate
Davis	Sub.	Whitaker
Roard		
Franke	Coach	E. Fosdick
Hass	Referee	
Barnett	Umpire	

The Radford Normal basketball team again defeated Harrisonburg Normal on the Harrisonburg Court. The final score was 29 to 7 in favor of Radford. The line-up was:

Harrisonburg		Radford
Roark	C	Noe
Wagstaff	SC	Baylor
Long	F	Coates
Brooks	F	Thomas
Rhodes	G	Shumate
Bonney	G	Gimbert
Franke	Coach	E. Fosdick
Hass	Referee	
Barnett	Umpire	

The Radford Normal basketball team met Farmville on the Farmville Court Saturday. March 25, and was defeated. The score was 11 to 9. The line-up was:

Farmville		Radford
Vaughan	C	C. Noe
Bell	SC	A. Baylor
Matthews	RF	J. Coates
Treakle	LF	L. Thomas
Sexton	RG	W. Shumate
Parsons	LG	A. Gimbert
Buford	Coaches	E. Fosdick
Barnett	Referee	

The last inter-collegiate basketball game made March 31st another Red-Letter Day in the Radford Normal Calendar. It was played with Farmville. The final score was 28 to 21 in favor of Radford.

Harrisonburg lost their fifth game with Radford, February 9, 1923, on their home court. The final score was 17 to 10. The line-up was:

Harrisonburg		Radford
Ada Long	F	Frances Herrick
Jesse Rosen	F	Lucinda Thomas
Mildred Belle	C	Celesta Whitaker
Helen Wagstaff	C	Audrey Baylor
Claris Coleman	G	Bill Shumate
Rose Hendricks	G	Annie Gimbert
Mr. Kromer	Umpire	
Mr. Stancer	Referee	

The Radford Normal girls' first defeat was met at the hands of the Harrisonburg Normal on April 23, 1923. This was the sixth game that the schools had played which made a tie for the season. The line-up was:

Harrisonburg		Radford
Roser	RF	Herrick
Clark	LF	Thomas
Bell	JC	Whitaker
Wagstaff	SC	Baylor
Coleman	RG	Shumate
Chinault	LG	Gimbert

A hard fought but brilliant game was played on Friday, March 9, when Radford defeated Farmville on the home court. The line-up was:

Radford		Farmville
Thomas	F	Treakle
Herrick	F	Matthews
Gimbert	JC	Whaley
Baylor	SG	Walton
Shumate	G	Sexton
Perry	G	Hall
Whitaker	Sub.	Bell
Showalter	"	Reed
		Hall
Scorekeepers		Mr. Barnett
		Miss Moore
Referee		Meredith
Umpire		Weddle

The opening game of the 1924 season was displayed with unusual ability. The Radford State Normal team defeated Concord by a large score of 68 to 6. The line-up was:

Concord	
Barley	LF
Lilly	RF
Karnes	SC
Holyrod	C
Farley	LG
Woodson	RG

On February 1, Radford won over Concord College 62 to 9. After the game a very enjoyable reception was given to the team by Concord. The line-up was:

Radford		Concord
Thomas	LF	Barle
Parsons	RF	Lilly
Parsons	C	Karnes
Showalter	S	Sampson
Hite	RG	Farley
Perry	LG	Woodson
Wolfenbarger	RG	Harlyrod
Herrick	LG	Smith

The Radford sextette was defeated at Harrisonburg on February 16, 1924. Radford added 27 points to her 174 for the season and lost the game by 4.

Mr. Sylvester McConnell who acted as assistant coach accompanied the team.

March 8, 1924 State Teachers College lost to their sister college, Harrisonburg. The final score being 25 to 16. This game closed the basketball season.

Charlsie Camper of the Freshman Class was elected Captain of the Varsity Team for 1924-1925.

On Friday, January 30, 1925, Radford played her first big game of the season. Her first opponents being the Virginia Polytechnic Institute Co-eds. At the end of the game the score stood 94 to 1 in favor of Radford.

February 5, 1925, Radford played Harrisonburg. The score was a tie 35 to 35.

On Tuesday evening, February 17, the Harrisonburg State Teachers College team holders of the State Championship for 1924 met an overwhelming defeat of 22 to 5 at the hands of the Radford Varsity on the home court. The Rotary Club of Radford and a large delegation of students from Virginia Polytechnic Institute attended the game in a body. The Radford team was coached by Miss Wanda Ellis, the Harrisonburg team by Mrs. J. C. Johnson. The officials of the game were Miss Rath of Roanoke and Miss Barclay of Bluefield.

Radford played two games with Concord, one at Concord and one on the home court. The first game ended with the score 94 to 1 in favor of Radford. The last game was also in favor of Radford with a score of 4 to 34.

On November 22, 1925 the Varsity team of the College had a banquet. Miss Jeannette Mears was announced captain for the year.

The Blacksburg court was a scene of overwhelming victory for the Radford State Teachers College Basketball team on December 5, 1925. The final score was 24 to 2. The line-up was:

Radford

Miller	F
Scott	F
Parsons	C
Jeannette Mears	SC
(Captain)	
Baylor	G
Williamson	G

Concord lost a basketball game here by score of 31 to 2 on February 12, 1926. The line-up was:

Concord		Radford
Burgess	F	Copper
B. Hale	F	Scott
Wells	JC	Zimmerman
Edmond	SC	Gobble
M. Hale	G	Worrell
Johnson	G	Fugate

The girls of Harrisonburg lost to Radford on February 13, in a score of 23 to 21. The line-up was:

Harrisonburg		Radford
Heiserman	F	Gilley
Rosen	F	Ogburn
Miller	JC	Parsons
Nickells	JC	Mears
Jackson	G	Baylor
Kelly	G	Williamson

On Thursday night February 18, 1926 Harrisonburg was defeated on their home court by the Radford State Teachers College girls. The final score was 34 to 16. The line-up was the same as the game played on February 13.

Once more a victory was written in the annals of Varsity history when Radford won over E. T. C. at Johnson City with a score of 34 to 12. February 27. The girls taking part in the game from R. S. T. C. were Ogburn, Gilley, Parsons, Fugate, Williamson, and Baylor.

December 9, 1926, the Virginia Polytechnic Co-eds lost a game to Radford by a score of 50 to 5.

V. P. I.		Radford
Vernon	F	Ogburn
Holdaway	F	Nida
Garner		Nunnally
Pillow	C	Fugate
Minix	G	Worrell
Thomas	G	Rhodes
Miss Farlow	Referee	

February 19, 1927 Harrisonburg and Radford met on the Radford floor. The game ended with a score of 8 to 10 in favor of Radford. The line-up was:

Radford			Harrisonburg
Ogburn	F		Doan
Etheridge	F		Smith
Camper	JC		Quesenberry
Mears	SC		Nichell
Baylor	G		Cockerill
Fugate	G		Miller

On January 29, Radford won a hard-fought game over E. S. T. C. The score was 62 to 9. The Radford line-up for the first half was:

Ogburn	F
Etheridge	F
Fugate	G
Worrell	G
Camper	JC
Mears	RC

Last Half

Ogburn	F
Gilley	F
Williamson	G
Baylor	G
Orr	JC
Fugate	RC

The game marking the close of the season of 1926-27 in which the team went undefeated was played with Farmville here at the college. This game closed with a score of 36 to 20. The line-up was:

Radford		Farmville
Ogburn	F	Hardy
Etheridge	F	Wilderson
Camper	JC	Gurley
Mears	SC	Palmer
Baylor	G	Hatchette
Fugate	G	Garry
Miss Tew, Washington, D. C.		Referee
Miss Bartlette, Bluefield, Va.		Umpire

On February 12, the Radford team met the Lynchburg team on the home court and gained another victory with the score of 32 to 16. The line-up was:

Radford		Lynchburg
Ogburn	F	Hunley
Etheridge	F	Keseh
Camper	JC	Mardux
Mears	S	Haye
Fugate	G	Gardner
Baylor	G	Smithson
Referee		Miss Taylor
		Lynchburg, Virginia
Umpire		Miss Tew, Washington, D. C.

On Saturday, February 4, the Radford team played Farmville on their home floor. The game ended with a score of 22 to 9 in favor of R. S. T. C. girls. Those playing this game from Radford were Ogburn, Etheridge, Camper, Mears, Fugate, and Baylor, Miss Tew of Washington, D. C.

The Radford College closed the 1926 season with a total score of 243 points without defeat in any of the eight games they easily vanquished their opponents and proved themselves to be the strongest team in the Virginia Girls' Colleges. The final game was played on the Lynchburg Court when they defeated the Lynchburg College with a score of 28 to 9.

On January 19, 1928, Radford played her first ball game of the year with Emory and Henry Co-eds. At the end of the game the score had reached the high point of 68 to 8 in favor of Radford.

On January 28, the Radford team went to Emory where they gained another victory in a score of 29 to 8 in their favor. The line-up was:

Radford		Emory & Henry
Ogburn	F	Sibly
Etheridge	F	Mason
Camper	C	Umbarger
Mears	C	Russell
Gimbert	G	Lewis
Myers	G	DeVault

On Saturday February 11, Harrisonburg defeated the Radford Varsity. When the final whistle blew the score stood 23 to 12 in Harrisonburg's favor. The line-up was:

Harrisonburg		Radford
Doan	F	Etheridge
Smith	F	Ogburn
Quesenberry	JC	Camper
Heitzer	SC	Mears
Compton	G	Gimbert
Miller	G	Hennesey
Stewart	Referee	
Thomas	Umpire	

On the evening of March 3, 1928 the Radford girls met the Farmville basketball team on Farmville's court. With excellent playing on both sides the game ended with a score of 28 points for Radford and Farmville.

Radford		Farmville
Ogburn	F	Smith
Etheridge	F	Smith
Camper	C	
Mears	SC	Jones
Gimbert	G	Hatchett
Carter	G	Coleman
Myers	Sub.	
Miss Doan	Umpire	
Richmond, Virginia		

From Farmville the team went to Harrisonburg where they played on the Monday night following. This was the first game ever played in their new gymnasium. There were over 1000 spectators assembled to see the game. The final score was 25 to 26 in favor of Radford. The line-up was:

Radford		Harrisonburg
Ogburn	F	Doan
Etheridge	F	Smith
Camper	JC	Quesenberry
Mears	SC	Nichell
Baylor	G	Cockernelle
Fugate	G	Miller
Miss Lincoln,	Referee	
Marion, Virginia		
Mr. Kiracofe	Umpire	

The college began the season in 1927 with two victories on the home court January 15, between Radford and the Co-eds of V. P. I. The final score stood 50 to 3. The outstanding players of Radford were: Ogburn, Gilley, Camper, and Fugate.

The Varsity squad held its last banquet Thursday evening, April 21, at 6:00 P. M.

The Athletic Association presented a play "At the End of the Rainbow" on Saturday, May 14.

On October 7, the members of the Athletic Association assembled in the gymnasium and enjoyed an old-fashioned square dance.

On March 10, two of the strongest teams in the State clashed for the second time. The first game which was on the court at Radford had ended in favor of Harrisonburg but this one ended with a score of 23 to 11 in favor of R. S. T. C. The line-up was:

Radford		Harrisonburg
Ogburn	F	Doan
Etheridge	F	Smith
Camper	JC	Quesenberry
Mears	RC	Heitzer
Carter	G	Cockrell
Gimbert	G	Miller

The Radford Varsity added another victory to its laurels when it played the V. P. I. Co-eds on January 31. The final score was 47 to 9.

In a close and exciting basketball game played on February 23, 1929, in the Lynchburg gymnasium the Radford team won its second victory over the Co-eds by a score of 37 to 23. Graham and Etheridge were the star players in this game.

Radford was given her second defeat of the season on March 2, by an ancient rival, Harrisonburg. The result of the game was 44 to 18. The line-up was:

Harrisonburg		Radford
Smith	RF	Graham
Sullivan	LF	Etheridge
Quesenbery	JC	Flanary
Ralston	SC	Mears
Miller	RG	Hennessey
Heiser	LG	Bopp

INTER-COLLEGIATE DEBATE CONTRACT

Radford - - - - - - - -Farmville - - - - - - - - - Harrisonburg

Article I

This contract is entered into by the respective Inter-collegiate Debate Councils of Radford State Teachers College, East Radford, Virginia; Farmville State Teachers College, Farmville, Virginia, and Harrisonburg State Teachers College, Harrisonburg, Virginia, for the purpose of arranging a triangular debate among the institutions for the session of 1925-1926.

Article II

The subject for debate shall be: "Resolved -

Article III

Each college shall be represented by two debating teams of two women each, there being one debate held at Radford, one at Farmville, and one at Harrisonburg College on the same evening. The visiting teams shall debate the negative side of the question. Radford shall send her negative team to Harrisonburg; Farmville shall send her negative to Radford, and Harrisonburg shall send her negative team to Farmville.

Article IV

The date of said debate shall be --
The contest shall be held in the evening--

Article V

Not later than fifteen days preceding the debate the entertaining college shall send the visiting college a list of six persons from which the judges of the contest are to be chosen. The visiting college shall have the right to challenge any of the judges submitted in which case the entertaining college shall submit additional names.

No relative of any contestant, no alumna of any institution participating and no person who has any official relation with either of the contesting colleges shall be eligible for a judge. The college submitting the list of names shall always report on the qualifications of the judges in the following respects: Occupation and where educated.

Article VI

Each contest shall be presided over by a chairman (chosen by the home college and acceptable to the visiting team) whose duties shall be to enforce the rules of debating.

Any undergraduate who is regularly enrolled for at least nine hours of academic work and is in good standing at her college shall be eligible to represent her institution.

Each team shall be allotted forty-two minutes time. Each debater shall be allowed twenty-one minutes. One woman may not use more than sixteen minutes in the main speech nor more than six minutes in rebuttal. The first main speech shall be by the affirmative and the first rebuttal by the negative. No new arguments shall be introduced in the rebuttal, the judges deciding this point.

Article VII

The decision shall be based on argument, diction, and delivery. Judges shall sit in different parts of the audience and shall cast their ballots without conference with any of the other judges. The ballots shall be sealed and delivered to the presiding officer who shall open them and announce the decision.

This article of the contract shall be read to the judges previous to the debate.

Article VIII

The visiting team shall bear its own traveling expenses.

The cost of advertising expenses of judges, and local entertainment for the visiting team shall be paid by the home college.

Article IX

Evening dresses shall be worn by the debaters of each institution.

Article X

Each college agrees to furnish to its opponents after the debate a true copy of the speeches of its teams, together with the bibliographical sheet which may be used as a permanent record of the contest.

Given under our hands, with date accompanying each signature.

President Radford Inter-collegiate Debate Council

President Farmville Inter-collegiate Debate Council

President Harrisonburg Inter-collegiate Debate Council

The first inter-collegiate debate for the Radford College was held under this contract on April 30, 1926. The question which had been proposed by Radford and accepted by the other colleges was: Resolved "That Virginia should concentrate her efforts upon the development of her rural possibilities rather than the development of a Metropolitan area around Hampton Roads". The Radford College was represented by Misses Sallie Vaughn Turner, Loraine Holstead; affirmative; Eula Porter, Estel Kilgore, negative. The affirmative team debated Farmville at Radford while the negative team debated at Harrisonburg on the same debate. Both Radford teams won over their opponents.

LIST OF SOME OUTSTANDING PLAYS
GIVEN AT COLLEGE

AMATEUR PRESENTATIONS

June 1914	Bibi, by the Senior Class.
December 4, 1914	Japanese Operetta.
May 31, 1915	Gypsy Operetta
1915	America's Aboard (Operetta), Written by Miss Baird, also presented at Virginia Polytechnic Institute.
June 1915	Education (Pageant), written by Miss Baird.
November 29, 1915	The Ministrel
December 18, 1915	Mother Goose Party
Spring 1916	The Princess
June 1916	The Rivals - Sheridan, by the Seniors.
March 1917	The Great Catastrophe, by the Seniors.
June 4, 1917	Milton's "Comus", by the Seniors.
December 11, 1920	A Christmas Carol, Dickens, by the Pocahontas Society.
1920	Womanless Wedding. (Doctor McConnell, the Bride).
December 10, 1921	When the Star Shone.
December 14, 1921	Sun Up, by the Pocahontas Literary Society.
1921	The Prince Chap
March 11, 1922	Life of Mary Draper Ingles, by the Ingles Literary Society
June 2, 1922	Crickett on the Hearth, by the Senior Class.
December 9, 1922	Christmas Light, by the Pocahontas Literary Society
October 14, 1922	Program with Roanoke Times, Ingles Literary Society
January 18, 1923	Virginia Tech Minstrel.
April 5, 1923	Woodcock's Little Game, by the Degree Students.
April 14, 1923	The Wild Rose, by the Ingles Literary Society.
June 1, 1923	Merrily Mary Ann, by the Senior Class.
December 15, 1923	The Birds Christmas Carol, by the Pocahontas Literary Society.
February 29, 1924	Clarence, by the Degree Class.
June 6, 1924	Under two Flags, by the Senior Class.
December 13, 1924	Why the Chimes Rang, by the Pocahontas Literary Society.
February 20, 1925	Three One-Act plays, by the Degree Class. (The Hour Glass (Spreading the News (Pierrot of the Menute
June 5, 1925	Mrs. Wiggs of the Cabbage Patch, by the Two-Year Class.
March 3, 1925	The Wishing Will, by Radford Alumnae
December 12, 1925	Pollyanna, by the Pocahontas Literary Society.

January 30, 1926	Ingles Log, by the Ingles Literary Society
March 6, 1926	The Romance of Hiawatha, by the Pocahontas Literary Society.
March 28, 1926	Little Women, by the Ingles Literary Society
March 13, 1926	Dady Long Legs
April 10, 1926	Adam and Eve, by the Senior Class.
June 4, 1926	The Whole Town's Talking, by the Sophomore Class.
December 13, 1926	The Goose Hangs High, by the Pocahontas Society.
January 14, 1927	Tom, Dick, and Harry, by the Roanoke College Harlequins.
March 5, 1927	The Romance of Pocahontas, by the Pocahontas Literary Society.
March 12, 1927	Green Stockings, by the Ingles Society.
October 8, 1927	Aladdin and the Magic Lamp, Inter-Society Reception
October 28, 1927	Why Not? Musical Comedy by the Athletic Association.
December 1927	Smiling Through, by the Pocahontas Literary Society.
March 3, 1928	The Gift of the Peace Pipe, by the Pocahontas Literary Society.
March 28, 1928	The Gypsy Rover, by the Glee Club.
March 30, 1928	Lamentable Tragedy of Julius Caesar, by the Men of the Faculty.
April 14, 1928	Rosemary, by the Ingles Literary Society.
Spring, 1928	Once There was a Princess, by the Roanoke-Radford Alumnae Chapter.
June 1, 1928	The Witching Hour, by the Degree Class.
August 18, 1928	She Stoops to Conquer, by the College Students.
1928	The Romance of Youth, by the Athletic Association.
1928	See You Later.
January 26, 1929	The Country Cousin, by the Pocahontas Society.
March 30, 1929	The Charm School, by the Ingles Literary Society.
April 1, 1929	The Haunted House, by the Washington and Lee Troubadours and the Southern Collegian Orchestra.
December 7, 1929	The Heartless House, by John Powell Glee Club.
March 15, 1930	A Mennonite Maid, by the Ingles Literary Society.
May 16, 1930	Riding Down the Sky, by the Radford Alumnae
June 6, 1930	The Rivals, by the Graduating Class

PROFESSIONAL AND VISITING AMATEUR ENTERTAINERS*
(Note: See text for some early entertainers)

April 11, 1921	Sir Edward Baxter Peery, gave a recital.
August 11, 1921	Powell Hale, Impersonator and Humorist.
October 27, 1921	Mrs. Frank Mebane, Lecturer on the Balkans.
January 20, 1922	Mr. Inman Johnson, gave a recital.
February 2, 1922	W. B. Cridlin, Originator of the Virginia Pageant.
February 1, 1923	Mr. Henry Olds, Silver Springs, Maryland, "Birds".
April 8, 1923	Evelyn Gurley Kane, Musical dramatization of the Book of Job.
January 8, 1923	Virginia Tech Minstrels.
April 26, 1923	Reverend Blackwelder of Roanoke presented an illustrated lecture of the Passion play on April 26, 1923.
October 25, 1923	Mr. Tom Skeyhill, Lecturer.
February 24, 1924	Virginia Tech Minstrels.
February 23, 1924	Cheif George Cook of the Pamunkey Indians.
July 25, 1924	Carl Jansen, Swedish Impersonater.
July 22, 1924	Franceska Kaspar Lawson, Singer of Washington, D. C.
August 7-8, 1924	Devereux Players.
November 13, 1924	Mr. W. P. Hote, notable impersonator on November 13, 1924
December 18, 1924	Miss Mary Barber, demonstrator for the Kellog Co.
January 14, 1925	Miss Ruth Egge, Educational director of the Sterling Silver Association Exhibit.
January 16, 1925	Dulcy, by the Roanoke College Harlequins.
January 24, 1925	Flapper Grandmother, American Legion.
March 12, 1925	"Empressario" by the Henshaw Company.
May 7, 1925	The Barber of Seville, by the Devereux Players.
October 20, 1925	"Elixir of Love" by the William Wade Henshaw Company.
November 30, 1925	Mr. and Mrs. Skoogoard, Danish Violinist.
April 12, 1926	Fiddling Powers and his Family.
April 23, 1926	Virginia Tech Minstrel.
May 5, 1926	McDonald Highlanders Band of St. Augustine, Florida.
October 26, 1926	Russian Cossack Chorus, under the direction of Sergi Socoloff.
November 11, 1926	The Rhond la Welsh Male Singers.
October 19, 1927	Miss Susanne Keener Metropolitan Opera Company
January 24, 1927	Tom, Dick, and Harry, by the Roanoke College Harlequins
February 18, 1927	Zimmer Harp Trio.
February 25, 1928	Virginia Polytechnic Institute Dramatic Club presented "Bumpstead Leigh".
February 2, 1928	Chief Nipo Strong Heart of the Yakima tribe.
March 21, 1928	The Troubadours of Washington and Lee presented "The Butter and Egg Man".
October 25, 1928	The Cordova Concertiers.

*This list is not complete, no record was kept prior to publication of Grapurchat from which this list is compiled.

November 1, 1927	"Romance of Youth", by the Devereux Players.
January 7, 1928	Ethelnyde Smith, Singer.
November 1, 1929	Honey, Biblical dramatization interpreter.
January 12, 1930	Doctor Charles Barker, Lecturer.
March 14, 1930	Ruth St. Dennis and the Denishon Dancers.
April 11, 1930	Chief Sunny Skis of the Iriquois Indians.
April 24, 1930	The Murder in the Red Barn by the Jitney Players.
July 18, 1930	Mr. and Mrs. Pierre Pelletion and the Elizabethian Players "Merchant of Venice".
July 30, 1930	Macbeth, presented by the Stratford Players.

SOME OF THE "BEGINNINGS" OF POLICIES, ACTIVITIES, ORGANIZATIONS
SPONSORED BY VARIOUS FACULTY MEMBERS AS STATED BY THEM[1]

———

I organized the Saturday afternoon Hiking Club.
                                        --Virginia Arnold.

I gave the name "Radnor" to the annual. It was an abbre-
viation of Radford Normal. I learned later that there was a
Radnor County in England adjacent to Montgomery County. I
coached debators on both sides for the first two annual debates
without either knowing the other points. It was upon my recommendation that: First, Courses of study were arranged in parallel, equivalent form. Second: A full quarter of Practice Teaching was required. Third: A system of typical training schools
were established. I was advisor of the Senior Classes graduating 1914, 1915. I organized and instituted Sunday School
Training Courses (Interdenominational).
                                        --Joseph Emory Avent.

Furnishing and equipping of new campus training school;
tentative plans for the opening.
                                        --Winifred E. Bain.

I wrote the Alma Mater, various class songs, one athletic
song, pageant, operetta, and one class play.
                                        --Florence C. Baird.

I prepared the manuscript of the History of Radford College.
                                        --Zella L. Blackard.

Organized the Mathematics Club; Director of Visual Education, managed the Motion Picture shows for years.
                                        --Wilson R. Bowers.

Charter member of the Pi Gamma Mu and Kappa Delta Pi Fraternities.
                                        --Ruth Bricker Painter.

Instituted tap dancing in the college.
                                        --Irene Brown Weaver.

Student Loan Fund, Dramatic Club, Annual Class Stunt night,
Annual Debating contest between the Literary Societies, various

[1]Based on questionnaire returns.

activities connected with commencement, including Vesper services, Story Tellers Club, The Radnor (one annual) was dedicated to me.

--Blanche Bulifant McFarland.

Organized the Alice Evans Biology Club; collected many local specimens for Biological collection.

--Paul Randolph Burch.

County Clubs, Virginia Music Teachers' State Association.
--Lizzie Faye James Carr.

Volunteer Bible Classes in the dormitories, pioneer in starting the Teacher Training work, both in the inter-denominational classes in the college and the various Sunday Schools of the town. I organized the Science section of the Educational Conference meeting with us in 1915. Mr. Heatewole thinks that was the first organization of Science in Virginia.

--Olive Flora Bryson.

The Ellen H. Richards Club had a spasmodic existence and I think it started at the time under the direction of Miss Moffett, Miss Smenner and myself.

--Mary W. Chapin.

For years I have cared for squirrels, peacocks, and other pets on the campus.

--Mary B. Clark.

The Alice Evans Biology Club.

--Elton C. Cocke.

The questionnaire in preparation for the Ingles first debate which was won in June 1919 and 1920 by the Ingles Literary Society.

--William Benjamine Coggin.

Organized the college orchestra.

--John W. Comstock.

By special appointment of national officers, I organized and installed the Radford Chapter of Pi Gamma Mu, also wrote the inaugural ceremony of officers, and the ritual for the candidates for membership. (See the minutes of the Secretary's book regarding the correspondence for the said organization and other matters pertaining to its organization). I was appointed by national officers to organize a chapter of Tri Sigma and other national sororities but on account of going to New York for the winter, the matter was left on the table for the time being.

--Mary Eolian Coppedge.

I helped the student teachers to make practical use of "tests and measurements" and graph results to show pupils the results of their work as well as student teachers.

--Flora J. Dungy Golding.

Developed a direct method of teaching Geometry in Radford High School, taught this to college student teachers.

--Alfred K. Eagle.

Organized and directed the Radford State Teachers' Choral Club in 1929, directed group who sang in the first Virginia Music Festival, at University, 1930.

--Mrs. John Einstein.

My activities were mostly in connection with programs given by the Literary Societies, the Allegaynianna; festivals, Y. W. C. A., Athletic Association and other organizations. My efforts were directed toward developing a type of physical education in which all students could participate.

--Wanda N. Ellis.

I inaugurated the "Better Speech" Club, 1919-1920.

--Lottie M. Evans.

I helped to start the Virginia School Messages, later became editor-in-chief; Second director of Extension Service.

--Francis B. Fitzpatrick.

Working toward the development of the Training School, member of the first Faculty of the Campus Training School, 1929; Principal, 1930.

--Kathryn Fritz.

Designed and started the Golf Course.

--Henry Emmett Fulcher.

I was instrumental in helping to organize the first Student Government organization, also the Pocahontas Literary Society.

--Ethel Garrett Robinson.

The first faculty member to arrive in Radford, forty days before September 17, 1913; Literary Societies, Building Student Activity Building; contest among High Schools of Virginia, building museum, organized the Book Supply Department; Student Government; Chairman of Public Exercise Committee; Chairman of Assembly

Committee.
                                    --William E. Gilbert.

        Organized and indexed the Bulletin Library.
                                    --H. C. Graybeal.

        I was the first full time librarian in 1915, 1916, Alum-
nae Association, helped to organize and also carried on necessary correspondence for the year.
                                    --Carrie Helen Green.

        Pi Gamma Mu; Tri Sigma; System of Class sponsors; First
president of the American Association of University Women; Policy of giving honors at commencement, cum laude, magna cum laude,
summa cum laude; Chairman of the committee to draft the plan for
giving the annual A. A. U. W. creative prizes.
                                    --Virginia O'Rear Hudson.

        Biology Club, helped to frame constitution, charter member
Kappa Delta Pi, First President.

                                    --Mae Kelly.

        Hostess in Helen Henderson Hall, 1929-1931.
                                    --Ruth Lewis.

        Student teaching, Home Economics in City High School, 1930;
cafeteria in Training School in 1931.
                                    --Luna M. Lewis.

        Cottage home for the students doing practice teaching at
Belspring.
                                    --Frances W. Long.

        Forensics; I have helped to organize forensic activities
here to the point of participation in Inter-collegiate debating
upon equal terms with the other standard colleges in Virginia;
the Forensic Council which I suggested, now controls such activities; The Question Mark Club is an honor society for recognition of successful debaters. It is now petitioning for a charter as a chpater of Tau Kappa Alpha, a national honor forensic
fraternity. During the first quarter of my service here I suggested to Doctor McConnell that our students were not given sufficient opportunity for, and impulse to social activity. He a-
greed and urged remedial measures. I have urged that the homes
of professors may help to supply social background and atmosphere
for the students.

                                    --William Stapleton Long.

I revived the Mathematics Club and gave it a higher standard than it had ever had; entertained the Club at my home once a month, inspired my students to go on for graduate work.

--Gertrude I. McCain.

In 1927 I helped to organize and directed a large Summer School Chorus.

--Clara J. McCauley.

On Student organization committee for several years; helped "put over" the "B" standard for office holding; one of the two men students to attend Radford during the regular session.

--John Paul McConnell.

Pi Gamma Mu Adviser in 1928 to 1931, Tri Sigma.

--Hermine Menzie.

Very closely associated with Doctor McConnell in development of all phases of the institution. That is why he had me write the history; Home Economics, all buildings, Dean of Women's responsibilities; Publicity.

--M'Ledge Moffett.

The size of the Grapurchat was changed during the time I acted as adviser; Writer's Club for one year and one summer.

--Mary Ethel NeSmith.

Long distance hiking, Inter-college Field Hockey Games.

--Louise Ninde Fisher.

Made up the first health record; taught special First Aid for Red Cross during the World War period; first class was in the City High School, several college teachers took this course, then I had classes at the College. One class of fifty-six at the College was reported to have been the largest in the country.--In the "Flu" epidemic of 1918 about seventy-per cent of the student body had the disease, not a case of pneumonia developed and no deaths. My method of treatment attracted attention and I was requested to write a paper on it to be read before the Southwestern Virginia Medical Society which I did at Bristol, Virginia, 1919. From 1913 to 1931 not a single death has occurred in the school.

--Joseph Alexander Noblin.

Art Club, student teas in dormitories, better English movements.

--Florence Belle Ogg.

The remarks about activities while in Radford are necessarily brief for a stay of one summer quarter, I enjoyed the work very much and should like to return for another summer.

                    --Loula McNeer Pangle.

      Helped organize Sigma, Sigma, Sigma.
                    --Susan E. Roberts.

      First President of the Radford Branch of American Federation
of Art; sponsored many art exhibits.

                    --Lillian Simmons.

      The Home Economics students and I re-decorated the Blue Gate
Tea Room and kept it in operation. The Tea Room had been opened
before I was associated with the College.

                    --Bess Smenner.

      The naming of Glee Clubs, Powell and Kelly, organizing of the
Glee Clubs as to classes; buying of vestments for Glee Clubs, purchase of Hymn books for Assembly (making money by presenting operetta given by two Glee Clubs, also presenting "Burlesque of Julius
Caesar by men of the Faculty"); instigator of book racks for song
books in Assembly; organized the Men's Faculty Quartet; organized
women double quartet from Faculty; instigator of the library of
Octaro Music, additional new material added last year.

                    --C. Edmee Smith.

      Public exhibits at close of session. Public exhibits in hall
of timely flora.

                    --William Day Smith.

      Helped organize the Pi Gamma Mu.
                    --C. B. Swaney.

      Virginia Celebration (Bimillinium); organized the Latin Club
and La Petite Academic Francaise.

                    --Gladys G. Tapley.

      Y. W. C. A., Yearly publication (annual).
                    --Eleanor Terry Noell.

      Was active in inaugurating the plan of intelligence testing
for Freshmen discussed at length in Faculty meetings several times
the Normal Curve of Distribution; framed a resolution which (I think)
was passed interpreting the meaning of grades, A, B, C, D, E, and F.

            A represents a student 2 or more S. D. above mean
            B represents a student between 1 or 2 S. D. above mean
            C.represents a student Mean and 1 S. D. above mean

D represents a student Mean and 1 S. D. below mean
E represents a student between 1 and 2 S. D. below mean
F represents a student 2 or more S. D. below mean
                                        --Minor Wine Thomas.

I was in the Training School work only the first half of the session of 1928 and 1929 and really had no part in the campus activities.
                                        --Eva Vaughan.

The English Club.
                                        --Mary Emile Windle.

SOME MEMORIES OF RADFORD

(Compiled from Questionnaires answered by Faculty Members)

Three rehearsals in one night with "no time off" for supper. This frequent occurrence brings only agreeable sensations today and happy memories.
                                        --Ina Addington Cox.

The only thing I seem to remember about teaching is the sage in my class room. I think I will come back some day and see what became of the last one.
                                        --Bonnie Jean Alderson.

The many activities and triumphs of my senior class .(the one of which I was advisor), their stunt which I planned and coached them in "A Holiday in a Lunatic Asylum" and their winning first prize on stunt night. Their Senior play which I advised, Dickens' "Cricket on the Hearth". Their graduation and class day when I sat on the stage with them and T. J. our delightful and efficient class president.
                                        --Elizabeth Sheffield Allen.

My most interesting Radford memories are my relations with the college faculty and student body.
                                        --John Lee Allison.

Class room teaching.
                                        --Mary Allison.

Twenty-five hours a week instruction, administration as Registrar.

—Joseph Emory Avent.

Golf, Picnics, Literary Societies, and teaching in tents are my most interesting Radford memories.

—Richard O. Bagby.

Some of my friends have said they remember me only as the pioneer woman making the trip to Belspring in the "covered wagon", provisions in a tin box, toilet accessories in a bag, and books and other teaching materials slipping from side to side about me. The former students remember only the days when I jumped from the bus in terror lest it overturn on roads which were under construction. The teachers who went to the Galax Convention think of me only as I crossed the Spring freshet with Professor Bowers and NeSmith in a row boat after the ferry had been washed away. I think most often of the red bud in the Spring, the snow in the winter and the many colored leaves in the fall on the everlasting hills.

—Winifred E. Bain.

I enjoyed my association with many of the students and most of the faculty very very much. The Dean's private swimming parties are a pleasant memory.

—Mary Elder Harwood Beebe.

Doctor McConnell's advice to teachers not to talk too much merely because they had run out of "soap grease". Helping to organize the "Faculty Follies".

—Walter Herman Bell.

My most interesting memories are my work with the children in the Training School and with the girls in the dormitory. The Porto Rican girls have been most interesting personalities. I shall always be amused when I think of Mr. Estes (Rabbit) who hid behind the hollyhocks, or shrubs (lest he be "bandered about") when an unusual event happened on the campus. He was always most complimentary of the way the hostesses handled affairs.

—Ercelle Bennett.

Talks in chapel by Doctor McConnell, Y. W. C. A. and Literary Society work. Friendships made with some of the girls, class work such as French.

—Margaret Fisher Black.

Contact with other faculty members. Informal and pleasant atmosphere of Radford. Brief sight seeing tours of Virginia and

neighboring States.

--Ruth Borders.

The memorable afternoon I spent convincing Doctor McConnell that I was not too young to teach in summer school. I worked hard to win; the Faculty basketball team which often went down to defeat; the Faculty Parties given by different members of the Faculty and Doctor and Mrs. McConnell's parties for the Faculty at their home. [Su]ch a perfect host and hostess! The night the Ingles Literary [So]ciety won the debating cup for the first time from the Pocahontas Society. I was adviser at the time and worked very hard with the girls helping them collect material and criticizing their speeches.

Hikes through fields and along the river, drives through the Southwest and most pleasant contacts with members of the Faculty both in homes and on the campus. Memories of the friendliness of people of the town.

--Mabel Bower.

As a student I enjoyed contact with the other students, work in the Literary Society, Glee Club, class and society plays. I enjoyed hours spent in the dormitory and there many friendships were established. I liked to study. I have found the faculty, for the most part, much more interesting out of the class room than in.

--Ruth Bricker Painter.

Taught one class per day in the open under the oak trees in front of the Administration Building. The competition with the Yard Engine on the Norfolk & Western just below is not to be forgotten.

--Earl B. Broadwater.

Bird life on the campus from the humming birds to the owls. One night while nursing Miss Bulifant two bats got into my room! Dramatic performance (stunt night) by Faculty, "Everybody works but Father".

--Bessie M. Brown.

Among my many pleasant memories of R. S. T. C. two impressions are outstanding; on the part of the students, a remarkable earnestness in their work, and effort to make college days indeed days of preparation; on the part of the administration, an exaltation of the ideals of true womanhood a constant challenge to the best.

--Hattie Edna Brown.

Association with the students and visits of Mr. Whitt and Dr. Bain.

--Julia Bryant.

Among my most interesting Radford memories are those connected with the work of my Sunday School Class and the associations brought about through the church. Some times I long to be able to help the Methodist ladies wash dishes in the kitchen of Grove Avenue Church and again enjoy the fellowship of thier jolly company forgetting that there are many papers to grade in the whole world. Then there were the early morning breakfasts, bacon bats with the Biology classes where we got cinders in the eggs and pulled sticks out of the coffee. Oh yes, there were hardships that brought out all the native wit of the participants. There was the winter that the "back campus" was scraped off to make it level and when it rained, which was all the time, the mud was deep and stiff. I, with Miss Brown and a number of girls lived in the "Old Dormitory" and the "Dismal Swamp" was a nightmare for us all winter. When we did not have time to go around the campus, we had to walk on the lower boards of the fence skirting the entire upper campus to reach the Administration Building. Often we would slip off and then scraping was next on the program. Once I was reproved by the President for having mud on my heel. The little lump was not any bigger than a black walnut. It is hard to please some people. When the men dug post holes along the path across the pasture where we had to walk, we fully expected to fall into one and break a limb. Miss B. said one day that she wished a pig would fall in and perhaps we could get them filled. The next Sunday one did fall in and the President pulled it out. I kept her in hot water for a month by almost telling what she said every time we were both in his presence. Then there was the time my Physics class wired the Administration Building for electric bells and one day while we were at the most interesting point crawling around in the attic the chapel bell rang and my white dress was so soiled that I did not dare go down. A South Carolinian lectured that day and I had to content myself with peeping over the bannisters with a handkerchief over my dirty face. I did not want her to go back and tell the neighbors what a mess she found me in but the bells rang and we were happy. There was the time that Mr. Worley generously offered to get candles from my laboratory for Miss M.'s party when the electric lights went out. He got them a dozen standard candles that could not be bought this side of Chicago and the work the next day was spoiled for want of them.

There was "Beautiful" the College Cat. She kept the rats down for me in the laboratories and in many ways appropriated my attentions. One day I was holding "Teddy Roosevelt", the Bricker Kitten, on my knee when she leaped up into my lap and used all the cat language she knew to induce me to put him down. Finally she slapped me with all claws exposed. When I returned the compliment she jumped down, stalked out of the house and refused to "speak" to me for two whole weeks. Yes, we had fun, hard work, disappointments, joys, sorrows, and all sorts of "ups and downs" everything that it takes to make a complete journey and I am glad that I came the Radford way.

--Olive Flora Bryson.

Among my Radford memories are: Doctor McConnell chewing paper during Faculty and other meetings. Doctor McConnell and his "apple-a-day" (only it was several apples a day), chapel in the fall of 1913, with students wrapped in blankets and faculty shivering on the stage. Mother Goose Party participated in by students and Faculty. Spring cleaning the campus, etc., 1914.

--Blanche Bulifant McFarland.

Faculty contacts and student contacts; watching the progress of the College; my family; contacts with various people of the community and success in my field profession are my interesting Radford memories.

--Paul Randolph Burch.

Chaperoning the girls at V. P. I. and having one of the boys ask me to tell him who the chaperon was so he might get permission to take a girl to a party.

--Myrtle Burnett.

When I think of Radford I always think of the spirit of the school always friendly and home like. My class in school gardening was an interesting experience. I made some good friends in Radford.

--Virginia Caldwell.

Trips to Mountain Lake, Tennis Matches, picnics, opening of the Lee Highway at Christiansburg; meeting of Southwestern Virginia Incorporated, etc. at Wytheville one Fourth of July.

--D. A. Cannaday.

Chapel hour with Doctor McConnell telling jokes; faculty picnics; friendly chats with Mr. and Mrs. Whitt, keeping tab on Miss Moffett and Miss Simmons; sewing buttons on Mr. Gilbert's overcoat.

--Lizzie Faye James Carr.

My summers spent at East Radford stand out as among the happiest of my life.

--Cornelia A. Carter.

The enrollment in the Summer quarters was very large so that the class rooms and halls were crowded. My husband taught a class on the lawn for lack of a class room.

--Mary Carter Broadwater.

The memories of Radford would fill a book. To mention them briefly, the enjoyment I had in my work; choir practice at the Baptist Church; my admiration for Miss Moffett; arguments and discussions that Sue Roberts, Hattie Brown, and I would have; walks to the Old Mill; our daily assemblies; Doctor McConnell's dignity and uneffected jokes; the literary society plays and programs; commencement festivities; swimming, both outdoors and indoor; basketball games.

--Mary Wright Chapin.

The memory I treasure most is that of the way I was welcomed into the College. Also the many banquets I attended were very enjoyable, knowing the faculty I also will always remember.

--Mary Ruhama Clem.

The year I spent in Radford was pleasant in every way, and I have many happy memories of the school and my friends made while there.

--Thelma Gluck Martin.

Organizing the rural schools across the New River. I visited the school every morning for almost nine months. My corns which grew from those walks are with me yet. The "blue-jay" corn plaster people have almost made a fortune out of me. The State still owes me money for the work I did in that school.

--William Benjamin Coggin.

Serving first meal to eighty people with only a barrel of glasses and we had to borrow every dish from the merchants of Radford.

--Mrs. Cecil Crockett.

One of the most interesting things I think of just now is the pleasure I got out of my class in the Middle Ages. It was a small class with some excellent students, and I thoroughly enjoyed teaching them.

--Sophie M. Dabbs.

Direct contact with children and student teachers; personal conversations with Doctor Moffett and Doctor McConnell, Programs and Receptions.

--Blanche Wilson Daniel.

Doctor McConnell's chapel addresses, Miss Moffett's executive ability, Mr. Gilbert's so-called hard classes, Mr. J. R. L. Johnson's criticisms, Mr. F. B. Fitzpatrick's psychology, Mr. W. R. Bowers and Sowder's "fatherliness"; the art classes with Miss Simmons, and that splendid example of the use of double letters as given by J. P. Whitt, "Up, up, Lucy and look at the moon", are all memories of Radford.

         --Enola Dobyns Jennings.

The first Alleganianna, first faculty follies, faculty picnics, Mr. Wyches' story telling on the campus (met him later in York, Pennsylvania) are interesting memories of Radford.

         --Jane Blachly Driver.

The most interesting memories at Radford are: my associations with Virginia girls in R. S. T. C.; pleasure of knowing very interesting faculty members, and joys of many happy week end trips.

         --Mrs. Flora Dungy Golding.

My experience in Radford was no Joke.

         --Gilbert H. Easley.

My associations in Radford are the most poignant of my memories. The diversity of activities in relation to physical education and health education were interesting and most helpful.

         --Wanda N. Ellis.

My one year at Radford College as Dietitian was a very pleasant one, of course there were hardships but the pleasure outweighed them in my memory. When a person is in love nothing can discourage them.

         --Parke Ferguson Wilcox.

All of my associations at Radford were pleasant and the memory of all is very dear.

         --Geraldine Fitzgerald Hagan.

Contacts made with faculty members and those not connected with the college.

         --Kathryn Fritz.

The serious attitude of the majority of the students with regard to their work.

         --Henry Emmett Fulcher.

Getting all the amino acids into my head was quite a big task. Putting up a good entertainment in a few hours was something I admired in R. S. T. C. The three weeks I spent at the hospital with pneumonia were very sad.

         --Teresa Funtane de Colon.

Most interesting work in Y. W. C. A., my hardships, walking

to Rockford; Doctor McConnell telling the student body at Chapel period that the "fools' eyes were at the end of the world"; teaching Mathematics to review students.

--Ethel Garrett Robinson.

Debates, Society work, May days, work on the "Beehive", Doctor Moffett in Orientation, feasts after "light boll", election day at Radford College, English and History classes, Doctor McConnell's idealism and advice are interesting memories of Radford.

--Genevieve Gertrude Giesen.

Buying the books and butter for the first year of school; helping to start several phases of work in the early years.

--William E. Gilbert.

The pleasure of teaching girls who were interested and anxious to be taught. The President and Faculty, I found ready and willing to cooperate, I enjoyed my work.

--Alice M. Gleaves.

During the spring quarter of 1920, Elizabeth was "the college baby". (The first and only baby to live in the dormitory.)

--Margaret Godby Smith.

I thoroughly enjoyed my work at Radford, the kindness everyone gave, and I shall always think of the days there as pleasant ones.

--Mrs. Madeline G. Phlegar.

The celebration of the announcement of Armistice and Judge Cassel speaking from a soap box near the station.

--J. L. Hardin.

The four and one-half years I spent in Radford as teacher in the high school were most pleasant. The greatest hardship was trying to secure a rooming and boarding place when I first arrived. After inquiring at six or more places I was "temporarily" taken in by the Barnetts where I remained the four and one-half years. My major interest in high school and I enjoyed so much the one class I taught at the "Normal" and the contacts I made there.

--Mrs. Gladys Howe Chamberlin.

Pleasures from nature and outings and vacations such as the summers of 1927 and 1930 spent in travel in Europe; personalities of Doctor McConnell, Professors Johnson, Gilbert, Sowder, Fitzpatrick; the work of Tennyson and Browning, Milton and Shakespeare, creative writing; hardships of cold in the rooming houses, etc.

--Virginia O'Rear Hudson.

Some of my most interesting experiences centered around
the teaching of History of the review students in summer sessions.
--Gladys Huffard Fillinger.

My work kept me very busy but happy and interested. School
and the Faculty parties are remembered with pleasure. Doctor
McConnell and Doctor Allison still are an inspiration to me and
will always be.
--Myrtle E. Hyre.

I enjoyed my work while at Radford.
--J. R. L. Johnson.

Associating with the people in that section of Virginia. The
serious attitude of the students toward their work.
--Obed Wilbur Johnson.

The contacts that I have had with a few of the Faculty members; my pleasantest memories will always be associated with the
one person who has meant more to me than any one else in my professional life, the Dean. I have always been happy with my pupils.
--Mae Kelly.

I recall as my most pleasant memories of the college the
association with so many people who are now close friends.
--Sena Kirby Lineberry.

The many lovely automobile trips I took through the State
I shall never forget. I always enjoyed my work at Radford College and the many friends I made among students and College Professors.
--Clara Georgine Langvick.

My most interesting work was teaching English 13, in the
summer of 1931 and conferences with student teachers in regular
session. The most interesting personalities are the members of
the Home Department and one or two other members of the Faculty.
--Ruth Lewis.

Hardship, when all but fourteen girls in the domitory were
in bed with Influenza in 1918; pleasures, Ingles Literary Society
work, helping the Class of 1918 work for a post office.
--Frances W. Long.

The friendliness of the Presbyterians and the Club women of
the town; the association with certain congenial faculty friends;
my rose garden; these are the bright spots.
--Gertrude I. McCain.

My most interesting memories of Radford consist in the happy recollection that all professors, students, and citizens were kind and helpful so much that I look back on my years then as some of my happiest ones.

--Clara J. McCauley.

It is difficult to recollect any one of the experiences as I had lived in the town from the time I was thirteen years old. So all the gradual change from its original setting into the present campus and arrangement of buildings, equipment and personnel possibly is the most interesting observation.

--John Paul McConnell.

Hardships; getting up before day to practice for a "Pokie" opening meeting; teaching the same Psychology lesson five times on Friday. Pleasures: enjoying the wholesomeness of the whole situation. Personalities: Miss Belle Wooding and her great knowledge of the Bible in contest with my little knowledge when I was a teacher and she a student. Doctor McConnell and his methods of handling the many personalities of the faculty; Mr. Whitt and his several-sided-self, interesting all; Jokes: The feeling that I had on reaching East Radford (Which that I had in every letter from Doctor McConnell was referred to as "the City") when I followed a drove of cows up the street to reach my boarding place. When Doctor McConnell looked the Faculty over and selected me to teach Bible because I have an uncle who is a minister. Work: When I tell you that although nearly nine years have passed since I left East Radford occassionally I hear from an old student, it must be seen that either my work or I made some "imprint". I shall be conceited enough to say that it was my work, I did my best.

--Mary H. McLees.

I have so many fond memories of my short stay at Radford that it will be impossible to enumerate them. I enjoyed the Faculty and student body associations thoroughly, and I can recall no unpleasant experience connected with my summer while there. The literary societies were the best that I have found at Colleges, I believe.

--Thomas Burton Meadows.

See the History, which is my story of Radford.
--M'Ledge Moffett.

Doctor McConnell's introduction and history of each student as diplomas were given at commencement. His memory seems most unusual. The beautiful sunset from the hill near the cemetery;

a Faculty meeting in which short skirts were discussed; the
marriage of Doctor McConnell's daughter in the auditorium of
the school, and a fresh corn roast on a nearby farm given for
the "Pocahontas Club" to which she belonged.

--Flora Neley.

"Remember the "flu".

--Mary Montague.

So many delightful personal associations among the faculty,
students, and townspeople, and dare I mention the strolling cows.
I often allowed right of way on the sidewalk while I stepped safely away in the street.

Louise Ninde Fisher.

My most interesting memory is that of baking cakes which the
other teachers cut at will and served to their friends. Then one
night I served a few slices which another teacher baked when complaint was made. I once won a cake at a school entertainment at
New River. I brought it back to the teacherage and the other
teachers ate it in my absence. It was always queer to me that
"sauce for the goose was not sauce for the gander" at the teacherage.

--Elizabeth Painter.

The Pokie and Ingles debates and the attendant complications
are some of my interesting Radford memories.

--Lavada Reed.

The wonderful climate, marvelous sunsets and mountains,
Southern hospitality.

--Rosetta Rhenke Gibbs.

Association with students and Faculty, especially "Tie-dying"
scarfs for the boys to present to their girl friends.

Stanley E. Rittase.

Visits of Mr. Whitt and Doctor Bain to the Training School
and encouragement they gave us.

--Daisy Robinson.

Some of my most pleasant memories are of the days I spent
working in Radford College, particularly the work done as Acting
Treasurer, the splendid cooperation not only of the officials of
the College but the Faculty and students also. My work was very
pleasant and has been of much help to me since that time.

--Mary S. Blankenbeckler.

I think I enjoyed most making a success of the "Blue Gate Tea Room".

--Bess Smenner.

Association with my students, being of service when called upon, helping those to see the finer things in music (the infinite). Do your best angels can do no better (slogan). The educating of one of my students brought me the greatest joy and pleasure while at Radford. Now the fulfillment of my joy is being realized seeing her (Caroline V. Honts) in the school room.

--C. Edmee Smith.

Teaching in tents, gathering fern herbarium and the field trips.

--William Day Smith.

Although I remember with pleasure my association with you and your Faculty I can hardly fill in a formal blank with my most vivid memories. One is of a casual chance meeting with Miss Moffett, another of strolling along to an early class one brilliant morning in June and loitering to watch two boys starting across the street in front of an approaching automobile. I was speculating on whether one was fool hardy to continue his way or the other over-cautious to return to the curb and wondering whether their actions at the moment were indicative of their respective characters when I turned lightly and saw Miss Moffett behind the stone wall among the hollyhocks watching the same scene with an expression of mingled amusement and understanding on your face.

My class room work at East Radford was the most satisfying I have ever done. Nowhere else have I found so ready a response from students. Their alertness, curiosity, and desire for knowledge, as well as, for information, were a delight to me after the mental lethargy of boarding school girls. Mrs. Burkett, Blanche Daniel, Mrs. Johnson, Lillian Smith, Cassie Rea and some whose faces are clear in my memory, but whose names have slipped from me made every hour an interesting one. My classes in Pre-Shakespearian and Shakespearian drama were the high lights of my teaching career.

--Gaynell Callaway Spivey.

My association with members of the Faculty at social gatherings, meals, etc. Association with the President and his family; associations with students in class room, on hikes, trips to Mountain Lake, etc. My hardship of a cold room to live in, such are my pleasant memories of Radford College.

--Dora A. States.

I think my most interesting memories at Radford were:
swimming class (students didn't know this member of the class
was on the Faculty), and the Blue Gate Tea Room.
                                        --Marion Struthers.

I like most to think of my work in French and Latin, from
the scholars viewpoint; all the lovely girls I taught, especially
those of the Latin Classes; of my friends at the Baptist Church;
of the marvelous mountain scenery of Radford; of the congenial
Faculty, the intimate fineness of the President and his family.
                                        --Gladys Tapley.

A picture is ever present. The Administration Building
without a front door, boards nailed up and down with snow drift-
ing in the cracks, the girls attending chapel with blankets
wrapped around them. I practically remember Lois Showalter
one cold morning.
                                        --Mrs. Eleanor Terry Noell.

Perhaps hardships while in the Training School--see Mae
Kelly. Generally speaking, personalities and associations.
                                        --Eva Vaughan.

A vividly and interesting memory of Southern hospitality
and Dean Moffett's kindly friendship, especially that Sunday
morning delicious breakfast I partook of as a guest.
                                        --Gladys J. Ward.

Most vivid recollection is being introduced by Jerry Whitt
either as Lena Stafford's husband or as the husband of the first
student of Radford College.
                                        --George Albert Williams.

My work in the History Department and my association with
the other members of the department was my most pleasant experience
in teaching.
                                        --Elizabeth Gertrude Wilson.

My most interesting memories of Radford are my class room
work and the supervisors conferences.
                                        --Edna Yeatts.

The music by Hampton Institution quartet, tennis with Professor Burch; leaving Radford one day never having been married
and returning the next day never to be single again.
                                        --Wilson H. Young.

MAJOR COMMUNITY INTERESTS OF MEMBERS OF THE RADFORD
FACULTY WHILE LIVING IN RADFORD

(Compiled from Questionnaires answered by Faculty members)

Taught Sunday School Class at the Methodist Church; took charge of the Junior League of the Methodist Church, put on programs.

--Ina Addington Cox.

Sang in the Christian Church choir.

--Ethel Akers Coleman.

Most of my time was occupied in grading plans to please "Sister Bulifant".

--Bonnie Jean Alderson.

Sang in the Presbyterian choir, joined the Presbyterian Church, worked in the diet kitchen in Emergency Hospital at West Radford during the "flu" epidemic; nursed the "flu" for a week in the dormitory during the "flu" epidemic.

--Elizabeth Sheffield Allen.

I was supply pastor of the Central Presbyterian Church for three years.

--John Lee Allison.

Teacher of College girls' Sunday School Class at the Baptist Church.

--Daisy L. Anderson.

Taught Sunday School Class several years; member of the Woman's Missionary Society, Grove Avenue Methodist Church.

--Pearl M. Andrews.

Superintendent of the Methodist Church Sunday School; wrote campaign handbook for city-manager campaign.

--Joseph Emory Avent.

The Rotary Club and Golf were my major community interests while living in Radford.

--Richard Bagby.

Sang in the Methodist, Baptist, and Presbyterian Churches; spoke at Parent Teachers Associations.

--Winifred E. Bain.

Sang in the Presbyterian Choir.

> --Mary Elder Harwood Beebe.

Church; faculty advisor on B. S. U. Council.

> --Ercelle Bennett.

Member of the Virginia Mae Chapter of Eastern Star organization.

> --Zella L. Blackard.

Taught in Bourne Memorial Methodist Sunday School.

> --Ruth Borders.

Sang in the Methodist choir; member of the General Board of Education; Superintendent of Sunday School from 1921 to the present time.

> --Wilson R. Bowers.

Member of the Radford Music Club; Sang in the Baptist Choir.

> --Ruth Bricker Painter.

Story Telling Club, Attendance at Music Club.

> --Bessie Brown.

Sunday School, Epworth League.

> --Elizabeth Brown.

Taught in Sunday School, served on Social Service Committee, Methodist Missionary Society; taught Mission Study Classes in Missionary Society, Sunday School Teacher Training, leader in Knitting Unit with College girls during the World War; served on the Red Cross Committee a number of years; Health Survey of the town.

> --Olive Flora Bryson.

Sang in the choir of the Episcopal Church, taught Bible Class in Episcopal Sunday School, directed telling of Bible stories by members of the Story Tellers Club in various churches of the community.

> --Mrs. Blanche B. McFarland.

Sunday School Teacher in the Methodist Church; Scoutmaster of Boy Scouts of America; member of the Isaac Walton League.

> --Paul R. Burch.

Connections with the Presbyterian Church.

> --Myrtle C. Burnette.

Teacher of a Sunday School Class.

--M. Grace Caldwell.

Teacher in the Lutheran Sunday School.

--Nellie B. Caldwell.

Native of the town, member of the First Baptist Church.

--D. A. Cannaday.

Sang in the Methodist choir, also the organist.

--Lizzie Faye James Carr.

Played the piano for the Baptist Church.

--Mary Wright Chapin.

Sang in the Baptist choir, pianist for the Men's Glee Club
of Radford.

--Mary Ruhama Clem.

Taught Sunday School Class at the First Baptist Church.

--Elton C. Cocke.

I play in the Methodist Church and occasionally in the
other Churches.

--John W. Comstock.

I was a teacher in the Baptist Sunday School at different
times and a member of the Red Cross organization.

--Mary Eolian Coppedge.

Sang in the Methodist Choir; Hi-League Counsellor.

--Blanche Wilson Daniel.

Taught a class in the Presbyterian Sunday School.

--Mattie C. Denny.

I was a teacher in the M. E. Church, South; helped serve
with the Red Cross, Community Welfare Work, Chest Clinics,
P. T. A., etc.

--Enola Dobyns Jennings.

Organist of the First Baptist Church for two years; organist
of the Methodist Church two years; member of the American Legion,
Forty and Eight, Rotary Club.

--Alfred K. Eagle.

Pastor of Church (Christian) Radford.

--Gilbert H. Easley.

Chairman of the Radford Music Club; member of Governing
Board, Director of Radford Music Glee Club; Director of Radford's
Episcopal Church choir.

--Edythe W. Einstein.

Preparation of programs for Music Club, Woman's Club, High
School Assembly, Sunday School Class at the Christian Church,
High School operetta, U. D. C., Kiwanis and Rotary Club.

--Wanda Ellis.

Taught College Class in Baptist Sunday School for fourteen
years.

--Lottie M. Evans.

Church interests, Red Cross, Kiwanis Club.

--Frances Burke Fitzpatrick.

Taking part in community plays.

--Kathryn Fritz.

Teacher of Sunday School Classes.

--Henry Emmett Fulcher.

Taught Sunday School Classes in the Christian Church, a
leader in the High School Young Women's Christian Association.

--Ethel Garrett Robinson.

Work in the Lutheran League of the Lutheran Church.

--Genevieve Gertrude Giesen.

Build up the town, change form of Government, serve in getting
Bond issued for schools, streets, etc., Mayor.

--William E. Gilbert.

Played the violin in all the churches, for entertainments,
music clubs, and in the homes.

--Alice M. Gleaves.

Sunday School teacher of the West Ward Christian Church.

--Stanley Godbey.

Organist for the Presbyterian church part of the time, sang
in the Presbyterian choir, also played and sang for the various
programs at the churches and high school.

--Madeline Guthrie Phlegar.

Pianist at the Christian Church, taught Sunday School class
there also.

--Mrs. Gladys H. Chamberlin.

Work in the D. A. R. as member and Regent of the General William Campbell Chapters; member of the Music Club, Woman's Club, Garden Club, Sing in the Presbyterian choir and have made many speeches before various organizations.

--Virginia O'Rear Hudson.

I had no major community interests save doing my work thoroughly while in Radford.

--John Lee Johnson.

Teaching Sunday School Class, Preaching, founder of men's Glee Club, member of the Board of Directors of Kiwanis Club; sang in the Episcopal choir.

--John W. Humphreys.

To learn the policies of the school, community, and city.
--Obed Wilbur Johnson.

Music Club, Church Organists.

--Elsie Hartwell Jones.

Attended the Lutheran Church in West Radford.
--Clara Georgine Langvick.

Sunday School Work in the Methodist Church, Community League Work.

--Mae Kelly.

A member of the Education Committee of American Association of University Women, giving toy and book exhibit; home visiting in an effort to bring about better relations between home and school, thus promoting the welfare of the child; church activities.
--Mildred Kocher.

Contributing to needs of especially poor families.
--Ruth Lewis.

Sang in the Presbyterian Choirs.
--Elizabeth Lloyd.

Belspring Community League Worker; helped get Chautauquas and new school building in Belspring.
--Frances W. Long.

Organized the Isaak Walton League Chapter; member of the Rotary Club; member of sub-committee of twenty-five of the civic improvement council; community fund committee.
--William Stapleton Long.

Sang in the Christian Church Choir.

--Annie Lucas Kennedy.

Taught in the "Radford College Class" in the Presbyterian Church in 1931.

--Grace Susan Martz.

President of a Garden Club, served on the program committees of the Woman's Club; taught the Bible Class and sang in the choir at the Presbyterian Church.

--Gertrude I. McCain.

Organ and choir work, teacher of girls' class in Sunday School in the Methodist Church.

--Mrs. W. C. McCarty.

Taught Sunday School Classes and aided in music work of the Methodist Church, Presbyterian Church, and Baptist Church.

--Clara J. McCauley.

Superintendent of Sunday School of the Christian Church for two years, member of the Rotary Internationals.

--John Paul McConnell.

Taught Ladies Bible Class at the Presbyterian Church.

--Mary H. McLees.

Member of the Presbyterian Central choir, substitute Teacher of Woman's Bible Class.

--Ethel McLeod.

I sang second tenor with the Male Quartet and at Sunday School a few times.

--Thomas Burton Meadows.

I sang in the Lutheran Church choir, actively interested in the Young Peoples work of the church.

--Sadie E. Miller.

Speaker, Woman's Club, Kiwanis, Church, Community life, Taught Sunday School several years, Presbyterian Church.

--M'Ledge Moffett.

Teacher in the Baptist Sunday School; Red Cross Work.

--Mary Wortley Montague.

Making speeches, Juding contests.

--Mary Ethel NeSmith.

Member of the Baptist choir for three years.
                                --Louise Ninde Fisher.

Local Norfolk and Western Railroad surgeon since 1910;
City Health Officer, Deacon of the Baptist Church; Rotarian.
                                --J. A. Noblin.

State Federation Contest in Music; Art Club, Music Club,
Woman's Club, Sunday School Class, Missionary Society, American
Association of University Women, Garden Club, College Quartette.
                                --Florence Belle Ogg.

Taught Class at the Christian Church; President of the Young
Peoples Organization (Christian Endeavor), Christian Church.
                                --Hallie Mae Otey.

Organized the Boy Scouts at Belspring, taught in the Presbyterian and Methodist Sunday Schools; helped in the Christian Endeavor.
                                --Elizabeth Painter.

Director of the Presbyterian Choir, member of the Music Club,
Accompanist for Mrs. Einstein's chorus.
                                --Harriette Perkins Danbury.

Secretary of Eastern Star Lodge.
                                --Ruby A. Shrader.

Church work in the Episcopal Church.
                                --Bess Smenner.

Sang in the Methodist choir two years, taught Sunday School
Class one year. Sang solos in various churches, college programs,
etc.
                                --C. Edmee Smith.

Taught Sunday School Class, and had charge of the Junior Endeavor.
                                --Dora A. States.

Member of the Men's Glee Club, occasionally supply pulpits
when there is no one else.
                                --C. B. Swaney.

Baptist Church.

                                --Gladys Tapley.

American Association of University Women.
                                --Jean E. Taylor.

Sang in the Episcopal Choir, Men's Glee Club, Rotarian.
--Minor Wine Thomas.

Church work, Rotary Club, American Legion, Bible School;
Deacon, First Christian Church, Teacher Men's Bible Class, First
Christian Bible School, member of the Board of Directors of the
Club; Historian, American Legion.
--George Albert Williams.

Member of the Woman's Christian Temperance Union, U. D. C.,
Garden Club, President of Radford Woman's Club, Secretary of
Radford Woman's Club, Sunday School Class, Missionary Society.
--Jaynie S. Whitt.

OFF-CAMPUS SERVICE OF THE MEMBERS OF THE RADFORD FACULTY
IN THE PROFESSIONAL LIFE OF VIRGINIA AND THE NATION[1]

Secretary-Treasurer of various State departments in the Educational Association. Talks at several State meetings.
--Ina Addington Cox

Gave readings and entertainments in nearly every town between Roanoke and Knoxville and thus advertised Radford College and the Department of Oratory in particular. Gave readings at Kiwanis (or Rotary) luncheons.
--Elizabeth Sheffield Allen

Grand Master of Odd Fellows for one year; made many addresses at Mason and Kiwanis Conventions, delivered many Literary Addresses and Commencement Sermons for High Schools and Colleges.

--John Lee Allison

Made numerous speeches before Teachers' Associations and at High School Commencements.
--Joseph Emory Avent

Supervisor of Extension Classes.
--Richard O. Bagby

Spoke at Division meeting of Virginia Teachers, Galax, Virginia; spoke at N. E. A. Annual Meeting in Atlanta, Georgia.
--Winifred E. Bain

Treasurer of College Club, Roanoke, Virginia; Member of the Board of Roanoke Woman's Club, one year; Junior Red Cross Work; Red Cross Nurse during the "flu" epidemic; Speech, Better Roads Program, Spies, North Carolina.
--Mary Elder Harwood Beebe

Preached once near Ashland, Virginia, twelve out of thirty-five in the congregation went to sleep; member of Cosmopolitan Club, Baltimore, Maryland; A few random talks, never twice in the same place.

--Walter Herman Bell

Secretary for the State Geography Association at Virginia Educational Conference in Richmond, November 1929.
--Ruth Borders

1. As reported in replies to questionnaires.

Vice-President of Virginia Education Association 1925-1927, President of the Mathematics Department, 1923-1925; Also 1929-1931; made commencement addresses in High Schools, speeches at Sunday School Conventions and Church.

--Wilson R. Bowers

National officer in Pi Gamma Mu Honor Fraternity(Recording Secretary), Delegate to two national conventions.

--Ruth Bricker Painter

President of Wise County Education Association 1921-1922; Vice-President of District "K", Virginia Education Association, 1928-1929; President of Albemarle County Education Association, 1929-1930; Member of Virginia Committee for Research in Secondary Education.

--Earl B. Broadwater

Professional services have been in the field of Religious Education rather than secular Education.

--Elizabeth Brown

President of the Science Section, State Teachers' Association; Secretary of Botany Section, Virginia Academy of Science, two years; Presented a paper at the first meeting of the Academy of Science at the College of William and Mary; Acting director of Educational work under the State Board of Health of Virginia; visiting the County Teachers' Institutes and talking in the interests of the West Law Course; Organizing Health Leagues.

--Flora Bryson

President of Geography Section of Virginia State Teachers Association, one year; President of Primary Section of Virginia State Teachers Association, several years; President of Primary Section of Southwest Virginia Teachers' Association; Speaker on State and Sectional programs many times, varied subjects; delegate and speaker, Episcopal Sunday School Convention; Congressional District Chairman of Committee which secured admission for women to University of Virginia

--Mrs. Blanche Bulifant
McFarland

Chairman of Zoology Section of Virginia Academy of Science, 1930-1931. Paper read at Lynchburg meeting of Virginia Academy of Science; Paper at the Williamsburg meeting of the Virginia Academy of Science; Various speeches for Kiwanis Club, High

School, and Church organizations; Scout Master of Troop Number
1, Radford, Virginia, Boy Scouts of America. Delegate, Isaac
Walton League, Lynchburg, Virginia.

--Paul Rudolph Burch

Vice-President of Virginia Home Economics Association, 1928,
Delegate to A. H. E. A. Meeting 1926; Talks to Clubs and Parent
Teachers Meetings on planning meals for adults and children on
budgeting. Extension classes for teachers stressing child care.

--Virginia G. Caldwell

Principal speaker at celebration of 100th Anniversary of
Andrew Johnson's arrival in Greenville, Tennessee; Addresses on
Tennessee History; Rotary and Kiwanis Clubs of Greenville and
Newport, Tennessee; Addresses on Southern Literature, various or-
ganizations of Greenville, Tennessee.

--D. A. Cannaday

Playing and singing for College Assembly, also doing solo
work for Kiwanis, Musicale and Rotary Clubs; Singing at the
Baptist, Presbyterian, Methodist, and other churches.

--Mary Ruhama Clem

Made commencement speeches at various points.

--Wm. Benjamin Coggin

Member of faculty, Summer quarter, George Peabody College
for Teachers, 1922; Member of faculty of Summer quarter at the
University of Virginia, 1929; Secretary-Treasurer of High School
Normal Training Department of Virginia State Teachers' Association, 1910-1911; President of High School Normal Training Department of Virginia State Teachers' Association, 1911-1916; Secretary-Treasurer of Kindergarten, Primary Department of Virginia
State Teachers' Association, 1918-1921; President of Virginia
Society of Geography Teachers, 1922-1925; Member of Committee
of the State Course of Study in Geography and Reading.

--Mary Eolian Coppedge

Community service clubs; served on the Co-Council of Defense in both Montgomery and Pulaski Counties in 1916-1917,
and put in many hours of hard service in that connection. The
work included conservation and Education for Women's and Chil-
drens Clubs, also much Educational work with the men's service
and commercial clubs.

--Mrs. Edna Cox Wolfe

President of the Geographic Society of Virginia; gave speeches before the County Teachers' Meetings.

--Blanche Wilson Daniel

"No offices, no orator" a calm observer of school and church activities, a willing helper with both hand and heart. Since leaving R. S. T. C. three years have been spent in Radford High as an instructor, one in Petersburg Public Schools, and three in Hillsville High School, Carroll County, Virginia.

--Mrs. Enola Dobyns
Jennings

Taught Extension Classes in East Ward School, after school hours at the College. In these classes were enrolled all Training School Supervisors. Some of the city teachers and the city school superintendents, Education 40 and 41.

--Mrs. Flora Dungy Golding

Paper read at Virginia Educational Conference 1930, on "New Methods in Plane Geometry."

--Alfred K. Eagle

Programs for Southwest Virginia Incorporated; Speech and activities in connection with the State Health and Physical Health Association; Activities in relation to County and State Basketball tournaments; Talks in High Schools in the interest of Radford College.

--Wanda M. Ellis

Director of District "C", 1918, 1919, 1920; Member of Executive Committee, 1931-1932; Member of Appalachian Foundation; Speaker for Cooperative Education Association; Contributor to Virginia Journal of Education.

--Lottie M. Evans

I have taken an active part in the life of the Virginia Education Association, served as President, Vice-President, Board of Directors, Executive Committee. I was a member of the Virginia Board of Examiners for six years. I have written many articles for the Virginia Journal, served as President of the Department of Rural Education for several years.

--Francis Burke Fitzpatrick

I took training at St. Lukes Hospital for thirty months, May, 1921 to November, 1924.

--Geraldine Fitzgerald Hagan

I made a speech on "Evaluation of Primary Arithmetic" at the District Teachers Meeting in Roanoke, 1930.
--Kathryn Fritz

Served one year as supervisor of a one-teacher school at Rockford; served four years as Principal of Belspring High School; attended two conferences at Blue Ridge, North Carolina, serving as Secretary; One Student Volunteer Conference at Farmville, Virginia.
--Mrs. Ethel Garrett Robinson

I have made speeches each year before District "K", Virginia Education Association Meetings (1929-1932); Director of all high school plays here, one College play (Bluefield College), and one Parent Teachers Association play; Coach of debate and public speaking at Graham High School. (I am proud to state that my debate team won B class State Championship (1930) at Charlottesville and my boy-speaker won State Championship in 1931).
--Genevieve Gertrude Giesen

Active member of the Virginia Education Association; Lieutenant-Governor, Capitol District, Kiwanis, made some six to ten commencement talks each year in high schools.
--William E. Gilbert

President of American Association of University Women, 1931-1932.
--Jonnie Gore

Judged Music(Piano and Voice) contests of Pearisburg and Pembroke High Schools.
--Madeline Guthrie Phlegar

Numerous speeches before Teachers of Radford, Belspring, the College Faculty, D. A. R., U. D. C., A. A. U. W., Woman's Club, etc. of an educational nature. Active work to improve the English of prospective teachers of Virginia and the nation. I have not been given the opportunity to appear on State or National Programs.
--Virginia O'Rear Hudson

Attended conventions, spoke before the Virginia Academy of Science, School addresses at close of year.
--John W. Humphreys

Have made several addresses at high schools, churches, and Parent Teachers' Meetings.
--Obed Wilbur Johnson

Have made several talks at State Meetings and District
Meetings.
--Mae Kelly

Treasurer of the American Association of University Women.
--Mildred Kocher

Several commencement addresses, two addresses before the English Section of the Virginia Education Association, many to the
Rotary, Kiwanis, U. D. C., and Elementary School Assemblies. Participation in the State Program for adult education by Extension
work for R. S. T. C. and for the University of Virginia. I helped
organize then served as an officer in the Association of the Izaak
Walton League Chapters in Virginia. I have been helping in the
State-wide Campaign for Conservation of National Resources.
--William Stapleton Long

Literary Editor of "The Buffalo" annual of Milligan College,
1917. On the Editorial Staff the four school years I taught at
Clifton Forge of "The Mountaineer" school magazines. One speech
worthy of mention, "Steps to the Temple of Fame".
--Annie Lucas Kennedy

I have made a number of speeches on "Causes of Pupil Fail-
ures", "The Value of the Social Program in Education", "The Art
of Collecting"and "Refining Curriculum Materials", at State
meetings and University Summer Schools, but not in Virginia and
I hesitate to say that these were of national interest.
--Grace Susan Martz

Made speeches over my County in Indiana during the campaign
for woman suffrage. Spoke and wrote to get a library in my home
town in Indiana; helped establish it; worked in all sorts of club
work and church and Sunday School work.
--Gertrude I. McCain

Accompanied Doctors Clarkton, McConnell, and Mr. Bryan in an
educational survey of Southwestern Virginia. Aided in setting
forth opportunities for music in education available at Radford.
--Clara J. McCauley

Numerous talks before community leagues as well as school
groups, commencement addresses in high and graded schools of the
section.
--John Paul McConnell

Spoke at the State Teachers Association in Richmond, Virginia.
--Mary H. McLees

Lay-Leader of the Methodist Church, South; speaker on education-al programs in Georgia, Alabama, Mississippi, Tennessee, Louisiana; speaker at various banquets; leader in Sunday School Teacher Train-ing; member of Educational Survey Staff of Peabody College; lec-tures at the University Professors; lectures at the Doctor's Acad-emy, etc.
--Thomas Burton Meadows

Speaker at County institutes, State meetings, National Associa-tion of Deans of Women (N. E. A.). Director(three terms) Virginia Education Association; President of Virginia Home Economics Associa-tion (two terms). Councillor of American Home Economics Association. Attended five meetings of N. E. A., speaker twice; State Chairman of Home Economics Federation of Women's Clubs.
--M'Ledge Moffett

Secretary of the English Section of Virginia Education Associa-tion; Director representing Southeastern Virginia; National Council of Teachers of English; Spoke once at Virginia Education Association, English; President of the American Association of University Women, Radford Branch; made two speeches before Radford P. T. A.
--Mary Ethel NeSmith

These opportunities limited to a few only.
--Florence Belle Ogg

When I was Supervisor of Rural Schools I made several speeches at Civic Leagues, but do not remember what they were.
--Elizabeth Painter

Paper, The Cult of Vesta in Early Roman Life, read before the Virginia Classical Association, November, 1930, Richmond, Virginia.
--Susan E. Roberts

Delegate to Institute of Public Affairs; member of Committee for Eradication of Illiteracy; member of Committee for Home Im-provement.
--Daisy Robinson

Chairman, Membership Committee, State Home Economics Associa-tion; talk at State Meeting, State Home Economics Association.
--Bess Smenner

Took Glee Clubs for programs, Floyd, and Eggleston, also to Emory and Henry College (operetta); helped in laying corner stone of High School in Radford, also the Legion Building. Took part in Operetta given in High School, sang for the Kiwanis program, etc.

--C. Edmee Smith

Principal of High School, Scottsville, twenty-five years; President of County Teachers Association.

--William Day Smith

State Teachers Association, Round Table Discussions, Rural Education Leader, Speeches at County Institute, regular sessions and through the visiting rural schools and rural supervisors.

--Dora States

Gave one address at District "I" meeting in Roanoke in 1931; make occasional commencement addresses.

--C. B. Swaney

Extension Courses.

--Jean E. Taylor

Occasional speeches at Teachers meetings; during the fall of 1930 I attended and addressed fifteen teachers meetings in twelve counties from September to Christmas; a member of the Survey Staff of Montgomery County, taught Extension Classes for thirty weeks in Montgomery County; special educational advisor for Montgomery County; member of the Survey Staff of Grayson County; Special consultant, Educational Survey at Wythe County; Director of Experimental work in individual instruction in Montgomery County; Author of the Montgomery County Plan of Individual Instruction.

--Minor Wine Thomas

Secretary of District "I" two years.

--Eva Vaughan

Member of the American Home Economics Association, Family Economics Section Committee; member of the National Safety Council Home Safety Division; made talks over Station W I L L, University of Illinois; made talks at P. T. A., Kiwanis Clubs, etc.

--Gladys J. Ward

Speaker on Scientific subjects at meetings of such organizations as, Virginia Education Association, American Chemical Society, Virginia Academy of Science, Hampton Roads Chemists Club, Society for Experimental Biology, and Medicine, etc. I broadcast

140-A

weekly(from 10:00 to 10:15 P. M. every Wednesday) from Station
W T A R Norfolk, on Chemical subjects of general interest, particularly on nutrition and chemistry of health, disease, and
diet.

--George A. Williams

Chairman of Division of Adult Education in Virginia Federation of Women's Clubs.

--Jaynie S. Whitt

Note: Those not quoted did not answer the question or did not
return the questionnaire.

HONOR STUDENTS

BACHELOR OF SCIENCE

1922 - Virginia Harwood
1924 - Virginia Porter
1925 - Helen Hill Haight (First)
      Maude Paine (Second)
1926 - India Covey (First)
      Margaret Black (Second)
1927 - Ethel Roberts (First)
      Laura Wine (Second)

SUMMA CUM LAUDE - 1928

1928 - Ruth Bricker
      Genevieve Gieson
      Conchita Santos
      Sallie Vaughan Turner

MAGNA CUM LAUDE

      Lina Dobyns
      Myrtle Ellis
      Cassie Gardner
      Mrs. Ethel Shockey

CUM LAUDE

      Nannie Hardy Clarke
      Anna Belle DeHart
      Frances Edwards
      Nora Garrett
      Hattie Ogburn
      Garnett Shufflebarger

SUMMA CUM LAUDE - 1929

      Ada Blanco
      Esther Large
      Kate Stanfield

MAGNA CUM LAUDE - 1929

      Anna Agnew
      Audrey Arthur

MAGNA CUM LAUDE - 1929 (Con.)

Marida Blanco
Doris Bell
Anne Jennings
Linwood Kinder
Jeannette Mears

CUM LAUDE - 1929

Jessie Britt
Lohren Davenport
Evelyn Fitzpatrick
Martha Garrett
Eva Jennings
Louise Mahaney
Nannie McConnell
Pauline Osborne

SUMMA CUM LAUDE - Summer 1929

Ercelle Bennett
Elinor Bryant
Blanche Daniel
Mae Kelly
Emile Nunn Windle

MAGNA CUM LAUDE

Champe Carter Douthat
Willis Douthat
Berta Hartman
Lucille Griener Johnson

CUM LAUDE
Mrs. Bertha Lee Chapman
Ida Einstein
Annie Mae Harrington
Margaret Miller
Ethel Rorer
Willie Lee Stowers

TWO-YEAR HONOR STUDENTS

1920 - Salutatorian - Emma Quesenberry
       Valedictorian - Sena Kirby
1921 - Clara McCauley
1922 - Ina Addington
1924-Virginia Perry
1925 - Alice Wolfersburger

INDEX

Arranged by Alma Mitchell

A

INDEX

INDEX

INDEX

INDEX

- E -

- F -

INDEX

INDEX

INDEX

INDEX

INDEX

INDEX

INDEX

Rinktum Ditty Club   367, 368
Roberts, Artie   230
Roberts Estate   32
Roberts, Ethel   381, 113, 114, 208
Roberts, Henry   229
Roberts, Lottie   101
Roberts Rules of Order   292
Roberts, Susan   113, 147, 241, 361
Roberts, Trula   295
Roberts, Virginia Mae   316
Roberts, (Mrs.) Walter   336, 351
Rockford School   207
Robinson, A. Stuart   69, 89
Robinson, Charles M.   47, 53
Robinson, Cora   134
Rogers, Edward   62
Rogers, Margaret   281
Room Assignments: Administrative offices   50
    Administration Building 1913   48, 49
    Classrooms in Madame Russell   58
    Major Changes in   49
Roop, Ed   38, 41, 45, 46, 47, 49
                                  52, 55, 58, 89, 92, 117
                                 127, 136, 192, 254, 288, 327,
                                 346, 373

Roop, Elizabeth   101, 102, 216
Ruffner, William H.   1, 2
Ruggles, Louise   64, 183, 206, 326
Rural Arts   174
Rural Education   207
Rural Schools   192, 193
Rural School Messages   215
Rusmisell, B. F.   46
Russell, E. H.   4

- S -

INDEX

INDEX

INDEX

INDEX

INDEX

INDEX

INDEX